# THE LEGAL
# RESEARCH
# AND WRITING
# HANDBOOK

ASPEN COLLEGE SERIES

SEVENTH EDITION

# THE LEGAL RESEARCH AND WRITING HANDBOOK

## A BASIC APPROACH FOR PARALEGALS

ANDREA B. YELIN

HOPE VINER SAMBORN

 Wolters Kluwer

Law & Business

Published by Wolters Kluwer Law & Business in New York.

Wolters Kluwer Law & Business serves customers worldwide with CCH, Aspen Publishers, and Kluwer Law International products. (www.wolterskluwerlb.com)

To contact Customer Service, e-mail customer.service@wolterskluwer.com, call 1-800-234-1660, fax 1-800-901-9075, or mail correspondence to:

> Wolters Kluwer Law & Business
> Attn: Order Department
> PO Box 990
> Frederick, MD 21705

Printed in the United States of America.

1 2 3 4 5 6 7 8 9 0

ISBN 978-1-4548-4081-7

**Library of Congress Cataloging-in-Publication Data**

Yelin, Andrea B. author
    The legal research and writing handbook: a basic approach for paralegals / Andrea B. Yelin, Hope Viner Samborn. — Seventh edition.
        p. cm.
    ISBN 978-1-4548-4081-7
1. Legal research—United States. 2. Legal composition. I. Samborn, Hope Viner, author. II. Title.
    KF240.Y45 2014
    340.072′073—dc23

                                                                    2014020448

# About Wolters Kluwer Law & Business

Wolters Kluwer Law & Business is a leading global provider of intelligent information and digital solutions for legal and business professionals in key specialty areas, and respected educational resources for professors and law students. Wolters Kluwer Law & Business connects legal and business professionals as well as those in the education market with timely, specialized authoritative content and information-enabled solutions to support success through productivity, accuracy and mobility.

Serving customers worldwide, Wolters Kluwer Law & Business products include those under the Aspen Publishers, CCH, Kluwer Law International, Loislaw, ftwilliam.com and MediRegs family of products.

**CCH** products have been a trusted resource since 1913, and are highly regarded resources for legal, securities, antitrust and trade regulation, government contracting, banking, pension, payroll, employment and labor, and healthcare reimbursement and compliance professionals.

**Aspen Publishers** products provide essential information to attorneys, business professionals and law students. Written by preeminent authorities, the product line offers analytical and practical information in a range of specialty practice areas from securities law and intellectual property to mergers and acquisitions and pension/benefits. Aspen's trusted legal education resources provide professors and students with high-quality, up-to-date and effective resources for successful instruction and study in all areas of the law.

**Kluwer Law International** products provide the global business community with reliable international legal information in English. Legal practitioners, corporate counsel and business executives around the world rely on Kluwer Law journals, looseleafs, books, and electronic products for comprehensive information in many areas of international legal practice.

**Loislaw** is a comprehensive online legal research product providing legal content to law firm practitioners of various specializations. Loislaw provides attorneys with the ability to quickly and efficiently find the necessary legal information they need, when and where they need it, by facilitating access to primary law as well as state-specific law, records, forms and treatises.

**ftwilliam.com** offers employee benefits professionals the highest quality plan documents (retirement, welfare and non-qualified) and government forms (5500/PBGC, 1099 and IRS) software at highly competitive prices.

**MediRegs** products provide integrated health care compliance content and software solutions for professionals in healthcare, higher education and life sciences, including professionals in accounting, law and consulting.

Wolters Kluwer Law & Business, a division of Wolters Kluwer, is headquartered in New York. Wolters Kluwer is a market-leading global information services company focused on professionals.

To David, Rachel, and Henry with all my love.

—ABY

To my youngest students and teachers, Eve, Sarah, and Benjamin, and to my favorite teacher and friend, Randy. You have all my love and thanks.

—HVS

# SUMMARY OF CONTENTS

| | |
|---|---|
| *Contents* | *xi* |
| *List of Illustrations* | *xxxiii* |
| *Preface* | *xxxix* |
| *Acknowledgments* | *xli* |

**PART 1 LEGAL RESEARCH**       **1**
**CHAPTERS**

| | | |
|---|---|---|
| 1 | Introduction to Legal Research | 3 |
| 2 | Legal Authorities and How to Use Them | 19 |
| 3 | Court Decisions | 35 |
| 4 | Digests | 73 |
| 5 | Validating | 119 |
| 6 | Secondary Authority | 151 |
| 7 | Constitutions and Statutes | 193 |
| 8 | Legislative History | 237 |
| 9 | Administrative Materials and Looseleaf Services | 251 |
| 10 | Commercial Databases | 279 |
| 11 | Practice Rules | 303 |
| 12 | Ethical Rules | 313 |
| 13 | Practitioner's Materials | 321 |
| 14 | Research Strategy | 329 |

**PART 2 LEGAL WRITING**                                               **343**
**CHAPTERS**
    15   Getting Ready to Write                                       345
    16   Clear Writing and Editing                                    355
    17   Writing Basics                                               365
    18   Case Briefing and Analysis                                   377
    19   The Legal Memorandum                                         419
    20   Questions Presented and Conclusions or Brief Answers         431
    21   Facts                                                        443
    22   The IRAC Method                                              465
    23   Synthesizing Cases and Authorities                           481
    24   Outlining and Organizing a Memorandum                        497
    25   Letter Writing                                               529

    *Appendix A*   *Shepardizing and Cite Checking*                   *553*
    *Appendix B*   *Citation*                                         *557*
    *Appendix C*   *Sample Memoranda*                                 *573*
    *Appendix D*   *Helpful Websites*                                 *583*

    *Index*                                                            *593*

# CONTENTS

List of Illustrations                                                    *xxxiii*
Preface                                                                    *xxxix*
Acknowledgments                                                              *xli*


## PART 1   LEGAL RESEARCH                                                      1

### CHAPTER 1   INTRODUCTION TO LEGAL
                RESEARCH                                                        3

*CHAPTER OVERVIEW*                                                              3

**A. INTRODUCTION TO LEGAL RESEARCH
   AND WRITING**                                                               4
   **1. The Role of the Paralegal in Legal Research and Writing**              4
   Why Do Paralegals Perform Research?                                         4
   What Tasks Do Paralegals Handle in the
      Research and Writing Process?                                            4

**B. INTRODUCTION TO THE U.S. LEGAL SYSTEM**                                   5
   **1. The Organization of the Legal System**                                5
   How Did the Federal and State Systems Originate?                           6
   **2. Components of the Federal System and Governing Law**                  6

a.  **The Legislative Branch**                                          6
How Is a Law Created?                                                   7
b.  **The Executive Branch**                                           7
c.  **The Judicial Branch**                                            9
Who Can Bring an Action in Federal Court?                             10
   *i.  The Trial Courts*                               11
   *ii. The Appellate Courts*                           11
   *iii. The Supreme Court*                             12
3.  **Relationship Between Federal and State Governments**            14
Can a Federal Court Decide an Issue of State Law?                     14
What Effect Does a Federal Decision Have on State Law?                14
Are Federal and State Agencies Part of One Governing Body?            14
4.  **Organization of State Governments**                             14
What Are the Duties of the State Courts?                              15
Can State Courts Decide Issues of Federal Law?                        16

*Chapter Summary*                                                     16
*Key Terms*                                                           17
*Exercises*                                                           17

## CHAPTER 2   LEGAL AUTHORITIES AND HOW TO USE THEM

                                                                  19

*CHAPTER OVERVIEW*                                                    19

A.  **DETERMINATION OF GOVERNING LAW**                               20
1.  **Jurisdiction**                                                 20
What Factors Determine Which Jurisdiction Governs Your Case?         20
2.  **Precedent**                                                    20
3.  **Hierarchy of Authorities**                                     21
a.  **Currency**                                                     21
b.  **Levels of Court**                                              22
c.  **Conflicting Decisions Between Circuits**                       23
d.  **State and Federal Decisions Concerning an Issue**              24
e.  **Conflicts in Federal and State Authority**                     24
f.  **State Court Decisions**                                        25
4.  **Dicta**                                                        25

B.  **TYPES OF LEGAL RESOURCES**                                     25
1.  **Primary Authority**                                            25
How Do You Determine Whether a Case Is Mandatory
  or Binding?                                               26
2.  **Secondary Authority**                                          27
3.  **Finding Tools**                                                28
4.  **Hybrid Sources of Authority**                                  29
5.  **Nonlegal Sources**                                             29

**C. USE OF AUTHORITIES OR SOURCES IN YOUR
   LEGAL WRITING**    29
  1. **Essential Sources to Cite**    29
  2. **Valuable Sources to Cite**    30
  3. **Sources Never to Cite**    30
  4. **Checklist**    30

*In-Class Exercise*    31
*Chapter Summary*    31
*Key Terms*    32
*Exercises*    32

**CHAPTER 3    COURT DECISIONS**    35

*CHAPTER OVERVIEW*    35

**A. REPORTERS**    35
  1. **Bench Opinions**    36
  2. **Slip Opinions**    36
     a. **Supreme Court Slip Opinions**    39
     b. **Other Slip Opinions**    39
     How Are Pending or Unreported Opinions Such as Slip
        Opinions Cited?    39
  3. **Advance Sheets**    40
  4. **Bound Reporters**    40
     a. **U.S. Supreme Court Decisions**    40
     Is U.S. Supreme Court Docket Information Available on the Internet?    43
     What Happens if the Language of a Decision in the Commercial
        Reporters Varies from the Language in *U.S. Reports?*    43
     Why Use the Commercial Reporters Rather Than the Official
        Reports?    43
     How Do You Locate a Reported Case?    47
     How Are U.S. Supreme Court Cases Cited?    53
     b. **Other Federal Case Reporters**    53
     Where Do You Find Decisions of Other Federal Courts?    53
     How Are *Federal Reporter* and *Federal Supplement* Decisions
        Cited?    55
     Are Decisions Published in Any Other Reporters?    55
  5. **Computerized Reporting**    55
     Can You Find Decisions on the Internet and Through Fee-Based
        Computer Services?    55
     How Do You Know Whether a Case Is Published or Only
        Available Online?    58
     How Are Decisions Reported Only on Westlaw or Lexis Cited?    58

**6. State Reporters**    59

Where Can You Find State Court Decisions?    59

Are There Any Unofficial Reports of State Cases?    59

Why Would You Use the Regional Reporter Rather Than the
Official State Reporter?    60

How Are State Cases Cited?    68

*Chapter Summary*    70

*Key Terms*    70

*Exercises*    71

**CHAPTER 4   DIGESTS**    73

*CHAPTER OVERVIEW*    73

**A. CONTENT OF DIGESTS AND ORGANIZATION**    74

What Are Digests, and What Do They Contain?    74

**1. Headnotes and Key Numbers**    75

**2. Types of Digests**    77

**3. Organization of Digests**    78

How Are Digest Systems Organized?    78

**B. STEP-BY-STEP GUIDE TO THE DIGEST SYSTEM**    83

How Do You Use a Digest System?    83

**1. Descriptive Word Index Method**    83

What Is the Descriptive Word Index Method?    83

**2. Topic Outline Method**    86

What Is the Topic Outline Method?    86

**3. One Good Case Method**    86

What Is the One Good Case Method?    86

Are There Any Other Ways to Find Cases in the Digests?    93

Once You Have a Relevant Topic or Key Number, What
Comes Next?    93

What Are Pocket Parts?    93

How Do You Use the Pocket Parts?    93

**4. Online Digest Search**    93

Can Digests Be Searched Online?    93

*Chapter Summary*    115

*Key Terms*    115

*Exercises*    115

## CHAPTER 5   VALIDATING                                             119

*CHAPTER OVERVIEW*                                                    119

**A.  *SHEPARD'S***                                                   119
What Is a Citator?                                                    119
What Do You Learn from Reviewing *Shepard's* Citations?              120
How Do You Use *Shepard's* in Print?                                 131
Which Citator Should You Consult for State Cases?                    135

**B.  *SHEPARD'S* ONLINE**                                           136
How Do You Use *Shepard's* Online?                                   136
Is *Shepard's* Online More Current Than *Shepard's* in Print?        136
How Is *Shepard's* Different Online Than in Hard Copy?               136

**C.  KEYCITE**                                                      140
What Is the Difference Between *Shepard's* and KeyCite?              145
Why Would You Use Both KeyCite and *Shepard's*?                      145
How Do I Access KeyCite?                                             145

**D.  GLOBALCITE**                                                   146

*Chapter Summary*                                                    147
*Key Terms*                                                          147
*Exercises*                                                          147


## CHAPTER 6   SECONDARY AUTHORITY                                    151

*CHAPTER OVERVIEW*                                                    151

**A.  SECONDARY AUTHORITY: WHAT IT IS AND
WHERE TO FIND IT**                                                   152
What Is Secondary Authority?                                         152
Why and When Do You Use a Secondary Source?                          152
What Are the Sources of Secondary Authority?                         153

**B.  DICTIONARIES**                                                 153
What Is a Legal Dictionary?                                          153
When Would a Legal Dictionary Be Used?                               154
How Would You Cite to a Legal Dictionary?                            154
Are Legal Dictionaries Available Online?                             154

**C.  THE LEGAL THESAURUS**                                          154
What Is a Thesaurus?                                                 154
Why Would You Use a Thesaurus?                                       157

**D. ENCYCLOPEDIAS**                                                                 157
  **1. Generally**                                                         157
    What Is a Legal Encyclopedia?                                 157
    Why Would You Use an Encyclopedia?                            157
    When Do You Cite an Encyclopedia as Authority?               158
  **2. *American Jurisprudence***                                          158
    What Is Contained in *American Jurisprudence*?                158
    How Do You Use Am. Jur.?                                      161
    What Is the Citation Format for Am. Jur.?                     165
  **3. *Corpus Juris Secundum***                                           165
    What Is Contained in *Corpus Juris Secundum*?                 165
    How Do You Use C.J.S.?                                        166
    How Is C.J.S. Cited?                                          166
  **4. State Law Encyclopedias**                                           170
    Are There Any Legal Encyclopedias for State Law?             170
  **5. Online Encyclopedia Services?**                                     170
    Are Legal Encyclopedias Available on Lexis or Westlaw?       170

**E. *AMERICAN LAW REPORTS***                                                       170
  What Are *American Law Reports*?                                          170
  How Do You Use A.L.R.?                                                    172
  Why Would You Use A.L.R.?                                                 177
  How Do You Cite to an A.L.R. Annotation?                                  177
  How Do You Update an A.L.R. Annotation?                                   178
  Can A.L.R. Annotations Be Shepardized?                                    178

**F. TREATISES AND HORNBOOKS**                                                      178
  What Are Treatises and Hornbooks?                                         178
  How Do You Find a Thorough Treatise or Hornbook?                          179
  Which Treatises Are Most Noteworthy?                                      179
  Why Do You Use a Treatise?                                                179
  How Do You Use a Treatise or Hornbook?                                    180
  Are Treatises Ever Relied on as Authority?                                180
  How Do You Cite to a Hornbook and a Treatise?                             180
  Are Treatises Available Online?                                           181
  How Are Treatises and Hornbooks Updated?                                  181

**G. RESTATEMENTS OF THE LAW**                                                      181
  What Are Restatements?                                                    181
  How Are the Restatements Updated?                                         182
  How Do You Use the Restatements?                                          182
  Can the Restatements Be Shepardized?                                      182
  Are the Restatements Available Online?                                    183
  How Are the Restatements Cited?                                           184

**H. LEGAL PERIODICALS**                                                            185
  What Are Legal Periodicals?                                               185
  Why Would You Use a Legal Periodical?                                     186

How Do You Obtain Relevant Legal Periodical Articles? 187
Are Legal Periodicals Available on Lexis and Westlaw? 188
How Do You Cite to a Law Review or Law Journal? 188
What Is a Blog? 188

*Chapter Summary* 189
*Key Terms* 189
*Exercises* 189


**CHAPTER 7   CONSTITUTIONS AND STATUTES** 193

*CHAPTER OVERVIEW* 193

**A. CONSTITUTIONS** 194
What Is a Constitution? 194
What Is the Relationship Between the Federal Constitution
and the State Constitutions? 194
Who Determines Whether a Statute Violates the U.S.
Constitution? 194
Can Federal and State Constitutions Be Validated? 194
Where Are Federal and State Constitutions Found? 194
How Do You Cite Federal or State Constitutions? 200
Are Constitutions Available on Lexis or Westlaw? 200
Are There Any Hard-Copy Digests or Other Finding Tools
That Assist with Researching Federal Constitutional Issues? 200

**B. STATUTES** 201
What Are Statutes? 201
**1. The Legislative Process** 201
How Is a Statute Created Through the Federal Legislative
Process? 201
What Are Slip Laws? 203
What Are Session Laws? 203
What Are the *Statutes at Large*? 203
What Is Codification? 204
**2. Reading and Understanding Statutes** 215
How Do You Read a Statute? 215
What Type of Legal Authority Are Statutes? 215
What is the Relationship Between Statutes and Case Law? 216
**3. How to Find Federal Statutes** 216
Where Are Federal Statutes Found? 216
How Often Is the U.S.C. Updated? 217
Is the U.S.C. the Only Codified Version of the Federal
Statutes? 217
What Do the Unofficial Codes Contain? 217

Is There Any Difference Between the U.S.C.S. and the
U.S.C.A.? 218
Why Would You Use an Annotated Set of the U.S.C.? 218
How Useful Are Annotated Statutes as Finding Tools? 219
What Are the Research Methods Used to Find Relevant Statutes? 219
How Do You Cite Federal Statutes? 221
**4. Validating and Updating Statutes** 226
How and Why Would You Validate Federal Statutes? 226
How Do You Update Statutes with Print Resources? 226
**5. How to Find State Statutes** 231
How Does State Statutory Research Compare with Federal
Statutory Research? 231
How Can You Tell Whether a State Code Is the Official or
the Unofficial Statutory Compilation? 232
**6. Researching Statutes Online** 234
Are the Federal Statutes Available on Lexis and Westlaw? 234
Are State Statutes Available on Lexis and Westlaw? 234
Can Statutes Be Validated on Lexis and Westlaw? 234
How Do You Update Federal Statutes Online? 234
Are Statutes Available on the Internet? 235

*Chapter Summary* 235
*Key Terms* 235
*Exercises* 235

**CHAPTER 8   LEGISLATIVE HISTORY** 237

*CHAPTER OVERVIEW* 237

**A. LEGISLATIVE INFORMATION** 237
**1. Finding the Text of Pending Legislation** 238
**2. Tracking Pending Legislation** 239

**B. LEGISLATIVE HISTORIES** 239
Where Do You Find Copies of Public Laws? 239
How Do You Research Legislative Histories of Laws That
Are Already Enacted? 240
How Do You Use U.S.C.C.A.N. in Conjunction with the
U.S.C.A.? 241
What Are Other Ways to Find Relevant Legislative
History in U.S.C.C.A.N.? 241
Is Legislative History Primary Authority? 245
How Do You Cite Legislative History Found in U.S.C.C.A.N.? 245
How Do You Cite to a Legislative History of a Statute? 245
What Are Some Other Sources of Legislative Information? 245

How Do You Research State Legislative Histories? 246
What Additional Sources for Legislative Information
  Are Available? 249


*Chapter Summary* 249
*Key Terms* 249
*Exercises* 249

## CHAPTER 9  ADMINISTRATIVE MATERIALS AND LOOSELEAF SERVICES

**CHAPTER 9  ADMINISTRATIVE MATERIALS AND
             LOOSELEAF SERVICES** 251

*CHAPTER OVERVIEW* 251

**A. INTRODUCTION** 252
  What Is Administrative Law? 252
  How Can Administrative Agencies Create Law When
    This Is the Job of Congress? 252
  How Do Administrative Agencies Operate? 252

**B. REGULATIONS** 253
  How Are Regulations Adopted? 253
  What Type of Authority Is an Administrative Regulation or Rule? 253

**C. FINDING ADMINISTRATIVE LAW** 253
  **1. Generally** 253
  Where Do You Find Federal Administrative Law? 253
  Where Do You Find State Administrative Law? 256
  **2. Specific Sources** 256
    **a. *Federal Register*** 256
  How Do You Use the *Federal Register* in Print? 257
  How Do You Search the *Federal Register* on the Internet? 263
  How Can You Use Lexis and Westlaw to Retrieve the *Federal
    Register*? 265
    **b. *Code of Federal Regulations*** 266
  How Often Is the C.F.R. Updated? 267
  How Do You Use the C.F.R. in Print? 267
  How Do You Search the C.F.R. on the Computer? 268
  Why Would You Use Old Regulations? 268
  How Do You Update and Validate Regulations? 268
  How Is the Updating Performed in Practice? 270
  How Do You Validate or Shepardize a C.F.R. Citation? 271
  How Are the C.F.R. and the *Federal Register* Cited? 274

**D. DECISIONS** 274
  What Else Do Administrative Agencies Do? 274
  What Kind of Authority Are Administrative Decisions? 275

Can Administrative Agency Decisions Be Shepardized? 275
Other Than the Agency Itself, Where Can You Find
  Administrative Agency Decisions? 275

**E. LOOSELEAF SERVICES** 275
  What Are Looseleaf Services? 275
  Can Looseleafs Be Retrieved Online? 276
  What Type of Authority Are Looseleaf Services? 276
  Researching Administrative Law: Summary 276

*Chapter Summary* 277
*Key Terms* 277
*Exercises* 278


**CHAPTER 10   COMMERCIAL DATABASES** 279

*CHAPTER OVERVIEW* 279

**A. INTRODUCTION** 280
  What Are the Benefits of Using Online Legal Research Systems? 281
  What Are the Major Disadvantages of Using Online Legal
    Research Systems? 282
  **1. Uses for Lexis, Westlaw, and Bloomberg Law** 282
  **2. Additional Features** 283

**B. SEARCHING WITH ONLINE LEGAL RESEARCH
  SYSTEMS** 284
  General Overview 284
  **1. The Basics** 285
  How Can You Filter the Information? 285
  **2. Search Formulation** 286
  What Is a Search or Query? 286
    **a. Connectors** 287
    **b. Quotations** 289
    **c. Plurals** 289
    **d. Irregular Plurals** 289
    **e. Hyphenated Words** 290
    **f. Noise Words or Articles** 290
    **g. Capitalizing Proper Nouns and Other Terms** 290
  **3. Other Ways to Restrict Your Search to Retrieve
    On-Point Information** 290
    **a. Date and Court Restrictors** 290
    **b. Other Restrictors** 291
    **c. Fields** 292
  Why Does Integrating Traditional and Computerized Resources
    Result in the Most Effective Computerized Legal Research? 292

4. **Retrieving the Results of Your Research** 293
   Are There Any Other Ways to Retrieve Documents? 294
5. **Point-and-Click Enhancements** 294
6. **Additional Features on Lexis and Westlaw** 294
7. **Comparing Lexis and Westlaw** 296
   a. **Differences Between Lexis and Westlaw** 296
   b. **Similarities Between Lexis and Westlaw** 296
   How Do You Use the Computer Most Efficiently? 297
   How Do You Cite to Cases Retrieved on Lexis and Westlaw? 297
   How Do You Cite a Decision Reported on Lexis? 297
   How Do You Indicate a Page or Screen Number for the Case? 298
   What Are the Other Sites for Computerized Legal Research? 298

*Chapter Summary* 299
*Key Terms* 300
*Exercises* 300


**CHAPTER 11   PRACTICE RULES** 303

*CHAPTER OVERVIEW* 303

A. **OVERVIEW OF RULES OF PRACTICE** 304
   What Are Rules of Practice? 304
   What Rules Govern Procedures in the Federal Courts? 304
   Do the Federal Rules Control Proceedings in State Courts? 304
   What Federal Courts Follow the Federal Rules of Civil Procedure? 304
   Are the Federal Trial Courts Governed by Any Other Rules? 304
   What Rules of Procedure Do Federal Appellate Courts Follow? 305
   What Rules Govern Practice Before the U.S. Supreme Court? 305

B. **RESEARCHING RULES OF PRACTICE** 306
   1. **Sources** 306
      Where Do You Find These Rules in the Print Materials? 306
      Are the Federal Rules Available Online? 306
   2. **Steps in Researching Rules and Court Decisions** 307
      How Do You Research a Federal Rule? 307
      How Do You Find Cases or Secondary Authorities That
         Interpret and Explain the Federal Rules? 307
      What Sources Are Available to Help Interpret These Rules? 308
      How Would You Cite the Various Federal Rules? 308
      How Would You Cite a Decision Contained in the
         *Federal Rules Decisions*? 309

C. **STATE RULES OF PRACTICE** 309
   What Rules Control the Conduct of State Proceedings? 309

Where Would You Find State Rules and Local Rules for
   State Courts?    309
Are Annotations for State Rules Available?    310
Are There Any Significant State Rule Treatises or Secondary
   Authorities?    310

**D. ENSURING CURRENCY**    310
How Do You Ensure That You Are Reviewing the Most Current
   Version of the Rule?    310
Can Federal Rules Be Validated Online?    311
Can State Rules Be Shepardized?    311
Can State Rules Be Shepardized Online?    311

*Chapter Summary*    311
*Key Terms*    311
*Exercises*    312


**CHAPTER 12    ETHICAL RULES**    313

*CHAPTER OVERVIEW*    313

**A. RULES OF PROFESSIONAL RESPONSIBILITY**    313
Is There a National Code of Ethics for Attorneys or Paralegals?    314
What Type of Authority Are These Rules and Cases?    314
When Would You Review the Rules for Ethical Conduct and the
   Applicable Cases?    315

**B. RESEARCHING ETHICAL QUESTIONS**    315
**1. Primary Sources and Annotated Sources**    315
What Is the Value of an Annotated Source for the Rules
   and Codes?    315
Where Can You Find the *ABA Model Rules of Professional Conduct?*    315
What Other Secondary Sources Are Useful for Ethics
   Researchers?    315
How Do You Use the Annotated Sources?    316
**2. Other Useful Authorities**    316
Do State Bar Associations Publish Ethics Opinions Similar to
   Those Prepared by the ABA?    316
**3. Research Process**    317
How Would You Research an Ethical Question?    317
Can You Find State Ethical Rules on Westlaw and Lexis?    317
Can Ethics Rules Be Validated?    317
**4. Sample Research Problem**    318
How Would You Cite an Ethics Rule Found in the *ABA
Model Rules of Professional Conduct?*    318
How Would You Cite an ABA Ethics Opinion?    318

*Chapter Summary*                                                    319
*Key Terms*                                                          319
*Exercises*                                                          319


## CHAPTER 13    PRACTITIONER'S MATERIALS                           321

*CHAPTER OVERVIEW*                                                   321

### A.  FORMS                                                        321
Where Can Forms Be Found?                                           322

### B.  OTHER PRACTITIONER'S MATERIALS                              323
   **1. Checklists**                                                323
   Do Any Publications or Websites Contain Lists of What Steps
       You Should Follow to Complete a Project?                     323
   **2. Continuing Legal Education Materials**                      323
   Are CLE Materials Available Online?                              324
   How Do You Find CLE Materials?                                   324
   **3. Handbooks**                                                 324
   What Other Valuable Practitioner's Materials Are Available?      324
   **4. Jury Instructions**                                         324
   What Are Pattern Jury Instructions, and How Do They Differ
       from Other Jury Instructions?                                324
   Do the Federal Courts Have Pattern Jury Instructions and Where
       Can They Be Found?                                           325
   What Type of Research Should Be Done Before You Draft
       Jury Instructions?                                           325
   **5. Other Tools**                                               325
   What Other Tools Might a Paralegal Use in Researching a
       Problem?                                                     325
   How Do You Locate Lawyers and Law Firms in Other States
       or Within a State?                                           326

*Chapter Summary*                                                    326
*Key Terms*                                                          327
*Exercises*                                                          327


## CHAPTER 14    RESEARCH STRATEGY                                  329

*CHAPTER OVERVIEW*                                                   329

### A.  DEFINE THE ISSUES AND DETERMINE AREA OF LAW                 330
Where Do You Begin Your Research?                                   330

**B. REFINING RESEARCH**    330

How Do You Refine Your Research Strategy?    330

**C. DIAGRAMMING THE RESEARCH PROCESS**    332

What Is the Purpose and Technique for Record Keeping?    332

Example of Record Keeping    333

**D. EXAMPLE OF RESEARCH STRATEGY**    334

   1. **How to Phrase the Issue If You Are Researching the Fur Labeling Problem**    334

   2. **First Steps**    334

   3. **What Sources to Consult and Why**    335

   4. **What to Do After Completing Your Research**    336

   5. **Combining Computerized Research Methods with Hard-Copy Method**    337

   6. **Using Online Services in the Fur Labeling Problem**    337

*Chapter Summary*    340

*Key Terms*    340

*Exercises*    340

# PART 2    LEGAL WRITING

343

# CHAPTER 15    GETTING READY TO WRITE

345

*CHAPTER OVERVIEW*    345

**A. WRITING GOALS AND HOW TO ACHIEVE THEM**    346

How Do You Plan Your Communication and Revise It?    346

**B. THE WRITING PROCESS**    346

   1. **Preparing to Write: Purpose and Audience**    346

How Do You Complete the Research Process and Make the Transition to Writing?    346

    a. **Purpose**    347

What Is the Purpose of the Document?    347

    b. **Audience**    348

To Whom Are You Speaking?    348

   2. **Drafting a Detailed Outline**    348

How Do You Organize Your Ideas?    348

   3. **Revision: The Final Part of the Process**    349

   4. **Example of Process Writing Techniques**    350

*Chapter Summary*                                                          351
*Key Terms*                                                                352
*Exercises*                                                                352


## CHAPTER 16   CLEAR WRITING AND EDITING                                 355

*CHAPTER OVERVIEW*                                                        355

### A.  PURPOSE OF EDITING                                                355

### B.  PROCESS OF EDITING                                                356

### C.  SPECIFIC ITEMS TO REVIEW WHILE EDITING                            357
  1. **Diction**                                                         357
     What Is Diction?                                                     357
     What Are Concrete Verbs?                                             357
     How Do You Avoid Legalese or Legal Speak?                           358
  2. **Voice**                                                           359
     What Is the Difference Between Active Voice and Passive Voice?       359
  3. **Paragraphs**                                                      360
  4. **Sentences**                                                       360
  5. **Other Key Rules**                                                 361
     **Revision Checklist**                                              362

*Chapter Summary*                                                         362
*Key Terms*                                                               362
*Exercises*                                                               363


## CHAPTER 17   WRITING BASICS                                            365

*CHAPTER OVERVIEW*                                                        365

### A.  PUNCTUATION                                                       366
  1. **Commas**                                                          366
  2. **Special Comma Rules**                                             367
  3. **Semicolons**                                                      368
  4. **Colons**                                                          368
  5. **Parentheses**                                                     369
  6. **Double Quotation Marks**                                          369
  7. **Single Quotation Marks**                                          369

### B.  MODIFIERS                                                         369

### C.  PARALLEL CONSTRUCTION                                             370

**D. SUBJECT AND VERB AGREEMENT** — 370

**E. RUN-ON SENTENCES** — 372

**F. SENTENCE FRAGMENTS** — 373

**G. THAT AND WHICH** — 373

*Chapter Summary* — 373
*Key Terms* — 374
*Exercises* — 374

**CHAPTER 18    CASE BRIEFING AND ANALYSIS** — 377

*CHAPTER OVERVIEW* — 377

**A. PURPOSE OF A CASE BRIEF** — 378

**B. DIAGRAM OF A DECISION** — 378

**C. ANATOMY OF A CASE BRIEF** — 381
  **1. Citation** — 381
  **2. Procedural History** — 384
  **3. Issues** — 386
  How Do You Determine the Legal Issue or Issues
    Presented When Examining a Client's Problem? — 386
  How Do You Draft a Statement of the Issue or Issues? — 386
  **4. Holding** — 388
  How Do You Draft a Holding? — 388
  **5. Facts** — 389
  What Are the Relevant Facts? — 389
  How Do You Organize Your Facts Statements? — 390
  **6. Reasoning** — 392
  **7. Dicta** — 394
  **8. Disposition** — 394

*In-Class Exercise* — 396

**D. CASE ANALYSIS** — 405
  **1. Sample Single Case Analysis** — 405
  **2. Sample Analysis Using Two Cases** — 412

*Chapter Summary* — 414
*Key Terms* — 415
*Exercises* — 415

## CHAPTER 19   THE LEGAL MEMORANDUM             419

*CHAPTER OVERVIEW*                                419

**A. THE LEGAL MEMORANDUM**                      420
    What Is an Objective Legal Memorandum and Why Is
      It Written?                                420

**B. AUDIENCE**                                  420
    Who Reads a Memorandum?                      420

**C. COMPONENTS OF A MEMORANDUM**                421
    What Is Included in a Memorandum?            421
    **1. Heading**                               423
    **2. Questions Presented or Issues**         425
    **3. Conclusion or Brief Answer**            425
    What Is the Difference Between a Conclusion and a
      Brief Answer?                            426
    **4. Facts**                                 426
    **5. Discussion**                            427

**D. STEPS IN DRAFTING A MEMORANDUM**            427
    What Steps Should You Take in Drafting a Memo?   427
    Checklist for Drafting a Memorandum          428
    **1. Memo Drafting Tips**                    429

*Chapter Summary*                                429
*Key Terms*                                      429
*Exercises*                                      430


## CHAPTER 20   QUESTIONS PRESENTED AND
##                        CONCLUSIONS OR BRIEF ANSWERS      431

*CHAPTER OVERVIEW*                                431

**A. QUESTIONS PRESENTED OR ISSUES**             431
    Who Reads the Questions Presented Statement?   432
    **1. First Draft**                           432
    What Are Legally Significant Facts?          433
    **2. Research the Issue and Revise It**       433
    **3. Specificity and Precision**             434

**B. BRIEF ANSWERS AND CONCLUSIONS**             435
    **1. Brief Answers**                         435

**2. Conclusions** 436
How Is a Conclusion Different from a Brief Answer? 436
**3. Drafting Conclusions** 436

*Chapter Summary* 439
*Key Terms* 439
*Exercises* 439

## CHAPTER 21   FACTS 443

*CHAPTER OVERVIEW* 443

**A. FACTS STATEMENT** 444
   **1. Defining** *Fact* 444
   **2. Legally Significant Facts** 444
   What Facts Should Be Included in the Facts Statement? 444
   **3. Fact Versus a Legal Conclusion** 446
   **4. Source of Information for a Facts Statement** 447

**B. ORGANIZING THE FACTS STATEMENT** 447
   What Are the Different Methods of Organizing a Facts Statement? 447
   **1. Chronological Organization** 447
   **2. Organization by Claim or Defense** 448
   **3. Organization by Party** 449
   **4. Combination of Chronological and Claim or Party Organization** 450

**C. WRITING THE FACTS STATEMENT** 453
   **1. Prepare a List of Facts and Preliminary Statement** 453
   **2. Research the Issue** 454
   **3. Revise to Include Only Legally Significant Facts** 455
   **4. Organize the Facts** 455
   **5. Rewrite the Facts Statement** 456

*Chapter Summary* 456
*Key Terms* 457
*Exercises* 457

## CHAPTER 22   THE IRAC METHOD 465

*CHAPTER OVERVIEW* 465

**A. PURPOSES OF IRAC** 466
   What Is IRAC? 466

**B. IRAC COMPONENTS**     466
What Does an IRAC Paragraph Look Like?     466
  **1. Issues**     468
    What Is the Difference Between the Question Presented
    and the Issues in IRAC Paragraphs?     468
  **2. Rules of Law**     469
    Why Is Citation Important?     470
  **3. Application of the Law to the Problem's Facts**     471
    How Do You Use the Legally Significant Facts?     471
  **4. Conclusion**     472

*Chapter Summary*     472
*Key Terms*     473
*Exercises*     473

**CHAPTER 23    SYNTHESIZING CASES AND
AUTHORITIES**     481

*CHAPTER OVERVIEW*     481

**A. SYNTHESIS**     482
What Is the Process of Synthesizing Legal Rules?     482
Why Do We Synthesize Legal Authority?     482

**B. TYPES OF SYNTHESIS**     483
What Are the Four Methods of Synthesizing Authority?     483

**C. STEP-BY-STEP PROCESS TO SYNTHESIZING LEGAL
RULES**     483

**D. EXAMPLES OF CASE SYNTHESIS**     485
How Do You Synthesize Two Sources of Statutory Authority?     492

*Chapter Summary*     494
*Key Terms*     494
*Exercises*     494

**CHAPTER 24    OUTLINING AND ORGANIZING
A MEMORANDUM**     497

*CHAPTER OVERVIEW*     497

**A. PURPOSE OF OUTLINING**     498

**B. STEPS TO OUTLINING**     498
   1. **Steps in Compiling a List of Legal Authorities**     498
   2. **Organize Issues**     501
     What Steps Should You Follow in Preparing Your Outline of
     Each of the Issues?     502
   3. **Draft a Thesis Paragraph**     502
   4. **Determine Which Element to Discuss First**     503
   5. **List Elements or Subissues**     503
   6. **Add Authority**     504
   7. **Refine Issues**     504
   8. **Arrange the Order of Elements**     504
   9. **Organize into IRAC Paragraph**     504

**C. MULTI-ISSUE MEMORANDUM**     505
     How Do You Organize a Multi-Issue Memorandum?     505

*In-Class Exercise*     517
*Chapter Summary*     519
*Key Terms*     520
*Exercises*     520

**CHAPTER 25   LETTER WRITING**     529

*CHAPTER OVERVIEW*     529

**A. BASICS OF LETTER WRITING**     530
     What Formats Are Used?     530

**B. COMPONENTS OF A LETTER**     530
   1. **Letterhead and Headers**     530
   2. **Date**     532
   3. **Method of Transmission**     532
   4. **Inside Address**     532
   5. **Reference Line**     533
   6. **Greeting**     533
   7. **Body of Letter**     533
   8. **Closing**     534
   9. **Copies to Others and Enclosures**     535

**C. TYPES OF LETTERS**     536
   1. **Confirming Letters**     536
   2. **Status Letters and Transaction Summary Letters**     536
   3. **Demand Letter**     542
   4. **Opinion Letters**     543
   5. **E-mail**     545
   6. **Social Media**     547

| | | |
|---|---|---:|
| *Chapter Summary* | | 548 |
| *Key Terms* | | 549 |
| *Exercises* | | 549 |
| | | |
| *Appendix A* | *Shepardizing and Cite Checking* | 553 |
| *Appendix B* | *Citation* | 557 |
| *Appendix C* | *Sample Memoranda* | 573 |
| *Appendix D* | *Helpful Websites* | 583 |
| | | |
| *Index* | | 593 |

# LIST OF
# ILLUSTRATIONS

| | | |
|---|---|---|
| 1-1 | U.S. and State Government Systems | 5 |
| 1-2 | The Government of the United States | 8 |
| 1-3 | Federal Judicial System | 10 |
| 1-4 | Circuit Map of the U.S. Courts of Appeals | 13 |
| 2-1 | Example of Ranking Authorities | 22 |
| 2-2 | Authorities and Finding Tools | 26 |
| 3-1 | A Portion of a Supreme Court Slip Opinion | 37 |
| 3-2 | Pages from *U.S. Reports, United Paperworkers Intl. Union, AFL-CIO, et al. v. Misco, Inc.*, 484 U.S. 29 (1987) | 41 |
| 3-3 | Pages from *Supreme Court Reporter, United Paperworkers Intl. Union, AFL-CIO, et al. v. Misco, Inc.*, 108 S. Ct. 364-365, 370 (1987) | 44 |
| 3-4 | *West's North Eastern Reporter, Thompson v. Economy Super Marts, Inc., 581 N.E.2d 885 (Ill. App. Ct. 1991)* | 48 |
| 3-5 | *West's Federal Reporter and Federal Supplement Coverage* | 54 |
| 3-6 | Finding a Case in Westlaw | 56 |
| 3-7 | Finding a Case in Lexis | 57 |
| 3-8 | West's Regional Reporters Coverage | 59 |
| 3-9 | West's National Reporter System | 60 |
| 3-10 | West Case Report, *Kellermann v. Car City Chevrolet-Nissan*, 713 N.E.2d 1285 (Ill. App. Ct. 1999) | 61 |
| 4-1 | West's Digest Topics | 74 |
| 4-2 | Assorted Digests | 77 |
| 4-3 | Sample Pages from *West's Illinois Digest* | 79 |
| 4-4 | Key Number Translation Table from *West's Illinois Digest 2d* | 82 |

| | | |
|---|---|---|
| 4-5 | Results of Brainstorming Session | 84 |
| 4-6 | Sample Page from West's *Illinois Digest 2d* Descriptive Word Index | 85 |
| 4-7 | *West's Illinois Digest 2d* Topic Outline | 87 |
| 4-8 | *West's Massachusetts Digest* Page | 92 |
| 4-9 | Pocket Part Page from *Illinois Digest 2d* | 94 |
| 4-10 | Westlaw Printout of Case *Green v. Jewel Food Stores* | 95 |
| 4-11 | Westlaw Key Number Search Page | 102 |
| 4-12 | Westlaw Online Topics | 103 |
| 4-13 | Expanded List of Westlaw Topics and Key Numbers for Premises Liability and Standard of Care | 104 |
| 4-14 | Sample Westlaw Custom Digest | 106 |
| 4-15 | Westlaw Key Number Search Page Using Terms and Sample Results | 108 |
| 4-16A | List of Lexis Legal Topics on Lexis | 109 |
| 4-16B | List of Lexis Legal Topics on Lexis Advance | 110 |
| 4-17 | Expanded List of Lexis Legal Topics for Torts and Premises Liability | 112 |
| 4-18 | Lexis Search Page from LexisNexis Library Express | 113 |
| 4-19 | Results of LexisNexis Search of Terms Business Invitee, Store Owner, and Premises Liability | 114 |
| 5-1 | *Shepard's Northeastern Reporter Citations*, 2007 Volume 12, *Thompson v. Economy Super Marts, Inc.*, 581 N.E.2d 885 | 121 |
| 5-2A | Lexis Online *Shepard's* Report for *Thompson v. Economy Super Marts*, 581 N.E.2d 885 | 122 |
| 5-2B | Lexis Advance Online *Shepard's* Report for *Thompson v. Economy Super Marts, Inc.*, 581 N.E.2d 885 | 127 |
| 5-3 | *Shepard's Northeastern Reporter Citations*, *Ward v. K-Mart Corp.*, 554 N.E.2d 223 (Ill. 1990) | 128 |
| 5-4 | *Shepard's* Case Citations | 132 |
| 5-5 | Front Cover of a *Shepard's* Cumulative Supplement Detailing Volumes and Pamphlets to Review | 133 |
| 5-6 | Page from *Shepard's Illinois Citations* | 134 |
| 5-7A | *Shepard's* Search Screen on LexisNexis | 136 |
| 5-7B | *Shepard's* Search Screen on Lexis Advance | 137 |
| 5-8 | *Shepard's* Online Signal Indications | 138 |
| 5-9 | Screen Shots of Westlaw KeyCite Result for *Thompson v. Economy Super Marts, Inc.* | 141 |
| 5-10 | Westlaw KeyCite Result Showing Secondary Sources to Review for *Thompson v. Economy Super Marts, Inc.* | 143 |
| 5-11 | Westlaw KeyCite Result Showing Appellate Court Documents to Review for *Thompson v. Economy Super Marts, Inc.* | 144 |
| 5-12 | Westlaw KeyCite Result Showing Trial Court Documents to Review for *Thompson v. Economy Super Marts, Inc.* | 145 |
| 5-13 | Loislaw GlobalCite Results for *Thompson v. Economy Super Marts, Inc.* | 146 |
| 6-1 | Definition of *Easement* in *Black's Law Dictionary* | 155 |

| | | |
|---|---|---|
| 6-2 | Topic Outline for Easements and Licenses at 25 Am. Jur. 2d 495 (2004) | 159 |
| 6-3 | Portion of Easement Entry at 25 Am. Jur. 2d § 90 (2004) | 161 |
| 6-4 | Cover and Sample Page Pocket Part for Volume 25 Am. Jur. 2d | 162 |
| 6-5 | Am. Jur. 2d General Index, Sample Pages | 164 |
| 6-6 | 28A C.J.S. Easements § 18 from Westlaw, current through December 2013 | 167 |
| 6-7 | Total Client-Service Library References at 36 A.L.R.4th 769 (1985) | 171 |
| 6-8 | Outline of Annotation at 36 A.L.R.4th 770 (1985) | 172 |
| 6-9 | Table of Cases, Laws, and Rules at 36 A.L.R.4th 771 (1985) from Westlaw | 173 |
| 6-10 | A.L.R. Index Entry | 175 |
| 6-11 | Sample Pages from Restatement (Second) of Contracts | 183 |
| 6-12 | Table of Contents from Restatement (Second) of Contracts | 185 |
| 7-1 | Sample Page, Retrieved from Lexis, Showing Analysis of Fourth Amendment with Citing Decisions | 195 |
| 7-2 | Page from Decision in *U.S. Reports* That Discusses the Fourth Amendment | 198 |
| 7-3 | Sample Session Law Published in *Statutes at Large* | 205 |
| 7-4 | Table of U.S.C. Titles from the U.S.C.S. | 206 |
| 7-5 | Sample Page Showing 15 U.S.C. § 68 (2012) | 207 |
| 7-6 | Sample Pages Showing 15 U.S.C.A. § 68 (West 2009) | 208 |
| 7-7 | Sample Pages Showing 15 U.S.C.S. § 68 Accessed on LexisAdvance.com | 211 |
| 7-8 | U.S.C.A. Popular Name Table | 220 |
| 7-9 | U.S.C.A. *Statutes at Large* and Public Law Numbers Table | 222 |
| 7-10 | U.S.C.A. General Index | 223 |
| 7-11 | Outline of Sections in Title 15 U.S.C.A., Commerce and Trade, §§ 68-68j, Labeling of Wool Products | 224 |
| 7-12 | Pages from *Decision in the Federal Reporter* That Cites to 15 U.S.C. § 68 | 227 |
| 7-13 | Sample Page from *Shepard's* on Lexis Showing Treatment of U.S.C. References | 229 |
| 7-14 | Pocket Part Entry for 15 U.S.C.A. § 68 | 230 |
| 7-15 | Sample Page Showing Vermont Statues Annotated, 9 V.S.A. § 2698, *available at* www.leg.state.vt.us/statutes | 233 |
| 8-1 | Sample Pages from U.S.C.C.A.N. Showing Pub. L. No. 96-242 | 242 |
| 8-2 | Sample Pages from U.S.C.C.A.N. Showing the Legislative History of Pub. L. No. 96-242 | 243 |
| 8-3 | Congress.gov Search Results for 113th Congress and Bills Containing "clothing textiles" | 247 |
| 9-1 | Sample Pages from the *Code of Federal Regulations* | 254 |
| 9-2 | Federal Digital System | 257 |
| 9-3 | Table of Contents Page of the *Federal Register* | 258 |
| 9-4A | Sample *Federal Register* Page | 259 |
| 9-4B | Sample *Federal Register* Page | 260 |

| | | |
|---|---|---|
| 9-5 | List of Federal Publications | 264 |
| 9-6 | Index Page from www.federalregister.gov | 265 |
| 9-7 | L.S.A. Monthly Pamphlet Page | 269 |
| 9-8 | Reader's Aids of the *Federal Register* Page with CFR Parts Affected Shown | 270 |
| 9-9 | CFR Parts Affected for the Month | 272 |
| 11-1 | Courts and the Applicable Rules | 305 |
| 18-1 | Sample Case, *Seymour v. Armstrong* | 379 |
| 18-2 | Sample Case, *King v. Miller* | 381 |
| 18-3 | Sample Case Brief, *King v. Miller* | 384 |
| 18-4 | Case Briefing Process | 395 |
| 18-5 | *Molitor v. Chicago Title & Trust Co.* | 396 |
| 18-6 | Case Brief for *Molitor v. Chicago Title & Trust Co.* | 400 |
| 18-7 | *Heuvelman v. Triplett Elec. Instrument Co.* | 401 |
| 18-8 | Case Brief for *Heuvelman v. Triplett Elec. Instrument Co.* | 403 |
| 18-9 | *Shila Morganroth, Plaintiff-Appellant v. Susan Whitall and The Evening News Association, Inc.* | 405 |
| 18-10 | Brief of *Morganroth v. Whitall* | 410 |
| 19-1 | Sample Memorandum | 421 |
| 19-2 | Sample Memorandum: McMillan Battery Action | 423 |
| 19-3 | Sample Memorandum Heading | 425 |
| 19-4 | Question Presented | 425 |
| 19-5 | Brief Answer | 426 |
| 19-6 | Conclusion | 426 |
| 19-7 | Facts Statement | 427 |
| 20-1 | Question Presented | 434 |
| 20-2 | Question Presented and Brief Answer | 435 |
| 20-3 | Brief Answer | 436 |
| 20-4 | Questions Presented and Conclusions | 438 |
| 21-1 | Chronological Organization | 448 |
| 21-2 | Reverse Chronological Order | 448 |
| 21-3 | Organization by Claim or Defense | 449 |
| 21-4 | Organization by Party | 450 |
| 21-5 | Chronological and Claim Organization | 451 |
| 21-6 | Chronological and Party Organization | 452 |
| 21-7 | Excerpt from a Client Interview | 453 |
| 21-8 | Sample Preliminary Facts Statement Based on the Client Interview | 454 |
| 21-9 | List of Legally Significant Facts | 455 |
| 21-10 | Sample Facts Statement for Slip-and-Fall Case | 456 |
| 24-1 | List of Authorities | 499 |
| 24-2 | Outline of Battery Discussion | 499 |
| 24-3 | Memorandum: McMillan Battery Action | 500 |
| 24-4 | Thesis Paragraph | 503 |
| 24-5 | Multi-Issue Memorandum: McMillan Battery Action | 507 |
| 24-6 | Multi-Issue Outline | 512 |
| 24-7 | Writing from an Outline | 516 |
| 24-8 | Sample Memorandum Slip-and-Fall Case | 517 |

| 25-1 | Full Block Letter | 531 |
| 25-2 | Letter Confirming Deposition | 535 |
| 25-3 | Letter Concerning Deposition Schedule | 537 |
| 25-4 | Letter Enclosing Deposition Transcript | 538 |
| 25-5 | Status Report Letter | 539 |
| 25-6 | Request for Information | 540 |
| 25-7 | Request to Produce Documents | 541 |
| 25-8 | Letter Accompanying Document | 542 |
| 25-9 | Letter Accompanying Check | 544 |
| 25-10 | Demand Letter | 545 |

# PREFACE

As paralegals, you can be invaluable to attorneys and clients when you have adequately mastered legal research and writing skills. This book is a step-by-step guide that explores the twists and turns of legal research and writing, teaching you how to avoid the dead ends and conquer obstacles along the way. Examples, exercises, and checklists help make it a smooth and enjoyable road.

Part 1 features an introduction to the legal system and legal authorities: the state and federal legislatures, the courts, and administrative agencies. It explains the relationship between state and federal governments and between other governing bodies.

The research component of Part 1 begins with print resources. Proficiency in hard-copy research will bring you greater success when performing research using a computer. You will also learn how to use online resources. All significant resources will be explored, and you will learn how they are interrelated and how to find the best sources for your particular project. Legal writing pointers are integrated throughout the research chapters where relevant.

Part 2 focuses on basic legal writing, with an emphasis on legal memoranda and letters—the most common documents that paralegals draft. Objective memos inform the attorney of all of the relevant law, both for and against the client's position. Having paralegals brief cases expedites the research process. Delegating research and writing tasks to the paralegal is cost-effective for the client and saves the client money.

Part 2 also guides you step-by-step through the legal writing process. You will be introduced to the case brief, the legal memorandum, the questions presented statement, the brief answer, and the facts statement. You will learn how to identify the legal issues and relevant facts of a case and how to

organize and present them in a written brief or memorandum. As the culmination of your legal writing skills, you will learn to synthesize—to distill a general legal concept that applies to a case and then state it in writing (citing more than one case or statute). Synthesis is essential to writing most case-related documents. A clear methodology—IRAC—will introduce you to the important components of synthesis: Issue, Rule, Application, and Conclusion. Using IRAC, you will learn to synthesize effectively and consistently.

A valuable reference tool, The Legal Research and Writing Handbook reviews letter writing, grammar, and editing—all essential skills you will use every day as a paralegal. Also, the examples and citation appendix will help you draft documents.

The Legal Research and Writing Workbook gives you hands-on exercises that reinforce the concepts in this textbook and provide you with practical applications for future work experiences. Practice pointers and ethics alerts included in this text are designed to guide you in your day-to-day work as a paralegal. This edition provides Net Notes to help you navigate the Internet to review points raised in the text. Computer resources, both paid and free, are integrated throughout the book.

You should view The Legal Research and Writing Handbook as a launching point from which to begin developing your research and writing skills. You will want to refer to the guidelines and concepts in this book throughout your career as you continue to expand in knowledge and experience.

July 2014

*Andrea B. Yelin*
*Hope Viner Samborn*

# ACKNOWLEDGMENTS

We would like to acknowledge all of the people who have helped us create this text and who have shaped its contents.

Thank you to Betsy Kenny for helping us to hone our continuing revisions of the text, the workbook, and the teacher's manual and for countless hours spent guiding us. Thanks to Lisa Wehrle for her great job copyediting the first and second editions of this text, and thanks to Tom Daughhetee of The Froebe Group for editing the seventh edition.

Thanks to Sylvia Rebert at Progressive Publishing Alternatives for her work on the sixth edition, to Julie Grady and Rebecca Logan for their assistance with the fifth edition, to Candice Adams for her assistance with the fourth edition, and to Peggy Rehberger, Melody Davies, Ellen Greenblatt, Curt Berkowitz, Suzanne Rapcavage, and Barbara Roth for their editing and additional help with the text. Thank you to Dave Herzig, Steve Silverstein, and Lou McGuire for their terrific marketing of the text.

Thanks to Loyola University Law School Library in Chicago, Thomson Reuters, Lexis/Nexis, Bureau of National Affairs, Shepard's, and the Arlington Heights Memorial Public Library for assistance in obtaining illustrations for this book.

Thanks also to Patricia Scott, Joe Mitzenmacher, Julie Grant, and Fred LeBaron of Loyola University Chicago Law School for all of your assistance past and present. A special debt of gratitude goes to Fred LeBaron, once again, for his invaluable wise counsel and professional guidance. Extra thanks to Matt Timko and Kaye Friberg for their help with the illustrations. Thank you to Eve Samborn, Ben Samborn, and Lauren Grodsky for their research contributions.

Thanks to our families and friends, whose continued support has helped us to revise this text.

We continue to be indebted to the people whose assistance, direction, and support led to the first edition of this text and ultimately this revised text as well as individuals who helped with our text Basic Legal Writing for Paralegals, a project that led to some of the revisions in this text.

To that end, we thank Jean Hellman Ryan, Director of the Loyola University Chicago, Institute for Paralegal Studies, who encouraged us to write our first book and who introduced us to Carolyn O'Sullivan of

Little, Brown and Company, the predecessor of Aspen. We cannot thank Carolyn O'Sullivan, Betsy Kenny, Lisa Wehrle, Joan Horan, John Lyman, and Katie Byrne Butcher enough for their assistance with our books.

We also thank our students who have helped us to hone the text and the exercises. Their writing and use of the exercises helped form the skeleton for the book and then mold its contents. Their continued use of the book assisted us in revising the text. Our students have taught us more than we ever could teach them, and we appreciate all that they have done. Some of our students who deserve special thanks for their critiques, suggestions, and encouragement include Kelly Barry, Amy Berezinski, Nanette Boryc, Mara Castello, Patricia Cochran, Jessie Cohen, Nan Crotty, Beverly Dombroski, Susanne Grant, Stephen Gromala, Chris Harrigan, Marion Kahle, Michael Luckey, Mitchell McClure, Brenda Mondul, Cheryl Morgan, Patricia Naqvi, Melissa Pederson, Shay Robertson, Louise Tessitore, and Amy Widmer.

Thanks to Terri Rudd, David Harris, Marc Steer, the late Debbie Freudenheim, and Linda Kahn for your insightful ideas and assistance.

We would also like to thank the reviewers listed below. Their careful review of the first manuscript and the Basic Legal Writing for Paralegals manuscript produced many valuable comments and suggestions. We greatly appreciate their efforts.

Jonathan H. Barker
George Washington University

Laura Barnard
Lakeland Community College

Suzanne Cascio
Manhattanville College

Charles E. Coleman
New York City Technical College

Holly L. Enterline
State Technical Institute at Memphis

Andrew T. Fede
Montclair State College

William J. Heimbuch
Montclair State College

Patricia Hohl
Boston University

Mary Holland
Manchester Community College

Paul Klein
Duquesne University

Gina-Marie Reitano
St. John's University

Brenda L. Rice, J.D.
Johnson County Community College

Kay Y. Rute
Washburn University

Helene Kulczycki
Briarcliffe, The College for Business and Technology

Adelaide Lagnese
University of Maryland

Cynthia B. Lauber
Denver Paralegal Institute

Sy Littman
Platt College

Judith M. McAuliffe
Quincy College

Robin O. McNeely
McNeese State University

Joy O'Donnell
Pima Community College

Eric Olson
Barry University

Elaine Puri
University of North Florida

Julia O. Tryk
Cuyahoga Community
College

Sue K. Varon
National Center for Paralegal
Training


Lastly, we would like to thank the following publishers for allowing us to reprint the illustrations listed below.

Illustrations 3-3, 3-4, and 3-6. Reprinted with permission of Thomson Reuters.

Illustration 3-7. Reprinted with the permission of LexisNexis.

Illustrations 3-9, 3-10, 4-1, 4-3, 4-4, 4-6, 4-7, 4-8, 4-9, 4-10, 4-11, 4-12, 4-13 4-14, and 4-15. Reprinted with permission of Thomson Reuters.

Illustrations 4-16A, 4-16B, 4-17, 4-18, 4-19, 5-1, 5-2A, 5-2B 5-3, 5-5, 5-6, 5-7A, 5-7B, and 5-8. Reprinted with the permission of LexisNexis. For Illustrations 4-19, 5-2A, 5-2B, and 5-7B, see online document for complete report.

Illustrations 5-9, 5-10, 5-11, and 5-12. Reprinted with permission of Thomson Reuters.

Illustration 5-13. Reprinted with permission of CCH INCORPORATED, a Wolters Kluwer Business. http://estore.loislaw.com/.

Illustrations 6-1, 6-2, 6-3, 6-4, 6-5, 6-6, 6-7, 6-8, 6-9, and 6-10. Reprinted with permission of Thomson Reuters.

Illustrations 6-11 and 6-12. Copyright © 1981 by the American Law Institute. Reprinted with permission. All rights reserved.

Illustration 7-1. Reprinted with the permission of LexisNexis. See online document for complete report.

Illustration 7-4. Reprinted with the permission of LexisNexis.

Illustration 7-6. Reprinted with permission of Thomson Reuters.

Illustration 7-7. Reprinted with the permission of LexisNexis.

Illustration 7-8, 7-9, 7-10, 7-11, and 7-12. Reprinted with permission of Thomson Reuters.

Illustration 7-13. Reprinted with the permission of LexisNexis. See online document for complete report.

Illustration 7-14 Reprinted with permission of Thomson Reuters.

Illustrations 8-1, 8-2, and 18-1. Reprinted with permission of Thomson Reuters.

Illustration 18-9. Reprinted with the permission of LexisNexis.

# PART 1

# LEGAL RESEARCH

## CHAPTER 1

# INTRODUCTION TO LEGAL RESEARCH

**A. INTRODUCTION TO LEGAL RESEARCH AND**     4
   **WRITING**
   1. The Role of the Paralegal in Legal Research and Writing     4
**B. INTRODUCTION TO THE U.S. LEGAL SYSTEM**     5
   1. The Organization of the Legal System     5
   2. Components of the Federal System and Governing Law     6
   3. Relationship Between Federal and State Governments     14
   4. Organization of State Governments     14

## *CHAPTER OVERVIEW*

Before you begin to research and to write about a legal problem, you must understand your role as a paralegal. You are an important member of a team. To function effectively, you must know which legal system governs and how that system operates. This chapter first considers your role in researching a legal problem and communicating it to your supervising attorney. Next, it discusses the legal system. It focuses on the organization of the U.S. federal government, which is divided into three separate branches: the legislative, the executive, and the judicial. It also provides a general explanation of how state governments are structured. Finally, the role of major governmental bodies is explored.

# A. INTRODUCTION TO LEGAL RESEARCH AND WRITING

## 1. The Role of the Paralegal in Legal Research and Writing

Legal research and legal writing are among the tasks paralegals can perform efficiently and cost-effectively for law firms and their clients. But to do so effectively, you must understand the legal system and a variety of legal concepts. You must be able to use all the research tools available to lawyers and their staffs. Paralegals retrieve information regarding the law as well as nonlegal information, such as financial information and test results.

### ▼ Why Do Paralegals Perform Research?

Often research is done to determine whether a client has a case. We write an office memo to predict an outcome for the client. This requires that we evaluate all relevant law for and against the client's position. Other times, paralegals must research a particular issue raised after a case has been filed. Some research is done to support motions to be filed with courts. Research also may be done when a client is involved in a transaction and the attorney must determine the law and the steps to take in the transaction.

### ▼ What Tasks Do Paralegals Handle in the Research and Writing Process?

In practice, paralegals act as an arm of an attorney. The amount of research and the type of assignments paralegals perform vary throughout the country.

In some law offices, paralegals undertake all of the research in preparation for the filing of motions but attorneys draft the motions. In others, paralegals research and prepare rough drafts of motions. Once a research project is completed, you must communicate your research results effectively. To do this, you must understand the fundamentals of legal writing and be able to write detailed, clear, and thoughtful memoranda. Paralegals often are asked to prepare memoranda that summarize their research results. Some paralegals who work with judges prepare rough drafts of court decisions. This book is designed to help you complete each of these tasks.

When you are assigned a research problem, you are expected to work as a professional. You should complete the assignment in a timely fashion. More important, however, the written research results must be accurate, complete, and current. This book teaches you how to analyze, organize, and communicate the results of a research project in a well thought out, well supported document.

---

*ETHICS ALERT*

Paralegals work under the supervision of attorneys, except in very limited, statutorily sanctioned situations. As a result, all research results and client memoranda should be submitted to an attorney before they are provided to a client. Work submitted to clients containing legal opinions should never be signed by a paralegal.

---

# B. INTRODUCTION TO THE U.S. LEGAL SYSTEM

## 1. The Organization of the Legal System

The United States consists of a multi-tiered system of government. The **federal government** and the **state governments** are the top two tiers. See Illustration 1-1.

Several lower-tier governmental bodies, including **city, village, township**, and **county governments**, exercise authority over the citizens of the United States. For the most part, your research will concern either federal or state law. Therefore, this book focuses its discussion on the federal and state systems and how to find the law they generate. The knowledge of these systems, the types of laws they adopt, and how to find legal standards for these systems later can be applied to any research you undertake concerning other government bodies and their laws.

**ILLUSTRATION 1-1.   U.S. and State Government Systems**

---

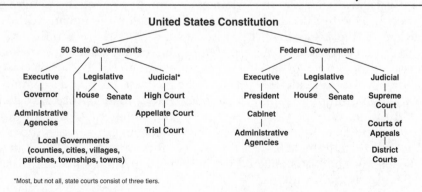

United States Constitution

50 State Governments

Executive — Legislative — Judicial*
Governor — House Senate — High Court
Administrative Agencies — Appellate Court
— Trial Court
Local Governments
(counties, cities, villages,
parishes, townships, towns)

Federal Government

Executive — Legislative — Judicial
President — House Senate — Supreme Court
Cabinet — Courts of Appeals
Administrative Agencies — District Courts

*Most, but not all, state courts consist of three tiers.

---

## ▼ How Did the Federal and State Systems Originate?

Representatives of the states adopted a **constitution** for the United States that is the framework for the operation of this federal/state system of government. To that end, the U.S. Constitution creates three branches of government and defines their powers. You can think of the Constitution as an umbrella over all of the United States' governing bodies as it covers questions of not only federal government powers, but some state powers as well. The Constitution reserves for the states all the remaining powers not specifically designated to the federal government bodies. In addition, the Constitution establishes the rules for the relationship between the federal and state governments. The U.S. Constitution is the supreme law of the United States. For example, Congress, the legislative body of the federal government, cannot enact a law that is contrary to the U.S. Constitution. The state legislatures similarly are prevented from adopting laws that violate provisions of the U.S. Constitution.

## 2. Components of the Federal System and Governing Law

The federal government consists of three branches of government: the legislative, the executive, and the judicial. The U.S. Constitution created each branch and defines the relationship between them. The Constitution establishes a system in which each branch of government can monitor the activities of the other branches to prevent abuses. Each branch has the ability to alter actions of another branch. In this way, the Constitution provides **checks** and **balances** concerning the actions of each branch of government.

In general, the legislative branch creates the laws, the executive branch enforces the laws, and the judicial branch interprets the laws.

### a. The Legislative Branch

The **legislative branch** of the federal government is called the **Congress.** It is comprised of two houses or chambers called the **Senate** and the **House of Representatives.** Both houses are comprised of individuals who are elected. The Congress creates laws called **statutes.** Some statutes are new rules of law. Other statutes supersede or adopt court-made law. Court-made law is referred to as **case law** or the **common law.** When Congress adopts common law as its own, the process is called **codification.** One pervasive example of this is patent law. Many laws were adopted based on court decisions concerning this area of the law. The statutes and the U.S. Constitution comprise one body of law called **enacted law.** The laws enacted by the federal government apply to all U.S. citizens and residents.

Congress.gov provides access to federal legislative information including House and Senate bills.

### ▼ How Is a Law Created?

Anyone can propose that Congress adopt a new law, and either chamber can introduce a law for consideration. When a proposed law is introduced, it is called a **bill.** Before the bill can become a law, both chambers must approve it. If both houses approve the same version of the bill, it is sent to the chief of the executive branch, our **president**. The president can sign or veto the bill or withhold action on it. If the president signs the bill, it becomes law. If the president does not act within ten days and the legislative session is still in progress, the bill becomes law. If the president vetoes the bill, Congress may override the veto by a two-thirds majority vote of each house.

If the president fails to act on the bill within the ten days and the legislature is out of session, the bill does not become law. This action is called a **pocket veto.**

### b. The Executive Branch

The **executive branch** of the government, headed by the president, is the primary enforcer of the law. The president appoints the cabinet and oversees many federal agencies. The executive branch is responsible for the day-to-day management of the federal government. With the assistance of the vice president, the cabinet members, and the heads of federal agencies, the president helps to guide the day-to-day operations of the government. The president can issue executive orders to direct the operations of various agencies and the actions of the citizens of the United States. In addition, the president is the commander in chief of the armed forces and with the advice and consent of the Senate, he can enter into treaties. Most federal administrative agencies are under direct control of the executive branch. See Illustration 1-2.

As the country's top executive, the president has the authority to control many administrative agencies. However, some administrative agencies are independent. For example, the Department of Justice that includes the Office of the Attorney General is part of the executive branch. However, the Federal Trade Commission is an independent agency.

# ILLUSTRATION 1-2.   The Government of the United States

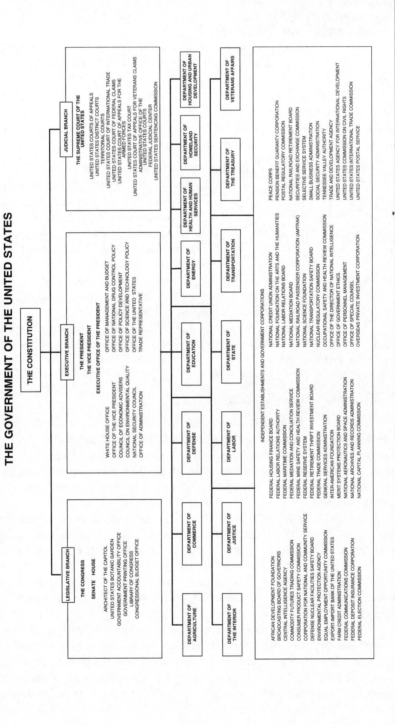

## THE GOVERNMENT OF THE UNITED STATES

**THE CONSTITUTION**

### LEGISLATIVE BRANCH

**THE CONGRESS**

**SENATE   HOUSE**

ARCHITECT OF THE CAPITOL
UNITED STATES BOTANIC GARDEN
GOVERNMENT ACCOUNTABILITY OFFICE
GOVERNMENT PRINTING OFFICE
LIBRARY OF CONGRESS
CONGRESSIONAL BUDGET OFFICE

### EXECUTIVE BRANCH

**THE PRESIDENT**

**THE VICE PRESIDENT**

**EXECUTIVE OFFICE OF THE PRESIDENT**

WHITE HOUSE OFFICE
OFFICE OF THE VICE PRESIDENT
COUNCIL OF ECONOMIC ADVISERS
COUNCIL ON ENVIRONMENTAL QUALITY
NATIONAL SECURITY COUNCIL
OFFICE OF ADMINISTRATION

OFFICE OF MANAGEMENT AND BUDGET
OFFICE OF NATIONAL DRUG CONTROL POLICY
OFFICE OF POLICY DEVELOPMENT
OFFICE OF SCIENCE AND TECHNOLOGY POLICY
OFFICE OF THE UNITED STATES
TRADE REPRESENTATIVE

### JUDICIAL BRANCH

**THE SUPREME COURT OF THE
UNITED STATES**

UNITED STATES COURTS OF APPEALS
UNITED STATES DISTRICT COURTS
TERRITORIAL COURTS
UNITED STATES COURT OF INTERNATIONAL TRADE
UNITED STATES COURT OF FEDERAL CLAIMS
UNITED STATES COURT OF APPEALS FOR THE
ARMED FORCES
UNITED STATES TAX COURT
UNITED STATES COURT OF APPEALS FOR VETERANS CLAIMS
ADMINISTRATIVE OFFICE OF THE
UNITED STATES COURTS
FEDERAL JUDICIAL CENTER
UNITED STATES SENTENCING COMMISSION

---

DEPARTMENT OF
AGRICULTURE

DEPARTMENT OF
COMMERCE

DEPARTMENT OF
DEFENSE

DEPARTMENT OF
EDUCATION

DEPARTMENT OF
ENERGY

DEPARTMENT OF
HEALTH AND HUMAN
SERVICES

DEPARTMENT OF
HOMELAND
SECURITY

DEPARTMENT OF
HOUSING AND URBAN
DEVELOPMENT

DEPARTMENT OF
THE INTERIOR

DEPARTMENT OF
JUSTICE

DEPARTMENT OF
LABOR

DEPARTMENT OF
STATE

DEPARTMENT OF
TRANSPORTATION

DEPARTMENT OF
THE TREASURY

DEPARTMENT OF
VETERANS AFFAIRS

---

### INDEPENDENT ESTABLISHMENTS AND GOVERNMENT CORPORATIONS

AFRICAN DEVELOPMENT FOUNDATION
BROADCASTING BOARD OF GOVERNORS
CENTRAL INTELLIGENCE AGENCY
COMMODITY FUTURES TRADING COMMISSION
CONSUMER PRODUCT SAFETY COMMISSION
CORPORATION FOR NATIONAL AND COMMUNITY SERVICE
DEFENSE NUCLEAR FACILITIES SAFETY BOARD
ENVIRONMENTAL PROTECTION AGENCY
EQUAL EMPLOYMENT OPPORTUNITY COMMISSION
EXPORT-IMPORT BANK OF THE UNITED STATES
FARM CREDIT ADMINISTRATION
FEDERAL COMMUNICATIONS COMMISSION
FEDERAL DEPOSIT INSURANCE CORPORATION
FEDERAL ELECTION COMMISSION

FEDERAL HOUSING FINANCE BOARD
FEDERAL LABOR RELATIONS AUTHORITY
FEDERAL MARITIME COMMISSION
FEDERAL MEDIATION AND CONCILIATION SERVICE
FEDERAL MINE SAFETY AND HEALTH REVIEW COMMISSION
FEDERAL RESERVE SYSTEM
FEDERAL RETIREMENT THRIFT INVESTMENT BOARD
FEDERAL TRADE COMMISSION
GENERAL SERVICES ADMINISTRATION
INTER-AMERICAN FOUNDATION
MERIT SYSTEMS PROTECTION BOARD
NATIONAL AERONAUTICS AND SPACE ADMINISTRATION
NATIONAL ARCHIVES AND RECORDS ADMINISTRATION
NATIONAL CAPITAL PLANNING COMMISSION

NATIONAL CREDIT UNION ADMINISTRATION
NATIONAL FOUNDATION ON THE ARTS AND THE HUMANITIES
NATIONAL LABOR RELATIONS BOARD
NATIONAL MEDIATION BOARD
NATIONAL RAILROAD PASSENGER CORPORATION (AMTRAK)
NATIONAL SCIENCE FOUNDATION
NATIONAL TRANSPORTATION SAFETY BOARD
NUCLEAR REGULATORY COMMISSION
OCCUPATIONAL SAFETY AND HEALTH REVIEW COMMISSION
OFFICE OF THE DIRECTOR OF NATIONAL INTELLIGENCE
OFFICE OF GOVERNMENT ETHICS
OFFICE OF PERSONNEL MANAGEMENT
OFFICE OF SPECIAL COUNSEL
OVERSEAS PRIVATE INVESTMENT CORPORATION

PEACE CORPS
PENSION BENEFIT GUARANTY CORPORATION
POSTAL REGULATORY COMMISSION
NATIONAL RAILROAD RETIREMENT BOARD
SECURITIES AND EXCHANGE COMMISSION
SELECTIVE SERVICE SYSTEM
SMALL BUSINESS ADMINISTRATION
SOCIAL SECURITY ADMINISTRATION
TENNESSEE VALLEY AUTHORITY
TRADE AND DEVELOPMENT AGENCY
UNITED STATES AGENCY FOR INTERNATIONAL DEVELOPMENT
UNITED STATES COMMISSION ON CIVIL RIGHTS
UNITED STATES INTERNATIONAL TRADE COMMISSION
UNITED STATES POSTAL SERVICE

**Administrative agencies** enforce many of the laws of the United States. These agencies are responsible for the daily regulation of activities controlled by federal law. For a listing of some of the many administrative agencies, see Illustration 1-2.

Congress creates the agencies and delegates some of its own power to them because it alone is unable to handle the day-to-day enforcement of the overwhelming number of federal laws. Agencies, however, have the staff and often the technical expertise to deal with the daily enforcement of Congress's enacted laws. To do this, agencies often make rules that explain in detail how individuals should act to comply with congressional mandates. In some cases, agencies hold hearings to enforce the law. These agencies, therefore, function in quasi-judicial and quasi-legislative roles.

For example, Congress enacted the Consumer Product Safety Act and delegated its enforcement power to the U.S. Consumer Product Safety Commission. Congress charged the commission with the responsibility for the daily enforcement of that act. As part of the commission's duties, it adopts rules or regulations. It also has administrative hearings, which often result in decisions.

In some cases, agencies use their **police powers** to enforce the law. For example, the U.S. Environmental Protection Agency will assist in prosecuting individuals or corporations that violate the Clean Air Act or other laws designed to protect the environment.

Search for federal agencies and information about a particular agency at search.usa.gov. Details about cabinet members, proclamations, executive orders, and issues facing the executive branch can be found at www.whitehouse.gov. Another government source of information is www.usa.gov.

## c. The Judicial Branch

The third branch of government is the **judicial branch.** The federal judicial system includes three levels of courts that resolve disputes. See Illustration 1-3.

The entry-level court is the **trial court.** In that court, disputes are heard and decided by either a judge or a jury. The second level or intermediate level of courts is called **appellate courts.** These courts consider appeals of decisions of the trial court. The final level is the **U.S. Supreme Court.** Its decisions cannot be appealed to any court.

**ILLUSTRATION 1-3.    Federal Judicial System**

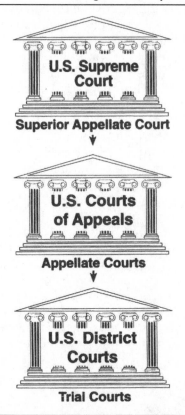

The website www.uscourts.gov provides links to all the U.S. appellate and district courts and U.S. bankruptcy courts, as well as the U.S. Supreme Court. Information is provided about judges, court personnel, locations, and court rules.

### ▼ Who Can Bring an Action in Federal Court?

A court can only consider a case if it has **jurisdiction** to hear it, that is, if the court is authorized to consider such cases. The federal court can consider all cases involving issues of federal law. In addition, it may hear cases involving disputes between parties of different states. Such cases

are called **diversity cases.** Cases in which both the plaintiff, who is the party bringing the lawsuit, and the defendant are citizens of different states are examples of diversity cases. Diversity cases often involve issues of state law.

---

### ETHICS ALERT

If you are assisting an attorney in preparing a claim, be certain that the claim is made in a court that has jurisdiction over such a claim.

---

### PRACTICE POINTER

State and federal courts can decide issues of state or federal law.

---

### i. The Trial Courts

The **trial court** is the court that hears the facts concerning a dispute. It is generally the first place in which a party can seek a remedy in federal court. In that way, it is considered a court of **original jurisdiction.** However, this court also hears appeals from some administrative agencies and the federal bankruptcy courts. Some administrative agency decisions, however, are appealed directly to the appellate courts.

In the federal system, the trial courts are known as the **district courts.** These courts decide disputes when a party (which can be a person, corporation, or other entity) brings an action against another party. In such cases, the trial courts often are asked to interpret congressional enactments such as statutes, ordinances, charters, or executive branch-created laws, including agency rules or decisions. When a court interprets a statute or regulation, it is overseeing the actions of other government branches. Courts often consult a body of law called the common law before rendering any decisions. Common law is court-created law found in the judicial opinions or cases; it is not found in the statutes.

### ii. The Appellate Courts

The federal trial courts' decisions can be appealed to one of the 13 **federal appellate courts** known as the **U.S. Courts of Appeals.** See Illustration 1-3. This second tier of federal courts is broken into numbered and named **circuits.** Eleven circuits are known as the First

through Eleventh. The remaining circuits are the Federal Circuit and the District of Columbia Circuit. The circuits are geographic, except for the Federal Circuit. See Illustration 1-4. An online map is available at www.uscourts.gov. These courts decide issues of law posed in appeals of trial court decisions located within its circuit. These courts do not consider new factual evidence. Witnesses are not brought before these courts. The Court of Appeals for the Federal Circuit has nationwide jurisdiction to hear appeals in specialized cases such as those arising from decisions of the Court of Federal Claims or the Court of International Trade. Decisions of the federal appellate courts can be appealed to the U.S. Supreme Court.

### iii. The Supreme Court

The U.S. Supreme Court is the highest court in the United States. See Illustration 1-3. The U.S. Constitution establishes this court. Today nine justices, appointed by the president and confirmed by the U.S. Senate, sit on this tribunal. The U.S. Supreme Court has discretion to consider many issues. This discretion is called **certiorari.** If the court decides not to hear an issue, it denies certiorari. The effect is that the decision of the appellate court is final. If the U.S. Supreme Court decides to hear an issue, it grants certiorari. It then will consider whether the appellate court's decision should stand. By law, the U.S. Supreme Court alone has the authority to hear appeals of a state court of last resort decision when a substantial federal constitutional issue is presented. The U.S. Supreme Court also may hear a dispute between two states. The Supreme Court also has original jurisdiction—that is the right—to directly take actions and proceedings in which ambassadors, other public ministers, consuls, or vice consuls of foreign states are parties. It also has original jurisdiction in all controversies between the United States and a state. The U.S. Supreme Court site, www.supremecourt.gov, is an excellent resource for recent decisions, and to monitor the status of pending decisions. Many opinions are posted the same day that they are decided. Additionally, the site allows access to the briefs for the U.S. Supreme Court cases. The Supreme Court briefs are terrific resources for the researcher.

The Federal Judicial Center provides information about the federal judiciary and its history. See www.fjc.gov.

# ILLUSTRATION 14. Circuit Map of the U.S. Courts of Appeals

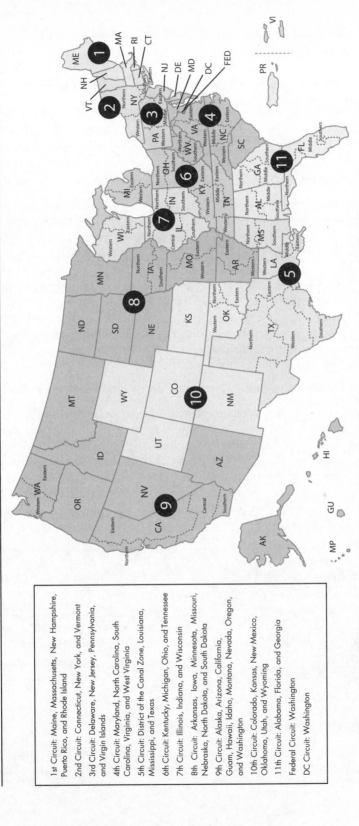

1st Circuit: Maine, Massachusetts, New Hampshire, Puerto Rico, and Rhode Island

2nd Circuit: Connecticut, New York, and Vermont

3rd Circuit: Delaware, New Jersey, Pennsylvania, and Virgin Islands

4th Circuit: Maryland, North Carolina, South Carolina, Virginia, and West Virginia

5th Circuit: District of the Canal Zone, Louisiana, Mississippi, and Texas

6th Circuit: Kentucky, Michigan, Ohio, and Tennessee

7th Circuit: Illinois, Indiana, and Wisconsin

8th Circuit: Arkansas, Iowa, Minnesota, Missouri, Nebraska, North Dakota, and South Dakota

9th Circuit: Alaska, Arizona, California, Guam, Hawaii, Idaho, Montana, Nevada, Oregon, and Washington

10th Circuit: Colorado, Kansas, New Mexico, Oklahoma, Utah, and Wyoming

11th Circuit: Alabama, Florida, and Georgia

Federal Circuit: Washington

DC Circuit: Washington

Found at the U.S. Courts website, www.uscourts.gov.

13

## 3. Relationship Between Federal and State Governments

### ▼ Can a Federal Court Decide an Issue of State Law?

Yes. A federal court can decide an issue of state law if the state issue is presented with a related federal issue or if the state question is raised in a dispute between parties of different states in a case called a diversity action.

### ▼ What Effect Does a Federal Decision Have on State Law?

A federal court decision generally cannot change state law. It may persuade the state courts to review state law, but its decision usually does not force any change in the law. These decisions, therefore, are advisory for future litigants but must be followed by the parties directly involved in the case in which the decision was rendered. Because states are separate sovereigns, in almost all cases only the state governing bodies can change state law. One exception to this rule does exist. The U.S. Supreme Court can determine whether state law violates the U.S. Constitution. If such a violation is found, the decision of the U.S. Supreme Court could invalidate state law.

### ▼ Are Federal and State Agencies Part of One Governing Body?

No. The federal government is one sovereign or governing body and the state is a separate governing body or sovereign. That means that the state cannot control the federal government agencies or change federal law. In general, the federal government branches cannot control the state government or change state law. However, the U.S. Constitution, the umbrella, can limit actions of the state government. The Constitution prohibits the states from making any laws that are contrary to its provisions.

---

## *PRACTICE POINTER*

Often attorneys choose to bring a case in a federal rather than state court or the other way around for tactical reasons. More often the reason for bringing an action in a particular court is based solely on the law that serves as the basis for the claim.

---

## 4. Organization of State Governments

Most state governments are organized in a manner similar to that of the federal government. State governments are governed by constitutions.

That constitution defines the organization of the state's government and the relationship between the branches of government. The states have legislative, executive, and judicial branches.

The legislative branches operate in a manner similar to that of Congress and often feature two chambers. Some legislatures enact enabling laws that create administrative agencies and provide such agencies with the responsibility for the daily enforcement of state laws. The chief executive in each state is a governor.

Each state has a judicial system. However, not all state systems mirror the federal government's three-tier court system. Each state establishes which courts can hear different disputes. Some states have a three-tier system similar to that of the federal judicial branch. In some states, the intermediate appellate court is eliminated. The following systems do not include an intermediate appellate court: Delaware, District of Columbia, Maine, Montana, Nevada, New Hampshire, Rhode Island, South Dakota, Vermont, West Virginia, and Wyoming. The creation of such a court in Nevada is being studied.

---

## *PRACTICE POINTER*

The Supreme Court may not be the highest court in a state. This is the case in New York. Check the *Bluebook*, Table 1, for state court information.

---

**NET NOTE**

For more information about the state trial courts, see the National Center for State Courts website, www.ncsc.org. Information about court structures and links to the court are provided.

---

### ▼ What Are the Duties of the State Courts?

In most state court systems, trial courts determine the facts and legal issues of a case. A trial court might include a family, a municipal, or a small claims court. The jurisdiction of these courts is generally limited, sometimes according to the amount of money in dispute.

The next level generally is an appellate level court. However, as noted above, some states do not have this level. As in the federal court system, this court usually does not hear new facts or evidence. Instead, it decides whether the lower court erred in deciding

substantive law or procedural issues. Finally, most states have another appellate level court, similar to the U.S. Supreme Court, which is the final arbiter of disputes. In some states, there are two such courts—one for criminal cases and the other for civil cases. Texas and Oklahoma are two states that have such courts.

---

## *PRACTICE POINTER*

An appellate court may hear facts and evidence if it is the court of original jurisdiction.

---

### ▼ Can State Courts Decide Issues of Federal Law?

Yes, state courts can decide issues of federal law. Although a state court decision concerning federal law does not change the federal law, it may persuade federal governing bodies to change federal law. The state court decision's impact is limited to the case in which the federal issue was presented, and therefore only parties involved in that case are bound or required to follow that ruling.

The federal government controls all issues of federal law. The state governments exercise authority over all issues of state law. These areas are not always well defined. In some areas, both the state and federal governments exercise authority. For example, both the state and federal governments control how industries dispose of their wastes. Do not be discouraged if you have difficulty separating state and federal issues in some cases. Many times courts struggle with these issues.

## CHAPTER SUMMARY

In this chapter, you learned about the branches of the U.S. government and their functions, as well as the general structure of the state governments. The United States has three branches of government: the legislative, the executive, and the judicial. All of these branches were created by the U.S. Constitution, which guides their activities. In addition, administrative agencies enforce the laws created by the legislature.

The legislature, which consists of the House of Representatives and the Senate, creates laws called statutes.

The executive branch enforces the laws of the United States, and the judicial branch resolves disputes and interprets the laws.

The judicial branch is comprised of a three-tier court system. The highest court is the U.S. Supreme Court; the middle courts are the U.S. Courts of Appeals; the trial or lowest courts are the U.S. District Courts. All three branches of government create law.

# KEY TERMS

administrative agencies

appellate courts

balances

bill

case law

certiorari

checks

circuits

city government

codification

common law

Congress

constitution

county government

district courts

diversity cases

enacted law

executive branch

federal appellate court

federal government

House of Representatives

judicial branch

jurisdiction

legislative branch

original jurisdiction

pocket veto

police powers

president

Senate

state governments

statutes

township government

trial court

U.S. Courts of Appeals

U.S. Supreme Court

village government

# EXERCISES

1. Draw a diagram of your state government.
2. How many houses does your legislature have? What are the names of each chamber?
3. Diagram your state court system. Is there an intermediate court?
4. Draw a flow chart of the federal bill process.
5. Draw a flow chart of the state bill process for your state.
6. Who is the chief executive?
7. Go to the National Center for State Courts website and review the structure of your state court.
8. What are the monetary requirements for filing an action in the trial court in your state?
9. Go to www.usa.gov and click around the site to find links to the Congressional Budget Office and the Domestic Policy Council.
10. What are the branches of the U.S. government and what are the responsibilities of each branch?
11. What are Congress-created laws called?
12. What is the body of law created by the courts called?
13. Name the judges on your high court. Where did you find this information?
14. Find your state's website. Note it.
15. Find a website for your state courts. Note it.
16. Find a website for your state legislature. Note it.

## CHAPTER 2

# LEGAL AUTHORITIES AND HOW TO USE THEM

| | |
|---|---|
| **A. DETERMINATION OF GOVERNING LAW** | 20 |
| 1. Jurisdiction | 20 |
| 2. Precedent | 20 |
| 3. Hierarchy of Authorities | 21 |
| 4. Dicta | 25 |
| **B. TYPES OF LEGAL RESOURCES** | 25 |
| 1. Primary Authority | 25 |
| 2. Secondary Authority | 27 |
| 3. Finding Tools | 28 |
| 4. Hybrid Sources of Authority | 29 |
| 5. Nonlegal Sources | 29 |
| **C. USE OF AUTHORITIES OR SOURCES IN YOUR LEGAL WRITING** | 29 |
| 1. Essential Sources to Cite | 29 |
| 2. Valuable Sources to Cite | 30 |
| 3. Sources Never to Cite | 30 |
| 4. Checklist | 30 |

## CHAPTER OVERVIEW

In researching legal issues, you must have goals and understand the value of the legal authorities you find. This chapter explains the concept of legal authority and the determination of governing law.

It discusses the value of various authorities and how authorities inter-relate with each other. You will learn which authorities should determine the outcome of a case and which authorities merely provide persuasive support for a case. You will learn how to determine which authorities to use in documents you write.

# A. DETERMINATION OF GOVERNING LAW

To determine what law controls your case, you must first determine the jurisdiction. Next, you must identify the current law that applies to your case. To do this, you must examine the hierarchy of authorities. You then consider relevant precedent and dicta.

## 1. Jurisdiction

**Jurisdiction** is a complex concept that has several different definitions. In the broadest sense, jurisdiction is the right of a state or of the federal government to apply its laws to a dispute and to exercise control over a conflict. Jurisdiction also is defined as a geographic area such as a state that has the right to interpret and to apply its law to a particular case. When a court or a governing body has jurisdiction over a case or situation, it has the authority to control the case or outcome of the situation.

### ▼ What Factors Determine Which Jurisdiction Governs Your Case?

A variety of factors affect which jurisdiction governs a claim in a particular case, including where the dispute arose, the parties involved in the case, and the nature of the dispute. Sometimes making this determination is a complex task. Ask the assigning attorney to assist you in making this determination. Various statutes, procedural rules, and cases also can assist you in understanding which court has jurisdiction. For example, federal court jurisdiction is specified by federal law.

## 2. Precedent

You already have learned that the courts generate decisions of cases that become law. The basic rule of law decided by the court is the **holding.** If the court is presented with more than one issue, the decision includes more than one holding. The holding also is called the **precedent.**

Theoretically, the lower courts must follow decisions or precedents of the higher courts in their jurisdiction. This theory is called **stare decisis.** The idea behind it is that parties should be able to rely on what the courts have done in the past. Doing so allows parties to predict how a court is likely to rule in their cases.

The doctrine of stare decisis makes your job as a researcher important. You must determine what the courts have decided in the past to assist the attorneys in predicting what the court is likely to do, or likely

to be persuaded to do, in your case. Sometimes a court will not follow precedent. Even though stare decisis and precedent are the controlling doctrines, courts often decide cases based on the facts before them and the changes in society. This allows the law, through the holdings, to evolve and to meet contemporary needs. Holdings are what you must consider after reviewing the theories of hierarchy of authorities.

## 3. Hierarchy of Authorities

Once you have determined the jurisdiction, you then must identify the current law that applies to the case. To determine what law applies to your case, you must determine the **hierarchy of authorities.** This is a system in which legal authorities such as court decisions, statutes, administrative rules and decisions, and constitutions are ranked according to the effect they have in controlling the law of a governing body. You can think of this in part as a chain of command. For example, U.S. Supreme Court cases outrank federal appeals and trial courts concerning issues of federal law. Determining the hierarchy of authorities can be simple or complex depending in large part on the system of government and structure of the courts, the law applicable to the dispute, and the underlying claim The currency of an authority and competing laws within a jurisdiction are other factors that help researchers determine whether one authority outranks another.

### a. Currency

You must first determine which authority is most current. Suppose you find that the law governing your case is a federal law and the case involves a question of federal constitutional law. At first glance the highest legal authority would appear to be the U.S. Constitution because it is the supreme law of the United States and because the legal issue in question is constitutional in nature. However, if the U.S. Supreme Court has interpreted the Constitution on the issue presented in your case, its decision is more current and would therefore be the highest legal authority.

In another case that does not involve a constitutional issue, a federal statute might be the highest authority. This would depend on whether a court had interpreted the statute. If a federal court had interpreted the statute's language and that language affected the issue involved in your case, you would need to determine whether the court decision or the statute is more recent. The most current authority is the highest authority.

### EXAMPLE OF THE HIERARCHY QUESTION BETWEEN A STATUTE AND A CASE

Your case involves a legal issue that was addressed in a statute that was enacted on December 1, 2013. The court cases you have found that may have a bearing on this legal issue involved in this case were decided before December 1, 2013. Therefore, the statute—the most current

authority—is the highest authority concerning this issue. For another example, see Illustration 2-1.

## b. Levels of Court

Next, you must consider the level of each authority, that is, where the court or government body ranks in order of its authority. The trial courts, appellate courts, and U.S. Supreme Court do not carry the same weight. For example, a decision of the highest court, the U.S. Supreme Court, would be at the top of the hierarchy of authorities of federal court decisions. Its decisions would trump those of other federal courts.

Except for the U.S. Supreme Court, all the federal courts are within defined groups called **circuits.** Within each circuit are a group of district courts and one circuit court of appeals. The key to the relationship between the federal courts is that the district courts, which are the entry-level courts, must follow decisions of the U.S. Circuit Court of Appeals within its circuit. A district court does not have to follow decisions of appellate courts that are outside of its circuit. A Texas district court is within the Fifth Circuit. Appeals of its decisions generally are made to the U.S. Court of Appeals for the Fifth Circuit. Therefore, the Texas district court must follow the precedents established in the decisions of the U.S. Court of Appeals for the Fifth Circuit. It does not have to follow the precedents set in the decisions of the U.S. Court of Appeals for the Sixth Circuit. For a review of the circuit divisions, review Chapter 1. Decisions of appellate courts outside of a circuit, however, often are used to persuade an appellate court to make a certain decision if it has not addressed that issue earlier. Such a decision is **persuasive authority** discussed later in this chapter.

## ILLUSTRATION 2-1.   Example of Ranking Authorities

The problem presented is whether the U.S. constitutional provision that requires due process applies to aliens held under the USA Patriot Act.

> Applicable law:
>
> U.S. Constitution
>
> The USA Patriot Act (2001)
>
> Supreme Court case 2013 determining that the Due Process Clause of the U.S. Constitution is not applicable to persons held under the USA Patriot Act

Rank of authorities and reason for the ranking:

1. Supreme Court case 2013 interpreting the Constitution and the USA Patriot Act would be first. It is the most current authority.
2. The next authority is likely to be the USA Patriot Act if it directly addresses this point. It is the second most current authority.

---

*PRACTICE POINTER*

For each jurisdiction in which you often undertake research, create a chart that lists the primary and secondary authorities to consider.

---

### c. Conflicting Decisions Between Circuits

Each circuit is independent of the other circuits. Therefore, their decisions may conflict. Each appellate court can make its decision independent of any decisions concerning the same issue rendered by other appellate courts. If two appellate courts have conflicting decisions concerning the same issue, how can you, as a researcher, decide what law governs? You must determine what circuit court authority is **mandatory authority** for your case. If the question is a particularly significant federal issue, check if the U.S. Supreme Court has decided the issue or is about to render a decision concerning such an issue. If so, a decision of the Supreme Court—the highest level of court—will be at the top of the hierarchy of authority.

Often, however, one appellate court may be guided in its decision by the decision of another appellate court. Review the example below.

### *EXAMPLES OF HIERARCHY BETWEEN COURTS*

The U.S. District Court for the Northern District of Illinois, which is in Chicago, falls in the Seventh Circuit. See Illustration 1-4. If the federal district court in Illinois was asked to determine whether federal law permitted a union to charge a fee to nonmembers for activities that benefit nonmembers, it would be bound to follow any U.S. Seventh Circuit Court of Appeals decision concerning this issue. This is because this appellate court is a higher court than the district court within the Seventh Circuit. Appeals from the Illinois district court generally are taken to the Seventh Circuit Court of Appeals. If the U.S. Sixth Circuit Court of Appeals in Cincinnati handed down a decision on this issue that conflicted with the Seventh Circuit Court of Appeals, the District Court for the Northern District of Illinois, a trial court, would be bound to follow the decision of the Seventh Circuit Court of Appeals, as it is within the Seventh Circuit and the Seventh Circuit Court of Appeals is above the Illinois district court in rank and status. The Illinois court is not within the Sixth Circuit. Therefore, the Sixth Circuit Court of Appeals is not above the Illinois district court in rank and status. The Illinois court would not be bound to follow the decision of the U.S. Court of Appeals for the Sixth Circuit in Cincinnati. However, the Seventh Circuit decision would be considered **mandatory binding authority** for the Illinois court. The Sixth Circuit opinion would be

primary persuasive authority. The Sixth Circuit decision would be very persuasive authority if the Seventh Circuit appellate court had not already ruled on the same issue of law. The Illinois district court facing a decision in a union fee case or even the Seventh Circuit Court of Appeals may be guided by the Sixth Circuit opinion, a persuasive authority rather than mandatory or binding authority.

The U.S. District Court for the Northern District of Ohio, based in Cleveland, falls within the Sixth Circuit. See Illustration 1-4. That district court must follow decisions of the Sixth Circuit appellate court, not those of the Seventh Circuit Court of Appeals in Chicago, because decisions of the Sixth Circuit Court would be mandatory binding authority for the Ohio court. Decisions of the Seventh Circuit would be primary persuasive authorities for the Ohio court.

### d. State and Federal Decisions Concerning an Issue

What happens if the issue in your case involves both state and federal decisions? How do you make sense of the hierarchy of authorities in such cases? The key is to determine which court has jurisdiction or the right to hear the case. The court systems of the state and federal governments operate in tandem. As explained above, the federal courts may decide issues of both federal or state law. For example, a federal diversity case may involve a negligence issue—a state law issue.

Next, you must determine whether federal or state law applies. If you find this difficult, ask the assigning attorney. The federal courts must look to decisions of the highest court of the state to make a determination of state law. The federal court decision, however, does not bind later state court decisions.

State courts also may decide issues of either federal or state law. The state court decisions concerning federal law are merely persuasive authority, however, because federal courts are not required to follow these decisions. State courts will look to federal courts for guidance in deciding issues of federal law. However, they are not bound to follow those decisions. Similarly, a state court may decide a federal age discrimination issue, but the federal courts can disregard that decision when facing the same question.

### e. Conflicts in Federal and State Authority

Although the federal and state governments are independent governments, they sometimes regulate some of the same areas, such as environmental pollution. In some cases, the federal government by congressional action will control an area extensively, and a state will attempt to monitor the same area. Who controls varies. Often, a determination of which of the **conflicting authorities** governs is decided by reviewing the Constitution. Other times, federal or state law might specify which law governs.

The federal courts sometimes are asked to decide who controls. The courts may look to the Constitution for guidance or may consider who has pervasively regulated an area. For example, if a case involves a section of the U.S. Constitution, the U.S. Supreme Court is the final authority. In other cases, it depends on the area being regulated.

### f. State Court Decisions

Each group of state courts is a separate court system. State courts of one state are not required to follow decisions made by courts of other states. Often, however, state courts consider other states' court decisions for guidance in how to decide a case. Decisions of one state's courts are merely advisory or persuasive decisions for another state's courts, not decisions that control the law of the first state.

## 4. Dicta

Often a court addresses an issue that is not directly presented by the parties. In such cases, a court states what it would do if it was presented directly with the issue. When the court makes such statements, they are called **dicta.** Dicta do not have the same force and effect as holdings. They are not authoritative, and lower courts are not bound to follow such statements.

You might use dicta when no court has ever been asked directly to decide the issue addressed. The dicta explain how the court would decide the issue if it was directly presented to the court. Because of this, the dicta might help you to predict how a court might decide an issue. Dicta also can be used to persuade a court to decide an issue in a certain manner. Although dicta may be helpful, finding dicta is not the goal of your research.

# B. TYPES OF LEGAL RESOURCES

Your task is to find primary authority "on point" or "on all fours" with your case, in other words, cases that are similar in fact and in legal issue to your case and whose holdings address an issue presented in your case.

## 1. Primary Authority

**Primary authority** is law generated by a government body. Cases decided by any court are primary authority. Legislative enactments such as constitutions, statutes, ordinances, or charters are primary authorities. See Illustration 2-2. Administrative agency rules and decisions are primary authorities.

These authorities often are published chronologically. However, statutes are arranged by subject. Some sources of primary authorities

## ILLUSTRATION 2-2.   Authorities and Finding Tools

| Primary Authorities | Secondary Authorities | Finding Tools |
|---|---|---|
| Court decisions | Encyclopedias | Digests |
| Statutes | *American Law Reports* | Citators |
| Agency rules and regulations | Periodicals | Updaters |
| Constitutions | Law reviews | Case and Statute Annotations |
| Charters | Dictionaries | |
| Ordinances | Thesauri | |
| Adopted pattern jury instructions | Model codes | |
| | Unadopted uniform laws | |
| Court rules | Treatises | |
| State-adopted model code provisions | Restatement of the Law | |
| State-adopted uniform laws | | |

will be more appropriate for your research than others. In some cases, primary authority is mandatory or binding authority because a government body must follow that authority when it makes future decisions. The words *mandatory* and *binding* are interchangeable.

### ▼ How Do You Determine Whether a Case Is Mandatory or Binding?

To determine whether a case is mandatory or binding, you must consider the rank of the authorities. Follow the steps below.

1. Determine the jurisdiction that applies to your case. Then, look to the hierarchy of the courts within that jurisdiction.
2. Note what court decided the case you are reviewing.
3. Determine whether this is a court within the jurisdiction that applies to your case.
4. If the court is within the appropriate jurisdiction, you must determine the level of that court within the court system. Is it a trial court or an appellate court? Is it the highest court of the system? States often have rules that specify the effect of a court decision on other courts within the same system. In general, the lower courts in a system must follow the decisions of the highest court in the system. The rules concerning which courts must follow the decisions of the intermediate-tier courts vary by jurisdiction. Consult the rules for that jurisdiction.

An authority is mandatory only if it controls or shapes the law of a particular jurisdiction. Examples of such authorities include state appellate court opinions or state statutes.

An authority is persuasive when it is made by a court outside of a particular jurisdiction. Decisions of one state court are not binding on courts of other states. Decisions of the Arizona Supreme Court are mandatory or binding on the lower courts in Arizona, but these decisions are merely persuasive primary authority in Michigan.

A decision is also persuasive rather than mandatory if it is made by a court whose decisions according to the law do not bind other courts. For example, decisions of the federal trial courts do not have to be followed by other federal courts.

Persuasive authority can be invaluable in persuading a court. This is especially true in decisions concerning statutory interpretation that involve statutes that are identical. For example, Kansas and Ohio adopted the same comparative negligence statute at different times. Kansas courts faced challenges concerning the statutory language. The decisions were highly persuasive authority when Ohio courts faced similar challenges years later, particularly since it was likely that the Ohio legislators were aware of the Kansas interpretations when they adopted the Ohio statute.

---

### *PRACTICE POINTER*

Use persuasive authority if you do not have primary authority on point. For statutory disputes, determine whether legislators would have been aware of the persuasive authority when the statute was adopted.

---

## 2. Secondary Authority

Another type of authority is **secondary authority.** Such authority is not generated by government bodies. Instead, secondary authority includes commentary written by attorneys or other experts. Secondary authority is persuasive only, and it is never binding or mandatory. In general, an attorney would not base an argument to a court on a secondary authority.

Secondary sources are helpful in understanding an issue of law, in discovering other issues, and in finding primary authorities. Sometimes secondary authorities help to interpret primary authority for you and the court. Secondary sources include treatises, Restatements of the Law, dictionaries, encyclopedias, legal periodicals, *American Law Reports*, books, and thesauri. See Illustration 2-2. Often these sources direct you to cases, statutes, and other primary authorities.

Some secondary authorities are more persuasive than others. Many Restatements and treatises are authoritative and can be noted in court documents and legal reports called memoranda addressed to attorneys.

However, most secondary authorities should not be noted in these reports.

Uniform codes are a type of secondary authority often mistaken for a primary authority. Many uniform codes exist throughout the country. These are suggested laws, often devised by experts. If a state adopts the uniform code in total or in part, its adopted statute, not the underlying uniform code, is primary authority, but the recommended or uniform code remains as a very persuasive secondary authority.

---

*PRACTICE POINTER*

If you have a primary authority on point, do not cite a secondary authority to make the same point.

---

*PRACTICE POINTER*

Secondary authorities are rarely cited in court documents. However, some secondary authorities carry significant persuasive weight, for example, commentaries to uniform laws.

---

## 3. Finding Tools

To find primary and secondary resources, often you need to consult **finding tools**, such as digests and citators. See Illustration 2-2. These finding tools are neither primary nor secondary authority. They should never be noted or cited in memoranda or court documents. Among the finding tools are **digests**, which are books containing case abstracts arranged according to publisher-assigned topics rather than in chronological order. **Annotated statutes** also include case abstracts written by the publishers. **Citators**, such as *Shepard's®*, provide you with listings of cases and some secondary authorities.

---

*PRACTICE POINTER*

Attorneys do not look favorably on paralegals who cite finding tools as authority.

## 4. Hybrid Sources of Authority

**Hybrid sources of authority** contain primary authorities, secondary authorities, regulations, cases, and finding tools. Hybrid sources of authority include looseleaf services, formbooks, and proof of facts. These resources can be useful in finding multiple authorities. However, be certain that you distinguish the primary and secondary authorities and finding tools and that in most cases, you cite only the primary authorities.

## 5. Nonlegal Sources

You often must consult nonlegal sources, such as newspapers or corporate information statements. These sources are not authoritative. Never use nonlegal sources to determine the law that governs a case. However, they can assist you in your work. Sometimes it is necessary to cite these sources as relevant **factual authority** in a motion or a brief. These sources often provide insight into the purpose behind a court decision or the enactment of a law.

# C. USE OF AUTHORITIES OR SOURCES IN YOUR LEGAL WRITING

## 1. Essential Sources to Cite

Primary authority is the key type of authority you should use in any form of legal writing such as a legal memorandum (discussed in detail later in this book). As explained earlier, primary authority is the highest authority in the chain of command. In particular, you should use primary, binding authority for the jurisdiction in which your action will be filed or is pending. Primary, binding authority that is tailored to your case— that is, one that is similar in fact and legal issues to your case—is best. However, do not ignore primary, binding authority that does not support your client's case. If you have not found any primary, binding authority that matches your case facts or legal issues, then consider primary, persuasive authority that matches your case facts or legal issues. For example, if you are working on a case in the federal district court in Florida and you cannot find a U.S. Supreme Court or an Eleventh Circuit appellate court decision on point, you can use a case from the federal Second Circuit Court of Appeals if it has considered a similar case. If, however, you are writing a legal memorandum for an attorney, you should mention all primary, persuasive authorities, both for and against a particular case if you cannot find any primary, binding authorities. An attorney needs to know the cases that support his or her client's position as well as those that oppose it.

## 2. Valuable Sources to Cite

Primary, persuasive authorities are valuable sources to cite if you do not have primary, binding authority that is similar in fact and law to your case. However, some secondary authorities such as Restatements of Law or treatises are very persuasive and can be cited when you lack primary authority on point. Restatements and treatises are discussed in detail in Chapter 6. When you cite these secondary authorities, you need to be careful to note, however, that you did not have any primary authority on point.

## 3. Sources Never to Cite

Do not cite digests, the annotations in secondary authorities, or the case abstracts listed in the annotated statutes. Citing these nonauthorities can result in serious consequences, including ethical violations. Non-legal sources such as newspapers should not be cited to support a legal issue. Only cite these sources to support factual statements.

## 4. Checklist

- Review all of your sources of authority.
- Divide the sources into primary and secondary authorities and finding tools.
- Make a list of all of the primary authorities.
- Separate primary authorities that are applicable to the jurisdiction that applies in the case you are handling.
- Make a ranking of those primary authorities—determine which are binding and which are merely persuasive. To rank these authorities, determine which authority is highest in the chain of command as explained in the hierarchy of authority section of this chapter. Consider which authority is most current and which authority is precedential in value rather than merely dicta.
- Determine whether these binding authorities match your facts or legal issues.
- Determine whether the primary persuasive authorities match your facts or legal issues.
- Make a ranking of the secondary authorities and determine whether these match your facts or legal issues.
- Start your analysis and written summary with the primary, binding authorities that match your facts and legal issues.
- Next incorporate primary, persuasive authorities that match your facts and legal issues. However, you should use these authorities only if the primary, binding authority does not match your facts or legal issues in total.
- Finally, consider incorporating secondary authorities into your writing if none of the primary authorities address your facts or legal issues.

- Never cite a secondary authority when you have a primary binding authority on point.
- Never cite a newspaper article or a finding tool to support a legal issue. Nonlegal sources such as newspapers should be cited only to support a factual issue.

## IN-CLASS EXERCISE

### FACTS

You are a paralegal in the state in which you live. You have been assigned to research whether an individual can bring an action in state court against a car dealer and the car manufacturer of a car that has been trouble-ridden since the individual purchased it eight months ago.

### RESEARCH RESULTS

You have found a statute that explains lemon law actions in your state; two cases in your state that interpret the statute; a federal case that explains the lemon law's application in your state; a case from another state that explains the lemon law; an encyclopedia explanation of the statute; a periodical article in a bar journal about lemon law actions in your state; and a newspaper article that explains how to bring a lemon law action and what actions are barred.

### DISCUSSION QUESTIONS FOR THE CLASS

**a.** What type of authority is the lemon law statute in your state?
**b.** What type of authority are the two cases from your state?
**c.** What type of authority is the case from another state?
**d.** What type of authority is the federal case?
**e.** What type of authority is the encyclopedia reference to the statute?
**f.** What type of authority is the periodical article?
**g.** What type of authority is the newspaper article?
**h.** Which, if any, authorities might be binding or mandatory authorities?
**i.** Which authorities might be noted in a memorandum to a court?

Determine whether the authorities are primary mandatory, primary persuasive, or secondary authorities, and rank authorities according to which authorities the students would use first, second, third, and so on, if at all.

## CHAPTER SUMMARY

In this chapter, you learned that determining governing law involves examining jurisdiction and the hierarchy of authorities. You also learned how precedent and dicta influence governing law. As a researcher, your goal is to find cases that are similar to yours in fact and legal issue and whose holdings

address an issue presented in your case. In reaching this goal, you first seek primary authorities because these authorities carry more weight with the courts than secondary authorities. Primary authorities include court decisions, statutes, court rules, constitutions, and administrative rules and regulations.

Some primary authorities are binding. If an authority is binding, a court must follow that authority. Other authorities are merely persuasive. Such authorities provide guidance to the courts and often are followed by the decision-making tribunal.

As you are researching, you often will refer to secondary authorities. Secondary authorities provide you with information to understand primary authorities. Generally, secondary authorities are commentaries prepared by experts in a particular field. These authorities often include citations to primary authorities. Secondary authorities are persuasive only. Therefore, you would rely on a primary authority rather than a secondary authority. Secondary authorities include encyclopedias, treatises, and legal periodicals.

Finding tools are designed to assist you in your research, but they are not considered authorities. These tools provide you with citations to primary and secondary authorities. Finding tools include annotated statutes, digests, and citators.

Finally, you learned how to incorporate these authorities into your legal writing. You learned that primary, binding authority is the best authority to use to support a legal proposition. Primary, persuasive and some secondary authority also may be cited. Finding tools and nonlegal sources should not be used to support a legal theory.

## KEY TERMS

annotated statutes

binding authority

circuits

citators

conflicting authorities

dicta

digests

factual authority

finding tools

hierarchy of authorities

holding

hybrid sources of authority

jurisdiction

mandatory authority

persuasive authority

precedent

primary authority

secondary authority

stare decisis

## EXERCISES

### COURT SYSTEMS

**Exercises**

1. What is the highest court of your state? Where can you find this information on the Internet? Give a website.
2. Within your state's court system, what type of authority are decisions made by the highest court named in question 1?

    a. primary binding
    b. primary persuasive
    c. secondary binding
    d. secondary persuasive

3. What is the name of the trial court of your state?
4. Are the trial court's decisions binding on the highest court of the state?
5. What is the highest court of the federal system of government?
6. Within the federal system of government, what type of authority are decisions made by the highest court named in question 5?
    a. primary binding
    b. primary persuasive
    c. secondary binding
    d. secondary persuasive
7. What is the name of the trial court of the federal government?
8. Are decisions of any federal trial court binding on any federal appellate court?
9. Are all federal appellate court decisions binding on every federal trial court? Why or why not?
10. Can state courts decide issues of federal law?
11. Can federal courts decide issues of state law?
12. What is primary authority?
13. What is binding or mandatory authority?
14. When would you use primary authority?

## Research Strategy

15. Can the Arizona Legislature adopt a law that contradicts the U.S. Constitution?
16. Must the U.S. Circuit Court of Appeals for the Ninth Circuit follow a decision of the U.S. Supreme Court concerning a federal issue?
17. Must an Arkansas trial court follow a decision of the U.S. Supreme Court concerning an issue of federal law?
18. You are a paralegal assigned to research the components necessary to create a valid will in your state. List in order the types of authorities you would consult and why. Next, rank the authorities according to whether they are primary mandatory, primary persuasive, or secondary.
19. You are a paralegal who has just researched what constitutes a breach of contract in a case involving the delivery of dairy products in Wisconsin. Rank the following authorities and list whether each is a primary binding, primary persuasive, or secondary authority.
    a. a Wisconsin Supreme Court case involving a breach of contract dispute
    b. a Wisconsin statute that defines breach of contract
    c. a Wisconsin statute that defines the term *delivery* in a contract
    d. a Wisconsin trial court case involving a breach of contract dispute
    e. an Illinois Supreme Court case involving a breach of contract dispute
    f. a Uniform Commercial Code section concerning breach of contract. (The Wisconsin statute is derived in part from this section but does not adopt it in total.)
20. You are researching the question of whether a company that employs 50 individuals is an employer under the federal law regulating age

discrimination in employment. Your case is pending in the federal district court in Toledo, Ohio. You learn that the definitions in the age discrimination statute were derived from those already in the sex discrimination statute. Rank the following authorities and list whether each is a primary binding, primary persuasive, or secondary authority.

a. the federal age discrimination in employment statute that defines the term *employer*

b. the federal sex discrimination in employment statute that defines the term *employer*

c. a U.S. Supreme Court case that interprets the definition of *employer* contained in the federal age discrimination in employment statute

d. a U.S. Supreme Court case that interprets the definition of *employer* contained in the federal sex discrimination in employment statute

e. a decision of the Northern District Court of Ohio, Western Division, concerning the definition of *employer* under the federal age discrimination in employment statute

f. a law review article in the *University of Toledo Law Review* concerning the definition of *employer* contained in the federal age discrimination in employment statute

g. a section of an employment law treatise that explains the definition of *employer* under the federal age discrimination in employment statute

h. an Ohio Supreme Court case that explains the definition of *employer* under the federal age discrimination in employment statute
Which authorities would you use in a legal memorandum you are writing for an attorney and why?

21. You are asked to research the validity of a New York statute that bars high school students from wearing t-shirts bearing antigovernment slogans. Your case is pending in the state court of New York. Rank the following authorities and list whether each is a primary binding, primary persuasive, or secondary authority.

a. the New York statute in question

b. the U.S. Constitution's First Amendment regarding free speech

c. a U.S. Supreme Court case that prohibits states from banning the wearing of symbols by high school students because such a ban violates the U.S. Constitution

d. a case decided by the highest court in New York that holds that the statute is invalid

e. a California case involving an identical statute adopted in California that holds that the statute is valid

f. an encyclopedia entry that states that such bans are invalid

g. a newspaper article in *The National Law Journal* that predicts that the U.S. Supreme Court will invalidate the New York statute
Which authorities would you use in a legal memorandum you are writing for an attorney and why?

## CHAPTER 3

# COURT DECISIONS

| | |
|---|---|
| **A. REPORTERS** | 35 |
| 1. Bench Opinions | 36 |
| 2. Slip Opinions | 36 |
| 3. Advance Sheets | 40 |
| 4. Bound Reporters | 40 |
| 5. Computerized Reporting | 55 |
| 6. State Reporters | 59 |

## *CHAPTER OVERVIEW*

In Chapters 1 and 2, you learned about our system of government and were introduced to the concept of legal authorities. This chapter focuses on one of those legal authorities—case law, which is a primary authority. The chapter describes where to find U.S. Supreme Court cases and other federal court decisions as well as the location of many state court opinions. It also explains where you can find the most recent court decisions. You are then introduced to a topical system for locating cases and are shown how to use this system.

## A. REPORTERS

Court decisions are often referred to as **case law.** Case law is one of the primary sources of our law, on both the state and the federal levels.

Finding and reading past court decisions is therefore vital to any lawyer or paralegal working on a client's case.

Several publishers publish court decisions in various forms. Many publishers have devised **reporting systems** for organizing these court decisions. The major reporting system is called the **National Reporter System** and is published by West. It includes books called **reporters** that contain many federal and state decisions in chronological order. Several other companies and government agencies also publish court decisions in chronologically arranged reporters. In all cases, the decisions are selectively reported. Many decisions never appear in print or online.

## 1. Bench Opinions

The U.S. Supreme Court provides the text of **bench opinions** immediately after the Court announces an opinion from the bench. It is a pamphlet that has the opinion of the majority, the plurality, and any concurring or dissenting opinions written by the justices. These opinions are available electronically through Project Hermes. It is a subscription service and most subscribers are universities, news media outlets, and publishing houses.

## 2. Slip Opinions

The next *printed* version of a U.S. Supreme Court decision, and often the first printed version of other court decisions, is called a **slip opinion.** See Illustration 3-1. Sometimes, the slip opinion is the only report of a court's action because the case is never published in a reporter or other service. This is usually the case with trial court decisions, especially state court decisions. However, many court slip opinions, including those of the U.S. Supreme Court, are readily available to the public online at a court website. In some instances, you need to know the name of the case. Many court websites allow you to search by keyword. Most are available free or for a minimal charge. A list of some of the sources of these opinions is included in Appendix D. In addition, Westlaw, Lexis, and Loislaw, computerized legal research services, include many slip opinions online.

An official U.S. Supreme Court slip opinion contains a syllabus. See Illustration 3-1 point A. It is written by the Reporter of Decisions. It is not part of the decision.

---

### ETHICS ALERT

Newspaper reports of slip opinions of court cases also are quickly available; however, these should never be quoted in a memorandum for an attorney or in a motion to the court because such reports have no force within the law. In addition, they may be incorrect. Only quote or cite information that comes directly from the official court opinion.

---

## ILLUSTRATION 3-1.   A Portion of a Supreme Court Slip Opinion

---

(Slip Opinion)                OCTOBER TERM, 2007                1

Syllabus

NOTE: Where it is feasible, a syllabus (headnote) will be released, as is being done in connection with this case, at the time the opinion is issued. The syllabus constitutes no part of the opinion of the Court but has been prepared by the Reporter of Decisions for the convenience of the reader. See *United States* v. *Detroit Timber & Lumber Co.*, 200 U. S. 321, 337.

## SUPREME COURT OF THE UNITED STATES

Syllabus

(B) UNITED STATES *v.* RESSAM

CERTIORARI TO THE UNITED STATES COURT OF APPEALS FOR THE NINTH CIRCUIT

(C) No. 07–455.   (D) Argued March 25, 2008—(E) Decided May 19, 2008

After respondent gave false information on his customs form while attempting to enter the United States, a search of his car revealed explosives that he intended to detonate in this country. He was convicted of, *inter alia*, (1) feloniously making a false statement to a customs official in violation of 18 U. S. C. §1001, and (2) "carr[ying] an explosive during the commission of" that felony in violation of §844(h)(2). The Ninth Circuit set aside the latter conviction because it read "during" in §844(h)(2) to include a requirement that the explosive be carried "in relation to" the underlying felony.

*Held:* Since respondent was carrying explosives when he violated §1001, he was carrying them "during" the commission of that felony. The most natural reading of §844(h)(2) provides a sufficient basis for reversal. It is undisputed that the items in respondent's car were "explosives," and that he was "carr[ying]" those explosives when he knowingly made false statements to a customs official in violation of §1001. Dictionary definitions need not be consulted to arrive at the conclusion that he engaged in §844(h)(2)'s precise conduct. "[D]uring" denotes a temporal link. Bec⎡                        ⎤con-
temporaneous with his §1001│ A  Syllabus           │that
violation. The statute's histo│ B  Case name         │that
Congress did not intend a rel│ C  Docket number     │res-
ently written. Pp. 2–6 ⁴      │ D  Date argued       │
                              │ E  Date decided      │
474 F. 3d 597, reversed.      │ F  Summary of how the│
                              │    judges voted concerning│
   STEVENS, J., delivered the op│   the decision       │RTS,
C. J., and KENNEDY, SOUTER, G⎣                        ⎦d in
which SCALIA and THOMAS, JJ., [                 ]d an
opinion concurring in part and concurring in the judgment, in which
SCALIA, J., joined. BREYER, J., filed a dissenting opinion.

## ILLUSTRATION 3-1. *Continued*

---

Cite as: 553 U. S. ____ (2008)        1

Opinion of the Court

NOTICE: This opinion is subject to formal revision before publication in the preliminary print of the United States Reports. Readers are requested to notify the Reporter of Decisions, Supreme Court of the United States, Washington, D. C. 20543, of any typographical or other formal errors, in order that corrections may be made before the preliminary print goes to press.

# SUPREME COURT OF THE UNITED STATES

No. 07–455

## UNITED STATES, PETITIONER *v.* AHMED RESSAM

### ON WRIT OF CERTIORARI TO THE UNITED STATES COURT OF APPEALS FOR THE NINTH CIRCUIT

[May 19, 2008]

Ⓖ JUSTICE STEVENS delivered the opinion of the Court.

Respondent attempted to enter the United States by car ferry at Port Angeles, Washington. Hidden in the trunk of his rental car were explosives that he intended to detonate at the Los Angeles International Airport. After the ferry docked, respondent was questioned by a customs official, who instructed him to complete a customs declaration form; respondent did so, identifying himself on the form as a Canadian citizen (he is Algerian) named Benni Noris (his name is Ahmed Ressam). Respondent was then directed to a secondary inspection station, where another official performed a search of his car. The official discovered explosives and related items in the car's spare tire well.

Respondent was subsequently convicted of a number of crimes, including the felony of making a false statement to a United States customs official in violation of 18 U. S. C. §1001 (1994 ed., Supp. V) (Count 5) and carrying an explosive "during the commission of" that felony in violation of §844(h)(2) (1994 ed.) (Count 9). [G Body of the decision] als for the Ninth Circuit set aside his conviction on Count 9 because it read the word "during," as used in §844(h)(2), to

### a. Supreme Court Slip Opinions

For the U.S. Supreme Court, you can retrieve decisions from the court clerk or from its website. The U.S. Supreme Court slip opinions are available at www.supremecourt.gov/opinions/slipopinions.aspx. Cases and the docket files can be searched by keywords. The government also offers Supreme Court slip opinions through its PACER Service, www.pacer.gov. The public can access case files 24 hours a day through this service. Users must register to use this service and pay minimal fees for items retrieved. Cases can be searched by court, case number, party name, and filing date. A full docket for a case can be displayed by clicking on a hyperlink. To view documents associated with a particular docket entry, click on the hyperlink that appears next to the entry. If requested, e-mail updates of case activity will be sent.

*United States Law Week*, long-time a service of the Bureau of National Affairs, now called Bloomberg BNA, allows you to access the full text of U.S. Supreme Court opinions daily through the Internet as soon as they are issued. It provides summaries, official and publisher-created headnotes of cases, and a list of cases docketed, decided, and denied review. A case summary will provide some information about the topic addressed in the opinion, the docket number, a brief case history, the summary of the ruling of the case on appeal, and the attorneys involved in the case. *U.S. Law Week* also provides information about other newsworthy legal developments. This fee-based subscription service provides highlights of significant state, administrative and federal court decisions nationwide at bna.com. Web reports are archived since June 1997. *U.S. Law Week* continues to appear in print. *U.S. Law Week* also provides some synopsis of arguments and analysis of significant opinions complete with headnotes and citations to electronic links. *U.S. Law Week* and the *Supreme Court Today*, another BNA product, are e-mailed daily to subscribers in addition to weekly updates.

### b. Other Slip Opinions

Slip opinions for other federal courts can be secured from the court, the Internet, Westlaw, Lexis, and Loislaw. State court slip opinions also are easily accessible from Westlaw, Lexis, Loislaw, or the Internet at the court's website, but the electronic coverage may not be complete. Contact the state court if you cannot find its opinion elsewhere. Many courts will also e-mail slip opinions to registered users.

### ▼ How Are Pending or Unreported Opinions Such as Slip Opinions Cited?

Slip opinions are cited according to **Rule 10.8.1** of *The Bluebook: A Uniform System of Citation* (19th ed. 2010) or **Rule 12.15** of the *ALWD Guide to Legal Citation* (5th ed. 2014). Updates for *The Bluebook* can be found at www.legalbluebook.com. Users must register to receive

these updates. The fifth edition of the *ALWD Guide to Legal Citation* (formerly the *ALWD Citation Manual: A Professional System of Citation*), published in April 2014, also has an online companion at its website, www.alwd.org/publications/citation-manual. Both citation manuals yield the same citation in this case. In either case, you should provide the docket number, the court, and the full (but abbreviated) date of the most recent disposition of the case.

**slip opinion cite:**    Gillespie v. Willard City Bd. of Educ., No. C87-7043 (N.D. Ohio Sept. 28, 1987)

**with page cite:**    Gillespie v. Willard City Bd. of Educ., No. C87-7043, slip op. at 3 (N.D. Ohio Sept. 28, 1987)

---

## ETHICS ALERT

Always check the local court rules to see if unpublished cases can be cited.

---

## 3. Advance Sheets

After a U.S. Supreme Court slip opinion is released, it is published in **advance sheets.** Many other court opinions also may appear in advance sheets. Advance sheets, often distributed as pamphlets, contain the full text of a decision and often are paginated using the same page numbers that will be used when the decision is published in the bound reporter. Many advance sheets contain publisher's notes called **headnotes** that are designed to assist readers. These notes summarize points of law in a case and have a topic and number assigned to them. These topics and numbers assist you in finding additional cases. The timing of the publication of advance sheets varies by publisher. After decisions appear in advance sheets, they are published in the bound reporters. Many print advance sheet publications are being phased out as many courts and fee-based online services now send users slip opinions via e-mail.

## 4. Bound Reporters
### a. U.S. Supreme Court Decisions

A U.S. Supreme Court case is first presented as a bench opinion (also called a preliminary print), published as a slip opinion, then as an advance sheet, and finally as a report in a bound volume. For U.S. Supreme Court cases, the official, government-printed reporter is *United States Reports*. See Illustration 3-2. Illustration 3-2 includes a syllabus or summary of the case. It is not part of the court's decision and

**ILLUSTRATION 3-2.** Pages from *U.S. Reports, United Paper-workers Intl. Union, AFL-CIO, et al. v. Misco, Inc.*, 484 U.S. 29 (1987)

## UNITED PAPERWORKERS INTERNATIONAL UNION, AFL–CIO, ET AL. *v.* MISCO, INC.

### CERTIORARI TO THE UNITED STATES COURT OF APPEALS FOR THE FIFTH CIRCUIT

(1) No. 86–651. Argued October 13, 1987—Decided December 1, 1987 (2)

Respondent employer's collective-bargaining agreement with petitioner union authorizes the submission to binding arbitration of any grievance that arises from the interpretation or application of the agreement's terms, and reserves to management the right to establish, amend, and enforce rules regulating employee discharge and discipline and setting forth disciplinary procedures. One of respondent's rules listed as causes for discharge the possession or use of controlled substances on company property. Isiah Cooper, an employee covered by the agreement who operated a hazardous machine, was apprehended by police in the back-seat of someone else's car in respondent's parking lot with marijuana smoke in the air and a lighted marijuana cigarette in the frontseat ash-tray. A police search of Cooper's own car on the lot revealed marijuana (3) gleanings. Upon learning of the cigarette incident, respondent discharged Cooper for violation of the disciplinary rule. Cooper then filed a grievance which proceeded to arbitration on the stipulated issue whether respondent had just cause for the discharge under the rule and, if not, the appropriate remedy. The arbitrator upheld the grievance and ordered Cooper's reinstatement, finding that the cigarette incident was insufficient proof that Cooper was using or possessed marijuana on company property. Because, at the time of the discharge, respondent was not aware of, and thus did not rely upon, the fact that marijuana had been found in Cooper's own car, the arbitrator refused to accept this fact into evidence. However, the District Court vacated the arbitration award and the Court of Appeals affirmed, ruling that reinstatement would violate the public policy "against the operation of dangerous machinery by persons under the influence of drugs." The court held that the cigarette incident and the finding of marijuana in Cooper's car established a violation of the disciplinary rule that gave respondent just

1 Docket number
2 Decision date
3 Syllabus written by reporter

...eeded the limited authority possessed by
...'s award entered pursuant to a collective-

## ILLUSTRATION 3-2.   *Continued*

PAPERWORKERS v. MISCO, INC.                    31

29                        Opinion of the Court

framed under the approach set out in *W. R. Grace*, and the violation of
such policy must be clearly shown.   Here, the court made no attempt to
review existing laws and legal precedents, but simply formulated a policy against the operation of dangerous machinery under the influence of
drugs based on "general considerations of supposed public interests." ④
Even if that formulation could be accepted, no violation of the policy
was clearly shown, since the assumed connection between the marijuana
gleanings in Cooper's car and his actual use of drugs in the workplace is
tenuous at best.   It was inappropriate for the court itself to draw that
inference, since such factfinding is the task of the arbitrator chosen by
the parties, not the reviewing court.   Furthermore, the award ordered
Cooper's reinstatement in his old job or an equivalent one for which he
was qualified, and it is not clear that he would pose a threat to the
asserted public policy in every such alternative job.   Pp. 42–45.

768 F. 2d 739, reversed.

⑤ WHITE, J., delivered the opinion for a unanimous Court.   BLACKMUN,
J., filed a concurring opinion, in which BRENNAN, J., joined, *post*, p. 46.

*David Silberman* argued the cause for petitioners.   With ⑥
him on the briefs were *Lynn Agee*, *Michael Gottesman*, and
*Laurence Gold*.

*A. Richard Gear* argued the cause and filed a brief for
respondent.*

JUSTICE WHITE delivered the opinion of the Court.

The issue for decision involves several aspects of when a ⑦
federal court may refuse to enforce an arbitration award rendered under a collective-bargaining agreement.

I

Misco, Inc. (Misco, or the Company), operates a paper con-
~~~~~~~~~~~~~~~~~~~~~~~~~ isiana.   The Company is a party
~~~~~~~~~~~~~~~~~~~~~~~ reement with the United Paper-
~~~~~~~~~~~~~~~ a, AFL–CIO, and its union local
~~~~~~~~~~~~~~~ covers the production and main-

~~~~~~~ *. Murphy* filed a brief for the National
~~~~~~~ *curiae* urging reversal.
~~~~~~~ *R. Stein* filed a brief for Northwest Air-
~~~~~~~ rging affirmance.

**4 Syllabus**
**5 Judicial author of opinion
and concurring opinions**
**6 Attorneys representing
the parties**
**7 The start of the Court's opinion**

should not be quoted in any documents submitted to the court. It has no force of law. This illustration also indicates the author of the opinion and whether any judges concurred or dissented. The attorneys representing the parties are noted. Then the decision begins. This reporter, however, is not published quickly, nor does it contain any research aids. Because of this delay, commercial publishers have created reporter systems that contain the same decisions as those published in *U.S. Reports.*

Commercial publishers produce these decisions as well. One commercial publisher, West, publishes all U.S. Supreme Court decisions in its reporter called the *Supreme Court Reporter.* See Illustration 3-3. LexisNexis (Lexis) prints the same full text of U.S. Supreme Court decisions in its reporter called *United States Supreme Court Reports, Lawyers' Edition 2nd.* Most people simply call it the *Lawyers' Edition.*

Within both reporters, the case opinions are identical to the decisions that appear in the official *U.S. Reports.* The reports in these commercially published reporters, however, also contain references prepared by the publishers to assist you in your research. These references direct you to other sources that may help you understand a point of law. For example, a publisher may direct you to a treatise that contains commentary about a point of law raised in the case reported. In addition, these references may assist you in locating other cases on point.

### ▼ Is U.S. Supreme Court Docket Information Available on the Internet?

Yes. For U.S. Supreme Court docket, schedules, general information, and links to decisions, see www.supremecourt.gov. This site also provides oral argument transcripts and argument audio in recent cases. As of October 2013, the Court now provides full text of bound volumes of the fourth generation of the Court's opinions.

### ▼ What Happens if the Language of a Decision in the Commercial Reporters Varies from the Language in *U.S. Reports?*

If the decision text contained in either the *Supreme Court Reporter* or the *Lawyers' Edition* varies from the official, government-printed report, the language in *U.S. Reports* governs.

### ▼ Why Use the Commercial Reporters Rather Than the Official Reports?

You should review U.S. Supreme Court cases in either the *Supreme Court Reporter* or in the *U.S. Supreme Court Reports, Lawyers' Edition.* They contain a variety of publisher's headnotes or case abstracts that assist you in your research. Often they include additional references, such as encyclopedia cite. These headnotes summarize points of law found in a case. They also include a publisher's topic designation and number. These topics and numbers tie into the commercial publisher's indexes of legal

**ILLUSTRATION 3-3.   Pages from *Supreme Court Reporter, United Paperworkers Intl. Union, AFL-CIO, et al. v. Misco, Inc.*, 108 S. Ct. 364-365, 370 (1987)**

①

②**364**                    **108 SUPREME COURT REPORTER**                    484 U.S. 29

③        ④
484 U.S. 29, 98 L.Ed.2d 286

⑤ UNITED PAPERWORKERS INTERNA-
TIONAL UNION, AFL-CIO, et
al., Petitioners

v.

MISCO, INC.

⑥    No. 86–651.

Argued Oct. 13, 1987.

Decided Dec. 1, 1987.

⑦ After arbitrator determined that employee did not violate employer's rule regarding use or possession of marijuana on
company property, and ordered reinstatement of employee, the United States District Court for the Western District of Louisiana, Tom Stagg, Chief Judge, vacated
arbitration award.  On appeal, the Court of
Appeals for the Fifth Circuit, Gee, Circuit
Judge, 768 F.2d 739, affirmed, and determined that reinstatement would violate
public policy against operation of dangerous machinery by persons under influence
of drugs.  On writ of certiorari, the Supreme Court, Justice White, held that: (1)
Court of Appeals was not free to refuse
enforcement of arbitrator's award on basis
that it found arbitrator's fact-finding improvident; (2) arbitrator was entitled to
refuse to consider evidence unknown to
company at time employee was fired; (3)
formulation of public policy set up by
Court of Appeals did not comply with requirement that such policy must be ascer-
tained by reference to laws and legal precedence and not from general considerations
of supposed public interests; and (4) even
if Court of Appeals' formulation of public
policy was accepted, no violation of that
policy was clearly shown.

Reversed.

Justice Blackmun filed concurring
opinion in which Justice Brennan joined.

⑧ **1. Arbitration** ⬅73.7(3) ⑨
Courts play only limited role when
asked to review decision of arbitrator;
courts are not authorized to reconsider
merits of award even though parties may
allege that award rests on errors of fact or
on misinterpretation of collective bargaining contract.

**2. Labor Relations** ⬅416.1
Courts have jurisdiction to enforce collective bargaining contracts, but where
contract provides grievance and arbitration
procedures, those procedures must first be
exhausted and courts must order resort to
private settlement mechanism without dealing with merits of dispute. ⑩

**3. Labor Relations** ⬅485
To resolve disputes about application
of collective bargaining agreement, arbitrator must find facts and court may not
reject those findings simply because it dis-
agrees with them.

**4. Labor Relations** ⬅462, 479
Arbitrator may not ignore plain lan-

1 *Supreme Court Reporter*
   volume number
2 *Supreme Court Reporter*
   page number
3 Citation to official reporter
4 Citation to unofficial reporter
5 Case name
6 Docket number
7 Syllabus by reporter editor,
   labeled in current editions as
   background and holding
8 West topic
9 West key number
10 West headnotes
11 Number of page of official
    reports
12 Syllabus written by
    Supreme Court's reporter

## ILLUSTRATION 3-3.  *Continued*

**7. Labor Relations ⊜479**

Arbitral decisions pertaining to collective bargaining agreements which are procured by parties through fraud or through arbitrator's dishonesty need not be enforced.

**⑧8. Labor Relations ⊜479 ⑨**

Arbitrator's decision, which was rendered pursuant to collective bargaining agreement, that evidence was insufficient to prove that discharged employee had possessed or used marijuana on company property in contravention of company's rule could not be reversed on basis that appellate court found fact-finding by arbitrator to be improvident.

**9. Labor Relations ⊜479**

Appellate court could not refuse to enforce arbitrator's award which required ⑩company to reinstate employee who had been discharged for allegedly violating company rule pertaining to use of marijuana on company property because arbitrator, in deciding whether there was just cause to discharge, refused to consider evidence unknown to company at time of discharge; arbitrator's approach was consistent with collective bargaining agreement, and with practice followed by other arbitrators, and further, even if arbitrator erred in refusing to consider disputed evidence, error was not in bad faith so as to justify setting aside award. 9 U.S.C.A. § 10(c).

**10. Labor Relations ⊜479**

Court's refusal to enforce arbitrator's award under collective bargaining agreement because it is contrary to public policy is specific application of more general doctrine, rooted in common law, that court may refuse to enforce contracts that violate law or public policy.

**11. Labor Relations ⊜264**

Courts may only refuse to enforce collective bargaining agreement when specific terms contained in agreement violate public policy.

**12. Labor Relations ⊜479**

Formulation of public policy based only on general considerations of supposed public interest is not type of public policy that permits court to set aside arbitration award that was entered in accordance with valid collective bargaining agreement.

**13. Master and Servant ⊜47**

Even if public policy considerations against operation of dangerous machinery while under influence of drugs existed, no violation of that policy was shown in case where traces of marijuana had been found in terminated employee's car; assumed connection between marijuana gleanings and employee's actual use of drugs in workplace provided insufficient basis for holding that his reinstatement would actually violate public policy.

**14. Labor Relations ⊜483**

Appellate court's conclusion that since marijuana had been found in terminated employee's car, employee had ever been or would ever be under influence of marijuana while he was on job and operating dangerous machinery was improper exercise in fact-finding about employee's use of drugs and his amenability to discipline, which exceeded authority of court which was asked to overturn arbitration award; parties did not bargain for facts to be found by court, but rather, fact-finding was to be made by arbitrator chosen by parties who had more opportunity to observe employee and to be familiar with workplace and its problems.

⑫ *Syllabus* *

Respondent employer's collective-bargaining agreement with petitioner union authorizes the submission to binding arbitration of any grievance that arises from the interpretation or application of the agreement's terms, and reserves to management the right to establish, amend,

---

* The syllabus constitutes no part of the opinion of the Court but has been prepared by the Reporter of Decisions for the convenience of the reader. See *United States v. Detroit Lumber Co.*, 200 U.S. 321, 337, 26 S.Ct. 282, 287, 50 L.Ed. 499.

# ILLUSTRATION 3-3.   *Continued*

**370**   108 SUPREME COURT REPORTER   484 U.S. 36

peals but alternatively argues that the judgment below should be affirmed because of erroneous findings by the arbitrator. We deal first with the opposing alternative arguments.

## A

[1] Collective-bargaining agreements commonly provide grievance procedures to settle disputes between union and employer with respect to the interpretation and application of the agreement and require binding arbitration for unsettled grievances. In such cases, and this is such a case, the Court made clear almost 30 years ago that the courts play only a limited role when asked to review the decision of an arbitrator. The courts are not authorized to reconsider the merits of an award even though the parties may allege that the award rests on errors of fact or on misinterpretation of the contract. "The refusal of courts to review the merits of an arbitration award is the proper approach to arbitration under collective bargaining agreements. The federal policy of settling labor disputes by arbitration would be undermined if courts had the final say on the merits of the awards." *Steelworkers v. Enterprise Wheel & Car Corp.*, 363 U.S. 593, 596, 80 S.Ct. 1358, 1360, 4 L.Ed.2d 1424 (1960). As long as the arbitrator's award "draws its essence from the collective bargaining agreement," and is not merely "his own brand of industrial justice," the award is legitimate. *Id.*, at 597, 80 S.Ct., at 1361.

"The function of the court is very limited when the parties have agreed to submit all questions of contract interpretation₃₇ to the arbitrator. It is confined to ascertaining whether the party seeking 🔟 tration is making a claim which on its face is governed by the contract. Whether the moving party is right or wrong is a question of contract interpretation for the arbitrator. In these circumstances the moving party should not be deprived of the arbitrator's judgment,

when it was his judgment and all that it connotes that was bargained for.

"The courts, therefore, have no business weighing the merits of the grievance, considering whether there is equity in a particular claim, or determining whether there is particular language in the written instrument which will support the claim." *Steelworkers v. American Mfg. Co.*, 363 U.S. 564, 567–568, 80 S.Ct. 1343, 1346, 4 L.Ed.2d 1403 (1960) (emphasis added; footnote omitted).

See also *AT & T Technologies, Inc. v. Communications Workers*, 475 U.S. 643, 649–650, 106 S.Ct. 1415, 1418–1419, 89 L.Ed.2d 648 (1986).

[2–7] The reasons for insulating arbitral decisions from judicial review are grounded in the federal statutes regulating labor-management relations. These statutes reflect a decided preference for private settlement of labor disputes without the intervention of government: The Labor Management Relations Act of 1947, 61 Stat. 154, 29 U.S.C. § 173(d), provides that "[f]inal adjustment by a method agreed upon by the parties is hereby declared to be the desirable method for settlement of grievance disputes arising over the application or interpretation of an existing collective-bargaining agreement." See also *AT & T Technologies*, *supra*, at 650, 106 S.Ct., at 1419. The courts have jurisdiction to enforce collective-bargaining contracts; but where the contract provides grievance and arbitration procedures, those procedures must first be exhausted and courts must order resort to the private settlement mechanisms without dealing with the merits of the dispute. Because the parties have contracted to have disputes settled by an arbitrator chosen by the 🔟 ther than by a judge, it is the arbitrator's view of the facts and of the meaning₃₈ of the contract that they have agreed to accept. Courts thus do not sit to hear claims of factual or legal error by an arbitrator as an appellate court does in reviewing decisions of lower courts. To resolve disputes about the application of a collective-bargaining agree-

issues called **digests.** These digests are organized by topic and numbers. These digests will be discussed in detail in Chapter 4.

Cases published in the *Supreme Court Reporter* also contain headnotes. See Illustration 3-3. Similar to the cases published in the *Lawyers' Edition,* the *Supreme Court Reporter* cases include topics and numbers, which West calls **key numbers.** In Illustration 3-3, the first headnote includes the topic Arbitration and the key number 73.7(3). Also included in the text is the publisher's case abstract of a point of law. West has devised a system of organizing federal and state cases according to topics coupled with key numbers. See Chapter 4 for a more detailed explanation of this system. Across the top of the page in Illustration 3-3 is the citation to the *Supreme Court Reporter.* Above the name of the case is the official citation to the *U.S. Reports* and a citation to the *Lawyers' Edition* report of this case. In addition to the official syllabus of the court, West provides a summary of each case called a **syllabus.** This syllabus should not be cited because it is not authoritative.

Note the small numbers in front of some words in Illustration 3-3. Those numbers indicate the page number in which that text would appear in the official reports.

West also includes a research aid called **West Codenotes.** These indicate whether a statute cited in the case has been ruled unconstitutional, preempted, or modified in one of 25 ways. These are placed between the headnotes and the opinion's text.

The *Lawyers' Edition* also includes headnotes, or the publisher's summaries of points of law presented in each case. These headnotes are arranged by publisher-designated topics and numbers in a series of volumes called *United States Supreme Court Digest, Lawyers' Edition.* Headnotes and digests are explained in detail later in Chapter 4. You should not quote from these headnotes because they are not authoritative.

### ▼ How Do You Locate a Reported Case?

Cases have citations that are similar to addresses. For example, "108 S.Ct. 364" is a citation. The number "108" is the volume of the reporter that contains the case. "S.Ct." is the abbreviation for the *Supreme Court Reporter* that contains the case and finally, "364" is the first page the case appears on within the reporter. See Illustration 3-3. Another example of a citation is "581 N.E.2d 885." The number "581" indicates the volume that contains the case. "N.E.2d" is the abbreviation for the reporter, the *North Eastern Reporter Second Series.* The last number, "885," is the first page of the case. This citation identifies the case, *Thompson v. Economy Super Marts.* See Illustration 3-4.

At the top of Illustration 3-4, next to the circled 1 is this same *West's North Eastern Reporter* citation. Above the name of the case, you can find the official (that is, state government-printed) citation and a citation to *West's Illinois Decisions Reporter.*

## ILLUSTRATION 3-4.    *West's North Eastern Reporter, Thompson v. Economy Super Marts, Inc., 581 N.E.2d 885 (Ill. App. Ct. 1991)*

THOMPSON v. ECONOMY SUPER MARTS, INC.        Ill.  **885**
Cite as 581 N.E.2d 885 (Ill.App. 3 Dist. 1991) ———①

provided for both of them on the instrument. Therefore, the defendant argues, since the intention of the Bank was to obtain a mortgage of the premises from both joint tenants and only one joint tenant signed the mortgage, the instrument should be found to be unenforceable as was the contract in *Dineff.*

*Dineff* is clearly distinguishable from the instant case. In *Dineff*, the plaintiff was attempting to enforce an agreement to convey the entire interest in the jointly held property without the signatures of both cotenants. The court pointed out that there was no prayer for partial performance against the cotenant who had signed the agreement. (*Dineff*, 27 Ill.2d at 482, 190 N.E.2d at 311.) It is well established that one cotenant cannot convey the interest of another cotenant without proper authority.

Here, however, the plaintiff is not attempting to foreclose on the entire interest in the property. The foreclosure complaint is against only the undivided one-half interest of the joint tenant who signed the mortgage.

[4] We disagree with the defendant's argument that the clear intention of the parties required the defendant's signature

that the names of both husband and wife appear in the body of the instrument and in the acknowledgment. The rule seems to be general that a deed naming two or more parties as grantors, executed by only a portion of them, is valid as to

those executing it." *Heckmann*, 283 Ill. at 513, 119 N.E. at 642.

It is clear that Mr. Stauffenberg intended to mortgage the real estate. There is nothing in the mortgage to indicate that it was not to be binding unless the defendant signed it also. We see no reason to deviate from the established rule that when a property owner attempts to convey a greater interest in the property than he actually has, that the conveyance is valid to the extent of his interest and void only as to the excess.

For the reasons stated above, the order of the trial court dismissing the complaint is reversed. This cause is remanded for further proceedings.

Reversed and remanded.

GORMAN and McCUSKEY, JJ., concur.

221 Ill.App.3d 263 ②
③
163 Ill.Dec. 731

**Cherryl E. THOMPSON,**
**Plaintiff–Appellant,**

v.

**ECONOMY SUPER MARTS, INC., a Division of Weems & Bruns Corp., a Corporation, and Weems & Bruns Corp., a Corporation, Defendants–Appellees.** ④

No. 3–90–0662. ⑤

Appellate Court of Illinois,
Third District.

Nov. 8, 1991.

Customer allegedly injured when she slipped on lettuce leaf in produce section of grocery store brought negligence action against store owners. The Circuit Court, 12th Judicial Circuit, Will County, Michael H. Lyons, J., granted defendants' posttrial motion for judgment notwithstanding verdict after jury found customer to be 55% contributorily negligent and awarded her ⑥

---

1  Citation to *West's North Eastern Reporter*
2  Citation to official reporter
3  Citation to unofficial reporter
4  Case name
5  Docket number
6  Syllabus by reporter editor
7  West key numbers and headnotes
8  *Ward* case cited in Illustration 5-3

# ILLUSTRATION 3-4.   *Continued*

⑥ damages. the Appellate Court, Haase, J., held that: (1) where foreign substance causing slip of business invitee is on premises due to negligence of proprietor or his servants, it is not necessary to establish their actual or constructive knowledge of the substance, but if substance is on premises through acts of third persons, time element during which substance was present is material factor to establish knowledge of, or notice to, proprietor; (2) even where there is proof that foreign substance causing slip of business invitee was related to defendant's business, where no further evidence is offered other than presence of substance and occurrence of injury, defendant is entitled to directed verdict, as such evidence is insufficient to support necessary inference of negligence; and (3) evidence of negligence of grocery store was not sufficient to permit customer to recover from store owners.

Affirmed.

⑦ **1. Negligence ⬥32(2.8)**

Defendant owes business invitee on defendant's premises duty to exercise ordinary care in maintaining premises in reasonably safe condition.

**2. Negligence ⬥44, 48**

Where business invitee is injured by slipping on premises, liability may be imposed if substance causing slip was placed by negligence of proprietor or his servants; or if substance was on premises through acts of third persons or there is no showing how it got there, liability may be imposed if it appears that proprietor or his servant knew of presence of substance, or that substance was there sufficient length of time so that in exercise of ordinary care its presence should have been discovered.

**3. Negligence ⬥48**

Where foreign substance causing slip of business invitee is on premises due to negligence of proprietor or his servants, it is not necessary to establish their actual or constructive knowledge of the substance, but if substance is on premises through acts of third persons, time element during which substance was present is material

factor to establish knowledge of, or notice to, proprietor.

**4. Negligence ⬥136(22)**

Where there is proof that foreign substance causing slip of business invitee was product sold or related to defendant's operations and invitee offered some further evidence, direct or circumstantial, however slight, such as location of substance or business practices of defendant from which it could be inferred that it was more likely that defendant or his servants, rather than a customer, dropped the substance on the premises, trial court should allow negligence issue to go to jury.

**5. Negligence ⬥121.1(8)**

Even where there is proof that foreign substance causing slip of business invitee was related to defendant's business, where no further evidence is offered other than presence of substance and occurrence of injury, defendant is entitled to directed verdict, such evidence being insufficient to support necessary inference of negligence.

**6. Negligence ⬥134(5)**

Evidence of negligence of grocery store was not sufficient to permit customer allegedly injured when she slipped on lettuce leaf in produce section of store to recover from store, even though leaf was described as wilted and was found near unsupervised produce section where vegetables were packed on ice; no direct or circumstantial evidence made it more likely that store's servants, rather than customer, dropped the leaf, and customer presented no evidence that ice which packed produce was directly above water spot or any evidence regarding how ice was packed or how easy it might have been to jar ice loose and spill it to the floor.

---

James J. Morici, Jr., argued, Anesi, Ozmon & Rodin, Ltd., Chicago, for Cherryl E. Thompson.

Kenneth T. Garvey, Robert Spitkovsky, Jr. and Kevin P. O'Connell, argued, Bresnahan & Garvey, Chicago, for Economy Super Marts, Inc.

# ILLUSTRATION 3-4. *Continued*

**THOMPSON v. ECONOMY SUPER MARTS, INC.**    Ill. **887**

Cite as 581 N.E.2d 885 (Ill.App. 3 Dist. 1991)

Justice HAASE delivered the opinion of the Court.

The plaintiff, Cherryl E. Thompson, brought this negligence action against the defendants, Economy Super Marts, Inc. and Weems & Bruns Corp., to recover damages for personal injuries she sustained when she slipped on a lettuce leaf in the produce section of the defendants' grocery store. A jury awarded the plaintiff $12,974.96 in recoverable damages after finding that she was 55% contributorily negligent. Thereafter, the trial court granted the defendants' post-trial motion for a judgment notwithstanding the verdict. The plaintiff appeals from that decision.

The plaintiff testified at trial that on July 3, 1986, she picked up a watermelon in the produce section of the defendants' store and began to walk through the produce aisle. At that point, she slipped and fell on a lettuce leaf and water. She had not seen the leaf or the water before her fall and did not know how long they were there. She noted that the lettuce leaf was green and brown, had dirt on it, and appeared beat up. According to the plaintiff, her fall occurred about two or three feet to the left of the produce aisle. She also stated that the fruits and vegetables in the produce aisle were kept on ice.

Terida Thompson, the plaintiff's daughter, substantially corroborated the plaintiff's testimony. Additionally, she stated that the lettuce leaf looked old and like it had been there awhile. She further stated that she had walked through the produce aisle once before the accident occurred and did not see any water or a lettuce leaf on the floor prior to the plaintiff's fall.

Gene Pesavento, the assistant store manager, testified that it was his duty to make sure that all areas in the grocery store were clear and free of debris. He agreed that the produce department requires constant surveillance to ensure that debris is not left on the floor. He also agreed that debris poses a tripping hazard.

Pesavento further testified that no one was specifically charged with the responsibility of constantly monitoring the floor of the produce department. He explained that the defendants' employees knew that they were supposed to keep an eye on the entire store, and not specifically one area.

Phil Woock, the store's general manager, testified that he was not working at the time of the plaintiff's accident. He stated that the store's floor was dry mopped and swept every night in July, 1986. In addition, the floors were swept during the day as needed, and spills were cleaned as needed. The floors were professionally mopped and waxed every Wednesday night, and the plaintiff's accident occurred on a Thursday. Woock further testified that a part-time employee was on duty in the produce department at the time of the accident, but he could have been working in the back room when it occurred. Woock also testified that all store workers have the responsibility of keeping the floor clean if no one is working in the produce department at a particular time.

Donald Schreiner and Rubin Amazan each testified that they were working at the store at the time of the plaintiff's accident, but did not witness the fall. They both stated that they did not observe a lettuce leaf on the floor after inspecting the floor following the accident.

Based on the foregoing evidence, the jury found that the plaintiff suffered $28,833.24 in damages, but it awarded her only $12,974.96 because it found that she was 55% contributorily negligent. Thereafter, the defendants filed a post-trial motion requesting that the trial court enter a judgment notwithstanding the verdict. The trial court subsequently granted the defendants' motion, finding that: (1) no evidence was presented that the defendants had actual or constructive notice of the lettuce leaf and water for a sufficient length of time that its presence should have been discovered; and (2) the jury's award of damages was a compromise verdict and could not be sustained.

On appeal, the plaintiff initially argues that the trial court erred in granting a judgment notwithstanding the verdict. She contends that the court mistakenly found that she did not present any evidence that

# ILLUSTRATION 3-4.  *Continued*

**888** Ill.        **581 NORTH EASTERN REPORTER, 2d SERIES**

the defendants had actual or constructive notice of the lettuce leaf.

**[1–3]** It is well-settled that a defendant owes a business invitee on the defendant's premises a duty to exercise ordinary care in maintaining the premises in a reasonably safe condition. (*Ward v. K Mart Corp.* (1990), 136 Ill.2d 132, 143 Ill.Dec. 288, 554 N.E.2d 223; *Perminas v. Montgomery Ward & Co.* (1975), 60 Ill.2d 469, 328 N.E.2d 290.) Where a business invitee is injured by slipping on the premises, liability may be imposed if the substance was placed there by the negligence of the proprietor or his servants, or, if the substance was on the premises through acts of third persons or there is no showing how it got there, liability may be imposed if it appears that the proprietor or his servant knew of its presence, or that the substance was there a sufficient length of time so that in the exercise of ordinary care its presence should have been discovered. (*Olinger v. Great Atlantic & Pacific Tea Co.* (1961), 21 Ill.2d 469, 173 N.E.2d 443; *Wroblewski v. Hillman's, Inc.* (1963), 43 Ill.App.2d 246, 193 N.E.2d 470.) Thus, where the foreign substance is on the premises due to the negligence of the proprietor or his servants, it is not necessary to establish their knowledge, actual or constructive; whereas, if the substance is on the premises through acts of third persons, the time element to establish knowledge or notice to the proprietor is a material factor. *Blake v. Dickinson* (1975), 31 Ill.App.3d 379, 332 N.E.2d 575.

**[4, 5]** Where there is proof that the foreign substance was a product sold or related to the defendant's operations, and the plaintiff offers some further evidence direct or circumstantial, however slight, such as the location of the substance or the business practices of the defendant, from which it could be inferred that it was more likely that the defendant or his servants, rather than a customer, dropped the substance on the premises, the trial court should allow the negligence issue to go to the jury. (*Donoho v. O'Connell's, Inc.* (1958), 13 Ill.2d 113, 148 N.E.2d 434.) However, even where there is proof that the foreign substance was related to the defendant's business, but no further evi-

dence is offered other than the presence of the substance and the occurrence of the injury, the defendant is entitled to a directed verdict, such evidence being insufficient to support the necessary inference. *Olinger v. Great Atlantic & Pacific Tea Co.* (1961), 21 Ill.2d 469, 173 N.E.2d 443; *Wroblewski v. Hillman's, Inc.* (1963), 43 Ill. App.2d 246, 193 N.E.2d 470.

**[6]** The plaintiff argues that she satisfied the requirements set forth in *Donoho* of introducing "further evidence, however slight, such as the location of the substance or the business practice of the defendant, from which it could be inferred that it was more likely that the defendant or his servants, rather than a customer, dropped the substance on the premises." She contends that evidence of the wilted lettuce leaf and the fact that it was found near the unsupervised produce section where vegetables were packed on ice was sufficient to allow the case to go to the jury under *Donoho*.

We disagree. The Illinois Supreme Court in *Donoho* undertook an extensive analysis of the circumstances under which negligence could be inferred from the conduct of the defendant when it was uncertain who was responsible for the foreign substance dropped on the premises. In *Donoho*, the plaintiff slipped and fell on an onion ring at the defendant's restaurant. It was unknown who dropped the onion ring. Yet, the court found that from the circumstantial evidence, it could be reasonably inferred that it was more likely that the onion ring was on the floor through the acts of the defendant's servants rather than a customer. The court based its decision on the additional circumstantial evidence that the onion ring on which the plaintiff slipped was located by a table cleared by a bus boy, under the bus boy's practice of clearing tables food particles could drop to the floor, and testimony that after the bus boy cleared the table in question no one else ate there before the plaintiff fell.

In the present case, however, there was no direct or circumstantial evidence indicating that it was more likely that the defendants' servants dropped the item than a customer. Furthermore, the plaintiff did not present any evidence that the ice, which

## ILLUSTRATION 3-4. *Continued*

PEOPLE v. SOLANO      Ill. **889**

Cite as 581 N.E.2d 889 (Ill.App. 3 Dist. 1991)

packed the produce, was directly above the water spot. Nor did she present any evidence regarding how the ice was packed or how easy it might have been to jar it loose spilling it to the floor. Moreover, there was no specific evidence that the plaintiff's business practice was unusual or created any special hazard.

The plaintiff also relies on *Perminas v. Montgomery Ward & Company* (1975), 60 Ill.2d 469, 328 N.E.2d 290, in support of her position. In *Perminas*, the plaintiff slipped on a skateboard-like object in an aisle of the defendant's store. There, one of the defendant's employees actually had knowledge that the object was creating a dangerous condition. The court imposed liability on the defendant because the defendant, after receiving notice through its employee that its product was creating a dangerous situation, failed to return its premises to a safe condition or warn its customers.

We find that the plaintiff's reliance on *Perminas* is misplaced. In the present case, unlike *Perminas*, the defendants did not have actual or constructive knowledge of the situation. Furthermore, the record in the instant case does not contain any evidence regarding the length of time the substance was on the floor from which it could be inferred that the defendants had constructive notice.

After reviewing the evidence in the aspect most favorable to the plaintiff, we conclude that the evidence so overwhelmingly favored the defendants that no contrary verdict could ever stand. Accordingly, we find that the trial court properly granted the defendants' motion for a judgment notwithstanding the verdict. Our resolution of the foregoing issue renders the parties' remaining issues moot.

The judgment of the circuit court of Will County is affirmed.

Affirmed.

McCUSKEY, J., and STOUDER, P.J., concur.

221 Ill.App.3d 272

163 Ill.Dec. 735

**The PEOPLE of the State of Illinois, Plaintiff–Appellee,**

v.

**Juan SOLANO, Defendant–Appellant.**

No. 3–91–0067.

Appellate Court of Illinois, Third District.

Nov. 8, 1991.

Sixteen-year-old defendant was convicted of reckless homicide and driving under the influence of alcohol by the 13th Judicial Circuit Court, LaSalle County, James Lanuti, J., and he appealed. The Appellate Court, McCuskey, J., held that: (1) degree of harm to passenger in defendant's car was aggravating factor that trial judge could consider in imposing sentence, and (2) trial judge could likewise consider defendant's prior underage drinking and level of alcohol in defendant's blood.

Affirmed.

**1. Criminal Law** ⟜1147, 1208.2

Sentencing is matter of judicial discretion and, absent abuse of discretion by trial court, sentence may not be altered on review.

**2. Criminal Law** ⟜986.2(1)

Defendant's history, character and rehabilitative potential, along with the seriousness of defendant's offense, need to protect society, and need for deterrence and punishment, must be equally weighed at sentencing.

**3. Criminal Law** ⟜986(3), 1144.17

Sentencing judge is presumed to have considered mitigating circumstances before court, and there is no requirement that judge recite and assign value to each circumstance presented.

**4. Automobiles** ⟜359

Trial judge sufficiently considered motorist's rehabilitative potential, young age,

Reprinted with permission of Thomson Reuters.

## ▼ How Are U.S. Supreme Court Cases Cited?

Cite U.S. Supreme Court cases according to *Bluebook* Rule 10, especially Table T1.1. Once a U.S. Supreme Court case is published in an advance sheet of the *U.S. Reports*, the *U.S. Reports* citation, and only the *U.S. Reports* citation, is the proper citation. Do not include parallel citations with the official *U.S. Reports* cite.

**correct:**      *Erie R.R. v. Tompkins*, 304 U.S. 64 (1938)

**incorrect:**    *Erie R.R. v. Tompkins*, 304 U.S. 64, 58 S. Ct. 817, 82 L. Ed. 1188 (1938)

The citation would be the same based on *ALWD* **Rule 12.4(c)**.

However, if a Supreme Court opinion has been published in the *West's Supreme Court Reporter* but not yet in the *U.S. Reports*, the *Supreme Court Reporter* citation should be used. *See Bluebook* **Table T1.1** and *ALWD* **Rule 12.4(c)**.

If a Supreme Court opinion has not yet been published in *U.S. Reports*, the *Supreme Court Reporter*, or *Lawyers' Edition*, then you should cite to *United States Law Week*. *See Bluebook* **Table T1.1** and *ALWD* **Rule 12.4**.

**U.S.L.W. cite:**    *Ashcroft v. The Free Speech Coalition*, 70 U.S.L.W. 4237 (US April 16, 2002).

Place the court designation for U.S. Supreme Court, "U.S.," in parentheses with the full date following. See *Bluebook* **Rule 10.5**.

Again, the same rules apply for *ALWD* citation, so the citation would be the same.

### b. Other Federal Case Reports

#### ▼ Where Do You Find Decisions of Other Federal Courts?

Many opinions of the U.S. Courts of Appeals can be found in *West's Federal Reporter*, *now in the third series*. In addition to printing the decisions of the U.S. Courts of Appeals, the current series contains some decisions of the Temporary Emergency Court of Appeals. See Illustration 3-5 for court coverage during specific years.

*West's* **Federal Supplement,** now in the second series, is a publication started in 1932 to connect with the *Federal Reporter*. It includes decisions of the U.S. District Courts, the U.S. Court of Claims from 1932 to 1960, the U.S. Court of International Trade (formerly known as the U.S. Customs Court), and the Judicial Panel on Multidistrict Litigation. See Illustration 3-5.

In 2001, West started publishing *West's* **Federal Appendix.** It is an offshoot of the *Federal Reporter*. It contains U.S. Court of Appeals

**ILLUSTRATION 3-5.**    *West's Federal Reporter and Federal Supplement Coverage*

| *West's Federal Reporter Coverage* (F., F.2d, F.3d) | |
| --- | --- |
| U.S. Circuit Courts | 1880 to 1912 |
| Commerce Court of the United States | 1911 to 1913 |
| U.S. District Courts | 1880 to 1932 |
| U.S. Court of Claims (1960 to 1982) | 1929 to 1932 |
| U.S. Court of Appeals (formerly United States Circuit Court of Appeals) | 1891 to date |
| U.S. Court of Customs and Patent Appeals | 1929 to 1982 |
| U.S. Emergency Court of Appeals | 1943 to 1961 |
| Temporary Emergency Court of Appeals | 1972 to 1993 |
| | |
| *West's Federal Supplement Coverage* (F. Supp., F. Supp. 2d) | |
| U.S. District Courts | 1932 to date |
| U.S. Court of Claims | 1932 to 1960 |
| U.S. Court of International Trade (formerly U.S. Customs Court) | 1956 to date |
| Judicial Panel on Multidistrict Litigation | 1968 to date |

decisions that are not designated by the court for publication. Similar to the other West reporters, both the print and online cases included in this publication contain headnotes and other West enhancements. Its advance sheets are combined with the *Federal Reporter* advance sheets.

Not all federal appellate court or district court decisions are published. In some instances, the judges of these courts determine whether to submit their decisions to the publishers. In other cases, the publishers selectively print decisions. Unpublished opinions are available from the courts. In 2006, the Federal Rules of Appellate Practice were amended to allow for citation to unpublished cases in court documents. Individual circuits, however, may determine how to deal with unpublished cases issued on or after January 1, 2007, based upon Federal Rule of Appellate Procedure 32.1.

---

*PRACTICE POINTER*

Check all applicable rules whenever you plan to use an unpublished case as an authority for a point of law.

▼ How Are *Federal Reporter* and *Federal Supplement* Decisions Cited?

Cite *Federal Reporter* and *Federal Supplement* decisions according to *Bluebook* **Rules 10.1** through **10.6** and **Table T.1** or *ALWD* **Rule 12**. The case name is placed first and underlined. Next, place the volume number. The reporter abbreviation is next. Note that for the *Federal Reporter*, the abbreviation is "F." If the *Federal Reporter* cited belongs to the second or third series, "2d" or "3d" should be placed next to the "F." For the *Federal Supplement*, the reporter is abbreviated "F. Supp." or "F. Supp. 2d." The page number follows the abbreviation for the reporter. Next, in parentheses you should place an abbreviation that denotes the appropriate court and then the date of the decision. Be certain to include a geographic designation for the district courts.

**Federal Reporter case**     *Zimmerman v. N Am. Signal Co.*, 704 F.2d 347 (7th Cir. 1983)—*Bluebook* format

**Federal Supplement case:**  *Musser v. Mountain View Broad.*, 578 F. Supp. 229 (E.D. Tenn. 1984)—*Bluebook* format

The *ALWD* citations would be similar for these cases based upon **Rule 12**. The only difference is "Mountain" would be abbreviated "Mt." in the second citation.

▼ Are Decisions Published in Any Other Reporters?

Several publishers of looseleaf services and specialized reporters also publish some federal decisions. Sometimes they duplicate opinions found in the West series. West also publishes some specialized reporters, such as the **Federal Rules Decisions** (F.R.D.). This reporter contains decisions in which a federal rule of civil or criminal procedure is at issue. *Federal Rules Decisions* includes not only cases but speeches, articles, and reports of judicial conferences. Another specialized reporter is *West's Education Law Reporter*. It is a compilation of selected state and federal education-related decisions from 1982 to date.

## 5. Computerized Reporting

▼ Can You Find Decisions on the Internet and Through Fee-Based Computer Services?

Yes. Many published and unpublished federal and state decisions are online on Westlaw, Lexis, Loislaw, VersusLaw, and through the Internet. Many courts provide online decisions free or for a nominal fee. For example, the PACER service provides access to federal court decisions for a modest fee. Many state courts provide these decisions as well. Although online cases found at court websites can be accessed at a

## ILLUSTRATION 3-6. Finding a Case in Westlaw

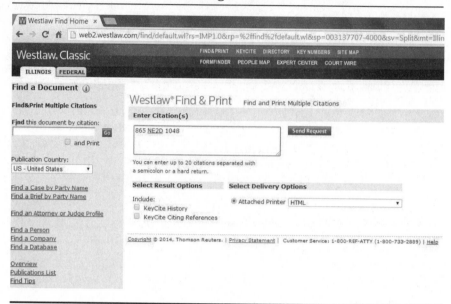

Reprinted with permission of Thomson Reuters.

low cost 24 hours a day, these cases often lack research aids and may be difficult to locate.

On Westlaw, Lexis, Loislaw, and VersusLaw, cases are organized into databases or files and can be accessed through keyword and other searches. Unlike most cases that may be found on the Internet, cases that appear within Westlaw or Lexis databases contain publishers' research aids such as headnotes and West Codenotes.

To access Web-based cases through the Internet, go directly to a court's website. Review Appendix D.

The United States courts also provide the public with electronic access to case and docket information of the federal appellate, district, and bankruptcy case. Most court information can be obtained through the Internet and PACER, discussed above.

If you know the case citation, you can easily find the case on Westlaw, Lexis, or Loislaw provided that it is available in the database. On Westlaw, begin at the search page. Westlaw search pages may vary in display depending on the subscription. Find the tab or box labeled "Find by Citation." See Illustration 3-6. To find the case, 865 NE2d 1048, you would enter the citation as shown. Click on the go button and the case would appear. West's newest service, WestlawNext, a substantially modified version of Westlaw, allows users to enter a

citation in a search box similar to that found on a Google search page. Users can search multiple databases at once in a search that is similar in feel to a Google search.

Now view Illustration 3-7. It is the Lexis search page. You can search by citation or by party name. To search by citation, enter the citation in the search box and click on the search button. The same type of search can be done on Loislaw. You do not need to be in a database to retrieve cases using these search tools.

---

## *PRACTICE POINTER*

Check court rules for citing and relying on opinions available on the Internet. Many courts may prohibit researchers from citing a Web case if it is available in a reporter, an online database, or a printed source, such as a looseleaf.

---

## ILLUSTRATION 3-7. **Finding a Case in Lexis**

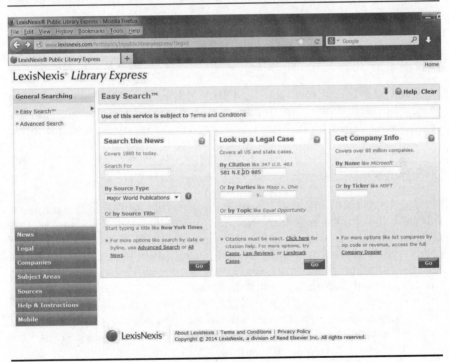

Reprinted with the permission of LexisNexis.

## ▼ How Do You Know Whether a Case Is Published or Only Available Online?

Westlaw and Lexis provide the citations for all cases that are published in print. If this information is absent or the publisher indicates that it is not published, it is not. Instead, Westlaw provides its own citation for this case. Lexis also indicates its own citation for cases it publishes only online.

## ▼ How Are Decisions Reported Only on Westlaw or Lexis Cited?

*Bluebook* **Rule 18** and *ALWD* **Rule 12** explain how you should cite an unpublished decision found only on either Westlaw or Lexis. (If a decision is published in a hard-copy reporter, you should not use the Westlaw or Lexis citation.)

For both Westlaw and Lexis, the *Bluebook* citation would first state the case name. After the case name is the docket number. In the example that follows, that number is "No. 82-C-4585." Next is the year of the decision. For Westlaw cases, the next item would be "WL" for Westlaw. The Westlaw number assigned to the case follows that. If a spot cite is provided, precede the screen or page number with an asterisk. Finally, in the parentheses, place the court and the full date.

**Westlaw cite:**    *Clark Equip. Co. v. Lift Parts Mfg. Co.*, No. 82-C-4585, 1985 WL 2917, at *1 (N.D. Ill. Oct. 1, 1985)

The *ALWD* citation based on **Rule 12**, especially **Rule 12.13(b)**, would be as follows: the docket number and the abbreviation for company is dropped because it is the second business designation:

*Clark Equip. Co. v. Lift Parts Mfg.*, 1985 WL 2917, at *1 (N.D. Ill. Oct. 1, 1985)

For Lexis citations, the *Bluebook* requires that you state the name of the case, the docket number, the year of the decision, the name of the Lexis file that contains the case, the name "LEXIS" to indicate that the case is found on Lexis, and the document number. Last, place the court and the full date in parentheses. However, the *ALWD* citation allows for the docket number to be omitted.

**Lexis cite:**    *Barrett Indus. Trucks v. Old Republic Ins. Co.*,
**Bluebook** citation:    No. 87-C-9429, 1990 U.S. Dist. LEXIS 142, at *1 (N.D. Ill. Jan. 9, 1990)

**ALWD** citation:    *Barrett Indus. Trucks v. Old Republic Ins.*, 1990 U.S. Dist. LEXIS 142, at *1 (N.D. Ill. Jan. 9, 1990)

# 6. State Reporters

▼ Where Can You Find State Court Decisions?

Many states continue to publish state decisions in their own reporters. In those states, the state publication is the official reporter. Some states authorize private publishers to publish the official reports for them. For example, West's regional reporters have been adopted as official state reporters in various states.

▼ Are There Any Unofficial Reports of State Cases?

Yes. In addition to its publication of some states' official reporters, West publishes seven **regional reporters** that contain state cases. See Illustrations 3-8 and 3-9. The regional reporters are not based on actual geographic regions. For example, Illinois is in the American Midwest region, but the regional reporter that contains Illinois decisions is the *North Eastern Reporter*.

The regional reporters contain decisions from several different states. Some states have designated the West regional reporter as the official reporter of their state decisions.

## ILLUSTRATION 3-8.  West's Regional Reporters Coverage

| *Regional Reporter* | *States Covered* |
| --- | --- |
| *West's Atlantic Reporter* (A. or A.2d) | Connecticut, Delaware, Maine, Maryland, New Hampshire, New Jersey, Pennsylvania, Rhode Island, Vermont, and the District of Columbia |
| *West's North Eastern Reporter* (N.E. or N.E.2d) | Illinois, Indiana, Massachusetts, New York, and Ohio |
| *West's North Western Reporter* (N.W. or N.W.2d) | Iowa, Michigan, Minnesota, Nebraska, North Dakota, South Dakota, and Wisconsin |
| *West's Pacific Reporter* (P. or P.2d) | Alaska, Arizona, California, Colorado, Hawaii, Idaho, Kansas, Montana, Nevada, New Mexico, Oklahoma, Oregon, Utah, Washington, and Wyoming |
| *West's South Eastern Reporter* (S.E. or S.E.2d) | Georgia, North Carolina, South Carolina, Virginia, and West Viginia |
| *West's South Western Reporter* (S.W. or S.W.2d) | *Arkansas, Kentucky, Missouri, Tennessee, and Texas* |
| *West's Southern Reporter* (So. or So. 2d) | *Alabama, Florida, Louisiana, and Mississippi* |

**ILLUSTRATION 3-9.    West's National Reporter System**

Reprinted with permission of Thomson Reuters.

---

*PRACTICE POINTER*

In theory, the text of a case published in the state reporter should be identical to that in the regional reporter. If the two differ, then the language of the official version governs.

---

▼ Why Would You Use the Regional Reporter Rather
Than the Official State Reporter?

The regional reporter contains the publisher's headnotes designed to assist you. See Illustrations 3-4 and 3-10. These notes guide you to the publisher's topical index of cases called a digest. You also might use the

## ILLUSTRATION 3-10.   West Case Report, *Kellerman v. Car City Chevrolet-Nissan*, 713 N.E.2d 1285 (Ill. App. Ct. 1999)

①   KELLERMANN v. CAR CITY CHEVROLET–NISSAN    Ill.  **1285**

Cite as 713 N.E.2d 1285 (Ill.App. 5 Dist. 1999)

the trade or commerce of selling real estate'" within the intended scope of the Act. *Zimmerman*, 156 Ill.App.3d at 168–69, 109 Ill.Dec. 541, 510 N.E.2d 409. The court concluded: "We find no support in Illinois law for the proposition that an individual selling his own home is liable to a purchaser under the Consumer Fraud Act." *Zimmerman*, 156 Ill.App.3d at 168, 109 Ill.Dec. 541, 510 N.E.2d 409. The Appellate Court, Third District, followed *Zimmerman* in *Anderson v. Stowell*, 183 Ill.App.3d 862, 863–64, 132 Ill.Dec. 289, 539 N.E.2d 852 (1989).

[5] Although the language of the Act does not express the distinction established in *Zimmerman*, the legislature has apparently accepted that interpretation of the Act's intended coverage. The legislature has amended the Act several times since *Zimmerman* was decided more than a decade ago, but it has taken no action to abrogate that case. See *Scarsdale Builders, Inc. v. Ryland Group, Inc.*, 911 F.Supp. 337, 339 (N.D.Ill.1996) (noting the continuing viability of the *Zimmerman* exception to the Act's scope). When the legislature chooses not to amend a statute to reverse a judicial construction, we must presume that it has acquiesced in the court's statement of legislative intent. *People v. Drakeford*, 139 Ill.2d 206, 215, 151 Ill.Dec. 337, 564 N.E.2d 792 (1990). By failing to so amend the Act after *Zimmerman*, the legislature has implicitly

claim, and the trial court properly dismissed it.

The Smiths have asked us to determine that this appeal is frivolous and to impose sanctions upon plaintiffs pursuant to Supreme Court Rule 375(b) (155 Ill.2d R. 375(b)). A frivolous appeal is one that is not reasonably well-grounded in fact and not warranted by existing law or a good-faith argument for the extension, modification, or reversal of existing law. 155 Ill.2d R. 375(b); *Gunthorp v. Golan*, 184 Ill.2d 432, 441, 235 Ill.Dec. 21, 704 N.E.2d 370 (1998).

[6, 7] Rule 375(b) sanctions are penal and should be applied only to cases that fall strictly within the terms of the rule. *Beverly v. Reinert*, 239 Ill.App.3d 91, 101, 179 Ill.Dec. 789, 606 N.E.2d 621 (1992). We find that plaintiffs made a good-faith argument based upon a reasonable interpretation of the language of the Act, and we therefore decline to find that this appeal is frivolous.

For these reasons, the order of the circuit court of Du Page County is affirmed.

Affirmed.

INGLIS and McLAREN, JJ., concur.

②

306 Ill.App.3d 285

239 Ill.Dec. 435 ③

|1285|Kevin E. KELLERMANN and ④
Kathleen A. Kellermann,
Plaintiffs–Appellants.

v.

CAR CITY CHEVROLET–NISSAN,
INC. Defendant–Appellee.

⑤ No. 5–98–0142.

Appellate Court of Illinois,
Fifth District.

July 21, 1999.

Rehearing Denied Aug. 5, 1999.

⑥

Visitor who slipped and fell on snow at auto sales lot sued lot owner for negligence. The Circuit Court, Clinton County, John W.

---

1 Citation to the West's
  *North Eastern Reporter*
2 Citation to official reporter
3 Citation to unofficial reporter
4 Case name
5 Docket number
6 Syllabus by reporter editor
7 West key numbers
8 West topic
9 Headnote text
10 Bracketed number refers
   to headnote
11 Page in official case report

## ILLUSTRATION 3-10. *Continued*

**1286** Ill.    713 NORTH EASTERN REPORTER, 2d SERIES

McGuire, J., dismissed claim. Appeal was taken. The Appellate Court, Welch, J., held that natural-accumulation rule precluded owner's liability for injuries.

Affirmed.

Goldenhersh, J., filed a dissenting opinion.

**1. Appeal and Error** ⚯893(1)

Appellate Court reviews de novo the dismissal of a complaint for failure to state a cause of action.

**2. Appeal and Error** ⚯895(2)

Under a de novo standard of review, Appellate Court need not give deference to the circuit court's decision.

**3. Negligence** ⚯210

In a negligence action, one of the essential elements is the existence of a duty to exercise reasonable care.

**4. Negligence** ⚯1692

Question of whether a duty is owed is a question of law.

**5. Negligence** ⚯1037(4), 1040(3)

As general rule, a landowner or a possessor of land has a duty to an invitee or a licensee to exercise ordinary or reasonable care in maintaining his premises in a reasonably safe condition.

**6. Negligence** ⚯1095

Where a business invitee is injured by slipping and falling on defendant's premises, liability may be imposed if the substance was placed there by the negligence of the proprietor or his servants or, if the substance was on the premises through acts of third persons or there is no showing how it got there, liability may be imposed if the proprietor or his servant knew of its presence or if the substance was there a sufficient length of time so that in the exercise of ordinary care its presence should have been discovered.

**7. Negligence** ⚯1076

"Natural-accumulation rule" provides that a landowner does not have a duty to a business invitee to remove natural accumulations of snow and ice.

> See publication Words and Phrases for other judicial constructions and definitions.

**8. Negligence** ⚯1134

If the snow or ice on which a business invitee slips and falls was produced or accumulated by artificial causes or if the snow or ice was produced or accumulated in an unnatural way because of landowner's own use of the area concerned, liability will be imposed on landowner.

**9. Negligence** ⚯1133

Pursuant to natural-accumulation rule, owner of outdoor automobile sales lot was not liable for injuries to visitor who slipped on accumulated snow and ice, regardless of allegation that slip-and-fall occurred in a display area, that owner encouraged potential customers to go there, and that owner directly benefitted from having a display area.

**10. Negligence** ⚯210, 213

In determining whether a duty exists, court must consider the following factors: (1) the reasonable foreseeability of the injury, (2) the likelihood of injury, (3) the magnitude of the burden of guarding against it, and (4) the consequences of placing that burden upon the defendant.

**11. Negligence** ⚯1133

Reason for rule protecting landowners from liability for injuries arising from naturally accumulated snow and ice is because it would be unreasonable, in a climate where those conditions are common, to force a landowner to expend the money and labor necessary to constantly keep the areas safe.

**12. Constitutional Law** ⚯70.1(9)

Request to overrule rule protecting landowners from liability for injuries resulting from natural accumulations of ice and snow should be addressed to the legislature, not to the Appellate Court.

―――――

₁₂₈₆James B. Wham, Jennifer W. Price, Wham & Wham Attorneys, Centralia, for Appellants.

# ILLUSTRATION 3-10.  *Continued*

## KELLERMANN v. CAR CITY CHEVROLET–NISSAN  Ill. **1287**
### Cite as 713 N.E.2d 1285 (Ill.App. 5 Dist. 1999)

Stephen C. Mudge, Tara English, Reed, Armstrong, Gorman, Coffey, Gilbert & Mudge, P.C., Edwardsville, for Appellee.

Justice WELCH delivered the opinion of the court:

Plaintiffs, Kevin E. Kellermann and Kathleen A. Kellermann, appeal the circuit court of Clinton County's dismissal of counts IV and V of their second amended complaint filed against defendant, Car City Chevrolet–Nissan, Inc. (Car City). Counts IV and V of the complaint allege that due to defendant's negligence, plaintiffs sustained injuries when Kevin slipped and fell on snow which had accumulated on defendant's sales lot. The circuit court applied the natural-accumulation rule, finding that defendant was not liable for injuries incurred by plaintiffs when Kevin slipped and fell on snow which had |₁₂₈₇naturally accumulated on defendant's lot. Plaintiffs now appeal the dismissal of counts IV and V of their amended complaint, arguing that the natural-accumulation rule should not apply. For the following reasons, we affirm the decision of the circuit court.

On January 18, 1997, Kevin Kellermann and his wife, Kathleen, were walking on the auto sales lot of Car City in Centralia, Illinois. The lot is outdoors and contains numerous automobiles and trucks that are placed on display to allow an inspection by potential customers. According to the complaint, snow accumulated on the lot, making the lot "slick, icy[,] and hazardous." Plaintiffs do not allege that the accumulation of snow was unnatural or that a dangerous condition was created by defendant. The complaint does not describe the size of the auto sales lot, the size of the display area on the auto sales lot, or whether Kevin was distracted by anything on the lot.

In their complaint, plaintiffs allege that defendant was negligent for (1) failing to maintain a safe car-sales lot, (2) failing to remove the accumulation of snow and ice, (3) failing to place salt or cinders on the snow and ice, (4) failing to barricade the area containing the slick snow and ice, (5) failing to prevent customers' access to the area containing the snow and ice, (6) failing to warn the customers of the snow and ice, and (7) displaying the vehicles on the snow and ice when defendant knew that potential customers would go upon the area to examine the vehicles.

On January 17, 1998, the circuit court conducted a hearing concerning plaintiffs' second amended complaint. Although plaintiffs apparently requested that the circuit court create an exception to the natural-accumulation rule, the circuit court stated, "Perhaps such an exception should and may some day be created by the higher courts[;] however[,] at this time it appears clear to this court that under the general rule stated in *Timmons v. Turski*, 103 Ill.App.3d 36, 58 Ill.Dec. 884, 430 N.E.2d 1135 (1981), a property owner is not liable for injuries resulting from an icy condition which is a natural one." Accordingly, the circuit court dismissed plaintiffs' second amended complaint with prejudice. We shall now review this decision by the circuit court and address plaintiffs' arguments on appeal.

[1, 2] We review *de novo* the circuit court's dismissal of plaintiffs' complaint for the failure to state a cause of action. See *Kotarba v. Jamrozik*, 283 Ill.App.3d 595, 596, 218 Ill.Dec. 659, 669 N.E.2d 1185 (1996). Under a *de novo* standard of review, we need not give deference to the circuit court's decision. See *Von Meeteren v. Sell–Sold, Ltd.*, 274 Ill.App.3d 993, 996, 211 Ill.Dec. 115, 654 N.E.2d 577 (1995).

[3, 4] In the instant case, plaintiffs allege that defendant was negligent in maintaining its sales lot. In a negligence action, one of the essential elements is the existence of a duty to exercise|₁₂₈₈reasonable care. See *Unger v. Eichleay Corp.*, 244 Ill.App.3d 445, 449, 185 Ill.Dec. 556, 614 N.E.2d 1241 (1993). The question of whether a duty is owed is a question of law. See *Roberson v. J.C. Penney Co.*, 251 Ill.App.3d 523, 526, 191 Ill.Dec. 119, 623 N.E.2d 364 (1993). If defendant does not owe a duty to plaintiffs to exercise reasonable care, then no cause of action for negligence will exist. See *Sparacino v. Andover Controls Corp.*, 227 Ill.App.3d 980, 986, 169 Ill.Dec. 944, 592 N.E.2d 431 (1992).

[5, 6] It is the general rule in Illinois that a landowner or a possessor of land has a duty to an invitee or a licensee to exercise ordi-

## ILLUSTRATION 3-10. *Continued*

**1288** Ill.      **713 NORTH EASTERN REPORTER, 2d SERIES**

nary or reasonable care in maintaining his premises in a reasonably safe condition. See *Thompson v. Economy Super Marts, Inc.,* 221 Ill.App.3d 263, 265, 163 Ill.Dec. 731, 581 N.E.2d 885 (1991). Accordingly, where a business invitee is injured by slipping and falling on defendant's premises, liability may be imposed if the substance was placed there by the negligence of the proprietor or his servants or, if the substance was on the premises through acts of third persons or there is no showing how it got there, liability may be imposed if the proprietor or his servant knew of its presence or if the substance was there a sufficient length of time so that in the exercise of ordinary care its presence should have been discovered. See *Thompson,* 221 Ill.App.3d at 265, 163 Ill.Dec. 731, 581 N.E.2d 885.

[7, 8] There is also a rule in Illinois known as the natural-accumulation rule. The natural-accumulation rule provides that a landowner does not have a duty to a business invitee to remove natural accumulations of snow and ice. See *Watson v. J.C. Penney Co. Inc.,* 237 Ill.App.3d 976, 978, 178 Ill.Dec. 929, 605 N.E.2d 723 (1992). Even if the snow and ice remain on the property for an "unreasonable" length of time, it has been held that no liability will be imposed on the proprietor as long as the snow and ice is a natural accumulation. See *Foster v. George J. Cyrus & Co.,* 2 Ill.App.3d 274, 279, 276 N.E.2d 38 (1971) (where this court rejected a rule that would require property owners to remove natural accumulations of snow and ice after a reasonable length of time or be liable for injuries suffered by their tenants). However, if the snow or ice was produced or accumulated by artificial causes or if the snow or ice was produced or accumulated in an unnatural way because of defendant's own use of the area concerned, liability will be imposed. See *McCann v. Bethesda Hospital,* 80 Ill.App.3d 544, 548, 35 Ill.Dec. 879, 400 N.E.2d 16 (1979).

The natural-accumulation rule was first recognized in Illinois by our supreme court in *Graham v. City of Chicago,* 346 Ill. 638, 178 N.E. 911 (1931). In *Graham,* plaintiff sued the City of Chicago when she slipped and fell on a patch of ice that had formed on a city

sidewalk. The Illinois Supreme Court adopted the natural-accumulation rule, holding that it would be "unreasonable to compel a city to expend the money and perform the labor necessary to keep its walks reasonably free from ice and snow during winter months." *Graham,* 346 Ill. at 643, 178 N.E. 911.

$|_{289}$This rule was later extended beyond cities and municipalities to allow landlords to escape liability for injuries incurred by tenants who slipped and fell on naturally accumulated snow and ice while on the landlord's premises. In *Cronin v. Brownlie,* 348 Ill. App. 448, 109 N.E.2d 352 (1952), a tenant slipped and fell on a walk that was covered with naturally accumulated snow and ice. This court applied the natural-accumulation rule and stated:

"In our northern climate where ice and snow come frequently and are accepted by all, it appears to us that the [natural-accumulation] rule adopted by the majority of the states finding no liability against the landlord is more reasonable and persuasive * * *. * * * [I]t appears to us to be unreasonable and somewhat impractical to require a landlord to remove ice and snow from sidewalks used jointly by his tenants where the ice and snow arise from natural causes." *Cronin,* 348 Ill.App. at 456, 109 N.E.2d 352.

Since *Cronin,* Illinois courts have consistently applied the natural-accumulation rule to all types of businesses. *Riccitelli v. Sternfeld,* 1 Ill.2d 133, 115 N.E.2d 288 (1953) (natural-accumulation rule applied to path through snow on sidewalk adjoining filling station); *Galivan v. Lincolnshire Inn,* 147 Ill.App.3d 228, 101 Ill.Dec. 18, 497 N.E.2d 1331 (1986) (natural-accumulation rule applied to parking lot at an Inn); *Thompson v. Tormike, Inc.,* 127 Ill.App.3d 674, 82 Ill.Dec. 919, 469 N.E.2d 453 (1984) (natural-accumulation rule applied to parking lot of restaurant); *Smalling v. LaSalle National Bank of Chicago,* 104 Ill.App.3d 894, 60 Ill.Dec. 671, 433 N.E.2d 713 (1982) (natural-accumulation rule applied to parking lot at shopping center); *Lohan v. Walgreens Co.,* 140 Ill.App.3d 171, 94 Ill.Dec. 680, 488 N.E.2d 679 (1986) (natural-accumulation rule applied to snow

# ILLUSTRATION 3-10. *Continued*

---

KELLERMANN v. CAR CITY CHEVROLET–NISSAN    Ill. **1289**
Cite as 713 N.E.2d 1285 (Ill.App. 5 Dist. 1999)

and ice that naturally accumulated outside store but had been tracked inside). In addition, Illinois courts have applied the natural-accumulation rule to all areas on a defendant's property (*i.e.*, on a sidewalk, on a parking lot, inside a store, or on the step of an entranceway (see *Gehrman v. Zajac*, 34 Ill.App.3d 164, 340 N.E.2d 184 (1975) ( tenant))). Plaintiffs fail to cite a single case that has created an exception to the natural-accumulation rule on the basis of where the fall occurred or on the basis of what kind of business was being conducted on the property.

[9] In the instant case, plaintiffs request that we not apply the natural-accumulation rule because Kevin slipped and fell on a display area on defendant's property. Plaintiffs contend that because defendant encourages plaintiffs to go to the display area, defendant should maintain that area as "a safe place for customers to come upon and inspect the automobiles displayed for sale." Furthermore, plaintiffs contend that because defendant directly benefits from having the display area, it should shoulder the burden of keeping that area safe or close the area in the presence of snow and ice.

[10, 11] |₂₉₀In determining whether a duty exists, the court must consider the following factors: (1) the reasonable foreseeability of the injury, (2) the likelihood of injury, (3) the magnitude of the burden of guarding against it, and (4) the consequences of placing that burden upon the defendant. See *Maschhoff v. National Super Markets, Inc.*, 230 Ill.App.3d 169, 172, 172 Ill.Dec. 304, 595 N.E.2d 665 (1992). The reason our courts have consistently found that a landowner does not have a duty to keep premises safeguarded against the potential dangers of naturally accumulated snow and ice is because it would be unreasonable in our climate to force a defendant to expend the money and labor necessary to constantly keep the areas safe. See *Graham v. City of Chicago*, 346 Ill. 638, 178 N.E. 911 (1931); *Cronin v. Brownlie*, 348 Ill.App. 448, 109 N.E.2d 352 (1952). A similar rationale is explained in American Jurisprudence Second:

"[I]n a climate where there are frequent snowstorms and sudden changes in temperature, these dangerous conditions appear with a frequency and suddenness which defy prevention, and usually, correction; consequently, the danger from ice and snow in such locations is an obvious one, and the occupier of the premises may expect that an invitee on his premises will discover and realize the danger and protect himself against it." 62A Am.Jur.2d *Premises Liability* § 699 (1990).

Based on the reasons noted above, Illinois courts have consistently determined that no duty exists for a defendant to remove, monitor, or exercise reasonable care in making reasonably safe an area which contains naturally accumulated snow and ice.

In the instant case, we shall not depart from Illinois's well-established natural-accumulation rule. We believe that defendant owes no duty to plaintiffs to exercise reasonable care toward protecting its outdoor display area from the hazards associated with the natural accumulation of snow and ice. As we have repeatedly noted, in our northern climate, snow and ice can occur frequently and unpredictably. Furthermore, snow and ice is a hazard in this part of the country, and that hazard is known to all. As our courts have consistently found it an unreasonable burden for a business to keep small areas such as parking lots, sidewalks, and entryways safe from naturally accumulated snow and ice, we believe that it would be even more burdensome to require an automobile dealership to monitor its entire display area. Is not almost every automobile that is for sale on defendant's lot on display? Although plaintiffs fail to describe the dimensions of the display area, common sense tells us that such an automotive display area is normally much larger than an average parking lot, sidewalk, or entryway. Our acceptance of plaintiffs' request would effectively require all outdoor businesses to constantly |₂₉₁monitor its entire business activity area or close its entire business activity area at the first sign of snow or ice. We believe that to place such expense and burden on a property owner is unreasonable.

[12] Therefore, we believe that the natural-accumulation rule is applicable to the in-

## ILLUSTRATION 3-10.    *Continued*

stant case. A result different would essentially overrule the natural-accumulation rule. As this court has previously stated, we are not the proper forum in which the natural-accumulation rule should be overruled. See *Watson v. J.C. Penney Co.*, 237 Ill.App.3d 976, 978–79, 178 Ill.Dec. 929, 605 N.E.2d 723 (1992) (this court stated that the plaintiff's request to overrule the natural-accumulation rule should be addressed "to the legislature, which formulates the public policy of this State and which could change this 'antiquated rule' if it wished."). Accordingly, the circuit court correctly applied the natural-accumulation rule and properly dismissed plaintiffs' complaint.

On another matter, on September 30, 1998, we entered an order indicating that we would take with this appeal a motion filed by defendant to strike portions of plaintiffs' reply brief. For the reasons explained in plaintiffs' response to the motion to strike, we deny said motion.

For the foregoing reasons, the dismissal by the circuit court of counts IV and V is hereby affirmed.

Affirmed.

RARICK, P.J., concurs.

Justice GOLDENHERSH, dissenting:

I respectfully dissent. The circuit court ruled, and Car City urges us to agree, that the natural-accumulation rule would apply to the instant case and that adhering to plaintiff's position would result in an abrogation of this longstanding rule. Plaintiffs, on the other hand, contend that they are not attempting to abrogate the natural-accumulation rule but, rather, that under these particular circumstances the general rule of premises liability concerning the duty of a possessor of land toward its business invitees should be the rule of law applied by the courts. I agree with plaintiffs' position.

The courts have specifically imposed a duty on the possessor of land in situations where a hazard was open and obvious but the harm to an invitee may reasonably be anticipated, such as when an invitee's attention is distracted by goods on display or for some other reason the invitee is not focused on the

hazard. See *Ward v. K mart Corp.*, 136 Ill.2d 132, 143 Ill.Dec. 288, 554 N.E.2d 223 (1990). In *Ward*, our supreme court determined such duties as follows:

⌐₂₉₂"A rule more consistent with an owner's or occupier's general duty of reasonable care, however, recognizes that the 'obviousness' of a condition or the fact that the injured party may have been in some sense 'aware' of it may not always serve as adequate warning of the condition and of the consequences of encountering it. It is stated in Prosser & Keeton on Torts:

'[I]n any case where the occupier as a reasonable person should anticipate an unreasonable risk or harm to the invitee notwithstanding his knowledge, warning, or the obvious nature of the condition, something more in the way of precautions may be required. This is true, for example, where there is reason to expect that the invitee's attention will be distracted, as by goods on display, or that after a lapse of time he may forget the existence of the condition, even though he has discovered it or been warned; or where the condition is one which would not reasonably be expected, and for some reason, such as an arm full of bundles, it may be anticipated that the visitor will not be looking for it.' W. Keeton, Prosser & Keeton on Torts, § 61, at 427 (5th ed.1984).

See also 5 F. Harper, F. James & O. Gray, The Law of Torts, § 27.13, at 244–47 (2d ed.1986); J. Page, The Law of Premises Liability, § 4.6, at 80–85 (2d ed.1988).

This is the position taken by the Restatement (Second) of Torts, section 343A (1965). That section provides in pertinent part:

'(1) A possessor of land is not liable to his invitees for physical harm caused to them by any activity or condition on the land whose danger is known or obvious to them, *unless the possessor should anticipate the harm despite such knowledge or obviousness.*' (Emphasis added.)

Comment *e* of section 343A(1) states the general rule that the owner or occupier may reasonably assume that invitees will

# ILLUSTRATION 3-10. *Continued*

exercise reasonable care for their own safety, and that ordinarily he need not take precautions against dangers which are known to the visitor or so obvious that the visitor may be expected to discover them. Comment *f,* however, explains that reason to expect harm to visitors from known or obvious dangers may arise 'where the possessor has reason to expect that the invitee's attention may be distracted, so that he will not discover what is obvious, or will forget what he has discovered, or fail to protect himself against it. \* \* \* In such cases the fact that the danger is known, or is obvious, is important in determining whether the invitee is to be charged with contributory negligence, or assumption of risk. It is not, however, conclusive in determining the duty of the possessor, or whether he has acted reasonably under the circumstances.' Restatement (Second) of Torts, § 343A, comment *f,* at 220 (1965).

⌊293The manifest trend of the courts in this country is away from the traditional rule absolving, *ipso facto,* owners and occupiers of land from liability for injuries resulting from known or obvious conditions, and toward the standard expressed in section 343A(1) of the Restatement (Second) of Torts (1965)." *Ward,* 136 Ill.2d at 148–50, 143 Ill.Dec. 288, 554 N.E.2d 223.

This court applied *Ward* and section 343A in *Maschhoff v. National Super Markets, Inc.,* 230 Ill.App.3d 169, 172 Ill.Dec. 304, 595 N.E.2d 665 (1992) (delivery man slipped and fell on liquid buildup in store). After citing *Ward* and quoting extensively from comment *f* of 343A, this court concluded that the injury was reasonably foreseeable, that plaintiff could have been distracted from the obvious conditions, and that, therefore, the questions of the defendant's breach of duty and the plaintiff's comparative negligence were properly submitted to the jury.

As directed by our supreme court in *Ward,* we must consider whether in the instant case the imposition of a duty meets with the following factors:

"We recognize that the Restatement speaks to the more general question of liability, and not specifically to the existence of a duty. But we think the principles expressed there are consistent with the general duty of reasonable care owed to invitees and licensees, and they are relevant to the resolution of whether an injury was reasonably foreseeable. We emphasize, however, that since the existence of a duty turns in large part on public policy considerations, the magnitude of the burden of guarding against the injury, and the consequences of placing that burden upon the defendant, as well as the likelihood of injury and the possible serious nature of such an injury[,] must also be taken into account." *Ward,* 136 Ill.2d at 151, 143 Ill.Dec. 288, 554 N.E.2d 223.

The standards of premises-liability duty, as delineated in *Ward,* appropriately apply in the instant case. We have a situation in which the possessor of land is aware of the hazards posed by ice and snow and with such knowledge seeks to bring the invitee into the business-activity part of its premises with the intent of, and taking actions toward, diverting the invitee's attention and changing the invitee's focus to the goods and services offered by the possessor of land. Under those circumstances, it is reasonably foreseeable by the possessor of land that an injury such as this might occur, and under these circumstances, it is both reasonable and appropriate that the burden should fall on the possessor of land. It is not an onerous burden on that possessor to alleviate the hazardous conditions so that the attention and focus of the invitee might safely be focused on the possessor's business activities. In comparison, the circumstances of the instant case pose a substantial likelihood of injury. I also note that the activities of diverting the invitee's attention and focus are for the benefit of the possessor₂₉₄ of land, and accordingly, it is not unreasonable to place this duty on that party.

Choosing to apply the duties delineated in *Ward* and the *Restatement,* rather than the natural-accumulation rule, does not constitute an abrogation of the natural-accumulation rule. That doctrine is quite alive and well, as noted in the cases cited by the majority. In those instances involving injuries on business premises, the rule has been readily applied to those areas adjacent to and

## ILLUSTRATION 3-10.  *Continued*

---

1292  Ill.          713 NORTH EASTERN REPORTER, 2d SERIES

utilized in the approaching of the area of commercial activity (sidewalks, parking lots), whereas the instant case involves the actual area of business activity.  We may infer from these cases that the possessor of the business property has no reason to, and is not likely to, make any effort to divert the attention of a prospective customer who is approaching his commercial-activity area.  In the instant case, however, the prospective customer who has entered the business-activity area is in the midst of an obvious hazard known to the property owner, and the property owner is actively diverting the customer's attention and focus to his commercial activities.  We should be hard put to conclude that under these circumstances the type of injury as occurred in this case would not be reasonably foreseeable.  Concurrently, we should rea-

sonably conclude that removing the hazard the invitee faces when engaging in the possessor's business activity is a minor burden on that possessor of land, given the hazard's foreseeability and the commercial benefits from successful engagement with the invitee. The difference between the approaches to business establishment and the commercial-activity area of that business are clear, qualitative, and crucial.  The *Ward*/Restatement rule appropriately applies.

---

Reprinted from *West's North Eastern Reporter* with permission of Thomson Reuters.

regional reporter because it is published sooner than the official reporter.

### ▼ How Are State Cases Cited?

Cite a state case according to *Bluebook* **Rule 10**. Note especially *Bluebook* **Rule 10.3.1** and **Table T.1**, which instruct on which state reporter to cite and when.

    If you are citing a state case in a document submitted to a court in the same state, you should provide the citations required by local rule. That is often both the official citation, if one exists, and the regional citation. The official citation should be listed first. Some states now require a public domain citation rather than a citation to an official print reporter.

    When you cite a state case in a memorandum addressed to a federal court or to a court of a different state, you should include only the regional citation, according to both the *Bluebook* and the *ALWD* manuals. If you are only using the regional citation, you must remember to place the abbreviation for the deciding court in parentheses. See *Bluebook* **Rule 10.4** and ALWD **Rule 12.6**. You can remember this if you consider the reasoning behind it. Most libraries outside of the state have no need to purchase materials that are merely persuasive because of the cost involved and the space necessary to store the reports.

Therefore, they are likely only to have the regional reporter—a more economic version of out-of-state cases.

The following are *Bluebook* examples of how an Illinois Appellate Court case would be cited in a brief prepared for the Illinois Supreme Court and in one prepared for the U.S. District Court for the Northern District of Illinois.

**Illinois Supreme Court**   *Thompson v. Econ. Super Marts,* 221
**brief:**   Ill. App. 3d 263, 581 N.E.2d 885,
163 Ill. Dec. 731 (1991)

**U.S. District Court**   *Thompson v. Econ. Super Marts,* 581
**(N.D. Ill.) brief:**   N.E.2d 885 (Ill. Ct. App. 1991)

However, the cite for the *Thompson* case under *ALWD* rules would be as follows:

*Thompson v. Econ. Super Marts,* 221 Ill. App. 3d 263, 581 N.E.2d 885 (1991).

The Illinois Appellate 3d citation must be included because local Illinois rules require parties to cite to the official reporter for all cases decided before July 1, 2011. Similar to other states, Illinois recently amended the Illinois Supreme Court Rules to direct the courts to assign public domain case designator numbers to all opinions. The new rules require that cases decided on or after July 1, 2011 have public domain numbers, and it requires citation to the public domain case citation rather than the Illinois official reporter for all cases decided on or after July 1, 2011.

These public domain or neutral citations allow researchers to find their case in a computerized system that does not rely on commercial publishers. Cites to commercial reporters such as West's may be used to augment public domain citations.

*Bluebook* **Rule 10.3.3** requires that you cite public domain citations as follows: case name, followed by the year of the decision, the deciding court, the sequential number of the decision. In some jurisdictions, the sequential number of the decision is the docket number. If available, a parallel cite must be listed. To cite to a specific portion of the decision, you may add a reference to the paragraph.

**public domain citation:**   State v. Kienast, 1996 S.D. 111 ¶ 2, 553
N.W.2d 254

Cite to what *ALWD* refers to as neutral citations rather than public domain citations, according to **Rule 12.17** of the *ALWD* guide. First, use the format specified by the court or include the case name, the year of the decision, the state's two-letter postal code abbreviation, the court abbreviation if decided by a court other than the state's high court, the

opinion number, and then a pinpoint citation reference. The above case would be cited as follows:

State v. Kienast, 1996 SD 111, 553 NW2d 254.

## CHAPTER SUMMARY

In this chapter, you learned about case law and about the reporters that contain Supreme Court, federal, and state decisions. Case law consists of court-adopted decisions. These decisions are primary authorities. These authorities generally are organized chronologically. Several publishers have established case reporters that are books, usually in series format, which contain court decisions.

Decisions are first published in slip opinions, generally a typed set of pages. Next, advance sheets are published. These decisions usually look similar to the final case reporter version of a decision.

Next, bound reporters that carry the case decision reports are published. For the Supreme Court decisions, three reporters are available. The *United States Reports* is published by the government. The *United States Supreme Court Reports, Lawyers' Edition* is published by Lexis. The *Supreme Court Reporter* is published by West. The commercial publishers' reports include publishers' notes and annotations, such as headnotes designed to assist you in your research.

Many other federal court decisions are published in *West's Federal Supplement, West's Federal Reporter*, and *West's Federal Appendix*. State court decisions often are found in a state-published case reporter and in West's regional reporters. Some looseleaf publishers also report decisions, and West reports some opinions in specialized reporters. These commercial reporters have headnotes that assist you in your research. These headnotes contain case abstracts concerning a point of law raised in a case and a topic and number that refer you to a topical system for finding additional similar cases discussed in the next chapter.

Today, slip and other opinions often are available free of charge or for a nominal fee on the Internet from official court sites.

## KEY TERMS

advance sheets
bench opinion
case law
digests
*Federal Appendix*
*Federal Reporter*
*Federal Rules Decision*
*Federal Supplement*
headnotes
key numbers
*Lawyers' Edition*

*National Reporter System*
regional reporter
reporters
reporting systems
slip opinion
Supreme Court Reporter
syllabus
*U.S. Law Week*
*U.S. Reports*
West Codenotes

# EXERCISES

## REPORTER EXERCISES

1. List the three reporters that contain the decision in Illustration 3-4.
2. What reporter or reporters would you look in to find a published Illinois Supreme Court decision?
3. What reporter or reporters would you look in to find a published U.S. Court of Appeals decision decided in 1991?
4. What reporter or reporters would you look in to find a U.S. District Court decision from 1930?
5. What is contained in the *Federal Rules Decisions?*
6. What sources would you look in to find a U.S. Supreme Court decision one to two weeks after the case was decided by the Court? (List at least four sources.)
7. What is the advantage of using the *Lawyers' Edition* to review a Supreme Court case?
8. What is the advantage of using a West's regional reporter in researching rather than the *Illinois Reports?*
9. When you are beginning a research assignment, what is the first thing that you should determine? How is this determined?
10. Are headnotes cited? Why, or why not?

## TREASURE HUNT

11. Find 507 F. Supp. 1091. What is the key number and topic for the second headnote?
12. Find 825 F.2d 257. What court decided this case?
13. Find 819 F.2d 630. What is the docket number for this case? List the names of the attorneys who argued this case.
14. Find 373 N.E.2d 1371. List the presiding judge and the date the case was decided.
15. Find 432 N.E.2d 1123. List the official citation for this case, the name of the plaintiff, and the name of the defendant.
16. Find 222 N.E.2d 561. List the name of the judge who wrote the opinion.
17. Using the Internet, find the *Kellerman v. Car City Chevrolet-Nissan* case shown in Illustration 3-10. Where did you find it?
18. Find the Government Printing Office's U.S. Supreme Court decisions on the Internet. What is the website address?
19. Go to the U.S. Courts website. What links to other courts are available? Please provide the websites for at least three links.
20. Go to the U.S. 5th Circuit Court of Appeals website. Find the court's local rules. What is the Web address for these rules?
21. Find 2002 WL1592517 (CA 7. Ill.).
    a. What does this say about publication in the Federal Reporter?
    b. Who is the trial judge?
    c. What is the date the case was argued?
    d. What is the date it was decided?

## CHAPTER 4

# DIGESTS

| | | |
|---|---|---|
| **A. CONTENT OF DIGESTS AND ORGANIZATION** | | 74 |
| 1. Headnotes and Key Numbers | | 75 |
| 2. Types of Digests | | 77 |
| 3. Organization of Digests | | 78 |
| **B. STEP-BY-STEP GUIDE TO THE DIGEST SYSTEM** | | 83 |
| 1. Descriptive Word Index Method | | 83 |
| 2. Topic Outline Method | | 86 |
| 3. One Good Case Method | | 86 |
| 4. Online Digest Search | | 93 |

## *CHAPTER OVERVIEW*

This chapter focuses on the use of **digests**, topically organized indexes. You will be taught how to use the West's digests, the largest and most diverse digest system. The skills you learn will help you to use other publishers' digests. Topical searching, as well as research, using headnotes and key numbers will be explored.

# A. CONTENT OF DIGESTS AND ORGANIZATION

## ▼ What Are Digests, and What Do They Contain?

Publishers have developed systems called digests that index the law by topics or legal issues. For example, West's digests contain at least 450 topics. A list of some of the topics is shown in Illustration 4-1.

## ILLUSTRATION 4-1.   West's Digest Topics

THOMSON REUTERS
### WESTLAW™

WESTLAW® CLASSIC
QUICK REFERENCE GUIDE

## West Key Number System®
Numerical List of Digest Topics

| | | | | | |
|---|---|---|---|---|---|
| 1 | Abandoned and Lost Property | 31 | Appearance | 69 | Cancellation of Instruments |
| 2 | Abatement and Revival | 34 | Armed Services | 70 | Carriers |
| 4 | Abortion and Birth Control | 35 | Arrest | 71 | Cemeteries |
| 5 | Absentees | 36 | Arson | 72 | Census |
| 6 | Abstracts of Title | 37 | Assault and Battery | 73 | Certiorari |
| 7 | Accession | 38 | Assignments | 74 | Champerty and Maintenance |
| 8 | Accord and Satisfaction | 40 | Assistance, Writ of | 75 | Charities |
| 9 | Account | 41 | Associations | 76 | Chattel Mortgages |
| 10 | Account, Action on | 42 | Assumpsit, Action of | 76A | Chemical Dependents |
| 11 | Account Stated | 43 | Asylums and Assisted Living Facilities | 76D | Child Custody |
| 11A | Accountants | | | 76E | Child Support |
| 12 | Acknowledgment | 44 | Attachment | 76H | Children Out-of-Wedlock |
| 13 | Action | 45 | Attorney and Client | 78 | Civil Rights |
| 14 | Action on the Case | 46 | Attorney General | 79 | Clerks of Courts |
| 15 | Adjoining Landowners | 47 | Auctions and Auctioneers | 80 | Clubs |
| 15A | Administrative Law and Procedure | 48 | Audita Querela | 82 | Collision |
| | | 48A | Automobiles | 83 | Commerce |
| 16 | Admiralty | 48B | Aviation | 83H | Commodity Futures Trading Regulation |
| 17 | Adoption | 49 | Bail | | |
| 18 | Adulteration | 50 | Bailment | 83T | Common Interest Communities |
| 19 | Adultery | 51 | Bankruptcy | 84 | Common Lands |
| 20 | Adverse Possession | 52 | Banks and Banking | 85 | Common Law |
| 21 | Affidavits | 54 | Beneficial Associations | 89 | Compromise and Settlement |
| 23 | Agriculture | 55 | Bigamy | 90 | Confusion of Goods |
| 24 | Aliens, Immigration, and Citizenship | 56 | Bills and Notes | 91 | Conspiracy |
| | | 58 | Bonds | 92 | Constitutional Law |
| 25 | Alteration of Instruments | 59 | Boundaries | 92B | Consumer Credit |
| 25T | Alternative Dispute Resolution | 60 | Bounties | 93 | Contempt |
| 26 | Ambassadors and Consuls | 61 | Breach of Marriage Promise | 95 | Contracts |
| 27 | Amicus Curiae | 63 | Bribery | 96 | Contribution |
| 28 | Animals | 64 | Bridges | 96H | Controlled Substances |
| 29 | Annuities | 65 | Brokers | 97C | Conversion and Civil Theft |
| 29T | Antitrust and Trade Regulation | 66 | Building and Loan Associations | 98 | Convicts |
| | | 67 | Burglary | 99 | Copyrights and Intellectual Property |
| 30 | Appeal and Error | | | | |

For assistance using Westlaw Classic , call **1-800-WESTLAW** (1-800-937-8529).

For free reference materials, visit **legalsolutions. thomsonreuters.com/ guides**.

THOMSON REUTERS WESTLAW
Thomson Reuters Westlaw comprises industry leading online research, print products, software, tools, and services that help legal professionals perform their work faster and more efficiently, every day.

**THOMSON REUTERS™**

# ILLUSTRATION 4-1.   *Continued*

| | | | | | | | |
|---|---|---|---|---|---|---|---|
| 100 | Coroners | 136 | Dower and Curtesy | 178 | Food | 220 | Internal Revenue |
| 101 | Corporations and Business Organizations | 141 | Easements | 179 | Forcible Entry and Detainer | 221 | International Law |
| | | 141E | Education | | | 222 | Interpleader |
| 102 | Costs | 142 | Ejectment | 180 | Forfeitures | 223 | Intoxicating Liquors |
| 103 | Counterfeiting | 142T | Election Law | 181 | Forgery | 224 | Joint Adventures |
| 104 | Counties | 143 | Election of Remedies | 183 | Franchises | 226 | Joint Tenancy |
| 105 | Court Commissioners | 145 | Electricity | 184 | Fraud | 227 | Judges |
| | | 146 | Embezzlement | 185 | Frauds, Statute of | 228 | Judgment |
| 106 | Courts | 148 | Eminent Domain | 186 | Fraudulent Conveyances | 229 | Judicial Sales |
| 107 | Covenant, Action of | 149 | Entry, Writ of | 187 | Game | 230 | Jury |
| 108 | Covenants | 149E | Environmental Law | 188 | Gaming | 231 | Justices of the Peace |
| 108A | Credit Reporting Agencies | 149T | Equitable Conversion | 189 | Garnishment | 231E | Kidnapping |
| | | | | 190 | Gas | 231H | Labor and Employment |
| 110 | Criminal Law | 150 | Equity | 191 | Gifts | | |
| 111 | Crops | 151 | Escape | 192 | Good Will | 233 | Landlord and Tenant |
| 113 | Customs and Usages | 152 | Escheat | 193 | Grand Jury | 234 | Larceny |
| | | 154 | Estates in Property | 195 | Guaranty | 237 | Libel and Slander |
| 114 | Customs Duties | 156 | Estoppel | 196 | Guardian and Ward | 238 | Licenses |
| 115 | Damages | 157 | Evidence | 197 | Habeas Corpus | 239 | Liens |
| 116 | Dead Bodies | 158 | Exceptions, Bill of | 198 | Hawkers and Peddlers | 240 | Life Estates |
| 117 | Death | 159 | Exchange of Property | | | 241 | Limitation of Actions |
| 117G | Debt, Action of | | | 198H | Health | 242 | Lis Pendens |
| 117T | Debtor and Creditor | 160 | Exchanges | 200 | Highways | 244H | Lobbying |
| 118A | Declaratory Judgment | 161 | Execution | 201 | Holidays | 245 | Logs and Logging |
| | | 162 | Executors and Administrators | 202 | Homestead | 246 | Lost Instruments |
| 119 | Dedication | | | 203 | Homicide | 247 | Lotteries |
| 120 | Deeds | 163 | Exemptions | 205 | Husband and Wife | 248 | Malicious Mischief |
| 122A | Deposits and Escrows | 164 | Explosives | 205H | Implied and Constructive Contracts | 249 | Malicious Prosecution |
| 123 | Deposits in Court | 164T | Extortion | | | | |
| 124 | Descent and Distribution | 166 | Extradition and Detainers | 206 | Improvements | 250 | Mandamus |
| | | 167 | Factors | 207 | Incest | 251 | Manufactures |
| 125 | Detectives and Security Guards | 168 | False Imprisonment | 208 | Indemnity | 252 | Maritime Liens |
| 126 | Detinue | 169 | False Personation | 209 | Indians | 253 | Marriage |
| 129 | Disorderly Conduct | 170 | False Pretenses | 210 | Indictment and Information | 256 | Mayhem |
| 130 | Disorderly House | 170A | Federal Civil Procedure | | | 257 | Mechanics' Liens |
| 131 | District and Prosecuting Attorneys | 170B | Federal Courts | 211 | Infants | 257A | Mental Health |
| | | 171 | Fences | 212 | Injunction | 258A | Military Justice |
| 132 | District of Columbia | 172 | Ferries | 213 | Innkeepers | 259 | Militia |
| 133 | Disturbance of Public Assemblage | 174 | Fines | 216 | Inspection | 260 | Mines and Minerals |
| | | 175 | Fires | 217 | Insurance | 265 | Monopolies |
| 134 | Divorce | 176 | Fish | 218 | Insurrection and Sedition | 266 | Mortgages |
| 135 | Domicile | 177 | Fixtures | | | 267 | Motions |
| 135H | Double Jeopardy | | | 219 | Interest | | |

2    West Key Number System

# 1. Headnotes and Key Numbers

These topics are continually being revised. In the digest, you find **headnotes** or case abstracts in which the publishers assign a topic and number to a point of law. The headnotes assist you in finding other cases that are

## ILLUSTRATION 4-1. *Continued*

WESTLAW CLASSIC **QUICK REFERENCE GUIDE**

| | | | | | | | |
|---|---|---|---|---|---|---|---|
| 268 | Municipal Corporations | 313 | Process | 346 | Scire Facias | 382T | Trademarks |
| 269 | Names | 313A | Products Liability | 347 | Seals | 384 | Treason |
| 271 | Ne Exeat | 314 | Prohibition | 348 | Seamen | 385 | Treaties |
| 272 | Negligence | 315 | Property | 349 | Searches and Seizures | 386 | Trespass |
| 273 | Neutrality Laws | 315H | Prostitution | 349A | Secured Transactions | 387 | Trespass to Try Title |
| 274 | Newspapers | 315P | Protection of Endangered Persons | 349B | Securities Regulation | 388 | Trial |
| 275 | New Trial | 315T | Public Amusement and Entertainment | 350 | Seduction | 390 | Trusts |
| 276 | Notaries | 316E | Public Assistance | 350H | Sentencing and Punishment | 391 | Turnpikes and Toll Roads |
| 277 | Notice | 316H | Public Contracts | 351 | Sequestration | 392 | Undertakings |
| 278 | Novation | 317 | Public Lands | 352 | Set-Off and Counterclaim | 392T | Unemployment Compensation |
| 279 | Nuisance | 317A | Public Utilities | 353 | Sheriffs and Constables | 393 | United States |
| 280 | Oath | 318 | Quieting Title | 354 | Shipping | 394 | United States Magistrates |
| 281 | Obscenity | 319 | Quo Warranto | 355 | Signatures | 395 | United States Marshals |
| 282 | Obstructing Justice | 319H | Racketeer Influenced and Corrupt Organizations | 356 | Slaves | 396 | Unlawful Assembly |
| 283 | Officers and Public Employees | 320 | Railroads | 356H | Social Security | 396A | Urban Railroads |
| 284 | Pardon and Parole | 321 | Rape | 357 | Sodomy | 398 | Usury |
| 285 | Parent and Child | 322 | Real Actions | 358 | Specific Performance | 399 | Vagrancy |
| 286 | Parliamentary Law | 323 | Receivers | 359 | Spendthrifts | 400 | Vendor and Purchaser |
| 287 | Parties | 324 | Receiving Stolen Goods | 360 | States | 401 | Venue |
| 288 | Partition | 325 | Recognizances | 361 | Statutes | 402 | War and National Emergency |
| 289 | Partnership | 326 | Records | 362 | Steam | 403 | Warehousemen |
| 290 | Party Walls | 327 | Reference | 363 | Stipulations | 404 | Waste |
| 291 | Patents | 328 | Reformation of Instruments | 365 | Submission of Controversy | 405 | Water Law |
| 294 | Payment | 330 | Registers of Deeds | 366 | Subrogation | 406 | Weapons |
| 295 | Penalties | 331 | Release | 367 | Subscriptions | 407 | Weights and Measures |
| 296 | Pensions | 332 | Religious Societies | 368 | Suicide | 408 | Wharves |
| 297 | Perjury | 333 | Remainders | 369 | Sunday | 409 | Wills |
| 298 | Perpetuities | 334 | Removal of Cases | 370 | Supersedeas | 410 | Witnesses |
| 300 | Pilots | 335 | Replevin | 371 | Taxation | 411 | Woods and Forests |
| 302 | Pleading | 336 | Reports | 372 | Telecommunications | 413 | Workers' Compensation |
| 303 | Pledges | 337 | Rescue | 373 | Tenancy in Common | 414 | Zoning and Planning |
| 305 | Possessory Warrant | 338 | Reversions | 374 | Tender | 450 | Merit Systems Protection |
| 306 | Postal Service | 339 | Review | 375 | Territories | | |
| 307 | Powers | 340 | Rewards | 377E | Threats, Stalking, and Harassment | | |
| 307A | Pretrial Procedure | 341 | Riot | 379 | Torts | | |
| 308 | Principal and Agent | 342 | Robbery | 380 | Towage | | |
| 309 | Principal and Surety | 343 | Sales | 381 | Towns | | |
| 310 | Prisons | 344 | Salvage | | | | |
| 311 | Private Roads | | | | | | |
| 311H | Privileged Communications and Confidentiality | | | | | | |

West Key Number System    **3**

Reprinted with permission of Thomson Reuters.

relevant to the issues presented in your case. Cases are read by editors, and each issue is put into a topic category. The specific legal issue is then assigned a number to accompany the topic. This enables you to match cases discussing the same issues of law. Digests also contain references to the publisher's other resources and law review articles.

The most comprehensive digest system is published by West. The **West key number system** is divided into digest topics, such as bankruptcy, civil rights, criminal law, negligence, double jeopardy, and damages. LexisNexis publishes a digest for U.S. Supreme Court cases and a series covering state cases called *U.S. Supreme Court Digest, Lawyers' Edition.* Other publishers also prepare state digests. West's state digests contain references to decisions of federal courts sitting within that state that pertain to the state's legal issues. West's regional digests do not contain federal cases. In addition to these digests, West and other publishers print topical digests, such as the *West's Education Law Digest.*

## 2. Types of Digests

The *West American Digest System* is a comprehensive set of all of West's reported federal and state cases. See Illustration 4-2. This system includes the *Century Digest,* which contains cases decided between 1658 and 1897. It does not contain key numbers. However, a West index allows you to cross-reference cases in the first and second *Decennial Digest* to convert them to the equivalent key number.

### ILLUSTRATION 4-2.   Assorted Digests

**American Digest System**
*West's General Digests*
*Century Digest*
*Decennial Digests*
*General Digests*

**Digests that Abstract All U.S. Supreme Court Cases**
*U.S. Supreme Court Digest* (West)
*U.S. Supreme Court Digest, Lawyer's Edition*

**Other Federal Court Digests**
*Federal Digest*
*Modern Federal Practice Digest*
*West's Federal Practice Digest 2d*
*West's Federal Practice Digest 3d*
*West's Federal Practice Digest 4th*
*West's Federal Practice Digest 5th* contains all of the federal court
cases reported by West, including U.S. Supreme Court cases

**State Cases**
*West Regional Digests:* indexes cases reported in the reporter bearing the
same name
   *North Western Digest*
   *South Eastern Digest*

## ILLUSTRATION 4-2.   *Continued*

*Pacific Digest*
*Atlantic Digest*

West does not publish a digest for the *North Eastern Reporter*, the *Southern Reporter*, or the *South Western Reporter*

*Individual State Digests:* West publishes digests for most of the 50 states and the District of Columbia; however, it publishes a combined digest for South Dakota and North Dakota and a combined digest for West Virginia and Virginia. It does not publish separate digests for Utah, Delaware, and Nevada. Digest summaries for those cases appear in their respective regional digest products.

**Specialized Digests**

*Federal Sentencing Guidelines Digest*
*West's Bankruptcy Law Digest*
*Annotated Patent Digest*
*West's Military Justice Digest*
*West's U.S. Federal Claims Digest*
*West's Education Law Digest*

---

The *Decennial Digests* is a multiple-volume digest that includes state and federal court cases from all U.S. jurisdictions between 1997 to date. Presented in ten-year increments, it contains points of law that are summarized in headnotes and classified using the West Key Number System. Older *Decennial Digests* contain all of the abstracts from West's regional, state, and federal digests. *General Digests* also are included in this system. These also include all West cases and are presented in one-year increments. These types of print digests, however, are falling out of favor; instead, researchers are turning to Westlaw, WestlawNext, Lexis, and Loislaw to search for cases involving multiple jurisdictions.

United States Supreme Court opinions are indexed in a digest called the *United States Supreme Court Digest*, in *West's Supreme Court Digest*, and in *West's Federal Practice Digest* series.

## 3. Organization of Digests

▼ How Are Digest Systems Organized?

Most digest systems are organized by topic. Case abstracts of points of law are prepared by the publisher, and these points of law are then assigned topics. Within each topic, points of law are assigned numbers. In the West system, this match of a topic and a number is called a "key number." Key numbers are the cornerstones of the West system. Key numbers correspond to specific points of law presented in a case. See Illustrations 3-4 and 3-10. The case abstracts are not authoritative and should never be cited. These case abstracts contain a publisher's summary of a point of law, the case name, and a citation. See Illustration 4-3.

# ILLUSTRATION 4-3.   Sample Pages from *West's Illinois Digest*

① ②

⚷1076  NEGLIGENCE                                      38A Ill D 2d—128

**For later cases, see same Topic and Key Number in Pocket Part**

Storekeeper is not insurer of his customer's safety.

> Mick v. Kroger Co., 224 N.E.2d 859, 37 Ill.2d 148, 21 A.L.R.3d 926.

**Ill. 1961.** Store owner owed business invitee duty of exercising ordinary care to maintain premises in a reasonably safe condition.

> Olinger v. Great Atlantic & Pacific Tea Co., 173 N.E.2d 443, 21 Ill.2d 469.

A proprietor of a store is not an insurer against all accidents and injuries to customers coming to his place of business.

> Olinger v. Great Atlantic & Pacific Tea Co., 173 N.E.2d 443, 21 Ill.2d 469.

**Ill. 1958.**      Restaurant    proprietor owes a business invitee duty of exercising ordinary care in maintaining premises in reasonably safe condition.

> Donoho v. O'Connell's, Inc., 148 N.E.2d 434, 13 Ill.2d 113.

**Ill. 1955.** Where operator of bowling alley maintained adjacent to the bowling alley an automobile parking lot for use of its patrons, and a patron was injured in the parking lot, relation of injured patron to operator of bowling alley was that of a "business invitee" to whom operator of bowling alley owed duty to exercise reasonable care for safety of patron while he was on the parking lot.

> Geraghty v. Burr Oak Lanes, 125 N.E.2d 47, 5 Ill.2d 153.

Where operator of bowling alley maintained an automobile parking lot adjacent to the bowling alley for the use of its patrons, operator of bowling alley owed p̲a̲t̲r̲o̲n̲ ̲w̲h̲o̲ ̲l̲e̲f̲t̲ ̲h̲i̲s̲ automobile in the p̲a̲[ 1 Key number ]̲ exercise ordinary c̲a̲[ 2 Topic ]̲g̲ lot in a reasonab̲l̲e̲ ̲w̲a̲y̲ ̲f̲o̲r̲ ̲h̲i̲s̲ ̲use in a manner consistent with purpose of the invitation, or at least not to lead patron into a dangerous trap, or expose him to unreasonable risk, and to give him adequate and timely notice and warning of any latent or concealed perils, which were known to operator of bowling alley but not to patron.

> Geraghty v. Burr Oak Lanes, 125 N.E.2d 47, 5 Ill.2d 153.

**Ill. 1948.** The general rule is that the owner is not liable for negligence where the invitee is using a portion of the premises to which invitation has not been extended and which the owner would not reasonably expect the invitee to use in connection with the conduct of business on the premises.

> Briney v. Illinois Cent. R. Co., 81 N.E.2d 866, 401 Ill. 181.

**Ill.App. 1 Dist. 2003.** Duty of reasonable care of store owner, based on distraction exception to open and obvious rule, encompassed risk that customer, while exiting store, would be distracted by unattended shopping cart and trip and fall over irregular pavement.

> Green v. Jewel Food Stores, Inc., 278 Ill.Dec. 875, 799 N.E.2d 740, 343 Ill.App.3d 830, rehearing denied.

A business operator generally owes his customers a duty to exercise reasonable care to maintain his premises in a reasonably safe condition.

> Green v. Jewel Food Stores, Inc., 278 Ill.Dec. 875, 799 N.E.2d 740, 343 Ill.App.3d 830, rehearing denied.

**Ill.App. 1 Dist. 2003.** A tavern operator is not an insurer of its patrons.

> Sameer v. Butt, 277 Ill.Dec. 697, 796 N.E.2d 1063, 343 Ill.App.3d 78, rehearing denied.

**Ill.App. 1 Dist. 2002.** In an action based upon negligence, general rule regarding duty of a business occupier of any premises is that it must provide a reasonably safe means of ingress to and egress from premises, but ordinarily it will not be held liable for any injuries incurred on a public sidewalk under control of municipality, even though sidewalk may also be used for ingress or egress to premises.

> Friedman v. City of Chicago, 267 Ill. Dec. 627, 777 N.E.2d 430, 333 Ill. App.3d 1070.

**Ill.App. 1 Dist. 2002.** Store, tavern, or restaurant owners owe a duty of ordinary care to their business invitees.

> Salazar v. Crown Enterprises, Inc., 262 Ill.Dec. 906, 767 N.E.2d 366, 328 Ill.App.3d 735, appeal denied 266 Ill.Dec. 447, 775 N.E.2d 9, 199 Ill.2d 579.

**Ill.App. 1 Dist. 1999.** Person is a "business invitee" on the land of another if (1) the person enters by express or implied invitation, (2) the entry is connected with

† **This Case was not selected for publication in the National Reporter System**
**For legislative history of cited statutes, see West's Smith-Hurd Illinois Compiled Statutes Annotated**

# ILLUSTRATION 4-3. *Continued*

---

**①☞1076 NEGLIGENCE ②**        38 Ill D 2d—420

**For later cases, see same Topic and Key Number in Pocket Part**

to such licensee is to not wilfully or wantonly injure him.

> Wesbrock v. Colby, Inc., 43 N.E.2d 405, 315 Ill.App. 494.

Where plaintiff, after making some purchases in defendant's store, was injured when she fell down basement steps as she attempted to make use of telephone located in stairway of store which was not intended for public use, and there was no evidence that clerk who showed plaintiff where telephone was had authority to give plaintiff permission to use it, plaintiff at time she received her injuries was a "licensee", and not an "invitee", and hence could not recover for her injuries, in absence of any willful or wanton misconduct by defendant.

> Wesbrock v. Colby, Inc., 43 N.E.2d 405, 315 Ill.App. 494.

**Ill.App. 2 Dist. 1942.** Although one operating a business to which the public is invited is not an "insurer" of safety of patrons, he has the duty to use reasonable care to keep premises in a reasonably safe condition so that patrons will not be injured by reason of any unsafe condition of the premises, and a failure to do so is actionable negligence in case an injury results therefrom.

> Crump v. Montgomery Ward & Co., 39 N.E.2d 411, 313 Ill.App. 151.

An owner of store in propping open the doors at entrance of store owed the same duty to its invitees to use reasonable care for their safety as it did to provide safe equipment.

> Crump v. Montgomery Ward & Co., 39 N.E.2d 411, 313 Ill.App. 151.

**Ill.App. 2 Dist. 1939.** The law raises on the part of a proprietor of a store an implied invitation to the public to come into his building or upon his premises should they seek to do business with him, and he is under a legal obligation to exercise ordinary and reasonable care to make his premises safe for the protection of his customers.

> Todd v. S. S. Kresge Co., 24 N.E.2d 899, 303 Ill.App. 89.

A proprietor of a store is not an insurer against all accidents and injuries to customers coming to his place of business.

> Todd v. S. S. Kresge Co., 24 N.E.2d 899, 303 Ill.App. 89.

**Ill.App. 3 Dist. 1993.** Person is "business invitee" on land of another if that person enters land by express or implied invitation, if entry is connected with owner's business or with activity conducted by owner on land, and if owner receives benefit.

> Leonardi v. Bradley University, 192 Ill.Dec. 471, 625 N.E.2d 431, 253 Ill.App.3d 685, appeal denied 198 Ill.Dec. 544, 633 N.E.2d 6, 155 Ill.2d 565.

**Ill.App. 3 Dist. 1993.** Store owner did not assume duty to remove all tracked-in water from its store when it placed two mats near its outside entrance; owner's duty extended only to maintaining with reasonable care the mats it installed.

> Roberson v. J.C. Penney Co., 191 Ill.Dec. 119, 623 N.E.2d 364, 251 Ill.App.3d 523.

**④Ill.App. 3 Dist. 1991.** Defendant owes business invitee on defendant's premises duty to exercise ordinary care in maintaining premises in reasonably safe condition.

> Thompson v. Economy Super Marts, Inc.,**③** 163 Ill.Dec. 731, 581 N.E.2d 885, 221 Ill.App.3d 263.

**Ill.App. 3 Dist. 1987.** A "business invitee" is one who enters upon the premises of another in response to an express or implied invitation for the purpose of transacting business in which the parties are mutually interested.

> Simmons v. Aldi-Brenner Co., 113 Ill.Dec. 594, 515 N.E.2d 403, 162 Ill.App.3d 238, appeal denied 119 Ill.Dec. 398, 522 N.E.2d 1257, 119 Ill.2d 575.

The owner or occupier of land owes to persons present on the premises as business invi[tee] ... and reas... are reas... es. ... ec. ...38, ...22 ...ers must be founded on fault.

> **1 Key number**
> **2 Topic**
> **3 *Thompson* case**
> **4 Deciding court**

> Simmons v. Aldi-Brenner Co., 113 Ill.Dec. 594, 515 N.E.2d 403, 162 Ill.App.3d 238, appeal denied 119 Ill.Dec. 398, 522 N.E.2d 1257, 119 Ill.2d 575.

**Ill.App. 3 Dist. 1985.** Storekeeper is not insurer of customer's safety.

> Nicholson v. St. Anne Lanes, Inc., 91 Ill. Dec. 9, 483 N.E.2d 291, 136 Ill.App.3d 664, appeal denied.

**Ill.App. 3 Dist. 1982.** Duty of owner of commercial enterprise to provide reasonably safe means of ingress and egress from place of business for use of his patrons is not abrogated by presence of accumulation of ice or snow which is natural.

> Kittle v. Liss, 64 Ill.Dec. 307, 439 N.E.2d 972, 108 Ill.App.3d 922.

**Ill.App. 3 Dist. 1980.** Duty owed to business invitee is to exercise ordinary care in maintaining premises in a reasonably safe condition.

> Hayes v. Bailey, 36 Ill.Dec. 124, 400 N.E.2d 544, 80 Ill.App.3d 1027.

**For legislative history of cited statutes**

Illustration 4-3 shows pages from *West's Illinois Digest.* On the second page of the illustration, the *Thompson* case is noted in the second column by the circled 3. Note that the case abstract contained on this digest page is identical to the first headnote contained in Illustration 3-4. However, the key number is different. At the top of Illustration 4-3 is the word *Negligence.* This indicates the topic. Next to it is a key and the number 1076. This is the key number. The deciding court and the year of the decision are noted at the beginning of the abstract. See the court next to the circled 4 in Illustration 4-3.

The West key number system is altered frequently. Recently, the Negligence key numbers were changed substantially. Go to Illustration 3-4, the *Thompson v. Economy Super Marts* case. On page 886 of the case, the first headnote contains a notation of 32.8. That is the key number assigned to that headnote topic. When the headnote topics were revised, that number changed. To find the current headnote number that corresponds to a topic, you would review a table such as the one shown in Illustration 4-4. That is a "Key Number Translation Table" found in the digest. In Illustration 4-4, go to Key Number 32.(2.8) in the table. It indicates that the new number is 1076-1078.

The theory of the key number system is that if you have a good case on point and you want to find similar cases on point, you look under the topic and the key number assigned to the point in your case. The case abstracts listed under that topic and key number should be similar to your case. To find cases similar to the point of law noted in the first headnote of the *Thompson* case, you would review Negligence key number 1076 in the current digest as well as pamphlets and pocket parts that update the digest. One of the cases that is found in the digest under that key number is *Kellermann v. Car City Chevrolet–Nissan,* 306 Ill. App.3d 285, 713 N.E.2d 1285 (1999) shown in Illustration 3-10. See headnote 7 of that case. It is Negligence 1076. Review the language of the case that corresponds to that headnote and compare it with case language that corresponds with headnote 1 of the *Thompson* case. To find the case language that corresponds to the headnote, find the bracketed numbers in the case text. The two cases address similar issues. However, note that the headnotes are not identical. They summarize what the court in each case said about this topic.

A case generally has multiple key numbers because a case abstract and a corresponding topic and key number are prepared for each point of law raised in a case. See Illustration 3-10.

*PRACTICE POINTER*

The same West digest system is used for all states. Therefore, you can find a good case in one state and look up the relevant key number in another state's digest. That will lead you to cases that are similarly decided in the second state.

## ILLUSTRATION 4-4.    Key Number Translation Table from
*West's Illinois Digest 2d*

---

NEGLIGENCE                                              38 Ill D 2d—52

### TABLE 1

### KEY NUMBER TRANSLATION TABLE

### FORMER KEY NUMBER TO PRESENT KEY NUMBER

---

The topic NEGLIGENCE in the American Digest System has been extensively revised to reflect current developments in the law.

This table indicates the location, in the revised topic, of cases formerly classified to the earlier Key Numbers.

In many instances there is no one-to-one relation between the Key Numbers, new and old. This table recognizes only significant correspondence. When there is more than one new Key Number to which headnotes formerly under a particular number have been reclassified, the new Key Numbers are listed in numerical order, with the most significant correspondence indicated in bold type. For the present classification of a particular case, see the Table of Cases.

The absence of a Key Number indicates that there is no useful parallel.

| Former Key Number | Present Key Number | Former Key Number | Present Key Number |
|---|---|---|---|
| 1 | 200, 202 | 32(2.7) | 1204(1, 3, 6), 1205(7, 9) |
| 2 | 210, 220 | 32(2.8) | 1076–1078 |
| 3 | 230, 231 | 32(2.9) | 1037(8) |
| 4 | 232, 233 | 32(2.10) | 1037(7), 1204(1) |
| 5 | 236, 322 | 32(2.11) | 1204(8) |
| 6 | 222, 238, 259 | 32(2.12) | 1040(2–4) |
| 7 | 216, 237, 257 | 32(2.13) | 1040(4), 1079 |
| 8 | 281–285 | 32(2.14) | 1037(7) |
| 9 | 200, 210, 233 | 32(2.15) | 1037(2), 1076 |
| 10 | 213 | 32(2.16) | 1037(7), 1076, 1102 |
| 11 | 274, 275 | 32(2.17) | 1060, 1076 |
| 12 | 291–295 | 32(2.18) | 570, 1060, 1315 |
| 13 | 273 | 32(3) | 1037(1), 1052, 1076 |
| 14 | 481, 483 | 32(4) | 1016, 1066, 1076 |
| 15 | 484 | 33(1) | 1045(3, 4) |
| 16 | 305 | 33(2) | 1045(2) |
| 17 | 236, 342; R R 277.5 | 33(3) | 1067 |
| 18 | 222, 259, 341, 343 | 34 | 1071, 1151 |
| 19 | 303(1–3), 306 | 35 | 1071, 1152 |
| 20 | 253, 307 | 36 | 1125–1127 |
| 21 | 341–344 | 37 | 1191–1197 |
| 22 | 305–307 | 38 | 1010, 1140 |
| 22.5 | Autos 181(1, 2, 4); Mun Corp 705(3) | 39 | 1172–1178 |
| 23(1) | 1172–1176 | 41 | 1130 |
| 23(2) | R R 277.5 | 42 | 1140, 1204(2), 1205(7) |
| 24 | 212, 251, 253, 302 | 43 | 1119, 1125, 1151, 1204(2) |
| 25 | 221, 332 | 44 | 1076, 1104(6, 8) |
| 26 | 253, 351–355 | 45 | 1117 |
| 27 | Prod Liab 41, 47, 49 | 46 | 1010, 1013 |
| 28 | 1032, 1033 | 47 | 1037(4), 1040(3) |
| 29 | 1011, 1204(1) | 48 | 1088, 1089, 1104(6) |
| 30 | 1104(8) | 50 | 1024, 1037(4), 1076, 1078, 1162 |
| 31 | 1025, 1204(5–7) | 51 | 1140, 1205(7) |
| 32(1) | 1037(4), 1040(3), 1076 | 52 | 1020, 1037(4), 1040(3), 1076 |
| 32(2) | 1040(2), 1050 | | |
| 32(2.1) | 1050 | 54 | 1011, 1263 |
| 32(2.2) | 1040(2, 3) | 55 | 1205(7–9) |
| 32(2.3) | 1037(2, 4), 1076 | 56(1) | 370, 375 |
| 32(2.4) | 1037(6), 1050 | 56(1.1) | 371, 373 |
| 32(2.5) | 1076 | 56(1.2) | 375, 379 |
| 32(2.6) | 1040(2) | 56(1.3) | 372 |

1 Old key number
2 New key number

Reprinted with permission of Thomson Reuters.

# B. STEP-BY-STEP GUIDE TO THE DIGEST SYSTEM

### ▼ How Do You Use a Digest System?

You might use one of several methods for finding cases within a digest: the descriptive word index method, the topic outline method, and the one good case method.

## 1. Descriptive Word Index Method

### ▼ What Is the Descriptive Word Index Method?

One method you might use is the **descriptive word index method.** This index is included in each West digest. Other digest series have similar indexes. Before you review the digest, brainstorm for words that might be indexed. You must separate the facts into various categories. These categories will assist you in brainstorming.

To categorize the materials, first review the facts. Select only the important or relevant facts. How do you determine which facts are relevant? Facts are relevant if they might have a bearing on the outcome of a case. These are facts that the courts will look at to make their determinations of the law.

Let's suppose that you are asked to research the claims a client might have against a supermarket for a slip and fall accident in a grocery store. In this case, your client slipped on a banana peel in the produce section of the supermarket while she was speaking on a cell phone.

First, determine what facts are legally relevant. How do you as a researcher make this determination? You must first determine the legal issues presented. Negligence is one theory. The question posed is, Was the store owner negligent? The second question to consider is, Was the woman also negligent? Negligence is a broad area of the law.

Next, you should brainstorm to develop a list of possible words to review in the digest. Brainstorming is important because a publisher might index a subject differently than you would index it. For example, slip and fall accidents at hotels or motels are not indexed under hotel or motel in the West digest. Instead, they are found under the topic Innkeepers.

Consider the people, the places, and the things involved in your case, as well as the basis for any action and any defenses. These are manageable categories. Consider also the relationships between people. In this case, we have a grocer and a patron. Next, think about the location of the incident. Where did the accident occur? It occurred in the produce section of a grocery store. Finally, determine what happened. A woman slipped on a banana peel while talking on a cell phone.

Next, develop a relationship between the facts to one another. For example, does the grocer owe a duty to his patron to prevent the patron from slipping and falling inside his store? Does the patron owe a duty to herself to ensure that she does not fall?

Once you have determined these relationships, you should find synonyms for the words you plan to research. Use a thesaurus or an encyclopedia to find synonyms and other additional search words. For example, *grocer* might be indexed. But other words might be used in its place. Try *store owner, market owner,* or *shopping center owner.* For *patron,* an index might contain the words *customer, shopper,* or *invitee,* a legal term of art. Cases may have dealt with a shop owner's liability for a slip and fall accident, but banana peels may not have been involved. Research slip and fall accidents that occurred on surfaces covered with food or other slippery items such as snow or water as well as those that occurred on dry surfaces.

Now frame the legal issues: Did the owner clean the floor? If so, did he do it in a timely fashion? Did the owner ensure his patrons' safety? Was the woman negligent because she walked while talking on the telephone?

The results of your brainstorming session for the grocery slip and fall might be recorded as indicated in Illustration 4-5.

Once you have brainstormed, review the descriptive word index. Look under the most obvious topics first, such as negligence, slip and fall, customer, or grocery store. Once you have reviewed these words, the digest will lead you to topics and key numbers. See Illustration 4-6.

## ILLUSTRATION 4-5.  Results of Brainstorming Session

| *People or Parties* | *Place* | *Things* |
| --- | --- | --- |
| Customer | Grocery store | Banana peel |
| Patron | Shopping center | |
| Buyer | Supermarket | |
| Purchaser | Shop | |
| Shopper | Store | |
| Grocer | | |
| Supermarket | | |
| Grocery store | | |
| Store | | |
| Shop | | |
| Shopping center | | |

| *Activity* | *Action* | *Defense* |
| --- | --- | --- |
| Slip | Negligence | Contributory negligence |
| Fall | Negligence | Comparative negligence |

## ILLUSTRATION 4-6. Sample Page from *West's Illinois Digest 2d* Descriptive Word Index

66A Ill D 2d–45

**PREMISES**

References are to Digest Topics and Key Numbers

**PREMISES LIABILITY**—Cont'd
**STATUS of entrant**—Cont'd

Exceeding invitation or license, **Neglig** ⟸ 1052

Invitee. See subheading INVITEE, under this heading.

Licensee. See subheading LICENSEE, under this heading.

Rejection of status distinctions, **Neglig** ⟸ 1053

Relative degrees of care, **Neglig** ⟸ 1051

Standard of care dependent on status, **Neglig** ⟸ 1036

Trespasser. See subheading TRESPASSERS, under this heading.

**STATUTES, Neglig** ⟸ 1002

**STATUTORY requirements,**
Duty of care, **Neglig** ⟸ 1025

Safe workplace laws. See subheading SAFE workplace laws, under this heading.

Standard of care, **Neglig** ⟸ 1079

Violation of requirements in general,
Building and structures in general, **Neglig** ⟸ 1101

Firefighters, **Neglig** ⟸ 1210

Plaintiff's conduct or fault, **Neglig** ⟸ 1295

Police, **Neglig** ⟸ 1210

Stairs and ramps, hand and guard rails, **Neglig** ⟸ 1110(3)

Swimming pools, **Neglig** ⟸ 1129

**STORE and business proprietors,**
Breach of duty,
Criminal acts of third persons, **Neglig** ⟸ 1162

Displays and shelves, **Neglig** ⟸ 1119

Falling merchandise, **Neglig** ⟸ 1119

Third persons, acts of, **Neglig** ⟸ 1162

Business invitee. See subheading BUSINESS invitee, under this heading.

Duty of care,
Generally, **Neglig** ⟸ 1022-1024

Criminal acts of third persons, **Neglig** ⟸ 1024

Discovery, **Neglig** ⟸ 1023

Foreseeability, **Neglig** ⟸ 1022

Ice and snow, **Neglig** ⟸ 1022

Inspection, **Neglig** ⟸ 1023

Third persons, acts of, **Neglig** ⟸ 1024

Warning, **Neglig** ⟸ 1022

Standard of care,
→ Generally, **Neglig** ⟸ 1076-1078

Criminal acts of third persons, **Neglig** ⟸ 1078

Discovery, **Neglig** ⟸ 1077

Inspection, **Neglig** ⟸ 1077

**PREMISES LIABILITY**—Cont'd
**STORE and business proprietors**—Cont'd
**Standard of care**—Cont'd

Insurer of safety, **Neglig** ⟸ 1076  ◄—

Third persons, acts of, **Neglig** ⟸ 1078

**STRICT liability,**
Buildings and structures in general, **Neglig** ⟸ 1101

Floors, cleaning or waxing, **Neglig** ⟸ 1104(8)

**STRUCTURAL work laws,**
Safe workplace laws, **Neglig** ⟸ 1204(7)

**SUBCONTRACTORS,**
Construction, demolition and repairs, **Neglig** ⟸ 1205(9)

Injury or loss, **Neglig** ⟸ 1251

**SUPPLIERS,**
Construction, demolition and repairs, **Neglig** ⟸ 1205(10)

**SWIMMING pools,**
Attractive nuisance doctrine, **Neglig** ⟸ 1177

Breach of duty, **Neglig** ⟸ 1129

Complaint, **Neglig** ⟸ 1524(4)

Evidence,
Burden of proof, **Neglig** ⟸ 1565

Presumptions and inferences, **Neglig** ⟸ 1596

Weight and sufficiency, **Neglig** ⟸ 1671

Hotels and motels, **Inn** ⟸ 10

Jury instructions, **Neglig** ⟸ 1737

Jury questions and directing verdict, **Neglig** ⟸ 1709

Plaintiff's conduct or fault, **Neglig** ⟸ 1290

Proximate cause, **Neglig** ⟸ 1234

Violation of statutory requirements, **Neglig** ⟸ 1129

**THEATERS. See heading THEATERS AND SHOWS, generally.**

**THIRD persons, acts of,**
Breach of duty,
Generally, **Neglig** ⟸ 1161-1162

Store and business proprietors, **Neglig** ⟸ 1162

Duty of care,
Generally, **Neglig** ⟸ 1019

Store and business proprietors, **Neglig** ⟸ 1024

Plaintiff's conduct or fault, **Neglig** ⟸ 1292

Standard of care,
Generally, **Neglig** ⟸ 1070

Store and business proprietors, **Neglig** ⟸ 1078

Reprinted with permission of Thomson Reuters.

Illustration 4-6 is a sample page from *West's Illinois Digest 2d* Descriptive Word Index. Under the word *premises liability* and *stores and business proprietors,* you see a variety of subtopics such as Standard of Care and Insurer of Safety. Many of these subtopics refer you to the Negligence topic with the designation "Neglig." The number next to the topic designation is the key number. Under the subtopics Standard of Care and Insurer of Safety, the notation is "Neglig 1076." This topic and key number should have cases that are relevant. After reviewing this page, you would retrieve the volume with the Negligence topic (each volume's binding gives an alphabetical range of topics) and follow the numbers to the key numbers suggested in the descriptive word index. In this case, you would review Negligence key number 1076. Reading the case abstracts (such as those found in Illustration 4-3), you could determine the cases relevant to your own. Each digest case abstract contains a notation of the deciding court, a publisher's statement concerning the issue of law, and a citation. Under key number 1076, you would find a case abstract that refers to headnote 1 of the *Thompson v. Economy Super Marts* case.

## 2. Topic Outline Method

### ▼ What Is the Topic Outline Method?

Another method you can use to locate cases is the **topic outline method.** If you were asked to research a slip and fall problem similar to the one noted above, you might already suspect that negligence is the designated topic. You then would find the negligence topic in the appropriate volume of the digest series. At the beginning of the topic, you would review a topic outline, which is similar to a table of contents. See Illustration 4-7. Review the outline and note the key numbers that might be relevant to your case. Note any related topics. You might want to consider them if you decide that this topic is not appropriate. Premises liability seems appropriate and was the heading in the descriptive word index. Review the topics and key numbers below those words. The words "Standard of Care" appear as they did in the index. Scan down the list of key numbers and topics below those words. Note key number 1076 is for the "general" standard of care information. Note that number 1075 pertains to "care required of store and business proprietors." Both key numbers are relevant to the issue you are researching.

## 3. One Good Case Method

### ▼ What Is the One Good Case Method?

You also can use the **one good case method** to find cases when you already have found a case on point. If you have a West report of the case, the report will contain headnotes or abstracts with topic and key number designations. See Illustrations 3-4 and 3-10. Note the topic and

# ILLUSTRATION 4-7. *West's Illinois Digest 2d* Topic Outline

## NEGLIGENCE

### SUBJECTS INCLUDED

General civil negligence law and premises liability, including duty, standards of care, breach of duty, proximate cause, injury, defenses, and comparative fault, whether based on the common law or statute, as well as procedural aspects of such actions

General civil liabilities for gross negligence, recklessness, willful or wanton conduct, strict liability and ultrahazardous instrumentalities and activities

Negligence liabilities relating to the construction, demolition and repair of buildings and other structures, whether based on the common law or statute

General criminal negligence offenses and prosecutions

### (1) SUBJECTS EXCLUDED AND COVERED BY OTHER TOPICS

Accountants or auditors, negligence of, see ACCOUNTANTS ☞8, 9

Aircraft, accidents involving, see AVIATION ☞141–153

Attorneys' malpractice liability, see ATTORNEY AND CLIENT ☞105–129.5

Banks, liabilities of, see BANKS AND BANKING ☞100

Brokers, securities and real estate, liabilities of, see BROKERS

Car and highway accidents, see AUTOMOBILES

Common carriers, liabilities to passengers, see CARRIERS

**1 Related subjects**

Domestic animals, injuries by or to, see ANIMALS

Dram Shop liability and other liabilities for serving alcohol, see INTOXICATING LIQUORS ☞282–324

Drugs, liabilities relating to manufacture, sale and dispensing of, see DRUGS AND NARCOTICS ☞17–22

Educational institutions and personnel, liabilities of, see SCHOOLS and COLLEGES AND UNIVERSITIES

Electricity-related injuries, see ELECTRICITY ☞12–19(13)

Elevators, liabilities of owners to passengers, see CARRIERS

Employers, liabilities for injuries to their own employees, see EMPLOYERS' LIABILITY

Employers, liabilities for acts committed by their employees or for negligent hiring or retention of employees, see MASTER AND SERVANT ☞300–313

Exculpatory clauses prospectively waiving negligence liability, see CONTRACTS ☞114, 189

Explosion, fireworks and blasting injuries, see EXPLOSIVES ☞6–12

Firearms, injuries inflicted with, see WEAPONS ☞18

Food, injuries caused by, see FOOD ☞25

Flooding others' lands or polluting others' water supply, see WATERS AND WATER COURSES

Governments, negligence liability of, see COUNTIES, DISTRICT OF COLUMBIA, MUNICIPAL CORPORATIONS, STATES, TOWNS, TERRITORIES, and UNITED STATES

## ILLUSTRATION 4-7.   *Continued*

---

38 Ill D 2d—33                                                        **NEGLIGENCE**

Homicide by negligence, see AUTOMOBILES and HOMICIDE

Hospitals, liabilities of, see HOSPITALS ⬳7

Hotels, motels, inns and boarding houses, liabilities of, see INNKEEPERS ⬳10–11(12), 14.1

Insurers, liabilities of, see INSURANCE and WORKERS' COMPENSATION

Lease of personal property, liabilities relating to, see BAILMENT

Lease of real property, liabilities relating to, see LANDLORD AND TENANT

Manufacture, sale or distribution of products, liabilities relating to, see PRODUCTS LIABILITY and SALES

Maritime accidents and injuries, see ADMIRALTY, COLLISION, FERRIES, PILOTS, SALVAGE, SEAMEN, SHIPPING and WHARVES

Medical malpractice and liabilities of health care professionals in general, see PHYSICIANS AND SURGEONS ⬳14–18.130

Mines and quarries, injuries in excavation and operation of, see MINES AND MINERALS ⬳118

Natural gas and propane, injuries from escape or explosion of, see GAS ⬳14.50–20(6)

Negligence as measure of criminal intent generally, see CRIMINAL LAW ⬳23

Negligent misrepresentation, see FRAUD ⬳13(3)

Nursing homes, day care centers and similar group homes, injuries in, see ASYLUMS ⬳6, 7

Pesticides, herbicides and fertilizers, liabilities involving, see AGRICULTURE ⬳7, 9.13

Railroads, liabilities to non-passengers, see RAILROADS and URBAN RAILROADS

Release from liability after injury, see RELEASE

Security personnel and private investigators, see DETECTIVES ⬳4

Sports and public amusements, liabilities of proprietors, managers, and sponsors, see THEATERS AND SHOWS

Wrongful death actions, procedural aspects of, see DEATH

**For detailed references to other topics, see Descriptive-Word Index**

---

                                          **2 Key numbers**

*Analysis*

**②**

I. **IN GENERAL,** ⬳200–205.

II. **NECESSITY AND EXISTENCE OF DUTY,** ⬳210–222.

III. **STANDARD OF CARE,** ⬳230–239.

XVII. **PREMISES LIABILITY,** ⬳1000–1320.

    (A) IN GENERAL, ⬳1000–1004.

    (B) NECESSITY AND EXISTENCE OF DUTY, ⬳1010–1025.

---

key number designations for the points contained in the case that are relevant to your research; next, go to the relevant digest. For example, if you were researching an issue of federal law, you would review first the *Federal Practice Digest, Fifth.* However, if you are researching a question of

## ILLUSTRATION 4-7. *Continued*

---

(C) STANDARD OF CARE, ⟲1030–1079.

(D) BREACH OF DUTY, ⟲1085–1162.

(E) ATTRACTIVE NUISANCE DOCTRINE, ⟲1172–1178.

(F) RECREATIONAL USE DOCTRINE AND STATUTES, ⟲1191–1197.

(G) LIABILITIES RELATING TO CONSTRUCTION, DEMOLITION AND REPAIR, ⟲1201–1205.

(H) STATUTORY CAUSES OF ACTION FOR POLICE AND FIREFIGHTERS, ⟲1210.

(I) PROXIMATE CAUSE, ⟲1220–1247.

(J) NECESSITY AND EXISTENCE OF INJURY, ⟲1250–1251.

(K) PERSONS LIABLE, ⟲1260–1269.

(L) DEFENSES AND MITIGATING CIRCUMSTANCES, ⟲1280–1320.

**XVIII. ACTIONS,** ⟲1500–1750.

    (A) IN GENERAL, ⟲1500–1508.

    (B) PLEADING, ⟲1510–1542.

    (C) EVIDENCE, ⟲1550–1685.

        1. BURDEN OF PROOF, ⟲1550–1573.

        2. PRESUMPTIONS AND INFERENCES, ⟲1575–1604.

        3. RES IPSA LOQUITUR, ⟲1610–1625.

        4. ADMISSIBILITY, ⟲1630–1642.

        5. WEIGHT AND SUFFICIENCY, ⟲1650–1685.

    (D) QUESTIONS FOR JURY AND DIRECTED VERDICTS, ⟲1691–1719.

    (E) INSTRUCTIONS, ⟲1720–1747.

    (F) VERDICT AND FINDINGS, ⟲1750.

**XIX. CRIMINAL NEGLIGENCE,** ⟲1800–1809.

---

**I. IN GENERAL.**

    ⟲200. Nature.

    201. Distinction between negligence and intentional conduct.

    202. Elements in general.

    203. Constitutional, statutory and regulatory provisions.

    204. What law governs.

    205. Preemption.

**II. NECESSITY AND EXISTENCE OF DUTY.**

    ⟲210. In general.

**XVI. DEFENSES AND MITIGATING CIRCUMSTANCES.**—Continued.

    570. —— Professional rescuers; "firefighter's rule".

    575. Imputed contributory negligence.

**XVII. PREMISES LIABILITY.**

    (A) IN GENERAL.

    ⟲1000. Nature.

    1001. Elements in general.

    1002. Constitutional, statutory and regulatory provisions.

    1003. What law governs.

    1004. Preemption.

---

Massachusetts law, you should review West's *Massachusetts Digest.* See Illustration 4-8. Review the cases under the Negligence key number 1076. Compare Illustrations 4-3 and 4-8. Note that the case abstracts found in the *Massachusetts Digest* are similar to those found in the Illinois Digest for the same Negligence key number. Review the case

## ILLUSTRATION 4-7.   *Continued*

(B) NECESSITY AND EXISTENCE OF DUTY.

☞1010. In general.

1011. Ownership, custody and control.

1012. Conditions known or obvious in general.

1013. Conditions created or known by defendant.

1014. Foreseeability.

1015. Duty as to children.

1016. —— In general.

1017. —— Trespassing children.

1018. Duty to inspect or discover.

1019. Protection against acts of third persons in general.

1020. Duty to warn.

1021. Duty of store and business proprietors.

1022. —— In general.

1023. —— Duty to inspect.

1024. —— Protection against acts of third persons.

1025. Duty based on statute or other regulation.

(C) STANDARD OF CARE.

☞1030. In general.

1031. Not insurer or guarantor.

1032. Reasonable or ordinary care in general.

1033. Reasonably safe or unreasonably dangerous conditions.

1034. Status of entrant.

1035. —— In general.

1036. —— Care dependent on status.

1037. —— Invitees.

(1). In general.

(2). Who are invitees.

(3). Not insurer as to invitees.

(4). Care required in general.

(5). Public invitees in general.

(6). Implied invitation.

(7). Persons working on property.

(8). Delivery persons and haulers.

1040. —— Licensees.

(1). In general.

(2). Who are licensees.

## XVII. PREMISES LIABILITY.—Continued.

(C) STANDARD OF CARE.—Continued.

☞1040. —— Licensees.—Continued.

(3). Care required in general.

(4). Social guests.

1045. —— Trespassers.

(1). In general.

(2). Who are trespassers.

(3). Care required in general.

(4). Knowledge, discovery or acquiescence.

1050. —— Distinctions between types of entrants.

## ILLUSTRATION 4-7. *Continued*

1051. —— Relative degrees of care.
1052. —— Change of status; exceeding scope of invitation or license.
1053. —— Rejection of status distinctions.
1060. Police, firefighters and other public servants.
1065. Care as to children.
1066. —— In general.
1067. —— Trespassing children.
1070. Protection against acts of third persons generally.
1071. Off-premises injuries.
1075. Care required of store and business proprietors.
➤ 1076. —— In general.
1077. —— Inspection and discovery.
1078. —— Protection against acts of third persons.
1079. Standard established by statute or other regulation.

(D) BREACH OF DUTY.

☞1085. In general.
1086. Defect or dangerous conditions generally.
1087. Knowledge or notice in general.
1088. —— In general.
1089. —— Constructive notice.
1090. Miscellaneous particular cases.
1095. Slips and falls in general.
1100. Buildings and structures.
1101. —— In general.
1102. —— Doors, entryways and exits.
1103. —— Windows.
1104. —— Floors.
    (1). In general.
    (2). Knowledge of condition or danger.
    (3). Falls in general.
    (4). Inequalities in surface.
    (5). Rugs, carpets and mats.
    (6). Water and other substances.
    (7). Objects and debris.
    (8). Cleaning and waxing.

Reprinted with permission of Thomson Reuters.

abstracts. The case abstracts contained in the digests are identical to the headnotes. Compare Illustrations 3-4 and 4-3; note headnote 1 of the *Thompson* case and the case abstract on the digest page. They are identical.

## ILLUSTRATION 4-8.    *West's Massachusetts Digest* Page

18 Mass D 2d—209

NEGLIGENCE    ⟳1076

For references to other topics, see Descriptive-Word Index

**Mass. 1959.** Duty of store owner owed to a customer was to use reasonable care to keep in a safe condition that part of the premises to which customer was invited or at least warn her of dangers not known to her or obvious to a person of ordinary intelligence which were either known or should have been known to the owner in the exercise of reasonable care.

Rossley v. S. S. Kresge Co., 162 N.E.2d 26, 339 Mass. 654.

**Mass. 1958.** A business invitee has no complaint if the condition of the premises is incidental to the business there conducted and to be ordinarily expected by an invitee.

McKinstry v. New York, N. H. & H. R. Co., 153 N.E.2d 764, 338 Mass. 785.

**Mass. 1958.** Owners of shopping center owed to their invitees duty to use reasonable care to keep premises in reasonably safe condition for invitees' use according to invitation, and at least owed duty to warn invitees against any dangers, attendant upon use of shopping center, which were not known to them or obvious to any ordinarily intelligent person and which either were known, or in exercise of reasonable care ought to have been known, to shopping center owners.

Underhill v. Shactman, 151 N.E.2d 287, 337 Mass. 730.

**Mass. 1958.** Duty of a storekeeper to its invitees is to use due care to keep that portion of the premises provided for the use of its patrons in a reasonably safe condition, and to warn them of any dangers that might arise from such use by reason of a condition of the premises, which were not likely to be known to the patrons and of which storekeeper knew or ought to have known.

Young v. Food Fair, Inc., 149 N.E.2d 219, 337 Mass. 323.

**Mass. 1957.** Where plaintiff and her sister were watching operation of a money wheel in a tent on carnival grounds, and injury to plaintiff through collapse of portion of tent framework occurred before closing time, plaintiff had not lost her status as invitee merely because she had stood for an hour at booth without participating in game.

Di Roberto v. Lagasse, 145 N.E.2d 834, 336 Mass. 309.

**Mass. 1957.** Duty of due care of owner of grocery store extends to small children of customer.

Brady v. Great Atlantic & Pacific Tea Co., 145 N.E.2d 828, 336 Mass. 386.

**Mass. 1957.** A storekeeper owes duty to business invitee to use ordinary care to keep his premises in reasonably safe condition and must warn invitee of dangers of which he knew or ought to have known and of which invitee could not reasonably be expected to know.

Scully v. Joseph Connolly Ice Cream Sales Corp., 145 N.E.2d 826, 336 Mass. 392.

**Mass. 1957.** One who enters store to make purchases is business invitee to whom storekeeper owes duty to exercise reasonable care to keep in a safe condition that part of premises to which customer is invited or at least to warn customer against dangers which are not known to customer and are not obvious to an ordinarily intelligent person and are either known or ought to have been known to storekeeper.

Boehm v. S. S. Kresge Co., 145 N.E.2d 691, 336 Mass. 320.

**Mass. 1957.** A storekeeper owes to minor accompanying adult customer the same duty of care which must be exercised toward a customer whom the storekeeper invites upon his premises to trade.

Valunas v. J. J. Newberry Co., 145 N.E.2d 685, 336 Mass. 305.

**Mass. 1957.** A business invitee has no complaint if condition of premises is incidental to the business there conducted and to be ordinarily expected by an invitee.

Vance v. Wayside Inn, Inc., 141 N.E.2d 365, 335 Mass. 617.

**Mass. 1956.** Duty owed to a business invitee was to use due care to keep premises in a reasonably safe condition for use according to the invitation or to warn of dangers not obvious to the ordinary person, of which invitee would not be expected to know but which were known or should have been known to defendant.

Benjamin v. O'Connell & Lee Mfg. Co., 138 N.E.2d 126, 334 Mass. 646.

**Mass. 1956.** One who invites a business visitor to enter his premises owes to

† This Case was not selected for publication in the National Reporter System
For legislative history of cited statutes, see Massachusetts General Laws Annotated

### ▼ Are There Any Other Ways to Find Cases in the Digests?

Yes. If you have the name of a case on point but you do not have information about the key numbers contained in the case, you can look up the case name in the table of cases. It will list the case name and any applicable key numbers.

### ▼ Once You Have a Relevant Topic or Key Number, What Comes Next?

Once you find a relevant topic and key number using any of these methods, then you must be certain to check that topic and key number in the bound volume of the digest, in any pocket parts, and in any supplemental pamphlets.

### ▼ What Are Pocket Parts?

**Pocket parts** are pamphlets that are usually inserted in a slot at the back of a bound book. If the pocket part is too thick, the publishers often will print it as a small pamphlet. These pamphlets contain the most current cases and publisher references to related sources.

### ▼ How Do You Use the Pocket Parts?

To find cases in the pocket parts or in the pamphlets, you should find the topic that is listed alphabetically and then locate the appropriate key number. See Illustration 4-9. This is a pocket part page updating the second digest page shown in Illustration 4-3. Scan the page. At the bottom of the second column, you will find key number 1076. A number 1 is found next to the key number. Just below the key number, you will find a reference to *Green v. Jewel Food Stores, Inc.* A number 2 is next to the *Green* note in the pocket part. A Westlaw print out of the case is shown in Illustration 4-10. The first and fourth headnotes concern West key number 1076. Note the bracketed numbers and find number 1. That section of the case corresponds to the first headnote. Find number 4. That section of the case corresponds to the fourth headnote. The two headnotes are similar to one another and to those found for both the *Thompson* and the *Kellermann* cases. Review Illustration 3-4, headnote 1, and Illustration 3-10, headnote 7. A review of the three cases illustrates that they all deal with a similar negligence issue.

## 4. Online Digest Search

### ▼ Can Digests Be Searched Online?

You can search online for topics and key numbers on Westlaw only. However, topics and Lexis headnotes may be searched on Lexis. Because Westlaw is a West product, it has exclusive access to the key

## ILLUSTRATION 4-9.    Pocket Part Page from *Illinois Digest 2d*

🗝540   NEGLIGENCE                                                            476

the conduct of a third person, or some other causative factor, is the sole proximate cause of plaintiff's injuries.—Thomas v. Johnson Controls, Inc., 279 Ill.Dec. 798, 801 N.E.2d 90, 344 Ill. App.3d 1026, rehearing denied.

🗝570. —— Professional rescuers; "firefighter's rule".

**Ill.App. 2 Dist. 2003.** Because the grounding of fireman's rule is found in a compromise of rights between firemen and owners or occupiers, the rule cannot be expanded beyond its limited context of landowner/occupier liability.—Randich v. Pirtano Const. Co., Inc., 281 Ill.Dec. 616, 804 N.E.2d 581, opinion supplemented on denial of rehearing.

### XVII. PREMISES LIABILITY.

#### (A) IN GENERAL.

🗝1002. Constitutional, statutory and regulatory provisions.

**Ill.App. 2 Dist. 2003.** Under due process clause, statute providing that owner or occupier of premises owes fire fighters a duty of reasonable care in maintenance of premises could not be applied retroactively to cause of action that had accrued prior to effective date of statute. U.S.C.A. Const. Amend. 14; S.H.A. 425 ILCS 25/9f.—Randich v. Pirtano Const. Co., Inc., 281 Ill.Dec. 616, 804 N.E.2d 581, opinion supplemented on denial of rehearing.

#### (B) NECESSITY AND EXISTENCE OF DUTY.

🗝1010. In general.

**Ill.App. 1 Dist. 2003.** In premises liability cases, including those where a guest suffered injury while on hotel premises, Illinois courts determine whether a duty of care exists by considering the common law duty factors of (1) reasonable foreseeability of the injury; (2) likelihood of the injury; (3) magnitude of the burden on the defendant of guarding against the injury; and (4) consequences of placing the burden on the defendant.—Schmid v. Fairmont Hotel Company-Chicago, 280 Ill.Dec. 936, 803 N.E.2d 166, 345 Ill.App.3d 475.

🗝1012. Conditions known or obvious in general.

**Ill.App. 1 Dist. 2003.** In premises liability cases, the open and obvious nature of a condition generally affects whether the resulting harm was foreseeable, which, in turn, is relevant in determining whether a duty and proximate cause exist; in these cases, the open and obvious nature of a dangerous condition may preclude recovery, unless one of various exceptions is present.—Blue v. Environmental Engineering, Inc., 280 Ill.Dec. 957, 803 N.E.2d 187, 345 Ill.App.3d 455.

The exceptions to the rule that the open and obvious nature of a dangerous condition precludes recovery include: (1) the distraction exception—where the possessor of the property has reason to expect that an invitee's attention may be distracted and therefore he will not notice the danger; and (2) the deliberate encounter exception—where the possessor has reason to expect that the invitee will proceed to encounter the known or obvious danger because to a reasonable man in his position the advantages of doing so would outweigh the apparent risk. Restatement (Second) of Torts § 343A.— Id.

**Ill.App. 1 Dist. 2003.** A party who owns or controls land is not required to foresee injuries if the

**1 Key number**
**2 Court and year**
**3 Headnote**

potentially dangerous condition is open and obvious; the term "obvious" means that both the condition and the risk are apparent to and would be recognized by a reasonable person, in the position of the visitor, exercising ordinary perception, intelligence, and judgment.—Green v. Jewel Food Stores, Inc., 278 Ill.Dec. 875, 799 N.E.2d 740, 343 Ill.App.3d 830, rehearing denied.

In applying the distraction exception to the open and obvious doctrine, a court considers whether, despite the obviousness of a hazard, defendant should have anticipated the harm to plaintiff.—Id.

🗝1013. Conditions created or known by defendant.

**N.D.Ill. 2003.** Under Illinois law of negligence, building owner has duty to correct dangerous conditions on premises of which he knows or reasonably should know.—Ohio Cas. Group v. Dietrich, 285 F.Supp.2d 1128.

🗝1014. Foreseeability.

**Ill.App. 1 Dist. 2003.** In premises liability cases, including those where a guest suffered injury while on hotel premises, Illinois courts determine whether a duty of care exists by considering the common law duty factors of (1) reasonable foreseeability of the injury; (2) likelihood of the injury; (3) magnitude of the burden on the defendant of guarding against the injury; and (4) consequences of placing the burden on the defendant.—Schmid v. Fairmont Hotel Company-Chicago, 280 Ill.Dec. 936, 803 N.E.2d 166, 345 Ill.App.3d 475.

**Ill.App. 1 Dist. 2003.** A party who owns or controls land is not required to foresee injuries if the potentially dangerous condition is open and obvious; the term "obvious" means that both the condition and the risk are apparent to and would be recognized by a reasonable person, in the position of the visitor, exercising ordinary perception, intelligence, and judgment.—Green v. Jewel Food Stores, Inc., 278 Ill.Dec. 875, 799 N.E.2d 740, 343 Ill.App.3d 830, rehearing denied.

#### (C) STANDARD OF CARE.

🗝1037(4). Care required in general.

**Ill.App. 1 Dist. 2003.** The exceptions to the rule that the open and obvious nature of a dangerous condition precludes recovery include: (1) the distraction exception—where the possessor of the property has reason to expect that an invitee's attention may be distracted and therefore he will not notice the danger; and (2) the deliberate encounter exception—where the possessor has reason to expect that the invitee will proceed to encounter the known or obvious danger because to a reasonable man in his position the advantages of doing so would outweigh the apparent risk. Restatement (Second) of Torts § 343A.—Blue v. Environmental Engineering, Inc., 280 Ill.Dec. 957, 803 N.E.2d 187, 345 Ill.App.3d 455.

🗝1076. —— In general.

►**Ill.App. 1 Dist. 2003.** Duty of reasonable care of store owner, based on distraction exception to open and obvious rule, encompassed risk that customer, while exiting store, would be distracted by unattended shopping cart and trip and fall over irregular pavement.—Green v. Jewel Food Stores, Inc., 278 Ill.Dec. 875, 799 N.E.2d 740, 343 Ill. App.3d 830, rehearing denied.

A business operator generally owes his customers a duty to exercise reasonable care to maintain his premises in a reasonably safe condition.—Id.

† **This Case was not selected for publication in the National Reporter System**

**ILLUSTRATION 4-10.   Westlaw Printout of Case** *Green v. Jewel Food Stores*

---

westlaw.

799 N.E.2d 740                                                                                          Page 1
343 Ill.App.3d 830, 799 N.E.2d 740, 278 Ill.Dec. 875
**(Cite as: 343 Ill.App.3d 830, 799 N.E.2d 740, 278 Ill.Dec. 875)**

▷

Appellate Court of Illinois,
First District, Second Division.
Robert GREEN and Doris Green, Plaintiffs-Appellants,
v.
JEWEL FOOD STORES, INC., Defendant-Appellee.

No. 1-02-1856.
Sept. 9, 2003.
Rehearing Denied Oct. 10, 2003.

Customer brought negligence action against corporation seeking damages for injuries sustained when she fell while exiting corporation's store. The Circuit Court, Cook County, David G. Lichtenstein, J., granted corporation's motion for summary judgment. Customer appealed. The Appellate Court, Cahill, J., held that duty of reasonable care of corporation, based on distraction exception to open and obvious rule, encompassed risk that customer would be distracted by unattended shopping cart and trip and fall over irregular pavement.

Reversed and remanded.

West Headnotes

① [1] Negligence 272 ⬤⟿1076

**1 Headnote 1 Case Reference
to Key Number 1076**

272 Negligence
   272XVII Premises Liability
     272XVII(C) Standard of Care
       272k1075 Care Required of Store and Business Proprietors
        272k1076 k. In General. Most Cited Cases

**Negligence 272 ⬤⟿1291(3)**

272 Negligence
   272XVII Premises Liability
     272XVII(L) Defenses and Mitigating Circumstances
       272k1281 Plaintiff's Conduct or Fault
        272k1291 Exterior Grounds
         272k1291(3) k. Parking Lots and Driveways. Most Cited Cases
   Duty of reasonable care of store owner, based on distraction exception to open and obvious rule, encompassed risk that customer, while exiting store, would be distracted by unattended shopping cart and trip and fall over irregular pavement.

[2] Negligence 272 ⬤⟿202

272 Negligence
   272I In General

© 2011 Thomson Reuters. No Claim to Orig. US Gov. Works.

---

number system. West's online search tools allow researchers to use this key number system to access a broad range of cases. Researchers can use several different methods to design their online searches.

To browse online for key numbers, you can access the West Key Number Digest. To do this, click on the words "Key Numbers" at the

## ILLUSTRATION 4-10.   *Continued*

343 Ill.App.3d 830, 799 N.E.2d 740, 278 Ill.Dec. 875
(Cite as: 343 Ill.App.3d 830, 799 N.E.2d 740, 278 Ill.Dec. 875)

272k202 k. Elements in General. Most Cited Cases
Plaintiff states a cause of action for negligence by establishing: (1) that defendant owed a duty of care to plaintiff; (2) defendant breached the duty; (3) an injury occurred; and (4) the injury was proximately caused by defendant's breach.

[3] Judgment 228 ⬤⟿181(33)

228 Judgment
    228V On Motion or Summary Proceeding
        228k181 Grounds for Summary Judgment
            228k181(15) Particular Cases
                228k181(33) k. Tort Cases in General. Most Cited Cases
Whether a duty of care exists for negligence action is a question of law which may be decided on a motion for summary judgment.

**②**   [4] Negligence 272 ⬤⟿1076

> **2 Headnote 4 Case Reference to Key Number 1076**

272 Negligence
    272XVII Premises Liability
        272XVII(C) Standard of Care
            272k1075 Care Required of Store and Business Proprietors
                272k1076 k. In General. Most Cited Cases
A business operator generally owes his customers a duty to exercise reasonable care to maintain his premises in a reasonably safe condition.

[5] Negligence 272 ⬤⟿210

272 Negligence
    272II Necessity and Existence of Duty
        272k210 k. In General. Most Cited Cases
To decide whether a duty exists court considers: (1) foreseeability that defendant's conduct will result in injury to another; (2) likelihood of injury; (3) burden of guarding against injury; and (4) consequences of placing that burden on defendant.

[6] Negligence 272 ⬤⟿1012

272 Negligence
    272XVII Premises Liability
        272XVII(B) Necessity and Existence of Duty
            272k1012 k. Conditions Known or Obvious in General. Most Cited Cases

Negligence 272 ⬤⟿1014

272 Negligence
    272XVII Premises Liability
        272XVII(B) Necessity and Existence of Duty
            272k1014 k. Foreseeability. Most Cited Cases

top of any Westlaw page. A screen similar to the one shown in Illustration 4-11 will appear. There is a link to search West's Key Numbers. By clicking on that link, you can browse the digest topics.

Westlaw provides an extensive alphabetical listing of topics. See a sample of the topics in Illustration 4-12. If you scroll down the alphabetical list on Westlaw, you will find an arrow next to the notation "272 NEGLIENCE" with a small plus sign next to it. This is a

# ILLUSTRATION 4-10. *Continued*

343 Ill.App.3d 830, 799 N.E.2d 740, 278 Ill.Dec. 875
(Cite as: 343 Ill.App.3d 830, 799 N.E.2d 740, 278 Ill.Dec. 875)

A party who owns or controls land is not required to foresee injuries if the potentially dangerous condition is open and obvious; the term "obvious" means that both the condition and the risk are apparent to and would be recognized by a reasonable person, in the position of the visitor, exercising ordinary perception, intelligence, and judgment.

[7] Negligence 272 ☞1012

272 Negligence
    272XVII Premises Liability
        272XVII(B) Necessity and Existence of Duty
            272k1012 k. Conditions Known or Obvious in General. Most Cited Cases

Negligence 272 ☞1286(3)

272 Negligence
    272XVII Premises Liability
        272XVII(L) Defenses and Mitigating Circumstances
            272k1281 Plaintiff's Conduct or Fault
                272k1286 Knowledge of Danger
                    272k1286(3) k. Forgetfulness, Inattention or Distraction. Most Cited Cases
    In applying the distraction exception to the open and obvious doctrine, a court considers whether, despite the obviousness of a hazard, defendant should have anticipated the harm to plaintiff.

**741*830***876 Roosevelt Thomas of Westrate & Holmstrom, P.C., Dowagiac, MI, for Appellant.

Paul A. Tanzillo and Andrew T. Fleishman, of McBreen, Kopko, McKay & Nora, Chicago, for Appellee.

*831 Justice CAHILL delivered the opinion of the court:
    Plaintiffs Robert and Doris Green appeal from an order of summary judgment entered in favor of defendant, Jewel Food Stores, Inc. Plaintiffs contend that the trial court erred in disposing of their negligence complaint by finding that defendant owed no duty to the plaintiffs. We believe the undisputed facts of this case fall within the distraction exception set out in *Ward v. K mart Corp.*, 136 Ill.2d 132, 143 Ill.Dec. 288, 554 N.E.2d 223 (1990), and require that the question of duty be resolved against defendant. We reverse and remand.

    The Greens filed a complaint seeking damages for injuries sustained when Doris fell while exiting defendant's store in Oaklawn, Illinois. Plaintiffs alleged that defendant negligently maintained an inherently unsafe environment at the store's exit where there were unattended shopping carts and a one-inch ridge in the pavement. Doris claimed that the unsafe conditions were the proximate cause of her injury, a broken patella (kneecap). Her husband Robert sought damages for loss of consortium. The trial court granted defendant's motion for summary judgment, finding: (1) defendant did not breach a duty of care owed to plaintiffs; (2) the record was uncontested with no unanswered questions of fact; and (3) there was no unreasonably unsafe condition on defendant's property as a matter of law.

    The pleadings, depositions and photographs of record show that Doris and her husband's cousin, Eleanor Hastie, entered defendant's store at about 9:30 a.m. on **742 ***877 November 16, 1997. Doris was visiting from Michigan and had not previously shopped at that store. Robert waited in the car while the women shopped.

broad topic. When you click on the plus sign, the entry expands under the Negligence topic as shown in Illustration 4-13. The list shows additional specific Negligence key number ranges. Next to the A is the notation "premises liability, K1000-K1320." Those key numbers deal with that topic. In a negligence case involving a slip and fall on a premises or at a store, these would be relevant. If you click on that plus sign,

## ILLUSTRATION 4-10.   *Continued*

343 Ill.App.3d 830, 799 N.E.2d 740, 278 Ill.Dec. 875
(Cite as: 343 Ill.App.3d 830, 799 N.E.2d 740, 278 Ill.Dec. 875)

Doris exited the store, carrying her purse over her shoulder and a plastic shopping bag containing one or two items in her hand. Hastie was behind Doris. A customer exiting in front of Doris pushed an empty shopping cart toward a cart storage area. When Doris noticed the cart was rolling down a slope toward the parking lot, she grabbed it by the handle to stop it. She then fell.

In a recorded statement on November 20, 1997, Doris said as she and Hastie exited the store, a man ahead of them "just gave his cart a shove." Doris said, "I grabbed for [the cart] so it wouldn't be out in the cars or hit a car." When asked why she thought she fell, Doris replied, "I really don't know what caused it * * * unless it was this bump that [Robert] said was there." The bump referred to a ridge between the cement sidewalk and the asphalt paving of the parking lot that Robert noticed and photographed when he returned to the scene the next day. Doris later stated in a discovery deposition on September 19, 2000, "[t]here was a ridge, but I think [it was] the cart that made me fall." She estimated the ridge to have been about one inch high.

*832 Robert also gave a deposition on September 19, 2000. He said he saw Doris exit the store and then saw her on the ground. He did not see her fall but believed she fell because "when she grabbed that cart I think she didn't notice this little ridge" where the cement was "a little higher" than the asphalt. He said he did not notice the ridge until he returned to the scene the next day.

Hastie gave a deposition on May 23, 2001. She said she was walking 10 to 12 feet behind Doris and she believed Doris fell because she lost her balance as she reached out to grab the empty cart.

Ginger Lane, defendant's employee, gave a recorded statement on December 8, 1997, in which she said she saw Doris after the fall. Lane said Doris was on the ground on an incline that was dry and clean with no cracks in the pavement.

The standard of review of a trial court's grant of a motion for summary judgment is *de novo*. *Morris v. Margulis*, 197 Ill.2d 28, 35, 257 Ill.Dec. 656, 754 N.E.2d 314 (2001). We construe all evidence strictly against the moving party and liberally in favor of the nonmoving party. *Espinoza v. Elgin, Joliet & Eastern Ry. Co.*, 165 Ill.2d 107, 113, 208 Ill.Dec. 662, 649 N.E.2d 1323 (1995).

**(3)** [1][2][3] ▨ **3 Headnote 1 Case Reference** ▨ of action for negligence by establishing: (1) that the defendant owed a duty of care ▨ ▨ fendant breached the duty; (3) an injury occurred; and (4) the injury was proximately ▨ ▨ breach. *Curatola v. Village of Niles*, 154 Ill.2d 201, 207, 181 Ill.Dec. 631, 608 N.E.2d 8▨ ▨ of care exists is a question of law which may be decided on a motion for summary jud▨ ▨ at 207, 181 Ill.Dec. 631, 608 N.E.2d 882.

**(4)** [4][5][6] ▨ **4 Headnote 4 Case Reference** ▨ rally owes his customers a duty to exercise reasonable care to maintain his premises ▨ ition. *Ward*, 136 Ill.2d at 141, 143 Ill.Dec. 288, 554 N.E.2d 223. To decide whether ▨ : (1) the foreseeability that the defendant's conduct will result in injury to another; (2) ▨ ) the burden of guarding against injury; and (4) the consequences of placing that bur▨ ▨ *atola*, 154 Ill.2d at 214, 181 Ill.Dec. 631, 608 N.E.2d 882. A party who owns or con▨ *878 required to foresee injuries if the potentially dangerous condition is open and obvious. *Bucheleres v. Chicago Park District*, 171 Ill.2d 435, 447-48, 216 Ill.Dec. 568, 665 N.E.2d 826 (1996). The term " obvious" means that " 'both the condition and the risk are apparent to and would be recognized by a reasonable [person], in the position of the visitor, exercising ordinary perception, intelligence, and judgment.' " *Deibert v. Bauer Brothers Construction Co.*, 141 Ill.2d 430, 435, 152 Ill.Dec. 552, 566 N.E.2d 239 (1990), quoting Restatement (Second) of Torts § 343A, Comment *b*, at 219 (1965). In *Deibert*, however, the su-

additional key numbers will appear. See pages 2 and 3 of Illustration 4-13. On page 2, note the arrow next to Standard of Care. That is the issue raised in the negligence case involving a slip and fall. When you expand that entry, the results are shown on page 3 of this illustration. Locate the arrow on page 3. The arrow is next to the entry k1075. That entry is "Care required of store and business proprietors." Below that is k1076,

# ILLUSTRATION 4-10.   *Continued*

---

343 Ill.App.3d 830, 799 N.E.2d 740, 278 Ill.Dec. 875
(Cite as: 343 Ill.App.3d 830, 799 N.E.2d 740, 278 Ill.Dec. 875)

preme court noted that, even though a deep rut in the ground at a *833 construction site was an obvious hazard, it was foreseeable that the injured employee's attention would be distracted by the possibility of construction debris being thrown from an adjacent balcony. *Deibert,* 141 Ill.2d at 438, 152 Ill.Dec. 552, 566 N.E.2d 239.

Plaintiffs rely on the reasoning that governed our supreme court's decision in *Ward,* 136 Ill.2d at 147, 143 Ill.Dec. 288, 554 N.E.2d 223. Plaintiffs argue that open and obvious conditions do not necessarily relieve a defendant of a duty of reasonable care. In *Ward,* the supreme court held that a property owner owed a duty of care to a customer even though the customer was injured after encountering an obvious condition, if the defendant should reasonably anticipate that the plaintiff would be distracted. There, the plaintiff was injured when, while carrying a large mirror he had just purchased at defendant's store, he walked into a concrete post located just outside the store entrance. *Ward,* 136 Ill.2d at 138, 143 Ill.Dec. 288, 554 N.E.2d 223. The court concluded that the defendant owed the plaintiff a duty of care because it was reasonable to expect that the plaintiff's attention might be distracted from the pole, an obvious condition, as he carried a large item from the store. *Ward,* 136 Ill.2d at 149-50, 143 Ill.Dec. 288, 554 N.E.2d 223, adopting the reasoning in Restatement (Second) of Torts, § 343A, Comment *f,* at 220 (1965). The Restatement provides:

> "Such reason to expect harm to the visitor from known or obvious dangers may arise, for example, where the possessor [of land] has reason to expect that the invitee's attention may be distracted, so that he will not discover what is obvious, or will forget what he has discovered, or fail to protect himself against it. Such reason may also arise where the possessor has reason to expect that the invitee will proceed to encounter the known or obvious danger because to a reasonable man in his position the advantages of doing so would outweigh the apparent risk. In such cases the fact that the danger is known, or is obvious, is important in determining whether the invitee is to be charged with contributory negligence, or assumption of risk. [Citation.] It is not, however, conclusive in determining the duty of the possessor, or whether he has acted reasonably under the circumstances." Restatement (Second) of Torts, § 343A, Comment *f,* at 220 (1965).

The court in *Ward* held that the proper inquiry in deciding whether the distraction exception applies to the open and obvious doctrine is "whether the defendant should reasonably anticipate injury to those entrants on his premises who are generally exercising reasonable care for their own safety, but who may reasonably be expected to be distracted, as when carrying large bundles, or forgetful of the condition after having momentarily encountered it." *Ward,* 136 Ill.2d at 152, 143 Ill.Dec. 288, 554 N.E.2d 223. Whether the hazardous condition itself operated as adequate notice of its presence or whether additional precautions were required *834 to satisfy the defendant's **744 ***879 duty of care are questions properly left to the trier of fact. *Ward,* 136 Ill.2d at 156, 143 Ill.Dec. 288, 554 N.E.2d 223.

The narrow question in this case is, should defendant have reasonably anticipated that a shopper would be momentarily distracted from an open and obvious danger-the ridge or bump-by the sudden motion of an errant cart? Our reversal is informed by cases reliant on *Ward: Buchaklian v. Lake County Family Young Men's Christian Ass'n,* 314 Ill.App.3d 195, 200-01, 247 Ill.Dec. 541, 732 N.E.2d 596 (2000); *Maschhoff v. National Super Markets, Inc.,* 230 Ill.App.3d 169, 172-73, 172 Ill.Dec. 304, 595 N.E.2d 665 (1992).

[7] In *Buchaklian,* a YMCA member tripped and fell while walking across uneven mats on the floor of the defendant's facility. The trial court granted the defendant's motions for summary judgment, finding that no question of fact existed as to the open and obvious nature of the uneven mats. In denying the plaintiff's motion for reconsideration, the trial court further found that the defendant had no notice of the alleged condition and the defendant owed the plaintiff no duty as a matter of law. *Buchaklian,* 314 Ill.App.3d at 199, 247 Ill.Dec. 541, 732

---

which corresponds to the key number involved in the *Green* case shown in Illustration 4-10. That case also involved a fall.

As Illustration 4-4, the Key Number Translation Table, showed you, key number 1076 replaced 32(2.8), the key number that is shown in the *Thompson* case, which is presented in Illustration 3-4. This is the same key number that is referenced in the print digest shown in Illustration 4-3. By looking at each of these illustrations, you can see how the cases,

## ILLUSTRATION 4-10.   *Continued*

343 Ill.App.3d 830, 799 N.E.2d 740, 278 Ill.Dec. 875
(Cite as: 343 Ill.App.3d 830, 799 N.E.2d 740, 278 Ill.Dec. 875)

N.E.2d 596. We reversed, holding that the existence of an open and obvious condition is not a *per se* bar to finding a legal duty. *Buchaklian,* 314 Ill.App.3d at 204, 247 Ill.Dec. 541, 732 N.E.2d 596. In applying the distraction
exception to the open and obvious doctrine, we consider whether, despite the obviousness of a hazard, the defendant should have anticipated the harm to the plaintiff. *Buchaklian,* 314 Ill.App.3d at 204, 247 Ill.Dec. 541,
732 N.E.2d 596. The court acknowledged that a pedestrian cannot look up to avoid colliding with other pedestrians and, at the same time, look down to protect herself from tripping. *Buchaklian,* 314 Ill.App.3d at 202-03, 247
Ill.Dec. 541, 732 N.E.2d 596. "In sum, we hold that where reasonable persons could draw divergent inferences
from the undisputed material facts or where reasonable minds could differ as to a material fact, such as whether
a condition is open and obvious, summary judgment should be denied and the issue decided by the trier of fact."
*Buchaklian,* 314 Ill.App.3d at 205, 247 Ill.Dec. 541, 732 N.E.2d 596.

In *Maschhoff,* the plaintiff was injured while delivering milk to the defendant's store. *Maschhoff,* 230
Ill.App.3d at 170, 172 Ill.Dec. 304, 595 N.E.2d 665. The plaintiff said he was not sure why he fell inside defendant's dairy cooler where he was unloading crates of milk from a pallet, but he described the floor as covered with
a "buildup" of milk or water or grime. The defendant's dairy manager was standing about five feet away from
the plaintiff when the plaintiff fell. *Maschhoff,* 230 Ill.App.3d at 171, 172 Ill.Dec. 304, 595 N.E.2d 665. In reviewing a jury verdict in the plaintiff's favor, we concluded that the plaintiff's injury was reasonably foreseeable
and the defendant owed a duty of care under *Ward. Maschhoff,* 230 Ill.App.3d at 173, 172 Ill.Dec. 304, 595
N.E.2d 665. It was foreseeable that the plaintiff might be distracted from the slippery *835 condition, despite its
obviousness, while concentrating on stacking the crates and talking to the defendant's dairy manager, momentarily forgetting the slippery floor. *Maschhoff,* 230 Ill.App.3d at 174, 172 Ill.Dec. 304, 595 N.E.2d 665.

We discern little if any difference between the case before us and the facts in *Ward, Buchaklian* and *Maschhoff.* In *Ward,* the distraction was the large bundle and the proximate cause of injury was the concrete post. In
*Buchaklian,* the distraction was the other pedestrians and the proximate cause of injury was the uneven **745
***880 mats. In *Maschhoff,* the distraction was the job of stacking crates and the proximate cause of injury was
the slippery floor. Here, the distraction was the unattended cart and the proximate cause of injury was the uneven pavement.

We conclude that defendant owed a duty of care to plaintiffs because it was reasonably foreseeable that a
customer would be distracted by an unattended shopping cart and trip and fall over the irregular pavement. The
duty question having been resolved against defendant based on the distraction exception to the open and obvious
rule, it is for the trier of fact to determine whether the elements of negligence are present and, if so, whether
contributory negligence or risk assumption of plaintiff diminishes or negates liability. Reasonable persons could
draw different inferences from the facts in this case.

The judgment of the circuit court is reversed and the cause remanded.

Reversed and remanded.

McBRIDE, P.J., and GARCIA, J., concur.

Ill.App. 1 Dist.,2003.
Green v. Jewel Food Stores, Inc.
343 Ill.App.3d 830, 799 N.E.2d 740, 278 Ill.Dec. 875

END OF DOCUMENT

Reprinted with permission of Thomson Reuters.

both in print and online, and the digests, both in print and online, all
tie together.

Another method of locating a key number is similar to the one good
case method used for the print digest. This type of search is particularly
invaluable when you are undertaking research for a state case and you

do not have access to that state's digest for a particular state. Suppose you are presented with the same slip and fall issue noted above. You need to find Florida law, but you have only the *Illinois Digest* or an Illinois case on point. You can use the key number you found in the case to search for the Florida case on the computer.

Look closely at Illustration 4-10. Under each of the headnotes is a number similar to the key number. For headnote 1, the number is 272k1076. That number is the key number needed to do a search on Westlaw for similar cases. You should enter 272k1076 into the Key Number Search page similar to the one shown in Illustration 4-11. Searching that number for a specific jurisdiction allows you to create a Custom Digest similar to that found in Illustration 4-14. It shows a Custom Digest for Negligence key number 1076 listed as 272k1076. That headnote focuses on the "care required of store and business proprietors" generally. It is the same headnote involved in the *Kellermann* and *Green* cases. It is the newer key number for the same topical headnote referenced in the *Thompson* case.

If you had found the *Green* case and you wanted to search for similar case, you would enter 272k1076 in the search field. For Westlaw, 272 is the numerical designation for negligence topics. Each West digest topic is assigned a numerical counterpoint for computerized searches. K is for key number and 1076 corresponds to the print key number.

Another way to search for a key number and topic is similar to the Topic Outline method. With that approach, you could review the *Illinois Digest* to find the appropriate key number. You then insert the key number and the numeric number for the West negligence topic, which is 272, into the key number search field and it will generate a Custom Digest of cases similar to that found in Illustration 4-14.

The final way to obtain a topic and key number is to insert terms in the West Key Number Search box shown in Illustration 4-15. The words "store owner duty of care to invitee" are listed in the search field. The jurisdiction is Illinois. The computer yields various Negligence topics and key numbers. 272K1076 is listed first in the results. Once you have that key number, you would click on it or enter the key number as shown in Illustration 4-13, and the Custom Digest similar to Illustration 4-14 would appear.

Review Illustration 4-14. Note that these cases are similar to *Green*, *Thompson*, and *Kellermann*. The first case listed is *Marshall v. Burger King Corp.*, 856 N.E.2d 1048. It is the most recent case that involves the relevant Negligence topic discussed in headnote 272k1076. Note the number 1 in Illustration 4-14. It is where the *Green* case appears in the Custom Digest. A number 2 is next to the *Kellermann* case (shown in Illustration 3-10). *Hills v. Bridgeview Little League Ass'n*, 713 N.E2d 616 (1999) is listed in the digest next to the number 3. Again, the digest tells the researchers that these Illinois court cases discuss the

## ILLUSTRATION 4-11.   Westlaw Key Number Search Page

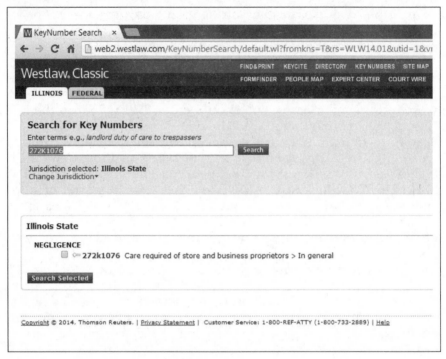

Reprinted with permission of Thomson Reuters.

definition of "business invitee." Note the number 4. It appears next to the *Thompson v. Economy Super Marts, Inc.*, 581 N.E.2d 885 (1991) shown in Illustration 3-4. It again discusses the question of the duty a business owes to an invitee. Now review the cases and note the similarities between them. They are not identical in facts or in the legal analysis. However, portions of the cases can be related to one another so that as a researcher you develop a better understanding of the relevant case law concerning the duty owed by a business to an invitee.

Lexis also offers the ability to search by topics. See Illustration 4-16A. It is a partial list of Lexis legal topics. The arrow highlights the Torts topic. You can drill down under premises liability to search for cases in a particular jurisdiction. The first page of Illustration 4-16B shows the topics for premises liability before they are expanded. The second page shows the topics on Lexis Advance after they have been expanded.

Another way to search is to use the Lexis search page, similar to the one shown in Illustration 4-17. You would select the jurisdiction and the sources and enter search terms similar to those entered in this

## ILLUSTRATION 4-12.   Westlaw Online Topics

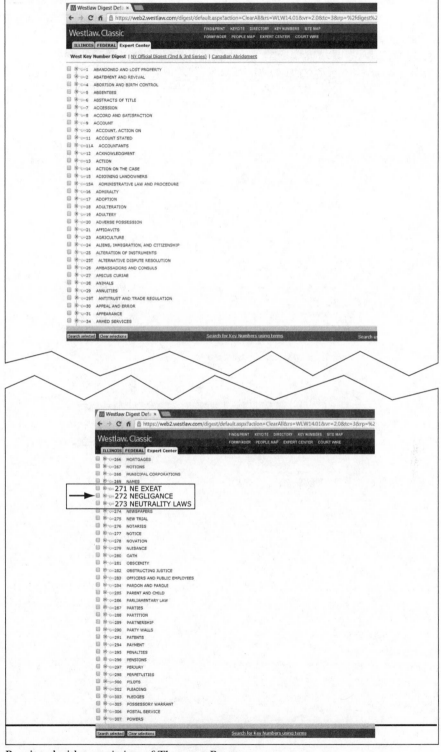

Reprinted with permission of Thomson Reuters.

## ILLUSTRATION 4-13.   Expanded List of Westlaw Topics and Key Numbers for Premises Liability and Standard of Care

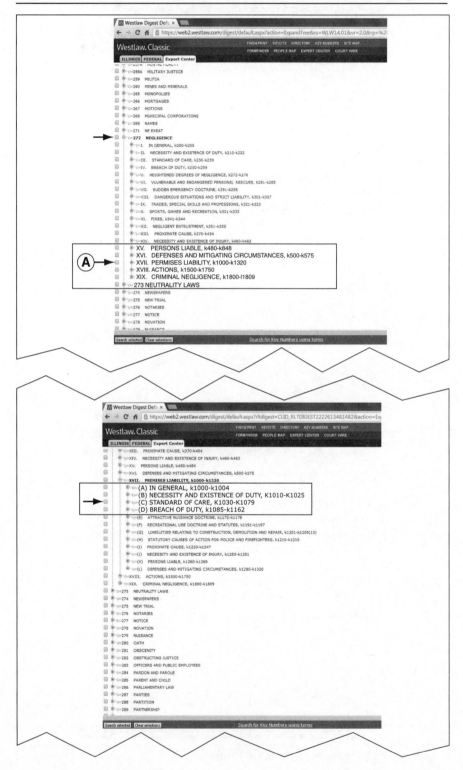

## ILLUSTRATION 4-13. *Continued*

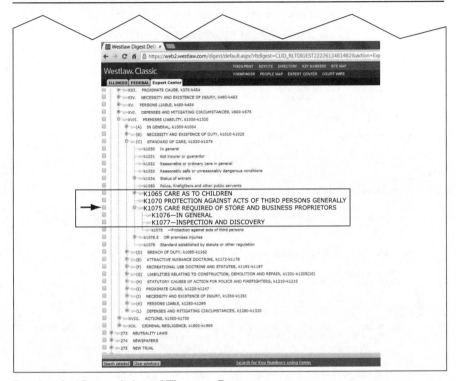

Reprinted with permission of Thomson Reuters.

illustration. You can enter specific terms or you can select the Natural Language method. Using that method, a researcher can enter terms without using Lexis search connectors. Lexis search techniques will be explained in detail in Chapter 10. By entering the terms "business invitee" and "store owner" and "premises liability" and searching the Illinois database on Lexis, the results are similar in part to those found on Westlaw using the key number 272k1070. See Illustration 4-19. One of the cases you will see there is *Kellermann v. Car City Chevrolet-Nissan*, 713 N.E.2d 1285 (1999). This case is also shown in the West Custom Digest shown in Illustration 4-14. If the entire custom digest and the full Lexis results were presented here, many of the same cases would be shown. Try this search on both Westlaw and Lexis and compare the results.

## ILLUSTRATION 4-14. Sample Westlaw Custom Digest

---

**Headnotes**

▷
Marshall v. Burger King Corp., 856 N.E.2d 1048
  272 NEGLIGENCE
    272XVII Premises Liability
      272XVII(C) Standard of Care
        272k1075 Care Required of Store and Business Proprietors

272k1076 k. In general.
Ill.,2006
Special relationship between a business invitor and invitee gives rise to an affirmative duty on the part of invitors to aid or protect invitees against unreasonable risk of physical harm; overruling *Stutz v. Kamm*, 204 Ill.App.3d 898, 149 Ill.Dec. 935, 562 N.E.2d 399. Restatement (Second) of Torts §§ 314A, 344.

▷
Marshall v. Burger King Corp., 856 N.E.2d 1048
Ill.,2006
Fast food restaurant, an establishment open to the general public for business purposes, was in a special invitor-invitee relationship with its customers, giving rise to duty to aid or protect customers against unreasonable risk of physical harm. Restatement (Second) of Torts §§ 314A, 344.

**c**
Pageloff v. Gaumer, 849 N.E.2d 1086
Ill.App.3.Dist.,2006
The operator of a business owes his invitees a duty to exercise reasonable care to maintain his premises in a reasonably safe condition for use by the invitees.

**c**
Pageloff v. Gaumer, 849 N.E.2d 1086
Ill.App.3.Dist.,2006
Campground and its owner did not have a duty to keep the ground clear of fallen walnuts and, thus, could not be liable to camper who tripped on a walnut that fell from a tree near her campsite for breach of such a duty; camper was aware of the existence of the walnuts and of the tripping danger posed by them, burden of guarding against injury caused by fallen walnuts would be extremely onerous, and imposing such a burden on campground owner would, as a practical matter, result in an inability to have walnut trees near campgrounds.

**o**
Pageloff v. Gaumer, 849 N.E.2d 1086
Ill.App.3.Dist.,2006
Campground and its owner had no duty to warn camper who tripped on a walnut that fell from a tree near her campsite of the danger posed by walnuts and other items on the ground in wooded campgrounds; campground customers were already well aware of the potential for a trip or fall caused by stepping on such items.

▷
Green v. Jewel Food Stores, Inc., 799 N.E.2d 740
Ill.App.1.Dist.,2003
(1) Duty of reasonable care of store owner, based on distraction exception to open and obvious rule, encompassed risk that customer, while exiting store, would be distracted by unattended shopping cart and trip and fall over irregular pavement.

# ILLUSTRATION 4-14. *Continued*

**H**
**(2)** Kellermann v. Car City Chevrolet-Nissan, Inc., 713 N.E.2d 1285
Ill.App.5.Dist.,1999
"Natural-accumulation rule" provides that a landowner does not have a duty to a business invitee to remove natural accumulations of snow and ice.
See publication Words and Phrases for other judicial constructions and definitions.

**(3)** Hills v. Bridgeview Little League Ass'n, 713 N.E.2d 616
Ill.App.1.Dist.,1999
Person is a "business invitee" on the land of another if (1) the person enters by express or implied invitation, (2) the entry is connected with either the owner's business or with an activity conducted by the owner on the land, and (3) the owner receives a benefit.
See publication Words and Phrases for other judicial constructions and definitions.

**(4)** Thompson v. Economy Super Marts, Inc., 581 N.E.2d 885
Formerly 272k32(2.8)
Ill.App.3.Dist.,1991
Defendant owes business invitee on defendant's premises duty to exercise ordinary care in maintaining premises in reasonably safe condition.

Reprinted with permission of Thomson Reuters.

## ILLUSTRATION 4-15. Westlaw Key Number Search Page Using Terms and Sample Results

**Search for Key Numbers**

Enter terms e.g., *landlord duty of care to trespassers*

| store owner duty of care | | Search |

Add Related Terms: HIDE STASH HOARD MARKET PURCHASER POSSESSOR HOLDER "DUE CARE" "ORDINARY CARE" "REASONABLE CARE" "STANDARD OF CARE" CAUTION PRUDENCE CUSTODY SUPERVISION [ SELECT ALL ]

Jurisdiction selected: **Illinois State**
Change Jurisdiction▾

West Key Number Digest Outlin

**Illinois State**

**NEGLIGENCE**

- ☐ **272k1076** **Care** required of **store** and business proprietors > In general
- ☐ **272k1022** **Duty** of **store** and business proprietors > In general
- ☐ **272k1289** Plaintiff's conduct or fault > Buildings and structures
- ☐ **272k1283(4)** Invitees > **Store** and business visitors
- ☐ **272k1077** **Care** required of **store** and business proprietors > Inspection and discovery
- ☐ **272k1024** **Duty** of **store** and business proprietors > Protection against acts of third persons
- ☐ **272k1670** Premises liability > Buildings and other structures
- ☐ **272k1119** Buildings and structures > Furniture, shelves, displays, carts and other accessories
- ☐ **272k1708** Premises liability > Buildings and other structures
- ☐ **272k1104(3)** Floors > Falls in general

**Additional Results from All Jurisdictions**

**NEGLIGENCE**

- ☐ **272k220** NECESSITY AND EXISTENCE OF **DUTY** > Protection against acts of third persons
- ☐ **272k1693** QUESTIONS FOR JURY AND DIRECTED VERDICTS > Negligence as question of fact or law generally

**ResultsPlus**

**Illinois Law & Practice: Negligence**
1. Duties Owed to Particular Class of Persons, Licensees and Invitees, **Duty** Owed to Persons on **Store** Premises a Invitees

**Restatement of Torts**
2. Liability of Possessors of Land to Persons on the Land, Title E. Special Liability of Possessors of Land to Invitees, Dangerous Conditions Known to or Discoverable by Possessor

**Restatement of Torts**
3. Liability of Possessors of Land to Persons on the Land, Title E. Special Liability of Possessors of Land to Invitees, Business Premises Open to Public: Acts of Third Persons or Animals

**Premises Liability**
4. Premises Liability Law, **Store** and Shopping Center Floors and Aisles, Floor Obstacles

**Causes of Action**
5. Cause of Action by Customer for Injury Suffered in Grocery **Store** Slip and Fall

**Am.Jur. Proof of Facts**
6. Dangerous Retail Floor Displays

**Corpus Juris Secundum: Negligence**

Reprinted with permission of Thomson Reuters.

# ILLUSTRATION 4-16A.   List of Lexis Legal Topics on Lexis

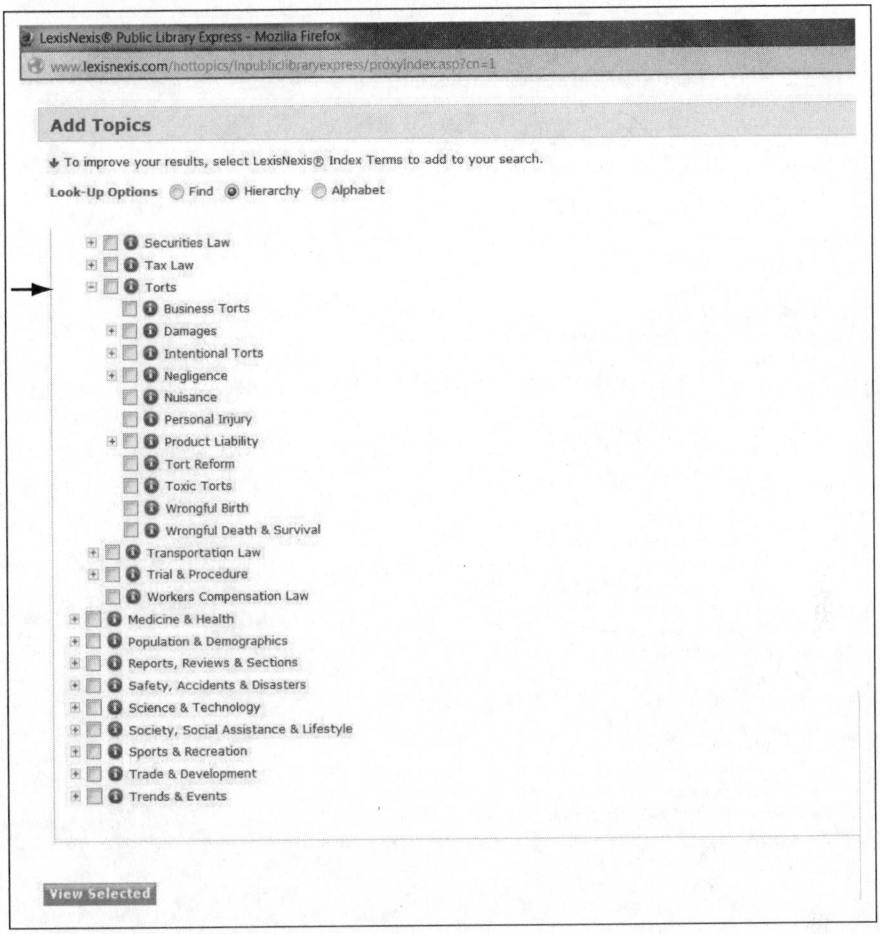

Reprinted with the permission of LexisNexis.

## ILLUSTRATION 4-16B.   List of Lexis Legal Topics on Lexis Advance

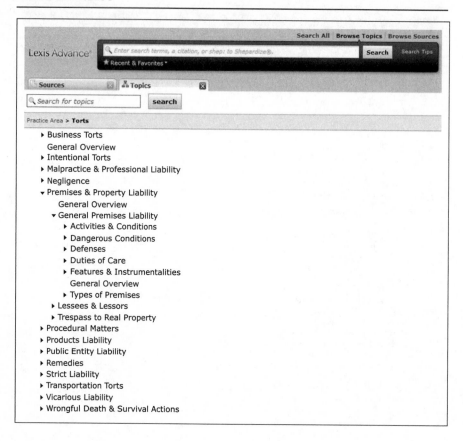

## ILLUSTRATION 4-16B. *Continued*

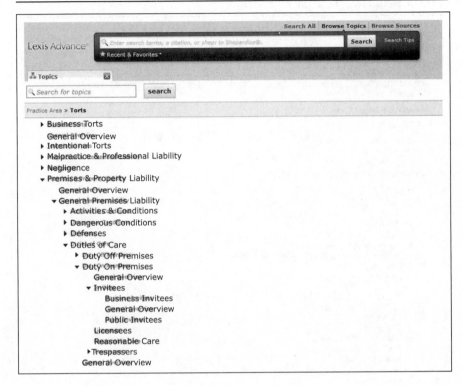

Reprinted with the permission of LexisNexis.

## ILLUSTRATION 4-17.   Expanded List of Lexis Legal Topics for Torts and Premises Liability

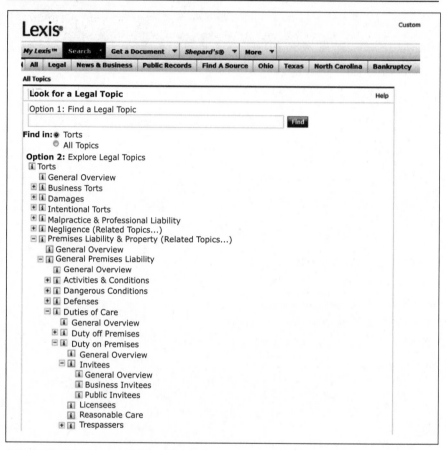

Reprinted with the permission of LexisNexis.

# ILLUSTRATION 4-18.   Lexis Search Page from LexisNexis Library Express

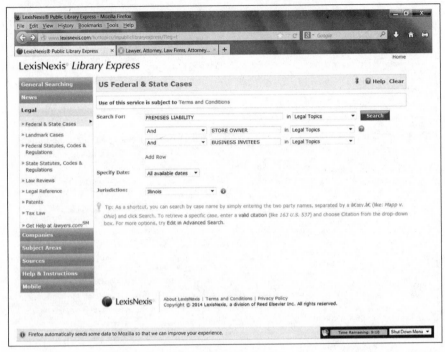

Reprinted with the permission of LexisNexis.

## ILLUSTRATION 4-19.    Results of LexisNexis Search of Terms Business Invitee, Store Owner, and Premises Liability

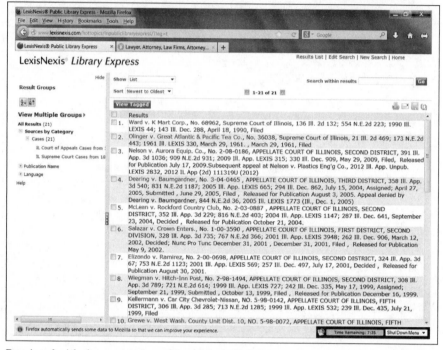

Reprinted with the permission of LexisNexis. Editor's Note: See online document for complete report.

# CHAPTER SUMMARY

In this chapter, you learned about digests that can assist you in locating similar cases on point. The digests are tied to the commercial reporters' headnotes that contact case abstracts concerning a point of law raised in a case. Each headnote contains a topic and a number that refer you to a topical system for finding additional similar cases. West's National Reporter System[TM] is linked to its digest system both in print and online. This system enables researchers to find applicable topics in one state and review the same topics in a different state digest to find similar cases. The online databases also allow researchers to research multiple states.

When you research a legal issue in a digest, you can review its index to find a relevant topic and number that directs you to cases on point. In the West system, the numbers are called key numbers. Another method for using the digest is to review the outline presented before each topic. You also might find a good case on point and locate other similar cases by using the digest topic and numbers listed in the publisher's headnotes that appear at the beginning of a case reporter.

In the next chapter, you will learn how to ensure that the cases you found are good law.

# KEY TERMS

descriptive word index method

digests

headnotes

one good case method

pocket parts

topic outline method

West American Digest system

West key number system

# EXERCISES

## DIGEST RESEARCH

1. Research the following issue in the appropriate digest.

    Your firm's client was fired from her job because she was 69 years old. She had worked for 40 years in this position. When she was fired, she was replaced with a 25-year-old woman. Your firm's client has a master's degree; the 25-year-old has a bachelor's degree.

    You only need to consider what federal law claims she might have against her former employer. Her case would be brought in the U.S. District Court for the Northern District of Ohio.

    *Brainstorm:* What words would you review? What topics and key numbers did you find? List them. List two relevant cases.

2. You must determine whether a former employee can assert the attorney-client privilege in your state when a third party, not the former employee, brings an action against the former employer.

    *Brainstorm:* What words would you review? What topics and key numbers did you find? List them. List two relevant cases.

3. Using the Pocket Parts in Illustration 4-9, do the following treasure hunt.
   Find a Northern District of Illinois opinion that relates to key number 1076 decided in 2003.
   a. What is the name?
   b. Are there any CA7th cases?
   c. Where in the federal digest would you find such cases?
4. Go to the federal digest.
   a. Find a 1990 Ninth Circuit case under key number 1013.
   b. Now find a 2006 District of Columbia case.
5. Now look at the key number translation table in the same digest. Review key number 1078. What were the old key numbers for that number?

## COMPUTER RESEARCH
### Portfolio Assignment for Digest Research
6. Read the following fact situation. Answer the questions following the situation.

## FACTS
Nate Late, a business owner, has two partners in the operation of Loose Cannon Manufacturing in Gurnee, Illinois. He owns 33 percent of a $3 million company. Late is ill, but not dying. He is grooming a 26-year-old, Ivan T. All, to run the business. He tells his family he likes All and wants to teach him the business. Nate Late dies.

The most current will leaves Late's estate to his wife of 24 years, Shirley Late, and his only son, Lou Sier. Mr. All tells Mrs. Late that her husband told All he intended to give the 26-year-old his one-third interest in Loose Cannon. This conversation took place in front of a bank president. No written record exists concerning Late's intention to give his stock to All. However, family members knew that Late intended for All to run the business and for All to get something if the business was sold. None of the family believed that Late intended to give the business to newcomer Ivan T. All. Late's shares of stock were never given to All. The shares were in the safety deposit box shared by Late and his wife.

Mrs. Late said that Mr. Late planned to give her the shares. He told her this when he opened the joint safety deposit box and gave her the key.

You work for a firm that has been retained by Mrs. Late. She would like to know if All can prove that Mr. Late gave All Mr. Late's interest in the company.

## DIGEST QUESTIONS
a. What digest is appropriate for this problem?
b. How would you find the appropriate digest topics? Note in detail two methods for finding the appropriate digest topics. Next, review two topics.
c. What topics did you review?

d. Did you find additional topics that should be reviewed? If so, review those now.

e. What topics and key numbers are relevant to this problem?

f. Review the case abstracts listed under one of the topics and key numbers. Which cases are relevant? Note two below. Copy the case abstract or photocopy the case abstracts. Review two cases.

## COMPUTER EXERCISES FOR DIGEST TOPICS

7. Search for Negligence key number 1076, cases in all 50 states. Print the search and the first page of the citation list of the cases.

8. Using the computer, prepare and list a headnote search of topic Bankruptcy 3079 in Minnesota. Print your search and the first page of the list of cases you find.

9. Find 713 N. E2d 1285. What is the topic number and key number for headnote 2?

10. Find 984 F.2d 214 online on Westlaw.
    a. What is the name of the case?
    b. Who are the plaintiffs?
    c. Who are the defendants?
    d. What is the topic number and key number for headnote number 4?
    e. What is the former key number for that headnote?
    f. Is the appellee's brief for this case available on Westlaw? If so, how would you find it?

11. Find 2013 WL 6452336.
    a. What is the name of the case?
    b. Who are the plaintiffs?
    c. Who are the defendants?
    d. Who is the deciding judge?
    e. What headnote involves the topic 272k1076?

## CHAPTER 5

# VALIDATING

| | |
|---|---|
| **A.** *SHEPARD'S* | 119 |
| **B.** *SHEPARD'S* ONLINE | 136 |
| **C.** KEYCITE | 140 |
| **D.** GLOBALCITE | 146 |

## *CHAPTER OVERVIEW*

This chapter teaches you how to ensure that a case that you find is good law and how to find additional cases using citators. To ensure that a case is current or is still good law, you must validate or update your research findings. A case is good law if its ruling has not been reversed or over-ruled by another court's decision. Validating or Shepardizing, as it is commonly called, is one of the most important tasks you must do as a researcher. It is also referred to as citechecking. To do this, you must review citators.

## A. *SHEPARD'S*

▼ What Is a Citator?

**Citators** are services that note when a court has mentioned or relied on a case. They also note when a law or statute is mentioned. The citator

may be found on the computer or in print. The ***Shepard's* citator system** is the most pervasive in print. It is found in printed form and on the Internet through Lexisnexis.com. KeyCite offered by Westlaw is the other widely used citator. Loislaw also provides a citator called GlobalCite.

Citators are used to validate an authority such as a case. In addition, you can use them to locate relevant primary authorities, including cases and statutes, and secondary authorities, such as law review articles and *American Law Reports*, that may assist you in finding additional primary authorities or in understanding the legal issues presented in your research. You also can review citators to determine the direct history of a case. This history describes the progress of a specific case and all of the decisions made by different courts pertaining to it.

## ▼ What Do You Learn from Reviewing *Shepard's* Citations?

*Shepard's* provides a list of parallel citations and the history of the case you are reviewing. The **case history** explains whether the case has been appealed and the results of that appeal. If it is a trial court case, *Shepard's* indicates whether it was appealed and lists the appellate citation. For state cases such as the *Thompson* case (discussed in Chapter 4), *Shepard's* in print contains parallel citations in parentheses. See Illustration 5-1. The parallel citations are reported the first time *Shepard's* reports a case in print; they are not reported in subsequent *Shepard's* print reports. In Illustration 5-1, the parallel citation is next to number 3. However, *Shepard's* online report of a case contains the parallel citations each time you review the case. See Illustrations 5-2A and 5-2B. Illustration 5-2A shows the report as it appears on Lexis. The first page summarizes the report. The second page of Illustration 5-2A shows many of the cases that cite the *Thompson* case. Illustration 5-2B shows the *Shepard's* report as it appears on Lexis Advance. Researchers can see that the Lexis Advance screen shows tabs similar to those found when using Internet search engines. The top screen shot shows the summary of the report. First the official citation, 221 Ill. App. 3d 263, is listed. It is followed by numerous parallel citations. The bottom screen shot shows the tab for citing decisions.

*Shepard's* lists all cases that mention or cite the case you are **Shepardizing.** For example, the *Thompson* decision shown in Illustration 3-4 mentions or cites *Ward v. K-Mart Corp.*, 136 Ill. 2d 132, 554 N.E.2d 223 (1990) on page 888 of the *Thompson* case. See Illustration 3-4. The *Shepard's* listing for the *Ward* case shown in Illustration 5-3 includes a notation that it is cited in the *Thompson* case, 581 N.E.2d 885, on page 888. Now review Illustrations 3-4 and 5-3.

Illustration 5-3 contains a *Shepard's* report for the *Ward v. K-Mart* case. The citation for the *Ward* case is 554 N.E.2d 223. This illustration is a page from the *Shepard's* volume that includes citations to the *Northeastern Reporter*. To find the *Ward* report in that *Shepard's* collection, you would search for citations for Volume 554 of the *Northeastern Reporter*. Next to the number 2, you will find the volume number.

## ILLUSTRATION 5-1. *Shepard's Northeastern Reporter Citations,* 2007 Volume 12, *Thompson v. Economy Super Marts, Inc.*, 581 N.E.2d 885

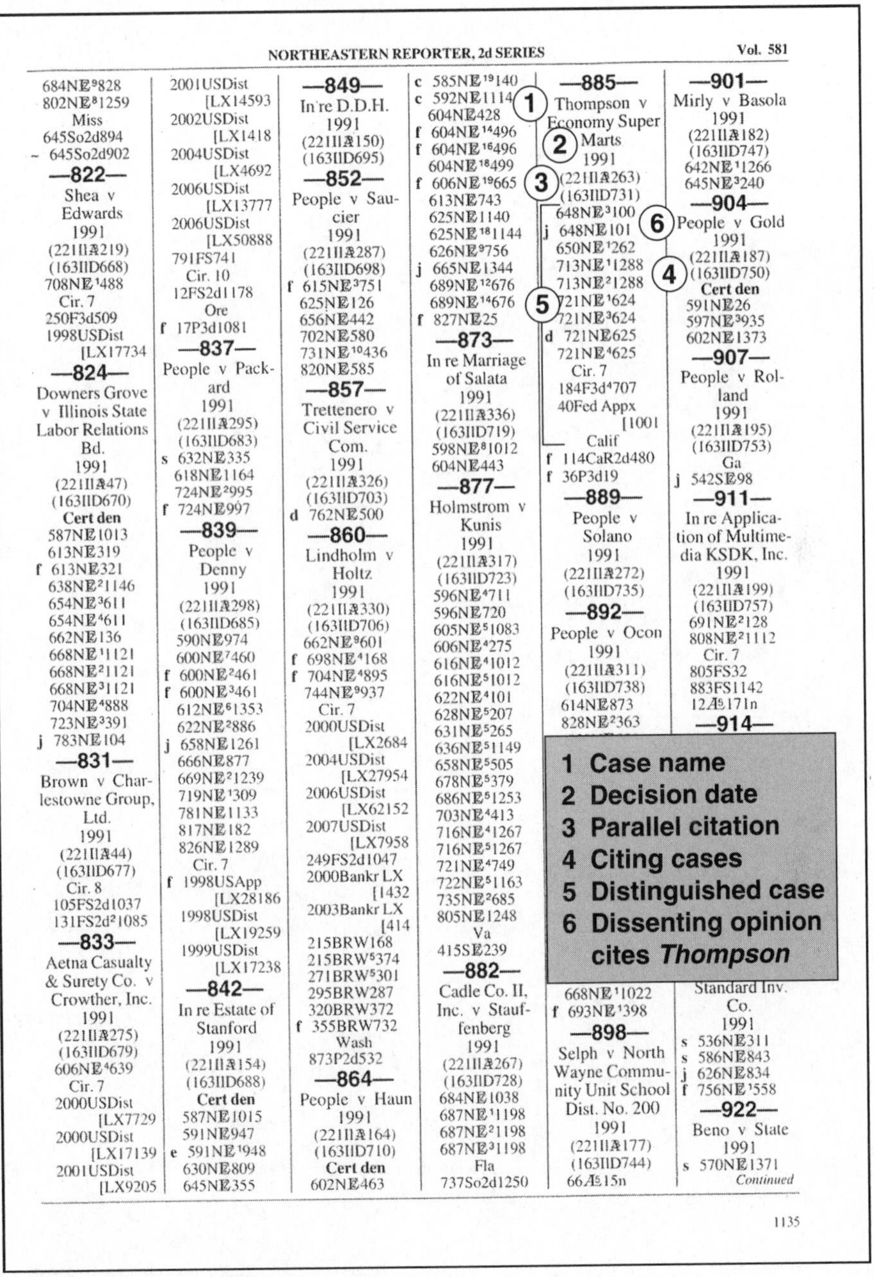

NORTHEASTERN REPORTER, 2d SERIES — Vol. 581

684NE[9]828
802NE[8]1259
Miss
645So2d894
~ 645So2d902
—822—
Shea v Edwards
1991
(221IlA219)
(163IlD668)
708NE[1]488
Cir. 7
250F3d509
1998USDist [LX17734
—824—
Downers Grove v Illinois State Labor Relations Bd.
1991
(221IlA47)
(163IlD670)
**Cert den**
587NE1013
613NE319
f 613NE321
638NE[2]1146
654NE[3]611
654NE[4]611
662NE136
668NE[1]1121
668NE[2]1121
668NE[3]1121
704NE[4]888
723NE[3]391
j 783NE104
—831—
Brown v Charlestowne Group, Ltd.
1991
(221IlA44)
(163IlD677)
Cir. 8
105FS2d1037
131FS2d[2]1085
—833—
Aetna Casualty & Surety Co. v Crowther, Inc.
1991
(221IlA275)
(163IlD679)
606NE[4]639
Cir. 7
2000USDist [LX7729
2000USDist [LX17139
2001USDist [LX9205

2001USDist [LX14593
2002USDist [LX1418
2004USDist [LX4692
2006USDist [LX13777
2006USDist [LX50888
791FS741
Cir. 10
12FS2d1178
Ore
f 17P3d1081
—837—
People v Packard
1991
(221IlA295)
(163IlD683)
s 632NE335
618NE1164
724NE[2]995
f 724NE997
—839—
People v Denny
1991
(221IlA298)
(163IlD685)
590NE974
600NE[7]460
f 600NE[2]461
f 600NE[3]461
612NE[6]1353
622NE[2]886
j 658NE1261
666NE877
669NE[2]1239
719NE[1]309
781NE1133
817NE182
826NE1289
Cir. 7
f 1998USApp [LX28186
1998USDist [LX19259
1999USDist [LX17238
—842—
In re Estate of Stanford
1991
(221IlA154)
(163IlD688)
**Cert den**
587NE1015
591NE947
e 591NE[1]948
630NE809
645NE355

—849—
In re D.D.H.
1991
(221IlA150)
(163IlD695)
—852—
People v Saucier
1991
(221IlA287)
(163IlD698)
f 615NE[3]751
625NE126
656NE442
702NE580
731NE[10]436
820NE585
—857—
Trettenero v Civil Service Com.
1991
(221IlA326)
(163IlD703)
d 762NE500
—860—
Lindholm v Holtz
1991
(221IlA330)
(163IlD706)
662NE[9]601
f 698NE[4]168
f 704NE[4]895
744NE[9]937
Cir. 7
2000USDist [LX2684
2004USDist [LX27954
2006USDist [LX62152
2007USDist [LX7958
249FS2d1047
2000Bankr LX [1432
2003Bankr LX [414
215BRW168
215BRW[5]374
271BRW[5]301
295BRW287
320BRW372
f 355BRW732
Wash
873P2d532
—864—
People v Haun
1991
(221IlA164)
(163IlD710)
**Cert den**
602NE463

c 585NE[19]140
c 592NE1114
604NE428
f 604NE[14]496
f 604NE[16]496
604NE[18]499
f 606NE[19]665
613NE743
625NE1140
625NE[18]1144
626NE[9]756
j 665NE1344
689NE[12]676
689NE[14]676
f 827NE25
—873—
In re Marriage of Salata
1991
(221IlA336)
(163IlD719)
598NE[8]1012
604NE443
—877—
Holmstrom v Kunis
1991
(221IlA317)
(163IlD723)
596NE[4]711
596NE720
605NE[5]1083
606NE[4]275
616NE[4]1012
616NE[5]1012
622NE[4]101
628NE[5]207
631NE[5]265
636NE[5]1149
658NE[5]505
678NE[5]379
686NE[5]1253
703NE[4]413
716NE[4]1267
716NE[5]1267
721NE[4]749
722NE[5]1163
735NE[2]685
805NE1248
Va
415SE239
—882—
Cadle Co. II, Inc. v Stauffenberg
1991
(221IlA267)
(163IlD728)
684NE1038
687NE[1]1198
687NE[2]1198
687NE[3]1198
Fla
737So2d1250

—885—
Thompson v Economy Super Marts
1991
(221IlA263)
(163IlD731)
648NE[3]100
j 648NE101
650NE[1]262
713NE[1]1288
713NE[2]1288
721NE[1]624
721NE[3]624
d 721NE625
721NE[4]625
Cir. 7
184F3d[4]707
40Fed Appx [1001
Calif
f 114CaR2d480
f 36P3d19
—889—
People v Solano
1991
(221IlA272)
(163IlD735)
—892—
People v Ocon
1991
(221IlA311)
(163IlD738)
614NE873
828NE[2]363
668NE[1]1022
f 693NE[1]398
—898—
Selph v North Wayne Community Unit School Dist. No. 200
1991
(221IlA177)
(163IlD744)
66A5 15n

—901—
Mirly v Basola
1991
(221IlA182)
(163IlD747)
642NE[1]1266
645NE[3]240
—904—
People v Gold
1991
(221IlA187)
(163IlD750)
**Cert den**
591NE26
597NE[3]935
602NE1373
—907—
People v Rolland
1991
(221IlA195)
(163IlD753)
Ga
j 542SE98
—911—
In re Application of Multimedia KSDK, Inc.
1991
(221IlA199)
(163IlD757)
691NE[2]128
808NE[2]1112
Cir. 7
805FS32
883FS1142
12A5171n
—914—
Standard Inv. Co.
1991
s 536NE311
s 586NE843
j 626NE834
f 756NE[1]558
—922—
Beno v State
1991
s 570NE1371
*Continued*

1 Case name
2 Decision date
3 Parallel citation
4 Citing cases
5 Distinguished case
6 Dissenting opinion cites *Thompson*

1135

Reprinted with the permission of LexisNexis.

## ILLUSTRATION 5-2A.   Lexis Online *Shepard's* Report for *Thompson v. Economy Super Marts, Inc.*, 581 N.E.2d 885

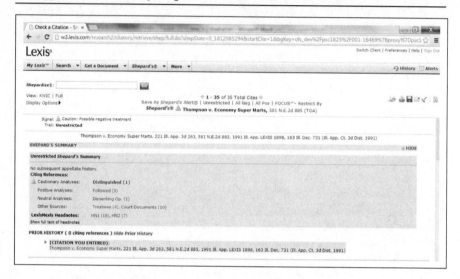

# ILLUSTRATION 5-2A. *Continued*

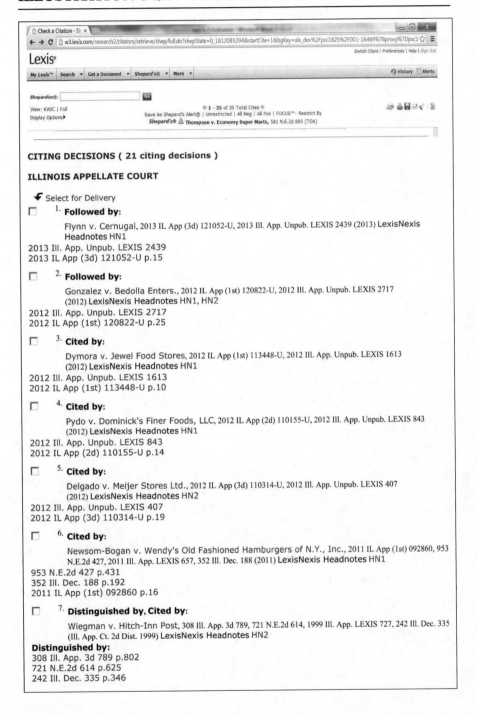

**Lexis®**

| My Lexis™ ▾ | Search ▾ | Get a Document ▾ | Shepard's® ▾ | More ▾ | | 🕓 History ☐ Alerts |

Shepardize®: [          ] [GO]

View: KWIC | Full
Display Options ▶

◆ **1 - 35** of 35 Total Cites ◆
Save As Shepard's Alert® | Unrestricted | All Neg | All Pos | FOCUS™- Restrict By
**Shepard's®** ⚠ Thompson v. Economy Super Marts, 581 N.E.2d 885 (TOA)

## CITING DECISIONS ( 21 citing decisions )

## ILLINOIS APPELLATE COURT

🕊 Select for Delivery

☐ **1. Followed by:**

Flynn v. Cernugal, 2013 IL App (3d) 121052-U, 2013 Ill. App. Unpub. LEXIS 2439 (2013) LexisNexis Headnotes HN1

2013 Ill. App. Unpub. LEXIS 2439
2013 IL App (3d) 121052-U p.15

☐ **2. Followed by:**

Gonzalez v. Bedolla Enters., 2012 IL App (1st) 120822-U, 2012 Ill. App. Unpub. LEXIS 2717 (2012) LexisNexis Headnotes HN1, HN2

2012 Ill. App. Unpub. LEXIS 2717
2012 IL App (1st) 120822-U p.25

☐ **3. Cited by:**

Dymora v. Jewel Food Stores, 2012 IL App (1st) 113448-U, 2012 Ill. App. Unpub. LEXIS 1613 (2012) LexisNexis Headnotes HN1

2012 Ill. App. Unpub. LEXIS 1613
2012 IL App (1st) 113448-U p.10

☐ **4. Cited by:**

Pydo v. Dominick's Finer Foods, LLC, 2012 IL App (2d) 110155-U, 2012 Ill. App. Unpub. LEXIS 843 (2012) LexisNexis Headnotes HN1

2012 Ill. App. Unpub. LEXIS 843
2012 IL App (2d) 110155-U p.14

☐ **5. Cited by:**

Delgado v. Meijer Stores Ltd., 2012 IL App (3d) 110314-U, 2012 Ill. App. Unpub. LEXIS 407 (2012) LexisNexis Headnotes HN2

2012 Ill. App. Unpub. LEXIS 407
2012 IL App (3d) 110314-U p.19

☐ **6. Cited by:**

Newsom-Bogan v. Wendy's Old Fashioned Hamburgers of N.Y., Inc., 2011 IL App (1st) 092860, 953 N.E.2d 427, 2011 Ill. App. LEXIS 657, 352 Ill. Dec. 188 (2011) LexisNexis Headnotes HN1

953 N.E.2d 427 p.431
352 Ill. Dec. 188 p.192
2011 IL App (1st) 092860 p.16

☐ **7. Distinguished by, Cited by:**

Wiegman v. Hitch-Inn Post, 308 Ill. App. 3d 789, 721 N.E.2d 614, 1999 Ill. App. LEXIS 727, 242 Ill. Dec. 335 (Ill. App. Ct. 2d Dist. 1999) LexisNexis Headnotes HN2

**Distinguished by:**
308 Ill. App. 3d 789 p.802
721 N.E.2d 614 p.625
242 Ill. Dec. 335 p.346

# ILLUSTRATION 5-2A. *Continued*

---

**Cited by:**
308 Ill. App. 3d 789 p.801
721 N.E.2d 614 p.624
242 Ill. Dec. 335 p.345

☐ 8. **Cited by:**

Kellermann v. Car City Chevrolet-Nissan, 306 Ill. App. 3d 285, 713 N.E.2d 1285, 1999 Ill. App. LEXIS 532, 239 Ill. Dec. 435 (Ill. App. Ct. 5th Dist. 1999) LexisNexis Headnotes HN1
306 Ill. App. 3d 285 p.288
713 N.E.2d 1285 p.1288
239 Ill. Dec. 435 p.438

☐ 9. **Cited by:**

Wind v. Hy-Vee Food Stores, 272 Ill. App. 3d 149, 650 N.E.2d 258, 1995 Ill. App. LEXIS 340, 208 Ill. Dec. 801 (Ill. App. Ct. 3d Dist. 1995) LexisNexis Headnotes HN1
272 Ill. App. 3d 149 p.155
650 N.E.2d 258 p.262
208 Ill. Dec. 801 p.805

☐ 10. **Cited in Dissenting Opinion at, Cited by:**

Miller v. National Ass'n of Realtors, 271 Ill. App. 3d 653, 648 N.E.2d 98, 1994 Ill. App. LEXIS 1471, 207 Ill. Dec. 642 (Ill. App. Ct. 1st Dist. 1994) LexisNexis Headnotes HN1, HN2
**Cited in Dissenting Opinion at:**
271 Ill. App. 3d 653 p.658
648 N.E.2d 98 p.101
207 Ill. Dec. 642 p.645

**Cited by:**
271 Ill. App. 3d 653 p.657
648 N.E.2d 98 p.100
207 Ill. Dec. 642 p.644

## 7TH CIRCUIT - COURT OF APPEALS

☐ 11. **Followed by, Cited by:**

Reid v. Kohl's Dep't Stores, Inc., 545 F.3d 479, 2008 U.S. App. LEXIS 19574 (7th Cir. Ill. 2008) LexisNexis Headnotes HN1
**Followed by:**
545 F.3d 479 p.482

**Cited by:**
545 F.3d 479 p.481

☐ 12. **Cited by:**

Varner v. Johnson, 40 Fed. Appx. 997, 2002 U.S. App. LEXIS 14696 (7th Cir. Ill. 2002) LexisNexis Headnotes HN2
40 Fed. Appx. 997 p.1001

☐ 13. **Cited by:**

Lane v. Hardee's Food Sys., 184 F.3d 705, 1999 U.S. App. LEXIS 16889 (7th Cir. Ill. 1999) LexisNexis Headnotes HN1
184 F.3d 705 p.707

## 7TH CIRCUIT - U.S. DISTRICT COURTS

☐ 14. **Cited by:**

Hamilton v. Target Corp., 2013 U.S. Dist. LEXIS 162801 (N.D. Ill. Nov. 15, 2013) LexisNexis Headnotes HN1
2013 U.S. Dist. LEXIS 162801

☐ 15. **Followed by:**

Zuppardi v. Wal-Mart Stores, Inc., 2013 U.S. Dist. LEXIS 132902 (C.D. Ill. Sept. 17, 2013) LexisNexis Headnotes HN2
2013 U.S. Dist. LEXIS 132902

# ILLUSTRATION 5-2A. *Continued*

☐ [16.] **Cited by:**

Breheny v. Fox's on Wolf, 2011 U.S. Dist. LEXIS 38392 (N.D. Ill. Apr. 7, 2011) LexisNexis Headnotes HN1

2011 U.S. Dist. LEXIS 38392

☐ [17.] **Cited by:**

Porges v. Wal-Mart Stores, Inc., 2011 U.S. Dist. LEXIS 26267 (N.D. Ill. Mar. 15, 2011) LexisNexis Headnotes HN1

2011 U.S. Dist. LEXIS 26267

☐ [18.] **Cited by:**

Jones v. Graphic Arts Finishing Co., 2010 U.S. Dist. LEXIS 3143 (N.D. Ill. Jan. 15, 2010) LexisNexis Headnotes HN2

2010 U.S. Dist. LEXIS 3143

☐ [19.] **Cited by:**

Byrd-Tolson v. Supervalu, Inc., 500 F. Supp. 2d 962, 2007 U.S. Dist. LEXIS 43096 (N.D. Ill. 2007) LexisNexis Headnotes HN1

500 F. Supp. 2d 962 p.970

☐ [20.] **Cited by:**

Jackson v. United States Postal Serv., 2007 U.S. Dist. LEXIS 33618 (N.D. Ill. May 2, 2007) LexisNexis Headnotes HN1

2007 U.S. Dist. LEXIS 33618

**CALIFORNIA SUPREME COURT**

☐ [21.] **Followed by:**

Ortega v. Kmart Corp., 26 Cal. 4th 1200, 114 Cal. Rptr. 2d 470, 36 P.3d 11, 2001 Cal. LEXIS 8479, 2001 Cal. Daily Op. Service 10516, 2001 D.A.R. 13099 (2001) LexisNexis Headnotes HN1

26 Cal. 4th 1200 p.1212
114 Cal. Rptr. 2d 470 p.480
36 P.3d 11 p.19

**TREATISE CITATIONS ( 4 Citing Sources )**

☐ [22.] 6-21 Personal Injury--Actions, Defenses, Damages @ 1

☐ [23.] 6-21 Personal Injury--Actions, Defenses, Damages @ 3

☐ [24.] 6-21 Personal Injury--Actions, Defenses, Damages @ 21.02

☐ [25.] 6-21 Personal Injury--Actions, Defenses, Damages @ 21.39

**BRIEFS ( 1 Citing Brief )**

☐ 26. ALEJANDRO TORRES v. TGI FRIDAY'S, 2007 U.S. 7th Cir. Briefs 1107, 2007 U.S. 7th Cir. Briefs LEXIS 40 (7th Cir. Apr. 20, 2007)

**MOTIONS ( 9 Citing Motions )**

☐ 27. REDDICK v. DILLARD STORE SERVS., 2008 U.S. Dist. Ct. Motions 331106, 2010 U.S. Dist. Ct. Motions LEXIS 11326 (S.D. Ill. July 27, 2010)

☐ 28. GENTRY v. SHOP 'N SAVE WAREHOUSE FOODS, 2009 U.S. Dist. Ct. Motions 988261, 2010 U.S. Dist. Ct. Motions LEXIS 9155 (C.D. Ill. Jan. 18, 2010)

## ILLUSTRATION 5-2A.   *Continued*

29. REDDICK v. DILLARD STORE SERVS., 2008 U.S. Dist. Ct. Motions 331106, 2009 U.S. Dist. Ct. Motions LEXIS 86567 (S.D. Ill. Dec. 1, 2009)

30. JONES v. GRAPHIC ARTS FINISHING CO., 2008 U.S. Dist. Ct. Motions 83327, 2009 U.S. Dist. Ct. Motions LEXIS 73562 (N.D. Ill. Oct. 16, 2009)

31. JONES v. GRAPHIC ARTS FINISHING CO., 2008 U.S. Dist. Ct. Motions 83327, 2009 U.S. Dist. Ct. Motions LEXIS 73561 (N.D. Ill. Oct. 2, 2009)

32. JONES v. GRAPHIC ARTS FINISHING CO., 2008 U.S. Dist. Ct. Motions 83327, 2009 U.S. Dist. Ct. Motions LEXIS 73560 (N.D. Ill. Sept. 2, 2009)

33. BUCHANAN v. WHOLE FOODS MKT. GROUP, 2007 U.S. Dist. Ct. Motions 74189, 2009 U.S. Dist. Ct. Motions LEXIS 8700 (N.D. Ill. Mar. 12, 2009)

34. BUCHANAN v. WHOLE FOODS MKT. GROUP, 2007 U.S. Dist. Ct. Motions 74189, 2009 U.S. Dist. Ct. Motions LEXIS 8699 (N.D. Ill. Feb. 12, 2009)

35. BUCHANAN v. WHOLE FOODS MKT. GROUP, 2007 U.S. Dist. Ct. Motions 74189, 2009 U.S. Dist. Ct. Motions LEXIS 8698 (N.D. Ill. Jan. 14, 2009)

Signal:

⚠ Caution: Possible negative treatment

Citation:

**581 N.E.2d 885** (Get this Document , Table of Authorities )

View:

Full

Trail:

• **Unrestricted**

Location:

1 - 35 of 35 Total Cites

Date/Time:

Monday, March 3, 2014 12:38:01 AM EST

* Signal Legend:

⬤ - Warning: Negative treatment is indicated

① - Warning: Negative case treatment is indicated for statute

Ⓠ - Questioned: validity questioned by citing refs

⚠ - Caution: Possible negative treatment

◆ - Positive treatment is indicated

Ⓐ - Citing Refs. With Analysis Available

ⓘ - Citation information available

* Click on any Shepard's editorial treatment code (e.g., distinguished, questioned) to view its definition.

⬤ LexisNexis® About LexisNexis | Privacy Policy | Terms & Conditions | Contact Us

Reprinted with the permission of LexisNexis. Editor's Note: See online document for complete report.

# ILLUSTRATION 5-2B.   Lexis Advance Online *Shepard's* Report for *Thompson v. Economy Super Marts, Inc.*, 581 N.E.2d 885

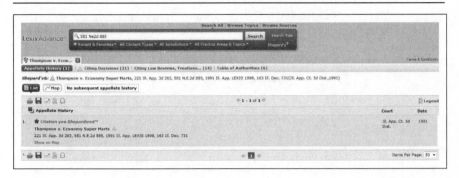

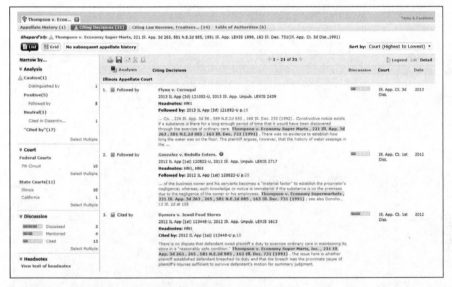

Reprinted with the permission of LexisNexis. Editor's Note: See online document for complete report.

## ILLUSTRATION 5-3. *Shepard's Northeastern Reporter Citations, Ward v. K-Mart Corp.*, 554 N.E.2d 223 (Ill. 1990)

④

**NORTHEASTERN REPORTER, 2d SERIES**   ②  Vol. 554

| | | | | |
|---|---|---|---|---|
| **—216—** | 2001IllApp LX | f 595NE⁷47 | 621NE⁶56 | 661NE416 | 724NE⁴202 |
| People v | [931 | 595NE⁹49 | 622NE³55 | 662NE⁶566 | f 725NE769 |
| Brown | 2006IllApp LX | f 595NE⁵0 | d 622NE57 | e 664NE³695 | 726NE³732 |
| 1990 | [1236 | 595NE⁸57 | 622NE⁸57 | 665NE831 | 726NE⁴732 |
| (136Il2d116) | 560NE²23 | f 595NE¹624 | 623NE³954 | f 665NE832 | 730NE1134 |
| (143IID281) | 560NE1102 | 595NE²667 | 625NE⁶776 | 665NE⁴836 | f 730NE⁹1215 |
| s 553NE455 | f 561NE²324 | 595NE³667 | 628NE⁴804 | 667NE¹679 | 730NE²1224 |
| 556NE901 | 562NE⁴403 | 595NE⁴667 | 628NE²876 | 667NE⁴1092 | 730NE³1224 |
| 556NE⁷902 | f 562NE⁹1060 | 595NE668 | 628NE³876 | 669NE²1191 | f 730NE⁹1225 |
| f 565NE⁴¹1353 | 563NE²1122 | e 595NE⁹1103 | 628NE⁴876 | 672NE315 | 732NE599 |
| f 565NE²1354 | 563NE³1122 | f 596NE⁵98 | d 628NE⁹877 | 672NE²372 | j 737NE298 |
| f 565NE³1354 | 563NE⁴1228 | 598NE²343 | d 629NE537 | 677NE⁴485 | 737NE676 |
| 587NE²1189 | j 563NE1229 | 598NE⁴344 | 629NE¹537 | 677NE²1316 | f 740NE450 |
| 587NE³1189 | f 563NE⁵1229 | 598NE⁷344 | 629NE³537 | 677NE³1316 | 740NE³450 |
| 588NE⁴1179 | 565NE³689 | 599NE¹1014 | 629NE⁹538 | e 677NE1317 | 740NE⁷450 |
| 593NE³1017 | f 566NE241 | 599NE1142 | 630NE1020 | 677NE⁴1317 | 747NE⁵382 |
| f 599NE²948 | 566NE⁴243 | f 600NE²876 | 631NE¹269 | 679NE1295 | 751NE³147 |
| f 599NE³948 | 567NE426 | f 600NE³876 | 634NE²391 | d 679NE1296 | 753NE1010 |
| f 603NE²599 | f 567NE⁹427 | 600NE⁴876 | 634NE1112 | 679NE⁹1296 | 753NE1127 |
| 606NE³284 | 569NE21⁵ | d 600NE⁹880 | 634NE²1139 | j 679NE1298 | 758NE³486 |
| 608NE606 | d 569NE⁷216 | 600NE884 | 635NE1001 | f 680NE²412 | 758NE⁴486 |
| 610NE166 | d 569NE⁹216 | f 600NE²1252 | f 636NE⁴69 | 680NE²434 | 759NE33 |
| 611NE19 | 569NE²583 | 600NE⁴1281 | 636NE⁹69 | 682NE²415 | 760NE995 |
| 612NE³901 | 569NE³583 | 602NE²21 | 636NE962 | f 688NE316 | 763NE³796 |
| 613NE²1279 | 570NE³1222 | 602NE³22 | f 636NE⁹964 | 688NE⁴317 | 763NE⁹796 |
| 613NE³1279 | e 571NE⁴481 | f 602NE²57 | f 637NE²515 | 689NE³157 | 766NE³1123 |
| f 614NE²1338 | 571NE817 | f 602NE³57 | 637NE³515 | f 689NE²370 | f 766NE⁴1124 |
| 615NE822 | d 571NE⁵818 | d 602NE58 | 637NE⁴515 | 692NE³1361 | 768NE³51 |
| 619NE²222 | f 571NE²1112 | 602NE⁴58 | 638NE²691 | f 692NE⁵1362 | 768NE⁴51 |
| 620NE631 | f 571NE³1112 | 602NE³899 | 638NE³692 | d 692NE1363 | 772NE223 |
| 626NE418 | f 571NE⁴1112 | 602NE⁴899 | 638NE⁴692 | 693NE⁴504 | d 772NE⁹224 |
| 626NE²423 | 572NE²989 | e 602NE⁶901 | 638NE⁵694 | 694NE1040 | 774NE³854 |
| 629NE²564 | 578NE²602 | 603NE²17 | 640NE688 | 694NE⁵1041 | 778NE⁸289 |
| 631NE²475 | 579NE1020 | d 603NE¹18 | f 641NE1231 | 694NE⁹1041 | 778NE⁹289 |
| 631NE³475 | d 580NE⁸167 | 603NE²819 | 642NE⁴758 | f 694NE1042 | d 778NE290 |
| q 638NE²394 | d 580NE⁹167 | 603NE³819 | f 642NE830 | q 694NE1043 | 781NE³635 |
| d 639NE1366 | 581NE23 | 605NE³502 | j 642NE832 | 695NE57 | f 781NE⁴635 |
| 647NE917 | 581NE⁷888 | d 605NE725 | 643NE²861 | f 695NE⁴58 | 782NE³714 |
| 647NE1106 | 582NE³300 | j 605NE727 | 643NE³1360 | j 695NE59 | 782NE⁵716 |
| 665NE1280 | 583NE¹705 | 606NE388 | | | |
| 667NE¹163 | 584NE¹161 | 606NE³635 | | | |
| f 667NE²164 | 585NE170 | 606NE753 | | | |
| f 667NE³164 | 585NE173 | e 606NE1281 | | | |
| f 667NE⁴164 | 585NE⁴173 | 607NE¹274 | | | |
| 693NE²873 | 585NE¹228 | f 607NE⁴1286 | | | |
| f 703NE²955 | f 586NE²378 | 609NE⁸924 | | | |
| 709NE¹713 | f 586NE⁴379 | 612NE³532 | | | |
| f 742NE²1250 | e 587NE⁵13 | 612NE⁷889 | | | |
| 762NE²600 | 588NE⁵382 | 614NE105 | | | |
| 762NE³600 | j 588NE383 | 614NE²400 | | | |
| 768NE81 | 588NE441 | 614NE1244 | | | |
| 777NE²53⁷ | d 588NE⁹442 | 614NE⁴1378 | | | |
| Cir. 7 | 589NE²572 | 614NE1379 | | | |
| 360F3d²79⁶ | 589NE³572 | f 614NE1380 | | | |
| f 2002USDist | 589NE⁹575 | 614NE1382 | | | |
| [LX1102] | 589NE⁴578 | j 614NE1382 | | | |
| **—223—** | f 592NE³366 | d 615NE867 | | | |
| Ward v K Mart | 592NE⁴366 | 615NE⁸867 | | | |
| Corp. | f 592NE⁷366 | 616NE¹1304 | | | |
| 1990 | f 592NE367 | 617NE²535 | | | |
| (136Il2d132) | 593NE²607 | e 617NE⁵539 | | | |
| (143IID288) | 593NE616 | f 617NE²1352 | | | |
| s 540NE1036 | d 593NE994 | d 618NE688 | | | |
| 2007Ill LX433 | 594NE³318 | 618NE908 | | | |
| f 1999IllApp LX | 594NE⁴318 | 620NE⁴665 | | | |
| [705 | e 594NE⁹319 | 620NE1086 | | | |
| | 595NE³46 | 620NE⁴1087 | | | |

⑥ ⑦ ⑤ ⑨ ⑪ ① ③ ⑧

**1** Beginning of *Ward* Case Shepard Citations

**2** Volume number

**3** Case name

**4** Reporter

**5** *Thompson* case

**6** Headnote 7

**7** Case that distinguishes *Ward* involving headnote 7

**8** Parallel citations

**9** Circuit court cases are listed below circuit number

**10** Reference to ALR

**11** First page number of case

# ILLUSTRATION 5-3. *Continued*

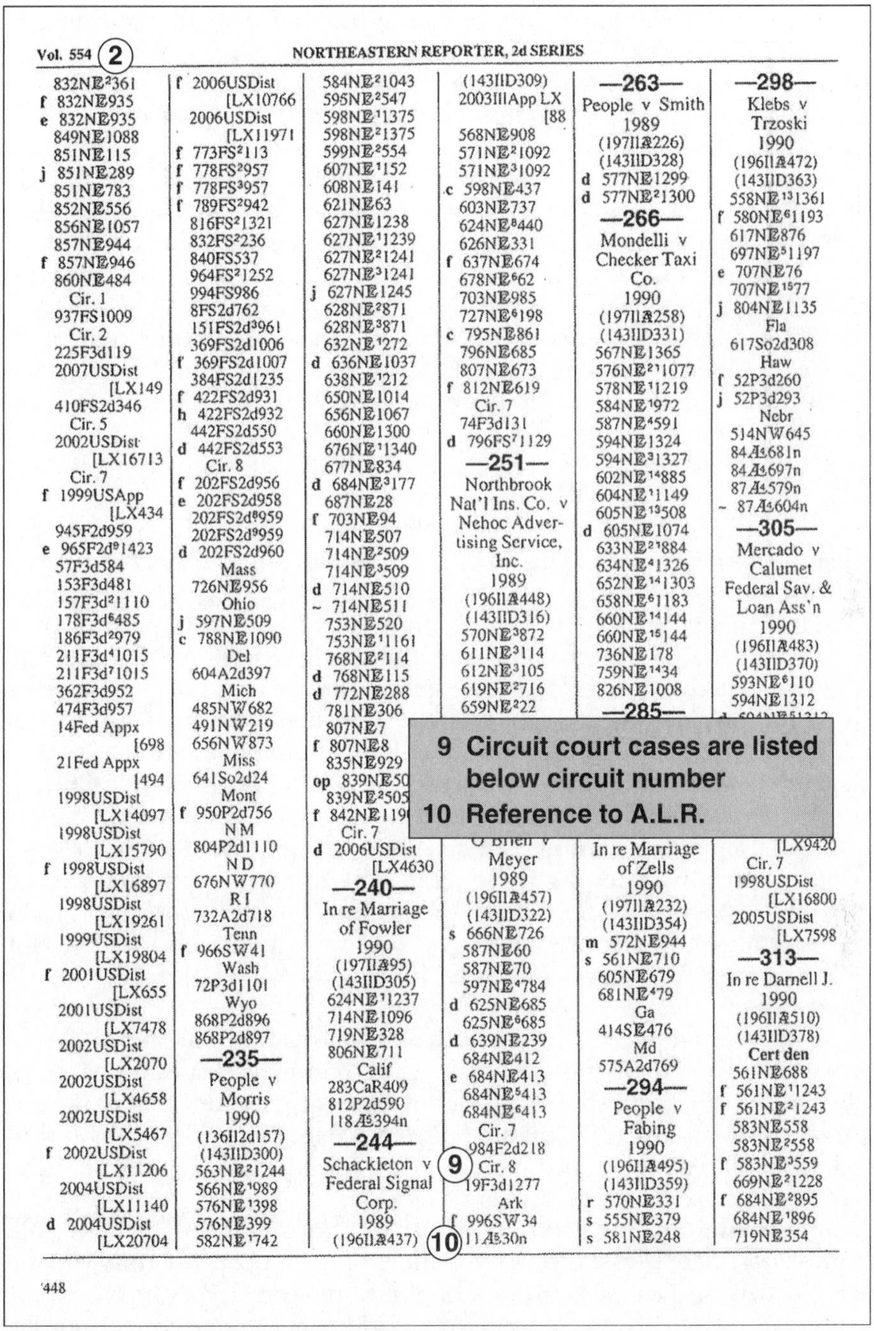
Vol. 554 (2) NORTHEASTERN REPORTER, 2d SERIES

832NE$^{2}$361
f 832NE935
e 832NE935
849NE1088
851NE115
j 851NE289
851NE783
852NE556
856NE1057
857NE944
f 857NE946
860NE484
Cir. 1
937FS1009
Cir. 2
225F3d119
2007USDist [LX149
410FS2d346
Cir. 5
2002USDist [LX16713
Cir. 7
f 1999USApp [LX434
945F2d959
e 965F2d$^{9}$1423
57F3d584
153F3d481
157F3d$^{2}$1110
178F3d$^{6}$485
186F3d$^{2}$979
211F3d$^{4}$1015
211F3d$^{7}$1015
362F3d952
474F3d957
14Fed Appx [698
21Fed Appx [494
1998USDist [LX14097
1998USDist [LX15790
f 1998USDist [LX16897
1998USDist [LX19261
1999USDist [LX19804
f 2001USDist [LX655
2001USDist [LX7478
2002USDist [LX2070
2002USDist [LX4658
2002USDist [LX5467
f 2002USDist [LX11206
2004USDist [LX11140
d 2004USDist [LX20704

f 2006USDist [LX10766
2006USDist [LX11971
f 773FS$^{2}$113
f 778FS$^{2}$957
f 778FS$^{3}$957
f 789FS$^{2}$942
816FS$^{2}$1321
832FS$^{2}$236
840FS537
964FS$^{2}$1252
994FS986
8FS2d762
151FS2d$^{3}$961
369FS2d1006
f 369FS2d1007
384FS2d1235
f 422FS2d931
h 422FS2d932
442FS2d550
d 442FS2d553
Cir. 8
f 202FS2d956
e 202FS2d958
202FS2d$^{8}$959
202FS2d$^{9}$959
d 202FS2d960
Mass
726NE956
Ohio
j 597NE509
c 788NE1090
Del
604A2d397
Mich
485NW682
491NW219
656NW873
Miss
641So2d24
Mont
f 950P2d756
N M
804P2d1110
N D
676NW770
R I
732A2d718
Tenn
f 966SW41
Wash
72P3d1101
Wyo
868P2d896
868P2d897
—235—
People v Morris
1990
(136Il2d157)
(143IlD300)
563NE$^{2}$1244
566NE$^{1}$989
576NE$^{1}$398
576NE399
582NE$^{1}$742

584NE$^{2}$1043
595NE$^{2}$547
598NE$^{1}$1375
598NE$^{2}$1375
599NE$^{2}$554
607NE$^{1}$152
608NE141
621NE63
627NE1238
627NE$^{1}$1239
627NE$^{2}$1241
627NE$^{3}$1241
j 627NE1245
628NE$^{2}$871
628NE$^{3}$871
632NE$^{1}$272
d 636NE1037
638NE$^{1}$212
650NE1014
656NE1067
660NE1300
676NE$^{1}$1340
677NE834
d 684NE$^{3}$177
687NE28
f 703NE94
714NE507
714NE$^{2}$509
714NE$^{3}$509
d 714NE510
~ 714NE511
753NE520
753NE$^{1}$1161
768NE$^{2}$114
d 768NE115
d 772NE288
781NE306
807NE7
f 807NE8
835NE929
op 839NE50
839NE$^{2}$505
f 842NE119
Cir. 7
d 2006USDist [LX4630
—240—
In re Marriage of Fowler
1990
(197IlA95)
(143IlD305)
624NE$^{1}$1237
714NE1096
719NE328
806NE711
Calif
283CaR409
812P2d590
118A5394n
—244—
Schackleton v Federal Signal Corp.
1989
(196IlA437)

(143IlD309)
2003IllApp LX [88
568NE908
571NE$^{2}$1092
571NE$^{3}$1092
c 598NE437
603NE737
624NE$^{8}$440
626NE331
f 637NE674
678NE$^{6}$62
703NE985
727NE$^{6}$198
c 795NE861
796NE685
807NE673
f 812NE619
Cir. 7
74F3d131
d 796FS$^{7}$1129
—251—
Northbrook Nat'l Ins. Co. v Nehoc Advertising Service, Inc.
1989
(196IlA448)
(143IlD316)
570NE$^{3}$872
611NE$^{3}$114
612NE$^{3}$105
619NE$^{2}$716
659NE$^{2}$22
O'Brien v
Meyer
1989
(196IlA457)
(143IlD322)
s 666NE726
587NE60
587NE70
597NE$^{4}$784
d 625NE685
625NE$^{6}$685
d 639NE239
684NE412
e 684NE413
684NE$^{5}$413
684NE$^{6}$413
Cir. 7
984F2d218
(9) Cir. 8
19F3d1277
Ark
f 996SW34
(10) 11A530n

—263—
People v Smith
1989
(197IlA226)
(143IlD328)
d 577NE1299
d 577NE$^{2}$1300
—266—
Mondelli v Checker Taxi Co.
1990
(197IlA258)
(143IlD331)
567NE1365
576NE$^{21}$1077
578NE$^{1}$1219
584NE$^{1}$972
587NE$^{4}$591
594NE1324
594NE$^{3}$1327
602NE$^{14}$885
604NE$^{1}$1149
605NE$^{13}$508
d 605NE1074
633NE$^{21}$884
634NE$^{4}$1326
652NE$^{14}$1303
658NE$^{6}$1183
660NE$^{14}$144
660NE$^{15}$144
736NE178
759NE$^{1}$434
826NE1008
—285—
In re Marriage of Zells
1990
(197IlA232)
(143IlD354)
m 572NE944
s 561NE710
605NE679
681NE$^{4}$79
Ga
414SE476
Md
575A2d769
—294—
People v Fabing
1990
(196IlA495)
(143IlD359)
r 570NE331
s 555NE379
s 581NE248

—298—
Klebs v Trzoski
1990
(196IlA472)
(143IlD363)
558NE$^{13}$1361
f 580NE$^{6}$1193
617NE876
697NE$^{5}$1197
e 707NE76
707NE$^{15}$77
j 804NE1135
Fla
617So2d308
Haw
f 52P3d260
j 52P3d293
Nebr
514NW645
84A5681n
84A5697n
87A5579n
~ 87A5604n
—305—
Mercado v Calumet Federal Sav. & Loan Ass'n
1990
(196IlA483)
(143IlD370)
593NE$^{6}$110
594NE1312
[LX9420
Cir. 7
1998USDist [LX16800
2005USDist [LX7598
—313—
In re Darnell J.
1990
(196IlA510)
(143IlD378)
Cert den
561NE688
f 561NE$^{1}$1243
f 561NE$^{2}$1243
583NE558
583NE$^{2}$558
f 583NE$^{3}$559
669NE$^{2}$1228
f 684NE$^{2}$895
684NE$^{1}$896
719NE354

9 Circuit court cases are listed below circuit number
10 Reference to A.L.R.

448

Reprinted with the permission of LexisNexis.

In this case, it is 554. The volume number will appear at the top of the page on either the right or left corner. The reporter name will appear at the top of the page in the middle. See number 4 in Illustration 5-3. To find the *Ward* case, you would look for the number of the first page of the *Ward* case—223. That appears in the third column of this *Shepard's* listing. A number 1 is next to the first page number of the *Ward* case. The *Ward* case *Shepard's* report begins next to the number 1. The first two citations in parentheses are the parallel citations for the *Ward* case. Following the parallel citations is the list of cases that mention or cite the *Ward* case. The *Thompson* case cites the *Ward* case. It appears next to the number 5. It tells the researcher that the citation appears on page 888 of the *Thompson* case.

Shepard's also references West's headnote system. In Illustration 5-3, the small raised 7 between the N.E.2d symbol and 888 in the *Thompson* notation of the *Ward Shepard's* report indicates that the citing case, *Thompson*, refers to the text found within the portion of the *Ward* case the publisher designated as headnote 7. See the numbers 5, 6, and 7 in Illustration 5-3.

The online version of *Shepard's* references these headnotes as well as LexisNexis headnotes. The print version does not note LexisNexis headnotes.

For some citing authorities, *Shepard's* provides additional information about the court's **treatment** of the citing case. For example, the *Shepard's* citation may include the letter *a* at the front of the citations list. That would indicate that the case has been affirmed on appeal *Shepard's* may indicate with other abbreviations whether a case has been dismissed, modified, reversed, criticized, explained, followed, limited, questioned, or overruled. A list of these treatments and their abbreviations and meanings can be found at the front of each *Shepard's* print volume. By reviewing these treatment notations, you can find the **negative history** of a case. These tell you how other courts have viewed the case and if any courts have cast doubt on the case's validity. Not all of these court cases, however, have a direct relationship to the cited case.

Shepard's can be used to research almost every federal and state case reported in print in the past 200 years. It now includes some cases considered unreported because they only appear online. However, these citations are only to unreported Lexis cases. See Illustration 5-3. Review the first column. Several cases contain an LX in the citation. Those cases are available only on Lexis.

Shepard's publishes a variety of citation books for federal and state authorities. See Illustration 5-4. Among the authorities that can be Shepardized are cases, statutes, constitutions, codes, jury instructions, administrative decisions, copyrights, trademarks, patents, and regulations as well as secondary authorities including Restatements and *American Law Reports*. More information about Shepardizing statutes can be found in Chapter 7. Most print *Shepard's* publications are

supplemented regularly. However, case law in many jurisdictions now requires that attorneys use *Shepard's* online to ensure that a cited case is valid. A daily update concerning a case of interest can be obtained via an e-mail. To receive this, you set up a *Shepard's* alert online. It can be done by clicking the words "save as Shepard's Alert" found at the top of the online *Shepard's* report. See Illustration 5-2.

The list of citing references in these print publications will vary because each publication pulls citations from different citing sources. For example, if you reviewed the *Thompson* or *Ward* cases in the *Shepard's Illinois Citations,* you might find a listing for an attorney general opinion or a law review article. However, the attorney general opinion and the law review citations would not be listed under the *Thompson* or the *Ward* case in the *Shepard's Northeastern Reporter Citations.* Each citator contains a list at the front of a volume of the sources that have been consulted to determine whether a case has been referred to within that source.

### ▼ How Do You Use *Shepard's* in Print?

First, you must determine which *Shepard's* series is the appropriate one to consult. *Shepard's* has multiple citators that might contain a particular case. For example, a state citator and a regional citator would contain the *Shepard's* report for a state case. For the *Thompson* case, you would look in the Illinois citator if you knew it was an Illinois case. Next, you must review the front cover of the most current pamphlet that accompanies the *Shepard's* citations. See Illustration 5-5. In Illustration 5-5, you can see the heading "What Your Library Should Contain." This lists all of the *Shepard's* volumes and supplements you must consider to complete your review of the *Shepard's* citations for a particular case. After you view the supplement cover, gather each of the volumes and supplements mentioned on the cover. The case citations are organized by reporter, volume, and page number. Find the appropriate reporter section. For the *Thompson* case, the *Shepard's Northeastern Reporter Second Series* is the correct division. To locate the bound volume number, look at the top corner of the page. You will find a bold number. That is the bound volume number. Now review Illustration 5-3. In this case, the volume number is 554. In the pamphlets that update the bound volume, reports from cases found in multiple case reporter volumes may be printed on the same page. See Illustration 5-6. Reports from volumes 581 and 582 of the *Northeastern Reporter* appear on this pamphlet page that updates the bound volume reports of cases found in those volumes. You may find when you use the pamphlets that the volume you wish to review is not listed in the corner, scan the page for your volume. Find the page number for the case. See Illustration 5-6. You then must repeat this procedure in each of the *Shepard's* volumes and pamphlets.

## ILLUSTRATION 5-4.  *Shepard's* **Case Citations**

---

**United States Citations**
Reports citations to decisions of the U.S. Supreme Court, the U.S.C., the U.S. Constitution, Court Rules, Federal Sentencing Guidelines, and other Federal Regulatory Law

**Shepard's Federal Citations**
Reports citations to decisions of the U.S. Courts of Appeal, the U.S. District Court, and the U.S. Court of Claims

**State, Puerto Rico, and District of Columbia cases**
Each state has a *Shepard's* citator, as does Puerto Rico and the District of Columbia

**Assorted Topical and Specialized Citators**
Such as *Shepard's Bankruptcy Citations, Shepard's Criminal Justice Citations, Shepard's Environmental Law Citations, Shepard's United States Administrative Citations, Shepard's Employment Law Citations*

**Shepard's Regional Citators**
Cases of all 50 states divided into nine regions that correspond to West's regional reporter system

---

Note that the *Shepard's* citations are not Bluebook abbreviations for the reporters and that the number for each series is placed on top of the reporter abbreviations.

**ILLUSTRATION 5-5.** Front Cover of a *Shepard's* Cumulative Supplement Detailing Volumes and Pamphlets to Review

VOL. 100          MAY 2008          NO. 5

# SHEPARD'S
# NORTHEASTERN
# REPORTER
# CITATIONS

Annual Cumulative Supplement

# PART A

### WHAT YOUR LIBRARY SHOULD CONTAIN

2007 Bound Volumes (Volumes 1–16)*

*Supplemented with:
  –May 2008 Annual Cumulative Supplement Vol. 100 No. 5
    (Parts A and B)

### DISCARD ALL OTHER ISSUES

LexisNexis®

Reprinted with the permission of LexisNexis.

## ILLUSTRATION 5-6. Page from *Shepard's Illinois Citations*

NORTHEASTERN REPORTER, 2d SERIES (Illinois Cases)    ① Vol. 582

```
—137—            —19—            —196—            —664—            689NE¹⁴676         —125—
Case 1           Cir. 7          683NE⁵519        1998IllAppLX                          s 1998Ill LX
s 1998           1998USDist                                [²297      —877—                      [361
   [IllAppLX194        [LX2459    —236—            682NE⁴104        678NE³379        1998Ill LX353
s 693NE426                        1998IllAppLX     682NE²1142       686NE⁴1253       1998IllAppLX
                 —44—                    [²191    682NE²1198                                [⁴⁷314
—139—            689NE359        1998IllAppLX     686NE²64         —882—
683NE¹⁸520       689NE379                [⁴191    Cir. 3           684NE1038        685NE906
                 Cir. 7          c 1998           976FS⁴296        687NE¹1198       688NE⁴⁷663
—191—            f 1998USDist          [IllAppLX191  Cir. 7         687NE²1198     j 688NE666
680NE¹⁴422             [LX1048    c 693NE436       121F3d³1105      687NE³1198
Cir. 7                                             1998USDist                         —173—
d 1998USDist     —67—            —275—                  [LX1726    —895—            e 685NE895
     [LX3988     691NE832        691NE⁸116        1998USDist       f 1998IllAppLX   687NE⁴1075
1998USDist                                              [LX6188           [³184
     [LX5095     —73—            —288—            979FS⁴654        f 693NE¹393      —196—
                 689NE²408       Cir. 7                                             682NE169
—586—                            127F3d¹579       —669—            —911—
1998IllAppLX     —90—                             Cir. 7           691NE²128        —200—
       [²236     1998IllAppLX    —293—            956FS⁸818                         f 688NE⁴690
693NE³510              [²138     cc 1998USDist    211BRW280        —1202—           Cir. 7
                 692NE²798              [LX4907                     691NE106         1998USDist
—619—            Cir. 7                           —678—            691NE¹107               [LX600
682NE435         1998USDist      —329—            f 1997IllAppLX
                       [LX2878   1998IllAppLX            [527                        —227—
—655—            967FS³1048            [³302      f 682NE⁴749      Vol. 582 ①        691NE³152
1997IllAppLX     967FS³1048                       682NE²749
       [539                      —367—            f 682NE750                         —265—
681NE³149        —118—           1998IllAppLX     682NE⁴750        —89— ②           689NE²230
684NE⁹820        1998IllAppLX           [²171     682NE⁶752        US cert den
                       [314      692NE²1290                        516US872         —271—
—887—            f 678NE⁴362                      —715—            680NE³306        f 679NE³430
f 678NE⁴1044     691NE⁴83        —383—            683NE1000        j 685NE907
                                 1998IllAppLX                                       —274—
—903—            —138—                  [156     —716—                              681NE²558
c 687NE³530      684NE¹801       692NE1226        683NE⁴457                          681NE⁴563
j 687NE532       685NE¹875                        683NE⁴457
                 685NE²875       —426—            683NE⁴457        1 Volume numbers
—1198—                           686NE²621        690NE³1029       2 Page numbers
Cir. 7           —145—           f 686NE622                                         679NE³94
962FS¹1053       1998IllAppLX                     —728—           1998IllAppLX      680NE⁴434
966FS749               [274      —637—            682NE218                [²216     681NE⁹2
d 1996Bankr LX                   Cir. 1                           j 1998IllAppLX    684NE²171
       [1202     —154—           954FS⁴436        —730—                   [216      687NE²546
                 d 690NE159                       f 688NE148       1998IllAppLX     689NE²261
—1220—                           —644—            688NE⁸148               [²302     690NE³1050
682NE1213        —158—           683NE⁹932                         678NE²28         691NE³397
682NE³1215       682NE99         683NE1271        —739—            678NE³52
57Æ15n           682NE303                         687NE³875        678NE⁴52         —308—
                 f 691NE³45      —648—                             678NE⁴52         688NE²128
—1246—           691NE⁵46       1998IllAppLX      —759—            680NE⁴434
687NE900                                [130⁄      681NE¹⁸567      681NE⁹1068       —317—
                 —175—           685NE427         f 681NE568       f 682NE⁴1243     e 1998
—1274—           1998IllAppLX    691NE98          c 681NE568       f 688NE⁸4             [IllAppLX³177
e 682NE²⁹1119          [³103     693NE869                          688NE²1175       e 692NE²831
                 679NE³434                         —819—           690NE⁴622
—1342—           692NE³717       —651—            684NE⁸828        j 693NE500       —685—
683NE153                         681NE¹547                         Cir. 7           Case 2
683NE1010        —180—           681NE²601        —860—            1998USDist       681NE162
                 f 683NE³1259                     Cir. 7                  [LX743     691NE30
Vol. 581 ①       Cir. 7          —656—            1997Bankr LX     1998USDist
                 979FS⁴739       1998IllAppLX            [1258            [LX2829    —690—
—1—                                     [⁴325     215BRW168                         687NE1123
f 1998IllAppLX   —191—           678NE⁸1105       215BRW⁹374       —120—            f 687NE1124
       [320      f 682NE1140     f 688NE³84       689NE¹²676       682NE³289        690NE³139
                                                                  682NE⁴289
```

459

Reprinted with the permission of LexisNexis.

Review Illustration 5-6. This is a page from a pamphlet that must be reviewed to completely Shepardize the *Thompson* citation. In Illustration 5-6, the volume number appears on the top of the page in the corner. It is volume number 582. Volume number 581 is in the middle of the page. The page numbers are found in bold in the middle of the page. All of the citations listed after the notation Vol. 581 refer to cases found in that volume of the *Northeastern Reporter*. If you needed to find a *Shepard's* report for a case contained in volume 580 of the *Northeastern Reporter*, you would review the citations listed before the notation Vol. 581. Now look for "885," the number referencing the first page of the *Thompson* case. Cases that cite to *Thompson* would be listed below that number as they are in Illustration 5-3. No new cases cite to the *Thompson* case in this illustration because "885" does not appear after the volume 581.

You can review cases by either official or parallel citations. For example, you can find the *Thompson* citation under the listings for *Northeastern Reporter Second Series, Illinois Appellate Reports Third Series,* or *Illinois Decisions*. A U.S. Supreme Court decision can be found based on its citation in *U.S. Reports, U.S. Supreme Court Reports, Lawyers' Edition,* and *U.S. Supreme Court* reporter. For your research to be complete, you must consult multiple citation services whenever possible. This ensures that you will review the different sources *Shepard's* reviewed to compile a citation list.

If you are only using *Shepard's* to validate an authority, your final step must be to review *Shepard's* online. That is the only way to ensure that an authority is still valid.

### ▼ Which Citator Should You Consult for State Cases?

For state cases, you should begin with the state *Shepard's*, if available to you.

Find the official citation, if one exists, and review it. Then review the regional citation. Next, if available, review the regional *Shepard's* citator that includes that state. If you have access to a relevant topical citator, review that citator.

---

*PRACTICE POINTER*

Update any print *Shepard's* with the most current online information. Case law in some states requires that attorneys use online resources such as Shepard's to ensure that an authority is valid.

---

# B. *SHEPARD'S* ONLINE

## ▼ How Do You Use *Shepard's* Online?

You can access *Shepard's* online at Lexisnexis.com during any point in your research. It cannot be accessed through Westlaw.

At the website, after you log on, with a click of a mouse you can access a box to enter a citation and ask the computer to find the *Shepard's* report. See Illustrations 5-7A and 5-7B.

## ▼ Is *Shepard's* Online More Current Than *Shepard's* in Print?

The online *Shepard's* on Lexis is more up to date than the print *Shepard's*. The online *Shepard's* is updated daily.

## ▼ How Is *Shepard's* Different Online Than in Hard Copy?

First, the online document provides you with a *Shepard's* listing only for the case you are reviewing. See Illustration 5-2. It provides the parallel citations. Compare Illustrations 5-1 and 5-2. The computer record of the *Shepard's* search is easier to read. Listing only one case eliminates the possibility of confusion, which often occurs with the print *Shepard's* materials. Computerized *Shepard's* also facilitates notetaking because the *Shepard's* can be printed, often on a single page, and does not involve the painstaking task of writing each notation. This also minimizes notetaking errors. One of the other advantages of *Shepard's*

**ILLUSTRATION 5-7A.** *Shepard's* **Search Screen on LexisNexis**

Reprinted with the permission of LexisNexis.

## ILLUSTRATION 5-7B.  *Shepard's* Search Screen on Lexis Advance

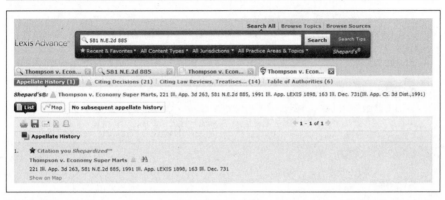

Reprinted with the permission of LexisNexis. Editor's Note: See online document for complete report.

online is that the computer automatically reviews all of the *Shepard's* volumes and provides one complete list of all the *Shepard's* citations.

As you learned earlier, a print search of the same citation would require you to review multiple volumes. The computer system is much easier to use because you only need to push a few buttons or click a mouse. It also is much quicker. In addition, the computer search will find *Shepard's* citations contained in different *Shepard's* citators. For example, a search online of the *Thompson* case produces the reports of the *Shepard's Illinois Citator* and the *Shepard's Northeastern Reporter Citations* because the computer searches multiple citators at one time. *Shepard's* online also provides a short summary of all of the data in the *Shepard's* report.

The publisher's *Shepard's* treatments also are easier to understand online because the publisher includes a full word and graphic signals to tell you the value of a case. These graphics are easier to read than the small abbreviations. *Shepard's* has signal aids to help you know whether to proceed in using an authority, to use the authority with caution, or to not use the authority. Review Illustration 5-2. At the top of the *Shepard's* result is a yellow triangle. That triangle indicates that a researcher should use caution before relying on the *Thompson* case. That is because of the possible negative treatment of this case.

If the *Shepard's* report has an orange Q, that indicates that opinions exist that question the validity or precedential value of the case. A red stop sign indicates that the case is no longer good law. See Illustration 5-8 for additional information about *Shepard's* signals. Although these signals can guide you in your legal research, you must determine for yourself whether a case is still good law. The signal may concern an issue that is different from the one you are researching. To thoroughly do your job as a researcher, you need to read the case yourself.

Another advantage is that you often can immediately access the citing cases online by clicking the mouse on the hyperlinked number.

## ILLUSTRATION 5-8.   *Shepard's* Online Signal Indications

**The *Shepard's* Signal™**

The *Shepard's* Signal Marker indicates the standing of your case or statute as treated by other cases (your **Cited Case** or **Cited Statute**).

**NOTE:**

The **Cited Case** or **Cited Statute** is the case or statute that you are *Shepardizing*™. The **Citing References** are citations in your *Shepard's* report that cite the case or statute that you are *Shepardizing*.

**Signal**
**Description**
**Detail**

Warning
Negative treatment indicated.
Includes the following analyses:

- Overruled by
- Superceded by
- Revoked
- Obsolete
- Rescinded

Warning
Negative case treatment is indicated for statute.

Includes the following analyses:

- Unconstitutional
- Void
- Invalid

Questioned

Validity questioned by citing references.

Includes the following analyses:

- Questioned by

## ILLUSTRATION 5-8. *Continued*

Caution

Possible negative treatment indicated.

Includes the following analyses:

- Limited
- Criticized by
- Clarified
- Modified
- Corrected

Positive

Positive treatment indicated.

Includes the following analyses:

- Followed
- Affirmed
- Approved

Citing References with Analysis

Other cases cited the case and assigned some analysis that is not considered positive or negative.

Includes the following analyses:

- Appeal denied by
- Writ of certiorari denied

Citation Information

References have not applied any analysis to the citation. For example the case was cited by case law or law reviews that do not warrant an analysis.

Includes the analysis Cited by.

**NOTE:**

Refer to the *Shepard's*® Citations Service Analysis Definitions for a complete list of analysis codes and definitions.

Reprinted with permission of LexisNexis.

After you retrieve the *Shepard's* cases, you will be able to perform word searches to narrow your results. The computer system allows you to design your *Shepard's* research so that you retrieve only the cases that have a negative impact on your case. You also can retrieve cases that contain only a particular headnote or are decided by a specific court. With Lexis, you would perform a **FOCUS** search. You also may filter your search results to include a particular jurisdiction, headnote, vital points of law or fact patterns, dates, or *Shepard's* treatments such as followed by or overruled.

---

### ETHICS ALERT

Some courts may sanction attorneys if they provide cases that are no longer good law to support their claims. Disciplinary action may be taken against an attorney who fails to use online resources to validate an authority.

---

*Shepard's* Alerts provide information about changes to already viewed reports. These alerts can be tailored to provide specific information only, such as the negative treatment of a case or changes to the citation.

## C. KEYCITE

Westlaw provides a service called **KeyCite** that competes with *Shepard's*. See Illustrations 5-9 and 5-10. KeyCite, however, is not offered in print.

KeyCite provides the direct history of a case as well as any case that impacts the precedential value of a case. See Illustration 5-9. It provides the direct history and lists any negative history at the top of the KeyCite report. With KeyCite you retrieve all citing references that are contained within Westlaw, including thousands of unpublished decisions as well as published cases, secondary sources, appellate briefs, trial motions, memoranda, and affidavits. In Illustration 5-10 you are directed to various *American Law Reports* and local encyclopedia references.

KeyCite also will provide a list and links to appellate court briefs as well as trial court motions, memoranda, and affidavits that cite to a case. See Illustrations 5-11 and 5-12.

KeyCite uses a system of colored flags to alert you to the history. A red case flag warns that the case is no longer good law for at least one of the points of law. A yellow flag warns that there is some negative history, but that the case has not been overruled or reversed. If the case has history that is not negative, it will have a blue H. A green C indicates that the case has citing references, but no direct or negative indirect history. Review Illustration 5-9. Note the flag at the top of

**ILLUSTRATION 5-9.   Screen Shots of Westlaw KeyCite Result for *Thompson v. Economy Super Marts, Inc.***

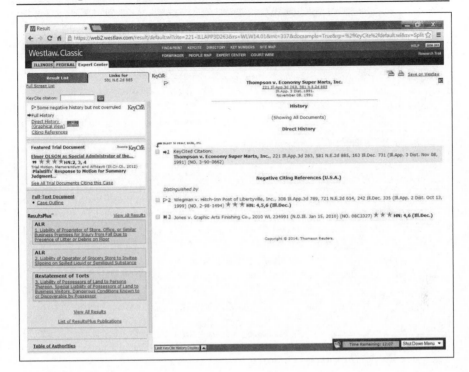

**ILLUSTRATION 5-9.** *Continued*

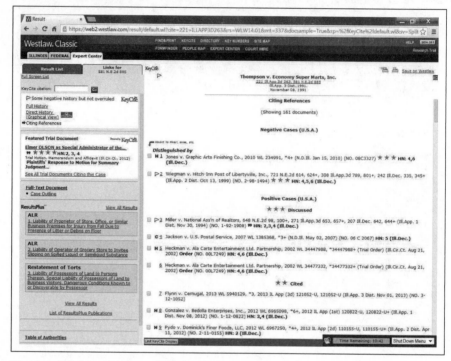

Reprinted with permission of Thomson Reuters.

## ILLUSTRATION 5-10.   Westlaw KeyCite Result Showing Secondary Sources to Review for *Thompson v. Economy Super Marts, Inc.*

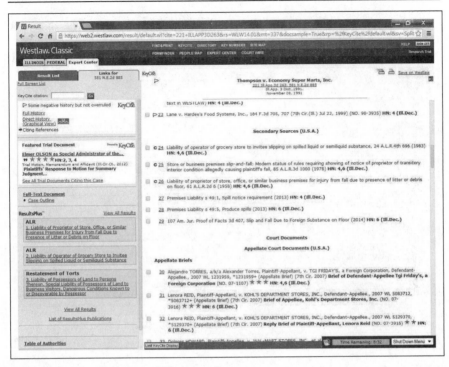

Reprinted with permission of Thomson Reuters.

Illustration 5-9. It is a yellow flag. It indicates that the case has some negative history.

In addition, Westlaw has developed a star system for noting the depth of the treatment a court provides to a case. Four stars means that the case was examined. Three stars mean it was discussed, and two stars indicate it was cited. One star means that the case was mentioned. Westlaw's headnotes and topics and key numbers also are incorporated into the KeyCite display. Note in Illustration 5-9 "HN: 4, 6" following the *Jones v. Graphic Arts Finishing Co.* case. That indicates that headnotes 4 and 6 of the *Jones* case are discussed. You can tailor your KeyCite search to focus on key numbers, topics, or jurisdictions.

Researchers can request that only certain documents, headnotes, or treatments be shown in the result. KeyCite allows you to receive automatic status updates concerning cases. You can indicate how often you would like to be updated and results can be sent to you via e-mail.

## ILLUSTRATION 5-11.   Westlaw KeyCite Result Showing Appellate Court Documents to Review for *Thompson v. Economy Super Marts, Inc.*

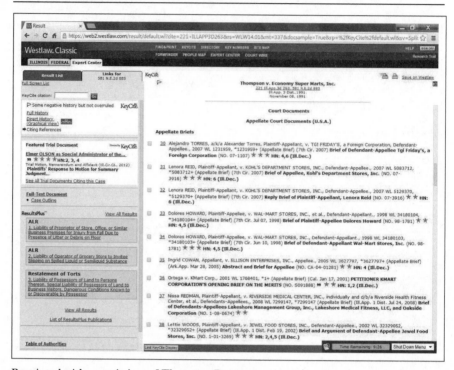

Reprinted with permission of Thomson Reuters.

**ILLUSTRATION 5-12.  Westlaw KeyCite Result Showing Trial Court Documents to Review for *Thompson v. Economy Super Marts, Inc.***

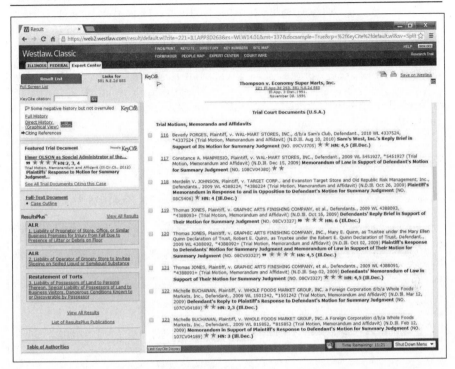

Reprinted with permission of Thomson Reuters.

### ▼ What Is the Difference Between *Shepard's* and KeyCite?

Researchers have noted recently that the services are very similar in nature. However, some citing references, such as some secondary authorities or treatises, may be unique to one system or the other.

### ▼ Why Would You Use Both KeyCite and *Shepard's?*

Using both services provides an additional check on the accuracy of the citation. Each also provides different references to secondary sources that might assist you in your research. For more information about secondary sources, consult Chapter 6.

### ▼ How Do I Access KeyCite?

From any Westlaw screen, point your mouse at the KeyCite button and type in the citation and press Enter. If you are already viewing a case, you merely click the status flag or H or the KeyCite button on the main screen and you can instantly KeyCite your citation.

## D. GLOBALCITE

**GlobalCite**, a service within Loislaw, allows you to search cases, statutes, regulations, and other sources within the Loislaw database to determine whether a document has been cited. GlobalCite can be accessed from the main screen or it can be done while reviewing a research document. Researchers can view all documents retrieved by the search or can limit the results to cases, statutes, or other documents. The results will list each citation of the document and a summary of the document found, and will allow you to hyperlink to the full text of those documents.

**ILLUSTRATION 5-13.   Loislaw GlobalCite Results for**
*Thompson v. Economy Super Marts, Inc.*

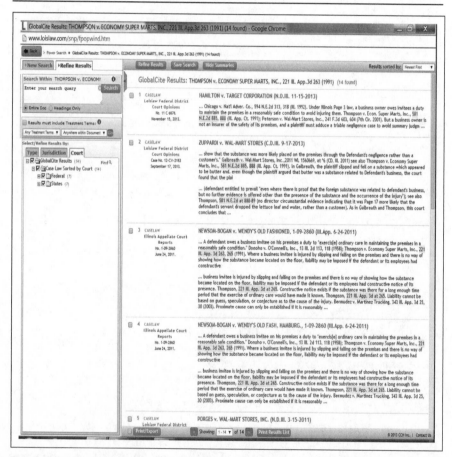

Reprinted with permission of CCH INCORPORATED, a Wolters Kluwer Business. http://estore.loislaw.com/.

Case treatment terms such as affirm, agree, distinguish, dismiss, overrule, and rescind will be highlighted in blue. Researchers must scan the cases to find these terms, however. They are not placed next to the case name in the GlobalCite search results. See Illustration 5-13.

Review the illustration. Although GlobalCite can be tailored to show only cases with negative treatments, the GlobalCite is not as easy to follow or as comprehensive as the other online citators. It, however, may be a valuable starting point for researchers who use Loislaw as their primary research database.

## CHAPTER SUMMARY

In this chapter, you learned that you must ensure that the law or authority you are citing is still current or valid. To determine this, you must validate or update your research findings. This process often is called *Shepardizing*. Citators not only assist you in validating the law but also provide you with citations to other authorities. You can validate an authority in both print and online.

The next chapter discusses resources called secondary authorities that help you understand legal issues and find primary authorities.

## KEY TERMS

case history

citators

FOCUS

GlobalCite

KeyCite

negative history

Shepardizing

*Shepard's* citator system treatment

## EXERCISES

### COMPUTER EXERCISES
#### Lexis
1. Shepardize the following citations:
   a. 64 N.W.2d 38
   b. 150 Ill. App. 3d 21
   c. 326 U.S. 310
2. For 326 U.S. 310, limit your treatment to negative treatment only. What are the results?

#### Westlaw
3. Perform a KeyCite search for the following citations:
   a. 64 N.W.2d 38
   b. 150 Ill. App. 3d 21
   c. 326 U.S. 310

## COMPUTER VALIDATING EXERCISES

4. Shepardize and KeyCite all of the following cases on the computer. Print out the first page of each result.
   a. *Consolidation Coal Co. v. Bucyrus-Erie Co.*, 89 Ill. 2d 103, 432 N.E.2d 250 (1982)
   b. *United States v. Upjohn*, 449 U.S. 383 (1981)
   c. *People v. Adam*, 51 Ill. 2d 46, 280 N.E.2d 205 (1972)
   d. *Cox v. Yellow Cab Co.*, 61 Ill. 2d 416, 337 N.E.2d 15 (1975)
   e. *Archer Daniels Midland Co. v. Koppers Co.*, 138 Ill. App. 3d 276, 485 N.E.2d 1301 (1985)

5. If available perform a GlobalCite search on the citations listed in number 4 above.

6. Perform GlobalCites for all of the cases in Number 3.

### Exercises

7. a. Shepardize the *Kellermann* case, 713 N.E.2d 1285. Note that it is cited by 754 N.E.2d 448. Now, go to that case. What is the name of that case?
   b. What headnote of the *Kellermann* case does the case you found relate to?
   c. What is the topic and key number?
   d. Now look at key numbers 22 and 23 of the case you found. What is the topic and key number?
   e. How do these paragraphs and key numbers differ from the *Kellermann* case?

8. Perform a KeyCite search for 507 F. Supp. 1091 on Westlaw. List some of cases that have yellow flags.

9. Perform a KeyCite for 2002 WL1592517 (CA 7. Ill.). Can you perform a KeyCite for this case on Westlaw? Can you Shepardize this case on *Shepard's* online?

10. Perform a KeyCite for 106 SCt 1415.
    a. What is the name of the case?
    b. Is there any signal indicating the validity of the case? If so, what is it?

11. Shepardize the following cases online.
    a. 816 F.2d 630
    b. 373 N.E.2d 1371
    c. 432 N.E.2d 1123
    d. 222 N.E.2d 561

12. Find 984 F.2d 218 online on Westlaw.
    a. Is there a signal that indicates whether the case is good law?
    b. If so, what is the signal and what does it indicate?
    c. Does it apply to the entire case? If no, what part of the case does it apply to?

13. Shepardize the citations listed below in hardcopy. List the steps you followed and the volumes you consulted and the page numbers. Be certain to Shepardize all citations for each case or statute. Then Shepardize each citation online.
    a. 361 N.E.2d 325

    b. 80 Ill. App. 3d 315

    c. 571 F. Supp. 1012

    d. 8 U.S.C. §1449

14. Shepardize the following citations in the *Shepard's* print citators and pro-vide the official citations. List the steps you followed and the volumes you consulted and the page numbers. Next Shepardize each citation online.

    a. 129 F.R.D. 515

    b. 432 N.E.2d 250

    c. 449 U.S. 383

    d. 423 F.2d 487

    e. Ill. S. Ct. Rule 201

15. Select a case from those listed above that has one headnote notation and write down the case and the headnote notation. Then select one case that has a *Shepard's* notation and note the case, the notation, and what the notation means.

## CHAPTER 6

# SECONDARY AUTHORITY

A. **SECONDARY AUTHORITY: WHAT IT IS AND WHERE**     152
   **TO FIND IT**
B. **DICTIONARIES**     153
C. **THE LEGAL THESAURUS**     154
D. **ENCYCLOPEDIAS**     157
   1. Generally     157
   2. *American Jurisprudence*     158
   3. *Corpus Juris Secundum*     165
   4. State Law Encyclopedias     170
   5. Online Encyclopedia Services     170
E. *AMERICAN LAW REPORTS*     170
F. **TREATISES AND HORNBOOKS**     178
G. **RESTATEMENTS OF THE LAW**     181
H. **LEGAL PERIODICALS**     185

## CHAPTER OVERVIEW

Secondary authorities are used to understand, analyze, and tie together primary authorities, or the law. Secondary authorities explain the law and the legal rules, and they provide insight into primary authorities. Cases, statutes, and administrative regulations—all primary

authorities—are frequently cited in secondary sources. Secondary authorities are useful tools for finding citations to law supporting a legal issue.

This chapter details the many sources of secondary authority, how to use the sources, and how to update them. Citation information is given for each source.

# A. SECONDARY AUTHORITY: WHAT IT IS AND WHERE TO FIND IT

### ▼ What Is Secondary Authority?

**Secondary authority** describes, analyzes, and comments on primary authority. Secondary authority provides commentary on the law. Any analytical or critical discussion of the law is considered secondary authority. Generally, individuals, institutions, and publishers create secondary sources.

Secondary authority compares and contrasts judicial opinions and indicates how the law is evolving. Also, a secondary source will often tell the researcher which cases are most important and which have little merit. If you do not understand a legal rule or are concerned about how to apply a legal rule, consult a secondary source for guidance. Secondary sources are easier to read than primary authority because they are written in a narrative format. Secondary sources discuss statutes and administrative materials expounding on the policy motivations for enacting legislation and the accompanying regulations.

### ▼ Why and When Do You Use a Secondary Source?

Secondary sources are used to explain the law or a particular legal concept. Secondary sources discuss the legal rules directly without requiring the reader to unearth the issues and the holdings from the texts of judicial decisions. Secondary authority provides insight into a legal topic by discussing the most important relevant cases and statutes and by explaining how that law is applied to the facts. Because secondary sources comment on, describe, and analyze primary sources, a researcher obtains citations to primary authority. By providing access to citations, secondary sources are great finding tools. A researcher uses secondary authority to gain insight into a legal topic as well as to obtain citations to primary sources.

Paralegals use secondary sources when they are unfamiliar with a legal issue or topic and need a broad overview of the concepts written in a text format that is easily understandable. Using secondary authority provides access to primary sources because of the great number of footnotes and citations found in the secondary source.

A tutorial for using secondary sources is available at www.law.georgetown .edu/library/research/guides/secondary.cfm.

### ▼ What Are the Sources of Secondary Authority?

Generally, any source that comments on, analyzes, criticizes, describes, or projects the status of the law is a secondary source. Any source that states what the law should be is a secondary source. Some secondary sources are considered more prestigious and carry more persuasive authority than others. For instance, the Restatements of Law are very well respected, as are scholarly law review articles. The major sources of secondary authority are dictionaries, thesauri, encyclopedias, American Law Reports (A.L.R.), hornbooks, treatises, Restatements, legal periodicals, and newspapers. We will discuss each source separately, give examples, and illustrate which research situation would mandate their respective use.

### *PRACTICE POINTER*

Secondary sources are great finding tools for primary authority, particularly case law. Use the secondary source to understand how case law fits together and to obtain citations. Always read the primary source that you find cited in the secondary authority—that is, the case, the statute, or the regulation—yourself to see if it is applicable to your research. Also, be sure to Shepardize or KeyCite any primary source before you rely on it as a source of authority.

## B. DICTIONARIES

### ▼ What Is a Legal Dictionary?

The **legal dictionary** provides the legal definition of a word or term. Sometimes a case is mentioned that contains the judicial definition of that word. The two most common legal dictionaries are *Black's Law Dictionary* and *Ballentine's Law Dictionary*.

### ▼ When Would a Legal Dictionary Be Used?

Researchers use a legal dictionary when they do not understand the **legal meaning** of a word or term. The emphasis is on the legal meaning because the legal definition of a word often differs from its lay meaning. Sometimes you will be assigned a research project where you cannot answer or resolve the issue without first figuring out what the terms mean.

### *EXAMPLE*

Ms. Associate asks you if Mr. Blackacre can obtain an easement by necessity to access his farm from the road by crossing his neighbor's property. You do not know what an easement is, nor do you know what an easement by necessity is. To research the issue effectively, you would use a legal dictionary to look up easement and easement by necessity.

Examples of dictionary entries of the word *easement* are provided in Illustration 6-1. The entries in the legal dictionary are in alphabetical order. Under the word *easement* are the various types of easements.

### ▼ How Would You Cite to a Legal Dictionary?

The correct citation format for dictionaries is found in *Bluebook* **Rule 15.8** and *ALWD* **Rule 22.1**.

Black's Law Dictionary 585 (9th ed. 2009)—*Bluebook* format

*Black's Law Dictionary* 712 (Bryan A. Garner, ed., 9th ed. 2009)— *ALWD* format

### ▼ Are Legal Dictionaries Available Online?

*Black's Law Dictionary* is available on Westlaw. The Directory screen, which changes constantly, indicates exactly where the dictionary is located within the Westlaw database. The contents of *Black's* online are identical to the hard-copy version. To search for a definition online, enter the word that you want to be defined. In our example, you would enter the word *easement.* A free online legal dictionary is available at dictionary.law.com. A plain English legal dictionary is at www.nolo.com/dictionary.

## C. THE LEGAL THESAURUS

### ▼ What Is a Thesaurus?

A **thesaurus** provides synonyms and antonyms for words. A legal thesaurus provides synonymous terms and opposite terms for legal words. A thesaurus is the same type of source for legal and nonlegal materials.

A common legal thesaurus is *Burton's Legal Thesaurus* by William C. Burton (McGraw-Hill, 5th edition 2013). Also, try Thesaurus.com for an online thesaurus accessible from your desktop.

# ILLUSTRATION 6-1.  Definition of *Easement* in *Black's Law Dictionary*

and experience. • Earning capacity is one element considered when measuring the damages recoverable in a personal-injury lawsuit. And in family law, earning capacity is considered when awarding child support and spousal maintenance (or alimony) and in dividing property between spouses upon divorce. — Also termed *earning power*. See LOST EARNING CAPACITY.

**earnings.** (16c) Revenue gained from labor or services, from the investment of capital, or from assets. See INCOME.

*appropriated retained earnings.* Retained earnings that a company's board designates for a distinct use, and that are therefore unavailable to pay dividends or for other uses. — Also termed *appropriated surplus*; *surplus revenue*; *suspense reserve*.

*earnings before interest and taxes. Corporations.* A company's income calculated without deductions for interest expenses and taxes, used as a measure of the company's ability to generate cash flow from ongoing operations.— Abbr. EBIT.

*earnings before interest, taxes, and depreciation. Corporations.* A company's income without deductions for interest expenses, taxes, depreciation expenses, or amortization expenses, used as an indicator of a company's profitabilty and ability to service its debt. — Abbr. EBITDA.

*future earnings.* See lost earnings.

*gross earnings.* See gross income under INCOME.

*lost earnings.* Wages, salary, or other income that a person could have earned if he or she had not lost a job, suffered a disabling injury, or died. • Lost earnings are typically awarded as damages in personal-injury and wrongful-termination cases. There can be past lost earnings and future lost earnings. Both are subsets of this category, though legal writers sometimes loosely use *future earnings* as a synonym for *lost earnings*. Cf. LOST EARNING CAPACITY. [Cases: Damages 37.]

*net earnings.* See net income under INCOME.

*normalized earnings. Corporations.* Earnings adjusted for inflation and to remove elements that are extraordinary, nonrecurring, nonoperating, or otherwise unusual.

*ongoing earnings.* See operating earnings.

*operating earnings.* Business income calculated in violation of generally accepted accounting principles by including income items and excluding various business expenses. • Many companies use operating earnings to favorably skew their price-earnings (P/E) ratios. Because the rationales for the underlying calculations vary from company to company, and from period to period within a company, operating earnings are almost always artificially inflated and unreliable. The term *operating earnings* is meaningless under generally accepted accounting principles. — Also termed *pro forma earnings*; *economic earnings*;

*core earnings*; *ongoing earnings*; *earnings excluding special items*. See PRICE-EARNINGS RATIO.

*pretax earnings.* Net earnings before income taxes.

*pro forma earnings.* See operating earnings.

*real earnings.* Earnings that are adjusted for inflation so that they reflect actual purchasing power.

*retained earnings.* A corporation's accumulated income after dividends have been distributed. — Also termed *earned surplus*; *undistributed profit*. [Cases: Corporations 151.]

*surplus earnings.* The excess of corporate assets over liabilities within a given period, usu. a year. [Cases: Corporations 152.]

**earnings and profits.** *Corporations.* In corporate taxation, the measure of a corporation's economic capacity to make a shareholder distribution that is not a return of capital. • The distribution will be dividend income to the shareholders to the extent of the corporation's current and accumulated earnings and profits. Cf. *accumulated-earnings tax* under TAX; *accumulated taxable income* under INCOME. [Cases: Internal Revenue 3830.1–3845.]

**earnings before interest and taxes.** See EARNINGS.

**earnings before interest, taxes, and depreciation.** See EARNINGS.

**earnings excluding special items.** See *operating earnings* under EARNINGS.

**earnings per share.** *Corporations.* A measure of corporate value by which the corporation's net income is divided by the number of outstanding shares of common stock. • Investors benefit from calculating a corporation's earnings per share, because it helps the investors determine the fair market value of the corporation's stock. — Abbr. EPS.

*fully diluted earnings per share.* A corporation's net income — assuming that all convertible securities had been transferred to common equity and all stock options had been exercised — divided by the number of shares of the corporation's outstanding common stock.

**earnings-price ratio.** See *earnings yield* under YIELD.

**earnings report.** See INCOME STATEMENT.

**earnings yield.** See YIELD.

**earnout agreement.** (1977) An agreement for the sale of a business whereby the buyer first pays an agreed amount up front, leaving the final purchase price to be determined by the business's future profits. • The seller usu. helps manage the business for a period after the sale. — Sometimes shortened to *earnout*.

**earwitness.** (16c) A witness who testifies about something that he or she heard but did not see. Cf. EYEWITNESS.

**easement** (eez-mənt). (14c) An interest in land owned by another person, consisting in the right to use or control the land, or an area above or below it, for a specific

## ILLUSTRATION 6-1.  *Continued*

limited purpose (such as to cross it for access to a public road). • The land benefiting from an easement is called the *dominant estate*; the land burdened by an easement is called the *servient estate.* Unlike a lease or license, an easement may last forever, but it does not give the holder the right to possess, take from, improve, or sell the land. The primary recognized easements are (1) a right-of-way, (2) a right of entry for any purpose relating to the dominant estate, (3) a right to the support of land and buildings, (4) a right of light and air, (5) a right to water, (6) a right to do some act that would otherwise amount to a nuisance, and (7) a right to place or keep something on the servient estate. See SERVITUDE (1). Cf. PROFIT À PRENDRE. — Also termed *private right-of-way.* [Cases: Easements ⟨⟩1.]

**access easement.** (1933) An easement allowing one or more persons to travel across another's land to get to a nearby location, such as a road. • The access easement is a common type of easement by necessity. — Also termed *easement of access; easement of way; easement of passage.*

**adverse easement.** See *prescriptive easement.*

**affirmative easement.** (1881) An easement that forces the servient-estate owner to permit certain actions by the easement holder, such as discharging water onto the servient estate. — Also termed *positive easement.* Cf. *negative easement.*

> "Positive easements give rights of entry upon the land of another, not amounting to profits, to enable something to be done on that land. Some are commonplace, examples being rights of way across the land of another and rights to discharge water on to the land of another. Others are more rare, such as the right to occupy a pew in a church, the right to use a kitchen situated on the land of another for the purpose of washing and drying clothes, and the right to use a toilet situated on the land of another." Peter Butt, *Land Law* 305 (2d ed. 1988).

**apparent easement.** (1851) A visually evident easement, such as a paved trail or a sidewalk. [Cases: Easements ⟨⟩22.]

**appendant easement.** See *easement appurtenant.*

**appurtenant easement.** See *easement appurtenant.*

**avigational easement.** An easement permitting unimpeded aircraft flights over the servient estate. — Also termed *avigation easement; aviation easement; flight easement; navigation easement.* [Cases: Aviation ⟨⟩3.]

**common easement.** (18c) An easement allowing the servient landowner to share in the benefit of the easement. — Also termed *nonexclusive easement.* [Cases: Easements ⟨⟩38.]

**continuous easement.** (1863) An easement that may be enjoyed without a deliberate act by the party claiming it, such as an easement for drains, sewer pipes, lateral support of a wall, or light and air. — Also termed (in Louisiana) *continuous servitude.* Cf. *discontinuous easement.* [Cases: Easements ⟨⟩38.]

**conservation easement.** *Property.* A recorded, perpetual, nonpossessory interest in real property held by a government entity or by a qualified nonprofit entity that imposes restrictions or affirmative obligations on the property's owner or lessee to retain or protect natural, scenic, or open-space values of real property, ensure its availability for agricultural, forest, recreational, or open-space use, protect natural resources and habitat, maintain or enhance air or water quality, or preserve the historical, architectural, archeological, or cultural aspects of the real property. — Also termed *conservation restriction; conservation servitude.*

**determinable easement.** An easement that terminates on the happening of a specific event.

**discontinuous easement.** (1867) An easement that can be enjoyed only if the party claiming it deliberately acts in some way with regard to the servient estate. • Examples are a right-of-way and the right to draw water. — Also termed *discontinuing easement; noncontinuous easement; nonapparent easement; (in Louisiana) discontinuous servitude.* Cf. *continuous easement.* [Cases: Easements ⟨⟩38.]

**easement appurtenant.** (1810) An easement created to benefit another tract of land, the use of easement being incident to the ownership of that other tract. — Also termed *appurtenant easement; appendant easement; pure easement; easement proper.* Cf. *easement in gross.* [Cases: Easements ⟨⟩3.]

**easement by estoppel.** (1907) A court-ordered easement created from a voluntary servitude after a person, mistakenly believing the servitude to be permanent, acted in reasonable reliance on the mistaken belief. [Cases: Estoppel ⟨⟩83(1), 87.]

**easement by implication.** See *implied easement.*

**easement by necessity.** (1865) An easement created by operation of law because the easement is indispensable to the reasonable use of nearby property, such as an easement connecting a parcel of land to a road. — Also termed *easement of necessity; necessary way.* [Cases: Easements ⟨⟩18.]

**easement by prescription.** See *prescriptive easement.*

**easement in gross.** (1866) An easement benefiting a particular person and not a particular piece of land. • The beneficiary need not, and usu. does not, own any land adjoining the servient estate. Cf. *easement appurtenant.* [Cases: Easements ⟨⟩3.]

**easement of access.** See *access easement.*

**easement of convenience.** An easement that increases the facility, comfort, or convenience of enjoying the dominant estate or some right connected with it.

**easement of natural support.** See *lateral support* under SUPPORT (4).

**easement of necessity.** See *easement by necessity.*

**easement of passage.** See *access easement.*

**easement of way.** See *access easement.*

**easement proper.** See *easement appurtenant.*

Reprinted with permission of Thomson Reuters.

▼ Why Would You Use a Thesaurus?

A paralegal uses a thesaurus when drafting a memo about a single topic, like easement. The memo becomes very dull if the term *easement* is used over and over again. After a while you lose the reader's attention. Substituting a synonymous term makes reading the memo much more interesting. Occasionally substituting *right of way* for *easement* keeps the reader's interest.

Unfortunately, the *Bluebook* and *ALWD* do not have an entry for citing to a thesaurus. A writer does not cite to *Roget's Thesaurus* when using a synonym found in that work, so the same principle applies when using a legal thesaurus.

# D. ENCYCLOPEDIAS

## 1. Generally

### ▼ What Is a Legal Encyclopedia?

Just as the *Encyclopedia Britannica* divides the realm of knowledge into subjects and discusses each subject broadly (for example, the subjects Insects and Cities), a **legal encyclopedia** divides the law into topics and offers a broad coverage of the legal rules pertaining to each topic. The discussion is thorough but not too detailed and is oriented to the reader with legal knowledge, though not necessarily of the particular subject in question. Encyclopedias provide generalized commentary on the law.

There are legal encyclopedias such as the *Encyclopedia of the American Constitution* that cover specialized subject areas. There are encyclopedias such as **American Jurisprudence** and **Corpus Juris Secundum** that are national in scope. Finally, there are state law encyclopedias such as *Illinois Law and Practice* and *Florida Jurisprudence Second*. There are legal encyclopedias for most states.

### ▼ Why Would You Use an Encyclopedia?

An encyclopedia is very helpful when beginning research in an area of the law in which you have no basic knowledge of the subject or the issues. Encyclopedias divide the law into topics and subtopics and provide a generalized, clearly written discussion of the issues and the general rules. A working vocabulary and a knowledge of the general rules are obtained when using an encyclopedia. In addition, encyclopedias give credit to every tenet mentioned, so they are a marvelous source for citations.

After reading the encyclopedia entry, you must always read for yourself the cases cited in the references to determine if they are relevant to your problem.

## ▼ When Do You Cite an Encyclopedia as Authority?

As a general rule, encyclopedias should never be cited as authority. Encyclopedias are not scholarly sources, and authorship is institutional rather than individual. This does not detract from their helpfulness in providing a broad overview of the legal topic and in providing citations to primary source materials.

A researcher should use primary source references, even from other jurisdictions, obtained from the encyclopedia rather than cite to the encyclopedia's text. Always read the case or statute that the encyclopedia cites and rely on the primary source for authority. It is better to analogize to the law from another jurisdiction than to use an encyclopedia as authority.

The two predominant encyclopedias that are national in scope are *American Jurisprudence*, commonly referred to as Am. Jur. and Am. Jur. 2d (second series), and *Corpus Juris Secundum*, known as C.J.S.

Both encyclopedias cover the individual legal disciplines in a generalized manner. Discussion is thorough but not overly detailed. The encyclopedias provide many more references to case law than to statutes and regulations. The footnotes and citations included in the sections provide citations to primary authorities. You must always read the primary source that you rely on, not only the encyclopedia's interpretation of it.

State encyclopedias also exist. In Illinois, *Illinois Law and Practice* is the encyclopedia that deals with issues of state law. *Illinois Law and Practice* is published by West and contains references to many other West publications, particularly the digests with the topics and key numbers. Check with your librarian for the encyclopedia in your state.

Boston University Law School Library has a guide on how to begin your research with legal encyclopedias available at www.bu.edu/lawlibrary/research/guides/encyclopedia.html.

## 2. *American Jurisprudence*

### ▼ What Is Contained in *American Jurisprudence*?

*American Jurisprudence*, commonly called Am. Jur., is published by West and references other publications such as the *American Law Reports* (A.L.R.). The encyclopedia is in the second edition. The entire set is divided into topics, and the topics are arranged alphabetically.

**ILLUSTRATION 6-2. Topic Outline for Easements and Licenses at 25 Am. Jur. 2d 495 (2004)**

EASEMENTS AND LICENSES

§ 83 Right of access to make repairs or improvements; secondary easements

C. ALTERATIONS

§ 84 Generally
§ 85 Where easement is owned in common

D. INTERFERENCE WITH EASEMENT; OBSTRUCTIONS

§ 86 Generally; rights of servient owner
§ 87 Structures on or over ways; generally
§ 88 —Gates
§ 89 Right to remove obstructions

VI. TRANSFER OF EASEMENT

→ § 90 Easements in gross
§ 91 Easements appurtenant, generally
§ 92 —On division of dominant tenement
§ 93 —On transfer of servient tenement; requirements as to notice

VII. DURATION, TERMINATION, AND REVIVAL

A. DURATION

§ 94 Generally
§ 95 Necessity of words of inheritance or limitation to create perpetual easement

B. TERMINATION OR EXTINGUISHMENT; REVIVAL

§ 96 Generally
§ 97 Occurrence of stated event or violation of conditions
§ 98 Abandonment
§ 99 Misuse
§ 100 Merger of dominant and servient estates
§ 101 Release; license
§ 102 Adverse possession
§ 103 Destruction or alteration of building or structure
§ 104 Foreclosure of mortgage or trust deed
§ 105 Sale for taxes; enforcement of special assessment
§ 106 Revival

VIII. ACTIONS TO ESTABLISH, ENFORCE, OR PROTECT EASEMENTS

A. IN GENERAL

§ 107 Generally

Reprinted with permission of Thomson Reuters.

Illustration 6-2 shows the topic outline for Easements and Licenses in Am. Jur. 2d. Notice that under the topics of Easements are various subtopics. The initial discussion of the subtopic Easements in Gross begins with a category entitled "Transfer of Easement."

The editors attempt to divide the entire body of American law into labeled topics. This gives the reader a subject approach to the law and permits the gathering of legal information, allowing the researcher to find out the general legal rules without reading the actual cases and statutes from which the rules are derived. The text explores each legal topic by providing the most important law that is relevant or the controlling legal doctrine, then discusses the exceptions to the general rules. The encyclopedia is considered to be a secondary source because it offers discussion and commentary on the law and synthesizes, or puts together, many cases. Of course, there is extensive footnoting to give proper credit or attribution to the authority discussed. This makes the encyclopedia a great finding tool, although not a substitute for reading the primary source material. The encyclopedia is a good place to begin research when you do not understand the topic and need a broad overview of the discipline. By virtue of reading about the topic, you will acquire case and statute citations to relevant materials.

Am. Jur. is organized by topic, and the volumes are updated with pocket parts. The pocket parts are called **Cumulative Supplements** and are generally published annually. Each volume of Am. Jur. is numbered, and the topics and sections contained within the volume are listed on the spine; for example, Volume 25 of Am. Jur. contains Domicil to Elections §§ 1-206. At the beginning of each topic is an outline listing every related subtopic. Each section within a topic refers to a subtopic; for example, under the topic of Easements and Licenses, captions indicate categories within the topics such as VI. Transfer of Easement. Under Transfer of Easement, § 90 is entitled "Easement in Gross." The text of Am. Jur. 2d repeats the topic and subtopic heading. See Illustration 6-3.

Notice that the topic or subtopic is first discussed generally, then the subissues are explored. To update the information found in the main volume, refer to the pocket part, or supplement, under the topic and then under the section. See Illustration 6-4. In our example, the supplement has no additional material updating § 90, but there is material updating other sections. Always check the pocket part, regardless of how recent the main volume publication date, to see if there are any new cases. For the purposes of illustration, see the new entries in the pocket part under *VI. Transfer of Easement*, § 91 *Easements appurtenant, generally.*

Narrative text generally is omitted in the pocket part, but new and updating citation references are included. This means that citations to new cases published that support the legal premises discussed in the main text are listed so that you can find the most recent authority for the legal premise. This is the same format as the pocket part in C.J.S.

Am. Jur. updates its topics with a volume entitled *New Topic Service* in which current topics, complete with text and footnotes, are contained. Am. Jur. also published the *Desk Book*, which contains facts, charts, tables, statistics, and court rules of interest to attorneys. The *Desk Book* is published annually.

**ILLUSTRATION 6-3. Portion of Easement Entry at 25 Am. Jur. 2d § 90 (2004)**

---

## VI. TRANSFER OF EASEMENT

**Research References**

West's Digest References

Easements ⬳24

Annotation References

A.L.R. Digest: Easements §§ 57 to 59, 59.7
A.L.R. Index: Easements

Forms References

Am. Jur. Legal Forms 2d, Pipelines §§ 203:48, 203:49

### § 90  Easements in gross

**Research References**

West's Key Number Digest, Easements ⬳24
Assignment permitted—Exception of right to construct additional pipelines. Am. Ju
Forms 2d, Pipelines § 203:48

Assignment prohibited—Exception of certain subsidiaries. Am. Jur. Legal Forms 2d, Pipelines
§ 203:49

An easement in gross, as a right personal to the one to whom it is granted, generally cannot be assigned or otherwise transmitted by him or her to another.[1] That is, because it is purely a personal right, an easement in gross is not assignable, absent evidence of the parties' intent to the contrary, and terminates upon the death of the individual for whom it was created.[2] However, there is some authority for the view that easements in gross that are taken for commercial purposes, especially those for public utility purposes such as railroads, telephone lines, and pipelines, are freely transferable,[3] and that easements in gross may be made assignable, however, by the terms of the instrument creating the right, particularly where the easement is of a commercial character, such as an easement for a pipeline, telegraph and telephone line, or railroad right-of-way.[4] When the evidence demonstrates that the parties clearly intended that an easement in gross be assignable, it is.[5]

---

Reprinted with permission of Thomson Reuters.

▼ How Do You Use Am. Jur.?

There are four basic methods of using Am. Jur. 2d.

1. **The index method.** This is the most efficient approach. At the end of the set is a multi-volume index that is printed annually. Entries are organized by descriptive word and topic and include subtopics as

**ILLUSTRATION 6-4.   Cover and Sample Page Pocket Part for Volume 25 Am. Jur. 2d**

# AMERICAN JURISPRUDENCE

### SECOND EDITION

## 2013 CUMULATIVE SUPPLEMENT

### ISSUED IN MAY 2013

Volume 25

**INSERT IN BACK OF BOUND VOLUME**

THOMSON REUTERS™

# ILLUSTRATION 6-4.    *Continued*

Consult the topic and section to see if there are new cases. The pocket part provides annotations to decisions that were published after the main volume was printed.

EASEMENTS AND LICENSES    § 91

Provisions of Restatement (Third) of Property: Servitudes, under which a court may modify a servitude to permit other uses under conditions designed to preserve the benefits of the original servitude, if the purpose of a servitude can be accomplished, but because of changed conditions the servient estate is no longer suitable for uses permitted by the servitude, would be rejected in favor of preventing the owners of servient estates from unilaterally relocating or terminating express easements. Restatement (Third) of Property Servitudes, §§ 4.8(3), 7.10(2). AKG Real Estate, LLC v. Kosterman, 2006 WI 106, 717 N.W.2d 835 (Wis. 2006).

### D.    INTERFERENCE WITH EASEMENT; OBSTRUCTIONS

§ 86  Generally; rights of servient owner

**Cases**

Remand was required for consideration as to whether surveillance cameras trained on beach access easement across lot owners' property placed an unreasonable burden on neighbors' use of the easement in light of lot owners' obligations in prior settlement agreement which provided that rightful users of the easement would not be photographed. Flaherty v. Muther, 2011 ME 32, 17 A.3d 640 (Me. 2011).

The owner of the dominant tenement is entitled to use the easement in a manner contemplated at the time of the conveyance, while the servient tenant is entitled the use and enjoyment of his property consistent with the terms and conditions of the reservation and may not obstruct the use of the easement. Rogers v. P-M Hunter's Ridge, LLC, 407 Md. 712, 967 A.2d 807 (2009).

If interference by the owner of the servient estate in an easement is slight and immaterial, it is not objectionable. Musselshell Ranch Co. v. Seidel-Joukova, 2011 MT 217, 362 Mont. 1, 261 P.3d 570 (2011).

Owner of a servient estate has the right to use its land in any manner that does not unreasonably interfere with the rights of the owners of an easement. Scappa v. Herzig, 92 A.D.3d 751, 938 N.Y.S.2d 346 (2d Dep't 2012).

The owner of a servient estate can fully exercise his rights of ownership in any manner and for any purpose not inconsistent with the easement and the dominant estate owner may not interfere with such use. Barrett v. Humphrey, 2012 OK CIV APP 28, 275 P.3d 959 (Div. 2 2012).

If the first easement is not exclusive, subsequent concurrent easements that are not unreasonably burdensome or inconsistent with the original easement are valid. McCarthy Holdings LLC v. Burgher, 282 Va. 267, 716 S.E.2d 461 (2011).

§ 87  Structures on or over ways; generally

**Cases**

Alternative access to dominant estate owners' property over servient estate did not diminish their rights in easement or allow servient estate owners to interfere with the dominant estate owners' ingress and egress over the easement. Whipple v. Hatcher, 283 Ga. 309, 658 S.E.2d 585 (2008).

Creation of 10 residential plots along length of ingress and egress easement did not unreasonably interfere with dominant estate owners' non-exclusive easement rights, as it did not interfere with the ability to pass over the driveway within the easement. Drees Co., Inc. v. Thompson, 868 N.E.2d 32 (Ind. Ct. App. 2007).

§ 88  Structures on or over ways; generally—Gates

**Cases**

Gate which lot owners placed across beach access easement did not unreasonably interfere with neighbors' use of the easement, although gate required neighbors to have a key; electronic gate access system was not uncommon, judgment in previous litigation between lot owners and homeowners association included provision that gate be erected, and any concerns about inconveniences created by gate, or potential for abuse, were speculative. Flaherty v. Muther, 2011 ME 32, 17 A.3d 640 (Me. 2011).

### VI.    TRANSFER OF EASEMENT

§ 91  Easements appurtenant, generally

**Cases**

As a non-possessory estate, town easement in gross, which allowed town to operate sewage pumping station on dominant estate, could not serve as dominant estate to appurtenant easement over servient estate, and thus dominant-estate owner could not convey appurtenant easement to town without transferring title to, or rightful possession of, a portion of dominant estate. Arcidi v. Town of Rye, 150 N.H. 694, 846 A.2d 535 (2004).

An express easement passes by a subsequent conveyance of the dominant estate without express mention in the conveyance. AKG Real Estate, LLC v. Kosterman, 2006 WI 106, 717 N.W.2d 835 (Wis. 2006).

A servient estate remains burdened by a recorded express easement even when the easement is not expressly mentioned in the conveyance, since the purchaser has constructive notice of the easement. AKG Real Estate, LLC v. Kosterman, 2006 WI 106, 717 N.W.2d 835 (Wis. 2006).

153

Reprinted with permission of Thomson Reuters.

cross-references. An example of the index from Am. Jur. 2d is shown in Illustration 6-5.

2. **The table method.** If you have a statutory cite, use the separate Am. Jur. 2d volume entitled *Table of Statutes, Rules and Regulations Cited.* If you have a relevant *United States Code* (U.S.C.) or U.S.C.S., *Code of Federal Regulations,* or uniform law citation, the tables will indicate the precise topic and section where it is discussed.

3. **The topic outline.** This is the least efficient method. In this method you review the topics outlined at the beginning of each topic section.

## ILLUSTRATION 6-5. Am. Jur. 2d General Index, Sample Pages

AMERICAN JURISPRUDENCE 2d

**DUST**—*continued*
Automobiles and highway traffic, visibility, **Autos** § 779
Cement plants, **Pollution** § 1858
Crop dusting. **Dusting Crops or Vegetation** (this index)
Entertainment and sports, **Pollution** § 1864
Grain and feed, **Pollution** § 1859, 1860
Highways, streets, and bridges, personal injuries, **Highways** § 482
Manufacturers, **Pollution** § 1863
**Mines and Minerals** (this index)
Refineries, **Pollution** § 1862
Stone quarries and rock crushers, **Pollution** § 1861
Transportation, **Pollution** § 1864
Workers' compensation, **Workers** § 350

**DUSTING CROPS OR VEGETATION**
Generally, **Agric** § 47
Actions and remedies, **Agric** § 58
Adjoining landowners, **Adjoining** § 40
Animals, injuries from crop spray to, **Animals** § 106
Personal injuries, **Aviation** § 167

**DUTCH AUCTION TENDER**
Corporate takeovers, **Corporatns** § 2178

**DUTIES**
**Customs Duties and Import Regulations** (this index)

**DUTY-FREE ARTICLES OR PROVISIONS**
**Customs Duties and Import Regulations** (this index)

**DUTY OF CARE**
**Negligence** (this index)

**DWELLING**
**House or Home** (this index)

**DWI**
Driving under influence. **Automobiles and Highway Traffic** (this index)

**DYES**
Barbers and cosmetologists, **Barbers** § 22
**Laundries, Dyers, and Dry Cleaners** (this index)

**DYING DECLARATIONS**
Generally, **Evidence** § 843, 844
**Homicide** (this index)
**Instructions to Jury** (this index)
Products liability, **ProductsLi** § 1699
Wrongful death, **Death** § 364

**DYNAMITE**
**Explosions and Explosives** (this index)

**EAGLES**
Indian lands, **Indians** § 65

**EAJA**
**Equal Access to Justice Act (EAJA)** (this index)

**EAR INJURIES**
**Ears or Hearing** (this index)

**EARLIER**
**Prior Acts and Matters** (this index)

**EARLIER ASSIGNMENT RULE**
Mortgages, **Mortgages** § 967

**EARLIER MATURITY RULE**
Mortgages, **Mortgages** § 966

**EARLY RETIREMENT**
**Pensions and Retirement** (this index)
**Social Security** (this index)

**EARLY TERMINATION**
**Bankruptcy** (this index)

**EARMARKING DOCTRINE**
**Bankruptcy** (this index)

**EARNED INCOME**
**Pensions and Retirement** (this index)
**Supplemental Security Income (SSI)** (this index)

**EARNEST MONEY**
**Auctions** (this index)
**Brokers** (this index)

**EARNING CAPACITY**
**Alimony** (this index)
**Damages** (this index)
**Divorce and Separation** (this index)

**EARNINGS**
**Profits or Income** (this index)

**EARNINGS RECORDS**
**Social Security** (this index)

**EARS OR HEARING**
**Deaf or Mute Persons** (this index)
Disability benefits, **Insurance** § 1482

**EARTH**
**Soil or Earth** (this index)

**EASEMENTS** ◄—
See also **Licenses in Real Property** (this index)
Generally, **Easements** § 1 to 126
Abandonment, **Easements** § 98
Access to make repairs or improvements, **Easements** § 83
Actions and remedies
  generally, **Easements** § 107 to 116
  burden of proof, **Easements** § 116

**EASEMENTS**—*continued*
Actions and remedies—*continued*
  damages, below
  defenses, **Easements** § 115
  evidence, **Easements** § 116
  injunctions, **Easements** § 110
  landlord and tenant, **Easements** § 109
  limitation of actions, **Easements** § 115
  parties, **Easements** § 108, 109
  pleadings, **Easements** § 114
  punitive damages, **Easements** § 112
  standing, **Easements** § 108, 109
  title and ownership, **Easements** § 109
  weight and sufficiency of evidence, **Easements** § 116
Adjoining Landowners (this index)
Adverse or hostile use. Prescription, below
Adverse possession
  prescription, **Easements** § 49
  termination or extinguishment, **Easements** § 102
Affirmative easements, **Easements** § 6
Agreement, creation by, **Easements** § 17
Airspace, avigation easements as defense to trespass, **Aviation** § 8
Alterations
  generally, **Easements** § 84
  access to make repairs or improvements, **Easements** § 83
  building or structure, alteration of, **Easements** § 103
  common easements, **Easements** § 85
Apparent easements
  generally, **Easements** § 7
  preexisting uses, **Easements** § 26
Appurtenant easements
  generally, **Easements** § 8
  easements in gross distinguished, **Easements** § 10
  transfer of easements
    generally, **Easements** § 91
    dominant tenement, division of, **Easements** § 92
    notice, **Easements** § 93
    servient tenement, division of, **Easements** § 93
Buildings or structures
  destruction of building or structure, **Easements** § 103
  interference with easements, structures on or over ways, **Easements** § 87, 88
Canals, **Canals** § 7
Change of location, **Easements** § 69
Classifications of easements, **Easements** § 5 to 10
Color of title, prescription, **Easements** § 57
Common easements, **Easements** § 85
Consent
  location by agreement of parties, **Easements** § 67
  permissive use. Prescription, below

For assistance using this index call 1-800-328-4880

4. **Access Am. Jur. on Lexis or Westlaw.** Although costly, you can search by word or term. This is particularly helpful when you have an unusual term. Also, all updates are integrated into the page or section retrieved so that you do not have to consult pocket part supplements.

## ILLUSTRATION 6-5. *Continued*

GENERAL INDEX

**EASEMENTS**—*continued*
Construction and interpretation, **Easements** § 18, 73
Contingencies, **Easements** § 97
Continuous use
  preexisting uses, **Easements** § 28
  prescription, continuous and uninter-
    rupted use, **Easements** § 61 to 63
Contract, creation by, **Easements** § 17
Cotenancy and joint ownership, **Cotenancy** § 103
Court, location fixed by, **Easements** § 68
**Covenants of Title** (this index)
**Covenants** (this index)
Creation of easements, **Easements** § 11 to 63
Damages
  generally, **Easements** § 111
  punitive damages, **Easements** § 112
Declaratory judgments, **DeclJuds** § 156
**Deeds and Conveyances** (this index)
Defenses, **Easements** § 115
**Definition, Easements** § 1
Destruction of building or structure, **Easements** § 103
Deviation from route, **Easements** § 70
Dominant and servient rights
  interference with easements, rights of
    servient owner, **Easements** § 86
  merger of dominant and servient estates,
    **Easements** § 100
**Drains and Drainage Systems** (this index)
Duration, **Easements** § 94, 95
Ejectment, **Ejectment** § 4
Electricity, **Energy** § 167, 168
**Eminent Domain** (this index)
Estoppel, creation by, **Easements** § 13
Evidence
  presumptions and burden of proof,
    below
  weight and sufficiency of evidence,
    **Easements** § 116
Exception, creation by, **Easements** § 16
Exclusive use, prescription, **Easements** § 53
Existing way, **Easements** § 65
Extinguishment. Termination or extinguish-

**EASEMENTS**—*continued*
Implied easements—*continued*
  light, air, and view, **Adjoining** § 97, 98
  location, **Easements** § 65
  maps and plats, **Easements** § 21
  preexisting uses, below
  use of easements, **Easements** § 79
  ways of necessity, below
Improvements, access to make, **Easements** § 83
Indefinite easements, **Easements** § 72
In gross, easements
  generally, **Easements** § 9
  appurtenant easements distinguished,
    **Easements** § 10
  transfer of easements, **Easements** § 90
Inheritance, **Easements** § 95
Injunctions, **Easements** § 110
Interference with easements
  generally, **Easements** § 86 to 89
  gates, **Easements** § 88
  removal of obstructions, **Easements** § 89
  rights of servient owner, **Easements** § 86
  structures on or over ways, **Easements** § 87, 88
Interrupted use, prescription, **Easements** § 62
**Irrigation** (this index)
**Judicial Sales** (this index)
Knowledge. Notice or knowledge, below
**Landlord and Tenant** (this index)
Lateral support, excavations affecting, **Adjoining** § 67
Licenses in real property distinguished, **Easements** § 2, 117
**Light, Air, and View** (this index)
Limitation of actions, **Easements** § 115
Limitations and restrictions on use, **Easements** § 71
Lis pendens, **LisPend** § 29
Location
  generally, **Easements** § 64 to 70
  agreement of parties, location by, **Easements** § 67

**EASEMENTS**—*continued*
Municipal corporations, drains and sewers, **MuncCorp** § 503
Navigable waters, land bordering, **Easements** § 38
Necessity
  preexisting uses, **Easements** § 29
  ways of necessity, below
Negative easements
  generally, **Easements** § 6
  restrictive covenants, reciprocal negative
    easements, **Covenants** § 155, 156
Nonapparent easements, **Easements** § 7
Notice or knowledge
  prescription, below
  transfer of easements, **Easements** § 93
Notorious use. Visible, open, and notorious
  use, below
Nuisances, **Nuisances** § 377
Obstructions. Interference with easements,
  above
Open use. Visible, open, and notorious use,
  below
Owner of fee, **Easements** § 11
Parties, **Easements** § 108, 109
Partition, **Partition** § 16
**Party Walls** (this index)
Permanency of preexisting uses, **Easements** § 27
Permissive use. Prescription, below
Perpetual easements
  generally, **Easements** § 95
  rule against perpetuities, **Perpet** § 46
**Pipes and Pipelines** (this index)
Place or location. Location, above
Pleadings, **Easements** § 114
Preexisting uses
  generally, **Easements** § 22 to 29
  apparentness of use, **Easements** § 26
  basis of rule, **Easements** § 24
  continuous uses, **Easements** § 28
  implied reservation, **Easements** § 23
  necessity of use, **Easements** § 29
  permanent uses, **Easements** § 27

▼ What Is the Citation Format for Am. Jur.?

*Bluebook* **Rule 15.8** and *ALWD* **Rule 22.3** cover legal encyclopedias. A cite for easements in § 90 would be as follows:

    25 Am. Jur. 2d <u>Easements and Licenses</u> § 90 (2004 & Supp. 2013)

## 3. *Corpus Juris Secundum*

▼ What Is Contained in *Corpus Juris Secundum*?

*Corpus Juris Secundum,* commonly known as C.J.S., is the other predominant encyclopedia that is national in scope. C.J.S. is a West publication, and other West materials are referred to in its text. The most notable reference in C.J.S. is to the West topics and key numbers tying the encyclopedia to the West National Reporter system and the West

Digests. See Illustration 6-6. This attribute makes C.J.S. a very powerful research tool.

C.J.S. is organized by titles, which are the individual legal subjects. At the beginning of each title is a section analysis that outlines the legal issues and subissues within the subject. The volumes are numbered and contain the various titles in alphabetical order. Footnotes within the text refer the reader to case citations, as in Am. Jur. 2d. Each volume of C.J.S. is updated by a pocket part that contains subsequent citations and references to support the legal premises discussed in the main volume. The pocket parts also have Library References at the beginning of various sections that indicate the correlating topic and key number in the West Digest system. C.J.S. is updated in the same manner as Am. Jur.

C.J.S. has a multivolume general index that is replaced annually. The general index is located in the last volumes of the set.

### ▼ How Do You Use C.J.S.?

There are three methods of using C.J.S.

1. **The general index method.** This is the most efficient method. Look up the appropriate subject in the set's general index just as you would in any encyclopedia's index to obtain references to titles and sections. If nothing is relevant, you may be given a *See also* instruction indicating that you should look up the subject using a different word.
2. **Title analysis method.** Review the title outline at the beginning of the subject or title and read the entry under the appropriate section. This is the least efficient method.
3. **On Westlaw.** Westlaw is the only commercial database that has the full text of selected sections of CJS in the CJS database. Accessing CJS on Westlaw permits key word searching. Updates to all entries are integrated into the document retrieved so there is no need to consult a pocket part supplement. See Illustration 6-6 for sample pages showing 28A C.J.S. *Easements* §18 accessed on Westlaw.

### ▼ How Is C.J.S. Cited?

*Bluebook* **Rule 15.8** and *ALWD* **Rule 22.3** for cover legal encyclopedias. A citation to easements in § 18 would be as follows:

28A C.J.S. <u>Easements</u> § 18 (2008 & Supp. 2013)

A cite to C.J.S. on Westlaw, according to *ALWD* **Rule 26.1**, would be as follows:

28A C.J.S. *Easements* § 18 (WL current through December 2013)

## ILLUSTRATION 6-6.   28A C.J.S. Easements § 18 from Westlaw, current through December 2013

---

§ 18.Easements in gross, 28A C.J.S. Easements § 18

28A C.J.S. Easements § 18

**(3)** Corpus Juris Secundum

Database updated December 2013

**(1)** Easements

Romualdo P. Eclavea, J.D., William Lindsley, J.D., Tom Muskus, J.D., Eric Surette, J.D.

II. Classes of Easements and Right in Nature of Easements

B. Easements Appurtenant or In Gross

Topic Summary   References   Correlation Table

§ 18. Easements in gross **(2)**

**West's Key Number Digest**

**West's Key Number Digest, Easements** ⊛ 3(1)
**West's Key Number Digest, Easements** ⊛ 3(2)

An easement in gross is a mere personal interest in or right to use another's lan[...]
the occupancy of the land. It differs from an easement appurtenant in that it do[...]
is not assignable or inheritable.

There is a class of rights which one may have in another's land without their bei[...]
of other lands, and they are called rights or easements in gross.[1] An easemen[...]
of another's land, but it is a mere personal interest.[2] An easement in gross is [...]
a mere personal interest in or right to use the land of another;[3] it is created t[...]
ownership or possession of specific land.[4] Simply stated, an easement in gross, sometimes called a personal easement, is an
easement which is not appurtenant to any estate in land, but in which the servitude is imposed upon land with the benefit thereof
running to an individual.[5] An easement in gross grants to the holder the right to enter and make use of the property of another
for a particular purpose.[6] An easement in gross attaches to the person and not to land.[7] An easement in gross is an easement
benefiting a particular person and not a particular piece of land.[8] An easement in gross is personal only to the grantee and,
therefore, cannot be apportioned to another unless the owner of the fee intended to permit apportionment.[9]

The principal distinction between an easement proper, that is an easement appurtenant, and a right in gross is found in the fact
that in the first there is and in the second there is not a dominant estate.[10] An "easement in gross" is an easement with a servient
estate but no dominant estate.[11] There is a servient estate created by an easement in gross, but no dominant estate, because the
easement benefits its holder whether or not the holder owns or possesses other land.[12]

It is a general rule that an easement in gross cannot extend beyond the life of the grantee;[13] unlike easements appurtenant, an
easement in gross is personal and ordinarily cannot be assigned or transmitted by descent.[14] However, there is authority that
an easement in gross is an alienable, and thus a transferable, property right.[15] It has also been held that parties to an easement
in gross may create an assignable easement through an express assignment provision.[16]

---

1. Title - Easements
2. Section
3. C.J.S. on Westlaw integrates all updates and is current through stated date so no need to consult pocket parts for updates.

## ILLUSTRATION 6-6.   *Continued*

> **1 Rule from case**
> **2 Footnote number indicates citation to case**

§ 18.Easements in gross, 28A C.J.S. Easements § 18

Easements in gross, whether affirmative or negative, are by statute recognized interests in real property, rather than merely personal covenants not capable of being disposed of by deed or will.[17] ②

An easement in gross is of a commercial character when the use authorized by it results primarily in economic benefit rather than personal satisfaction.[18]

#### *Easement in gross becoming easement appurtenant.*

When an instrument purports to create an easement in favor of a grantee to facilitate some other parcel of land which the grantee does not presently own but subsequently acquires, the easement is an easement in gross until the land is acquired, at which time it becomes an easement appurtenant.[19]

Footnotes

1    Wash.—Roggow v. Haggerty, 27 Wash. App. 908, 621 P.2d 195 (Div. 3 1980).

**Not incident of possession**

The benefit of an easement in gross is not an incident of the possession of land, because the uses authorized do not benefit a possessor of land in the use of the land possessed.

Ind.—Consolidation Coal Co. v. Mutchman, 565 N.E.2d 1074 (Ind. Ct. App. 1990).

**Agreements for signs**

Although invariably labeled "leases," agreements for the erection of advertising signs or for the placement of such signs on walls or fences are easements in gross.

N.Y.—XAR Corp. v. Di Donato, 76 A.D.2d 972, 429 N.Y.S.2d 59 (3d Dep't 1980).

2    N.H.—Tanguay v. Biathrow, 937 A.2d 276 (N.H. 2007), as modified on denial of reconsideration, (Dec. 4, 2007).

**Nonpossessory interest in land**

Tex.—Farmer's Marine Copper Works, Inc. v. City of Galveston, 757 S.W.2d 148 (Tex. App. Houston 1st Dist. 1988).

**Incorporeal nonpossessory right**

N.H.—Burcky v. Knowles, 120 N.H. 244, 413 A.2d 585 (1980).

3    U.S.—U.S. v. Turoff, 701 F. Supp. 981 (E.D. N.Y. 1988).

Ark.—Merriman v. Yutterman, 291 Ark. 207, 723 S.W.2d 823 (1987).

Cal.—Moylan v. Dykes, 181 Cal. App. 3d 561, 226 Cal. Rptr. 673 (3d Dist. 1986).

Idaho—Abbott v. Nampa School Dist. No. 131, 119 Idaho 544, 808 P.2d 1289, 67 Ed. Law Rep. 296 (1991).

Kan.—Allingham v. Nelson, 6 Kan. App. 2d 294, 627 P.2d 1179 (1981).

Mich.—Evans v. Holloway Sand and Gravel, Inc., 106 Mich. App. 70, 308 N.W.2d 440 (1981).

R.I.—McAusland v. Carrier, 880 A.2d 861 (R.I. 2005).

**Right to maintain water pipes**

Where interests reserved under plat, which dedicated streets but reserved to dedicator, his associates and assigns, the exclusive right to maintain water pipes and water mains and other items in such streets, was not created to benefit dedicator as possessor of tract of land, but was reserved to him for commercial purposes, such interest was not an appurtenant easement, but, rather, was an easement in gross.

Or.—Sunset Lake Water Service Dist. v. Remington, 45 Or. App. 973, 609 P.2d 896 (1980).

4    Ariz.—Ammer v. Arizona Water Co., 169 Ariz. 205, 818 P.2d 190 (Ct. App. Div. 1 1991).

Ill.—Schnabel v. DuPage County, 101 Ill. App. 3d 553, 57 Ill. Dec. 121, 428 N.E.2d 671 (2d Dist. 1981).

# ILLUSTRATION 6-6. *Continued*

§ 18.Easements in gross, 28A C.J.S. Easements § 18

Ind.—Consolidation Coal Co. v. Mutchman, 565 N.E.2d 1074 (Ind. Ct. App. 1990).
Mo.—Henley v. Continental Cablevision of St. Louis County, Inc., 692 S.W.2d 825 (Mo. Ct. App. E.D. 1985).
N.H.—Burcky v. Knowles, 120 N.H. 244, 413 A.2d 585 (1980).
5   Va.—U.S. v. Blackman, 270 Va. 68, 613 S.E.2d 442 (2005).
6   N.H.—Tanguay v. Biathrow, 937 A.2d 276 (N.H. 2007), as modified on denial of reconsideration, (Dec. 4, 2007).
7   N.C.—Woodring v. Swieter, 180 N.C. App. 362, 637 S.E.2d 269 (2006).
8   Ill.—Kankakee County Bd. of Review v. Property Tax Appeal Bd., 226 Ill. 2d 36, 312 Ill. Dec. 638, 871 N.E.2d 38 (2007).
    Mich.—Heydon v. MediaOne, 275 Mich. App. 267, 739 N.W.2d 373 (2007).
9   Ohio—Walbridge v. Carroll, 172 Ohio App. 3d 429, 2007-Ohio-3586, 875 N.E.2d 144 (6th Dist. Wood County 2007).
10  U.S.—U.S. v. Turoff, 701 F. Supp. 981 (E.D. N.Y. 1988).
    Ala.—Weeks v. Wolf Creek Industries, Inc., 941 So. 2d 263 (Ala. 2006).
    Idaho—Nelson v. Johnson, 106 Idaho 385, 679 P.2d 662 (1984).
    Kan.—Allingham v. Nelson, 6 Kan. App. 2d 294, 627 P.2d 1179 (1981).
    Mo.—Henley v. Continental Cablevision of St. Louis County, Inc., 692 S.W.2d 825 (Mo. Ct. App. E.D. 1985).
    R.I.—McAusland v. Carrier, 880 A.2d 861 (R.I. 2005).
    Utah—Crane v. Crane, 683 P.2d 1062 (Utah 1984).
    Va.—Virginia Elec. and Power Co. v. Northern Virginia Regional Park Authority, 270 Va. 309, 618 S.E.2d 323 (2005).
11  R.I.—McAusland v. Carrier, 880 A.2d 861 (R.I. 2005).
    Va.—Virginia Elec. and Power Co. v. Northern Virginia Regional Park Authority, 270 Va. 309, 618 S.E.2d 323 (2005).
12  N.H.—Tanguay v. Biathrow, 937 A.2d 276 (N.H. 2007), as modified on denial of reconsideration, (Dec. 4, 2007).
13  N.H.—Burcky v. Knowles, 120 N.H. 244, 413 A.2d 585 (1980).
14  Cal.—Moylan v. Dykes, 181 Cal. App. 3d 561, 226 Cal. Rptr. 673 (3d Dist. 1986).
    Mo.—Hodges v. Lambeth, 731 S.W.2d 880 (Mo. Ct. App. E.D. 1987).
    N.H.—Burcky v. Knowles, 120 N.H. 244, 413 A.2d 585 (1980).
    Tex.—Farmer's Marine Copper Works, Inc. v. City of Galveston, 757 S.W.2d 148 (Tex. App. Houston 1st Dist. 1988).
15  Mich.—Heydon v. MediaOne, 275 Mich. App. 267, 739 N.W.2d 373 (2007).
16  Tex.—Farmer's Marine Copper Works, Inc. v. City of Galveston, 757 S.W.2d 148 (Tex. App. Houston 1st Dist. 1988).
**③** 17  Va.—U.S. v. Blackman, 270 Va. 68, 613 S.E.2d 442 (2005).
18  Utah—Crane v. Crane, 683 P.2d 1062 (Utah 1984).
19  Wash.—Beebe v. Swerda, 58 Wash. App. 375, 793 P.2d 442 (Div. 1 1990).

**End of Document**                                                    © 2014 Thomson Reuters. No claim to original U.S. Government Works.

**3 Citation
supporting rule
in footnote 17**

Reprinted with permission of Thomson Reuters.

## 4. State Law Encyclopedias

▼ Are There Any Legal Encyclopedias for State Law?

Yes, almost every jurisdiction has a legal encyclopedia. Illinois, for example, has *Illinois Law and Practice*, commonly known as I.L.P. I.L.P. is published by West and refers the reader to the other West resources such as the key numbers and the digests. West publishes many state encyclopedias such as *Florida Jurisprudence Second* and *Texas Jurisprudence Third*.

## 5. Online Encyclopedia Services

▼ Are Legal Encyclopedias Available on Lexis or Westlaw?

Legal encyclopedias are available online. Am. Jur. is on Lexis. Selected portions of C.J.S. are on Westlaw. Am. Jur. is on Westlaw as well. Cornell University Legal Information Institute has a free legal encyclopedia called Wex. Wex can be accessed at topics.law.cornell.edu/wex.

# E. *AMERICAN LAW REPORTS*

▼ What Are *American Law Reports*?

The *American Law Reports* (A.L.R.), published by West, contain annotations on narrow, well-defined legal topics. Each volume contains at least a half dozen annotations, or in-depth articles, about a legal issue as well as the pivotal case that prompted the examination of the issue inspiring the editors to write the annotation. Subjects common to A.L.R. are torts, property, contracts, sales, and criminal law. Federal and state law are combined in A.L.R. until 1969. A.L.R. Federal (A.L.R. Fed.) began to be published in 1969. A.L.R. is in its 6th series. In print and updated with pocket part supplements are A.L.R., A.L.R.2d, A.L.R.3d, A.L.R.4th, A.L.R.5th, and A.L.R.6th. A.L.R. is published sequentially, just like case reporters, so that when a number of annotations are written, although they may bear no subject relationship to one another (just as with opinions), a volume of A.L.R. is published. A new volume is published about every six weeks.

Each volume of A.L.R. contains cases and annotations. The first section in each volume is a list entitled Subjects Annotated in this Volume. This provides a cross-reference for the annotations in the volume. The next section is Table of Cases Reported, which lists the full text decisions in the volume. Because every annotation is developed from a pivotal legal decision, A.L.R. reprints the full text of that decision before the annotation. Beginning with A.L.R.5th, the decisions are now found in the back of each volume.

As an example, let's look at the annotation entitled *Locating Easement of Way Created by Necessity*. The first page containing library references

leads you to many other relevant practice aids. See Illustration 6-7. The next entry is a detailed outline of the annotation so that if you are interested in only a portion of the discussion, you can focus your research efforts. There is also an index, just for each annotation, so that you can see which subjects are discussed by section. See Illustration 6-8. Following the annotation's index is the Table of Jurisdictions Represented. Then Illustration 6-9 on page 173 shows the Table of Cases, Laws, and Rules accessed on WestlawNext. The Table of Cases, Laws, and Rules makes A.L.R. a unique resource because each annotation includes every relevant statute or case from all of the appropriate jurisdictions. Think of an annotation as a survey of law on a particular issue. This is a windfall for the researcher. If possible, obtain this table on either Lexis or Westlaw because all of new cases are included weekly.

**ILLUSTRATION 6-7.   Total Client-Service Library References at 36 A.L.R.4th 769 (1985)**

---

ANNOTATION

**LOCATING EASEMENT OF WAY CREATED BY NECESSITY**

*by*

*William B. Johnson, J.D.*

---

**TOTAL CLIENT-SERVICE LIBRARY® REFERENCES**

25 Am Jur 2d, Easements and Licenses §§ 64–69

Annotations: See the related matters listed in the annotation, infra.

9 Am Jur Pl & Pr Forms (Rev), Easements and Licenses, Forms 41–48

3 Am Jur Proof of Facts 2d 647, Abandonment of Easement; 5 Am Jur Proof of Facts 2d 621, Intent to Create Negative Easement; 33 Am Jur Proof of Facts 2d 669, Extent of Easement Over Servient Estate

22 Am Jur Trials 743, Condemnation of Easements

L Ed Index to Annos, Real Property; Trespass

ALR Quick Index, Access; Adjoining or Abutting Landowners; Easements; Ingress and Egress; Place or Location; Right of Way; Trespass; Way by Necessity

Federal Quick Index, Adjoining Landowners and Property; Easements and Right of Way; Ingress; Place and Location; Trespass

Auto-Cite®: Any case citation herein can be checked for form, parallel references, later history, and annotation references through the Auto-Cite computer research system.

Reprinted with permission of Thomson Reuters.

**ILLUSTRATION 6-8.   Outline of Annotation at 36 A.L.R.4th 770 (1985)**

---

EASEMENT OF WAY BY NECESSITY—LOCATION      36 ALR4th
36 ALR4th 769
**Locating easement of way created by necessity**

I. PRELIMINARY MATTERS

§  1. Introduction:
    [a] Scope
    [b] Related matters
§  2. Summary and comment:
    [a] Generally
    [b] Practice pointers

II. AT COMMON LAW

A. GENERAL PRINCIPLES

§  3. Existing way as that intended
§  4. Right of servient owner to designate location
§  5. Right of dominant owner to designate location
§  6. Requirement of consent to change location

B. APPLICATION IN PARTICULAR SITUATIONS

§  7. Where there was prior use of one way:
    [a] Location along way used in past
    [b] Location along other route
§  8. Where there was prior use of multiple ways:
    [a] Location along route preferred, or to be selected, by servient owner
    [b] Location along route preferred by dominant owner

III. UNDER STATUTE

§  9. Initial location:
    [a] Location along existing way supportable
    [b] Location along existing way not established
§ 10. Relocation

---

**INDEX**

Acquiescence, generally, §§ 6, 7[a]
Aerial photographs, § 9[a]
Agricultural land, §§ 7-9
Alternative ways, preferred location, §§ 8, 9
Apartment building, § 7[a]
Barriers, §§ 5, 7[a], 8[b], 9[a]
Bridges, §§ 7[a], 9[a]
Burial grounds, §§ 7[a], 8[a]
Cattle grazing area, §§ 7, 9[a]
Cemeteries, §§ 7[a], 8[a]
Change or relocation, §§ 6, 10
Child-parent conveyances or inheritances, §§ 7[a], 8[b], 9[a]

Comment and summary, § 2
Common law, §§ 3-8
Consent to change location, § 6
Covenant against encumbrances, § 7[a]
Decedents' estates, §§ 7[a], 8[b], 9[a]
Deed covenant against encumbrances, § 7[a]
Deed reservation of right-of-way, § 7[a]
Designation of location, generally, §§ 4, 5, 8
Estates, §§ 7[a], 8[b], 9[a]
Expert testimony, § 9[a]
Family burial grounds, §§ 7[a], 8[a]
Family conveyances and inheritances,

**770**

---

Reprinted with permission of Thomson Reuters.

▼ How Do You Use A.L.R.?

There are four basic methods of using A.L.R.

1. **The index method.** A.L.R. has a subject index for A.L.R.2d through A.L.R.5th, A.L.R.6th, A.L.R. Fed., A.L.R. Fed. 2d, and *U.S. Supreme Court Reports, Lawyers' Edition.* See Illustration 6-10. It also contains a *Table of Statutes, Rules, and Regulations.* A.L.R. (first series) has a separate index. The index method requires that you find descriptive words for the issue or topic you are researching in one of A.L.R.'s

# ILLUSTRATION 6-9. Table of Cases, Laws, and Rules at 36 A.L.R.4th 771 (1985) from Westlaw

**Table of Cases, Laws, and Rules**

**Arkansas**
> Nation v. Ayres, 340 Ark. 270, 9 S.W.3d 512 (2000) — 9[a]
> White v. Grimmett, 223 Ark. 237, 265 S.W.2d 1 (1954) — 10

**California**
> Kripp v. Curtis, 71 Cal. 62, 11 P. 879 (1886) — 4, 5, 7[a]

**Colorado**
> De Reus v. Peck, 114 Colo. 107, 162 P.2d 404 (1945) — 2[b]

**Louisiana**
> Bandelin v. Clark, 7 La. App. 64, 1927 WL 3637 (1st Cir. 1927) — 9[a]
> Breeden v. Lee, 2 La. App. 126, 1925 WL 3669 (1st Cir. 1925) — 2[b], 9[b]
> Broussard v. Etie, 11 La. 394, 1837 WL 818 (1837) — 9[b]
> Bulliard v. Delahoussaye, 481 So. 2d 747 (La. Ct. App. 3d Cir. 1985) — 9[b]
> Collins v. Reed, 316 So. 2d 134 (La. Ct. App. 3d Cir. 1975) — 9[a]
> Dickerson v. Coon, 71 So. 3d 1135 (La. Ct. App. 2d Cir. 2011) — 6.5
> Howes v. Howes, 499 So. 2d 314 (La. Ct. App. 1st Cir. 1986) — 9[a]
> Inabnet v. Pipes, 241 So. 2d 595 (La. Ct. App. 2d Cir. 1970) — 10
> Littlejohn v. Cox, 15 La. Ann. 67, 1860 WL 5503 (1860) — 9[b]
> Martini v. Cowart, 23 So. 2d 655 (La. Ct. App. 2d Cir. 1945) — 9[a]
> Mercer v. Daws, 186 So. 877 (La. Ct. App. 2d Cir. 1939) — 9[a], 10
> Morgan v. Culpepper, 324 So. 2d 598 (La. Ct. App. 2d Cir. 1975) — 9[b]
> Rieger v. Norwood, 401 So. 2d 1272 (La. Ct. App. 1st Cir. 1981) — 9[a]
> Roberson v. Reese, 376 So. 2d 1287 (La. Ct. App. 2d Cir. 1979) — 9[b]
> Watson v. Scott, 349 So. 2d 982 (La. Ct. App. 2d Cir. 1977) — 9[a], 9[b]

**Tennessee**
> McMillan v. McKee, 129 Tenn. 39, 164 S.W. 1197 (1914) — 4, 5, 8[a]
> Pearne v. Coal Creek Min. & Mfg. Co., 90 Tenn. 619, 18 S.W. 402 (1891) — 7[a], 7[b]

**Texas**
> Grobe v. Ottmers, 224 S.W.2d 487 (Tex. Civ. App. San Antonio 1949) — 4, 5, 6, 7[a]
> Missouri-Kansas-Texas Ry. Co. of Texas v. Cunningham, 273 S.W. 697 (Tex. Civ. App. Amarillo 1925) — 4, 5, 6
> Parker v. Bains, 194 S.W.2d 569 (Tex. Civ. App. Galveston 1946) — 6, 8[b]
> Samuelson v. Alvarado, 847 S.W.2d 319 (Tex. App. El Paso 1993) — 4, 6

**Vermont**
> Jenne v. Piper, 69 Vt. 497, 38 A. 147 (1897) — 4, 7[a]

Reprinted with permission of Thomson Reuters.

indexes. The index is very detailed and has a pocket part supplement to update it. This is a very efficient method. A.L.R. also has a separate index entitled the *Quick Index,* which covers the broadest topics and index entries for A.L.R.3rd through A.L.R.6th.

The A.L.R. Index is available on Westlaw and WestlawNext. You can access the index on WestlawNext by clicking Secondary Sources, then selecting "ALR". On the right side of the screen, you will see "Tools and Resources". Under "Tools and Resources" click ALR Index, then enter your terms in the search bar. If you have a specific phrase or group of words, then you may consider entering the terms in quotes. For the example in illustration 6-10, the search terms were: "easement of way created by necessity." The phrase is in quotation marks because the exact phrase is searched. The online index is easy to use, you can use phrases that may appear in an annotation or any relevant term, it is updated frequently, and you can link to the annotation with a click. See Illustration 6-10.

NET NOTE

Boston University Law School Library has an online guide on how to use A.L.R., which is available at www.bu.edu/lawlibrary/research/guides/alr.html.

2. **The digest method.** The A.L.R. Digest is organized like any other digest in topics and sections. Each section stands for a point of law. Under the digest entry is an encyclopedia reference to Am. Jur., if relevant, and to the case that stands for that premise of law. If a case is given a digest entry, then you may assume that an annotation will follow the case in the A.L.R. volume. This is a very good way to find multiple cases and multiple annotations dealing with related legal issues. This method is best when you find a good case that forms the basis for an annotation. Not every library has the A.L.R. Digest, so check.

3. **The computerized method.** This is the best method of accessing A.L.R. annotations when available. Lexis has the full text of A.L.R. online, as does Westlaw. Using online access permits you to search for relevant annotations using the words that you think would appear in an annotation on point.

4. *Shepard's.* This is also an excellent way to find A.L.R. annotations. *Shepard's* lists any A.L.R. citations in which the case you are Shepardizing is cited. When you Shepardize a case, check to see if there are any A.L.R. references; they would appear at the end of the citation list.

# ILLUSTRATION 6-10.   A.L.R. Index Entry

EASEMENTS, A.L.R. Index

A.L.R. Index

American Law Reports
Index updated January 2013

Index to Annotations
EASEMENTS

EASEMENTS

Abandonment of property
    loss of private easement by nonuse, 25 ALR2d 1265, 62 ALR5th 219
    private easement in way vacated, abandoned, or closed by public, 150 ALR 644
Access
    misuse of easement, what constitutes, and remedies for, misuse of easement, 111 ALR5th 313
    roads. Access roads, in this topic
    scope of prescriptive easement for access (easement of way), 79 ALR4th 604
Access roads
    grant which does not specify location, 24 ALR4th 1053, § 5, 8, 13(b)
    inadequate access, way of necessity where a means of access does exist, but is claimed to be inadequate, inconvenient, difficult, or costly, 10 ALR4th 447
    locating **easement** of **way created** by **necessity**, 36 ALR4th 769
    part of land is inaccessible, 10 ALR4th 500
Adoption as period of prescription for easement the period prescribed by statute of limitations with reference to adverse possession as including condition of color of title or right or other conditions imposed by that statute, 112 ALR 545
Adverse possession
    boundaries, easement by prescription for use of land near boundary line, 58 ALR 1037
    building, adverse possession based on encroachment of building or other structure, 2 ALR3d 1005, § 3(a, b), 8 to 11
    loss of private easement by nonuser or adverse possession, 25 ALR2d 1265, 62 ALR5th 219
    prescriptive easements, adoption as period of prescription for easement the period prescribed by statute of limitations with reference to adverse possession as including condition of color of title or right or other conditions imposed by that statute, 112 ALR 545
    prescriptive easements, in this topic
    presumptions and evidence respecting identification of land on which property taxes were paid to establish adverse possession, 36 ALR4th 843, § 6(a)
    private easement, loss by adverse possession or nonuse, 25 ALR2d 1265, 62 ALR5th 219
Aerial photographs
    admissibility of evidence of aerial photographs, 85 ALR5th 671
    locating **easement** of **way created** by **necessity**, 36 ALR4th 769, § 9(a)
Alleys
    location, easement of way created by grant which does not specify location, 24 ALR4th 1053, § 9(a)
    maps, conveyance with reference to map or plat as giving purchaser rights in indicated streets, alleys, or areas not

## ILLUSTRATION 6-10. *Continued*

EASEMENTS, A.L.R. Index

environmental impact statements, necessity and sufficiency of environmental impact statements under § 102(2)(C) of National Environmental Policy Act of 1969 (42 U.S.C.A. § 4332(2)(C)) in cases involving logging, mining, and related projects, 74 ALR Fed 702, § 3(b)

private easement, loss by nonuse, 62 ALR5th 219, § 10, 30(a), 42(a), 49(a), 55, 59, 25 ALR2d 1320

railroads, deed to railroad company as conveying fee or easement, 6 ALR3d 973, § 6(b), 7, 8

Loss of easements

adverse possession, loss of easement by adverse possession, or nonuser, 25 ALR2d 1265, 62 ALR5th 219

logs and timber, private easement, loss by nonuse, 62 ALR5th 219, § 10, 30(a), 42(a), 49(a), 55, 59, 25 ALR2d 1320

Lots and parcels, roadway or pathway used at time of severance of tract as visible or apparent easement, 164 ALR 1001

Maps and plats

conveyance with reference to map or plat as giving purchaser rights in indicated streets, alleys, or areas not abutting his lot, 7 ALR2d 607

grant, easement of way created by grant which does not specify location, 24 ALR4th 1053, § 9(a), 14

necessity, easement of way created by necessity, locating, 36 ALR4th 769, § 9(a)

private easement, loss by nonuse, 62 ALR5th 219

Marketable record title statutes, construction and effect of, 31 ALR4th 11, § 7

Mechanic's lien for labor or material for improvement of easement, 77 ALR 817

Mines and minerals

crops, construction and effect of provision for payment of damages to crops or growing crops in mineral deed or lease, or in conveyance of pipeline or other underground easement, 87 ALR2d 235

private easement, loss by nonuse, 62 ALR5th 219

private easement as to mineral and quarry rights, loss by nonuser, 25 ALR2d 1320

reservation of right, effect, as between lessor and lessee, of provision in mineral lease purporting to except or reserve a previously granted right of way or other easement through, over, or upon the premises, 49 ALR2d 1191

Misuse

abandonment, waiver, or forfeiture of easement on ground of misuse, 16 ALR2d 609

forfeitures

abandonment, waiver, or forfeiture of easement on ground of misuse, 16 ALR2d 609

misuse of easement, or violation of conditions of its enjoyment, as ground of forfeiture, 78 ALR 1222

what constitutes, and remedies for, misuse of easement, 111 ALR5th 313

Mortgages

appurtenances, easement appurtenant to land, created subsequent to mortgage of dominant estate, as inuring to the benefit of the mortgagee or of purchaser at foreclosure sale and his subsequent grantees, 116 ALR 1078

foreclosure of mortgage or trust deed as affecting easement claimed in, over, or under property, 46 ALR2d 1197

Motor vehicles, parking on private way, 37 ALR2d 944

Moving and relocation

assistance, validity, construction, and application of state relocation assistance laws, 49 ALR4th 491, § 11

necessity, locating easement of way created by necessity, 36 ALR4th 769, § 6, 10

private parties, relocation (other than those originally arising by necessity); rights as between private parties, 80 ALR2d 743

Navigable water, easement by way of necessity where property is accessible by navigable water, 9 ALR3d 600

Necessity, way of

accessibility, way of necessity over another's land where a means of access does exist, but is claimed to be inadequate, inconvenient, difficult, or costly, 10 ALR4th 447

cessation of easement of way by necessity upon cessation of necessity, 103 ALR 993

grade of land, in this topic

highways and streets, in this topic

## ILLUSTRATION 6-10. *Continued*

EASEMENTS, A.L.R. Index

> hills, in this topic
>> inadequate access, way of necessity over another's land, where a means of access does exist, but is claimed to be inadequate, inconvenient, difficult, or costly, 10 ALR4th 447
>> locating **easement** of **way created** by **necessity**, 36 ALR4th 769
>> navigable water, way by necessity where property is accessible by navigable water, 9 ALR3d 600
>> part of land, way of necessity where only part of land is inaccessible, 10 ALR4th 500
>> private easement, loss by nonuse, 62 ALR5th 219
>> unity of title, what constitutes unity of title or ownership sufficient for creation of an easement by implication or way of necessity, 94 ALR3d 502
> Nonuse, loss of private easement by nonuser or adverse possession, 25 ALR2d 1265, 62 ALR5th 219
> Notice of easement, physical conditions which will charge purchaser of servient estate with notice of easement, 74 ALR 1250
> Nuisances, acquisition of easement or other property right by prescription, predicated upon acts amounting to a private

Reprinted with permission of Thomson Reuters.

### ▼ Why Would You Use A.L.R.?

A.L.R. is best consulted when you are researching a narrow, well-defined issue, similar to how you might use a law review article. The major difference between A.L.R. and a law review article is that A.L.R. provides you with indexed terms, an outline, a table of law from other jurisdictions, and library references to encyclopedias, form books, and digest topics. A.L.R., however, is not considered nearly as scholarly as a law review article. An A.L.R. annotation will provide you with a good understanding of a narrow, well-defined legal issue if an annotation is available on point. A.L.R. annotations are great finding tools because you are led to relevant primary authority, which you then must read.

It is best not to cite A.L.R. annotations and to not rely on them as authority unless absolutely necessary. Cite to the primary source materials that A.L.R. annotations provide after reading the primary authority to determine its relevance.

### ▼ How Do You Cite to an A.L.R. Annotation?

Citation style for the hard-copy A.L.R. is found in *Bluebook* **Rule 16.7.6** and *ALWD* **Rule 22.6**, as follows:

> William B. Johnson, Annotation, <u>Locating Easement of Way Created by Necessity</u>, 36 A.L.R.4th 769 (1985 & Supp. 2013).

*ALWD* requires italicizing the article title.

For the online version, *ALWD* format:

William B. Johnson, Annotation, *Locating Easement of Way Created by Necessity,* 36 A.L.R.4th 769 (1985) (accessed on Westlaw current through January 2014).

### ▼ How Do You Update an A.L.R. Annotation?

A.L.R. (first series) Volumes 1 to 175 are updated in the *Blue Book of Supplemental Decisions.* This is a separate set of books that comes out every two years that updates the annotations in Volumes 1 to 175. It also indicates where annotations have been superseded or supplemented in later editions or series of the A.L.R. Entries are organized by volume and page numbers.

A.L.R.2d is updated by using the separate set entitled the *A.L.R.2d Later Case Service.* All entries are found by volume and page numbers.

To update A.L.R.3d, 4th, 5th, 6th, or Fed. Annotations, consult the pocket part supplement to the volume to see if additional annotations and new statute and case law references are mentioned. Pocket parts are issued at least annually.

For any annotation, if using hard copy resources, consult the Annotation History Table in the Tables volume to see if the annotation is superseded.

The best and easiest way to update an A.L.R. annotation is to access the annotation on either Westlaw or Lexis. This may be costly in practice, so it is still important to know how to use the books. When you retrieve the annotation on a commercial database, weekly additions of new cases integrate the updates into the annotations. You will also be told if the annotation is superseded.

### ▼ Can A.L.R. Annotations Be Shepardized?

A.L.R. annotations can be Shepardized to see where they are cited in reported opinions and to see if a case reprinted in the A.L.R. has a parallel cite in a reporter. This information is found in *Shepard's Citations for Annotations.* Most researchers do not Shepardize annotations because they are not primary authority but rather lead you to primary sources on point.

## F. TREATISES AND HORNBOOKS

### ▼ What Are Treatises and Hornbooks?

Both hornbooks and treatises are secondary sources because they provide commentary, analysis, and criticism of the law and are written by private parties. Treatises and hornbooks help the researcher to understand the topic and, through cited references, provide citations to cases and statutes. **Treatises** are scholarly works, generally multivolume sets, that

examine one legal topic, such as contracts, in great detail and with very broad coverage. **Hornbooks**, also scholarly but designed for the student of law, are generally one-volume works providing an overview of a single legal topic. The authors of hornbooks and treatises are legal scholars.

### ▼ How Do You Find a Thorough Treatise or Hornbook?

The best place to look for a hornbook or treatise is in the law library. The librarian will be able to refer you to the treatises that are best for the legal topic you are researching. There is a treatise for almost every legal subject. Many hornbooks are published by West Publishing Co. At the beginning of a West hornbook is a list entitled *Hornbook Series and Basic Legal Texts*, which provides all of the hornbooks categorized by legal subject.

**NET NOTE**

The Harvard Law School Library provides a comprehensive list of treatises by subject at guides.library.harvard.edu/legaltreatises.

### ▼ Which Treatises Are Most Noteworthy?

The following example treatises are well known and respected.

> Corbin, *Contracts*
> Herzog, *Bankruptcy Forms and Practice*
> LaFave, *Principles of Criminal Law*
> McCormick, *Evidence*
> Rotunda and Nowak, *Constitutional Law*
> Prosser, *Torts*

### ▼ Why Do You Use a Treatise?

There are a few approaches to using a treatise. Because the treatise covers a single legal topic and is written like a text, rather than like a case opinion, it is easy to find relevant information. The amount of relevant information may present the only problem when using a treatise: so much detail is provided that you may lose sight of the focus of your research. A treatise is used to find a very detailed analysis of a point of law or a legal rule. A hornbook is used to find an overview of a point of law or a legal rule. Both sources provide the general rules of law, its exceptions, and information on how the law is evolving. Often, a treatise

or hornbook offers discussion of how the legal rules are applied in specific situations or in specific factual scenarios. You should use a treatise or a hornbook to educate yourself in a legal discipline or when an encyclopedia does not offer adequate detail in the discussion of a topic.

---

*PRACTICE POINTER*

You can use Google Scholar, at scholar.google.com, to find books too.

---

### ▼ How Do You Use a Treatise or Hornbook?

There are three methods of using a treatise or a hornbook.

1. **The table of contents method.** Treatises and hornbooks have detailed tables of contents that serve as outlines of the legal topics covered. A chapter or a subchapter often discusses the area you are researching.
2. **The table method.** Hornbooks and treatises contain tables of cases and tables of statutes. Use the relevant table when you have an excellent case or statute on point and want to understand the significance of the primary source in the context of the subject as a whole.
3. **The index method.** A subject index is found at the end of every treatise and hornbook. The index is a good place to start if you have found a word like *easement* and want to find out its relevance in property law.

### ▼ Are Treatises Ever Relied on as Authority?

Treatises are occasionally relied on as authority in a document when no primary authority is available on point and when it is necessary to show the progression or evolution of the law. Because scholars write treatises, they are considered to be very prestigious sources of secondary authority. Hornbooks should not be relied on for authority because they are designed for the student and are one-volume versions of treatises that support the study of the particular legal discipline.

### ▼ How Do You Cite to a Hornbook and a Treatise?

*Bluebook* **Rule 15.1** covers citation style for treatises and hornbooks. *ALWD* **Rule 20.1** uses the same format.

Wayne LaFave, *Search and Seizure: A Treatise on the Fourth Amendment* (4th ed. 2004 & Supp. 2010).

### ▼ Are Treatises Available Online?

More and more treatise titles are appearing online. Westlaw, because it is part of West, makes an increasing number of treatise titles available online, and its list is growing. Often updates are available online so that you can access the newest case references. Lexis also has an expanding number of treatises available. The benefit of using a treatise online is that you can perform full text searching whereby you construct a query and retrieve relevant information with your own selection of terms rather than relying on any of the traditional research methods. Some treatises are now available on the Internet.

### ▼ How Are Treatises and Hornbooks Updated?

Treatises are updated in two ways: pocket parts or supplements, which are published at least annually, and new editions. Always check to see that you are working with the most recent edition available and to see if there is a pocket part or updating supplement.

## G. RESTATEMENTS OF THE LAW

### ▼ What Are Restatements?

**Restatements of the Law**, published by the American Law Institute, are the most prestigious source of secondary authority. The subjects covered are agency, conflict of laws, contracts, foreign relations, judgments, property, restitution, security, torts, and trusts. There is a Restatement on Security, but this set is only in the first edition. Each of the legal disciplines mentioned comprises a separate set of the Restatements. The authors of the Restatements write every rule of law from these legal disciplines in a form that resembles a code and not a judicial opinion. The drafters of the Restatements are "restating" the law. The purposes are to codify the common law holdings so that a researcher does not have to unearth the legal rule from the text of an opinion and to make common law principles straightforward and succinct, like statutes. The Comments and the Illustrations are most helpful in understanding the application of the rule. The Reporter's Note, following the Illustrations, contains case references in which the Restatement section has been cited. See Illustration 6-11.

Washburn University has an excellent research guide for the Restatements at washburnlaw.edu/library/research/guides/restatements.html.

## ▼ How Are the Restatements Updated?

Most of the Restatements are in their second series. A few, such as Trusts, are in the third series. The rules, the codified-type versions of the legal principles, are updated in the appendix. Additional case references are also included in the appendix. The appendix is organized by section in the same order as the main text. The appendix is updated annually by pocket part supplements that are organized in the same manner as the main volume, by section. Also, the *Cumulative Annual Supplement* lists newer cases citing to the particular Restatement provision.

## ▼ How Do You Use the Restatements?

1. **The table of contents method.** Every set of the Restatements begins with a table of contents. See Illustration 6-12. The table of contents is an outline of the entire legal discipline, by topic and then within the topic, by rule. This is not a very efficient method, but it gives the researcher insight into where the section fits into the legal discipline. For instance, § 235 of the Restatement (Second) of Contracts is entitled Effect of Performance as Discharge & of Non-Performance as Breach. This section falls under Topic 2, Effect of Performance & Non-Performance, which is part of Chapter 10.
2. **The index method.** Use the index at the end of the set by looking up various descriptive words pertaining to your issue.
3. **The table of cases method.** When you have an excellent case on point, use the table of cases, organized in alphabetical order by plaintiff, to find references in the Restatements. This is the most efficient method when you have a specific case on point. Be sure to check the pocket part to locate references to newer cases.
4. **The online method.** The Restatements are available on Lexis and Westlaw. This is an efficient method to use when you know the significant vocabulary words that describe the subject. If you are unfamiliar with the terminology or the words used to describe the legal principles, then the online method is very costly and not very efficient. However, case citations for Restatement sections are kept current online and are easy to use.

## ▼ Can the Restatements Be Shepardized?

Yes, the Restatements can be Shepardized in the *Shepard's Restatement of Law Citations*. The *Shepard's* for the Restatements does not in any way validate the authority because the Restatements are secondary sources. *Shepard's*, in this instance, is a citator telling the researcher which cases contain citations to the particular Restatement section. Finding a case that cites your Restatement section may be helpful because a court may adopt the language from the Restatement section. On Lexis, you can Shepardize the Restatement provision when the section is on the screen.

**ILLUSTRATION 6-11.   Sample Pages from Restatement (Second) of Contracts**

---

**Ch. 10   PERFORMANCE AND NON-PERFORMANCE   § 235**

on Illustration 6 to former § 267. Beach v. First Fed. Sav. & Loan Ass'n, 140 Ga. App. 882, 232 S.E.2d 158 (1977). Illustration 5 is adapted from Illustration 7 to former § 267.

*Comment c.* See former § 272. Illustration 6 is based on Illustration 1 to former § 268 and on Kane v. Hood, 30 Mass. (13 Pick.) 281 (1832). Illustration 7 is based on Illustration 2 to former § 268.

*Comment d.* This Comment replaces former § 273. See 3A Corbin, Contracts § 689 (1951); 6 Williston, Contracts § 887C (3d ed. 1962). Illustration 8 is based on Illustration 2 to former § 273 and on Beecher v. Conradt, 13 N.Y. (3 Kern.) 108 (1855); see also Kennelly v. Shapiro, 222 A.D. 488, 226 N.Y.S. 692 (1928).

*Comment e.* On the origin of the principle, see 6 Williston, Contracts §

830 (3d ed. 1962); Murray, Contracts § 162 (2d rev. ed. 1974). That a substantial failure to make timely progress payments is a material breach when the payments are required by a construction contract, see United States ex rel. Micro-King Co. v. Community Science Technology, Inc., 574 F.2d 1292, 1295 n.3 (5th Cir. 1978).

*Comment f.* Illustration 9 is based on Stewart v. Newbury, 220 N.Y. 379, 115 N.E. 984 (1917). See also Illustration 1 to former § 270. Illustration 10 is based on Clark v. Gulesian, 197 Mass. 492, 84 N.E. 94 (1908). The facts in Illustration 11 are taken from New Era Homes v. Forster, 299 N.Y. 303, 86 N.E.2d 757 (1949). Illustration 12 is based on Comment *a* to former § 270 and Illustration 1 to former § 268.

### TOPIC 2.   EFFECT OF PERFORMANCE AND NON-PERFORMANCE

**§ 235.   Effect of Performance as Discharge and of Non-Performance as Breach**

(1) Full performance of a duty under a contract discharges the duty.

(2) When performance of a duty under a contract is due any non-performance is a breach.

**Comment:**

a. *Discharge by performance.* Under the rule stated in Subsection (1), a duty is discharged when it is fully performed. Nothing less than full performance, however, has this effect and any defect in performance, even an insubstantial one, prevents discharge on this ground. The defect need not be wilful or even negligent. Although a court may ignore trifling departures, performance that is merely substantial does not result in discharge under Subsection (1). See Comment *d* to § 237. A duty may, of course, be discharged on some other ground. See Chapter 12. For example, a duty that has not been fully

See Appendix for Court Citations and Cross References

211

---

▼ Are the Restatements Available Online?

Yes, as mentioned earlier, the Restatements are available online on both Lexis and Westlaw. The advantage of searching the Restatements online is that you do not have to rely on indexing terms. However, using

## ILLUSTRATION 6-11. *Continued*

performed may be discharged on the ground of impracticability of performance. See Chapter 11.

**Illustration:**

1. A contracts to build a house for B for $50,000 according to specifications furnished by B. A builds the house according to the specifications. A's duty to build the house is discharged.

*b. Effect of non-performance.* Non-performance is not a breach unless performance is due. Performance may not be due because a required period of time has not passed, or because a condition has not occurred (§ 225), or because the duty has already been discharged (Chapter 12) as, for example, by impracticability of performance (Chapter 11). In such a case non-performance is justified. When performance is due, however, anything short of full performance is a breach, even if the party who does not fully perform was not at fault and even if the defect in his performance was not substantial. Non-performance of a duty when performance is due is a breach whether the duty is imposed by a promise stated in the agreement or by a term supplied by the court (§ 204), as in the case of the duty of good faith and fair dealing (§ 205). Non-performance includes defective performance as well as an absence of performance.

**Illustrations:**

2. The facts being otherwise as stated in Illustration 1, A builds the house according to the specifications except for an inadvertent variation in kitchen fixtures which can easily be remedied for $100. A's non-performance is a breach.

3. A contracts with B to manufacture and deliver 100,000 plastic containers for a price of $100,000. The colors of the containers are to be selected by B from among those specified in the contract. B delays in making his selection for an unreasonable time, holding up their manufacture and causing A loss. B's delay is a breach. His duty of good faith and fair dealing (§ 205) includes a duty to make his selection within a reasonable time.

4. A contracts with B to repair B's building for $20,000, payment to be made "on the satisfaction of C, B's architect, and the issuance of his certificate." A makes the repairs but does not ask C for his certificate. B does not pay A. B's non-performance is not a breach. It is justified on the ground that performance is not due because of the non-occurrence of a condition. See Illustration 6 to § 227.

the Restatements online can be very expensive if you are unfamiliar with the legal terms used.

### ▼ How Are the Restatements Cited?

*Bluebook* **Rule 12.9.5** indicates that Restatements are cited as follows:

Restatement (Second) of Contracts § 235 (1979).

The year that the Restatement section was published is on the title page of every Restatements volume.

When citing to a Comment or Illustration that follows the Restatement section, **Rule 3.4** of the *Bluebook* applies:

**ILLUSTRATION 6-12.   Table of Contents from Restatement (Second) of Contracts**

Section
153.  When Mistake of One Party Makes a Contract Voidable
154.  When a Party Bears the Risk of a Mistake
155.  When Mistake of Both Parties as to Written Expression Justifies
       Reformation
156.  Mistake as to Contract Within the Statute of Frauds
157.  Effect of Fault of Party Seeking Relief
158.  Relief Including Restitution

Chapter 7

MISREPRESENTATION, DURESS AND
UNDUE INFLUENCE

Introductory Note

TOPIC 1.   MISREPRESENTATION

Introductory Note
159.  Misrepresentation Defined
160.  When Action Is Equivalent to an Assertion (Concealment)
161.  When Non-Disclosure Is Equivalent to an Assertion
162.  When a Misrepresentation Is Fraudulent or Material
163.  When a Misrepresentation Prevents Formation of a Contract
164.  When a Misrepresentation Makes a Contract Voidable
165.  Cure by Change of Circumstances
166.  When a Misrepresentation as to a Writing Justifies Reformation
167.  When a Misrepresentation Is an Inducing Cause
168.  Reliance on Assertions of Opinion
169.  When Reliance on an Assertion of Opinion Is Not Justified
170.  Reliance on Assertions as to Matters of Law
171.  When Reliance on an Assertion of Intention Is Not Justified
172.  When Fault Makes Reliance Unjustified
173.  When Abuse of a Fiduciary Relation Makes a Contract Voidable

TOPIC 2.   DURESS AND UNDUE INFLUENCE

Introductory Note
174.  When Duress by Physical Compulsion Prevents Formation of a
       Contract
175.  When Duress by Threat Makes a Contract Voidable
176.  When a Threat Is Improper
177.  When Undue Influence Makes a Contract Voidable

Volume 2

Chapter 8

UNENFORCEABILITY ON GROUNDS OF PUBLIC POLICY

Introductory Note

Copyright © 1981 by the American Law Institute. Reprinted with permission. All rights reserved.

Restatement (Second) of Contracts § 235 cmt. a, illus. 2 (1979).

Note that this is the date adopted.

*ALWD* **Rule 23.1** format, for citing to a comment that follows the Restatement section, requires that the year be the date of the volume publication. For example:

*Restatement (Second) of Contracts* § 235 cmt. a (1981).

# H. LEGAL PERIODICALS

## ▼ What Are Legal Periodicals?

**Legal periodicals** are secondary sources ranging from very prestigious to very practical forms of authority. Scholarly law review articles are

considered the most prestigious, and bar journals and commercial publications are considered the most pragmatic. The major categories of legal periodicals are:

1. academic law reviews
2. bar journals and practitioner's periodicals
3. commercial journals and newsletters
4. legal newspapers

Every conceivable subject is covered in a legal periodical. Some legal periodicals focus on a particular practice area, like estate planning. The different forms of legal periodicals have different attributes. Although not scholarly, legal blogs are a source of very current commentary on legal events and legislation.

## ▼ Why Would You Use a Legal Periodical?

Legal periodicals are published quickly and keep abreast of new legal issues and laws. They are a terrific place to obtain articles discussing the impact of a Supreme Court decision or the enactment of new legislation because such information is published very quickly, far faster than any text could be printed. Also, certain legal periodicals (for example, the practitioner's journals, the journals that pertain to specific bar association sections, the commercial journals, and newsletters) cover discrete legal subject areas and enable paralegals, practitioners, and researchers to keep up with all of the new developments in their respective practice areas. The website for a particular legal periodical or journal is also a terrific resource. You can also use Google to search for blogs and publications on a particular topic. When using a search engine such as Google, you may receive an abundance of hits that may not all be relevant.

The legal newspapers provide up-to-date information about the legal profession, the courts and significant opinions, the federal and state legislatures and significant laws, and information about law firms and the business of law. Legal newspapers also write about major and interesting cases and clients. Legal newspapers provide great insight into the realities of legal practice. Additionally, national newspapers such as *The New York Times, The Washington Post,* and *The Wall Street Journal* offer up-to-the-minute coverage of legal events with timely articles on seminal cases, U.S. Supreme Court activity, and pending legislation. National newspapers are a terrific resource to follow activity in the U.S. Congress. The papers' websites are updated very frequently and often provide links to the legislation or court decision under discussion.

Academic law review articles are very scholarly and are excellent finding tools because of the voluminous number of cited references in each article. Academic law review articles are often theoretical and discuss the application of a particular legal doctrine or a trend in the law. Sometimes authors of law review articles suggest how the law should hold

on certain issues. Because the academic law reviews are a very prestigious source of secondary authority, sometimes these resources are relied on for persuasive purposes when no primary authority is available on point.

▼ How Do You Obtain Relevant Legal Periodical Articles?

First, the researcher must decide the type of information needed. For example, is scholarly material required, or is practical information on drafting a will needed? After deciding on the type of information required for the project, the source should be selected accordingly. If scholarly material is required, then an academic law review would be appropriate. If practical information is needed, then a practitioner's journal, bar association section newsletter, or commercial publication dealing with the legal discipline is appropriate. If the researcher needs information about a law firm, a client, or a very recent (two-week-old) Supreme Court decision, then a legal newspaper is the ideal source.

Almost all legal periodicals, regardless of format, are indexed. The major indexes are:

*Current Law Index* (1980 to present): the most comprehensive hard-copy index. Published monthly, by Gale.

*LegalTrac* is the Web-based version of *Current Law Index.*

*Current Index to Legal Periodicals.*

*Index to Foreign Legal Periodicals* (1960 to present).

HeinOnline: an easy-to-use subscription database.

LexisWeb.com: a free searchable database. You will obtain summaries and citations, but then you will have to sign on to Lexis, with a subscription account, to read most articles in full-text.

Google Scholar at scholar.google.com: a free search engine for citations to legal articles and law journals. It provides abstracts of articles.

NET NOTE

Many law reviews have their own websites. Start with the law school website. Also, you can do a full-text search of journals on the Web at lawreview.org. The University Law School Project sponsors this site. Findlaw also has journal access at stu.findlaw.com/journals. Another free resource is www.hg.org/journals.html.

### ▼ Are Legal Periodicals Available on Lexis and Westlaw?

Yes, legal periodicals are available online on both Lexis and Westlaw. Both databases have full text articles, cover to cover, of an increasing number of law reviews. Also, the NEWS library on Lexis contains the full text copies of legal newspapers. Westlaw has the full text articles from an increasing number of law reviews. Most law reviews have websites, so you may be able to access the journal directly. For Lexis and Westlaw this may be a costly way to obtain a citation to a law review article.

### ▼ How Do You Cite to a Law Review or Law Journal?

*Bluebook* **Rule 16**, with **Table 13** for abbreviations, and *ALWD* **Rule 21**, with **Appendix 5** for abbreviations, cover the citation form:

Mitchell N. Berman, *Justification and Excuse, Law and Morality*, 53 Duke L.J. 1 (2003).

A legal newspaper is cited according to *Bluebook* **Rule 16.6** and *ALWD* **Rule 21.3**. For example:

Wayne Smith, *Remote Access: Striking a Balance*, Law Tech. News, Jan. 2005, at 11.

Using all formats of secondary sources can be reinforced with the tutorial found at www.law.georgetown.edu/library/research/guides/secondary.cfm.

### ▼ What Is a Blog?

Blogs are a very current source of information. The material may or may not be verified or edited. You will often not have links to primary authority. However, blogs can not be overlooked for their up-to-the-minute commentary and policy coverage.

To cite to a blog, consult **Rule 18.1** in the *Bluebook*, also called dynamic webpages. Sometimes blogs are called Direct Internet Resources because they do not have any print equivalent. The citation formats for Direct Internet Resources are in *Bluebook* **Rule 18.2.2** and *ALWD* **Rule 31.3**.

# CHAPTER SUMMARY

Secondary authorities describe, analyze, and criticize primary sources. You use secondary authorities to educate yourself about a legal topic and to find citations to primary sources.

The major sources of secondary authority are dictionaries, thesauri, encyclopedias, *American Law Reports* (A.L.R.), hornbooks, treatises, Restatements of the Law, and legal periodicals.

The dictionary and the thesaurus are used to find definitions and synonyms. Encyclopedias are used to educate yourself about a legal topic. *American Law Reports* contain articles called annotations that explore a legal issue in depth. Hornbooks are written for the student of law and cover a single legal subject. Treatises cover a single legal subject but go into great detail. Restatements of the Law, produced by the American Law Institute, attempt to organize common law holdings from cases into a format resembling statutes. Legal periodicals include academic law reviews, bar association and legal specialty publications, and legal newspapers. Law reviews are the most scholarly form of legal periodicals. Law review articles contain many citations to primary authority and are known for research accuracy.

Updating and correctly citing secondary authorities are important in your research process. Generally, it is best to rely on primary authority when writing a memo or a brief. Rely on secondary authority when there is no primary authority on point.

# KEY TERMS

*American Jurisprudence*
*American Law Reports*
*Corpus Juris Secondum*
Cumulative Supplements
hornbooks
legal dictionary
legal encyclopedia

legal meaning
legal periodicals
Restatements of the Law
secondary authority
thesaurus
treatises

# EXERCISES

## COMPARING SECONDARY AUTHORITIES

1. Look up the word *easement* in a legal dictionary. Now look up the same word in a thesaurus. Compare the two sources and the information provided. What is different?

   Now look up the word *easement* in your state legal encyclopedia (if you do not have a state legal encyclopedia available, use Am. Jur. or C.J.S.). How is the term treated in an encyclopedia? How is this different from a dictionary?

## ENCYCLOPEDIA RESEARCH

2. Locate the section in Am. Jur. 2d discussing *easements by necessity*. First, try to locate the section by using the index method, then by the topic outline method. Go to the encyclopedia volume for the sections that you found. Examine the treatment of *easements by necessity*. Do you see any cases from your state? Now update the section in the pocket part. Are there any new case references?

   Repeat this exercise using C.J.S. How do the encyclopedias differ? How are they similar?

3. Look up Pawnbroker in the index of C.J.S. or Am. Jur. 2d. Are there any encyclopedia sections discussing pawnbrokers? Now look up *Pawnbroker* in your state legal encyclopedia. Are there any relevant cases or statutes from your state?

4. Look up *gaming* in C.J.S. How is the topic organized?

   Go to the index for C.J.S. and look up *casinos*. Where can you find discussion of *casinos* in C.J.S.? In the index entry *casinos*, are there references to sections outside the topic of *gaming*?

   Now, go to the pocket part at the end of the volume containing the topic *gaming*. Does the pocket part contain updates to the topic of *gaming*?

   List one recent case mentioned in the pocket part. Is it a state case or a federal case?

   What do topic updates in the pocket part look like? How are they different, in general, than the entries in the main volume for the topic?

5. Use Am. Jur. 2d. Is there a topic called *gaming*? What similar topic covers the subject of gaming in Am. Jur. 2d?

   Go to the index in Am. Jur. 2d and look up *gaming*. Where are you led to?

   Compare the text in the main volume of Am. Jur. 2d that covers a topic similar to the *gaming* topic in C.J.S. How are the topics similar and how are they different?

   Does Am. Jur. 2d have a pocket part to the main volume that updates the topics?

   Using the index to Am. Jur. 2d, look up *casinos*. What do you find?

6. How are Am. Jur. 2d and C.J.S. similar? How are they different?

   What research benefits do you obtain when consulting a legal encyclopedia?

   Do either Am. Jur. 2d or C.J.S. lead you to other library resources or research tools? List two of the additional research tools.

7. Look up *negligence* in a law dictionary. Look up *negligence* in either C.J.S. or Am. Jur. 2d. What did you find in each source? How do the sources differ in their treatment of *negligence*?

### Assignment for Encyclopedia Research

8. Read the following fact situation, which you first encountered in Chapter 4. Answer the questions following the situation.

FACTS

Nate Late, a business owner, has two partners in the operation of Loose Cannon Manufacturing in Gurnee, Illinois. He owns $33\frac{1}{3}$ percent of a $3 million company. Late is ill, but not dying. He is grooming a 26-year-old, Ivan T. All, to run the business. He tells his family he likes All and wants to teach him the business. Nate Late dies.

The most current will leaves Late's estate to his wife of 24 years, Shirley Late, and his only son, Lou Sier. Mr. All tells Mrs. Late that her husband told All he intended to give the 26-year-old his one-third interest in Loose Cannon. This conversation took place in front of a bank president. No written record exists concerning Late's intention to give his stock to All. However, family members knew that Late intended for All to run the business and for All to get something if the business was sold. None of the family believed that Late intended to give the business to newcomer Ivan T. All. Late's shares of stock were never given to All. The shares were in the safe deposit box shared by Late and his wife.

Mrs. Late said that Mr. Late planned to give her the shares. He told her this when he opened the joint safety deposit box and gave her the key.

You work for a firm that has been retained by Mrs. Late. She would like to know if All can prove that Mr. Late gave All Mr. Late's interest in the company.

    a. What topics might be relevant to this question?

    b. How would you determine where to find those topics?

    c. List the steps that you would take.

    d. Take those steps. Note what you find.

    e. Select two topics for review. Review those topics. Which topics were most relevant?

    f. What additional information did you find to determine the answer to Mrs. Late's question?

    g. Where did you find that information?

9. Use Google Scholar to find a citation to an article about using Facebook as evidence for a divorce.

10. Use LexisWeb.com to find the citation to an article discussing "Cybercrime."

11. Consult Google Scholar. Is there a citation to an article on the topic of easements to make repairs?

12. On Westlaw, search Pennsylvania legal encyclopedia or *Pennsylvania Jurisprudence* for an entry on easements concerning "Private Ways and Alleys."

13. Consult *Florida Jurisprudence Second* on Westlaw. List citations to sections concerning easements, alleys, and rights-of-way.

## CHAPTER 7

# CONSTITUTIONS AND STATUTES

| | |
|---|---|
| **A. CONSTITUTIONS** | 194 |
| **B. STATUTES** | 201 |
| 1. The Legislative Process | 201 |
| 2. Reading and Understanding Statutes | 215 |
| 3. How to Find Federal Statutes | 216 |
| 4. Validating and Updating Statutes | 226 |
| 5. How to Find State Statutes | 231 |
| 6. Researching Statutes Online | 234 |

## *CHAPTER OVERVIEW*

Constitutions and statutes occupy the highest rung in the hierarchy of authority. Constitutions are the highest form of legal authority, only to be followed by statutes. In ordinary legal dilemmas, statutes are often the controlling law. In our society statutes govern relationships like marriage and adoption, transactions like banking, and behavior like criminal acts. Learning how to find relevant statutes and constitutional provisions is very important for effective legal research.

This chapter details the research methods used to find, to cite, and to validate constitutions and statutes. The legislative process that charts the path that a statute takes from initial sponsorship through codification is outlined. This chapter gives you the skills you need to perform constitutional and statutory research.

## A. CONSTITUTIONS

### ▼ What Is a Constitution?

A **constitution** is a document that establishes the legal structure of a state or nation and the basic legal principles that control the operation of the government and the conduct of its citizens.

### ▼ What Is the Relationship Between the Federal Constitution and the State Constitutions?

The U.S. Constitution is, in essence, the supreme law of the land. The state constitutions are the supreme law of each particular state. The federal constitution takes precedence over any state constitution. What does this mean? Only the U.S. Congress can repeal or redraft legislation or amend the U.S. Constitution. If a federal court determines that a state constitutional provision violates the U.S. Constitution, then the court must deem that section of the state constitution unconstitutional.

### ▼ Who Determines Whether a Statute Violates the U.S. Constitution?

Federal courts determine whether a statute violates the U.S. Constitution, and state courts determine if their respective state constitutions are being violated. Although courts determine if a statute violates the constitution, courts cannot rewrite or repeal statutes; only legislatures can.

### ▼ Can Federal and State Constitutions Be Validated?

Yes, federal and state constitutions can be validated. KeyCite, *Shepard's on Lexis,* and *Shepard's United States Citations* indicate if a court of law has interpreted or applied a section of the U.S. Constitution in question. KeyCite and *Shepard's* serve to validate the authority and are finding tools to obtain relevant case law decisions applying the constitutional section or amendment at issue in your research. See Illustration 7-1. Illustration 7-2 (see page ●●●) shows the *Go-Bart* decision and where the Fourth Amendment is discussed in the case (see arrow in Illustration 7-1 indicating cases citing the Fourth Amendment, including *Go-Bart.*). State constitutions are validated in the particular state code *Shepard's* or on KeyCite. For a full discussion of how to validate authority, see Chapter 5.

### ▼ Where Are Federal and State Constitutions Found?

The full text of the current version of the U.S. Constitution as well as all the amendments are contained in the first volume of the annotated versions of the *United States Code* (U.S.C.), the *United States Code Service* (U.S.C.S.), and the *United States Code Annotated* (U.S.C.A.).

**ILLUSTRATION 7-1. Sample Page, Retrieved from Lexis, Showing Analysis of Fourth Amendment with Citing Decisions**

Copyright 2014 SHEPARD'S(R) - 101 Citing references

**U.S. Const. amend. 4**

Restrictions: *U.S. Supreme Court; Restrict prior to year 1934*
FOCUS(TM) Terms: *No FOCUS terms*
Print Format: *FULL*
Citing Ref. Signal: *Hidden*

**SHEPARD'S SUMMARY**

| Restricted *Shepard's* Summary:   U.S. Supreme Court; Restrict prior to year 1934 |
| --- |
| **Citing References:** |

| Unrestricted *Shepard's* Summary | |
| --- | --- |
| **Citing References:** | |
| Positive Analyses: | Concurring Opinion (865), Followed (236) |
| Citing Decisions: | Construes (311), Dissenting Op. (2223), Interprets (318), Not Applicable (465), Quest. Precedent (196) |
| Other Sources: | Law Reviews (883), Secondary Sources (87), Other Citations (13) |

**LEGISLATIVE HISTORY** ( 7 citing references )

1. **Cited by:**
   *1945 Fla. Laws*
   1945C23176 ~16

2. **Cited by:**
   *1953 Fla. Laws*
   1953C28884 ~46

3. **Cited by:**
   *1955 Fla. Laws*
   1955p915

4. **Cited by:**
   *1961 Fla. Laws*
   1961C1866 ~48

## ILLUSTRATION 7-1. *Continued*

---

SHEPARD'S® - U.S. Const. amend. 4 - 101 Citing References

5. **Cited by:**
   *1927 Minn. Laws*
   1927C66~11

6. **Cited by:**
   *1933 Minn. Laws*
   1933C408 ~15

7. **Cited by:**
   *1963 Minn. Laws*
   1963C849~1

**CITING DECISIONS** ( 94 citing decisions )

**U.S. SUPREME COURT**

8. **Cited by:**
   *Nathanson v. United States*, 290 U.S. 41, 54 S. Ct. 11, 78 L. Ed. 159, 1933 U.S. LEXIS 961 (1933)
   290 U.S. 41 *p.41*
   78 L. Ed. 159 *p.159*
   54 S. Ct. 11 *p.11*

9. **Cited by:**
   *Sgro v. United States*, 287 U.S. 206, 53 S. Ct. 138, 77 L. Ed. 260, 1932 U.S. LEXIS 13, 85 A.L.R. 108
   (1932)
   287 U.S. 206 *p.206*
   53 S. Ct. 138 *p.138*
   77 L. Ed. 260 *p.260*

10. **Cited by:**
    *Grau v. United States*, 287 U.S. 124, 53 S. Ct. 38, 77 L. Ed. 212, 1932 U.S. LEXIS 9 (1932)
    287 U.S. 124 *p.124*
    77 L. Ed. 212 *p.212*
    53 S. Ct. 38 *p.38*

11. **Cited by:**
    *Taylor v. United States*, 286 U.S. 1, 52 S. Ct. 466, 76 L. Ed. 951, 1932 U.S. LEXIS 593 (1932)
    286 U.S. 1 *p.1*
    76 L. Ed. 951 *p.951*
    52 S. Ct. 466 *p.466*

12. **Cited by:**

# ILLUSTRATION 7-1.  *Continued*

SHEPARD'S® - U.S. Const. amend. 4 - 101 Citing References

*United States v. Lefkowitz*, 285 U.S. 452, 52 S. Ct. 420, 76 L. Ed. 877, 1932 U.S. LEXIS 446, 82 A.L.R. 775 (1932)
    285 U.S. 452 *p.452*
    52 S. Ct. 420 *p.420*
    76 L. Ed. 877 *p.877*

13. **Cited by:**
*Crowell v. Benson*, 285 U.S. 22, 52 S. Ct. 285, 76 L. Ed. 598, 1932 U.S. LEXIS 773, 1932 A.M.C. 355 (1932)
    285 U.S. 22 *p.37*
    52 S. Ct. 285 *p.287*
    76 L. Ed. 598 *p.604*

14. **Cited by:**
*Blackmer v. United States*, 284 U.S. 421, 52 S. Ct. 252, 76 L. Ed. 375, 1932 U.S. LEXIS 882 (1932)
    284 U.S. 421 *p.441*
    52 S. Ct. 252 *p.256*
    76 L. Ed. 375 *p.385*

15. **Cited by:**
*Husty v. United States*, 282 U.S. 694, 51 S. Ct. 240, 75 L. Ed. 629, 1931 U.S. LEXIS 37, 74 A.L.R. 1407 (1931)
    282 U.S. 694 *p.694*
    51 S. Ct. 240 *p.240*

16. **Cited by:**
*Alford v. United States*, 282 U.S. 687, 51 S. Ct. 218, 75 L. Ed. 624, 1931 U.S. LEXIS 36 (1931)
    75 L. Ed. 624 *p.629*

17. **Cited by:**
➤ *Go-Bart Importing Co. v. United States*, 282 U.S. 344, 51 S. Ct. 153, 75 L. Ed. 374, 1931 U.S. LEXIS 842 (1931)
    282 U.S. 344 *p.345*
    75 L. Ed. 374 *p.375*
    51 S. Ct. 153 *p.154*

18. **Cited by:**
*Sinclair v. United States*, 279 U.S. 263, 49 S. Ct. 268, 73 L. Ed. 692, 1929 U.S. LEXIS 339 (1929)
    279 U.S. 263 *p.293*
    73 L. Ed. 692 *p.698*
    49 S. Ct. 268 *p.272*

19. **Cited by:**
*Olmstead v. United States*, 277 U.S. 438, 48 S. Ct. 564, 72 L. Ed. 944, 1928 U.S. LEXIS 694, 66 A.L.R. 376

Reprinted with the permission of LexisNexis. Editor's Note: See online document for complete report.

**ILLUSTRATION 7-2.** Page from Decision in *U.S. Reports* That Discusses the Fourth Amendment

---

344         OCTOBER TERM, 1930.

Syllabus.         282 U. S.

to do business within a state. In those cases the judgment of this Court in no way restricts the further exercise of the legislative power of the state in any constitutional manner. Here the Commission is ousted from the exercise of power which Congress has given it, and an order is sanctioned authorizing an issue of securities which it cannot be said the Commission has approved, and which this Court does not purport to say is appropriate under the statute.

MR. JUSTICE HOLMES and MR. JUSTICE BRANDEIS concur in this opinion.

---

GO-BART IMPORTING COMPANY ET AL. *v.* UNITED STATES.

CERTIORARI TO THE CIRCUIT COURT OF APPEALS FOR THE SECOND CIRCUIT.

No. 111. Argued November 25, 1930.—Decided January 5, 1931.

1. A warrant issued by a United States Commissioner, addressed only to the Marshal and his deputies, and based upon, and reciting the substance of, a complaint that was verified merely on information and belief and that did not state an offense,—*held* invalid on its face, and no authority to prohibition officers to make an arrest. P. 355.
2. Acting under color of an invalid warrant of arrest, and falsely claiming to have a search warrant, prohibition agents entered the office of a company, placed under arrest two of its officers, and made a general search of the premises. They compelled by threats of force the opening of a desk and safe, and seized therefrom and from other parts of the office, papers and records belonging to the company and its officers. The officers of the company were arraigned before a United States Commissioner, and by him held on bail further to answer the complaint (U. S. C., Title 18, § 591), while the seized papers were held under the control of the United States Attorney in the care and custody of the prohibition agent in charge. The company, and its two officers individually, before

**ILLUSTRATION 7-2.** *Continued*

344 Syllabus.

an information or indictment had been returned against them;
applied to the District Court for an order to enjoin the use of the
seized papers as evidence and directing their return. On a rule
against the United States to show cause, the United States Attorney
appeared and opposed the motion and an affidavit of the agent in
charge was also filed in opposition. The applications were denied.
*Held:*

(1) In the proceedings before him, the Commissioner acted
merely as an officer of the District Court in a matter of which it
had authority to take control at any time. P. 353.

(2) Notwithstanding the order to show cause was addressed to
the United States alone, the proceeding was in substance and effect
against the United States Attorney and the prohibition agent in
charge, the latter being required by the Prohibition Act to report
violations of it to the former and being authorized by the statute,
subject to the former's control, to conduct such prosecutions; and
both these officers were subject to the proper exertion of the disciplinary powers of the court. P. 354.

(3) The District Court had jurisdiction summarily to determine
whether the evidence should be suppressed and the papers returned
to the petitioners. P. 355.

(4) The company being a stranger to the proceedings before
the Commissioner, the order of the District Court as to it was
final and appealable. P. 356.

(5) There being no information or indictment against the officers
of the company when the application was made, and nothing to
show that any criminal proceeding would ever be instituted in that
court against them, it follows that the order was not made in or
dependent upon any case or proceeding pending before the court,
and therefore the order as to them was appealable. *Id.*

(6) The Fourth Amendment forbids every search that is unreasonable, and is to be liberally construed. P. 356.

(7) Assuming that the facts of which the arresting officers had
been previously informed were sufficient to justify the arrests
without a warrant, nevertheless the uncontradicted evidence requires a finding that the search of the premises was unreasonable.
*Marron* v. *United States*, 275 U. S. 192, distinguished. P. 356.

(8) The District Court is directed to enjoin the United States
Attorney and the agent in charge from using the papers as evidence
and to order the same returned to petitioners. P. 358.

40 F. (2d) 593, reversed.

Encyclopedias are also sources of unannotated versions of the U.S. Constitution. Additionally, the full text of the U.S. Constitution is at www.usconstitution.net/const.html.

State constitutions are located in the first volume of the respective state code. Both the unannotated and the annotated state codes contain the state constitutions.

### ▼ How Do You Cite Federal or State Constitutions?

*Bluebook* **Rule 11** and *ALWD* **Rule 13** outline the format. The U.S. Constitution cite includes the particular article, section, and clause.

U.S. Const. art. II, § 2, cl. 1

This cite is used when you are referring to the body of the Constitution. A special citation format is required when you are referring to an amendment.

U.S. Const. amend. II

State constitutions are indicated by the name of the state in the *Bluebook* abbreviated format. *Bluebook* **Table 1** and *ALWD* **Appendix 1** indicate the accepted state name abbreviation. The postal abbreviation is not always used. The state of Washington's postal abbreviation is WA, but the citation abbreviation is Wash. A section of the Washington state constitution would be cited as follows:

Wash. Const. art. I, § 2

Years or dates are not included in citations to federal or state constitutions that are current. Parenthetical notations after the citation indicate the year only if a constitutional provision was repealed or amended. An example is the Eighteenth Amendment to the U.S. Constitution prohibiting the sale of liquor. This amendment was later repealed by the Twenty-First Amendment. *Bluebook* **Rule 11** and *ALWD* **Rule 13** use this example for the Prohibition amendment:

U.S. Const. amend. XVIII (repealed 1933)—*Bluebook* format

U.S. Const. amend. XVIII, *repealed by* U.S. Const. amend XXI—*ALWD* format

### ▼ Are Constitutions Available on Lexis and Westlaw?

The full text of the U.S. Constitution, in its current format, is available on Lexis. Westlaw has the full text of the current U.S. Constitution as well. The individual state constitutions are available on both Lexis and Westlaw.

### ▼ Are There Any Hard-Copy Digests or Other Finding Tools That Assist with Researching Federal Constitutional Issues?

Yes, the *United States Supreme Court Digest* (for a detailed explanation of how to use digests, see Chapter 3). Also, *Shepard's* and KeyCite are

terrific finding tools in that they provide cases and secondary sources citing to the particular part of the constitution you are researching. There are annotations discussing constitutional issues in the *American Law Reports Federal.*

Do not overlook hornbooks and treatises. Two excellent treatises on constitutional law are:

*Hornbook on Constitutional Law* by Nowak and Rotunda
*American Constitutional Law* by Fisher and Harriger

A treatise is the best place to start researching a constitutional law issue. Treatises explain the legal issues and indicate which cases are the most important. Treatises are particularly helpful in the area of constitutional law because the issues are very complex and require a high level of analysis. For more information on secondary sources, see Chapter 6.

# B. STATUTES

### ▼ What Are Statutes?

**Statutes** are the laws enacted by either a federal or a state legislature. The business of the legislature is to enact laws. Statutes, both state and federal, as well as municipal and county ordinances and charters, are primary authority.

## 1. The Legislative Process

### ▼ How Is a Statute Created Through the Federal Legislative Process?

Anyone can propose **legislation.** Very often special interest groups and law firms propose legislation. Once the legislation is proposed, a **sponsor** in the ranks of Congress must be found to introduce the legislation.

Legislation is generally introduced in the U.S. House of Representatives, but it can be introduced in the U.S. Senate. For purposes of our discussion, assume the legislation is introduced in the House. Once introduced, it is called a slip bill. The **slip bill** is given a numerical designation and is referred to the appropriate **House committee** and then often referred to a **subcommittee.** A committee print of the bill is created. Hearings are conducted on the bill to determine its impact and effectiveness. Various experts may testify at the hearings to give input as to the possible effects of the legislation or to offer insight as to the purpose the legislation will serve. The tangible result of the hearings is the transcript of the testimony. This records the testimony of experts and lobbyists and their exhibits.

The next stage is the presentation of the committee's report. The **committee report** is a very informative resource because it generally includes the purpose of the bill and the public policies that the bill

addresses. The bill is then debated on the floor of the House. The *Congressional Record*, which prints all activity occurring on the floor of both the House and the Senate, prints the transcripts of the debates. More policy information can be gathered from the debates. Flaws in the legislation can also be discerned from the text of the debates. The bill must pass by vote in the chamber of Congress in which it was initiated. In our example, the bill began in the House, so it would have to pass in the House before going to the Senate for approval.

When a bill is passed by the House and sent to the Senate, it must be referred to the appropriate committee and follow the identical route as it did in the first chamber. When the Senate passes its version of the bill, it may differ from the original House bill. Before the bill can become law, both chambers must pass the same version of the bill. If the House and the Senate pass different versions of the bill, the bill is referred to a **conference committee**, which issues a conference committee report and the conference committee version of the bill. The conference committee version is then submitted for votes in both chambers.

If both congressional chambers approve the same version, the bill is sent to the president for signing. If the president signs the bill, it becomes a slip law. If the president **vetoes** the bill, that is, refuses to approve it, the bill goes back to the Congress, and Congress may override the veto by a two-thirds majority vote in both the House and the Senate. If the president does not sign or veto the bill within ten days and the legislature is still in session, the bill automatically becomes law. Occasionally, the president uses a pocket veto. A **pocket veto** occurs when there are fewer than ten days left in the legislative session and the president neither signs nor vetoes the bill, but merely waits for the session to expire. If the session expires before the president acts on the bill, the bill dies because it did not survive the legislative session. If the sponsors are still interested in passing this legislation, it must be reintroduced, in either chamber, at the beginning of the next legislative session. If both chambers pass the bill in the same exact version, then it is sent again to the president for signing. The president has the same choices: sign or veto. If the president signs the bill, it becomes a slip law.

Consult www.gpo.gov/fdsys for a host of legislative information beginning with the 103rd Congress. This site is updated daily when bills are passed.

## ▼ What Are Slip Laws?

**Slip laws** are the first written presentation of enacted laws from a legislative body. Slip laws are identified by numbers, for example, Pub. L. No. 96-242. This cite is for a federal session law, or **public law**, for the amendments (to include the definition of "recycled wool") to the statute with the popular name: the Wool Products Labeling Act of 1939. The 96 indicates the congressional or legislative session, in this case the 96th Congress. The 242 indicates that it is the 242nd law passed by the 96th Congress. The slip laws are published in the order that they are enacted.

Slip laws can be obtained at federal government depository libraries (many university and large city libraries are government depository libraries), Congress.gov, or www.gpo.gov/fdsys, or purchased from the U.S. Government Printing Office. Slip laws can also be obtained from the law's sponsor in Congress. The annotated versions of the *United States Code* and the *United States Code Congressional and Administrative News* have advance services that publish the slip laws. Advance services are paperbound volumes that contain updated information published in advance of the bound volume or supplement.

## ▼ What Are Session Laws?

At the end of a congressional session, all of the laws created during the course of the session are numbered and given the designation of **session laws.** Session laws on the federal level, also known as public laws, are added to the *Statutes at Large* and receive a *Statutes at Large* citation. See Illustration 7-3 for the amendment to the Wool Products Labeling Act in the *Statutes at Large* at 94 Stat. 344. The text for the amendment to the Act, to include "recycled wool" in the *Statutes at Large* is identical to what is found in the earlier slip law.

## ▼ What Are the *Statutes at Large*?

The ***Statutes at Large*** are the compilation of the slip laws from the session of Congress that just ended. After each congressional session ends, the slip laws from that session are bound into at least one volume to form the *Statutes at Large*. The laws are published in chronological order rather than codified like the statutes because they document all legislation enacted during the congressional session. Unfortunately, the *Statutes at Large* volumes are not produced immediately after a congressional session. The *Statutes at Large* contain the public laws, or slip laws, as well as presidential proclamations and private laws. The wording of the session laws in the *Statutes at Large* is identical to the public law. The federal codes have tables indicating the *Statutes at Large* citation for a public law. See Illustration 7-3 for a reprint of the *Statutes at Large*. *Statutes at Large*, beginning with the 82nd Congress, is available at

www.gpoaccess.gov/statutes/index.html. See Illustration 7-9 for an example of the *Statutes at Large* and Public Law Numbers Table.

## ▼ What Is Codification?

Finally, the session laws are codified. **Codification** means that the session laws are grouped by subject and placed in the statutes according to their titles, which contain particular subject areas of the law. Unlike cases, which are published as the opinions are written, federal statutes are arranged by a defined group of 51 subject categories called titles. See Illustration 7-4 on page 206 for the list of titles. Statutes are updated during the course of a legislative session if the legislature proposes amendments or revisions. For instance, The Wool Products Labeling Act of 1939 was amended. The best finding tool for the appropriate statute, after it is codified, is a good index in an annotated statute set because we rely on unofficial codes for up-to-date information, editorial enhancements, and detailed indices. A new version of the official *United States Code* appears approximately every six years. In the interim, the Code is updated by slip laws and session laws. The *United States Code Annotated* on Westlaw and the *United States Code Service* on Lexis are updated weekly to include all new Congressional activity impacting the statute section you are researching. When accessing the relevant code section on either Lexis or Westlaw, there is no need to consult a pocket part supplement as all of the updates are integrated into the material retrieved. (See Illustration 7-7, for example.)

Constant updating is an essential component of statutory research. For instance, Pub. L. No. 96-242 (1996) updated the Wool Products Labeling Act of 1939 by amending the language of the statute to include recycled wool. Look carefully at Illustrations 7-5, 7-6, and 7-7 for amendments following the statute. These illustrations show how different publications provide information. Illustration 7-5 shows the text of the statute in the official United States Code for 2012. The official code does not show research enhancements or citing references. Looking at the unofficial codes in Illustrations 7-6 and 7-7, you will see legislative history references, relevant *Code of Federal Regulations* citations, research aids including practice materials and secondary sources, as well as cases citing the code section.

Staying current is essential when using statutory authority, because Congress passes new legislation continually during its sessions. Always check the year of the code volume and the year of the supplement, or pocket part, when researching statutory authority. The best way to make sure that the statute is in its most current form is to use the most recent compilation of an annotated statute and to update it with the pocket part supplements and the advance sheets for the code section, or pull up the statute section on Westlaw or Lexis to have all the updates. Now look at Illustration 7-15, which is the relevant page from the pocket part showing the sections. Note that § 68 is not included. This means that there are no new cases citing to § 68 and that § 68 has no new

# ILLUSTRATION 7-3. Sample Session Law Published in
## *Statutes at Large*

---

94 STAT. 344    PUBLIC LAW 96–242—MAY 5, 1980

Public Law 96–242
96th Congress

## An Act

May 5, 1980
[H.R. 4197]

To amend the Wool Products Labeling Act of 1939 with respect to recycled wool.

Wool Products
Labeling Act,
amendment.
15 USC 68.

*Be it enacted by the Senate and House of Representatives of the United States of America in Congress assembled,* That (a) section 2(c) of the Wool Products Labeling Act of 1939 (54 Stat. 1128) is amended to read as follows:

"(c) The term 'recycled wool' means (1) the resulting fiber when wool has been woven or felted into a wool product which, without ever having been utilized in any way by the ultimate consumer, subsequently has been made into a fibrous state, or (2) the resulting fiber when wool or reprocessed wool has been spun, woven, knitted, or felted into a wool product which, after having been used in any way by the ultimate consumer, subsequently has been made into a fibrous state.".

Repeal.

(b) Subsection (d) of section 2 of the Wool Products Labeling Act of 1939 is repealed.

(c) Subsections (e), (f), (g), (h), and (i) of section 2 of the Wool Products Labeling Act of 1939 and all references thereto are redesignated as subsections (d), (e), (f), (g), and (h), respectively.

(d) Section 2(d) of such Act, as redesignated by subsection (c) of this section, is amended by striking out ", reprocessed wool, or reused wool" and inserting in lieu thereof "or recycled wool".

15 USC 68b.

SEC. 2. Section 4(a)(2)(A) of the Wool Products Labeling Act of 1939 is amended—

(1) by striking out "(2) reprocessed wool; (3) reused wool" and inserting in lieu thereof "(2) recycled wool";

(2) by striking out "(4)" and inserting in lieu thereof "(3)"; and

(3) by striking out "(5)" and by inserting in lieu thereof "(4)".

Effective date.
15 USC 68 note.

SEC. 3. The amendments made by this Act shall take effect with respect to wool products manufactured on or after the date sixty days after the date of enactment of this Act.

Approved May 5, 1980.

---

LEGISLATIVE HISTORY:

HOUSE REPORT No. 96–795 (Comm. on Interstate and Foreign Commerce).
SENATE REPORT No. 96–655 (Comm. on Commerce, Science, and Transportation).
CONGRESSIONAL RECORD, Vol. 126 (1980):
    Mar. 11, considered and passed House.
    Apr. 23, considered and passed Senate.

## ILLUSTRATION 7-4.   Table of U.S.C. Titles from the U.S.C.S.

### TITLES OF UNITED STATES CODE

---

* 1. General Provisions

2. The Congress

* 3. The President

* 4. Flag and Seal, Seat of Government and the States

* 5. Government Organization and Employees; Appendix

6. Domestic Security

7. Agriculture

8. Aliens and Nationality

* 9. Arbitration

* 10. Armed Forces

* 11. Bankruptcy

12. Banks and Banking

* 13. Census

* 14. Coast Guard

15. Commerce and Trade

16. Conservation

* 17. Copyrights

* 18. Crimes and Criminal Procedure; Appendix

19. Customs Duties

20. Education

21. Food and Drugs

22. Foreign Relations and Intercourse

* 23. Highways

24. Hospitals and Asylums

25. Indians

26. Internal Revenue Code

27. Intoxicating Liquors

* 28. Judiciary and Judicial Procedure; Appendix

29. Labor

30. Mineral Lands and Mining

* 31. Money and Finance

* 32. National Guard

33. Navigation and Navigable Waters

† 34. [Navy]

* 35. Patents

* 36. Patriotic and National Observances, Ceremonies, and Organizations

* 37. Pay and Allowances of the Uniformed Services

* 38. Veterans' Benefits

* 39. Postal Service

* 40. Public Buildings, Property, and Works

* 41. Public Contracts

42. The Public Health and Welfare

43. Public Lands

* 44. Public Printing and Documents

45. Railroads

* 46. Shipping

47. Telegraphs, Telephones, and Radiotelegraphs

48. Territories and Insular Possessions

* 49. Transportation

50. War and National Defense; Appendix

* 51. National and Commercial Space Programs

---

\* This title has been enacted as positive law. However, any Appendix to the title has not been enacted as law.

† This title has been superseded by the enactment of Title 10 as positive law.

Titles of the United States Code which have been enacted into positive law are legal evidence of the general and permanent laws, while nonpositive law titles only establish prima facie the laws of the United States (1 USCS § 204(a)).

Reprinted with the permission of LexisNexis.

# ILLUSTRATION 7-5. Sample Page Showing 15 U.S.C. § 68 (2012)

---

## § 66. Short title

This subchapter may be cited as the "Webb-Pomerene Act".

(Apr. 10, 1918, ch. 50, § 6, as added Pub. L. 94–435, title III, § 305(c), Sept. 30, 1976, 90 Stat. 1397.)

### SUBCHAPTER III—LABELING OF WOOL PRODUCTS

## § 68. Definitions

As used in this subchapter—

(a) The term "person" means an individual, partnership, corporation, association, or any other form of business enterprise, plural or singular, as the case demands.

(b) The term "wool" means the fiber from the fleece of the sheep or lamb or hair of the Angora or Cashmere goat (and may include the so-called specialty fibers from the hair of the camel, alpaca, llama, and vicuna) which has never been reclaimed from any woven or felted wool product.

(c) The term "recycled wool" means (1) the resulting fiber when wool has been woven or felted into a wool product which, without ever having been utilized in any way by the ultimate consumer, subsequently has been made into a fibrous state, or (2) the resulting fiber when wool or reprocessed wool has been spun, woven, knitted, or felted into a wool product which, after having been used in any way by the ultimate consumer, subsequently has been made into a fibrous state.

(d) The term "wool product" means any product, or any portion of a product, which contains, purports to contain, or in any way is represented as containing wool or recycled wool.

(e) The term "Commission" means the Federal Trade Commission.

(f) The term "Federal Trade Commission Act" means the Act of Congress entitled "An Act to create a Federal Trade Commission, to define its powers and duties, and for other purposes", approved September 26, 1914, as amended, and the Federal Trade Commission Act approved March 21, 1938.

(g) The term "commerce" means commerce among the several States or with foreign nations, or in any Territory of the United States or in the District of Columbia, or between any such Territory and another, or between any such Territory and any State or foreign nation, or between the District of Columbia and any State or Territory or foreign nation.

(h) The term "Territory" includes the insular possessions of the United States and also any Territory of the United States.

(Oct. 14, 1940, ch. 871, § 2, 54 Stat. 1128; Pub. L. 96–242, § 1, May 5, 1980, 94 Stat. 344.)

### REFERENCES IN TEXT

The Act of September 26, 1914, referred to in subsec. (f), is act Sept. 26, 1914, ch. 311, 38 Stat. 717, as amended, which is classified generally to subchapter I (§ 41 et seq.) of this chapter. For complete classification of this Act to the Code, see section 58 of this title and Tables.

The Federal Trade Commission Act approved March 21, 1938, referred to in subsec. (f), is act Mar. 21, 1938, ch. 49, 52 Stat. 111, as amended. For complete classification of this Act to the Code, see Tables.

### AMENDMENTS

1980—Subsec. (c). Pub. L. 96–242, § 1(a), substituted "recycled wool" for "reprocessed wool" as term defined, designated existing definition as cl. (1), and added cl. (2).

Subsecs. (d) to (i). Pub. L. 96–242, § 1(b)–(d), redesignated subsecs. (e) to (i) as (d) to (h), respectively, and, in subsec. (d) as so redesignated, substituted "containing wool or recycled wool" for "containing wool, reprocessed wool, or reused wool". Former subsec. (d), which defined term "reused wool", was struck out.

### EFFECTIVE DATE OF 1980 AMENDMENT

Pub. L. 96–242, § 3, May 5, 1980, 94 Stat. 344, provided that: "The amendments made by this Act [amending this section and section 68b of this title] shall take effect with respect to wool products manufactured on or after the date sixty days after the date of enactment of this Act [May 5, 1980]."

### EFFECTIVE DATE

Act Oct. 14, 1940, ch. 871, § 12, 54 Stat. 1133, provided that: "This Act [this subchapter] shall take effect nine months after the date of its passage."

### SHORT TITLE OF 2006 AMENDMENT

Pub. L. 109–428, § 1, Dec. 20, 2006, 120 Stat. 2913, provided that: "This Act [amending section 68b of this title and enacting provisions set out as a note under section 68b of this title] may be cited as the 'Wool Suit Fabric Labeling Fairness and International Standards Conforming Act'."

### SHORT TITLE

Act Oct. 14, 1940, ch. 871, § 1, 54 Stat. 1128, provided that: "This Act [this subchapter] may be cited as the 'Wool Products Labeling Act of 1939'."

### SEPARABILITY

Act Oct. 14, 1940, ch. 871, § 13, 54 Stat. 1133, provided that: "If any provision of this Act [this subchapter], or the application thereof to any person, partnership, corporation, or circumstance is held invalid, the remainder of the Act and the application of such provision to any other person, partnership, corporation, or circumstance shall not be affected thereby."

### TRANSFER OF FUNCTIONS

For transfer of functions of Federal Trade Commission, with certain exceptions, to Chairman of such Commission, see Reorg. Plan No. 8 of 1950, § 1, eff. May 24, 1950, 15 F.R. 3175, 64 Stat. 1264, set out under section 41 of this title.

## § 68a. Misbranding declared unlawful

The introduction, or manufacture for introduction, into commerce, or the sale, transportation, or distribution, in commerce, of any wool product which is misbranded within the meaning of this subchapter or the rules and regulations hereunder, is unlawful and shall be an unfair method of competition, and an unfair and deceptive act or practice, in commerce under the Federal Trade Commission Act; and any person who shall manufacture or deliver for shipment or ship or sell or offer for sale in commerce, any such wool product which is misbranded within the meaning of this subchapter and the rules and regulations hereunder is guilty of an unfair method of competition, and an unfair and deceptive act or practice, in commerce within the meaning of the Federal Trade Commission Act.

This section shall not apply—

(a) To any common carrier or contract carrier in respect to a wool product shipped or delivered

**ILLUSTRATION 7-6.   Sample Pages Showing 15 U.S.C.A. § 68 (West 2009)**

---

**15 § 68**                                          **COMMERCE AND TRADE   Ch. 2**

**§ 68.   Definitions**

As used in this subchapter—

(a) The term "person" means an individual, partnership, corporation, association, or any other form of business enterprise, plural or singular, as the case demands.

(b) The term "wool" means the fiber from the fleece of the sheep or lamb or hair of the Angora or Cashmere goat (and may include the so-called specialty fibers from the hair of the camel, alpaca, llama, and vicuna) which has never been reclaimed from any woven or felted wool product.

(c) The term "recycled wool" means (1) the resulting fiber when wool has been woven or felted into a wool product which, without ever having been utilized in any way by the ultimate consumer, subsequently has been made into a fibrous state, or (2) the resulting fiber when wool or reprocessed wool has been spun, woven, knitted, or felted into a wool product which, after having been used in any way by the ultimate consumer, subsequently has been made into a fibrous state.

(Oct. 14, 1940, c. 871, § 2, 54 Stat. 1128;  May 5, 1980, Pub.L. 96–242, § 1, 94 Stat. 344.)

18

# ILLUSTRATION 7-6. *Continued*

Ch. 2  FEDERAL TRADE COMMISSION  **15 § 68**

## HISTORICAL AND STATUTORY NOTES

① **Revision Notes and Legislative Reports**
**1980 Acts.** Senate Report No. 96–655, see 1980 U.S. Code Cong. and Adm. News, p. 782.

**References in Text**
The Federal Trade Commission Act, referred to in subsec. (f), is Act Sept. 26, 1914, c. 311, 38 Stat. 717, as amended, which is classified generally to subchapter I (section 41 et seq.) of this chapter. For complete classification of this Act to the Code, see section 58 of this title and Tables.

**Amendments**
**1980  Amendments.** Subsec. (c). Pub.L. 96–242, § 1(a), substituted "recycled wool" for "reprocessed wool" as the term defined, designated the existing definition as cl. (1), and added cl. (2).

Subsec. (d).  Pub.L. 96–242, § 1(b) to (d), redesignated subsecs. (e) to (i) as (d) to (h), respectively, and, in subsec. (d) as so redesignated, substituted "containing wool or recycled wool" for "containing wool, reprocessed wool, or reused wool". Former subsec. (d), which defined the term "reused wool", was struck out.

**1940 Acts.** Section 12 of Act Oct. 14, 1940, provided that: "This Act [this subchapter] shall take effect nine months after the date of its passage."

**Transfer of Functions**
All executive and administrative functions of the Federal Trade Commission were, with certain reservations, transferred to the Chairman of such Commission by 1950 Reorg. Plan No. 8, § 1, eff. May 24, 1950, 15 F.R. 3175, 64 Stat. 1264, set out as a note under section 41 of this title.

**Separability of Provisions**
Section 13 of Act Oct. 14, 1940, provided that: "If any provision of this Act [this subchapter], or the application thereof to any person, partnership, corporation, or circumstance is held invalid, the remainder of the Act and the application of such provision to any other person, partnership, corporation, or circumstance shall not be affected thereby."

**Short Title**
**2006  Amendments.** Pub.L. 109–428, § 1, Dec. 20, 2006, 120 Stat. 2913, provided that: "This Act [amending 15

1 Citation to legislative history
2 References to administrative regulations
3 References to relevant secondary sources

## CODE OF FEDERAL REGULATIONS

② Regulations under specific acts of Congress—
Textile Fiber Products Identification Act, see 16 CFR § 303.1 et seq.
Wool Products Labeling Act, see 16 CFR § 300.1 et seq.

## Research References

**ALR Library**
③ 16 ALR, Fed. 361, Jurisdiction of Federal District Court to Entertain Attacks on Federal Trade Commission's Actions.
65 ALR 2nd 225, What Constitutes False, Misleading, or Deceptive Advertising or Promotional Practices Subject to Action by Federal Trade Commission.
149 ALR 349, Justiciable Controversy within Declaratory Judgment Act as Predicable Upon Advice, Opinion, or Ruling of Public Administrative Officer.
79 ALR 1200, Validity and Construction of Statute Creating Federal Trade Commission.
**Encyclopedias**
Am. Jur. 2d Monopolies, Restraints of Trade, etc. § 1301, Enforcement.

19

# ILLUSTRATION 7-6.    *Continued*

---

**15  § 68**                              COMMERCE AND TRADE    Ch. 2

61 Am. Jur. Proof of Facts 3d 501, Proof of Identity of Fiber, Fabric, or Textile.
24 Am. Jur. Trials 1, Defending Antitrust Lawsuits.

Forms

Federal Procedural Forms § 65:216, Introduction.
Federal Procedural Forms § 65:219, Labeling Requirements--Wool Products.
Federal Procedural Forms § 65:251, FTC Complaint--Wool Products Not Labeled,
    or Deceptively Labeled [15 U.S.C.A. §§ 45(A)(1), 68, 68a, 68b(A)(1),

Treatises and Practice Aids

Callmann on Unfair Compet., TMs, & Monopolies § 25:10, Jurisdiction of the
    Commission under the Wool and Fur Products Labeling Acts and Textile
    Fiber Products Identification Act.
Callmann on Unfair Compet., TMs, & Monopolies App 15 § 15:1, Wool Products
    Labeling Act of 1939.
Callmann on Unfair Compet., TMs, &amp;     **4 Case annotations for cases
                                          citing to the statute**                er

### WESTLAW ELECTRONIC RESEARCH

See Westlaw guide following the Explanation pages of this volume.

### Notes of Decisions

Purpose  1
Reprocessed wool  2
Wool product  3

**(4)** ——————

**1.  Purpose**

Sections 68 to 68j of this title were intended to protect consumers against concealment of substitutes for wool in products claimed to be made wholly or partially of wool. Marcus v. F. T. C., C.A.2, 1965, 354 F.2d 85. Antitrust And Trade Regulation ⧆ 164

**2.  Reprocessed wool**

To the extent that woven or felted wool waste entered into garnetter's operation,

his garnett was "reprocessed wool" and not a product of reprocessed wool within §§ 68 to 68j of this title. Carr v. F. T. C., C.A.1, 1962, 302 F.2d 688. Antitrust And Trade Regulation ⧆ 164

**3.  Wool product.**

Garnett, composed exclusively of ordinary wool waste which had never been processed was not a "wool product" within §§ 68 to 68j of this title and producer of garnett was not covered. Carr v. F. T. C., C.A.1, 1962, 302 F.2d 688. Antitrust And Trade Regulation ⧆ 164

20

---

## ILLUSTRATION 7-7. Sample Pages Showing 15 U.S.C.S. § 68 Accessed on LexisAdvance.com

---

### 15 USCS § 68

Current through PL 113-74, with a gap of PL 113-73, approved 1/16/2014

United States Code Service - Titles 1 through 51 > TITLE 15. COMMERCE AND TRADE > CHAPTER 2. FEDERAL TRADE COMMISSION; PROMOTION OF EXPORT TRADE AND PREVENTION OF UNFAIR METHODS OF COMPETITION > LABELING OF WOOL PRODUCT

| § 68. Definitions

As used in this Act

> Congress continually enacts new Public Laws. This statute is current through Public Law (PL) 113-74. 113 is the 113th Congress and 74 is the 74th law passed by the 113th Congress.

(a) The term "person" means an individual, partnership, corporation, business enterprise, plural or singular, as the case demands.

(b) The term "wool" means the fiber from the fleece of the sheep or Cashmere goat (and may include the so-called specialty fibers fro and vicuna) which has never been reclaimed from any woven or

(c) The term "recycled wool" means (1) the resulting fiber when wool has been woven or felted into a wool product which, without ever having been utilized in any way by the ultimate consumer, subsequently has been made into a fibrous state, or (2) the resulting fiber when wool or reprocessed wool has been spun, woven, knitted, or felted into a wool product which, after having been used in any way by the ultimate consumer, subsequently has been made into a fibrous state.

(d) The term "wool product" means any product, or any portion of a product, which contains, purports to contain, or in any way is represented as containing wool or recycled wool.

(e) The term "Commission" means the Federal Trade Commission.

(f) The term "Federal Trade Commission Act" means the Act of Congress entitled "An Act to create a Federal Trade Commission, to define its powers and duties, and for other purposes," approved September 26, 1914, as amended, and the Federal Trade Commission Act approved March 21, 1938.

(g) The term "commerce" means commerce among the several States or with foreign nations, or in any Territory of the United States or in the District of Columbia, or between any such Territory and another, or between any such Territory and any State or foreign nation, or between the District of Columbia and any State or Territory or foreign nation.

(h) The term "Territory" includes the insular possessions of the United States and also any Territory of the United States.

| History

(Oct. 14, 1940, ch 871, § 2,54 Stat. 1128; May 5, 1980, P.L. 96-242, § 1, 94 Stat. 344.)

**Effective date of section:**

This section became effective nine months after enactment on October 14, 1940, as provided by § 12 of Act Oct. 14, 1940, which appears as a note to this section.

## ILLUSTRATION 7-7. *Continued*

> **Amendments to the original statute that are incorporated.**

15 USCS § 68

**Amendments:**

**1980** .Act May 5, 1980 (effective as provided by § 3 of such Act, which appears as a note to this section) substituted subsec. (c) for one which read: "The term 'reprocessed wool' means the resulting fiber when wool has been woven or felted into a wool product which, without ever having been utilized in any way by the ultimate consumer, subsequently has been made into a fibrous state."; deleted former subsec. (d), which read: "The term 'reused wool' means the resulting fiber when wool or reprocessed wool has been spun, woven, knitted, or felted into a wool product which, after having been used in any way by the ultimate consumer, subsequently has been made into a fibrous state."; redesignated former subsecs. (e)-(i), as subsecs. (d)-(h), respectively; and in redesignated subsec. (d), substituted "or recycled wool" for ", reprocessed wool, or reused wool".

**Case Notes**

1. Generally
2. Purpose
3. Wool
4. Recycled wool
5. Wool product

> **Case annotations for cases citing to the statute.**

**1. Generally**

Wool Products Labeling Act is applicable only to wool products, and not to wool itself or reprocessed wool itself. *Carr v Federal Trade Com. (1962, CA1) 302 F2d 688.*

**2. Purpose**

In passing Wool Products Labeling Act (*15 USCS §§ 68-68j*), Congress intended to protect consumers against concealment of substitutes for wool in products claimed to be made wholly or partially of wool. *Marcus v Federal Trade Com. (1965, CA2) 354 F2d 85, 1965* CCH Trade Cases P 71633.

**3. Wool**

Garnett composed exclusively of ordinary wool waste which has never been processed constitutes wool and not wool product. *Carr v Federal Trade Com. (1962, CA1) 302 F2d 688.*

# ILLUSTRATION 7-7. *Continued*

15 USCS § 68

**4. Recycled wool**

Garnett of wool which has been processed is no more than reprocessed wool. *Carr v Federal Trade Com. (1962, CA1) 302 F2d 688.*

Because the Wool Products Labeling Act, *15 USCS §§ 68* et seq., requires recycled garments and fabrics, including cashmere, to be labeled as such, whenever a label represents that a garment contains the unqualified term "cashmere," the law requires that the garment contain only virgin cashmere; thus Act, is essentially telling consumers that garments labeled "cashmere" can be presumed to be virgin cashmere as if it had been explicitly stated. *Cashmere & Camel Hair Mfrs. Inst. v Saks Fifth Ave. (2002, CA1 Mass) 284 F3d 302, 2002-1* CCH Trade Cases P 73628, cert den *(2002) 537 US 1001, 123 S Ct 485, 154 L Ed 2d 396.*

> The U.S.C.S. includes references to administrative regulations.

**Research References & Practice Aids**

**Code of Federal Regulations:**

Federal Trade Commission--Rules and regulations under the Wool Products Labeling Act of 1939, *16 CFR 300.1* et seq.

Federal Trade Commission--Rules and regulations under the Textile Fiber Products Identification Act, *16 CFR 303.1* et seq.

**Am Jur:**

*54A Am Jur 2d, Monopolies, Restraints of Trade, and Unfair Trade Practices §§ 1237, 1239.*

**Am Jur Proof of Facts:**

61 Am Jur Proof of Facts 3d, Proof of Identity of Fiber, Fabric, or Textile, p

> Citations to secondary sources.

13 Am Jur Proof of Facts, Textile Identification and Clothing Hazards, p. 649.

**Corporate and Business Law:**

5 Antitrust Laws and Trade Regulation, 2nd Edition (Matthew Bender), ch 76, Enforcement by the Federal Trade Commission: An Overview § 76.02.

5 Antitrust Laws and Trade Regulation, 2nd Edition (Matthew Bender), ch 81, Remedial Powers of the Federal Trade Commission § 81.03.

5 Antitrust Laws and Trade Regulation, 2nd Edition (Matthew Bender), ch 83, Judicial Review and Enforcement of Federal Trade Commission Actions § 83.03.

4 Antitrust Counseling and Litigation Techniques (Matthew Bender), ch 48, Federal Trade Commission Investigations § 48.01.

*6 Kintner, Federal Antitrust Law (Matthew Bender), ch 44, The Federal Trade Commission Organization § 44.5.*

## ILLUSTRATION 7-7.  *Continued*

15 USCS § 68

*6 Kintner, Federal Antitrust Law (Matthew Bender), ch 45, The Federal Trade Commission Investigation and Enforcement Procedures § 45.114.*

*7 Kintner, Federal Antitrust Law (Matthew Bender), ch 49, Unfair or Deceptive Acts or Practices § 49.34.*

*7 Kintner, Federal Antitrust Law (Matthew Bender), ch 51, Product Description, Composition and Origin §§ 51.16, 51.19.*

*8 Kintner, Federal Antitrust Law (Matthew Bender), ch 64, Special Labeling Statutes Administered by the Federal Trade Commission §§ 64.2, 64.26.*

**Annotations:**

Supreme Court's views regarding consent judgments, decrees or orders in proceedings under federal antitrust laws or Federal Trade Commission Act. *43 L Ed 2d 807.*

Temporary relief against unfair trade practices under *15 USCS § 53*. *34 ALR Fed 507.*

Propriety of Federal Trade Commission order under *15 USCS § 45* applying to all products sold by party, or to all products in broad category, where Commission has found false advertising of only one product or group of products sold by party. *45 ALR Fed 612.*

Power of Federal Trade Commission to issue order requiring corrective advertising. *46 ALR Fed 905.*

Consumer product warranty suits in federal court under Magnuson-Moss Warranty--Federal Trade Commission Improvement Act (*15 USCS §§ 2301* et seq.). *59 ALR Fed 461.*

Reciprocal dealing as violation of Sherman Antitrust Act (*15 USCS §§ 1* et seq.) and Clayton Antitrust Act (*15 USCS §§ 12* et seq.). *69 ALR Fed 330.*

Award of attorneys' fees in actions under state deceptive trade practice and consumer protection acts. *35 ALR4th 12.*

Coverage of leases under state consumer protection statutes. *89 ALR4th 854.*

**Texts:**

2 The Law of Advertising (Matthew Bender), ch 17, The Jurisdiction of the Federal Trade Commission in Advertising § 17.02.

2 The Law of Advertising (Matthew Bender), ch 26, Representations as to Quality § 26.03.

3 The Law of Advertising (Matthew Bender), ch 33, Consent Agreement Procedure § 33.01.

UNITED STATES CODE SERVICE

amendments or legislative activity that would impact the text of the section. The pocket part provides important updating information for the statute section. The pocket parts are important to check when updating your research.

Alternatively, if cost is not an issue, access the code section on either Lexis or Westlaw, and the updates will be integrated into the statute cite retrieved. This is shown in Illustration 7-7, 15 USCS § 68 accessed on Lexis. When accessing either the USCA on Westlaw or the USCS on Lexis, there is no need to use pocket parts or advance sheets, because all of the amendments, legislative updates, and citing references are updated weekly.

## 2. Reading and Understanding Statutes

### ▼ How Do You Read a Statute?

Each word of a statute is read for its plain meaning. Statutes are drafted using as few words as possible to state the law. The courts resolve any ambiguities that arise when applying a statute. Often litigation involves the application or interpretation or violation of a statute. When a statute has not been applied in a case previously, it is a case of first impression. Remember that the text of the statute does not discuss policy issues but policy and political climate influence how a statute will be applied. Think of the goals that the government seeks to further and this will provide insight into relevant policy arguments concerning the application of a particular statutory provision.

The focus of statutory analysis is that legislation is adopted to apply to situations that will arise after the legislation goes into effect. An activity that existed prior to the passage of the particular legislation is **grandfathered** if the legislation includes language that does not prohibit this existing activity from continuing. For instance, suppose a city passes an ordinance forbidding the operation of commercial businesses in residentially zoned neighborhoods. Under a grandfather clause, an existing business would be permitted to continue its operation; the legislation would apply only to businesses opened after the legislation took effect.

### ▼ What Type of Legal Authority Are Statutes?

Statutes are primary authority because codes and statutes are the laws created by the legislature. Statutes are the authority to rely on when researching. When researching, first determine the relevant jurisdiction and then check the appropriate code to see if there is a statute on point. If there is a relevant statute on point, the statute takes precedence over case law holdings that were decided prior to the statute's enactment. Statutes are enacted to control conduct like criminal acts, relationships like marriage and adoption, and transactions like banking that occur frequently in our society. Court decisions applying and interpreting statutes already enacted must be consulted to assess how a statute has been applied and analyzed.

### ▼ What Is the Relationship Between Statutes and Case Law?

Most cases today revolve around the application or the interpretation of a statute. Courts determine whether an individual or an institution—public, private, or government—violated a statute or whether the statute itself is unconstitutional. People, institutions, municipalities, and even state governments go to court to determine if a statute is unconstitutional.

## 3. How to Find Federal Statutes

### ▼ Where Are Federal Statutes Found?

The official, government-issued compilation of the federal statutes is the *United States Code*, or U.S.C. See Illustration 7-5, the 2012 version of 15 U.S.C. § 68. The most cost-effective way to access the *United States Code* is at www.gpo.gov/fdsys. The official code is published only every six years, so you would have to search the section at uscode.house.gov/browse.xhtml to obtain information about subsequent legislative activity. Of course, you would not obtain any of the research enhancements or annotations, but the ease of use is remarkable, especially if you know the code section or a key word in the provision. Here you can search "wool labeling and recycled wool." The U.S.C. contains most of the laws created by the U.S. Congress. The U.S. Government Printing Office publishes the U.S.C. Another terrific Internet resource for federal and state codes is Cornell's Legal Information Institute at www.law.cornell.edu.

The U.S.C. is organized by title. There are now 51 titles. Each title covers a specific subject area over which the U.S. Congress has authority to draft legislation. For example, Title 15 contains all statutes dealing with commerce and trade. When a new piece of legislation is enacted that pertains to commerce and trade, which includes labeling provisions, it is placed in Title 15. Changes to a statute are called amendments. In our example, the original statute was amended in Pub. L. No. 96-242 to include language regarding recycled wool. When new statutes are enacted that replace existing statute sections, the older sections are then superseded. This differs from case law because new decisions over-rule prior decisions' holdings; they do not supersede them. Sometimes only a portion of an existing statute changes when a new public law is enacted, as in our example with the addition of new language to change "reprocessed wool" to "recycled wool." A statute is repealed when it is revoked and is no longer in force.

Go to the Law Library of Congress site at www.loc.gov/law/help/statutes .php for a helpful chart on how to find statutes.

### ▼ How Often Is the U.S.C. Updated?

An official version of the U.S.C. is published every six years. Supplements updating the existing Code are published annually. During the course of the six years, new legislation is passed all of the time. It is not included in the official code until the annual supplement is published. There may be a great time lag between the law's enactment and the production of the annual supplement. New legislation retains the slip format until it becomes a session law and gets a *Statutes at Large* citation. It is important to check to see if the legislation has been repealed or superseded by a slip law or a session law in the intervening years between publications of the official code and during the time between publications of the annual supplements. You will notice that Congress updates statutes with the same steps (slip law, session law, public law) as it employs to enact new legislation, as discussed earlier in this chapter.

### ▼ Is the U.S.C. the Only Codified Version of the Federal Statutes?

No. There are two unofficial versions of the U.S.C., the **United States Code Annotated** (U.S.C.A.) published by West and the **United States Code Service** (U.S.C.S.) published by LexisNexis. Both the U.S.C.A. and the U.S.C.S. contain the text of the laws found in the U.S.C. and also include case law annotations and excellent updating services. Unlike case law where the official and the unofficial reporters have different volume numbers and different pagination for the same case, the citations for the unofficial codes have the same title and section designations as the U.S.C. cite. For example, the following are citations to the identical statute:

26 U.S.C. § 61 (2012)

26 U.S.C.A. § 61 (West 2012)

26 U.S.C.S. § 61 (LexisNexis 2012)

### ▼ What Do the Unofficial Codes Contain?

NET NOTE

A free source to search the *United States Code* can be found at uscode.house .gov/search/criteria.shtml. This site includes updates, but always see if your code section is current by using a commercial annotated set, either the U.S.C.A. or the U.S.C.S., and then validate the cite with either *Shepard's* or KeyCite.

The unofficial codes contain references to cases that construe and apply the code section. See Illustrations 7-6 and 7-7. They are called annotated codes because they contain the case law annotations. The unofficial codes contain references to law review articles dealing with the particular code section as well as ties to the respective publisher's resources. The U.S.C.A. and U.S.C.S. are excellent research tools. See Illustrations 7-5, 7-6, and 7-7 for a comparison of the official and the unofficial codes.

The U.S.C.A., because it is published by Thomson-Reuters, the publisher of West and Westlaw products, links the researcher to all of the other West publications. See Illustration 7-6. References are given to topic and key numbers, if they are available, so that the subject covered by the code section can be examined in the *West Digests* to find pertinent case law. (See Chapter 4 for a detailed discussion of digests.) References to West secondary sources and law journals are given as well. (See Chapter 6.) References to the *United States Code Congressional and Administrative News* (U.S.C.C.A.N.), published by West and containing compilations of legislative histories for major public laws since the 1950s, are contained in the U.S.C.A. (The U.S.C.C.A.N. is discussed fully in Chapter 8.) Also, references to administrative laws, the *Code of Federal Regulations*, are provided for certain statutes. (Administrative materials are discussed in Chapter 9.)

The U.S.C.S., published by LexisNexis, provides references to other publications that are relevant to the particular code section. See Illustration 7-7. This illustration was downloaded from Lexis.com, USCS library. Note how the updating is integrated into the material retrieved. Westlaw has a similar feature in the U.S.C.A. database. The U.S.C.S. included related statute citations and pertinent secondary source references as well as case annotations. U.S.C.S. has consistent references to the *Code of Federal Regulations*. (See Chapter 9.)

Aside from providing excellent updates, case law annotations, and law review citations, the annotated or unofficial federal codes provide the researcher with an entry into the entire research network created by the respective publisher.

### ▼ Is There Any Difference Between the U.S.C.S. and the U.S.C.A.?

The U.S.C.S. provides consistent references to relevant *Code of Federal Regulations* (C.F.R.) citations; the U.S.C.A. does not consistently include administrative law citations. Overall, then, the U.S.C.S. is better for researching administrative issues. The U.S.C.A. provides key numbers and topics relating to the West Digest System as well as electronic searching tips for Westlaw query formulation.

### ▼ Why Would You Use an Annotated Set of the U.S.C.?

As mentioned earlier, the annotated codes offer a host of references to secondary source publications produced by the respective code's

publisher as well as case law annotations. You would use an annotated, or unofficial code, because the updating through pocket parts, bound supplements, and advance session law pamphlets is very timely. Between publication of the official statutes every six years, consult an unofficial version of the U.S.C. to determine if a statute has been updated, modified, amended, or superseded. The unofficial versions contain references to any new legislation that relates to the code section, even if it is a session law. Always check the volume's pocket part for updates as well as the advance pamphlets. The indexes of the unofficial codes are also superior to the index of the U.S.C.

### ▼ How Useful Are Annotated Statutes as Finding Tools?

Annotated codes are excellent finding tools for retrieving cases that interpret the statute section in question. You do not cite to the research points and abstracts following the code section, although they are very helpful in your research. When using an annotated code section on point, you are also linked to many other resources produced by the particular code's publisher. For example, within the U.S.C.A. you would find citations to encyclopedia sections. In addition, because of the excellent updating services, the annotated codes allow you to find subsequent legislation that relates to the statute section.

### ▼ What Are the Research Methods Used to Find Relevant Statutes?

The research methods are the same for the U.S.C., the U.S.C.A., and the U.S.C.S. The following methods are listed in order of efficiency.

1. **Popular name table.** The popular name table is found in a separate set of volumes, generally paperbound, in the unofficial codes. Almost every statute passed in Congress has a popular name; it is either a last name of the sponsor or a description of the act's intent. If you have a popular name but not a title and section number, you can use the popular name table. The popular name table will tell you where to find the act in the *United States Code.* The Popular Name Table in Illustration 7-8 indicates that the Wool Products Labeling Act is codified at 15 U.S.C. § 68 et seq. All of the popular names for all of the code sections are listed in alphabetical order with the corresponding title and section numbers of the act, the public law numbers, and the *Statutes at Large* citations. The popular name table is an excellent research tool for finding public law numbers quickly. In Illustration 7-8, the 1980 amendments for the Wool Products Labeling Act of 1939, where recycled wool is included, is Pub. L. No. 96-242. The 2013 U.S.C.A. Popular Name Table also shows that there are new Public Laws amending the Wool Products Labeling Act, since 1980. The Popular Name Table is a good source for updated information.

## ILLUSTRATION 7-8. U.S.C.A. Popular Name Table

---

### POPULAR NAME TABLE
1592

**Wool Manufacturer Payment Clarification and Technical Corrections Act—Continued**
  Collateral or Related Acts:
  Trade Act of 2002

**Wool Products Labeling Act of 1939**
Oct. 14, 1940, ch. 871, 54 Stat. 1128
Short title, see 15 USCA § 68 note
  Current USCA classifications:

| Section of ch. 871 | USCA Classification |
|---|---|
| 2 | 15 USCA § 68 |
| 3 | 15 USCA § 68a |
| 4 | 15 USCA § 68b |
| 5 | 15 USCA § 68c |
| 6 | 15 USCA § 68d |
| 7 | 15 USCA § 68e |
| 8 | 15 USCA § 68f |
| 9 | 15 USCA § 68g |
| 10 | 15 USCA § 68h |
| 11 | 15 USCA § 68i |
| 14 | 15 USCA § 68j |

*This list contains only sections enacted by this Public Law. For all sections affected by this law, see Act Oct. 14, 1940, ch. 871 in the USCA-TABLES database and the enacting credit set out below.*
Table of Contents for current USCA classifications:
15 USCA §§ 68, 68a to 68j
**Enacting law:**
Oct. 14, 1940, ch. 871, 54 Stat. 1128 (15 §§ 68, 68a to 68j)
**Amending laws:**
May 5, 1980, Pub.L. 96–242, §§ 1, 2, 94 Stat. 344 (15 §§ 68, 68b)
Sept. 24, 1984, Pub.L. 98–417, Title III, §§ 304 to 306, 98 Stat. 1604, 1605 (15 §§ 68b, 68c)
Dec. 20, 2006, Pub.L. 109–428, § 2(a), 120 Stat. 2913 (15 § 68b)

**Wool Suit and Textile Trade Extension Act of 2004**
Pub.L. 108–429, Title IV, Dec. 3, 2004, 118 Stat. 2600
Short title, see 7 USCA § 7101 note
  *This Public Law enacted no currently effective sections. For sections affected by this law, see Pub.L. 108–429 in the USCA-TABLES database and the enacting credit set out below.*
**Enacting law:**
Pub.L. 108–429, Title IV, Dec. 3, 2004, 118 Stat. 2600 (7 § 7101 note)
**Amending laws:**
Pub.L. 109–280, Title XIV, § 1633(b)(1), Aug. 17, 2006, 120 Stat. 1166
Pub.L. 110–343, Div. C, Title III, § 325(b)(1), Oct. 3, 2008, 122 Stat. 3875
**Collateral or Related Acts:**
Emergency Protection for Iraqi Cultural Antiquities Act of 2004
Miscellaneous Trade and Technical Corrections Act of 2004

**Wool Suit Fabric Labeling Fairness and International Standards Conforming Act**
Pub.L. 109–428, Dec. 20, 2006, 120 Stat. 2913
Short title, see 15 USCA § 68 note
  *This Public Law enacted no currently effective sections. For sections affected by this law, see Pub.L. 109–428 in the USCA-TABLES database and the enacting credit set out below.*
**Enacting law:**
Pub.L. 109–428, Dec. 20, 2006, 120 Stat. 2913 (15 §§ 68 note, 68b)

**Work Hours Act of 1962**
See Work Hours and Safety Act of 1962

**Work Hours and Safety Act of 1962 (Work Hours Act of 1962)**
Pub.L. 87–581, Aug. 13, 1962, 76 Stat. 357
  *This enactment was repealed and now has provisions contained in a Revised Title: see 40 USCA §§ 3701 to 3708.*
**Enacting law:**
Pub.L. 87–581, Aug. 13, 1962, 76 Stat. 357 (See 40 §§ 3701 to 3708)
**Amending laws:**
Pub.L. 91–54, Aug. 9, 1969, 83 Stat. 96 (40 §§ 327 note, 333)

Reprinted with permission of Thomson Reuters.

2. **Conversion table.** The conversion table is also at the end of the U.S.C. set, in the tables volume, as well as in the tables volume in the U.S.C.A. and in the U.S.C.S., and lets you find the U.S.C. citation if you have a *Statutes at Large* citation. In Illustration 7-9, using the conversion table in the U.S.C.A., you are able to convert the public law number into a *Statutes at Large* citation. For example, you would obtain the citation of 94 Stat. 344 from Pub. L. No. 96-242. The table also converts the public law number into a U.S.C.A. citation. (The public law number helps you find the legislative history of the act in the U.S.C.C.A.N. also. See Chapter 8 for more information on the U.S.C.C.A.N.)

3. **The index method.** First try to find the relevant code section by using the index. You can also find a relevant statute by checking under some of the significant terms from the act. Very often a word from the popular name of the statute is cited in the index. The index is in alphabetical order. In Illustration 7-10 on page 223, from the U.S.C.A., our example focuses on the subject heading: Wool, subheading: Labels. Note that the index entry contains some of the terms describing the subject matter of the statute.

4. **The title outline.** If you know the particular title where the statute section is located but don't know the section number, you can look at the title outline to see if any entry in the particular title is appropriate. Illustration 7-11 on page 224 shows the outline of some subchapters and sections in U.S.C.A. Title 15. You must have a very clear idea of what you are looking for and knowledge about the statute's language to use the title outline method effectively. Use this method only if you cannot find a statute section by any other means.

## ▼ How Do You Cite Federal Statutes?

Always cite to the official statutory compilation, if it is the most current version. The first entry in the citation is the title number, then the abbreviation for the statutory compilation, and then the section or paragraph number. *Bluebook* **Rule 12** and *ALWD* **Rule 14** detail the various rules on citing statutes and codes, state or federal. For example, Title 12, § 211 of the U.S.C. would be cited as:

12 U.S.C. § 211 (2012).

You always cite to the official code, the U.S.C., unless you are relying on an unofficial code for updating purposes.

The year included in the citation is the year that the code volume was published, not the year that the statute was enacted. The publication date is printed either on the title page of the bound volume or on the back of the title page. If a pocket part supplement is used, include that date as well.

## ILLUSTRATION 7-9.   U.S.C.A. *Statutes at Large* and Public Law Numbers Table

| | | | |
|---|---|---|---|
| **1980** | | | **96–249** |

| | | | | |
|---|---|---|---|---|
| | § 401(c)(2)(B) | 94 Stat 300 | 26 prec. 1031 | |
| | § 401(c)(3) | 94 Stat 300 | 26 § 2614 | Elim. |
| | § 401(d) | 94 Stat 300 | 26 § 1014 nt | |
| | § 401(e) | 94 Stat 301 | 26 § 1023 nt | |
| | § 402 | 94 Stat 301 | 19 § 1862 | |
| | § 403(a)(1) | 94 Stat 302 | 26 § 473 | |
| | § 403(a)(2) | 94 Stat 304 | 26 prec. 471 | |
| | § 403(a)(3) | 94 Stat 304 | 26 § 473 nt | |
| | § 403(b)(1) | 94 Stat 304 | 26 § 336 | Rep. |
| | § 403(b)(2)(A) | 94 Stat 304 | 26 § 337 | Rep. |
| | § 403(b)(2)(B) | 94 Stat 305 | 26 § 453 | Rep. |
| | § 403(b)(4) | 94 Stat 305 | 26 § 336 nt | |
| | § 404(a) | 94 Stat 305 | 26 § 116 | Rep. |
| | § 404(b)(1) | 94 Stat 306 | 26 prec. 101 | |
| | § 404(b)(2) | 94 Stat 306 | 26 § 265 | |
| | § 404(b)(3) | 94 Stat 306 | 26 § 584 | |
| | § 404(b)(4) | 94 Stat 306 | 26 § 643 | |
| | § 404(b)(5) | 94 Stat 307 | 26 § 702 | |
| | § 404(b)(6) | 94 Stat 307 | 26 § 854 | |
| | § 404(b)(7) | 94 Stat 307 | 26 prec. 851 | |
| | § 404(b)(8) | 94 Stat 307 | 26 § 857 | |
| | § 404(c) | 94 Stat 308 | 26 § 116 nt | Rep. |
| | | 94 Stat 309 | – § — | Uncl. |
| Apr. 3, 1980 ... 96–224 | — | 94 Stat 310 | 50 App. § 2166 | |
| 96–225 | — | | | |
| 96–226 | § 1 | 94 Stat 311 | 31 § 1 nt | Elim. |
| | § 101 | 94 Stat 311 | 31 § 67 | Rev.T. 31 |
| | § 102 | 94 Stat 312 | 31 § 54 | Rev.T. 31 |
| | § 103 | 94 Stat 314 | 31 § 53 | Rev.T. 31 |
| | § 104(a) | 94 Stat 314 | 31 § 42 | Rev.T. 31 |
| | § 104(b)(1) | 94 Stat 315 | 31 § 43 | Rev.T. 31 |
| | § 104(b)(2) | 94 Stat 315 | 31 § 43 nt | Elim. |
| | § 201 | 94 Stat 315 | 42 § 3523 | Rep. |
| | § 202 | 94 Stat 315 | 42 § 7138 | Rep. |
| 96–227 | § 1 | 94 Stat 317 | 25 § 761 nt | |
| | § 2 to 9 | 94 Stat 317 to 322 | 25 § 761 to 768 | |
| 96–228 | — | 94 Stat 323 | – § — | Uncl. |
| Apr. 7, 1980 ... 96–229 | § 2(d) | 94 Stat 327 | 42 § 4363a | |
| | § 2(e) | 94 Stat 327 | 42 § 4363 | |
| | § 4 | 94 Stat 328 | 42 § 4369a | |
| | § 5 | 94 Stat 328 | 42 § 4370 | |
| Apr. 8, 1980 ... 96–230 | — | 94 Stat 329 | 5 § 905 | |
| 96–231 | — | 94 Stat 330 | – § — | Uncl. |
| Apr. 10, 1980 ... 96–232 | — | 94 Stat 331 | – § — | Uncl. |
| 96–233 | — | 94 Stat 332 | – § — | Uncl. |
| Apr. 11, 1980 ... 96–234 | § 1, 2 | 94 Stat 333 | 7 § 1445e | |
| | § 3 | 94 Stat 333 | 15 § 714b | |
| Apr. 12, 1980 ... 96–235 | — | 94 Stat 335 | – § — | Uncl. |
| Apr. 22, 1980 ... 96–236 | § 1 to 6 | 94 Stat 336 to 337 | 7 § 3601 to 3606 | |
| Apr. 24, 1980 ... 96–237 | — | 94 Stat 338 | – § — | Uncl. |
| 96–238 | — | 94 Stat 339 | – § — | Uncl. |
| Apr. 30, 1980 ... 96–239 | § 1 | 94 Stat 341 | 29 § 1461 | |
| May 1, 1980 ... 96–240 | — | 94 Stat 342 | – § — | Uncl. |
| May 3, 1980 ... 96–241 | § 1 | 94 Stat 343 | 5 § 5312 nt | Elim. |
| | § 2 | 94 Stat 343 | 22 § 2651 nt | |
| → May 5, 1980 ... 96–242 | § 1 | 94 Stat 344 | 15 § 68 | |
| | § 2 | 94 Stat 344 | 15 § 68b | |
| | § 3 | 94 Stat 344 | 15 § 68 nt | |
| May 16, 1980 ... 96–243 | — | 94 Stat 345 | 7 § 2014 nt | |
| May 19, 1980 ... 96–244 | § 1 | 94 Stat 346 | 16 § 470h–1 | |
| | § 2 | 94 Stat 346 | 16 § 470t | |
| May 21, 1980 ... 96–245 | — | 94 Stat 347 | 29 § 161 | |
| May 23, 1980 ... 96–246 | — | 94 Stat 348 | 16 § 1535 | |
| 96–247 | § 1 | 94 Stat 349 | 42 § 1997 nt | |
| | § 2 | 94 Stat 349 | 42 § 1997 | |
| | § 3 to 12 | 94 Stat 350 to 354 | 42 § 1997a to 1997j | |
| 96–248 | § 1 | 94 Stat 355 | 16 § 1132 nt | |
| May 26, 1980 ... 96–249 | § 1 | 94 Stat 357 | 7 § 2011 nt | |
| | § 101(a) | 94 Stat 357 | 7 § 2012 | |
| | § 101(b) | 94 Stat 357 | 7 § 2019 | |
| | § 102, 103 | 94 Stat 357 | 7 § 2014 | |
| | § 104 | 94 Stat 358 | 7 § 2014, 2014 nt | Rep. |
| | § 105 | 94 Stat 358 | 7 § 2014, 2014 nt | Rep. |
| | § 106 | 94 Stat 358 | 7 § 2014, 2014 nt | |
| | § 107, 108 | 94 Stat 358 | 7 § 2014 | |
| | § 109, 110 | 94 Stat 359 | 7 § 2015 | |
| | § 111 | 94 Stat 360 | 7 § 2012 | |
| | § 112 | 94 Stat 361 | 7 § 2014 | |
| | § 113 | 94 Stat 361 | 7 § 2020 | |
| | § 114, 115 | 94 Stat 361 | 7 § 2015 | |
| | § 116 to 120 | 94 Stat 361 | 7 § 2020 | |
| | § 121 | 94 Stat 363 | 7 § 2025 | |
| | § 122, 123 | 94 Stat 363 | 7 § 2020 | |
| | § 124 | 94 Stat 363 | 7 § 2024 | |
| | § 125, 126 | 94 Stat 364 | 7 § 2025 | |

1525

# ILLUSTRATION 7-10. U.S.C.A. General Index

## WOODSY
1166

**WOODSY OWL**—Cont'd
Official symbol, environmental quality, 16 § 580p–3
Property, United States, 16 § 580p–1
Royalties, 16 § 580p–3
Secretary of Agriculture, royalties, 16 § 580p–3
Slogans, 16 § 580p
  Character, name, manufacturers and manufacturing, reproduction, 18 § 711a

## WOOL
  Generally, 15 § 68 et seq.
Advertisements, fraud, 15 § 68b
Analyses, 15 § 68d
Antitrust laws. Monopolies and combinations, generally, post
Appeal and review, loans, 7 § 7996
Base acres, payment, 7 § 7901 et seq.
Boards and commissions. Commission, generally, post
Bonds (officers and fiduciaries),
  Condemnation, 15 § 68e
  Exports and imports, 15 § 68f
  Injunctions, 15 § 68e
Brands, marks and labels. Labels, generally, post
Carbonizing, 19 § 1562
Cashmere, 15 § 68b
Charges. Rates and charges, generally, post
Combinations. Monopolies and combinations, generally, post
Commerce, definitions, 15 § 68
Commission, 15 § 68 et seq.
  Condemnation, 15 § 68e
  Definitions, 15 § 68
  Injunctions, 15 § 68e
  Labeling Act, 15 § 68d
  Misdemeanors, 15 § 68h
Commodity Exchanges, generally, this index
Continuing guarantees, 15 § 68g
Contracts, payment, 7 § 7917
Countercyclical payments, 7 § 7901 et seq.
Death, payment, transfers, 7 § 7915
Deceit. Fraud, generally, post
Deficiencies, markets and marketing, loans, payment, 7 § 7935
➤ Definitions, 7 § 7102; 15 § 68
  Actions and proceedings, loans, 7 § 7996
  Payment, 7 § 7901
Destruction, 15 § 68e
Direct payments, 7 § 7901 et seq.
Disposal,
  Condemnation, 15 § 68e
  Surplus property, 40 § 547
Double cropping, payment, 7 § 7911

**WOOL**—Cont'd
Elections, payment, 7 §§ 7911, 7912
Examinations and examiners, 15 § 68d
Exemptions, payment, transfers, 7 § 7915
Exports and imports,
  Application of law, 15 § 68a
  Assessments, 7 § 7104
  Fraud, 15 § 68f
  Invoices, 15 § 68f
Federal Trade Commission. Commission, generally, ante
Fees, grading, 7 § 415c
Fibers,
  Exports and imports, 15 § 68f
  Misbranded products, 15 § 68b
  Records and recordation, 15 § 68d
Fines and penalties, Labeling Act, 15 §§ 68d, 68h
Fraud, 15 § 68a et seq.
  Advertisements, 15 § 68b
  Exports and imports, 15 § 68f
  Guarantees, 15 § 68g
  Invoices, 15 § 68f
  Misbranding, 15 § 68a et seq.
  Stamps, 15 § 68c
  Tags, 15 § 68c
Grading, fees, 7 § 415c
Grazing, markets and marketing, loans, payment, 7 § 7936
Guaranty, 15 § 68g
Hosiery, misbranding, 15 § 68b
Identity and identification, 15 § 68a et seq.
Injunctions, 15 § 68e
Inspections, 15 § 68d
Insurance, actions and proceedings, 7 § 7996
Invoices, exports and imports, 15 § 68f
Labels, 15 § 68a et seq.
  Affixing labels, 15 § 68c
  Cashmere, 15 § 68b
  Guarantees, 15 § 68g
  Imported products, 15 § 68f
  Misbranding, 15 § 68a et seq.
  Mutilation, 15 § 68c
  Removal, 15 § 68c
Loans,
  Actions and proceedings, 7 § 7996
  Markets and marketing, 7 § 7931 et seq.
Mail orders, fraud, 15 § 68b
Markets and marketing,
  Actions and proceedings, loans, 7 § 7996
  Loans, 7 § 7931 et seq.
    Actions and proceedings, 7 § 7996
  Loss assistance, 7 § 1421 nt
Mental health, payment, transfers, 7 § 7915
Misbranding, 15 § 68a et seq.
Misdemeanors, Labeling Act, 15 § 68h

Reprinted with permission of Thomson Reuters.

**ILLUSTRATION 7-11.   Outline of Sections in Title 15 U.S.C.A., Commerce and Trade, §§ 68–68j, Labeling of Wool Products**

---

COMMERCE AND TRADE

| Chapter | | Section |
|---|---|---|
| 98. | Public Company Accounting Reform and Corporate Responsibility | 7201 |
| 99. | National Construction Safety Team | 7301 |
| 100. | Cyber Security Research and Development | 7401 |
| 101. | Nanotechnology Research and Development | 7501 |
| 102. | Fairness to Contact Lens Consumers | 7601 |
| 103. | Controlling the Assault of Non–Solicited Pornography and Marketing | 7701 |
| 104. | Sports Agent Responsibility and Trust | 7801 |
| 105. | Protection of Lawful Commerce in Arms | 7901 |
| 106. | Pool and Spa Safety | 8001 |
| 107. | Protection of Intellectual Property Rights | 8101 |

### CHAPTER 2—FEDERAL TRADE COMMISSION; PROMOTION OF EXPORT TRADE AND PREVENTION OF UNFAIR METHODS OF COMPETITION

#### SUBCHAPTER I—FEDERAL TRADE COMMISSION

Sec.
41.     Federal Trade Commission established; membership; vacancies; seal.
42.     Employees; expenses.
43.     Office and place of meeting.
44.     Definitions.
45.     Unfair methods of competition unlawful; prevention by Commission.
45a.    Labels on products.
46.     Additional powers of Commission.
46a.    Concurrent resolution essential to authorize investigations.
47.     Reference of suits under antitrust statutes to Commission.
48.     Information and assistance from departments.
49.     Documentary evidence; depositions; witnesses.
50.     Offenses and penalties.
51.     Effect on other statutory provisions.
52.     Dissemination of false advertisements.
53.     False advertisements; injunctions and restraining orders.
54.     False advertisements; penalties.
55.     Additional definitions.
56.     Commencement, defense, intervention and supervision of litigation and appeal by Commission or Attorney General.
57.     Separability clause.
57a.    Unfair or deceptive acts or practices rulemaking proceedings.
57a–1.  Omitted.
57b.    Civil actions for violations of rules and cease and desist orders respecting unfair or deceptive acts or practices.
57b–1.  Civil investigative demands.
57b–2.  Confidentiality.
57b–2a. Confidentiality and delayed notice of compulsory process for certain third parties.
57b–2b. Protection for voluntary provision of information.

4

# ILLUSTRATION 7-11. *Continued*

**COMMERCE AND TRADE**

**Sec.**
57b–3. Rulemaking process.
57b–4. Good faith reliance on actions of Board of Governors.
57b–5. Agricultural cooperatives.
57c. Authorization of appropriations.
57c–1. Staff exchanges.
57c–2. Reimbursement of expenses.
58. Short title.
59 to 60. Reserved.

### SUBCHAPTER II—PROMOTION OF EXPORT TRADE

61. Export trade; definitions.
62. Export trade and antitrust legislation.
63. Acquisition of stock of export trade corporation.
64. Unfair methods of competition in export trade.
65. Information required from export trade corporation; powers of Federal Trade Commission.
66. Short title.

### SUBCHAPTER III—LABELING OF WOOL PRODUCTS

68. Definitions.
68a. Misbranding declared unlawful.
68b. Misbranded wool products.
68c. Stamp, tag, label, or other identification.
68d. Enforcement of subchapter.
68e. Condemnation and injunction proceedings.
68f. Exclusion of misbranded wool products.
68g. Guaranty.
68h. Criminal penalty.
68i. Application of other laws.
68j. Exceptions from subchapter.

### SUBCHAPTER IV—LABELING OF FUR PRODUCTS

69. Definitions.
69a. Violations of Federal Trade Commission Act.
69b. Misbranded fur products.
69c. False advertising and invoicing.
69d. Fur products imported into United States.
69e. Name guide for fur products.
69f. Enforcement of subchapter.
69g. Condemnation and injunction proceedings.
69h. Guaranty.
69i. Criminal penalty.
69j. Application of other laws.

### SUBCHAPTER V—TEXTILE FIBER PRODUCTS IDENTIFICATION

70. Definitions.
70a. Violations of Federal Trade Commission Act.
70b. Misbranded and falsely advertised textile fiber products.
70c. Removal of stamp, tag, label, or other identification.
70d. Records.
70e. Enforcement.

5

Reprinted with permission of Thomson Reuters.

15 U.S.C.A. § 68 (West 2009 & Supp. 2013).

In this example, the first year mentioned, 2009, is the year that the particular volume of the code was published. The second date, 2013, is the year of the pocket part supplement that updates the code volume.

If a code section is well known by a popular name, then include the name in the citation:

Wool Products Labeling Act of 1939, 15 U.S.C. §§ 68-68j (2012).

## 4. Validating and Updating Statutes

▼ How and Why Would You Validate Federal Statutes?

Remember, it is important to validate and update statutes. You cannot rely on a particular statute until you have both updated and validated it. We discussed updating earlier in this chapter; it concerns finding any new legislative activity that impacts the statute section. Validating tells you how a court interpreted or applied a statute. *Shepard's* and KeyCite provide citations to cases and secondary sources that cite the statute section. *Shepard's* and KeyCite also provide the analytical treatment indicating how a court of law interprets or applies a statute section. *Shepard's* contains analysis that tells you whether the statute is constitutional, unconstitutional, valid, or invalid. See Illustration 7-12 for a portion of a case applying a statute and Illustration 7-13 on page 229 for the corresponding *Shepard's* entry indicating the analytical treatment. Validating indicates whether a court deems the statute constitutional or unconstitutional, valid or invalid.

Shepardizing statutes also includes information indicating whether the statute has been repealed or amended. You must update statutory authority by using the code's pocket part supplement and advance sheets. Most important, *Shepard's* for codes indicates the judicial treatment or interpretation of a statute, meaning how courts of law have looked at a statute's application and at whether its application was discriminatory or affected too broad or too narrow a group of people. Judges then determine if the statute has been complied with or if the statute is unconstitutional or constitutional in whole or in part. See Illustration 7-13 for *Shepard's* treatment of 15 U.S.C. § 68 and Illustration 7-12 where 15 U.S.C. § 68 is cited in a case listed in *Shepard's*.

▼ How Do You Update Statutes with Print Resources?

To update statutes to ensure that you have the most recent version, you must take the following steps.

**ILLUSTRATION 7-12.  Pages from *Decision in the Federal Reporter* That Cites to 15 U.S.C. § 68**

---

302                    284 FEDERAL REPORTER, 3d SERIES

### IV.

The plaintiff also challenges on appeal the district court's analysis of his claim for damages arising out of the alleged malpractice. The district court, in an effort to provide a "complete record of factual findings," analyzed the case backwards, starting with an assessment of damages, then proceeding to causation, negligence, and duty, in that order. Although we understand why the court engaged in this method of analysis, rather than simply concluding its ruling after finding there was no duty to disclose, such analysis resulted in extraneous factual findings. Therefore, because the district court did not need to reach the issue of damages, any findings regarding damages are dicta; the district court did not actually award any damages. As a result, plaintiff's claims of error in computing the damages are premature. *See United States v. Ottati & Goss, Inc.,* 900 F.2d 429, 443 (1st Cir.1990) (refusing

in cases where there is a "trade-off" between the health of the mother and the child, "pregnant women routinely choose" and "should" choose a cesaren section "for the benefit of their fetuses," even though the risk to the woman is higher than from a vaginal delivery).

**8.** We emphasize that a duty to disclose, if it exists, does *not* necessarily indicate any duty to offer or to perform a C-section if the doctor

CASHMERE & CAMEL HAIR MANU-FACTURERS INSTITUTE, f/k/a Camel Hair & Cashmere Institute of America, Inc., and L.W. Packard & Co., Inc., Plaintiffs, Appellants,

v.

SAKS FIFTH AVENUE, Harve Benard, Ltd. and Filenes Basement, Defendants, Appellees.

No. 00-2341.

United States Court of Appeals, First Circuit.

Heard Dec. 6, 2001.

Decided April 1, 2002.

Fabric wholesaler and trade association brought action against garment manu-

does not consider one to be warranted in his medical judgment. *See Canterbury,* 464 F.2d at 781 (separating physician's duty "to treat [and diagnose] his patient skillfully" from his "obligation to communicate specific information to the patient"). The duty to disclose is intended to be limited, so as not to unduly burden the practice of medicine. *See Harnish,* 439 N.E.2d at 243.

## ILLUSTRATION 7-12. *Continued*

CASHMERE & CAMEL HAIR MFRS. v. SAKS FIFTH AVE.     **315**
Cite as 284 F.3d 302 (1st Cir. 2002)

Because defendants do not dispute that overstating cashmere content is a literal falsity claim, we apply a presumption of consumer deception in plaintiffs' favor on this claim. Based on this presumption, and defendants' failure to present evidence to rebut it, Packard has satisfied its burden of demonstrating consumer deception on its cashmere content claim.

[15, 16] Whether literal falsity is involved in plaintiffs' claim that defendants improperly labeled their goods as cashmere rather than recycled cashmere, however, is a contentious issue. Defendants argue that this claim is, by definition, one of implied falsity—that is, a representation that is literally true but in context becomes likely to mislead. *See Clorox*, 228 F.3d at 33 (defining an implied falsity claim as one in which the "advertisement, though explicitly true, nonetheless conveys a misleading message to the viewing public"). As further support for their argument, defendants offer a simple syllogism: all suits based on implied messages are im-

falsity claim. *See id.* However, we disagree with defendants' assertion that all claims that rely on implied messages are necessarily implied falsity claims. In *Clorox*, this Court noted that "[a]lthough factfinders usually base literal falsity claims upon the explicit claims made by an advertisement, they may also consider any claims the advertisement conveys by 'necessary implication.'" *Id.* at 34–35. We explained that "[a] claim is conveyed by necessary implication when, considering the advertisement in its entirety, the audience would recognize the claim as readily as if it had been explicitly stated." *Id.* at 35.

After drawing all reasonable inferences in favor of the nonmoving party, a rational factfinder could conclude that plaintiffs' recycled cashmere claim is one of literal falsity. The Wool Products Labeling Act, 15 U.S.C. § 68 *et seq.*, requires recycled garments and fabrics, including cashmere, to be labeled as such. As a result, whenever a label represents that a garment

---

**13.** Defendants also argue that before the presumption of consumer deception can apply to a literal falsity claim for damages, the plaintiff must demonstrate that the defendant intentionally deceived the consuming public. None of the five circuit cases cited *supra*, however, speaks of the intent to deceive as a prerequisite to applying a presumption of consumer deception on a literal falsity claim. As discussed in more detail below, the intent

to deceive is an independent basis for triggering a presumption of consumer deception. *See William H. Morris Co. v. Group W, Inc.*, 66 F.3d 255, 258 (9th Cir.1995) (ruling, on an implied falsity claim, that "[i]f [defendant] intentionally misled consumers, we would presume consumers were in fact deceived and [defendant] would have the burden of demonstrating otherwise").

Reprinted with permission of Thomson Reuters.

**ILLUSTRATION 7-13.** **Sample Page from** *Shepard's* **on Lexis Showing Treatment of U.S.C. References**

---

Page 1

Copyright 2014 SHEPARD'S(R) - 193 Citing references

**15 U.S.C. sec. 68**

Restrictions: *Comprehensive Report Unrestricted*
FOCUS(TM) Terms: *No FOCUS terms*
Print Format: *FULL*
Citing Ref. Signal: *Hidden*

**SHEPARD'S SUMMARY**

| **Unrestricted** *Shepard's* **Summary** | | |
|---|---|---|
| **Citing References:** | | |
| Citing Decisions: | **Citing decisions with no analysis assigned (43)** | |
| Other Sources: | **Law Reviews (24), Secondary Sources (2), Statutes (57), Treatises (53), Other Citations (1), Court Documents (14)** | |

**HISTORY** (Oct. 14, 1940, ch 871, § 2, 54 Stat. 1128; May 5, 1980, P.L. 96-242, § 1, 94 Stat. 344.)

**CITING DECISIONS** ( 43 citing decisions )

**U.S. SUPREME COURT**

1. **Cited by:**
   *Jacob Siegel Co. v. FTC*, 327 U.S. 608, 66 S. Ct. 758, 90 L. Ed. 888, 1946 U.S. LEXIS 3081, 42 F.T.C. 902, 69 U.S.P.Q. (BNA) 1 (1946)
   327 U.S. 608 *p.613*
   66 S. Ct. 758 *p.760*
   90 L. Ed. 888 *p.893*

**1ST CIRCUIT - COURT OF APPEALS**

2. **Cited by:**
   ➤ *Cashmere & Camel Hair Mfrs. Inst. v. Saks Fifth Ave.*, 284 F.3d 302, 2002 U.S. App. LEXIS 5361, 2002-1 Trade Cas. (CCH) P73628 (1st Cir. Mass. 2002)
   284 F.3d 302 *p.315*

3. **Cited by:**
   *Carr v. Federal Trade Com.*, 302 F.2d 688, 1962 U.S. App. LEXIS 6045, 1962 Trade Cas. (CCH) P70216

---

Reprinted with the permission of LexisNexis. Editor's Note: See online document for complete report.

## ILLUSTRATION 7-14.   Pocket Part Entry for 15 U.S.C.A. § 68

# UNITED STATES CODE ANNOTATED

## TITLE 15

## COMMERCE AND TRADE

| Chapter | Section |
|---|---|
| 108. State–Based Insurance Reform | 8201 |
| 109. Wall Street Transparency and Accountability | 8301 |
| 110. Restore Online Shoppers' Confidence | 8401 |

### CHAPTER 2—FEDERAL TRADE COMMISSION; PROMOTION OF EXPORT TRADE AND PREVENTION OF UNFAIR METHODS OF COMPETITION

SUBCHAPTER IV—LABELING
OF FUR PRODUCTS

Sec.
69.   Definitions.

Sec.
69a.   Violations of Federal Trade Commission
Act.

### SUBCHAPTER IV—LABELING OF FUR PRODUCTS

### § 69.   Definitions

As used in this subchapter—

*[See main volume for text of (a) to (c)]*

**(d)** The term "fur product" means any article of wearing apparel made in whole or in part of fur or used fur.

*[See main volume for text of (e) to (k)]*

(Aug. 8, 1951, c. 298, § 2, 65 Stat. 175; Nov. 9, 2000, Pub.L. 106–476, Title I, § 1443(b), 114 Stat. 2167; Dec. 18, 2010, Pub.L. 111–313, § 2(a), 124 Stat. 3326.)

#### HISTORICAL AND STATUTORY NOTES

**Amendments**

**2010 Amendments.** Subsec. (d). Pub.L. 111–313, § 2(a), struck out "; except that such term shall not include such articles (other than any dog or cat fur product to which section 1308 of Title 19 applies) as the Commission shall exempt by reason of the relatively small quantity or value of the fur or used fur contained therein" following "or used fur".

**Effective and Applicability Provisions**

**2010 Acts.** Pub.L. 111–313, § 2(b), Dec. 18, 2010, 124 Stat. 3326, provided that: "The

amendment made by subsection (a) [amending this section] shall take effect on the date that is 90 days after the date of the enactment of this Act [Dec. 18, 2010]."

**Short Title**

**2010 Acts.** Pub.L. 111–313, § 1, Dec. 18, 2010, 124 Stat. 3326, provided that: "This Act [amending this section and 15 U.S.C.A. § 69a and enacting provisions set out as notes under this section] may be cited as the 'Truth in Fur Labeling Act of 2010'."

#### LAW REVIEW AND JOURNAL COMMENTARIES

Drop dead stylish: Mitigating environmental impact of fur production through consumer protection in the Truth in Fur Labeling Act of 2010.

Comment, 19 Penn St. Envtl. L. Rev. 267 (Spring 2011).

#### Research References

**ALR Library**

79 ALR 1200, Validity and Construction of Statute Creating Federal Trade Commission.

152 ALR 1198, Decision or Ruling by Federal Trade Commission as Res Judicata.

1. Rely on an unofficial code, the U.S.C.A. or the U.S.C.S. After finding the appropriate code section, consult the pocket part supplement at the end of the volume or the separately published pamphlet that updates the particular volume. For example, 15 U.S.C.A. § 68 is viewed in the main volume. See Illustration 7-6. Then turn to the back of the volume containing the initial entry and open the pocket part supplement to see if § 68 is mentioned. The entries in the supplement are in numerical order just as they are in the main volume. If a section is not affected, it is just skipped over and the next affected section, in sequential order, is mentioned. Here, § 68 is not included so this indicates that there are no updates for the section. See Illustration 7-14. Note that sometimes the material updating the code volume contains too many pages to be included in a pocket part so that a supplementary pamphlet, a separate paperback-bound pamphlet, is published.

2. To further update a federal code section, scan the *United States Code Service Advance Service,* the U.S.C.C.A.N. advance sheets (the paperbound pamphlets that are issued monthly containing the session laws from the Congress), or the U.S.C.A. statutory supplement to find relevant slip laws from recent congressional sessions. Look for entries that are similar in name to the code section you are updating. This can also be done for state statutes by using the state session law reporter.

3. If a state statute is being updated, review the session law reporter for the legislature to see if any new session laws modify, repeal, supersede, or amend existing legislation. Also, consult the state legislative information website. You can obtain state legislative information at www.llsdc.org/state-legislation, which has an updated list of all 50 states' legislative telephone numbers and state legislature's websites, with separate access information for each chamber when available.

4. You can track pending legislation for the 50 states on Lexis and on Westlaw in the respective state bill tracking files.

5. Review the U.S.C.A. statutory supplement for federal statutes. This pamphlet indicates whether a section of the U.S.C. has been amended, repealed, or created.

6. KeyCite or Shepardize the statute to get updates too.

## 5. How to Find State Statutes

▼ How Does State Statutory Research Compare with Federal Statutory Research?

State statutory research closely parallels federal statutory research. To perform state statutory research, you would use the index method, the title outline method, the popular name table, or the conversion table approach, just as you would with the federal materials. You should start your research with the annotated statute set for the state to be sure

to obtain research enhancements and updates. Even the precise, succinct language of the state statutes is similar to the federal statutes because of the canons of construction and models of statutory parallelism that are adopted by drafters of legislation.

State statutes are enacted by the state legislatures in the same manner as federal statutes and appear in the slip law format first, then become session laws, and finally are codified and incorporated into the state statutory codes. Current state legislation also can be found in state bar bulletins, legal newspapers, and on the Internet, or at the particular state's legislative website found at thomas.loc.gov/home/state-legislatures.html. You can also search state legislation on Lexis or Westlaw. An overlooked resource for state legislative information is the newspaper of a large city in the state or the newspaper of the state capital.

---

### *PRACTICE POINTER*

Always read a statute according to its plain meaning; that is, interpret the language just as it is written. After reading a statute, summarize the language in a few sentences, in your own words. This will help when you then want to use the statute in a written document. Your language and the statutory language won't contrast so sharply. Remember to cite to all statutory authority that you rely on, even if it is written in your own language. Be sure that any statute that you rely on is updated.

---

### ▼ How Can You Tell Whether a State Code Is the Official or the Unofficial Statutory Compilation?

*Bluebook* **Table T.1** and *ALWD* **Appendix 1** answer this question. Under each state in **Table T.1** is the boldface heading **Statutory compilations**, with information indicating the official format of the state code. *ALWD* indicates the official code with a star. For example, under Wisconsin you find:

**Statutory compilations:** Cite to Wis. Stat. if therein.

This indicates that Wis. Stat., the *Bluebook* abbreviation for the *Wisconsin Statutes*, is the official statutory compilation for Wisconsin. Under the Statutory compilations heading, the names of the state code, in the official and the unofficial format, are listed along with the *Bluebook* abbreviation. Also, check the *Bluebook* and *ALWD* for guidance on citing to state statutes retrieved from a state website. See **Rule 18** of the *Bluebook* and **Rule 14.4** and **Appendix 1** of *ALWD*.

**ILLUSTRATION 7-15.  Sample Page Showing Vermont Statutes Annotated, 9 V.S.A. § 2698** *available at* **www.leg.state.vt.us/statutes**

---

# The Vermont Statutes Online

## Title 9: Commerce and Trade

### *Chapter 73: WEIGHTS AND MEASURES*

*Sub-Chapter 04: Specific Weights And Measures*

**9 V.S.A. § 2698. Textile products**

**§ 2698. Textile products**

A person shall not keep for the purpose of sale, offer or expose for sale, or sell, any textile yard goods put up or packaged in advance of sale in a bolt or roll, or any other textile product put up or packaged in advance of sale in any other unit, for either wholesale or retail sale, unless that bolt or roll, or such other unit, is definitely, plainly, and conspicuously marked to show its net measure in terms of yards or its net weight in terms of avoirdupois pounds or ounces, subject, however, to the following limitations and requirements:

(1) Any unit of twine or cordage may be marked to show its net measure in terms of feet. Ready-wound bobbins that are not sold separately shall not be required to be individually marked, but the package containing those bobbins shall be marked to show the number of bobbins contained therein and the net weight or measure of the thread on each bobbin. Any unit of sewing, basting, mending, darning, crocheting, tatting, handknitting, or embroidery thread or yarn, except nylon handknitting yarn, that is not composed in whole or in part of wool, the net weight of which is less than two ounces avoirdupois, shall be marked to show its net measure in terms of yards as unwound from the ball or from the spool or other holder. Any retail unit of a textile product, sold only for household use, consisting of a package containing two or more similar individual units that are not sold separately, shall be marked to show the number of individual units in the package and the net weight or net measure of the product in each individual unit, but this proviso shall not apply where the individual units are separately marked. Any unit of yarn, composed in whole or in part of wool, sold to consumers for handiwork, shall be marked to show the net weight of such yarn, except that any such unit of tapestry, mending, or embroidery yarn, the net measure of which does not exceed 50 yards, may be marked to show its linear measures only.

(2) The marking required by this section shall in all cases be in combination with the name and place of business of the manufacturer, packer, or distributor of the product, or a trademark, symbol, brand, or other mark that positively identifies such manufacturer, packer, or distributor. Any such trademark, symbol, brand, or other mark that is employed to identify the manufacturer, packer, or distributor shall be filed with the secretary.

(3) Reasonable tolerances may be permitted, and these may be included in regulations for the enforcement of this section that shall be issued by the secretary.

(4) This section shall not apply to the following textile products when sold at wholesale in bulk by net weight: cordage, agricultural bag sewing threads, twines, yarns that are to be processed, and yarns that are to be industrially converted into end use products. (1967, No. 102, § 32, eff. April 14, 1967; amended 1991, No. 227 (Adj. Sess.), § 7; 2003, No. 42, § 2, eff. May 27, 2003.)

Sometimes a state has more than one statutory compilation, or there is not official compilation. When this occurs, follow the *Bluebook* or *ALWD* for guidance when citing.

## 6. Researching Statutes Online

▼ Are the Federal Statutes Available on Lexis and Westlaw?

Yes, the complete texts of the U.S.C. and the U.S.C.A. (published by West) are available on Westlaw. The U.S.C.S. is available in full text on Lexis. See Illustration 7-7 for an example. Both Lexis and Westlaw have added the browse enhancement to the statutes databases, enabling you to view the code sections preceding and following the code section that you retrieved. The browse feature emulates flipping through code sections in a hardbound format because you often look at related code sections when you find the section of the statutes with information on point. If cost is a factor, check www.gpo.gov/fdsys or www.law.cornell.edu.

▼ Are State Statutes Available on Lexis and Westlaw?

Yes, the full text of all 50 state statutory compilations are available on both Westlaw and Lexis. On Lexis, you can search all 50 state codes simultaneously. Slip laws are available for all 50 states on Lexis and Westlaw in the respective state legislative service file.

Cornell's Legal Information Institute permits you to access and to search all 50 state statutory compilations at no charge. The site is www.law.cornell.edu/states.

▼ Can Statutes Be Validated on Lexis and Westlaw?

*Shepard's* for all statutes is now available on Lexis. You can validate statutes on Westlaw by using KeyCite.

▼ How Do You Update Federal Statutes Online?

Updating statutory authority online is achieved through the point-and-click method. Once you have the relevant statutory provision on the screen, there will be a caption indicating that the statute is current through a particular date or session law. Citations to any slip laws or session laws updating the statute will be given. Merely point and click

the identifying citation, and you will link to the updating document. Before you perform this on either Lexis or Westlaw, call customer service for guidance.

### ▼ Are Statutes Available on the Internet?

Yes, the U.S.C. is available on the Internet at uscode.house.gov, www.gpo.gov/fdsys, and www.law.cornell.edu. Remember to validate any statutory provision that you use to see how a court has applied it. Also, double-check to see if the provision is current by consulting the last date updated on the site. State legislative information is easily obtained at thomas.loc.gov/home/state-legislatures.html.

## CHAPTER SUMMARY

This chapter led you through the legislative process, where you learned the steps a bill goes through to become law. Also, this chapter detailed constitutional and statutory research on the state and federal levels. You learned how to find, to cite, and to validate pertinent constitutional provisions. You learned about the different ways to perform statutory research—federal and state—and how to update, validate, and cite statutes.

## KEY TERMS

codification
committee report
conference committee
constitution
grandfathered
House committee
legislation
pocket veto
public laws
session laws
slip bill

slip law
sponsor
statutes
*Statutes at Large*
Statutory compilations
subcommittee
*United States Code*
*United States Code Annotated*
*United States Code Service*
veto

## EXERCISES

### RESEARCHING BY POPULAR NAME

To answer questions 1–9, look up the Americans with Disabilities Act of 1990.

1. What date was the act enacted originally? Where is the information? List at least two places.
2. List the names of the four substantive titles of the act. What are they called in the codified version?
3. Provide the public law number for the act. List at least two places where this information is found.

4. Explain what the numbers included in the public law number mean.
5. Provide the U.S.C. citation for the act. List the steps you followed to find this information.
6. Provide the *Statutes at Large* citation for the act. List at least two places where this information is found.
7. What is the definition of *employer* under the act?
8. Does the definition of *employer* under Title I of the act differ in the U.S.C.A. from the definition found in the *Statutes at Large* when the law was originally enacted? If so, how?
9. Find the *United States Code* section for the Americans with Disabilities Act on the Internet at www.gpo.gov/fdsys.

For questions 10–16, look up the Energy Conservation and Production Act in the U.S.C.'s popular name table. Note in particular the section discussing State Utility Regulatory Assistance.

10. Write the U.S.C. citation in *Bluebook* format. (Remember to look at the most recent amendments.)
11. After you find the U.S.C. cite, look up the U.S.C.A. entry for the code section. Compare the entries and the annotations. Note the research enhancements that a West publication provides. Write down any key numbers and any U.S.C.C.A.N. references.
12. Look up the U.S.C.S. entry for the code section. Note the research aids that U.S.C.S. provides. Note that you see administrative regulation references in the U.S.C.S.
13. What C.F.R. citation is referred to in the code section? (Remember to use the supplements and the pocket parts to ensure that you are looking at the most current version of the statute.)
14. Are there any cases that discuss or interpret the statute? If so, look up two cases and see how the statute is treated in the opinions.
15. Shepardize the statute citation.
16. Find the statute on the Internet at www.gpo.gov/fdsys.

For questions 17–18, use your state statutes to find the sections that pertain to pawnbrokers and moneylenders.

17. Write the official state code cite in correct *Bluebook* format. Next, write the annotated cite if available. Compare the entries.
18. Are there any cases that discuss or interpret the statute? If so, look them up and see how the statute is treated in the opinion. Finally, Shepardize or KeyCite the statute citation.
19. Use www.gpo.gov/fdsys to find the *United States Code* section containing the provisions concerning the definition of personal income for tax purposes.
20. List three ways to find a statute online. Name the sites consulted.
21. Search either Congress.gov or www.gpo.gov/fdsys for any federal bills or resolutions in the current Congress concerning the registration of sexual offenders.

## CHAPTER 8

# LEGISLATIVE HISTORY

| | |
|---|---|
| **A. LEGISLATIVE INFORMATION** | 237 |
| 1. Finding the Text of Pending Legislation | 238 |
| 2. Tracking Pending Legislation | 239 |
| **B. LEGISLATIVE HISTORIES** | 239 |

## *CHAPTER OVERVIEW*

Paralegals are called on to monitor the status of bills and proposed legislation currently being considered on the federal and state levels and to compile legislative histories of laws already passed and codified to ascertain the policy or intended effect of the legislation. The process of compiling all of the components of the legislative process leading to the enactment of a statute, called **legislative history**, is growing in importance as the need for the interpretation of statutes in litigation increases.

## A. LEGISLATIVE INFORMATION

Researching a legislative history requires that you retrace the law making process of enacted law from the initial bill through the committee reports through the various versions of the bill to the final version and the enacted law. Legislative histories are very informative because the

information gathered from the committee reports and the speeches or legislative debates given on the floor of the legislative body provides insight into the purpose and intent of the legislation. Sometimes you may want to see an earlier version of a statute, even if that version is no longer in effect, because the statute is cited in an older case.

A useful source of information on legislative history, including many links, is at www.llsdc.org/sourcebook. Look at the various links—all are helpful!

## 1. Finding the Text of Pending Legislation

Bills currently going through the process of being enacted into law are classified as **pending legislation.** Paralegals are called on to monitor pending legislation and to make sure that the information is as current as possible.

Lexis and Westlaw have current federal and state bills online. Lexis has the text of current pending federal bills as well as the full text of federal committee and conference reports dating back to January 1990. The text of pending state bills from all 50 states is also available.

Westlaw has bills starting with the 104th Congress. Bill tracking in the BILLTRK database on Westlaw also has pending legislation and the text of bills for states and the U.S. Congress online.

On the state level, each state has a legislative library from which you can request the copy of the particular bill in question. If the librarian cannot provide a copy of the bill, he or she will generally direct you to the member of the state House or Senate who sponsored the bill or to the appropriate committee. Pending legislation for all 50 states can be tracked on Lexis and Westlaw. You can also contact the particular state legislature's library or the state representative directly.

The website for the U.S. House of Representatives is www.house.gov. This site contains committee reports. Committee activities from the past three days are posted here. This is a good site to bookmark when you are tracking legislation, for it links you to bills in full-text format. It has a directory of House members complete with addresses, both postal and e-mail, and telephone numbers. This site posts activity currently on the House floor.

## 2. Tracking Pending Legislation

On the federal level, the *Congressional Index* is updated weekly when Congress is in session and provides information on voting records and the status of bills during the prior week. The status of the bill means where the bill in question is in the legislative process, whether it is in committee or subcommittee hearings, or whether it is being debated on the floor. Note that *Congressional Index* does not print the text of the bills.

Another source for tracking pending federal legislation is the *CQ Weekly Report*. This source, available online by subscription, is helpful for policy information regarding bills currently being considered in Congress and for voting records.

Congress.gov has the capability to monitor pending federal legislation online at no cost.

On the state level, almost every state has either a state legislative website, a state bar association, or a state legislative library that provides information as to the status of bills that are currently being created and considered.

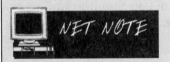

The Law Librarians' Society of Washington, D.C., has a handy website that links you to all 50 state legislatures, state databases, and the respective telephone numbers. This site, at www.llsdc.org/state-legislation, includes state legislative history information.

   Indiana University, Bloomington, Maurer School of Law Library has a state legislative history research guide, for all 50 states, at law.indiana .libguides.com/index.php. Scroll down to State Legislative History Research Guides and click.

# B. LEGISLATIVE HISTORIES

▼ Where Do You Find Copies of Public Laws?

**Public laws,** which are the federally enacted laws, can be obtained by contacting the law's sponsor in the House or the Senate. Also, the U.S. Government Printing Office issues pamphlets for each public law passed. In addition to U.S.C.C.A.N., these can be obtained at a government depository library. (Many university libraries and large city libraries are government depository libraries.) The *United States Code Service* (U.S.C.S.) publishes paperback advance sheets with the

public laws enacted during the prior month. The *United States Code Annotated* (U.S.C.A.) also prints paperback advance sheets each month that contain all of the public laws enacted during the prior month.

The steps for tracing federal legislation are located at www.law
.georgetown.edu/library/research/guides/legislative_history.cfm#bills.

Public laws starting with the 93rd Congress are available online, for no charge, at Congress.gov and at www.gpo.gov/fdsys.

### ▼ How Do You Research Legislative Histories of Laws That Are Already Enacted?

Commercial publishers compile the most accessible sources of legislative histories for laws that are already enacted. The most user-friendly hard-copy source of commercially compiled federal legislative histories is the *United States Code Congressional and Administrative News* (U.S.C.C.A.N.). U.S.C.C.A.N., which began publication in the 1950s, is published by West, and references to U.S.C.C.A.N. are provided in the U.S.C.A. Often a U.S.C.A. entry to a statute enacted since U.S.C.C.A.N.'s publication will contain a reference to the U.S.C.C.A.N. citation, which outlines the legislative process that the statute underwent prior to enactment.

U.S.C.C.A.N. is organized by congressional session; the congressional session is indicated on the spine of each volume. Each session's public laws, also indicated on the spine of each volume, and the legislative history of the public laws are arranged in numerical order according to public law number. See Illustrations 8-1 and 8-2 on pages 242 - 245.

U.S.C.C.A.N. is a good place to find legislative history and a copy of a public law, provided it is not too recent. For copies of recent public laws (one-month old), consult the pamphlets at the end of the U.S.C.A., U.S.C.S., and U.S.C.C.A.N. sets.

Legislative histories are also available on Westlaw in the LH database. The coverage begins in 1948.

Lexis has compiled legislative histories online for select, significant acts.

Congress.gov provides free access to legislative information, including public laws, beginning in the 93rd Congress. It also contains the Congressional Record beginning with the 101st Congress and committee reports starting with the 104th Congress as well as links to federal government websites. However, the full text of bills from before 1993, the 103rd Congress, is not currently available on Congress.gov. Use this site to find legislative information from the current Congress that may impact a particular federal statute. You can search by bill number, by popular name, or by word. You can view the actual bill in PDF.

### ▼ How Do You Use U.S.C.C.A.N. in Conjunction with the U.S.C.A.?

In Illustration 7-6, look at the reprint of 15 U.S.C.A. § 68 from the main code volume of the U.S.C.A. Notice the heading that follows the text of the statute: Historical and Statutory Notes. It is in this part of the U.S.C.A. that you obtain references to the public laws that created the statute and to the appropriate U.S.C.C.A.N. cite that contains the legislative history for the public law for the amendments to § 68.

We are interested in the amendments to the Wool Products Labeling Act of 1939 that concern the definition of recycled wool.

## PRACTICE POINTER

When retrieving a document from a government website, use your software's "Find" feature to locate relevant text within the document.

### ▼ What Are Other Ways to Find Relevant Legislative History in U.S.C.C.A.N.?

The popular name tables in the U.S.C., U.S.C.A., and U.S.C.S. provide references to the public law numbers for the statutes. If you have the public law number of a statute, then you can find the legislative history in U.S.C.C.A.N. because U.S.C.C.A.N. is organized by public law number.

## ILLUSTRATION 8-1.   Sample Pages from U.S.C.C.A.N. Showing Pub. L. No. 96-242

---

PUBLIC LAW 96–242 [H.R. 4197];   May 5, 1980

### WOOL PRODUCTS LABELING ACT OF 1939— RECYCLED WOOL

*For Legislative History of this and other Laws, see Table 1, Public Laws and Legislative History, at end of final volume*

**An Act to amend the Wool Products Labeling Act of 1939 with respect to recycled wool.**

*Wool Products Labeling Act, amendment. 15 USC 68.*

*Be it enacted by the Senate and House of Representatives of the United States of America in Congress assembled,* That (a) section 2(c) of the Wool Products Labeling Act of 1939 (54 Stat. 1128) is amended to read as follows:

"(c) The term 'recycled wool' means (1) the resulting fiber when wool has been woven or felted into a wool product which, without ever having been utilized in any way by the ultimate consumer, subsequently has been made into a fibrous state, or (2) the resulting fiber when wool or reprocessed wool has been spun, woven, knitted, or felted into a wool product which, after having been used in any way by the ultimate consumer, subsequently has been made into a fibrous state.".

*Repeal.*

(b) Subsection (d) of section 2 of the Wool Products Labeling Act of 1939 is repealed.

(c) Subsections (e), (f), (g), (h), and (i) of section 2 of the Wool Products Labeling Act of 1939 and all references thereto are redesignated as subsections (d), (e), (f), (g), and (h), respectively.

(d) Section 2(d) of such Act, as redesignated by subsection (c) of this section, is amended by striking out ", reprocessed wool, or reused wool" and inserting in lieu thereof "or recycled wool".

*15 USC 68b.*

Sec. 2. Section 4(a)(2)(A) of the Wool Products Labeling Act of 1939 is amended—

(1) by striking out "(2) reprocessed wool; (3) reused wool" and inserting in lieu thereof "(2) recycled wool";

(2) by striking out "(4)" and inserting in lieu thereof "(3)"; and

(3) by striking out "(5)" and by inserting in lieu thereof "(4)".

*Effective date. 15 USC 68 note.*

Sec. 3. The amendments made by this Act shall take effect with respect to wool products manufactured on or after the date sixty days after the date of enactment of this Act.

Approved May 5, 1980.

---

LEGISLATIVE HISTORY:

HOUSE REPORT No. 96-795 (Comm. on Interstate and Foreign Commerce).
SENATE REPORT No. 96-655 (Comm. on Commerce, Science, and Transportation).
CONGRESSIONAL RECORD, Vol. 126 (1980):
 Mar. 11, considered and passed House.
 Apr. 23, considered and passed Senate.

**94 STAT. 344**

Reprinted with permission of Thomson Reuters.

**ILLUSTRATION 8-2.   Sample Pages from U.S.C.C.A.N.**
**Showing the Legislative History of Pub. L. No. 96-242**

---

**LEGISLATIVE HISTORY**
P.L. 96–242

## WOOL PRODUCTS LABELING ACT OF 1939—
## RECYCLED WOOL

*P.L. 96–242, see page 94 Stat. 344*

**House Report (Interstate and Foreign Commerce Committee)**
**No. 96–795, Mar. 4, 1980 [To accompany H.R. 4197]**

**Senate Report (Commerce, Science, and Transportation Committee)**
**No. 96–655, Apr. 18, 1980 [To accompany H.R. 4197]**

**Cong. Record Vol. 126 (1980)**

**DATES OF CONSIDERATION AND PASSAGE**

**House March 11, 1980**

**Senate April 23, 1980**

**The Senate Report is set out.**

## SENATE REPORT NO. 96–655

[page 1]

The Committee on Commerce, Science, and Transportation, to which was referred the bill (H.R. 4197) to amend the Wool Products Labeling Act of 1939 with respect to recycled wool, having considered the same, reports favorably thereon without amendment and recommends that the bill do pass.

PURPOSE

H.R. 4197 would amend the Wool Products Labeling Act of 1939 by substituting the term "recycled wool" for the terms "reprocessed wool" and "reused wool" where these terms appear in the act. H.R. 4197 would also combine the definitions of "reprocessed wool" and "reused wool" into one definition for the term "recycled wool," and appropriately renumber subsections of the act accordingly. The amendments made by H.R. 4197 would beome effective 60 days after the date of enactment.

BACKGROUND AND NEED

The Wool Products Labeling Act of 1939, enacted October 14, 1940, provides for a system of labeling wool products introduced, manufactured for introduction, sale, transportation, or distribution in commerce. The failure to label wool products in accordance with the terms of the act is unlawful and is an unfair method of competition and an unfair and deceptive act or practice under the Federal Trade Commission Act.

[page 2]

The labeling terms required in the act are "wool," "reprocessed wool" and "reused wool." The term "wool" as used in the act means the fiber from the fleece of the sheep or lamb, or hair of angora or

**782**

## ILLUSTRATION 8-2.  *Continued*

---

**WOOL PRODUCTS LABELING ACT**
P.L. 96–242

cashmere goat (and may include the so-called specialty fiber from the hair of the camel, alpaca, llama, and vicuna) which has never been reclaimed from woven or felted wool products. The term "reprocessed wool" as used in the act means the resulting fiber when wool has been woven or felted into a wool product and which, without ever having been utilized in any way by the ultimate consumer, has subsequently been made into a fiber state. The term "reused wool" means the fiber which results when wool or reprocessed wool has been spun woven, knitted or felted into a wool product and which, after having been used in any way by the ultimate consumer, has subsequently been made into a fiber state again.

Since the fiber used in the production of "reprocessed wool" or "reused wool" goes through similar mechanical processes in order to be used in the remanufacture of wool products, the term "recycled" would be substituted for the terms "reprocessed" and "reused" since it more accurately describes the process involved.

The raw material for reprocessed wool comes from wool clippings and other wool products left over from manufacturing processes which is then recycled to its fibrous state. The raw material for reused wool stock comes from wool used in a wool product which has been used by the consumer and is then recycled to its fibrous state. The resulting fibers in each case are fibers of wool which are then made again into cloth, felt or some other wool product. As with wool or other fibers, that recycled wool fiber is frequently blended or combined with other fibers to produce the final product.

The steps in the recycling of wool are as follows:

Wool clippings and wool clothing or other wool products are sorted into more than 200 classifications before they are made into new cloth, felt, or other products. To prepare fibers for recycled wool, discarded wool products are first divided into those in good condition and those in poor condition. Products which are not suitable for fabrics are used for industrial purposes for roofing material.

The processed or used wool products are further graded. Knitted materials are separated from woven goods, woolens from worsteds. Pockets or linings of cotton or other materials are removed. The material is then sorted by color to permit its use where feasible without removing dyes. The material is usually carbonized which removes fibers and is thoroughly scoured to remove all soil and dirt. This makes the material sanitized.

After sorting has been completed, the products are placed in a machine that picks out the fibers used to produce wool stock. Clippings from cutting tables in garment plants are likewise sorted and graded in preparation for recycling.

Wool cloth, whether of 100-percent wool or recycled wool, is woven or otherwise fabricated in the same way. Wool stocks, both new wool and recycled wool, are blended to produce yarn which is then woven, knitted or blended for felt or other products. Fabrics are washed repeatedly to remove oil that is used to lubricate the fibers and all dirt that may be in the fabrics. The fabric is then dried in an oven at 240°F and sheared, finished, pressed, and ready for the manufacturer or home user.

[page 3]

After this processing, the wool fibers have been recycled, that is, entirely rebuilt into yarn, fabrics, and felt and subsequently into

# ILLUSTRATION 8-2. *Continued*

---

> **LEGISLATIVE HISTORY**
> P.L. 96–242
>
> products for apparel or industrial use. Recycled wools are used primarily in heavy winter clothing, gloves, caps, felts and blankets.
>    The Committee finds that the terms "reused wool" and "reprocessed wool" are unnecessary and often misleading to the consumer. Further, the terms also give a competitive advantage to foreign textile manufacturers who frequently do not comply with the rigid labeling requirements of the Wool Act.

Reprinted with permission of Thomson Reuters.

## ▼ Is Legislative History Primary Authority?

Legislative history is not primary authority but is considered to be secondary authority because it provides material to interpret the statutes. In the legislative branch of our government, primary authority is limited to constitutions, statutes, codes, charters, and ordinances.

## ▼ How Do You Cite Legislative History Found in U.S.C.C.A.N.?

Legislative history materials found in U.S.C.C.A.N. follow *Bluebook* **Rule 13.4** and *ALWD* **Rule 15.7(f)**. The correct cite for a U.S. Senate Report reprinted in U.S.C.C.A.N. is:

S. Rep. No. 13, 102d Cong., 2d Sess. 111 (1991), *reprinted in* 1991 U.S.C.C.A.N. 12.

## ▼ How Do You Cite to a Legislative History of a Statute?

*Bluebook* **Rule 13** and *ALWD* **Rule 15** detail the format for the components of the legislative process: the bill, the committee report, the debates, and the transcripts of the hearings.

## ▼ What Are Some Other Sources of Legislative Information?

**Congressional Information Service** (CIS) has been produced since 1970. CIS is a source of detailed compiled legislative histories. CIS has an index, which is published annually, that allows you to find the reference to the relevant public law. After you find the reference to the relevant legislation, you are instructed to consult the abstracts detailing the components of the legislative history for the relevant public law. The abstracts are very informative and should be consulted because you can find out if the information you need is found in the complete document. CIS is exhaustive in its coverage of legislative history information for public laws.

The CIS index and abstracts are also available online on Lexis. Many libraries have cancelled the hard copy subscription, so Lexis will provide your access to this resource.

The ***Congressional Record*** contains the text of all of the proceedings from the floor of the U.S. Congress. It is published every day that Congress is in session. The *Congressional Record* has been in print since the 1870s. It is currently available on Lexis and Westlaw. You can view today's *Congressional Record*, in PDF, at Congress.gov. The *Congressional Record* is available at www.gpo.gov/fdsys going back to 1994.

Sometimes it is necessary to consult a privately published legislative history. You should see your law librarian for this or contact the sponsor of the public law to find out more detailed information.

### ▼ How Do You Research State Legislative Histories?

Each state compiles legislative resources in a different manner, which complicates the task of research. Most states do not have commercially compiled legislative histories in hard-copy format. Some states have printed indexes, but the actual documents are on Microfiche or on the particular state's legislative website. Each state has a legislative library that you can call for more information. Large public libraries and university libraries, particularly law school libraries, are good places to obtain state legislative history information. Session law services are available for every state at the state legislature's website. Consult thomas.loc.gov/home/state-legislatures.html to obtain the state's legislative website.

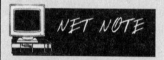

NET NOTE

To find Government Printing Office documents and links to the *Congressional Record, Congressional Bills*, and congressional publications, go to www.gpo.gov/fdsys.

The U.S. Senate website, at www.senate.gov, offers information about every Senate committee as well as a biographical directory of Senate members. This is also available for the House of Representatives at www.house.gov.

*PRACTICE POINTER*

Researching legislative histories can be time-consuming. Ask the attorney that you are working for about a time budget for the project before performing a legislative history. Also, contact a librarian at a large academic law library for assistance when performing legislative histories.

**ILLUSTRATION 8-3.** Congress.gov Search Results for 113th Congress and Bills Containing "clothing textiles"

---

II

113TH CONGRESS
1ST SESSION

# S. 1883

To extend duty-free treatment for certain trousers, breeches, or shorts imported from Nicaragua, and for other purposes.

---

## IN THE SENATE OF THE UNITED STATES

DECEMBER 20, 2013

Mrs. HAGAN introduced the following bill; which was read twice and referred to the Committee on Finance

---

# A BILL

To extend duty-free treatment for certain trousers, breeches, or shorts imported from Nicaragua, and for other purposes.

1    *Be it enacted by the Senate and House of Representa-*

2    *tives of the United States of America in Congress assembled,*

3    **SECTION 1. SHORT TITLE.**

4    This Act may be cited as the "Extending Incentives

5    for Exporting American Textiles Act of 2013".

6    **SEC. 2. EXTENSION OF DUTY-FREE TREATMENT FOR CER-**

7    **TAIN TROUSERS, BREECHES, OR SHORTS IM-**

8    **PORTED FROM NICARAGUA.**

9    (a) DUTY-FREE TREATMENT.—Notwithstanding the

10    termination of the tariff preference level program for im-

## ILLUSTRATION 8-3. *Continued*

2

1 ports of apparel articles from Nicaragua and subject to

2 subsection (b), eligible apparel articles shall enter the

3 United States free of duty if such eligible apparel articles

4 are accompanied by an earned import allowance certificate

5 for the amount of credits equal to the total square meter

6 equivalents of fabric in such eligible apparel articles, in

7 accordance with the program established under subsection

8 (c).

8

1      (4) ENTITY CONTROLLING PRODUCTION.—The

2 term "entity controlling production" means a person

3 or other entity or group that is not a producer and

4 that controls the production process in Nicaragua

5 through a contractual relationship or other indirect

6 means.

7      (5) FABRIC WHOLLY FORMED IN THE UNITED

8 STATES OF YARN WHOLLY FORMED IN THE UNITED

9 STATES.—The term "fabric wholly formed in the

10 United States of yarn wholly formed in the United

11 States" means fabric—

12      (A) woven in the United States from fibers

13      or from yarns, the constituent staple fibers of

14      which are spun in the United States or the con-

15      tinuous filament of which is extruded in the

16      United States;

17      (B) for which any dyeing, printing, or fin-

18      ishing is performed in the United States; and

19      (C) exported to Nicaragua on or after

20      April 1, 2014.

▼ What Additional Sources for Legislative Information Are Available?

The following sources provide additional assistance in researching legislative information.

www.house.gov: to find bill information, Representatives and House of Representatives personnel

www.senate.gov: to find legislative information, senators, and Senate staff

*The United States Government Manual:* searchable online at www.gpoaccess.gov/gmanual. Provides information about all agencies within all the branches of the federal government, including addresses and telephone numbers. Updated annually.

## CHAPTER SUMMARY

This chapter defined pending legislation and provided the tools to monitor pending legislation. U.S.C.C.A.N. is highlighted as the best and most efficient tool for compiling a legislative history of a federal statute. Both Congress.gov and www.gpo.gov/fdsys offer easy access to legislative information from the 93rd Congress to date and are very cost effective to use. You are also introduced to other resources to perform more detailed legislative histories, both federal and state.

## KEY TERMS

*Congress.gov*
Congressional Information Service
*Congressional Record*
www.gpo.gov/fdsys
legislative history

pending legislation
public laws
*United States Code Congressional and Administrative News*

## EXERCISES

1. Find the legislative history of the Brady Handgun Violence Prevention Act. This is a federal act. Cite the legislative history of the act in *Bluebook* format.
2. Find the legislative history of the Depository Library Act of 1964. This is a federal act. Cite the legislative history of the act in *Bluebook* format.
3. Name two components of a typical legislative history.
4. Why would you perform a legislative history of an act?
5. What information would you gather when performing a legislative history?
6. Search Congress.gov to see if there are any bills from the current Congress that update or address the Brady Handgun Act.
7. Search Congress.gov to find bills for the Rural America Energy Act of 2007.
8. Obtain any House or Senate bill numbers and the public law number for the Virginia Graeme Baker Pool and Spa Safety Act.

## CHAPTER 9

# ADMINISTRATIVE MATERIALS AND LOOSELEAF SERVICES

| | | |
|---|---|---|
| **A.** | **INTRODUCTION** | 252 |
| **B.** | **REGULATIONS** | 253 |
| **C.** | **FINDING ADMINISTRATIVE LAW** | 253 |
| | 1. Generally | 253 |
| | 2. Specific Sources | 256 |
| **D.** | **DECISIONS** | 274 |
| **E.** | **LOOSELEAF SERVICES** | 275 |

## CHAPTER OVERVIEW

In Chapter 7 you learned about the enactment of statutes and how to research them. Some statutes create administrative agencies and provide these agencies with a variety of powers. In this chapter, you learn about the creation of administrative agencies, the powers of these agencies, and the authority that they generate. You are shown how to locate these authorities as well as how to update and validate them. By the chapter's end, you will know how to use administrative materials and will understand their importance and relationship to other primary and secondary sources.

# A. INTRODUCTION

### ▼ What Is Administrative Law?

Administrative rules and regulations are essential to the practice of law in a variety of areas, such as taxation, environmental law, education, and health care law. Federal and state administrative agencies regulate many aspects of our lives ranging from the safety of the products we purchase to the amount of hazardous wastes that can be placed in our landfills.

### ▼ How Can Administrative Agencies Create Law When This Is the Job of Congress?

Congress delegates its power to create law to **administrative agencies** by enacting **enabling statutes.** With these statutes, Congress charges these agencies with the daily enforcement of detailed regulations. This is both more efficient for Congress and also allows the development of these regulations by individuals with more expertise in an area than individual congressional representatives. The agencies create these detailed regulations through a process that involves solicitation of public opinions.

### ▼ How Do Administrative Agencies Operate?

On the federal level, administrative agencies often fall under the control of the executive branch of the government. To determine which executives control a particular agency, several sources should be consulted. The *United States Government Manual* provides information about all federal government agencies as well as an organization chart. This information includes a brief description of the agency's functions, how it was created, and how it is controlled. Although every cabinet post has an agency beneath it, some agencies are not associated with cabinet posts, such as the National Aeronautics and Space Administration (NASA). Often, agency staff members, other than those who hold cabinet posts, are hired because of their expertise and qualifications in an area of law. These experts do not leave their posts at the end of a legislative term.

Agencies often are called bureaus, boards, commissions, corporations, or administrations. All agencies create law in the form of **rules** or **regulations.** Agencies may function in an **adjudicatory** or **quasi-judicial** manner when they hear cases involving the application of a particular regulation and then issue written opinions of their findings.

Agencies create rules or regulations regularly, conduct hearings concerning particular issues, make decisions, and enforce Congress's mandates. The agency regulations adopted, or promulgated, are similar to statutes except that they are far more detailed. The administrative

regulations explain how to apply the laws briefly outlined by Congress in the enabling legislation.

For example, Congress delegates to the U.S. Food and Drug Administration (FDA) authority to deal with the daily concerns regarding food products. FDA regulates the labeling of all consumer food products based on a Congress-adopted law that created that FDA. The regulations are very specific. Among the details specified is the definition of principal display panel and the fact that it should be "large enough to accommodate all the mandatory label information required to be placed thereon." See the regulation shown in Illustration 9-1.

# B. REGULATIONS

### ▼ How Are Regulations Adopted?

The process for adoption of regulations varies. The agency or the legislature determines what procedures must be followed before a regulation is adopted. In general, the agency requests comments from the public, conducts one or more hearings, and then decides whether to adopt a regulation. The agency concerns itself with the details. Agency regulations are revised, repealed, and created daily.

### ▼ What Type of Authority Is an Administrative Regulation or Rule?

The regulations and other documents adopted by federal agencies and published in the *Federal Register* and the *Code of Federal Regulations* (see next section) are primary authority because they are issued by a government body acting in its official law making capacity.

# C. FINDING ADMINISTRATIVE LAW

## 1. Generally

### ▼ Where Do You Find Federal Administrative Law?

Federal regulations are found in two official sources: the ***Code of Federal Regulations*** and the ***Federal Register.*** The *Code of Federal Regulations,* or the C.F.R. as it is known, contains all of the final administrative regulations. The C.F.R. is published annually, and different titles are published during different quarters of the year. The *Federal Register* is the daily newspaper for our administrative agencies and for our executive branch of the government. The *Federal Register* contains all of the proposed and final administrative regulations as well as executive orders and proclamations often issued by the president.

## ILLUSTRATION 9-1. Sample Pages from the *Code of Federal Regulations*

Pt. 101

of a food described in this section shall be exempt from declaration of the statements which paragraphs (a) and (b) of this section require immediately following the name of the food. Such exemption shall not apply to the outer container or wrapper of a multiunit retail package.

(e) All salt, table salt, iodized salt, or iodized table salt in packages intended for retail sale shipped in interstate commerce 18 months after the date of publication of this statement of policy in the FEDERAL REGISTER, shall be labeled as prescribed by this section; and if not so labeled, the Food and Drug Administration will regard them as misbranded within the meaning of sections 403 (a) and (f) of the Federal Food, Drug, and Cosmetic Act.

[42 FR 14306, Mar. 15, 1977, as amended at 48 FR 10811, Mar. 15, 1983; 49 FR 24119, June 12, 1984]

### PART 101—FOOD LABELING

#### Subpart A—General Provisions

Sec.
101.1 Principal display panel of package form food.
101.2 Information panel of package form food.
101.3 Identity labeling of food in packaged form.
101.4 Food; designation of ingredients.
101.5 Food; name and place of business of manufacturer, packer, or distributor.
101.9 Nutrition labeling of food.
101.10 Nutrition labeling of restaurant foods.
101.12 Reference amounts customarily consumed per eating occasion.
101.13 Nutrient content claims—general principles.
101.14 Health claims: general requirements.
101.15 Food; prominence of required statements.
101.17 Food labeling warning, notice, and safe handling statements.
101.18 Misbranding of food.

#### Subpart B—Specific Food Labeling Requirements

101.22 Foods; labeling of spices, flavorings, colorings and chemical preservatives.
101.30 Percentage juice declaration for foods purporting to be beverages that contain fruit or vegetable juice.

① 21 CFR Ch. I (4–1–08 Edition)

#### Subpart C—Specific Nutrition Labeling Requirements and Guidelines

101.36 Nutrition labeling of dietary supplements.
101.42 Nutrition labeling of raw fruit, vegetables, and fish.
101.43 Substantial compliance of food retailers with the guidelines for the voluntary nutrition labeling of raw fruit, vegetables, and fish.
101.44 Identification of the 20 most frequently consumed raw fruit, vegetables, and fish in the United States.
101.45 Guidelines for the voluntary nutrition labeling of raw fruit, vegetables, and fish.

#### Subpart D—Specific Requirements for Nutrient Content Claims

101.54 Nutrient content claims for "good source," "high," "more," and "high potency."
101.56 Nutrient content claims for "light" or "lite."
101.60 Nutrient content claims for the calorie content of foods.
101.61 Nutrient content claims for the sodium content of foods.
101.62 Nutrient content claims for fat, fatty acid, and cholesterol content of foods.
101.65 Implied nutrient content claims and related label statements.
101.67 Use of nutrient content claims for butter.
101.69 Petitions for nutrient content claims.

#### Subpart E—Specific Requirements for Health Claims

101.70 Petitions for health claims.
101.71 Health claims: claims not authorized.
101.72 Health claims: calcium and osteoporosis.
101.73 Health claims: dietary lipids and cancer.
101.74 Health claims: sodium and hyper-
101.75
101.76
101.77
nary heart disease.
101.78 Health claims: fruits and vegetables and cancer.
101.79 Health claims: Folate and neural tube defects.
101.80 Health claims: dietary noncariogenic carbohydrate sweeteners and dental caries.

**1 Title**
**2 Sections**
**3 Authority**
**4 *Federal Register* citation**
**5 Text**

10

# ILLUSTRATION 9-1.  *Continued*

---

**Food and Drug Administration, HHS**                               **§ 101.2**

101.81  Health claims: Soluble fiber from certain foods and risk of coronary heart disease (CHD).

101.82  Health claims: Soy protein and risk of coronary heart disease (CHD).

101.83  Health claims: plant sterol/stanol esters and risk of coronary heart disease (CHD).

**Subpart F—Specific Requirements for Descriptive Claims That Are Neither Nutrient Content Claims nor Health Claims**

101.93  Certain types of statements for dietary supplements.

101.95  "Fresh," "freshly frozen," "fresh frozen," "frozen fresh."

### Subpart G—Exemptions From Food Labeling Requirements

101.100  Food; exemptions from labeling.

101.105  Declaration of net quantity of contents when exempt.

101.108  Temporary exemptions for purposes of conducting authorized food labeling experiments.

APPENDIX A TO PART 101—MONIER-WILLIAMS PROCEDURE (WITH MODIFICATIONS) FOR SULFITES IN FOOD, CENTER FOR FOOD SAFETY AND APPLIED NUTRITION, FOOD AND DRUG ADMINISTRATION (NOVEMBER 1985)

APPENDIX B TO PART 101—GRAPHIC ENHANCEMENTS USED BY THE FDA

APPENDIX C TO PART 101—NUTRITION FACTS FOR RAW FRUITS AND VEGETABLES

APPENDIX D TO PART 101—NUTRITION FACTS FOR COOKED FISH

**(3)** AUTHORITY: 15 U.S.C. 1453, 1454, 1455; 21 U.S.C. 321, 331, 342, 343, 348, 371; 42 U.S.C. 243, 264, 271.

**(4)** SOURCE: 42 FR 14308, Mar. 15, 1977, unless otherwise noted.

EDITORIAL NOTE: Nomenclature changes to part 101 appear at 63 FR 14035, Mar. 24, 1998, 66 FR 17358, Mar. 30, 2001, and 66 FR 56035, Nov. 6, 2001.

### Subpart A—General Provisions

**§ 101.1  Principal display panel of package form food.**

**(5)** The term *principal display panel* as it applies to food in package form and as used in this part, means the part of a label that is most likely to be displayed, presented, shown, or examined under customary conditions of display for retail sale. The principal display panel shall be large enough to accommodate all the mandatory label information required to be placed thereon

by this part with clarity and conspicuousness and without obscuring design, vignettes, or crowding. Where packages bear alternate principal display panels, information required to be placed on the principal display panel shall be duplicated on each principal display panel. For the purpose of obtaining uniform type size in declaring the quantity of contents for all packages of substantially the same size, the term *area of the principal display panel* means the area of the side or surface that bears the principal display panel, which area shall be:

(a) In the case of a rectangular package where one entire side properly can be considered to be the principal display panel side, the product of the height times the width of that side;

(b) In the case of a cylindrical or nearly cylindrical container, 40 percent of the product of the height of the container times the circumference;

(c) In the case of any otherwise shaped container, 40 percent of the total surface of the container: *Provided, however,* That where such container presents an obvious "principal display panel" such as the top of a triangular or circular package of cheese, the area shall consist of the entire top surface. In determining the area of the principal display panel, exclude tops, bottoms, flanges at tops and bottoms of cans, and shoulders and necks of bottles or jars. In the case of cylindrical or nearly cylindrical containers, information required by this part to appear on the principal display panel shall appear within that 40 percent of the circumference which is most likely to be displayed, presented, shown, or examined under customary conditions of display for retail sale.

**§ 101.2  Information panel of package form food.**

(a) The term *information panel* as it applies to packaged food means that part of the label immediately contiguous and to the right of the principal display panel as observed by an individual facing the principal display panel with the following exceptions:

(1) If the part of the label immediately contiguous and to the right of the principal display panel is too small

11

## ▼ Where Do You Find State Administrative Law?

States have agencies similar to those of the federal government. Most states have administrative materials that are organized and published in the same manner as those of the federal government.

The amount of administrative materials states publish sometimes is quite voluminous. Some states have an administrative register but do not publish an administrative compilation. Other states have an administrative compilation but do not publish an administrative register. Many states provide their administrative codes only at a Web site.

One way to determine whether a state has an administrative compilation or an administrative register is to consult *The Bluebook: A Uniform System of Citation* (19th ed. 2010). The *Bluebook*'s **Table T.1**, United States Jurisdictions lists the administrative materials and the citation format for each state. By reviewing a particular state in the table, you also can determine whether a state has an administrative compilation. Another way is to review *The ALWD Guide to Legal Citation* (5th ed. 2014).

The major obstacle you face when researching state administrative law is the lack of uniformity among the 50 states' administrative materials in their format, scope, and editing. However, an increasing number of administrative compilations can be found on the Internet, and they are easy to search as many can be accessed by keywords.

Some of the state administrative codes overlap materials covered in the federal code. For example, both the federal government and the state of Michigan regulate food labeling.

The coverage of state administrative regulations on Lexis, Westlaw, and Loislaw is constantly changing. Therefore, check the directories. Using codes online, especially codes from other states, can be easier than trying to access print copies of the codes.

## 2. Specific Sources

### a. Federal Register

The *Federal Register*, a pamphlet published Monday through Friday except on legal holidays, contains all of the regulations adopted by the federal agencies, any regulations the agencies are considering adopting, and any agency notices. It often includes agency policy statements and discussions of comments received concerning agency actions. Executive orders and presidential proclamations also are found in the *Federal Register*. Documents are published in chronological order and are not codified. The *Federal Register* is available in print and on Westlaw, Lexis, and Loislaw, as well as on the Internet. The U.S. Government Printing Office provides the Federal Register, the Federal Digital System website shown in Illustration 9-2, and its federalregister .gov website.

## ILLUSTRATION 9-2. Federal Digital System

### ▼ How Do You Use the *Federal Register* in Print?

To use the *Federal Register,* you could review the table of contents or the index. See Illustration 9-3. The table of contents is found at the beginning of each volume of the *Federal Register* and is organized alphabetically by agency name. An index is published monthly and cumulated for 12 months. This table of contents also indicates that notices and proposed rules are printed in an edition for various agencies.

The table of contents or the index can be difficult to use because they are arranged by agency rather than by subject. Because of this organization, you first must determine what agency is responsible for regulating the conduct or activity you are researching. A review of the enabling statute should provide you with this information. Next, you should find the agency listing in the index and review any topics under each agency heading that are relevant to your research. For example, if you are researching regulations concerning prohibitions and restrictions on proprietary trading involving hedge funds and you know that the Commodity Futures Trading Commission is responsible for these operations, you would go to table of contents and look for that agency. Note Illustration 9-3. It is a page of the table of contents from the *Federal Register* published on January 31, 2014. Next to one of the arrows, it states that there are rules concerning prohibitions and restrictions on

proprietary trading involving hedge funds published in this edition of the *Federal Register*. The numbers next to the words are page numbers of the *Federal Register*.

**ILLUSTRATION 9-3.    Table of Contents Page of the** *Federal Register*

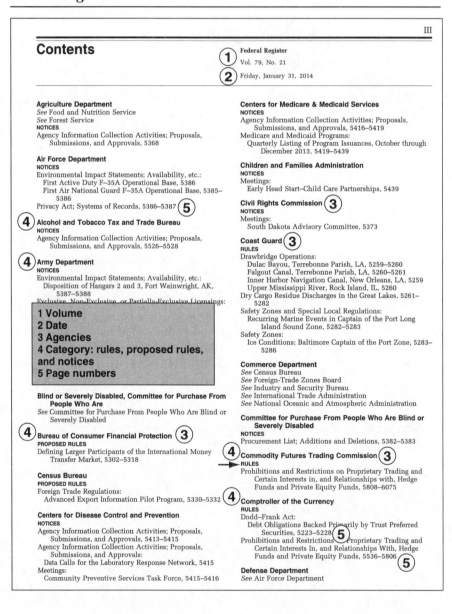

III

# Contents

Federal Register

Vol. 79, No. 21

Friday, January 31, 2014

**Agriculture Department**
*See* Food and Nutrition Service
*See* Forest Service
NOTICES
Agency Information Collection Activities; Proposals,
  Submissions, and Approvals, 5368

**Air Force Department**
NOTICES
Environmental Impact Statements; Availability, etc.:
  First Active Duty F–35A Operational Base, 5386
  First Air National Guard F–35A Operational Base, 5385–
  5386
Privacy Act; Systems of Records, 5386–5387

**Alcohol and Tobacco Tax and Trade Bureau**
NOTICES
Agency Information Collection Activities; Proposals,
  Submissions, and Approvals, 5526–5528

**Army Department**
NOTICES
Environmental Impact Statements; Availability, etc.:
  Disposition of Hangars 2 and 3, Fort Wainwright, AK,
  5387–5388
Exclusive, Non-Exclusive, or Partially-Exclusive Licensings:

> 1 Volume
> 2 Date
> 3 Agencies
> 4 Category: rules, proposed rules, and notices
> 5 Page numbers

**Blind or Severely Disabled, Committee for Purchase From People Who Are**
*See* Committee for Purchase From People Who Are Blind or
  Severely Disabled

**Bureau of Consumer Financial Protection**
PROPOSED RULES
Defining Larger Participants of the International Money
  Transfer Market, 5302–5318

**Census Bureau**
PROPOSED RULES
Foreign Trade Regulations:
  Advanced Export Information Pilot Program, 5330–5332

**Centers for Disease Control and Prevention**
NOTICES
Agency Information Collection Activities; Proposals,
  Submissions, and Approvals, 5413–5415
Agency Information Collection Activities; Proposals,
  Submissions, and Approvals:
  Data Calls for the Laboratory Response Network, 5415
Meetings:
  Community Preventive Services Task Force, 5415–5416

**Centers for Medicare & Medicaid Services**
NOTICES
Agency Information Collection Activities; Proposals,
  Submissions, and Approvals, 5416–5419
Medicare and Medicaid Programs:
  Quarterly Listing of Program Issuances, October through
  December 2013, 5419–5439

**Children and Families Administration**
NOTICES
Meetings:
  Early Head Start–Child Care Partnerships, 5439

**Civil Rights Commission**
NOTICES
Meetings:
  South Dakota Advisory Committee, 5373

**Coast Guard**
RULES
Drawbridge Operations:
  Dulac Bayou, Terrebonne Parish, LA, 5259–5260
  Falgout Canal, Terrebonne Parish, LA, 5260–5261
  Inner Harbor Navigation Canal, New Orleans, LA, 5259
  Upper Mississippi River, Rock Island, IL, 5260
Dry Cargo Residue Discharges in the Great Lakes, 5261–
  5282
Safety Zones and Special Local Regulations:
  Recurring Marine Events in Captain of the Port Long
  Island Sound Zone, 5282–5283
Safety Zones:
  Ice Conditions; Baltimore Captain of the Port Zone, 5283–
  5286

**Commerce Department**
*See* Census Bureau
*See* Foreign-Trade Zones Board
*See* Industry and Security Bureau
*See* International Trade Administration
*See* National Oceanic and Atmospheric Administration

**Committee for Purchase From People Who Are Blind or Severely Disabled**
NOTICES
Procurement List; Additions and Deletions, 5382–5383

**Commodity Futures Trading Commission**
RULES
Prohibitions and Restrictions on Proprietary Trading and
  Certain Interests in, and Relationships with, Hedge
  Funds and Private Equity Funds, 5808–6075

**Comptroller of the Currency**
RULES
Dodd–Frank Act:
  Debt Obligations Backed Primarily by Trust Preferred
  Securities, 5223–5228
Prohibitions and Restrictions on Proprietary Trading and
  Certain Interests In, and Relationships With, Hedge
  Funds and Private Equity Funds, 5536–5806

**Defense Department**
*See* Air Force Department

# ILLUSTRATION 9-4A.   Sample *Federal Register* Page

**⑥** **⑦** **⑧**

5808   Federal Register / Vol. 79, No. 21 / Friday, January 31, 2014 / Rules and Regulations

**①** COMMODITY FUTURES TRADING COMMISSION

**②** 17 CFR Part 75

RIN 3038–AD05

**⑤**

**Prohibitions and Restrictions on Proprietary Trading and Certain Interests in, and Relationships with, Hedge Funds and Private Equity Funds**

**①** **AGENCY:** Commodity Futures Trading Commission.

**③** **ACTION:** Final rule.

**④** **SUMMARY:** The Commodity Futures Trading Commission ("CFTC" or "Commission") is adopting a final rule to implement Section 619 of the Dodd-Frank Wall Street Reform and Consumer Protection Act (the "Dodd-Frank Act"), which contains certain prohibitions and restrictions on the ability of a banking entity and nonbank financial company supervised by the Board of Governors of the Federal Reserve System (the "Board") to engage in proprietary trading and have certain interests in, or relationships with, a hedge fund or private equity fund. Section 619 also requires the Board, the Federal Deposit Insurance Corporation, the Office of the Comptroller of the Currency, and the Securities and Exchange Commission to also issue regulations implementing section 619 and directs the CFTC and those four agencies to consult and coordinate with each other, as appropriate, in developing and issuing the implementing rules, for the purposes of assuring, to the extent possible, that such rules are comparable and provide for consistent application and implementation. To that end, although the Commission is adopting a final rule that is not a joint rule with the other agencies, the CFTC and the other agencies have worked closely together to develop the same rule text and supplementary information, except for information specific to the CFTC or the other agencies, as applicable. In particular, the CFTC's final rule is numbered as part 75 of the Commission's regulations, the rule text refers to the "Commission" instead of the "[Agency]" and one section of the regulations addresses authority, purpose, scope, and relationship to other authorities with respect to the Commission. Furthermore, it is noted that the supplementary information generally refers to the "Agencies" collectively when referring to deliberations and considerations in developing the final rule by the CFTC together with the other four agencies and references to the "final rule" should

be deemed to refer to the final rule of the Commission as herein adopted.

**DATES:** The final rule is effective April 1, 2014.

**FOR FURTHER INFORMATION CONTACT:** Erik Remmler, Deputy Director, Division of Swap Dealer and Intermediary Oversight ("DSIO"), (202) 418–7630, *eremmler@cftc.gov*; Paul Schlichting, Assistant General Counsel, Office of the General Counsel ("OGC"), (202) 418–5884, *pschlichting@cftc.gov*; Mark Fajfar, Assistant General Counsel, OGC, (202) 418–6636, *mfajfar@cftc.gov*; Michael Barrett, Attorney-Advisor, DSIO, (202) 418–5598, *mbarrett@ cftc.gov*; Stephen Kane, Research Economist, Office of the Chief Economist ("OCE"), (202) 418–5911, *skane@cftc.gov*; or Stephanie Lau, Research Economist, OCE, (202) 418–5218, *slau@cftc.gov*; Commodity Futures Trading Commission, Three Lafayette Centre, 1155 21st Street NW., Washington, DC 20581.

**SUPPLEMENTARY INFORMATION:**

**Table of Contents**

I. Background
II. Notice of Proposed Rulemaking: Summary of General Comments
III. Scope
IV. CFTC-Specific Comments
V. Overview of Final Rule
A. General Approach and Summary of Final Rule
B. Proprietary Trading Restrictions
C. Restrictions on Covered Fund Activities and Investments
D. Metrics Reporting Requirement
E. Compliance Program Requirement
VI. Final Rule
A. Subpart B—Proprietary Trading Restrictions
1. Section 75.3: Prohibition on Proprietary Trading and Related Definitions
a. Definition of "Trading Account"
b. Rebuttable Presumption for the Short-Term Trading Account
c. Definition of "Financial Instrument"
d. Proprietary Trading Exclusions
1. Repurchase and Reverse Repurchase Arrangements and Securities Lending
2. Liquidity management activities
3. Transactions of Derivatives Clearing Organizations and Clearing Agencies
4. Excluded Clearing-Related Activities of Clearinghouse Members
5. Satisfying an Existing Delivery Obligation
6. Satisfying an Obligation in Connection With a Judicial, Administrative, Self-Regulatory Organization, or Arbitration Proceeding
7. Acting Solely as Agent, Broker, or Custodian
8. Purchases or Sales Through a Deferred Compensation or Similar Plan
9. Collecting a Debt Previously Contracted
10. Other Requested Exclusions
2. Section 75.4(a): Underwriting Exemption
a. Introduction

b. Overview
1. Proposed Underwriting Exemption
2. Comments on Proposed Underwriting Exemption
3. Final Underwriting Exemption
c. Detailed Explanation of the Underwriting Exemption
1. Acting as an Underwriter for a Distribution of Securities
a. Proposed Requirements That the Purchase or Sale Be Effected Solely in Connection With a Distribution of Securities for Which the Banking Entity Acts as an Underwriter and That the Covered Financial Position Be a Security
i. Proposed Definition of "Distribution"
ii. Proposed Definition of "Underwriter"
iii. Proposed Requirement That the Covered Financial Position Be a Security
b. Comments on the Proposed Requirements That the Trade Be Effected Solely in Connection With a Distribution for Which the Banking Entity is Acting as an Underwriter and That the Covered Financial Position Be a Security
i. Definition of "Distribution"
ii. Definition of "Underwriter"
iii. "Solely in Connection With" Standard
c. Final Requirement That the Banking Entity Act as an Underwriter for a Distribution of Securities and the Trading Desk's Underwriting Position Be Related to Such Distribution
i. Definition of "Underwriting Position"
ii. Definition of "Trading Desk"
iii. Definition of "Distribution"
iv. Definition of "Underwriter"
v. Activities Conducted "In Connection With" a Distribution
2. Near Term Customer Demand Requirement
a. Proposed Near Term Customer Demand Requirement
b. Comments Regarding the Proposed Near Term Customer Demand Requirement
c. Final Near Term Customer Demand Requirement
3. Compliance Program Requirement
a. Proposed Compliance Program Requirement
b. Comments on the Proposed Compliance Program Requirement
c. Final Compliance Program Requirement
4. Compensation Requirement

b. Overview
1. Proposed Market-Making Exemption
2. Comments on the Proposed Market-Making Exemption

| 1 Agency |
| --- |
| 2 CFR Part |
| 3 Action |
| 4 Summary |
| 5 Contact person and contact information |
| 6 Federal register page numbers |
| 7 Volume |
| 8 Federal register date |

# ILLUSTRATION 9-4B.   Sample *Federal Register* Page

**⑥** 47154     Federal Register / Vol. 78, No. 150 / Monday, August 5, 2013 / Rules and Regulations

**⑦** **⑧**

> 1 Agency
> 2 CFR Part
> 3 Action
> 4 Summary
> 5 Contact person and contact information
> 6 Federal register page numbers
> 7 Volume
> 8 Federal register date
> 9 Supplemental information

[FR Doc. 2013–18844 Filed 8–2–13; 8:45 am]
**BILLING CODE 4810–AM–P**

**①** COMMODITY FUTURES TRADING COMMISSION

**17 CFR Part 37** **②**

**RIN 3038–AD18**

**Core Principles and Other Requirements for Swap Execution Facilities; Correction** **①**

**AGENCY:** Commodity Futures Trading Commission. **①**

**ACTION:** Final rule; correction. **③**

**SUMMARY:** The Commodity Futures Trading Commission is correcting a final rule that appeared in the **Federal Register** of June 4, 2013 (78 FR 33476). The final rule applies to the registration and operation of a new type of regulated entity named a swap execution facility, and implements provisions of the Dodd-Frank Wall Street Reform and Consumer Protection Act. **④**

**DATES:** The effective date of this correction is August 5, 2013.

**FOR FURTHER INFORMATION CONTACT:** Amir Zaidi, Special Counsel, Division of Market Oversight, Commodity Futures Trading Commission, Three Lafayette Center, 1155 21st Street NW., Washington, DC 20581; 202–418–6770; *azaidi@cftc.gov*. **⑤**

**SUPPLEMENTARY INFORMATION:** In FR Doc. 2013–12242 appearing on page 33476 in the **Federal Register** of Tuesday, June 4, 2013, the following corrections are made:

**§ 37.702   [Corrected]**

1. On page 33591, in the second column, in § 37.702 General financial integrity, paragraph (b) is corrected to read as follows:

(b) For transactions cleared by a derivatives clearing organization:

(1) By ensuring that the swap execution facility has the capacity to route transactions to the derivatives clearing organization in a manner acceptable to the derivatives clearing organization for purposes of clearing; and

(2) By coordinating with each derivatives clearing organization to which it submits transactions for clearing, in the development of rules and procedures to facilitate prompt and efficient transaction processing in accordance with the requirements of § 39.12(b)(7) of this chapter.

**Appendix B to Part 37—Guidance on, and Acceptable Practices in, Compliance With Core Principles [Corrected]**

2. On page 33600, in the second column, under the heading Core Principle 3 of Section 5h of the Act—Swaps Not Readily Susceptible to Manipulation, in paragraph (a)(3), correct the reference to "section c(5)" to read "section c(4)."

Dated: July 31, 2013.
Christopher J. Kirkpatrick,
*Deputy Secretary of the Commission.*
[FR Doc. 2013–18773 Filed 8–2–13; 8:45 am]
**BILLING CODE 6351–01–P**

---

**DEPARTMENT OF HEALTH AND HUMAN SERVICES**

**Food and Drug Administration**

**21 CFR Part 101** **②**

**[Docket No. FDA–2005–N–0404]**

**RIN 0910–AG84**

**Food Labeling; Gluten-Free Labeling of Foods**

**AGENCY:** Food and Drug Administration, HHS. **①**

**ACTION:** Final rule. **③**

**SUMMARY:** The Food and Drug Administration (FDA or we) is issuing a final rule to define the term "gluten-free" for voluntary use in the labeling of foods. The final rule defines the term "gluten-free" to mean that the food bearing the claim does not contain an ingredient that is a gluten-containing grain (e.g., spelt wheat); an ingredient that is derived from a gluten-containing grain and that has not been processed to remove gluten (e.g., wheat flour); or an ingredient that is derived from a gluten-containing grain and that has been processed to remove gluten (e.g., wheat starch), if the use of that ingredient **④**

results in the presence of 20 parts per million (ppm) or more gluten in the food (i.e., 20 milligrams (mg) or more gluten per kilogram (kg) of food); or inherently does not contain gluten; and that any unavoidable presence of gluten in the food is below 20 ppm gluten (i.e., below 20 mg gluten per kg of food). A food that bears the claim "no gluten," "free of gluten," or "without gluten" in its labeling and fails to meet the requirements for a "gluten-free" claim will be deemed to be misbranded. In addition, a food whose labeling includes the term "wheat" in the ingredient list or in a separate "Contains wheat" statement as required by a section of the Federal Food, Drug, and Cosmetic Act (the FD&C Act) and also bears the claim "gluten-free" will be deemed to be misbranded unless its labeling also bears additional language clarifying that the wheat has been processed to allow the food to meet FDA requirements for a "gluten-free" claim. Establishing a definition of the term "gluten-free" and uniform conditions for its use in food labeling will help ensure that individuals with celiac disease are not misled and are provided with truthful and accurate information with respect to foods so labeled. We are issuing the final rule under the Food Allergen Labeling and Consumer Protection Act of 2004 (FALCPA).

**DATES:** *Effective date:* The final rule becomes effective on September 4, 2013. *Compliance date:* The compliance date of this final rule is August 5, 2014. See section II.B.4 (comment 35 and response 35) for an additional explanation of the compliance date and implementation of this final rule.

**FOR FURTHER INFORMATION CONTACT:** Felicia B. Billingslea, Center for Food Safety and Applied Nutrition (HFS–820), Food and Drug Administration, 5100 Paint Branch Pkwy., College Park, MD 20740, 240–402–2371, FAX: 301–436–2636, email: *GlutenFreeFinalRule Questions@fda.hhs.gov*. **⑤**

**SUPPLEMENTARY INFORMATION:** **⑨**

**Executive Summary**

*Purpose of the Rule*

*Need for the rule:* Celiac disease is a hereditary, chronic inflammatory disorder of the small intestine triggered by the ingestion of certain storage proteins referred to as gluten occurring in wheat, rye, barley, and crossbreeds of these grains. Celiac disease has no cure, but individuals who have this disease are advised to avoid all sources of gluten in their diet to protect against adverse health effects associated with the disease. Many manufacturers currently label their food with a

# ILLUSTRATION 9-4B. *Continued*

**47178**    **Federal Register** / Vol. 78, No. 150 / Monday, August 5, 2013 / Rules and Regulations

*FoodScienceResearch/ RiskSafetyAssessment/UCM362401.pdf.*

25. Codex Alimentarius Commission, "Codex Standard for Foods for Special Dietary Use for Persons Intolerant to Gluten (Codex Standard 118–1979)," Rome, Italy, pp. 1–3, 2008; available at *http:// www.codexalimentarius.net/download/ standards/291/cxs_118e.pdf.*

26. The Commission of the European Communities, "Commission Regulation (EC) No 41/2009," *Official Journal of the European Union*, Brussels, Belgium, pp. L 16/3–L 16/5, January 20, 2009; available at *http://eur-lex.europa.eu/Lex UriServ/LexUriServ.do?uri=OJ:L:2009: 016:0003:0005:EN:PDF.*

27. Health Canada, Bureau of Chemical Safety, Food Directorate, Health Products and Food Branch "Health Canada's Position on Gluten-Free Claims," dated June 2012, available at *http://www.hc-sc. gc.ca/fn-an/alt_formats/pdf/securit/ allergy/cel-coe/gluten-position-eng.pdf.*

28. Government of Australia, "Australian New Zealand Food Standards Code: Chapter 1—General Food Standards, Part 1.2—Labelling and Other Information Requirements, Standard 1.2.8—Nutrition Information Requirements," pp. 2 and 14, 2012, available at *http://www. comlaw.gov.au/Details/F2012C00218.*

29. Armour, B., and T.B. Perry, Cream Hill Estates Ltd., Public comment letter Document ID: FDA–2005–N–0404–0399, submitted on November 19, 2005, to Docket No. 2005N–0279 pertaining to the Center for Food Safety and Applied Nutrition, Food and Drug Administration Public Meeting on Gluten-Free Food Labeling held in College Park, MD, pp. 1–3, August 19, 2005, available at *http://www.regulations.gov/#!document Detail;D=FDA-2005-N-0404-0399.*

30. Smith, S., Gluten Free Oats LLC, Public comment letter EMC301 submitted on March 20, 2006, to Docket No. 2005N– 0279 pertaining to the Center for Food Safety and Applied Nutrition, Food and Drug Administration Public Meeting on Gluten-Free Food held in College Park, MD, pp. 1–2, August 19, 2005.

31. Daou, C. and H. Zhang, "Oat Beta-Glucan: Its Role in Health Promotion and Prevention of Diseases," *Comprehensive Reviews in Food Science and Food Safety*, 11: 355–365, 2012.

32. Verrill, L., Y. Zhang, and C.T.J. Lin, Memorandum, "Consumer Studies' Comments on Alternative Terms for 'Gluten-Free' on The Food Label," Center for Food Safety and Applied Nutrition, Food and Drug Administration, College Park, MD, July 8, 2013.

33. FDA, "Guidance for Industry: Labeling of Certain Beers Subject to the Labeling Jurisdiction of the Food and Drug Administration; Draft Guidance," August 2009, available at *http://www.fda.gov/ Food/GuidanceRegulation/Guidance DocumentsRegulatoryInformation/ LabelingNutrition/ucm166239.htm.*

34. Verrill, L. and C.-T.J. Lin, Memorandum, "Consumer Studies' Comments on a Proposed Codicil in the 'Gluten-Free' Labeling Final Rule," Center for Food

Safety and Applied Nutrition, Food and Drug Administration, College Park, MD, July 8, 2013.

35. FDA/CFSAN, "Guidance for Industry: A Labeling Guide for Restaurants and Other Retail Establishments Selling Away-From-Home Foods," April 2008, available at *http://www.fda.gov/Food/ GuidanceRegulation/Guidance DocumentsRegulatoryInformation/ LabelingNutrition/ucm053455.htm.*

36. AOAC Research Institute, "Certificate of Performance Tested℠ Status, Certificate No. 120601," AOAC International, Gaithersburg, MD, 2013; available at *http://www.aoac.org/iMIS15_Prod/ AOAC_Docs/RI/RI_MethodsCert/2013_ 120601_certificate.pdf.*

37. Morinaga Institute of Biological Science, Inc., "Product: Food Allergen Kits: Food Allergen ELISA Kits," available at *http://www.miobs.com/english/product/ food_allergen_elisa_kits/index.html,* and Information Sheet Download "Wheat Protein ELISA Kit (Gliadin)," available at *http://www.miobs.com/english/product/ food_allergen_elisa_kits/dl/gdrev1.pdf.*

38. FDA/CFSAN, "Report to The Committee on Health, Education, Labor, and Pensions United States Senate and the Committee on Energy and Commerce United States House of Representatives, Food Allergen Labeling and Consumer Protection Act of 2004 Public Law 108– 282," available at *http://www.fda.gov/ downloads/Food/LabelingNutrition/Food AllergensLabeling/GuidanceCompliance RegulatoryInformation/UCM179390.pdf.*

39. FDA/CFSAN, "Gluten-Free Labeling of Foods, Final Regulatory Impact Analysis and Regulatory Flexibility Analysis," 2013.

## List of Subjects in 21 CFR Part 101

Food labeling, Nutrition, Reporting and recordkeeping requirements.

For the reasons discussed in the preamble, the Food and Drug Administration amends 21 CFR part 101 as follows:

## PART 101—FOOD LABELING

■ 1. The authority citation for 21 CFR part 101 continues to read as follows:

**Authority:** 15 U.S.C. 1453, 1454, 1455; 21 U.S.C. 321, 331, 342, 343, 348, 371; 42 U.S.C. 243, 264, 271.

■ 2. Section 101.91 is added to subpart F to read as follows:

**§ 101.91   Gluten-free labeling of food.**

(a) *Definitions.* (1) The term "gluten-containing grain" means any one of the following grains or their crossbred hybrids (e.g., triticale, which is a cross between wheat and rye):

(i) Wheat, including any species belonging to the genus *Triticum;*

(ii) Rye, including any species belonging to the genus *Secale;* or

(iii) Barley, including any species belonging to the genus *Hordeum.*

(2) The term "gluten" means the proteins that naturally occur in a gluten-containing grain and that may cause adverse health effects in persons with celiac disease (e.g., prolamins and glutelins).

(3) The labeling claim "gluten-free" means:

(i) That the food bearing the claim in its labeling:

(A) Does not contain any one of the following:

(*1*) An ingredient that is a gluten-containing grain (e.g., spelt wheat);

(*2*) An ingredient that is derived from a gluten-containing grain and that has not been processed to remove gluten (e.g., wheat flour); or

(*3*) An ingredient that is derived from a gluten-containing grain and that has been processed to remove gluten (e.g., wheat starch), if the use of that ingredient results in the presence of 20 parts per million (ppm) or more gluten in the food (i.e., 20 milligrams (mg) or more gluten per kilogram (kg) of food); or

(B) Inherently does not contain gluten; and

(ii) Any unavoidable presence of gluten in the food bearing the claim in its labeling is below 20 ppm gluten (i.e., below 20 mg gluten per kg of food).

(b) *Requirements.* (1) A food that bears the claim "gluten-free" in its labeling and fails to meet the requirements of paragraph (a)(3) of this section will be deemed misbranded.

(2) A food that bears the claim "no gluten," "free of gluten," or "without gluten" in its labeling and fails to meet the requirements of paragraph (a)(3) of this section will be deemed misbranded.

(3) A food that bears the term "wheat" in the ingredient list or in a separate "Contains wheat" statement in its labeling, as required by 21 U.S.C. 343(w)(1)(A), and also bears the claim "gluten-free" or a claim identified in paragraph (b)(2) of this section will be deemed misbranded unless the word "wheat" in the ingredient list or in the "Contains wheat" statement is followed immediately by an asterisk (or other symbol) that refers to another asterisk (or other symbol) in close proximity to the ingredient statement that immediately precedes the following: "The wheat has been processed to allow this food to meet the Food and Drug Administration (FDA) requirements for gluten-free foods."

(c) *Compliance.* When compliance with paragraph (b) of this section is based on an analysis of the food, FDA will use a scientifically valid method that can reliably detect the presence of 20 ppm gluten in a variety of food

## ILLUSTRATION 9-4B. *Continued*

---

Federal Register / Vol. 78, No. 150 / Monday, August 5, 2013 / Rules and Regulations   **47179**

matrices, including both raw and cooked or baked products.

(d) *Preemption.* A State or political subdivision of a State may not establish or continue into effect any law, rule, regulation, or other requirement that is different from the requirements in this section for the definition and use of the claim "gluten-free," as well as the claims "no gluten," "free of gluten," or "without gluten."

Dated: July 30, 2013.

**Leslie Kux,**

*Assistant Commissioner for Policy.*

[FR Doc. 2013–18813 Filed 8–2–13; 8:45 am]

BILLING CODE 4160–01–P

---

**DEPARTMENT OF STATE**

**22 CFR Part 126**

**RIN 1400–AD41**

[Public Notice 8409]

**Amendment to the International Traffic in Arms Regulations: Libya and UNSCR 2095**

AGENCY: Department of State.

ACTION: Final rule.

SUMMARY: The Department of State is amending the International Traffic in Arms Regulations (ITAR) to update the defense trade policy regarding Libya to reflect resolution 2095 adopted by the United Nations Security Council.

DATES: This rule is effective August 5, 2013.

FOR FURTHER INFORMATION CONTACT: Ms. Sarah J. Heidema, Acting Director, Office of Defense Trade Controls Policy, U.S. Department of State, telephone (202) 663–2809, or email *DDTCResponseTeam@state.gov.* ATTN: Regulatory Change, Libya.

SUPPLEMENTARY INFORMATION: On March 14, 2013, the United Nations Security Council adopted resolution 2095 ("UNSCR 2095"), which further modified the arms embargo against Libya put in place by the adoption in February and March of 2011 of resolutions 1970 and 1973, respectively, and modified by resolutions 2009 and 2016, adopted in September and October of 2011, respectively (for previous ITAR amendments regarding Libya defense trade policy, *see* "Amendment to the International Traffic in Arms Regulations: Libya," RIN 1400–AC83, 76 FR 30001, and "Amendment to the International Traffic in Arms Regulations: Libya and UNSCR 2009," RIN 1400–AC97, 76 FR 68313).

UNSCR 2095 removed the requirement for member states to notify the Committee of the Security Council concerning Libya ("the Committee") of exports of non-lethal military equipment, and the provision of any technical assistance or training, intended solely for security or disarmament assistance to the Libyan government. It also removed the requirement to seek the approval of the Committee for exports of non-lethal military equipment, and related technical assistance or training, for humanitarian and protective use. The Department of State is amending ITAR § 126.1(k) accordingly.

**Regulatory Analysis and Notices**

*Administrative Procedure Act*

The Department of State is of the opinion that controlling the import and export of defense articles and services is a foreign affairs function of the United States Government and that rules implementing this function are exempt from sections 553 (rulemaking) and 554 (adjudications) of the Administrative Procedure Act. Since the Department is of the opinion that this rule is exempt from 5 U.S.C. 553, it is the view of the Department that the provisions of section 553(d) do not apply to this rulemaking. Therefore, this rule is effective upon publication. The Department also finds that, given the national security issues surrounding U.S. policy towards Libya, notice and public procedure on this rule would be impracticable or unnecessary; for this reason also, this rule is effective upon publication.

*Regulatory Flexibility Act*

Since the Department is of the opinion that this rule is exempt from the provisions of 5 U.S.C. 553, there is no requirement for an analysis under the Regulatory Flexibility Act.

*Unfunded Mandates Reform Act of 1995*

This rulemaking does not involve a mandate that will result in the expenditure by state, local, and tribal governments, in the aggregate, or by the private sector, of $100 million or more in any year and it will not significantly or uniquely affect small governments. Therefore, no actions are deemed necessary under the provisions of the Unfunded Mandates Reform Act of 1995.

*Small Business Regulatory Enforcement Fairness Act of 1996*

This rulemaking has been found not to be a major rule within the meaning of the Small Business Regulatory Enforcement Fairness Act of 1996.

*Executive Orders 12372 and 13132*

This rulemaking will not have substantial direct effects on the States, on the relationship between the national government and the States, or on the distribution of power and responsibilities among the various levels of government. Therefore, in accordance with Executive Order 13132, it is determined that this rulemaking does not have sufficient federalism implications to require consultations or warrant the preparation of a federalism summary impact statement. The regulations implementing Executive Order 12372 regarding intergovernmental consultation on Federal programs and activities do not apply to this rulemaking.

*Executive Orders 12866 and 13563*

Executive Orders 12866 and 13563 direct agencies to assess costs and benefits of available regulatory alternatives and, if regulation is necessary, to select regulatory approaches that maximize net benefits (including potential economic, environmental, public health and safety effects, distributed impacts, and equity). These executive orders stress the importance of quantifying both costs and benefits, of reducing costs, of harmonizing rules, and of promoting flexibility. This rule has been designated a "significant regulatory action," although not economically significant, under section 3(f) of Executive Order 12866. Accordingly, this rule has been reviewed by the Office of Management and Budget (OMB).

*Executive Order 12988*

The Department of State has reviewed this rulemaking in light of sections 3(a) and 3(b)(2) of Executive Order 12988 to eliminate ambiguity, minimize litigation, establish clear legal standards, and reduce burden.

*Executive Order 13175*

The Department of State has determined that this rulemaking will not have tribal implications, will not impose substantial direct compliance costs on Indian tribal governments, and will not pre-empt tribal law. Accordingly, the requirements of Executive Order 13175 do not apply to this rulemaking.

*Paperwork Reduction Act*

This rule does not impose any new reporting or recordkeeping requirements subject to the Paperwork Reduction Act, 44 U.S.C. Chapter 35.

---

Now look at Illustration 9-4A. It is the *Federal Register* page 5808 that is noted in the table of contents in connection with the Commodity Futures Trading Commission's implementation of rules for hedge funds. The page also indicates the part of the *Code of Federal Regulations* in which this proposed rule would appear. It is 17 CFR part 75. It notes

the agency, the Commodity Futures Trading Commission. It summarizes the regulation. When the action involves a rule change, the *Federal Register* page will provide a brief summary and a more detailed summary of the agency's action. Next to the word "Action," you are told that this is a final rule. The effective date of the rule is provided. In addition, you are provided with a contact person for additional information as well as supplementary information. The rule change is included, however, it is not shown in this illustration. The *Federal Register* page includes a note regarding the section of the *United States Code* that provides the agency with authority to make this rule.

If this was a proposed rather than final rule, the public would have been invited to comment before action is taken. The dates for submitting comments would have been shown as well as the format and methods for submitting comments. An e-mail address as well as a regular mail address and other contact information would have been provided.

Illustration 9-4B also shows pages from the *Federal Register*. This is a lengthy entry so the first page and two of the pages near the end are shown. Similar to Illustration 9-4A, this entry details a final rule. This rule involves food labels for gluten free products. It will be incorporated into 21 CFR Part 101. A summary of the rule, the effective date, and contact information is provided on the first page of Illustration 9-4B. In the middle of the second page of Illustration 9-4B, the entry details how the new portion of this regulation should read and provides the U.S.C. authority for the regulation. It indicates that this language will be added to subpart F as Section 101.91.

The *Federal Register* begins a new volume each year. The issues are consecutively paginated from the first day that the government offices are open during the year through the last day that the government offices are open during the year. For example, a March 1 *Federal Register* might contain pages 2600-4200. The March 2 *Federal Register* would begin on page 4201. It is not uncommon for the page number in the last issue to be 60,000.

Dates are listed on the outside binding of the *Federal Register*. Therefore, you must determine the date of the *Federal Register* publication that contains the page that you are seeking. To do this, use the index table entitled Federal Register Pages and Dates. This table provides you with the date of the *Federal Register* that contains the relevant information. Another alternative is to consult a commercially prepared index to the *Federal Register*. Once you find the appropriate pamphlet, go to the *Federal Register* page.

▼ How Do You Search the *Federal Register* on the Internet?

The *Federal Register* now can be searched through the Federal Digital System www.gpo.gov/fdsys/search/home.action. Researchers can

perform simple keyword or citation searches or browse the publication. If you would like to browse a publication, click on the link in the upper left corner as shown in Illustration 9-2. A list of publications will appear as shown in Illustration 9-5 below. If you select the *Federal Register,* you will be asked to pick a year. After that you can select a month and date. Federal Registers from 1994 to the present can be searched.

Another way to search the *Federal Register* is to click on the advanced search function at the Federal Digital System home page. It will provide the page shown in Illustration 9-6. Select the publication you wish to search, in this case the *Federal Register.* Then enter your search keywords. The date could be restricted.

The www.federalregister.gov website allows users to search by date, sections, and keywords. Keyword searches can be limited to certain dates and document categories as well as other qualifiers. Users also can browse by agency and/or date.

This website also provides an easy to use index. See Illustration 9-6. The website details the last date contained within this index. You can browse through the agency listings. If you were searching for food labeling, you would click on the Food and Drug Administration. It allows you to see rules, proposed rules, and notices. Look under the section of

## ILLUSTRATION 9-5.  List of Federal Publications

**ILLUSTRATION 9-6.   Index Page from www.federalregister.gov**

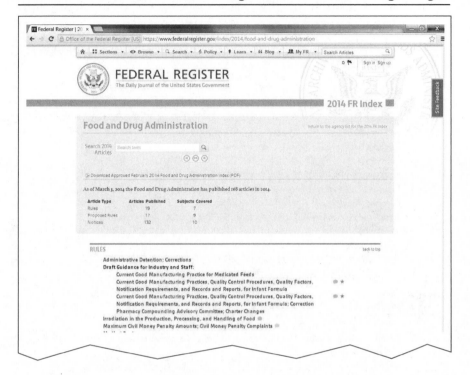

Proposed Rules in Illustration 9-6. Look at the note under the words "food labeling." It indicates that a revision was made concerning nutrition and supplement fact labels. It notes the date of the publication, 3/3/2014, and the *Federal Register* year—2014—and the page numbers 11879-11987. To see this proposed change, you would view the 2014 *Federal Register* pamphlet that contains those page numbers or review them online.

### ▼ How Can You Use Lexis and Westlaw to Retrieve the *Federal Register?*

Another simple method to retrieve *Federal Register* information concerning an adopted or proposed regulation is a computer search of either Lexis and Westlaw. You can search these *Federal Register* databases without regard to a publisher's choice of indexing terms. You may use your own terms to determine whether any regulations concerning your research topic are contained within the *Federal Register.*

## ILLUSTRATION 9-6.  *Continued*

Medical Devices:

Classification of the Neuropsychiatric Interpretive Electroencephalograph Assessment Aid
Electronic Submission Requirements ● ★

Immunology and Microbiology Devices; Classification of John Cunningham Virus
Serological Reagents

Pediatric Uses of Devices; Requirement for Submission of Information ● ★

Reports of Corrections and Removals; Technical Amendment

New Animal Drugs:

Argent Laboratories; Formalin; Tricaine Methanesulfonate; Withdrawal ⟨2⟩

Bambermycins; Clopidol; Ivermectin; et al.; Change of Sponsor; Change of Sponsor Address
Change of Sponsor

Zoetis Inc., et al.; Withdrawal of Approval; Combination Drug Medicated Feeds Containing ⟨2⟩
an Arsenical Drug

Premarket Approvals:

Transilluminator for Breast Evaluation and Sorbent Hemoperfusion System Devices for ●
Treatment of Hepatic Coma and Metabolic Disturbances; etc.

---

PROPOSED RULES                                                                back to top

Draft Guidance for Industry and Staff:

Current Good Manufacturing Practice and Hazard Analysis and Risk-Based Preventive ● ★
Controls for Food for Animals

Demonstration of the Quality Factor Requirements for Eligible Infant Formulas; Availability ●

Exempt Infant Formula Production; Current Good Manufacturing Practices, Quality Control
Procedures, Conduct of Audits, and Records and Reports; Availability

Focused Mitigation Strategies to Protect Food Against Intentional Adulteration; Meetings ●

Qualitative Risk Assessment of Risk of Activity/Animal Food Combinations for Activities
(Outside the Farm Definition) Conducted in a Facility Co-Located on a Farm

Sanitary Transportation of Human and Animal Food ● ●

Food Additive Petitions; Animal Use:

Lohmann Animal Health GMBH ●

Food Labeling:

Revision of the Nutrition and Supplement Facts Labels ● ★

➤ March      Published: 03/03/2014  FR Document: 2014-04387  Pages: 11879-11987(109  ● ★
                                                                  Pages)

Serving Sizes of Foods that Can Reasonably Be Consumed at One-Eating Occasion, etc. ● ★

Serving Sizes; Reference Amount and Serving Size Declaration for Hard Candies, Breath
Mints

~~Generic Drug User Fee Amendments:~~

## b. Code of Federal Regulations

During the course of the year, the regulations found in the *Federal Register* are incorporated into a codified version called the *Code of Federal Regulations* (C.F.R.). The code is comprised of 50 titles similar to the titles used in the statutory codes. However, not all 50 titles mirror the titles used in the *United States Code* (U.S.C.). Some titles, such as 26, the Internal Revenue Code, do follow the title of the U.S.C. Title

26 of the C.F.R. contains the Treasury regulations that instruct the researcher on how to apply the relevant statutory code section. The C.F.R. titles are organized by agency, not subjects. The C.F.R. is further divided into chapters, subchapters, parts, and sections. Check the back of each volume for a list of federal agencies and their C.F.R. titles and chapters.

The C.F.R. is prepared and published by the U.S. Government Printing Office. However, the C.F.R. is available online through the Government Printing Office and online services such as Westlaw, Lexis, and other fee-based companies.

### ▼ How Often Is the C.F.R. Updated?

The C.F.R. titles are updated quarterly. Titles 1 to 16 are updated January 1 of the cover year. Titles 17 to 27 are updated April 1 of that year, and titles 28 to 41 are updated on July 1 of that year. Titles 42 to 50 are updated on October 1 of the cover year.

### ▼ How Do You Use the C.F.R. in Print?

To use the C.F.R in print, consult the index that contains listings of subjects, agencies, and references to the regulations codified within the C.F.R. volumes. The index also provides a list of C.F.R. titles, chapters, subchapters, and parts, and an alphabetical list of the agencies in the C.F.R. This index is revised once a year as of January 1.

To research a particular topic in the index, you first must locate the name of the agency. Assume that you are looking for regulations concerning the food labeling of raw fruit, vegetables, and fish. First, you need to review the enabling statute to determine the agency responsible for such regulation. Once you have made that determination, you are ready to review the index. In this case, the responsible agency is the U.S. Food and Drug Administration. You would find that agency name listed in alphabetical order in the index. Next, you would review the topical listings below the agency name. In this case, the topic of possible interest is "labeling." An index page would refer you to title 21, part 101 of the C.F.R. for the labeling regulations.

The next step is to go to the C.F.R. volumes. The title and part numbers are listed on the binding. Review the appropriate part and chapter. Within the part, you will find a listing of the statutory authority that is the basis for the regulation. If you have not already consulted this statute, find the statute and review it.

Illustration 9-1 is the page of the C.F.R. referred to under the "labeling" topic in the index: title 21, part 101 of the C.F.R. concerning food labeling. You should scan the sections listed to find relevant sections. For example, suppose you are researching whether health claims may be made concerning raw fruit and the labeling required. You can scan the subpart list and see a listing for section 101.14 "Health Claims: general requirements" shown in Illustration 9-1. You would review

that section and any other relevant sections. The C.F.R. part also specifies the enabling statutes. In this case, the enabling statutes are the Fair Packaging and Labeling Act and the Federal Food, Drug, and Cosmetic Act. Citations to the U.S.C. for each act are included. In addition, the citation to the *Federal Register* publication is noted. Finally, the text of the regulation begins under the heading "Subpart A—General Provisions."

### ▼ How Do You Search the C.F.R. on the Computer?

Online computer searches may allow easier access to regulations than a print index. You can search the full text of the regulations at the government's website or on both the Westlaw and Lexis systems. With these searches you do not need to rely on the terms contained within the index. Current regulations, as well as many superseded regulations, can be searched online. If you go to the government website, you can search for a regulation by entering key words, a C.F.R. citation, or by browsing the titles at the Federal Digital System website and at www.federalregister.gov discussed above. In addition, the government offers an integrated version of the C.F.R. called ecfr at www.ecfr.gpoaccess.gov. This version is updated daily, but it is unofficial. It can be searched by browsing a C.F.R. title and indicates when the online C.F.R. was last updated.

### ▼ Why Would You Use Old Regulations?

Often a case will turn on a regulation that was in place at the time of the incident involved. For example, suppose you are representing a client involved in a car accident in 2012. The experts say that the accident occurred because the car manufacturer failed to use a safety device—one that was required by federal regulations. The car was manufactured in 2011. You must research the 2011 regulations to determine what safety regulations applied to that manufacturer.

### ▼ How Do You Update and Validate Regulations?

Updating is one of the most important tasks you must perform when you review agency regulations. This is especially important because the regulations change frequently. Because the C.F.R. is published annually with quarterly updates, you must determine the currentness of the document. The **List of CFR Sections Affected**, or L.S.A., enables you to update a C.F.R. citation. The L.S.A. identifies which sections have been changed, updated, or removed: in essence, which C.F.R. sections have been affected in any way. A monthly L.S.A. is published with the C.F.R. See Illustration 9-7. It is a page that details the parts that have changed between April 1, 2013 and December 31, 2013. The L.S.A. also appears daily in the Readers Aids section of the *Federal Register* in a section entitled "CFR Parts Affected." See Illustration 9-8. It is a page from the January 31, 2014 *Federal Register* that details only changes in

# ILLUSTRATION 9-7.   L.S.A. Monthly Pamphlet Page

AUTHENTICATED
U.S. GOVERNMENT
INFORMATION
GPO

## DECEMBER 2013                                    67

### CHANGES APRIL 1, 2013 THROUGH DECEMBER 31, 2013

718 Appendix A .............................35556
  Regulation at 78 FR 35556
  withdrawn ..............................53645
  Appendix C introductory text
  revised.....................................59115
725 Authority citation revised........35558
  Regulation at 78 FR 35558
  withdrawn ..............................53645
  Technical correction ..................60686
725.1 Revised...................................59115
725.2 Revised...................................59117
725.101 (a)(1), (2), (4), (32)(i)
  through (iv) and (b) amended
  ............................................ 59117
725.201 (a) revised; (b) removed;
  (c) and (d) redesignated as
  (b) and (c) ..............................59117
725.212 (a)(3) introductory text
  republished; (a)(3)(i) and (ii)
  revised.....................................59117
725.218 (a) introductory text republished; (a)(1) and (2) re-
  vised.......................................59117
725.222 (a)(5) introductory text
  republished; (a)(5)(i) and (ii)
  revised.....................................59118
725.309 Revised...............................59118
725.406 (a), (b), (c) and (e) revised
  ............................................ 35558
  Regulation at 78 FR 35558
  withdrawn ..............................53645
725.418 Revised...............................59118

### Proposed Rules:

404 ...30249, 38610, 46309, 53700, 69324, 76508
405.......................................................38610
416 .....................30249, 38610, 46309, 70244
638.......................................................19632
655.......................................................44054
670.......................................................19632
718.......................................................35575
725.......................................................35575

## TITLE 21—FOOD AND DRUGS

**Chapter I—Food and Drug Administration, Department of Health and Human Services (Parts 1—1299)**

1 Authority citation revised..........69543
1.1 (c) amended .............................69543
1.20 Introductory text corrected;
  CFR correction.......................54568
  Introductory text revised...........69543

1.281 Regulation at 76 FR 25545
  confirmed.................................32362
10.30 (b), (c), (d), (e)(3) and (g) revised.......................................76749
14.100 (f) removed; (g) redesig-
  nated as (f) ............................69992
16.1 (b)(2) amended.........................58817
21.61 (d) added................................39186
73 Technical correction .................42451
73.350 (c)(1) revised .......................35117
  Regulation at 78 FR 35117 con-
  firmed.....................................54758
73.530 Added...................................49120
  Regulation at 78 FR 49120 con-
  firmed.....................................68713
73.3100 Heading and (a) revised
  ............................................ 19415
  Regulation at 78 FR 19415 eff.
  date confirmed ........................37962
73.3106 (a) revised...........................19415
  Regulation at 78 FR 19415 eff.
  date confirmed ........................37962
101.91 Added...................................47178
123 Policy statement ......................69992
172.167 (b) revised...........................71461
172.320 Revised................................71461
172.345 (b) revised...........................71463
172.379 (b) revised...........................71463
172.380 (b) revised...........................71463
172.665 (d)(2) revised.......................71463
172.712 (b) revised...........................71463
172.736 (b)(2) revised.......................71463
172.780 (b) revised...........................71464
  (b) and (c) revised....................73437
172.800 (b)(2) revised.......................71464
172.804 (b) revised...........................71464
172.810 Introductory text revised
  ............................................ 71464
172.812 (a) revised...........................71464
172.831 (b) revised...........................71464
172.841 (b) revised...........................71464
172.862 (b)(1) revised.......................71465
172.867 (b) revised...........................71465
172.869 (b) introductory text and
  (6) through (11) revised.............71465
173.160 (d) revised...........................71466
173.165 (d) amended.........................71466
173.228 (a) revised; footnote 1 re-
  moved.....................................71466
173.280 (c) revised...........................71466
173.310 (c) table amended; (f)
  added.......................................71466
173.368 (c) revised...........................71467
175.300 (i) added .............................41843
175.320 correctly amended; CFR
  correction................................52429

that issue. This daily list of changes is found at the front of the *Federal Register*. At the back of the *Federal Register*, another CFR Parts Affected section details the changes that have occurred within the month of its publication. See Illustration 9-9. Therefore, you must check not only the monthly L.S.A. pamphlet, but also portions of a daily *Federal Register*. The L.S.A. is organized by title. See Illustration 9-7.

### ▼ How Is the Updating Performed in Practice?

Assume that you have found the regulation that defines the standard for labeling of food in the *Federal Register*. It is 21 C.F.R. § 101. Assume

### ILLUSTRATION 9-8. Reader's Aids of the *Federal Register* page with CFR Parts Affected Shown

VIII                 Federal Register / Vol. 79, No. 21 / Friday, January 31, 2014 / Contents

**CFR PARTS AFFECTED IN THIS ISSUE**

A cumulative list of the parts affected this month can be found in the Reader Aids section at the end of this issue.

**12 CFR**
44 (2 documents) ....5223, 5536
248 (2 documents) ...........5223,
                                    5536
255................................5223
351 (2 documents) ...........5223,
                                    5536
703................................5228
715................................5228
741................................5228
**Proposed Rules:**
1090..............................5302
**14 CFR**
39 (5 documents) ...5247, 5249,
              5251, 5254, 5257
**Proposed Rules:**
1......................................5318
39 (4 documents) ...5319, 5321,
                          5323, 5325
7Ch. 1 ............................5329
**15 CFR**
**Proposed Rules:**
30....................................5330
700..................................5332
**17 CFR**
75....................................5808
255..................................5536
**21 CFR**
**Proposed Rules:**
16....................................5353
121..................................5353
**33 CFR**
117 (4 documents) ..........5259,
                                    5260
151..................................5261
165 (2 documents) ..........5282,
                                    5283
**39 CFR**
111..................................5286
**Proposed Rules:**
3010................................5355
**40 CFR**
52 (3 documents) ...5287, 5291,
                                    5294
180..................................5294
**Proposed Rules:**
52 (2 documents) ..............5363
**47 CFR**
**Proposed Rules:**
79....................................5364
**50 CFR**
622..................................5300
**Proposed Rules:**
648..................................5364

also that it is February 1, 2014, and you want to determine if this regulation has been changed since it was last published. You want to be certain that you determine whether there have been any changes to the relevant section through the date of your search.

You should now review the current L.S.A. pamphlet. For our purposes, consult Illustration 9-7. This pamphlet discloses any changes to the regulations that occurred between April 1, 2013, and December 31, 2013. Find the title you want to update: in this case, title 21. It was last updated on April 1, 2013, based on the C.F.R. update schedule for its titles. Next review Illustration 9-7. Scan the sections column and determine whether section 101 has been changed since April 1. In this case, it has been altered. Note that section 101 has a five-digit number next to it. The five-digit number is the *Federal Register* page on which the changes appear. In this case, it is page 47178. That page is shown in Illustration 9-4A.

This pamphlet only includes changes through December 31, 2013. Therefore, you need to determine whether any changes were made to the section after that up until the date of your research, February 1, 2014. First, check the last *Federal Register* for January 2013. View the "Reader Aids" section entitled "CFR Parts Affected In January." See Illustration 9-9. Check to see if your citation is listed there. In this case, part 101 of title 21 was not listed, so it was not affected. If there had been changes, you would need to review those *Federal Register* pages to determine if any of the modifications are relevant to your research.

Next, you would check the daily CFR Parts Affected for February 1, 2014, if one was published. You would follow the same process you did when you reviewed Illustration 9-9. Since February 1, 2014 was a Saturday, no Federal Register was published and Illustration 9-9 shows the most current CFR Parts Affected.

The process is similar online. You can search for the relevant title by browsing or using search terms. You can check monthly pamphlets, the current list of C.F.R. parts affected, and the list of C.F.R. parts affected today. This is the most current search available.

On Lexis and Westlaw, the changes to the regulations already are incorporated.

### ▼ How Do You Validate or Shepardize a C.F.R. Citation?

Cases that construe an administrative regulation are compiled in the *Shepard's Code of Federal Regulations Citations*. The citations are organized by title and then by section. The publisher's analysis is similar to that given to statutes. (For a detailed explanation of how to Shepardize, consult Chapter 5 and Appendix A.) A court cannot repeal an administrative regulation. Shepardizing, however, indicates whether the regulation continues to be valid. However, Shepardizing an administrative regulation does not replace the need to update the regulation in the manner discussed in the prior sections. Updating the regulation

provides the most current version of the citation. In contrast, Shepardizing the cite reveals the judicial interpretations of the citation. Both tasks, Shepardizing and updating, must be performed for research to be thorough and complete.

## ILLUSTRATION 9-9.  CFR Parts Affected for the Month

i

### Reader Aids

Federal Register

Vol. 79, No. 21

Friday, January 31, 2014

#### CUSTOMER SERVICE AND INFORMATION

**Federal Register/Code of Federal Regulations**
General Information, indexes and other finding aids ... 202–741–6000
Laws ... 741–6000

**Presidential Documents**
Executive orders and proclamations ... 741–6000
The United States Government Manual ... 741–6000

**Other Services**
Electronic and on-line services (voice) ... 741–6020
Privacy Act Compilation ... 741–6064
Public Laws Update Service (numbers, dates, etc.) ... 741–6043
TTY for the deaf-and-hard-of-hearing ... 741–6086

#### ELECTRONIC RESEARCH

**World Wide Web**

Full text of the daily Federal Register, CFR and other publications is located at: **www.fdsys.gov**.
Federal Register information and research tools, including Public Inspection List, indexes, and Code of Federal Regulations are located at: **www.ofr.gov**.

**E-mail**

**FEDREGTOC-L** (Federal Register Table of Contents LISTSERV) is an open e-mail service that provides subscribers with a digital form of the Federal Register Table of Contents. The digital form of the Federal Register Table of Contents includes HTML and PDF links to the full text of each document.
To join or leave, go to **http://listserv.access.gpo.gov** and select *Online mailing list archives, FEDREGTOC-L, Join or leave the list (or change settings)*; then follow the instructions.
**PENS** (Public Law Electronic Notification Service) is an e-mail service that notifies subscribers of recently enacted laws.
To subscribe, go to **http://listserv.gsa.gov/archives/publaws-l.html** and select *Join or leave the list (or change settings)*; then follow the instructions.
**FEDREGTOC-L** and **PENS** are mailing lists only. We cannot respond to specific inquiries.
**Reference questions.** Send questions and comments about the Federal Register system to: **fedreg.info@nara.gov**
The Federal Register staff cannot interpret specific documents or regulations.
**Reminders.** Effective January 1, 2009, the Reminders, including Rules Going Into Effect and Comments Due Next Week, no longer appear in the Reader Aids section of the Federal Register. This information can be found online at **http://www.regulations.gov**.
**CFR Checklist.** Effective January 1, 2009, the CFR Checklist no longer appears in the Federal Register. This information can be found online at **http://bookstore.gpo.gov/**.

#### FEDERAL REGISTER PAGES AND DATE, JANUARY

| | | | |
|---|---|---|---|
| 1–324 | 2 | 3723–4072 | 23 |
| 325–528 | 3 | 4073–4264 | 24 |
| 529–748 | 6 | 4265–4388 | 27 |
| 749–1302 | 7 | 4389–4612 | 28 |
| 1303–1590 | 8 | 4613–4816 | 29 |
| 1591–1732 | 9 | 4817–5222 | 30 |
| 1733–2074 | 10 | 5223–6076 | 31 |
| 2075–2358 | 13 | | |
| 2359–2580 | 14 | | |
| 2581–2760 | 15 | | |
| 2761–3070 | 16 | | |
| 3071–3300 | 17 | | |
| 3301–3480 | 21 | | |
| 3481–3722 | 22 | | |

#### CFR PARTS AFFECTED DURING JANUARY

At the end of each month the Office of the Federal Register publishes separately a List of CFR Sections Affected (LSA), which lists parts and sections affected by documents published since the revision date of each title.

**3 CFR**

Proclamations:
| | |
|---|---|
| 9073 | 749 |
| 9074 | 751 |
| 9075 | 753 |
| 9076 | 3477 |
| 9077 | 3479 |
| 9078 | 3719, 4265 |

Executive Orders:
| | |
|---|---|
| 13656 | 4263 |

Administrative Orders:
Memorandums:
Memorandum of
  December 27,
  2013 ... 527
Memorandum of
  January 9, 2014 ... 2577
Memorandum of
  January 22, 2014 ... 4385
Notices:
Notice of January 21,
  2014 ... 3721
Presidential
Determinations:
No. 2014–07 of
  January 17, 2014 ... 4611

**5 CFR**
| | |
|---|---|
| 550 | 529 |
| 870 | 530 |
| 890 | 531 |
| 894 | 531 |
| 2641 | 1 |

Proposed Rules:
| | |
|---|---|
| 179 | 609 |
| 315 | 610 |
| 870 | 613 |

**6 CFR**
| | |
|---|---|
| 5 | 2 |

**7 CFR**
| | |
|---|---|
| 205 | 3301 |
| 210 | 325, 2761 |
| 271 | 5 |
| 272 | 5 |
| 274 | 5 |
| 276 | 5 |
| 277 | 5 |
| 400 | 2075 |
| 407 | 2075 |
| 457 | 2075 |
| 905 | 4817 |
| 915 | 2773 |
| 930 | 2775 |
| 987 | 4819 |
| 1222 | 3696 |

Proposed Rules:
| | |
|---|---|
| 319 | 4410 |
| 1211 | 2805 |
| 1216 | 3139 |

**9 CFR**
| | |
|---|---|
| 11 | 3071 |

Proposed Rules:
| | |
|---|---|
| 56 | 4538 |
| 94 | 3741 |
| 145 | 4538 |
| 146 | 4538 |
| 147 | 4538 |

**10 CFR**
| | |
|---|---|
| 218 | 16 |
| 429 | 500 |
| 430 | 500 |
| 431 | 16 |
| 490 | 16 |
| 601 | 16 |
| 820 | 16 |
| 824 | 16 |
| 851 | 16 |
| 1013 | 16 |
| 1017 | 16 |
| 1050 | 16 |

Proposed Rules:
| | |
|---|---|
| Ch. I | 3543 |
| 30 | 3328 |
| 40 | 3328, 4825 |
| 50 | 3328 |
| 52 | 3328 |
| 60 | 3328 |
| 61 | 3328, 4102 |
| 63 | 3328 |
| 70 | 3328, 4825 |
| 71 | 3328 |
| 72 | 3328, 4825 |
| 74 | 4825 |
| 150 | 4825 |
| 430 | 3742 |
| 431 | 2383 |

**11 CFR**
| | |
|---|---|
| 111 | 3302 |

**12 CFR**
| | |
|---|---|
| 44 | 5223, 5536 |
| 234 | 3666 |
| 237 | 340 |
| 248 | 5223, 5536 |
| 255 | 5223 |
| 351 | 5223, 5536 |
| 615 | 3543 |
| 652 | 3071 |
| 703 | 5228 |
| 715 | 5228 |
| 741 | 5228 |
| 1230 | 4389 |
| 1231 | 4394 |
| 1770 | 4389 |

Proposed Rules:
| | |
|---|---|
| 30 | 4282 |
| 170 | 4282 |
| Ch. II | 3329 |
| 201 | 615 |

# ILLUSTRATION 9-9. *Continued*

914.................................4414
917.................................4414
1006...............................2384
1090...............................5302
1236...............................4414
1239...............................4414
1710...............................4414
1720...............................4414

**13 CFR**

Ch. I.....................1303, 1309
115.................................2084

**14 CFR**

25 ..................1591, 2359, 2365
39 .......344, 532, 536, 540, 543,
   545, 549, 1315, 1733, 2366,
   3303, 3481, 4267, 4269,
   5247, 5249, 5251, 5254,
    5257
61......................................20
71 ..........346, 3305, 3315, 4073
73.................................3326
91.................................2088
95.................................2368
97.........................3072, 3073
121...............................2088
125...............................2088
141.................................20

**Proposed Rules:**

Ch. 1................................5318
25 .......1334, 1336, 1337, 1339,
   2384, 2387, 2388
39 .........65, 70, 72, 74, 76, 763,
   1772, 1774, 2391, 2593,
   2595, 2805, 3139, 3336,
   3339, 3341, 4300, 5319,
   5321, 5323, 5325
71 ......1341, 1342, 1344, 1345,
   1346, 1607, 3544, 3545,
    5329

**15 CFR**

732.................................4613
736.................................4613
740 ....................22, 264, 4613
742.................................22
744..........................22, 4613
752.................................4613
754.................................4613
758.................................4613
766.................................4613
770..........................22, 4613
772..........................22, 4613
774..........................22, 264

**Proposed Rules:**

30.................................5330
700.................................5332

**16 CFR**

1112...............................2581
1222...............................2581

**17 CFR**

42.................................2370
75.................................5808
200...............................1734
239...............................1316
240.........................1522, 2777
249.........................1522, 2777
255...............................5536
270...............................1316
274...............................1316
300...............................2779

**Proposed Rules:**

Ch. I.....................1347, 4104

150.........................2394, 3547
Ch. II...............................4638
230...............................3926
232...............................3926
239...............................3926
240...............................3926
260...............................3926

**18 CFR**

11.................................3075
35.........................755, 4075
40.................................3723
292...............................3483
1304...............................4620

**Proposed Rules:**

40.................................3547

**19 CFR**

12.........................2088, 2781

**Proposed Rules:**

7.................................2395
163...............................2395
168...............................2395
178...............................2395

**21 CFR**

14.................................2093
225...............................3738
510.........................2785, 2786
529.........................2785, 2786
814...............................1735
866...............................3739
876...............................3088
892...............................3088

**Proposed Rules:**

16.................................5353
25.................................3742
121...............................5353
870...............................765
1308.....................1776, 4429

**22 CFR**

120.................................26
121...........................26, 34
123...........................26, 34
124...........................26, 34
125.................................34
126.................................26

**23 CFR**

771...............................2107

**26 CFR**

1 ............755, 2094, 2589, 3094
31.........................4077, 4623
57.................................3483
602...............................3483

**Proposed Rules:**

1 ........3042, 3142, 3145, 4105,
   4302, 4826

**27 CFR**

**Proposed Rules:**

9.................................2399
478...............................774

**28 CFR**

**Proposed Rules:**

35.................................4839
36.................................4839
527.................................78

**29 CFR**

101...............................3483
102...............................3483

1630...............................4623
2700...............................3104
4007...............................347
4022...............................2591

**Proposed Rules:**

1904...............................778
1910...............................4641
1915...............................4641
1926...............................4641
4041A .............................4642
4231...............................4642
4281...............................4642

**32 CFR**

161...............................708

**Proposed Rules:**

767...............................620

**33 CFR**

110...............................2371
117 .....1741, 2098, 3495, 3496,
   4624, 5259, 5260
151...............................5261
165 .....2371, 3105, 3497, 3499,
   3502, 4077, 4401, 5282,
    5283

**Proposed Rules:**

140.........................1780, 2254
145...............................2254
146...............................1780
148...............................2254
149...............................2254
165 .....1789, 2597, 3552, 3555
401...............................4433

**34 CFR**

685...............................3108

**36 CFR**

**Proposed Rules:**

13.................................2608
242...............................1791

**37 CFR**

**Proposed Rules:**

1.........................3146, 4105
2.................................3750
3.................................3146
5.................................3146
6.................................3750
7.................................3750
11.................................3146

**38 CFR**

3.................................2099
4.................................2099
17.........................1330, 1332
36.................................2100
60.................................2099

**Proposed Rules:**

3.................................430
13.................................430

**39 CFR**

20.................................3327
111...............................5286
121...............................4079
775...............................2102

**Proposed Rules:**

111...............................375
121...............................376
3010...............................5355

**40 CFR**

9.................................350

30.................................4403
31.................................4403
52 ......47, 51, 54, 57, 364, 551,
   573, 577, 580, 1593, 1596,
   2375, 2787, 3120, 3504,
   3506, 4082, 4274, 4407,
   4820, 4821, 5032, 5287,
    5291, 5294
63.................................367
70.........................2787, 4274
98.................................3507
180 ........582, 1599, 3508, 3512,
   4624, 5294
228...............................372
260...............................350
261...............................350
300.................................61

**Proposed Rules:**

49.................................2546
52 ...378, 631, 784, 1349, 1350,
   1608, 1612, 1795, 2144,
   2404, 2808, 3147, 3757,
   4121, 4308, 4313, 4436,
    4862, 5363
60.........................1352, 1430
63 .........379, 1676, 3557, 4439
70.........................1430, 4313
71.................................1430
81.........................3757, 4121
98.........................1430, 2614
745...............................1799

**42 CFR**

85a.................................2789
412..........................61, 1741
413 ...................63, 1741, 1742
414...............................1741
419.................................61
424 ...................63, 1741, 1742
430...............................2948
431...............................2948
435...............................2948
436...............................2948
440...............................2948
441...............................2948
447...............................2948
482..........................61, 1741
485..........................61, 1741
489..........................61, 1741

**Proposed Rules:**

85a.................................2809
100...............................1804
409...............................1918
417...............................1918
422...............................1918
423...............................1918
424...............................1918

**44 CFR**

64.................................4085
67 ......2103, 3518, 4089, 4091,
   4094, 4097, 4100

**Proposed Rules:**

67.................................381

**45 CFR**

**Proposed Rules:**

160...............................298
162...............................298
164...............................784

**46 CFR**

30.................................2106
150...............................2106
153...............................2106

**Proposed Rules:**

4.................................1780

▼ How Are the C.F.R. and the *Federal Register* Cited?

Citations to the C.F.R. and the *Federal Register* should follow *Bluebook* **Rule 14.2**. Title 21 of the C.F.R., part 101 from 2010 is cited per the *Bluebook* as

21 C.F.R. pt. 101 (2013)

Title 21 of the C.F.R., § 101.62 from 2013 would be written as

21 C.F.R. § 101.62 (2013)

It will be the same based on *ALWD* **Rule 18.1**.

A *Federal Register* entry from volume 70 beginning on page 35030 from June 16, 2005, would be cited based on the *Bluebook* **Rule 14.2** as

Temporary Final Rule, 70 Fed. Reg. 35030 (June 16, 2005)

However, based on *ALWD* **Rule 18.3**, it would be cited as follows:

70 Fed. Reg. 35030 (June 16, 2005).

# D. DECISIONS

▼ What Else Do Administrative Agencies Do?

Agencies function in a quasi-judicial capacity when they conduct **hearings.** Hearings may resemble court proceedings. However, most hearings are informal. An **administrative law judge** (ALJ) hears cases involving the application of a particular regulation. Often these cases involve the violation of a regulation. After the hearing, the ALJ, who may be an agency employee or an independent attorney, issues an opinion that serves as primary authority. However, most agency decisions do not have the same binding effect as court decisions. Some agency decisions can be appealed in the courts if the parties are not satisfied with the results. Often, however, the federal courts follow agency decisions concerning areas in which the agencies have developed expertise. To determine whether a court will follow an agency ruling, you must review court and agency decisions.

## ETHICS ALERT

Some federal agencies permit paralegals to appear before them without an attorney present.

The Administrative Procedure Act requires agencies to publish their decisions and to make them available to the public. Researchers can contact a particular agency to obtain a decision. Administrative rulings are found frequently in the areas of labor, environmental, tax, securities, occupational safety and health, energy, and immigration law.

### ▼ What Kind of Authority Are Administrative Decisions?

Administrative decisions, like decisions of various courts, are primary authorities. Some of these decisions can be appealed to the courts after all agency remedies have been satisfied. For example, an ALJ will determine whether an individual is disabled and qualifies for Social Security. This decision is made following a hearing. The ALJ's decision then can be appealed to the U.S. District Court and subsequently to higher federal courts. The enabling statute defines the type of review each agency decision will be accorded. However, the precedential value of the agency's decision varies. Some agencies do not bind themselves to follow previous decisions. However, the courts may find that an agency's decision is very persuasive, particularly in areas in which an agency has developed an expertise.

### ▼ Can Administrative Agency Decisions Be Shepardized?

Yes, administrative agency decisions can be Shepardized. The citations are contained in *Shepard's U.S. Administrative Citations.*

### ▼ Other Than the Agency Itself, Where Can You Find Administrative Agency Decisions?

Sometimes a commercially published service prints administrative agency decisions. Many agency decisions are also available on Westlaw and Lexis. Looseleaf services covering a specific legal topic such as food and drug law or environmental law publish many of the decisions.

## E. LOOSELEAF SERVICES

### ▼ What Are Looseleaf Services?

**Looseleaf services** cover one topic thoroughly. The publishers compile administrative decisions, rules, regulations, and editorial comments within a single source. Looseleaf services are published in all areas covered by administrative law: environmental, labor, energy, and government contracts law. Many researchers think of looseleaf services as mini-libraries because they contain a variety of resources relating to a single legal topic.

Because the looseleafs are not bound volumes but are actually looseleaf notebooks, they are easily updated by adding and removing pages. Most looseleaf services are updated weekly, some more frequently. Once you become familiar with a practice area, particularly a heavily regulated area of the law, you quickly become familiar with the looseleaf services used in that area. The use of each looseleaf varies. Most contain directions at the beginning of the publication.

---

*PRACTICE POINTER*

Do not rely on the language of a primary authority you find in a looseleaf. Check the official version of the authority if one exists.

---

### ▼ Can Looseleafs Be Retrieved Online?

More and more looseleaf services are being used online. Subscriptions to looseleaf services are expensive, require shelf space, and are labor intensive to update and to maintain. Online use eliminates the subscription cost, permits the cost of its use to be charged to the client as online time, and avoids the labor required to update the looseleaf because the computerized version always is current.

Using the looseleaf services online is advantageous for the paralegal. The multiple indexes in the hard copy are difficult to use. You must use the terms selected by the indexer. In contrast, when accessing the service online, you have the benefit of full text searching. You can enter your query and select your own words. Another advantage of using looseleaf services online is that you can validate your research instantly at the terminal by using *Shepard's* online.

### ▼ What Type of Authority Are Looseleaf Services?

Looseleaf services as a whole are considered secondary authority because they are not published by a government body in its official law making capacity. However, looseleaf services contain primary resources such as agency decisions, and frequently a looseleaf service is the only hard-copy resource for the decision. When citing to an agency decision obtained in a looseleaf service, that decision is primary authority.

## RESEARCHING ADMINISTRATIVE LAW: SUMMARY

1. Find the enabling statute.
2. Find judicial opinions concerning the enabling statute.

3. Find agency regulations.
    a. Review the index for the appropriate title or look up title parallel-ing the statutory title and skim the contents.
    b. Or, look up the agency by name in the index. It will direct you to a C.F.R. part.
4. Find case adjudications. Consult looseleaf services, *Shepard's* and other citators, and the U.S.C.A. or U.S.C.S. annotations.
5. Validate and update your research.

## CHAPTER SUMMARY

Administrative agencies and their power and authority are created by the federal and state legislatures when they enact enabling statutes. These agen-cies operate on a daily basis to enforce these legislative mandates.

As part of their enforcement duties, the agencies adopt rules and regula-tions and hold quasi-judicial hearings.

Rules and regulations of the federal administrative agencies can be found in the *Code of Federal Regulations*. These regulations also are available online. A daily paper called the *Federal Register* also reports any new or proposed reg-ulations. States also have codes of regulations and generally a daily record of new and proposed administrative rules and regulations.

Updating these authorities is essential. You must use the *List of C.F.R. Sections Affected* (L.S.A.) to update a C.F.R. citation. These lists are organized by title and section and are included in the daily *Federal Register* publications. You must review both the monthly L.S.A. pamphlets and the *Federal Register* to update a C.F.R. section properly.

Decisions of administrative agencies also can be validated in a manner similar to other case decisions.

Looseleaf services focus on one area of the law. They contain both primary authorities such as statutes, administrative rules, and cases, and secondary authorities such as expert commentary. Some looseleaf services also have digests and citators and some can be found online.

The next chapter will explain how and when to use the computerized legal research systems.

## KEY TERMS

adjudicatory
administrative agencies
administrative law judge (ALJ)
*Code of Federal Regulations* (C.F.R.)
enabling statutes
*Federal Register*

hearings
*List of C.F.R. Section Affected* (L.S.A.)
looseleaf services
quasi-judicial
regulations
rules

## EXERCISES
### FEDERAL REGULATIONS

1. Find a federal regulation that concerns the number of parts of lead allowable in drinking water.
    a. List each source that might contain the regulation.
    b. Map out your search strategy.
    c. List at least two sources and how you would find a regulation in each.
    d. List topics you might consult.
    e. List at least one regulation.
    f. Update the regulation using the hard-copy materials. What steps did you take?
    g. List the citation in proper *Bluebook* and *ALWD* format.
2. Find a federal tax regulation that specifies how the value of estate property will be determined.
    a. List each source that might contain the regulation.
    b. Map out your search strategy.
    c. List at least two sources and how you would find a regulation in each.
    d. List topics you might consult.
    e. List at least one regulation.
    f. Update the regulation using the hard-copy materials. What steps did you take?
    g. List the regulation in proper *Bluebook* and *ALWD* format.

### STATE REGULATIONS

3. In your state, where would you look to find state regulations?
4. Find a state regulation that deals with the question of physician licensing
    a. List each source that might contain the regulation.
    b. Map out your search strategy.
    c. List at least two sources and how you would find a regulation in each.
    d. List topics you might consult.
    e. List at least one regulation.
    f. Update the regulation using the hard-copy materials. What steps did you take?
    g. List the citations in proper *Bluebook* and *ALWD* format.
5. You must find a federal regulation that concerns small toy parts and children.
    a. List each source that might contain the regulation.
    b. Map out your search strategy.
    c. List at least two sources and how you would find a regulation in each.
    d. List topics you might consult.
    e. List at least one regulation.
    f. Update the regulation using the hard-copy material. What steps did you take?
    g. List the citation in proper *Bluebook* and *ALWD* format.

## CHAPTER 10

# COMMERCIAL DATABASES

**A. INTRODUCTION**      280
  1. Uses for Lexis, Westlaw, and Bloomberg Law    282
  2. Additional Features    283
**B. SEARCHING WITH ONLINE LEGAL RESEARCH**    284
   **SYSTEMS**
  1. The Basics    285
  2. Search Formulation    286
  3. Other Ways to Restrict Your Search to Retrieve On-Point    290
    Information
  4. Retrieving the Results of Your Research    293
  5. Point-and-Click Enhancements    294
  6. Additional Features on Lexis and Westlaw    294
  7. Comparing Lexis and Westlaw    296

## CHAPTER OVERVIEW

This chapter explains the basic concepts of the use of Lexis Advance, WestlawNext, and Bloomberg Law and the way information is organized on the systems. The material in this chapter introduces you to the broad features of the systems. Even though we now all have experience searching the Internet, and even with new avenues for computer-assisted legal research, vendor training is still necessary. Vendor training is essential because the databases are very costly to use. Lexis Advance, WestlawNext, and Bloomberg Law provide valuable

editorial enhancements and accurate up-to-date information. All three have citators. Lexis Advance is the only online system with *Shepard's*. WestlawNext has KeyCite. Lexis Advance and WestlawNext tie the online resources to their respective print publications and research systems, and have coverage that goes back over 100 years.

Lexis Advance, WestlawNext, and Bloomberg Law now all use a "Google type" query bar that allows broad searching without terms and connectors and without the need to select the specific resource format or document type. Your search will yield more on-target hits if you incorporate a terms and connectors search and know the type of resource you are seeking, or at least are aware of the type of document your research requires. Preliminary research with secondary authorities will show you the vocabulary used in relevant documents and the proximity of the terms within the relevant documents. Instead of filtering the resources—for instance, for statutes or regulations—when you start the search, you can now filter after you obtain your documents. It is still imperative that you know the types of resources you are after.

The fundamental topics explored in this chapter include:

1. query formulation
2. finding content
3. validation of authority

Although this chapter focuses primarily on Lexis Advance and WestlawNext, using computer-assisted legal research in specific research situations is discussed throughout this book. Additionally, many cost-effective alternatives to Lexis Advance and WestlawNext have emerged, such as Fastcase and Loislaw. Free online websites for legal information are available at Cornell's Legal Information Institute (www.law.cornell.edu), the Government Printing Office site (gpo.gov), Justia, Findlaw, www.supremecourt.gov, and Google Scholar. Also, every state has its own website with state primary source documents. The depth of coverage varies greatly in all the cost-effective sites mentioned. The Lexis Advance and WestlawNext alternatives are good places to turn when you are looking for a particular case, statute, regulation, or journal article. However, these sites do not offer publishers' research enhancements, a wide variety of resources, or *Shepard's* or KeyCite. Research enhancements, such as key numbers and head notes, related resources produced by the publisher, updating, and validation services are essential for efficient legal research. For older material and a vast array of resources under one site, Lexis and Westlaw products are the way to go. The depth of coverage in both Lexis and Westlaw is vast and deep.

## A. INTRODUCTION

Lexis Advance is an online research system owned by Reed Elsevier, Inc., a British-Dutch publishing business. West, owned by Thomson

Reuters, a major legal publisher, also decided to create computerized legal databases and named their system WestlawNext. Bloomberg Law is produced by Bloomberg, the major online provider of business information. Additionally, Loislaw, owned by WoltersKluwer, is a legal database that offers research and updates for WoltersKluwer treatises. Lexis Advance and WestlawNext are the respective newer versions of Lexis and Westlaw.

A revolution in legal research occurred with the advent of computerized legal research. Researchers can now obtain documents, cases, statutes, bills, regulations, attorney general opinions, slip laws, and many other forms of information, legal and factual, from a myriad of jurisdictions and print it out in full text without leaving the office. In addition, researchers do not have to use an index when obtaining material online. Researchers can select terms or words that need to appear in the ideal document on point. The researcher can then combine the relevant terms in a query, which is used to search the appropriate databank for documents with those words or terms. Computerized research systems continually increase the amount of information and the variety of documents they contain.

Although commercial databanks are costly to use, they offer research enhancements that the scattered, free sites on the Internet often lack. Currently, though, www.gpo.gov/fdsys and Congress.gov are excellent updated resources for federal statutory and regulatory information.

Now you can access up-to-date versions of Lexis, Westlaw, and Bloomberg Law at the following URLS:

LexisAdvance.com
WestlawNext.com
Bloomberglaw.com

### ▼ What Are the Benefits of Using Online Legal Research Systems?

The greatest benefit of Lexis Advance, WestlawNext, Bloomberg Law, and LoisLaw is that all sources are reliable, accurate, and up to date. A vast variety of resources are accessible through a single computer terminal. You do not have to travel to various libraries to obtain the information that you need. Also, the material online is never off the shelf or checked out. Currentness is essential in legal research, and the commercial online databases keep everything as current as possible. (See Chapter 5, for example, on how to validate cases on Lexis and Westlaw.) Searching on the commercial databases is smooth. The database screens have many features to facilitate your search. In addition, *Shepard's* on Lexis and KeyCite on Westlaw permit you to validate the authority that you retrieve with a single click. (At the time of this edition, Bloomberg Law's **citatory**, BCite, only permits case validation.) It is essential to know that the authority is still good law before you

use it. Both Lexis and Westlaw tie you to their other research products, print and online, by showing you related sources, and both offer editorial enhancements in the form of headnotes, annotations, and summaries. Westlaw has the key number system and allows you to customize key number searches online for efficient research using the West Digest system. When you use one of these commercial databases, you never have to evaluate whether the site is trustworthy.

### ▼ What Are the Major Disadvantages of Using Online Legal Research Systems?

The first major disadvantage is cost. Lexis and Westlaw are still quite expensive, and the charges for searching, connect time, and subscribing add up very quickly. A half-hour search can easily cost well over $100. You can avoid some of the high fees by entering into a special contract with Lexis or Westlaw. Now many types of contracts can be negotiated, including contracts for single-state research or flat annual fees. Although the vendors have made online research easier and easier by adding many user-friendly features—like tool bar, menu-driven, and point-and-click searching—many skills must be developed to search in an efficient and cost-effective way. You must take the time to select your search terms to retrieve on-point information. What you enter will limit what you retrieve. Also, browsing through sources is difficult and costly.

---

### PRACTICE POINTER

Before using Lexis or Westlaw to perform any research or to cite check, ask the attorney assigning the project if it is permissible. Sometimes budgets are very restricted.

---

## 1. Uses for Lexis, Westlaw, and Bloomberg Law

Computerized legal research is a very powerful search tool to find cases that discuss unique fact patterns. For example, suppose you want to find cases that deal with a slip-and-fall issue on a shag carpet. An encyclopedia or digest index may have entries under "slip and fall" and possibly under "carpet," but it is very unlikely that there would be an index entry under "shag." Lexis and Westlaw permit you to search "shag carpet" to see where those words appear in a document.

With computerized legal research you also can find documents, cases, statutes, and articles when you only have some information from the cite but not the complete cite. Suppose you hear about a promising Florida Supreme Court case on point. You know the case was decided in April 2003 and the judge's name was Murphy, but you do

not have a clue as to the case name. Knowing the court, the year, and the judge will lead you to the case on Lexis or Westlaw.

---

*PRACTICE POINTER*

Some firms and companies still use the earlier versions of Lexis and Westlaw, simply called Lexis and Westlaw or Westlaw Classic. They are still available online.

---

## 2. Additional Features

Lexis Advance and WestlawNext are used very effectively for cite checking, updating, and validating authority. (See Chapter 5 for a full discussion of citators, *Shepard's*, and KeyCite.) The online systems enable you to obtain the subsequent history of a case. Retrieving updated statutory and administrative materials on Lexis and Westlaw is another valuable use of the systems' capabilities because you do not have to consult a number of hard-copy sources, pocket parts, and supplements to find the most current version of a statute or a regulation. Also, administrative and statutory materials have cumbersome and difficult-to-use indexes, and the full text search capabilities of Lexis Advance, WestlawNext, and Bloomberg Law permit you to obtain documents by combining the words and terms relevant to your research problem. Case law and code research from other jurisdictions is performed efficiently on the databases because you do not have to find out-of-state primary sources in hard-copy format. An underused feature of computerized legal research is to access looseleaf services online; subscription and filing fees are saved and the material is always current. Bloomberg Law now owns BNA publications, and their looseleaf services and portfolios are online. Lexis Advance has a related content feature on the screen display that provides links to related secondary sources. WestlawNext links the user to related West publications and the entire West key number system, indexing, and annotated statutes. Lexis Advance and WestlawNext provide integrated research so that the retrieval is actually expanded and is tied to the print publications so you can read the source in hard copy.

---

*PRACTICE POINTER*

Lexis and Westlaw have excellent online training. For Lexis, go to www .lexisnexis.com/en-us/support/lexis-advance/default.page, and for Westlaw, go to westelearning.com.

---

# B. SEARCHING WITH ONLINE LEGAL RESEARCH SYSTEMS

## ▼ General Overview

Lexis Advance, WestlawNext, and Bloomberg Law work in a similar fashion. The systems require careful query formulation and selection of search terms to obtain the most relevant information available. Both are **literal searching devices**, meaning that the computer searches for the appearance of the words or terms that you select to appear in the text of the document. You will retrieve a group of documents containing your search terms after executing a search.

The Internet is the gateway to the databanks so there is no need to download software and to update it. The systems are very intuitive and menu driven. You no longer have to locate the names of libraries or databases within the systems but merely have to point and click on the type of resource you want. The mechanics of using Lexis Advance and WestlawNext are now similar to using an Internet browser. Searching now does not require the user to know the database or library, for searching is performed with a series of clicks to narrow the retrieval potential with on-screen filters. Of course, you can type a variety of terms into the search box without connectors and without specifying the document type, but you will locate relevant sources more quickly with search enhancements and refinements.

Each system has iPad and smart phone search capability.

As stated earlier, although you can use a "Google type" search, the most efficient searching is performed with some traditional online research techniques. Begin the search by creating a list of words that would appear in the ideal document on point. (You should educate yourself on the topic before you get online so that you have a research vocabulary that includes synonymous terms.) Then you figure out the relationship between the ideal words or terms. How close together would they appear in the document? Would the words and terms appear in the same sentence? In the same paragraph? Within 100 words of one another? This involves thinking about the context of the words within the document's text and how those words should appear without losing their contextual significance.

The process of selecting the terms and determining the terms' contextual relationship is simpler now with natural language searching. Natural language lets you search in plain English using sentences and phrases without selecting connectors between the terms. (More on connectors later in the chapter.) The system then selects the significant terms from your search and looks for documents containing those terms. Whether you search using a group of words separated by connectors or use natural language, computerized legal research scans the databank for the appearance of those words and retrieves the documents for you.

Electronic retrieval systems do not replace traditional research sources. Electronic resources will not tell you if the source is relevant; you still must read the material to see if it applies. You also must validate any resource you rely on to make sure it is still good law. Even if a case is on Lexis Advance or WestlawNext, it may have been overruled. You must take the extra step to validate any primary source authority. Also, the databases are literal searching tools that cannot analyze or reach conclusions, legal or factual. The systems search for terms within the parameters that you specify, the connectors. The systems are excellent for searching terms that are not ordinarily included in traditional indexes. They are also good for searching for specific facts or legal terms. Remember that the most successful searching occurs after some preliminary research has been performed using secondary sources and digests and, if possible, primary authority. Preliminary research makes you aware of the vocabulary used in topic discussions and the wording in on-point opinions. *One warning:* The service is very costly when you are using it at a law firm or a corporation. Lexis Advance and WestlawNext are not suited to researching broad legal concepts like *breach of contract.* Use your judgment to determine if computerized or hard-copy research is the best route. Statutory research, especially if you have the books, is best started with the hard-copy format and then you can refine and narrow your research online. The best and most effective research uses a combination of hard-copy and computerized sources, drawing on the strengths of both. Computerized research is yet another tool in your arsenal of sources.

A comparison chart for Lexis Advance, WestlawNext, and Bloomberg Law is available at www.uakron.edu/law/library/docs/chart_comparing_3_research_systems.pdf.

## 1. The Basics

### ▼ How Can You Filter the Information?

Information on both Lexis Advance and WestlawNext can be filtered as follows:

1. by jurisdiction: individual states and federal cases and statutes;
2. by topic: for example, bankruptcy, tax, or contracts; or
3. by format: for example, cases, statutes, law reviews, looseleaf services, or news articles.

In the classic formats of Lexis and Westlaw, you can view the types of resources and then select where you want to search. The material, in the older versions, is organized by jurisdiction, by topic, and by format.

All three systems—Lexis, Westlaw, and Bloomberg Law—regardless of version, have state and federal primary authority—statutes, cases, and regulations—as well as secondary sources. The three systems allow you to do a survey of state statutory law on a topic. Lexis and Westlaw have many secondary sources that have a print equivalent such as the A.L.R., Am. Jur. 2d, C.J.S., and formbooks. Westlaw has the West Digest system and the topics and key numbers. Lexis has *Shepard's.* Bloomberg Law has an integrated search and retrieval capability to bring up relevant business information and corporate filings.

On Lexis Advance and WestlawNext, you can retrieve a document if you have the citation. Merely type the cite in the search bar. You can also type in the name of a specific source in the search bar to bring the source up.

---

## PRACTICE POINTER

Your employer will probably subscribe to one commercial database, and you can then focus your training on that system.

---

## 2. Search Formulation

Now that the systems use "Google type" searching, there is no need to learn the details of query formulation for each vendor. The new versions start with broad searches and then let you use the on-screen entries to filter your search. However, a basic understanding of a terms and connector type search will help you to construct a more precise search query.

### ▼ What Is a Search or Query?

Any group of terms or words that you type into the search bar is a query. The databases are literal searching systems. You must determine the words or terms that you want to appear in a document on point. Your **search** or **query** is the group of terms or words that you select, that you enter into the system to retrieve on-target information. If you use a terms and connectors search, the terms are separated by connectors. Suppose you want to find cases discussing Seminole Indians in Florida, particularly near St. Augustine, and their water, land, or property rights. The terms that you would select are:

Seminole Indian
St. Augustine

water right
land right
property right

These are the terms that would appear in the ideal opinion. Use a thesaurus to find synonymous terms to expand the number of documents you will retrieve. Next, if you use connectors, you must determine the placement of the terms in the document's text. Do you want the terms to be close together and to all fall in the same sentence? Do you want the terms to be anywhere in the document? In the same paragraph? Will the contextual meaning or significance of the terms be lost if they are too far apart? Will you fail to retrieve many documents if you indicate that they should be close together? Use connectors to indicate the proximity of the terms.

### a. Connectors

**Connectors** are the special words or symbols devised by Westlaw and by Lexis that link your search terms together to indicate your search terms' physical placement in the document's text. Now with the search bar on Lexis Advance, WestlawNext, and Bloomberg Law you do not have to use connectors when entering your terms. However, connectors will yield a more accurate search. Connectors tell Lexis and Westlaw the proximity of the search terms in relation to one another. Lexis uses the following connectors:

**and**—indicates that the terms are anywhere in the document but both terms must appear in the document. For example, in typing **seminole and indian**, the word *and* indicates that both terms must appear in the document.

**or**—indicates that one term or the other term or both terms must appear in the document. A blank space on Westlaw indicates "or." For example, on Lexis, typing **seminole or indian** would cause the retrieval system to look for the occurrence of either *Seminole* or *Indian* or both words in the document. To search for these synonymous terms on Westlaw, input **seminole indian.** The *or* connector is most frequently used for synonymous terms, like *car or vehicle or automobile.* This maximizes the possibility of retrieving a greater number of on-point documents.

**w/n**—means within *n* number of words. You determine how close the words should appear in relation to one another. In our example, you could use **seminole w/5 indian**, which would tell Lexis to search for the word *Seminole* to appear within 5 words of *Indian.*

**Pre/n**—This connector is unique to Lexis and is identical to *w/n* except that the first word must precede the second. You are able to set the spacing. For example, **seminole pre/5 indian** would search for the word *Seminole* to precede the word *Indian* by 5 words.

**w/s**—indicates that the two words must appear in the same sentence in any order. You can also use /s instead of *w/s.* **Seminole w/s indian** would search for the two terms to appear in the same sentence in any order.

**w/p**—instructs Lexis to search for the terms within the same paragraph in any order. You can also use /p instead of *w/p.* **Seminole w/p indian** would search for the appearance of those terms in the same paragraph in any order.

**and not**—excludes terms. Use it as your last connector. For example, **seminole and indian and not tribe** would retrieve documents with the words *Seminole* and *Indian* anywhere in the document but no documents with the word *tribe* would be retrieved.

Westlaw's connectors are very similar to those of Lexis, but as indicated earlier, Westlaw does have a few unique features:

**&**—identical to the Lexis **and.**

**[blank space]**—typing a blank space between two or more terms indicates *or.* For example, the search **auto car vehicle** translates into *auto or car or vehicle.* The **or** connector is most frequently used to indicate synonymous terms, but it is also used to link antonyms or opposites like *day or night.*

**/s**—Westlaw pioneered the within-the-same-sentence connector. It is very handy because you do not have to estimate the proximity of the words to one another. If the words fall in the same sentence, you retrieve the document. Sentences can vary in length, and **/s** approximates written English.

**+s**—indicates that the two words must appear in the same sentence, but the first term must precede the second. For example, **seminole +s indian** would search for *Seminole* and *Indian* to appear in the same sentence, but *Seminole* must precede *Indian.*

**/p**—indicates that the two terms appear within the same paragraph. The search **seminole/p indian** would search for those two terms' appearance in the same paragraph in any order.

**+p**—searches for two terms to appear in the same paragraph, but the first term must precede the second. In our example, **seminole +p indian** would retrieve documents with *Seminole* occurring before *Indian* in the same paragraph.

**/n**—you can customize the proximity of terms on Westlaw just as you can on Lexis. For example, **seminole/5 indian** would search for the word *Seminole* to appear within 5 words of *Indian.*

**+n**—this connector allows you to establish the number of words between terms, but the first term must appear before the second. For example, **seminole +5 indian** searches for documents with *Seminole* falling 5 words before *Indian.*

**%**—excludes the term following the connector.

The following table summarizes connectors.

| Description | Lexis | Westlaw |
|---|---|---|
| terms within the same document | and | & |
| either or both terms within the same document | or | [blank space] |
| terms appear within specified number of words of each other | w/n | /n |
| same as w/n but first term precedes second term | pre/n | +n |
| terms within the same sentence, any order | w/s | /s |
| terms within same sentence; first term precedes second term | – | +s |
| terms within same paragraph, any order | w/p | /p |
| excludes terms following the connector | and not | % |

## b. Quotations

If you want to search for a specific phrase or a complete name, enclose the terms in quotation marks. This technique is helpful with searching in the new versions of Lexis Advance, WestlawNext, and Bloomberg Law. Without enclosing the terms in quotations, the spaces between the words would be interpreted as *or* on Westlaw. Sometimes you want to search for a phrase that includes articles that are not terms located by either system. In these instances, place the phrase or name in quotations and the system will search for all the terms within the quotes as a unit. For example, you would use quotations to search for cases discussing Megan's Law or the Americans with Disabilities Act. If you do not use quotes, Westlaw would interpret *Megan's Law* to be *Megan's* or *Law*. To obtain the exact phrase in a document enter it as follows: "Americans with Disabilities Act."

## c. Plurals

Lexis and Westlaw automatically search for regular plurals. For example, if you enter the word *pattern, patterns* is automatically searched. Irregular plurals like *children* are not automatically searched when the singular term is entered.

## d. Irregular Plurals

Lexis and Westlaw have two symbols that assist you in searching for irregular plurals and for words that could have various endings

stemming from the root word. The symbol * is like a Scrabble blank: You use it to replace a letter in a term. For example, suppose you are searching for articles about women. Documents on point could have the term *woman* or *women*, so your query would be typed as **wom\*n** to increase the potential of retrieving on-point information. If you want documents about children, you could use the term **child\*\*\*** and retrieve documents with *child* or *children*. The word *childhood* would not appear, however, because you only reserved three spaces after the root of *child*. If you want all possible endings of a word following its root, regardless of the amount of letters, use !. In our example, **child!** would retrieve *children, childhood, child,* and *childish.*

### e. Hyphenated Words

If you place a space between two search terms on Lexis, the system will automatically search for the hyphenated version of the word. For example, if you are searching for documents containing the term *full-text,* and you enter **full text** as your query, you will retrieve documents with *full-text* as well as *full text*. On Westlaw, if you use **full-text** as your query, the system will search for the appearance of *full-text* and *full text*. Westlaw interprets a blank space as an *or*, so you must put phrases in quotes so that the system searches for the existence of the phrase or term. For example, you can enter **"full text"** and Westlaw will search for *full-text* and *full text*. The quotes are useful for phrases such as *res ipsa loquitor* so that the entire phrase will be searched for as a whole.

### f. Noise Words or Articles

Lexis and Westlaw do not search for the occurrence of articles. Omit *the, a, an,* and *and* from your search queries. The frequent appearance of articles (or "noise words") in text would slow down the computer system if it had to search for them.

### g. Capitalizing Proper Nouns and Other Terms

You do not have to worry about capitalization style on any commercial database. Lexis, Westlaw, and Bloomberg Law are not case sensitive, meaning that the databases do not discern between upper- and lowercase letters but search by matching words. Your query can be written as **united w/1 states**, and you will retrieve relevant documents.

## 3. Other Ways to Restrict Your Search to Retrieve On-Point Information

### a. Date and Court Restrictors

Date and court **restrictors** in your query help to narrow your search. In Lexis Advance, WestlawNext, and Bloomberg Law, you can filter your

retrieved documents by court and by date after you see the search results. You can also start with a date restriction in your search query, or you can filter the search results by date. On both Lexis and Westlaw, you can limit your search to look for documents from a particular time frame. On Lexis, you can restrict your search for information on the Seminole Indians to after 2010, before August 31, 2012, or to a specific date. The searches would look as follows: **seminole w/5 indian and date aft 2010** for documents after 2010; **seminole w/5 indian and date bef 8/31/12** for documents before August 31, 2012; or **seminole w/5 indian and date = 10/1/11** for documents pertaining to the date of October 1, 2011. Westlaw has the equivalent method of restricting the date in the search query. On Westlaw, you would search for documents after a certain date as follows: **seminole/5 indian and da(aft 2010)**; before a certain date: **seminole/5 indian and da(bef 8/31/12)**; from a specific date: **seminole/5 indian and da(10/1/11)**.

Court restrictors are another method of ensuring that the documents retrieved are pertinent. You can also restrict by court when you enter your search or when you look at the materials retrieved; you can then filter the results by court or by jurisdiction. On Westlaw, to retrieve cases from Florida courts enter the following: **co(florida)**. You can also search by level of court. If you want only Florida Supreme Court cases, your search would include the following on Westlaw: **seminole/5 indian & co(high)**. This search would ensure that you would only receive cases from Florida's highest court.

On Lexis you can limit the courts to only the jurisdictionally relevant ones by using the court segment in the query. An example of this is when you are searching all federal cases and want only those actually decided in a Florida state court or a federal court sitting in the state of Florida. A search using the court segment would look like this: **seminole w/5 indian and court(florida)**.

The systems now have field restrictors on the screen where you can plug in the specific term to look for in a particular part of the document. All the commercial systems have templates for the particular fields that you can search. Cases have set components that can be searched such as the judge's name, the court, the attorney, the party. For instance, on WestlawNext you can click on a field search when looking for cases to restrict the results. You may only want opinions written by Justice Scalia. You would then click: ju. Then you would enter Scalia in the box. Lexis and Bloomberg also have templates on the screen for segment searching. Also, you can filter your retrieved sources with on-screen clicks—by court and by jurisdiction—after you obtain your initial search results.

### b. Other Restrictors

The following table summarizes the symbols and abbreviations used for search query restriction.

| Description | Lexis | Westlaw |
|---|---|---|
| replaces a letter in a word or term | * | * |
| unlimited endings following the root of the word | ! | ! |

## c. Fields

Cases and other documents on Lexis contain **segments** and on Westlaw contain **fields** that can be searched. Date and court restrictors are examples of segments or fields. Lexis also has case name, judge, and counsel segments for cases, and Westlaw has counsel, judge, case name, and topic (from the West Digest topics). Every category of information on each database has different segments or fields. Lexis Advance and WestlawNext have point-and-click features. Just read the screen, point, and click. It is helpful to understand the underlying concepts to achieve more effective searching.

## ▼ Why Does Integrating Traditional and Computerized Resources Result in the Most Effective Computerized Legal Research?

Beginning your research with traditional sources allows you to become educated in the area of law and to learn the pertinent vocabulary used in decisions and in statutes. (See Chapter 6 for a complete discussion of secondary authorities.) A vocabulary of the words used in on-point opinions lets you construct your search queries most effectively. Online research is very costly, and you cannot afford to use the time online to educate yourself on a topic. It is, in fact, cost-effective to print out the citations and to read sources in hard copy if they are easily obtained.

### *EXAMPLE*

You are asked to find Florida cases discussing abuse of process. Your first reaction to the assignment is that you do not even know what abuse of process is. This is the strategy that you would follow:

1. Consult secondary source materials to educate yourself and to acquire a research vocabulary for search formulation.

2. Begin the education process with a dictionary. Abuse of process is a tort and occurs when the process of the courts is used for an improper purpose. Here's an example of abuse of process: An individual enters into a contract with another to purchase rare coins. The two parties draw up an installment contract specifying monthly payments for 10 years. After possessing the coins for 2 years and after making the agreed-on monthly payments, the buyer decides that the market value of the coins has fallen and does not want to continue to make the monthly payments. The buyer sues the seller for fraud, claiming that he was deceived as to the true value of the coins. The buyer sues for fraud

not because a fraud actually occurred but because he wants to get out of the contract. This is an abuse of process.

3. Decide the jurisdiction that the materials should be from. You can do a broad search and then filter the results after you retrieve the documents, or you can search for resources from a particular jurisdiction when you enter your query. You will need to know the relevant jurisdiction for your research. In our example, the supervising attorney requested Florida cases, so Florida is the appropriate jurisdiction. Determining the appropriate jurisdiction enables you to narrow your search results.

4. Determine the terms that would appear in the ideal opinion. *Abuse* and *process* would be the terms in this example.

5. Decide the relationship that the terms would have to one another in the text—the proximity of the terms. It is important to ensure that contextual meaning is not lost. This is where you decide what connectors you will use. We are looking for cases defining abuse of process. *Of* is a noise word, so we ignore it for purposes of listing terms for our query, but we know that it falls between two important words. The terms must be close together to retain their contextual meaning in the document. You select *w/3*. The query would be **abuse w/3 process**. If you do not know the proximity of the terms when you initially search, enter a natural language query and then read a few of the cases. Some cases will be on point. Examine the language in those opinions to draft a new, more precise query.

6. Your goal is to maximize the retrieval of on-point documents. A court can discuss the definition as abusing the process of the courts. To get this decision as well, use a root with a *!*. Your query would be **abus! w/3 process**.

7. You can view the most recent opinions by filtering the retrieval results by date after your search or by adding a date restrictor to your initial query. Use the drop-down menu to plug dates into the date field or segment.

8. If you are frustrated in your attempts to search, call Westlaw customer service at 1-800-Westlaw or Lexis customer service at 1-800-543-6862.

## 4. Retrieving the Results of Your Research

On Lexis Advance, WestlawNext, and Bloomberg Law, you can view the citations of documents found. The cite list, the list of documents retrieved from your search, has some text from the actual document with your terms. This allows you to quickly scan your cites to see what is most relevant. You can then select full text by merely pointing and clicking on a citation.

Viewing documents online in full text is time consuming and costly. It is best to obtain citations online and download the documents to a research folder.

▼ Are There Any Other Ways to Retrieve Documents?

On Lexis and Westlaw, you can retrieve a specific statute or a case if you know the citation. You can merely type the citation into the search bar. If you want to see the text of 121 So. 2d 319, you would type **121 so2d 319** and press **[enter]**. To view the text of a statute, you would type **28 usc 1485** and press **[enter]**.

## 5. Point-and-Click Enhancements

Not only do Lexis, Westlaw, and Bloomberg Law ensure that the information and search capabilities are current, they make searching easier with on-screen buttons to filter your research results. Additionally, both vendors have made the research services much easier to use by allowing you to use the commands of your Internet browser combined with point-and-click capability instead of learning the searching nuances of each system. The vendors have greatly simplified searching on the systems.

Lexis is at Lexis.com and Lexis Advance is at LexisAdvance.com. On Lexis, the source directory has replaced the libraries. Instead of constructing a query at the top of the page, you click on the terms box. Everything is completely menu driven. Also, just as on any other Web site, you can link to other resources. You can easily Shepardize on Lexis by merely clicking the "*Shepard's*" icon when a primary source document is on the screen. While reading a document you may see a cite to another document in the text. If the cite is highlighted in blue, you can click on the cite and you then go to the text of the cited document. To go back to the original source, just click your Web browser back.

Lexis.com has graphics at the beginning of each case to indicate the analysis that case has received. A red stop sign indicates that the case is no longer good law and that there is strong negative analysis. A blue circle means that the available analysis is neutral.

Westlaw, at Westlaw.com, and WestlawNext, at WestlawNext.com, are just as simple to use as Lexis.com. Westlaw also has point-and-click capabilities and hypertext links to cited authorities. Westlaw developed KeyCite, a case law validating service with graphics to indicate the strength of the authority. Westlaw relies on flags to indicate how a case has been treated by subsequent courts.

## 6. Additional Features on Lexis and Westlaw

*Shepard's* is available on Lexis, and online fees are incurred based on use. The beauty of online cite checking is that you do not have to worry about all of the books being on the shelf or about updating the material. The online services do it. In fact, Shepardizing on Lexis is now the main way that researchers use *Shepard's* citations. Additionally, Lexis permits customized *Shepard's* retrieval by court, jurisdiction, or analysis. Reed Elsevier, the parent company of Lexis, owns *Shepard's*, so *Shepard's* data is updated nightly online. Additionally, Lexis provides

the treatment that the citing case offers regarding the decision you are validating. *Shepard's* on Lexis has color-coded symbols to alert you to the treatment that the case received. Also, you can customize your *Shepard's* retrieval to select only negative or positive treatment.

You do not need a document on the screen to Shepardize online with Lexis. You can click on *Shepard's* when signing on. You can then type in the next citation and press **[enter]** while the *Shepard's* analysis is on the screen, and the information will reflect the analytical treatment of the succeeding document. You can go through entire lists of citations this way without entering a Lexis library.

Case validation on Westlaw is called **KeyCite**. KeyCite is as current as Westlaw. As soon as a case is placed on Westlaw, it receives KeyCite analysis and is included in that database. KeyCite includes thousands of unpublished opinions and references to law reviews. You can also customize your KeyCite search to focus on a particular jurisdiction, date ranges, and court level. Cases receive boxes to indicate the level of treatment in the cited case. Four boxes indicate that there is more than a page of treatment in the cited case, three boxes equal one page of discussion, two boxes have up to a paragraph, and one box indicates that your case is included in a string cite. The boxes immediately alert you to the depth of treatment in the citing case, which can be a big time saver during research.

A red flag pops up in KeyCite when a case has negative history. This visual clue indicates when a case is no longer good law for one of its points. A yellow flag means that the case has not been overruled but has received some criticism. A blue "H" means that the case has been discussed. You can KeyCite a case by pointing and clicking the KeyCite icon. You can KeyCite a wide range of primary and secondary sources in addition to cases and statutes. Additionally, KeyCite provides subsequent legislative activity for statutes. This is very handy when updating statutory authority. On Lexis, you can Shepardize a document on the screen by merely clicking on the *Shepard's* tab. (For a full discussion of cite checking, see Chapter 5.)

Westlaw and WestlawNext permit you to view a case as a PDF so that the case looks identical to its West Reporter version.

Lexis has NEWS resources, which were previously located in the NEXIS library. It is an excellent source for full-text news and periodical articles. It is updated daily and is invaluable when performing factual research on an individual, a corporation, or an event.

Dow Jones is also available on Westlaw. Westlaw Classic and WestlawNext also have a News database with hundreds of newspapers, journals, wire services, and blogs.

Both Lexis and Westlaw, in all versions, have many secondary sources online including legal encyclopedia, law journals, treatises, and formbooks.

Bloomberg Law links all searches to business information and news sources. Many legal matters are based on economic factors. This is one of Bloomberg Law's strengths. Bloomberg Law also has a citator, called BCite, BCite is currently limited only to cases.

Go to YouTube.com to view several engaging instructional video tutorials for using:

**Bloomberg Law** (in collaboration with the Washington & Lee University School of Law Library): www.youtube.com/playlist?list=PL2C5C40EFD2AA81B2;
**Lexis**: www.youtube.com/user/LexisNexisLawSchools/videos; and
**Westlaw**: www.youtube.com/user/WestlawInsider.

## 7. Comparing Lexis and Westlaw

### a. Differences Between Lexis and Westlaw

Lexis has News resources, which permit access to full text articles from hundreds of periodicals. It is an excellent way to perform factual research.

*Shepard's*, owned by Lexis, is updated nightly and covers all cases and statutes from the 50 states and federal government as well as many regulations and other resources.

Westlaw permits you to search the West Digest topics and key numbers online. This is very convenient because you can customize digest searching by adding date and court restrictors and significant fact terms. Just as Lexis links you to related sources, with Related Content, Westlaw links you to all West legal publishing resources.

News information on Westlaw can be searched as a whole by clicking on the News link on the screen. Dow Jones is part of this database. Westlaw contains hundreds of newspapers, newsletters, journals, and wire services. Westlaw has a new validation and citing service called KeyCite. KeyCite tells you the status of the case, its analytical treatment by subsequent courts, and the depth of the treatment.

Thomson Reuters West also publishes U.S.C.C.A.N., see Chapter 8—Legislative History, which provides the legislative history of selected Public Laws. Consequently, U.S.C.C.A.N. is available on Westlaw Classic and WestlawNext.

### b. Similarities Between Lexis and Westlaw

Both Lexis and Westlaw permit you to research myriad cases, statutes, administrative regulations, articles, factual information, and other documents online using natural language searches that eliminate the cumbersome restrictions imposed by indexes. Westlaw's natural

language searching capability is entered through a database. When it is time to construct your query, natural language will be an entry on the screen. You will have a choice of a terms and connectors search or a natural language search when entering your query. You can then construct your query as a phrase or sentence without connectors. Both Lexis and Westlaw have menu-driven searching systems with point-and-click capability so you can search effectively without becoming very familiar with the system. Both are kept up-to-date and permit you to find documents without having to travel from your keyboard. The accuracy of Lexis and Westlaw is reliable. Both databanks are tied to the respective publisher's hard-copy materials, complete with head notes, research aids, and practitioners' resources. In summary, Lexis and Westlaw are quite similar but competing products that are very powerful when put to use effectively.

### ▼ How Do You Use the Computer Most Efficiently?

As discussed earlier in the chapter, the most effective and efficient research is performed after you educate yourself on the topic using hard-copy resources. Doing traditional research gives you a vocabulary that you can use to construct your search queries. It is most efficient and cost-effective to obtain citations to relevant documents online and to read the documents in hard-copy format if they are readily available.

### ▼ How Do You Cite to Cases Retrieved on Lexis and Westlaw?

*Bluebook* **Rule 18.3.1** and *ALWD* **Rule 12.13(b)** explain how an unpublished decision found only on either Westlaw or Lexis should be cited. For Westlaw, first provide the name of the case and underline it. The next part of the citation is the docket number. In the example that follows, that number is No. 82-C4585. The next part of the citation is the year that the decision was issued. Next, indicate "WL" for Westlaw and finally the Westlaw number assigned to the case. Place the date in the parentheses.

**Westlaw example:**  Clark Equip. Co. v. Lift Parts Mfg. Co.,
  No. 82-C4585, 1985 WL 2917, (N.D. Ill. Oct. 1,
  1985)—*Bluebook* format

  Clark Equip. Co. v. Lift Parts Mfg. Co., 1985 WL
  2917 (N.D. Ill. Oct. 1, 1985)—*ALWD* format,
  **Rule 12.13(b)**

### ▼ How Do You Cite a Decision Reported on Lexis?

For Lexis citations, first state the name of the case, the docket number, the year of the decision, the name of the Lexis file that contains the

case, and the name LEXIS (in all capital letters) to indicate that the case is found on Lexis. Next place the date in parentheses.

**Lexis example:**     Barrett Indus. Trucks v. Old Republic Ins. Co.,
                          No. 87-C9429, 1990 U.S. Dist. LEXIS 142 (N.D.
                          Ill. Jan. 9, 1990)—*Bluebook* format
                          Barrett Indus. Trucks v. Old Republic Ins. Co.,
                          1990 U.S. Dist. LEXIS 142 (N.D. Ill. Jan. 9,
                          1990)—*ALWD* format

If a decision is published in a hard-copy reporter, you should not use the Westlaw or Lexis citation. This is stipulated in *Bluebook* **Rule 18.1** and *ALWD* **Rule 12**.

## ▼ How Do You Indicate a Page or Screen Number for the Case?

An asterisk should precede any screen or page numbers. See *Bluebook* **Rule 18.3.1** and *ALWD* **Rule 12.13(b)**.

**Westlaw screen**      Clark Equip. Co. v. Lift Parts Mfg. Co., No. 82-
**no.:**                    C4585, 1985 WL 2917, at *1 (N.D. Ill. Oct. 1,
                          1985)—*Bluebook* format
**Lexis screen no.:**   Barrett Indus. Trucks v. Old Republic Ins. Co.,
                          1990 U.S. Dist. LEXIS 142, at *1 (N.D. Ill. Jan.
                          9, 1990)—*ALWD* format

## ▼ What Are the Other Sites for Computerized Legal Research?

Loislaw, owned by WoltersKluwer, is a commercial database containing state and federal cases, statutes, and regulations. It is a cost-effective alternative to Lexis and Westlaw and is a particularly attractive commercial research option for small law firms. Loislaw also offers the ability to cite check statutes and cases. Loislaw is accessed via Loislaw .com. On the site, there are online tutorials that include tips for constructing searches. The site is very user friendly with on-screen icons for point-and-click search capability. Many firms have Loislaw subscriptions bundled with their purchases of WoltersKluwer treatises and looseleaf services. This enables users of these WoltersKluwer print products to update these resources continuously.

There are many sites for cost-effective legal research, such as Loislaw, described above, and Fastcase. Free legal resources are available at Justia.com, Cornell's Legal Information Institute at www.law.cornell .edu (one of the best and most reliable free sites), Google Scholar (excellent for finding law review articles), Findlaw (good for state

statutes and specific areas of state law), the Government Printing Office site at www.gpo.gov/fdsys/ (excellent for the Federal Register, Code of Federal Regulations, the United States Code, and congressional materials), and Congress.gov for federal legislative resources.

LexisWeb.com is a free search engine that scours legal websites and blogs. The search style is similar to most Internet search engines. Your hits will include documents available on Lexis that you must then sign on to Lexis to read. Think of LexisWeb.com as a free start to Lexis research.

All of these sites offer cost-effective alternatives to Lexis and Westlaw. However, the sites lack editorial enhancements such as headnotes and key numbers, links to related legal publications, validation, and citing services. You may find the searching to be a little less user-friendly, and the sites lack many of the on-screen buttons to filter the documents you retrieve. Additionally, many of these sites have materials only from the past 25 years, so they may lack the depth of coverage. If you do not need enhancements or validation and are looking for a specific case, statute, or rule, this may be the avenue to pursue. Always be sure to update and validate any primary source that you will use.

## CHAPTER SUMMARY

Computerized legal research opens up a vast realm of research possibilities for the paralegal. You are no longer limited to the resources available at your firm or school library. This chapter introduced you to the basic skills and concepts required to use Lexis Advance and WestlawNext, as well as the older versions of these services—Lexis and Westlaw, the two major online legal research systems. Also explored was Bloomberg Law, which is now an emerging player in the commercial legal database field. Additionally, Loislaw, a WoltersKluwer product, provides a cost-effective online research alternative. Lexis and Westlaw were also compared to highlight each system's distinguishing features.

Search query formulation is now very easy with natural language integrated into the search bar. This is a "Google type" search capability that we are all familiar with. You can filter the material you receive with on-screen buttons or you can refine your search query.

Effective research online comes with careful planning before accessing a commercial database. Learn the vocabulary for your topic. Evaluate whether the expense of online services is justified and within the budget. All the services allow you to manage your work product, and they permit you to save your information in folders to read off line.

Online research is not a panacea but an additional and powerful research tool.

## KEY TERMS

BCite

Bloomberg Law

Congress.gov

connectors

field

www.gpo.gov/fdsys

KeyCite

Lexis

Lexis Advance

literal searching devices

Loislaw

natural language searching

query

restrictors

search

segment

*Shepard's*

www.supremecourt.gov

Westlaw

WestlawNext

## EXERCISES

1. One fine autumn day, Jim and Jean decide to drive to the country in search of the perfect pumpkin. After driving an hour and a half, they pull into Pete's Pumpkin Patch, whose sign states "10,000 pumpkins—state's largest pumpkin patch!" Pete's Pumpkin Patch is packed with shoppers. Jim and Jean eye the perfect pumpkin. As Jim is reaching for the pumpkin, Bob reaches for the very same pumpkin. Bob is a little low on patience that day. Instead of offering to look for another pumpkin, Bob punches Jim right in the jaw. Jim wants to sue Bob for battery.

   The problem raises the issue of whether Bob has committed a battery by punching Jim. The attorney that you work for wants you to sign on to Lexis or Westlaw and find the statute for battery for your jurisdiction. If your jurisdiction does not have a battery statute, find a case discussing battery.

   a. How would you construct the query?

   b. What sources would you consult before going online to become aware of the terms or words that you would use in your query?

   c. How would you filter your search results to find the most relevant source?

   d. How would you validate the case?.

2. Imagine that you are employed as a paralegal at a law firm in Detroit. A partner in the firm has just finished interviewing a client who lives in Munster, Indiana. The partner requests that you find out for him whether the courts of Indiana recognize the "Totten" trust as a valid legal instrument in that state.

   a. How would you educate yourself before going online?

   b. Formulate a search query based on the given information.

   c. How would you filter your search results to limit the results to an Indiana statute?

   d. How would you update and validate the authority?

3. Mrs. Donahue comes to your firm because she wants to sue her dentist for malpractice. On April 27, 2014, Mrs. Donahue went to her dentist to have a chipped bridge removed and replaced. In removing her bridge, the dentist broke her tooth. Mrs. Donahue had considerable pain due to the broken tooth. In addition, Mrs. Donahue incurred substantial expenses to repair the broken tooth and to replace the bridge with dental implants.

      Now that you have done some research and have read some cases, you are familiar with the vocabulary used in relevant court decisions. You are now best equipped to perform online research economically and efficiently.

   a. Use Lexis or Westlaw to find two cases after 1990 that are relevant to Mrs. Donahue's problem.

   b. Download the cases to a folder to read later.

   c. Shepardize or KeyCite the cases and save these results.

4. Use either Lexis Advance, WestlawNext, or Bloomberg Law to find any cases from the U.S. Court of Appeals discussing Megan's Law.

   a. What is your query?

   b. Print out the list of citations.

   c. Shepardize the cites on Lexis, KeyCite the cites on Westlaw, or use BCite on Bloomberg Law to validate the cases.

5. Use either Lexis or Westlaw to search *American Jurisprudence 2d* for references to easements in gross. Try to find one reference that defines an "easement in gross."

## CHAPTER 11

# PRACTICE RULES

| | | |
|---|---|---|
| A. | **OVERVIEW OF RULES OF PRACTICE** | 304 |
| B. | **RESEARCHING RULES OF PRACTICE** | 306 |
| | 1. Sources | 306 |
| | 2. Steps in Researching Rules and Court Decisions | 307 |
| C. | **STATE RULES OF PRACTICE** | 309 |
| D. | **ENSURING CURRENCY** | 310 |

## *CHAPTER OVERVIEW*

This chapter provides an overview of practice rules, the sources that contain these rules, and how to find primary and secondary authorities that explain and interpret these rules. You also learn how to ensure that the rule you are relying on is valid. For our purposes, this chapter primarily focuses on the many rules that surround litigation because these rules are the most comprehensive ones you will review and research as paralegals. Most techniques useful for researching these litigation rules also are useful for investigating other rules, such as rules regarding patent and trademark proceedings, workers' compensation, and other administrative law areas as well as ethics rules.

# A. OVERVIEW OF RULES OF PRACTICE

### ▼ What Are Rules of Practice?

Rules govern the practice of law, especially litigation. Some of these rules also govern the conduct of the lawyers, the litigants, and the judges.

### ▼ What Rules Govern Procedures in the Federal Courts?

The most extensive set of procedural rules for litigation is the **Federal Rules of Civil Procedure.** These rules direct an attorney on how to conduct himself or herself in a court proceeding. They cover matters such as the filing of a complaint to begin an action, service of the complaint on the defendant, the answer to the complaint and subsequent motions, and the discovery of information. Postjudgment motions and appeals also are addressed in these rules.

### ▼ Do the Federal Rules Control Proceedings in State Courts?

The federal rules control the course of a civil case pending in federal court only. They do not govern proceedings in any of the state courts. Within the confines of the federal courts, these rules are **primary binding authorities.** Many state courts have patterned their procedural rules after the federal rules. Therefore, the decisions interpreting the federal rules that are similar in nature to the state court rules sometimes are very **persuasive authorities** in the state courts.

### ▼ What Federal Courts Follow the Federal Rules of Civil Procedure?

All U.S. trial courts follow the federal rules. These rules are not applicable to the U.S. appellate courts or the U.S. Supreme Court. Nor do these rules generally apply in administrative proceedings. See Illustration 11-1.

### ▼ Are the Federal Trial Courts Governed by Any Other Rules?

The federal district courts also follow the **Federal Rules of Evidence** for motion practice and trial proceedings, and, in criminal cases, the courts are governed by the **Federal Rules of Criminal Procedure.** In addition, many federal courts have adopted a set of rules called **local rules of court** that dictate the small details of practice before each court. For example, the local rules of one district specify the details concerning the electronic filing of documents and motions, including the amount of margin required on a page. You should carefully review the local rules any time you have an action pending in a federal court. In addition to a set of local rules, some courts have general orders that have the effect of local rules. Be sure to note whether the court has such rules. Local rules also can vary among judges within the same court.

## ILLUSTRATION 11-1. Courts and the Applicable Rules

*U.S. District Courts*
Federal Rules of Civil Procedure
Federal Rules of Criminal Procedure
Federal Rules of Evidence
Local Rules of Orders

*U.S. Appellate Courts*
Federal Rules of Appellate Procedure
Federal Rules of Evidence
Local Rules of Orders

*U.S. Supreme Court*
Rules of the Supreme Court
Federal Rules of Evidence

*U.S. Bankruptcy Courts*
Federal Rules of Bankruptcy Procedure
Federal Rules of Evidence
Local Rules of Orders

▼ What Rules of Procedure Do Federal Appellate Courts Follow?

The U.S. Courts of Appeals follow the **Federal Rules of Appellate Procedure.** These rules are similar in nature to the Federal Rules of Civil Procedure because they are primary binding authority and can be researched in the federal codes and online. Pending changes to the rules can also be found online.

▼ What Rules Govern Practice Before the U.S. Supreme Court?

The **Rules of the Supreme Court** control practice before that court. Again, these rules are primary binding authority.

---

## ETHICS ALERT

Courts may sanction attorneys for failing to follow court rules. Be certain to check not only federal or state rules for the court, but local rules as well.

---

## PRACTICE POINTER

If you are assisting with litigation, be sure that you know what general and local rules govern your work. Read those rules carefully.

# B. RESEARCHING RULES OF PRACTICE

## 1. Sources

### ▼ Where Do You Find These Rules in the Print Materials?

All federal rules of civil and criminal procedure, the evidentiary rules, the appellate procedure rules, and the Supreme Court rules, as well as the bankruptcy rules and official forms, are found in the *United States Code* (U.S.C.), the official federal code printed by the government, as well as annotated statutory codes, *United States Code Annotated* (U.S.C.A.), published by West, and *United States Code Service* (U.S.C.S.), a LexisNexis product. The U.S.C. is available at www.gpo.gov/fdsys/.

When you need an interpretation of a rule, these annotated code versions are the best sources to consult. The drafters' commentary is found in the official U.S.C. These codes are discussed in detail in Chapter 7. Several publishers produce the local federal court rules, including West, which publishes the Federal Local Court Rules 3d. These rules also can be found in a variety of other sources, including deskbooks and treatises.

**Attorney deskbooks**, as the name implies, generally are kept at each paralegal's or attorney's desk. These books usually are paperback and contain a full set of the federal rules, local rules, and sometimes the state rules for the state where the deskbook is set. These deskbooks are updated annually. However, many attorneys are now using online resources. In many cases, attorneys are using various tablet or phone applications that provide them with the full text of the Federal Rules of Civil Procedure.

### ▼ Are the Federal Rules Available Online?

The U.S. Courts website, www.uscourts.gov/RulesAndPolicies/rules .aspx, provides links to the Federal Rules of Civil Procedure as well as amendments and proposed amendments to the rules. In addition, it offers full PDF texts of the Federal Rules of Criminal Procedure, the Federal Rules of Appellate Procedure, and the Federal Rules of Bankruptcy Procedure. This court website also provides links to local federal court rules. Lexis, Westlaw, and Loislaw offer the Federal Rules of Civil Procedure, the Federal Rules of Appellate Procedure, the Federal Rules of Criminal Procedure, the Federal Rules of Evidence, and the Rules of the United States Supreme Court, as well as some state and local federal court rules. Links to district and appellate federal courts are found at www.uscourts.gov. In addition, information concerning the rulemaking process, proposed rule changes, and commentary are available at the U.S. Courts website. Most individual court websites provide their local rules.

*PRACTICE POINTER*

Be certain that the rules found on the Internet are from official rule sources before you rely on them.

## 2. Steps in Researching Rules and Court Decisions

▼ How Do You Research a Federal Rule?

First, review the rule in the U.S.C., U.S.C.A., or U.S.C.S. Each of these publications has an index that allows users to find rules by topic. Next, you will want to locate court decisions and possibly secondary authorities that explain and interpret the rule.

▼ How Do You Find Cases or Secondary Authorities That Interpret and Explain the Federal Rules?

The annotated codes contain excerpts of cases that explain and interpret the federal rules, as well as references to secondary sources such as encyclopedias and law review articles. See Chapter 7 for a complete discussion of the use of annotated codes.

One of the easiest ways to find cases is to look on the spine of the annotated code volumes for the volume that contains the rules you are researching. Turn to the page that contains the rule. Following the rule is an index of words that lists numbers indicating certain cases. The research strategy is similar to that involved in researching other statutory materials, explained in Chapter 7. Brainstorm for search words. Find the appropriate topic, and then review the case annotations. The annotations also are updated with pocket parts or supplementary pamphlets that should be reviewed for the most current citations to authorities.

Although some cases that deal with the federal rules are found in West's *Federal Supplement* or the *Federal Reporter*, many are published in a separate reporter called the **Federal Rules Decisions**. This reporter contains federal civil and criminal cases that focus on the federal rules. These cases have not been designated for publication in the Federal Supplement.

In addition to the annotated codes, selected secondary sources such as looseleaf services and treatises focus on the federal rules. The *Federal Procedure Rules Service*, published by West, contains the text of the federal civil rules, local district and appellate rules, and annotations concerning cases, law review articles, and other secondary sources that interpret and explain the rules. This service includes headnotes. The service has a topical digest system with headnotes and an index to

its digest similar to the digests discussed in Chapter 4. The *Federal Rules Digest 3d*, also published by West, helps you locate cases interpreting the federal rules.

The *Federal Rules of Evidence Service* can assist you in researching the evidence rules. Also published by West, this service includes a digest that includes civil and criminal cases that interpret the Federal Rules of Evidence. Headnotes are used as well as an index system. The *Federal Rules of Evidence Digest*, also published by West, is a valuable resource. For more information about how to use this digest, review Chapter 4.

### ▼ What Sources Are Available to Help Interpret These Rules?

Two multivolume treatises, *Federal Practice and Procedure*, known as Wright and Miller, its original authors, and published by West is widely regarded and very persuasive secondary authority that explain the federal rules and provide references to primary and secondary authorities.

Many circuits have handbooks that are prepared by local bar federal courts committees or the courts. These guides provide you with background and practical information about the courts as well as the time frame and procedure for filing appellate documents. If you are dealing with the Seventh Circuit Court of Appeals, a good reference book is the *Practitioner's Handbook for Appeals to the United States Court of Appeals for the Seventh Circuit*, found online at the court's website, www.ca7.uscourts.gov/rules/handbook.pdf. Other circuits have similar handbooks or instructions on their respective websites.

Another useful resource for you might be the federal rules committee comments concerning any changes in the rules or the committee's commentary regarding the purpose and origin of the rule.

Do not forget to consider resources such as encyclopedias, legal periodicals, and the A.L.R. series. For more information about these sources, see Chapter 6.

Consider a review of the federal digests under the topic Federal Civil Procedure for the federal civil rules and other related topics for other sets of federal rules. These digests provide citations to primary and secondary authorities. For a more detailed explanation of how to use the digests, consult Chapter 4.

### ▼ How Would You Cite the Various Federal Rules?

The federal rules should be cited in accordance with *Bluebook* **Rule 12.9.3** and *ALWD* **Rule 17** as follows:

> Fed. R. Civ. P. 56
> Fed. R. Crim. P. 1
> Fed. R. App. P. 26
> Fed. R. Evid. 803

Only include the year when the rule is no longer in force by providing the most recent year that it appeared and the year repealed. For example:

Fed. R. Civ. P. 9 (2006) (repealed 2008)—*Bluebook* **Rule 12.9.3**
Fed. R. Civ. P. 9 (repealed 2008)—*ALWD* **Rule 17.2**

## ▼ How Would You Cite a Decision Contained in the *Federal Rules Decisions?*

The abbreviation for the *Federal Rules Decisions* is F.R.D. in both the *ALWD* and the *Bluebook* citation guides. A case would be cited according to *Bluebook* and *ALWD* as follows:

Barrett Indus. Trucks v. Old Republic Ins. Co., 129 F.R.D. 515 (N.D. Ill. 1989).

# C. STATE RULES OF PRACTICE

### ▼ What Rules Control the Conduct of State Proceedings?

Most states have adopted rules of civil and criminal procedure. Many of these rules are patterned after the Federal Rules of Civil Procedure or the Federal Rules of Criminal Procedure. Some states have adopted evidence codes, while others rely on the common law and have not approved any evidentiary codes. Note that some of the states that have not adopted evidence codes rely on the Federal Rules of Evidence for guidance. The rules of the state courts control conduct similar to that dealt with in the federal rules. For example, the federal rules describe the procedure and the requirements for the dismissal of a case. Similarly under some state codes, the rules explain the circumstances that would allow a court to dismiss a case and the procedure to follow to obtain such an order. In addition to state codes, many state courts have local rules or orders similar to local rules issued by the federal courts. Again, check with these courts to determine whether such rules exist for each court.

### ▼ Where Would You Find State Rules and Local Rules for State Courts?

Many state court websites have links to the state and local rules. The states often include the rules of criminal and civil procedure and the evidentiary rules in their statutory codes. Many bar association websites also offer links to the rules, and several commercially published lawyers directories, in print and online, provide the state and local orders of courts in the area covered by the directory. For example,

if you want to find Ohio rules of court, go to www.sconet.state.oh.us/ LegalResources/Rules/. In addition, these rules are available on Westlaw, Lexis, and Loislaw. Several tablet and phone applications also provide full versions of state rules.

### ▼ Are Annotations for State Rules Available?

Yes, many annotated statutory codes contain references to cases and secondary authorities that explain or interpret the state procedural rules. These codes can be used in a manner similar to that of the federal annotated codes. For more information about how to use these annotated codes, see Chapter 7.

### ▼ Are There Any Significant State Rule Treatises or Secondary Authorities?

Each state's set of rules varies, as does the type and number of secondary authorities available to you as researchers. Check with your librarian for relevant materials. Consider reviewing the materials discussed above, such as federal treatises, and those discussed below, such as continuing legal education materials. These may be helpful because the states' rules often are patterned after the federal rules.

## D. ENSURING CURRENCY

### ▼ How Do You Ensure That You Are Reviewing the Most Current Version of the Rule?

If you are reviewing the rule in print, begin with the pocket parts and pamphlets that accompany the annotated codes. Next, you must use online resources to ensure that the rule is valid and current. First, you can Shepardize the rule in print and follow up with an online Shepard's search and perform a KeyCite search online. You should review both if possible. Validating a rule also helps you to find cases and other authorities that cite the rule. Validate both federal and state rules by following the same procedures used for the process for cases and statutes. For a more detailed explanation, consult Chapters 5 and 7.

For the federal rules, *Shepard's United States Citations* should be used because it includes citations for all federal rules. To use this in print, look for the rule number and set of rules listed at the top of the page. Then find the rule on the page. Citing sources such as cases will be listed. Note that the rules sometimes have subdivisions and that *Shepard's* lists citations below those subdivisions as well. Some libraries have *Shepard's Federal Rule Citations*, a specialized *Shepard's* devoted entirely to the federal rules and their citing authorities. The process for the use of this citator is similar to that of other *Shepard's* citators. *Shepard's* citatory will guide you to federal and state cases that cite the rules as well as law

review articles and A.L.R. annotations that may help you understand the rules.

### ▼ Can Federal Rules Be Validated Online?

Yes. You can validate rules found in the U.S.C. and U.S.C.A. on Westlaw using KeyCite and those found in the U.S.C.S. on Lexis using *Shepard's*. Loislaw provides GlobalCite to help validate federal rules. In addition, many court websites will provide information about pending rule changes and recent amendments. However, not all court websites may be up to date.

### ▼ Can State Rules Be Shepardized?

Yes. State rules are part of the specific state citator prepared by *Shepard's*. Use these in the same manner as the other *Shepard's* citators noted above.

### ▼ Can State Rules Be Shepardized Online?

Yes. States' rules can be Shepardized online as part of the individual state's codified statutes.

## CHAPTER SUMMARY

The rules that govern the conduct of cases brought before courts vary depending on the court in which an action is pending. Federal rules govern proceedings in the federal courts, and state rules control actions in the state courts.

These rules are primary authorities and generally can be found in statutory compilations. They also are contained in reference books called deskbooks. The statutory compilations can direct you to cases that interpret and explain these rules. Secondary authorities such as treatises and legal periodicals often explain these rules and provide you with citations to other primary authorities, including cases, that focus on the rules. Many rules are available online.

These rules are validated in a manner similar to statutes. When you validate a rule, you also find additional citing authorities.

The next chapter explains ethical rules and how to locate them, as well as how to find cases that interpret these rules. You also learn how to validate the rules.

## KEY TERMS

attorney deskbooks
Federal Rules of Appellate Procedure
Federal Rules of Civil Procedure
Federal Rules of Criminal Procedure
*Federal Rules Decisions*

Federal Rules of Evidence local rules
of court
persuasive authorities
primary binding authorities
Rules of the Supreme Court

## EXERCISES

1. Find Federal Rule of Civil Procedure 12 in an online source.
   a. What does this rule address?
   b. Where did you find this rule?
   c. Now find the rule online from an official source. Where did you find it?
2. If the U.S.C.A. was unavailable, where would you look for a Federal Rule of Evidence? List two other print sources.
3. What set or sets of rules or orders apply to cases pending in the U.S. District Court in your state or area?
4. What set or sets of rules or orders apply to motions and briefs in a case before the U.S. Circuit Court of Appeals in your state or area?
5. What set or sets of rules or orders apply to a trial in a federal court?
6. What set or sets of rules or orders apply to a trial in your state court?
7. What set or sets of rules apply to attorneys practicing in the bankruptcy courts generally?
8. What reference books would you use to find such bankruptcy rules? List four online sources that contain the U.S. bankruptcy rules.
9. What federal rule concerns a motion to dismiss for lack of jurisdiction?
10. What federal rule sets forth the criteria for a summary judgment motion?
11. What rules govern practice before the U.S. Supreme Court?
12. What sources contain citations to cases and other authorities that interpret or explain the federal rules?
13. Where would you find rules for the Indiana Supreme Court on the Internet?
14. Find rules on the Internet that concern juvenile procedure in Ohio.
15. Find a local rule concerning pro se parties in the family division of Florida's 11th Judicial Circuit Court. Explain the steps you took to find it and list where you found it. What is the rule number? What does number 1 in the rule specify?
16. List a phone or tablet application that provides the full text of practice rules.

## CHAPTER 12

# ETHICAL RULES

| | |
|---|---|
| **A. RULES OF PROFESSIONAL RESPONSIBILITY** | 313 |
| **B. RESEARCHING ETHICAL QUESTIONS** | 315 |
|     1. Primary Sources and Annotated Sources | 315 |
|     2. Other Useful Authorities | 316 |
|     3. Research Process | 317 |
|     4. Sample Research Problem | 318 |

## *CHAPTER OVERVIEW*

In Chapter 11, you learned about procedural rules. In this chapter, the discussion concerns ethical rules. You learn where to find these rules in print and online and how to retrieve primary and secondary authorities that explain or interpret these rules. You also are shown how to locate ethics opinions, both in print and online. Finally, you are taught about ensuring the currency of these rules.

## A. RULES OF PROFESSIONAL RESPONSIBILITY

For the practice of law, individual states determine the rules that regulate the conduct of lawyers. Some of those rules dictate an attorney's

**ethical behavior**, while others control an attorney's **ability to practice**, such as state licensing rules.

Each court has rules that govern the conduct of lawyers and litigants. Many state courts also have rules that regulate the activities of lawyers who never appear in court. For example, the high courts in many states have rules concerning licensing and registration of attorneys. You always should consider whether any rules exist that govern your conduct or the litigation process you are involved in. Some rules specify how attorneys must supervise paralegals.

Paralegals must be able to research ethical rules that control the conduct of attorneys and their staffs.

---

## ETHICS ALERT

Attorneys are responsible for ensuring that paralegals follow the rules that govern attorneys. However, you must know what rules to follow so that you do not jeopardize your supervising attorney or your job.

---

### ▼ Is There a National Code of Ethics for Attorneys or Paralegals?

No. Each state has its own set of rules that control the conduct of its attorneys. Lawyers must follow these rules of conduct and must supervise you and ensure that you also follow these rules. Most, but not all, state ethics rules are patterned after the American Bar Association's *Model Rules of Professional Conduct.* These rules govern issues such as conflicts of interest; client confidentiality; communications; fairness; responsibilities of supervisory lawyers, law firms, and associations regarding nonlawyer assistants; unauthorized practice of law; disqualification from a case; and the reporting of professional misconduct. In most cases, the rules require that attorneys ensure that paralegals follow the same rules designed for attorneys. Paralegals cannot be sanctioned for failing to follow the rules directed at attorney conduct. However, they offer paralegals some direction in how to conduct themselves. In addition to the rules of professional responsibility, cases that interpret the rules also govern the conduct of lawyers.

### ▼ What Type of Authority Are These Rules and Cases?

Rules adopted by a jurisdiction and the subsequent court decisions are primary binding authorities. The *ABA Model Rules of Professional Conduct* are secondary authorities, as are any of the drafters' comments about the origin and purpose of these rules. However, these ethics rules and comments are very persuasive secondary authorities because most state ethics codes or rules are patterned after the ABA models.

▼ When Would You Review the Rules for Ethical Conduct and the Applicable Cases?

You will be asked to review the ethical rules whenever issues involving ethics are presented. Self-interest also demands that you be familiar with the rules. You must follow the rules that govern attorneys. As clients, attorneys, and paralegals become more mobile, conflicts of interest have become a frequent topic for research.

# B. RESEARCHING ETHICAL QUESTIONS

## 1. Primary Sources and Annotated Sources

Many rules of professional responsibility are contained within the codifications of the state's statutes. To find cases, you would use the annotated sources. Most states' ethics rules and opinions are available online at the state court website.

▼ What Is the Value of an Annotated Source for the Rules and Codes?

The annotated rule sources are valuable in a manner similar to the annotated codes. These sources provide citations to primary authorities, such as court decisions, that interpret the rules and citations to secondary authorities such as treatises, and law review articles. See Chapter 7 for additional discussion of annotated codes. Some looseleaf publishers also publish ethics cases.

▼ Where Can You Find the *ABA Model Rules of Professional Conduct*?

An excellent secondary source for your research are the ABA Model Rules found in the *Annotated Model Rules of Professional Conduct* published by the American Bar Association. The annotated rules book contains the full text of the rules coupled with citations to any interpretations of the rules in court decisions or informal and formal ABA opinions. This source also includes the drafters' commentary about the purpose and design of each rule. These model rules and comments are available at the ABA website, www.americanbar .org/groups/professional_responsibility/publications/model_rules_ of_professional_conduct/model_rules_of_professional_conduct_table_ of_contents.html. These do not provide case annotations. The ABA also provides a downloadable app for phones and tablets that allows you to view an annotated version of the *ABA Model Rules of Professional Conduct*.

▼ What Other Secondary Sources Are Useful for Ethics Researchers?

In addition to the ABA annotated sources, many states have annotated guides for their rules of professional conduct. The ABA Center for Professional Responsibility provides online resources concerning attorneys' ethical obligations.

▼ How Do You Use the Annotated Sources?

The methods for using each of these sources generally involves a review of the table of contents or the index. The ABA annotated model rules, for example, lists each rule in the table of contents. This method is useful if you already know what rule you wish to review. Next to the rule is a list of the topics covered by the rule. You could read through each heading to see if the rule applies to your situation. However, it might be more efficient to review the alphabetical index at the back of the annotated rules. Within the index, you will find a variety of topics and cross-references to various subject areas, as well as citations to the rule.

## 2. Other Useful Authorities

The ABA and many state and local bar associations render **advisory ethics opinions** for attorneys. These opinions are secondary authorities. Although an **ABA opinion** is a secondary authority that has no force of law, in the ethics area, it is often a very persuasive authority because many ethics rules or codes that govern lawyers are based on the ABA models. The opinions generally are issued after a party requests that the ABA provide such an opinion.

The ABA Center for Professional Responsibility provides summaries of some of the most recent ABA ethics opinions online at americanbar.org/groups/professional_responsibility/publications/ethics_opinions.html. In some cases, the entire opinion is available. The indexes and full opinions can be obtained from the ABA. However, nonmembers will pay a fee for such opinions.

*PRACTICE POINTER*

Advisory ethics opinions often are excellent sources of rules and cases.

▼ Do State Bar Associations Publish Ethics Opinions Similar to Those Prepared by the ABA?

Yes. Some organizations publish pamphlets or books that contain their opinions while others can be found by reviewing continuing legal

education materials, which are discussed in Chapter 13. Some are accessible through the Internet, and others are available from online services.

## 3. Research Process

### ▼ How Would You Research an Ethical Question?

First, you would review the rule. Second, you should review any annotations, especially those found in the annotated codes or the annotated rule books or comments. Next, read any cases or informal and formal opinions. Shepardize the cases. Sometimes it is necessary to study a secondary authority to better understand an ethical dilemma. If necessary, perform a search of the rule on the computer to see if any additional cases can be found.

### ▼ Can You Find State Ethical Rules on Westlaw and Lexis?

You can review the ethical rules and perform searches for authorities that discuss these rules on both Lexis and Westlaw. You can access many state ethics rules on both services. For a detailed explanation of how to research using these fee-based services, see Chapter 10.

First, you should research the case databases. Next, you might want to search the ethics opinion databases. These databases will provide any informal or formal ethics opinions that may have been released by a state, county, or city bar association.

Next, you might want to review the ABA databases. These databases contain secondary authority that has not been adopted in total by any jurisdiction. However, this secondary authority is very persuasive because most states have patterned their ethics rules according to the ABA model rules or model code.

To find ethics information of particular interest for paralegals, see the National Association of Legal Assistants website, www.nala.org or the National Federation of Paralegal Association's website, paralegals.org.

### ▼ Can Ethics Rules Be Validated?

Yes. *Shepard's Professional and Judicial Conduct Citations* lists authorities that cite the ABA Model Code sections or the ABA Model Rules. Each ABA rule is listed in bold at the top of the page with a notation about whether it is a model rule or part of the model code. The ABA rules and code can be Shepardized as well as the Code of Judicial Conduct and opinions of the ABA Standing Committee on Ethics and Professional Responsibility. It draws from U.S. Supreme Court opinions, lower federal court decisions, state court decisions, ethics opinions, and articles in some law reviews. See Chapter 5 for more information concerning validating authorities.

## 4. Sample Research Problem

You have been asked to research a conflict of interest question. You work for an attorney who represented K. K. Industries in a matter against R. J. Enterprises in a contract dispute in 2014. R. J. Enterprises has now asked your boss to represent its company against Reynolds Wide Haulers in an unrelated contract dispute. Reynolds Wide Haulers, however, is the parent company of K. K. Industries. Your boss wants to know what rules govern such representation. Your firm is located in Ohio, which has adopted the *ABA Model Rules of Professional Conduct.*

First, brainstorm for possible search topics. Next, look in the index to the Ohio statutes. If you don't find any references concerning conflicts of interest, try the *ABA Model Rules.* One source would be the *ABA Annotated Model Rules of Professional Conduct.* You could look in the index under conflict of interest. You might find topics such as "existing client," "interest adverse to client," or "former client." You would then be directed to rules to review.

The text of each rule is contained in the annotated resource. After each rule is a comment section that explains the rule. Following the comments is a comparison of the model code and the model rules. Finally, there is a list of authorities, including primary authorities.

Next, you should review the authorities. Finally, you should validate the rule and authorities.

### ▼ How Would You Cite an Ethics Rule Found in the *ABA Model Rules of Professional Conduct?*

The rules for citation of ethics codes are found in *Bluebook* **Rule 12.9.6**. Rule 1.10 of the *ABA Model Rules of Professional Conduct* would be cited as follows:

Model Rules of Prof'l Conduct R.1.10 (2014)

The *ALWD* citation rules for the *ABA Model Rules of Professional Conduct* are found in **Rule 23.3** and would be cited as follows:

Model R. Prof. Conduct 1.10

### ▼ How Would You Cite an ABA Ethics Opinion?

The rules for citation of ethics opinions are contained in *Bluebook* **Rule 12.9.6**. A *Bluebook* citation of an ABA opinion would be as follows:

ABA Comm. on Prof'l Ethics and Grievances, Informal Op. 1526 (1988)

Based upon *ALWD* **Rule 16.2**, the *ALWD* citation for the same opinion would be as follows:

ABA Informal Ethics Op. 1526 (1988).

# CHAPTER SUMMARY

Each state has ethical rules that govern the conduct of lawyers and litigants. Many of these rules are patterned after the *ABA Model Rules of Professional Conduct.*

Often these rules are found in state statutory compilations or attorney deskbooks. The statutory codes provide references to other primary authorities, such as cases and related rules, and to secondary sources. A variety of secondary sources, such as treatises, legal periodicals, and A.L.R. annotations, explain and interpret these rules and include citations to primary authorities.

Many ethical rules are available online, as are some secondary sources that explain and interpret these rules.

In addition to state ethics opinions, the ABA and other bar associations issue advisory ethics opinions. These opinions are secondary authorities. However, they may be very persuasive authorities. These can be found in both print and online.

Both the ethics rules and opinions can be validated in print and online. The method for validating these authorities is similar to that used for cases, statutes, and rules governing court proceedings.

The next chapter will focus on practical resources that assist you in your research, such as continuing legal education materials, formbooks, and legal directories.

# KEY TERMS

ABA opinion
*Model Code of Professional Responsibility*
*Model Rules of Professional Conduct*

ability to practice
advisory ethics opinion
ethical behavior

# EXERCISES

You are working as a paralegal for a firm that is defending a personal injury action against a manufacturer of recreational bikes. The plaintiff, a resident of Findlay, Ohio, was injured while riding one of the bikes in an event known as the Hancock Horizontal Hundred. While working for the defendant's law firm, Cryer, Wolf and Nonnemaker, you attend depositions and strategy conferences between counsel representing the defendant and counsel representing the codefendant. You had many conferences with witnesses, transcribed statements, and prepared letters to clients after reviewing the files. Although you are working hard on this case, billable hours throughout the firm are down, and you are laid off. You are given two weeks to find a job.

A sole practitioner in Findlay, a town of 25,000, tentatively offers you a job, but you first must do some research. This attorney represents the plaintiff in the above-mentioned action. Before the practitioner will allow you to begin work, you must research whether his firm can hire

you and whether the firm can continue to represent the plaintiff in this action.

1. Map out your research plan. What sources will you consult?
2. For each source, note whether you will find secondary or primary authority or both.
3. As you list each print source, note your next step and why you would go to the next source.

## CHAPTER 13

# PRACTITIONER'S MATERIALS

| | |
|---|---|
| **A. FORMS** | 321 |
| **B. OTHER PRACTITIONER'S MATERIALS** | 323 |
|   1. Checklists | 323 |
|   2. Continuing Legal Education Materials | 323 |
|   3. Handbooks | 324 |
|   4. Jury Instructions | 324 |
|   5. Other Tools | 325 |

## CHAPTER OVERVIEW

In the preceding chapters, you have learned how to find primary and secondary authorities and how to use the resources that contain these authorities. This chapter focuses on some practical sources, such as formbooks and continuing legal education materials, for you to consider. In addition, you are taught about jury instruction sources and about how and when to use them.

## A. FORMS

Some courts, such as bankruptcy courts, require specific forms. Also, some types of legal documents must be drafted in the statutory form established by the state's legislature. For example, in many states that

have living will statutes, living wills must be drafted using the statute's "magic language" to be valid. To assist you in drafting such documents with the appropriate language, some publishers have compiled **forms.** These often include many federal and state court forms as well as examples of forms that contain the language appropriate for a particular statute. Other forms such as wills provide suggested draft documents for users. These forms can save you time and help in your drafting. However, you must be careful when using these standardized forms for drafting documents that are not standardized, such as wills. Ideally, these forms properly incorporate the language that would make the document legally valid in your state. That, however, is not always the case. Be careful to see whether the form is up to date.

---

### PRACTICE POINTER

You must know what language the current law requires or double-check with the court if you are using a court form. Do not substitute your independent judgment when you use these forms.

---

Some forms, such as those offered by West, include references to authorities and library sources such as key numbers and encyclopedia materials. However, these books are generally used only for forms.

▼ Where Can Forms Be Found?

Many publishers offer court formbooks. In the probate, real estate, and transaction areas, a variety of publishers issue forms. Some forms are available online through Westlaw and Lexis as well as at federal and state court and agency websites. Many can be downloaded in a format that allows the user to customize the form.

For example, the U.S. Court of Appeals for the Second Circuit provides easy access to forms from its home page, www.ca2.uscourts.gov/.

---

### ETHICS ALERT

If you use a form and change it substantially, be certain that an attorney reviews it. Otherwise, this could be considered the unauthorized practice of law.

---

### PRACTICE POINTER

Always check if a specific form is required by statute or rule.

# B. OTHER PRACTITIONER'S MATERIALS

## 1. Checklists

▼ Do Any Publications or Websites Contain Lists of What Steps You Should Follow to Complete a Project?

Many commercial publishers produce **checklists.** These checklists are for a variety of topics, such as estate planning, routine corporate matters, or matrimonial matters. Some checklists provide citations to authorities. Most are updated regularly.

In addition to the commercial checklists, many bar associations, such as the Georgia Bar Association, also offer free checklists on their websites. Continuing legal education materials often contain checklists and practical information that may be as valuable for paralegals as it is for lawyers.

Some courts now provide checklists. For example, the Utah Court of Appeals provides appellate court checklists in PDF format at www.utcourts.gov.

You can search the Internet for checklists. If you enter the term "legal checklists" into various search engines, you will find many such lists. Be careful to consider whether the source is reputable or not.

## 2. Continuing Legal Education Materials

**Continuing legal education (CLE) materials** generally explain an area of the law. They tend to be written by individual attorneys who are respected practitioners in a particular area. Within each state, a variety of continuing legal education materials are available. These are secondary authorities and have little or no persuasive value. Therefore, do not cite these materials to a court. However, they can be an invaluable tool in helping you learn about any area of the law. Unfortunately, many states do not update these quickly, and many of the materials lack adequate indexes. You generally must use the table of contents, which may not be comprehensive enough for your needs. However, for new areas of the law, these materials might be your only secondary source of information. Often bar associations present seminars with accompanying CLE materials whenever a major change in the law is made.

## ▼ Are CLE Materials Available Online?

Some national CLE publications can be found online on Westlaw and Lexis. Loislaw provides some state CLE publications. Some bar associations also provide these materials at their websites.

## ▼ How Do You Find CLE Materials?

Check with the law librarian or the attorney who assigned the project. You also could browse through the library catalog or the library shelves. Finally, you might call the local or state bar associations for guidance about their publications.

## 3. Handbooks

### ▼ What Other Valuable Practitioner's Materials Are Available?

Several publishers produce **handbooks** that provide you with special information about a specialized type of practice such as estate planning, real estate, or trial practice. Sometimes they contain research references and case citations as well as trial aids.

## 4. Jury Instructions

**Jury instructions** are provided to juries just after they are sworn in and before they deliberate in a case. These instructions explain to the jury members their duties and the applicable law in the case they are considering. In general, attorneys representing all litigants have an opportunity to draft jury instructions and work with a judge to develop a fair and accurate statement of the law that the jurors should be told to apply. Paralegals often assist in finding the appropriate instruction or in the drafting of the instructions. Improperly drafted jury instructions can affect the outcome of a case. Some jury instructions reference books are similar to formbooks because they provide you with sample instructions. Others, however, are pattern or approved instructions.

### ▼ What Are Pattern Jury Instructions, and How Do They Differ from Other Jury Instructions?

**Pattern** or **approved jury instructions** must be used in many states. In several states, practitioners must use their state's pattern instruction if one exists concerning a specific point. If an instruction does not exist or if it inaccurately states the current law, then an attorney can submit a proposed jury instruction that varies from the pattern instruction. Be certain that the jury instructions, especially criminal instructions, are up to date. Check the regular supplementary pamphlets. In all cases, review the law and the jury instructions in tandem. Some states have

"model" or sample jury instructions that they treat similar to pattern or approved instructions. Often verdict forms on which juries enter their findings are included in both the pattern and model jury instructions.

---

## *PRACTICE POINTER*

Always determine whether pattern or approved instructions are required.

---

## ETHICS ALERT

Failure to use pattern or approved jury instructions may result in sanctions for an attorney.

---

Jury instructions generally contain the text of the instruction and case or statutory authorities from which the instruction was derived.

### ▼ Do the Federal Courts Have Pattern Jury Instructions and Where Can They Be Found?

Federal courts have pattern or model jury instructions. These instructions can be found at the court's website. Westlaw, Lexis, and Loislaw also have a selection of jury instructions online.

### ▼ What Type of Research Should Be Done Before You Draft Jury Instructions?

First, you should be somewhat familiar with the case and the underlying law of the case. However, if you are just asked to retrieve a jury instruction this may not be necessary. Jury instructions are read to the juries deliberating a variety of cases. Some jury instructions include references to primary authorities that often are the basis for the instruction. Sometimes these sources can be useful in finding primary binding authority. However, you should carefully read the source to ensure that it in fact states the law as described in the jury instruction.

## 5. Other Tools

### ▼ What Other Tools Might a Paralegal Use in Researching a Problem?

Use your ingenuity when researching any problem. Often you are asked to research factual questions as well as legal questions. For example,

your firm may want some information about a corporation one of your clients hopes to acquire, and you have been asked to find as much information as possible. One source would be *Dun & Bradstreet Reports*, which provides information about the corporate officers, the date of incorporation, and capitalization. Additional information often can be obtained from the state's secretary of state.

## ▼ How Do You Locate Lawyers and Law Firms in Other States or Within a State?

A well-known source is the ***Martindale-Hubbell Law Directory***, which lists most attorneys nationwide. This is a voluntary directory, however, so some attorneys have chosen to be excluded. In addition to the free individual listings that include the person's name, address, degrees, and the name of the institute from which the person obtained his or her law degree, some firms pay to publish larger firm directories that list the firm, its areas of expertise, if any, the names of the individual attorneys, and a biography about each attorney. In addition, Martindale has a rating system for lawyers based on solicitations of confidential opinions of members of the bar. Martindale is available free at www.martindale.com. You can use the Lawyer Locator service in a variety of ways. You can search by lawyer, location and area of practice, by firm, by corporate law department, by U.S. Government Office, or by U.S. law faculty.

Other online lawyers' directories can be found on the Web.

## CHAPTER SUMMARY

Paralegals find that forms can be invaluable tools. These commercially published books provide guidance in drafting real estate contracts, court motions, estate plans, and the like. However, these are only guides, and the paralegal should always double-check the accuracy and timeliness of the forms they contain.

Practitioner's materials such as checklists and continuing legal education books can be of great assistance to paralegal researchers. Checklists offer step-by-step guidance for handling a variety of legal matters ranging from a real estate closing to the preparation of a will. CLE materials generally concentrate on individual areas of the law and are particularly good at explaining new or developing legal topics. The type and variety of continuing legal education materials available vary by state.

Jury instructions are drafted when a case is presented to a jury. Various books and online sources provide sample jury instructions concerning various legal issues. When a state or court has adopted pattern jury instructions, these instructions must be used.

Legal directories provide information about lawyers, their law firms, and their practices. Some directories also include information about local court phone numbers, rules, and court reporters. There are national and local legal directories.

# KEY TERMS

checklists
CLE materials
forms
handbooks

jury instructions
*Martindale-Hubbell Law Directory*
pattern jury instructions

# EXERCISES

## FORMS

1. Find a sample power of attorney for your state. What source did you review and why? Specify whether it was an online or print source.

## CHECKLISTS

2. Find a real estate closing checklist for a residential real estate closing. Where did you look and why?

## CLE MATERIALS

3. Find a continuing legal education book or materials other than those found at an attorney's website that covers estate planning in your state. Where did you look and why?

## JURY INSTRUCTIONS

4. Locate a civil jury instruction for nominal damages in your state.
5. Find a criminal jury instruction for reasonable doubt.
6. Find a criminal jury instruction for the definition of *recklessly* in your state.

## JURY INSTRUCTIONS ONLINE

7. Access a state's pattern instructions and find the instruction that defines *exemplary or punitive damages.* List the location of the jury instruction and how you found it.
8. Access a federal pattern instruction that defines circumstantial evidence. List the location of the jury instruction and how you found it.
9. Find a federal jury instruction that explains *retaliatory discharge.* List the location of the jury instruction and how you found it.

## USING THE *MARTINDALE-HUBBELL LAW DIRECTORY*

10. What is an AV rating in *Martindale-Hubbell?*

## CHAPTER 14

# RESEARCH STRATEGY

| | |
|---|---|
| **A. DEFINE THE ISSUES AND DETERMINE AREA OF LAW** | 330 |
| **B. REFINING RESEARCH** | 330 |
| **C. DIAGRAMMING THE RESEARCH PROCESS** | 332 |
| **D. EXAMPLE OF RESEARCH STRATEGY** | 334 |
| 1. How to Phrase the Issue If You Are Researching the Fur Labeling Problem | 334 |
| 2. First Steps | 334 |
| 3. What Sources to Consult and Why | 335 |
| 4. What to Do After Completing Your Research | 336 |
| 5. Combining Computerized Research Methods with Hard-Copy Method | 337 |
| 6. Using Online Services in the Fur Labeling Problem | 337 |

## *CHAPTER OVERVIEW*

Research involves planning. The more planning, the more effective the research. This chapter gives you step-by-step techniques to use when researching. You begin by educating yourself on a legal topic that pertains to the issue you are researching. You are then advised to note all of the pertinent information that you find during the research process so that you have a complete record of your findings and complete citations to those findings. Finally, you are reminded to update and to validate all of your findings.

Focusing on your issue and knowing when to stop researching are two skills that you must master. As a paralegal, you must always evaluate how much time it takes to research and to weigh cost with accuracy and thoroughness. This chapter helps you achieve the necessary balance required to effectively research a legal topic.

---

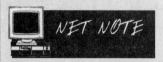

*NET NOTE*

At www.law.cornell.edu/wex/legal_research, Cornell's Legal Information Institute provides an overview of the main resource categories for legal research. Review this website's offerings to look at the "big picture" and to check on your thoroughness.

---

## A. DEFINE THE ISSUES AND DETERMINE AREA OF LAW

### ▼ Where Do You Begin Your Research?

First, gather all facts that are relevant to your problem and define the legal issues. The **facts** and the law guide your research. Ask a lot of questions of the client and of the attorney who assigns the problem. Clarify anything that is unclear. Frame the issue or review the issue framed by the attorney assigning the project.

Discerning the area of law is the second phase in beginning your research. The issues and the facts indicate what area of law is involved in the problem. If you are unclear as to the jurisdiction or the issues, ask the attorney. For example, will the question be resolved by tort law? By constitutional law? By the law of real property?

Make a list of important terms or words that describe the facts and the legal problem. These words help later when you are using an index. You may also want to use a legal dictionary to look up any word or term that sounds unfamiliar. (See Chapter 6 for a discussion on secondary sources.) Note unusual facts. An unusual fact may help you narrow your research later on.

## B. REFINING RESEARCH

### ▼ How Do You Refine Your Research Strategy?

After defining the legal issues and determining the area of law to research, you have to devise a systematic approach to the research process.

At times your knowledge of an area of law is not complete. The best way to gain an overview of the subject is to consult secondary sources. Hornbooks or textbooks about a particular subject are helpful because they explain the law in everyday language and indicate the legal rules and important cases. Generally, treatises are too detailed for the time constraints that you will be under; however, sometimes they may be valuable. (See Chapter 6 for a complete discussion of secondary sources.) Treatises may be valuable when you are searching for legal authority relating to an obscure issue.

A quick way to find the appropriate legal rule, particularly when the issue involves state law and you do not know whether a statute or a case governs the situation, is to consult a ***West's Law Finder.*** For example, *West's Texas Law Finder* can be used to find the controlling law relating to dramshops. The appropriate statute citation would be included. If a case is controlled in this instance, a citation to the case would be included.

Once you have educated yourself in the area of law, turn to a legal encyclopedia to obtain case citations. If a statute is involved, use an annotated statute for the relevant jurisdiction. This is particularly helpful when you are performing research for a problem dealing with state law. Additionally, annotated statutes provide many references to other resources from the same publisher. For instance, West's annotated codes also provide legislative history information. All annotated codes provide citations to cases that construe and apply the statute section and law review articles. The U.S.C.S. provides administrative code references.

For an overview of the law, in a format that is not too scholarly or detailed, use a legal encyclopedia. State legal encyclopedias are helpful in areas of state law research and enable you to find the general legal rule and citations to important cases quickly. Reading the pertinent encyclopedia section also helps you to create a **research vocabulary** that you can use when consulting indexes or constructing search strategies on Lexis and Westlaw. Legal encyclopedias can also provide you with citations to primary authority.

Once you find an excellent case or cases, go to the digests and use the one good case method. (See Chapter 4 for a detailed discussion on digest use.)

Most important, once you find pertinent authority to address the issue that you are researching, you must update and validate the authority. Updating and validating authority is performed by using *Shepard's* or KeyCite. *Shepard's* and KeyCite provide citations showing how subsequent courts viewed the decision to indicate whether the case or the statute that you are relying on is still good law. The cited cases in *Shepard's* or KeyCite are also newer cases that interpret the legal rule you are researching. Remember to update your *Shepard's* information by consulting the hard-copy supplements. If you are using Lexis to validate the authority, Shepardize the cites. If you are using Westlaw, use KeyCite. If time and money allow, use all of the updating and citing sources available online.

At this point, reexamine the issue that you formulated when you received the assignment. Review the vocabulary words that you listed to describe the legal issue and the factual scenario. Revise the issue to reflect your enhanced knowledge of the subject. Create an outline of the subissues. Remember three terms—reexamine, review, and revise—when you are performing research to find relevant information. Research involves educating yourself; as you learn more about an issue, your research becomes more focused and more precise.

Stay focused on your issue or issues. While gathering relevant information, it is easy to stray into related but inapplicable areas. Staying focused on your issues also is cost-effective because you do not waste valuable time on irrelevant information.

# C. DIAGRAMMING THE RESEARCH PROCESS

▼ What Is the Purpose and Technique for Record Keeping?

**Record keeping** and **note taking** are essential to effective legal research because they leave a written audit trail of all the sources consulted and the information derived from those sources. Records should also include sources consulted that did not contain pertinent information so that you do not reexamine those sources if you must expand your research at a later time. Another essential component of record keeping is to write the official *Bluebook* citation for each source that contains information helpful to your research. Establishing the complete citation at the time you are researching means you do not need to retrace your research steps to obtain citation information later on, particularly when you are writing.

Write out the proper *Bluebook* or *ALWD* citation for every source, document, case, and statute that you use. Take notes as you read and indicate in parentheses the page on which you found the information from within the text of the source. This is the pinpoint citation. For instance, if the case begins on page 1382, but the holding is on page 1389, write out the holding and then indicate parenthetically (1389) so that you know exactly where the information was found within the document. Noting the pinpoint citation, as you research, will save you time later.

Make a list of each source that you consult. List sources, citations, and any information obtained from the consulted source on a separate sheet. For example, you may find a useful A.L.R. annotation. Put the A.L.R. annotation at the top of the page in the correct *Bluebook* format. List all pertinent information relating to your research issue and the pages on which you found that information. Add any pertinent cites to cases and to statutes listed in the source to the sheet. The objective is to create a sheet of information that includes all of the relevant data obtained from the source consulted so that you do not have to go

back and review the source again. Also include information indicating whether you Shepardized the document and the date Shepardized or KeyCited so that you may redo it if too much time lapses. Note any significant information obtained from *Shepard's* or KeyCite about the document, for instance, if the case was criticized.

### *EXAMPLE OF RECORD KEEPING*

Below is an example of a case brief that supplies the primary authority for a legal memo addressing the topic of the effective rejection of a defective product. Some of the material in the brief has been created for the purpose of the example. The page numbers are noted for all the resources relied on including the parallel citations. The cites are not in *Bluebook* format.

CITATION
   Olson Rug Co. v. Smarto
   55 Ill. App. 2d 348, 204 N.E.2d 838 (App. Ct. 1965)

FACTS
   On March 16, 1962, Marty and Rose Smarto signed a contract with Olson Rug Company for the purchase of $450.62 worth of carpeting. They paid $120.00 as a down payment and agreed to pay the balance in monthly installments. The contract clearly stated that if the Smartos defaulted on payments, not only did the outstanding balance become immediately due, at Ill. App. 2d 349, 204 N.E.2d 839, but Olson Rug had irrevocable authority to have an attorney represent them and seek to have a judgment confessed against them. At N.E.2d 841. Prior to signing the agreement, Olson Rug assured the Smartos that the color and nap of the carpet would withstand their intended use for it. At Ill. App. 2d 350. Two weeks after installation of the carpet, the color faded and the nap lost its original shape. After two more weeks, the Smartos notified Olson Rug's agent and asked him to take the carpet back. At N.E.2d 842. He refused the request. The Smartos did not return the carpet, continued to use it, and apparently stopped paying installments. At Ill. App. 2d 351. Approximately one year later Olson Rug sought a judgment by confession against the Smartos for the outstanding balance and court costs. At Ill. App. 2d 351 and N.E.2d 842.

ISSUE
   Whether buyer's continued use of the carpet for more than one year after discovering that the seller delivered a defective product demonstrates effective rejection. At Ill. App. 2d 351 and N.E.2d 841.

HOLDING
   No, buyer's continued use of the carpet for more than one year after having discovered the defects does not indicate a timely rejection of the carpet or defective goods. At Ill. App. 2d 351 and N.E.2d 841.

RATIONALE

A buyer, upon discovering goods to be defective shortly after delivery, should soon thereafter return or offer to return the goods to the seller. The Smartos neither returned the carpeting nor offered to return it. For that reason, the court held that the Smartos, through their more than one-year-long delay, waived their right to rescind the carpet purchase contract. At Ill. App. 2d 350 and N.E.2d 840.

DISPOSITION

The appellate court affirmed the circuit court's decision to deny the defendants' motion to open or vacate the judgment confessed against them. At Ill. App. 2d 351 and N.E.2d 841.

All of the page numbers, indicating where the information is found within the text of the case, are included. This helps you when you are writing your memo and must include citation references to the case. You will not have to go back to the reporter and review the case again when your brief contains all of the page references and the complete *Bluebook* citation.

NET NOTE

The Gallagher Law Library's website, located at lib.law.washington.edu/ref/guides.html, provides terrific guides for using the specific resources as well as research guides for many legal disciplines.

# D. EXAMPLE OF RESEARCH STRATEGY

## *PROBLEM*

Mrs. Jones bought a fur coat from John J. Furriers. The coat was labeled 100 percent raccoon. One day Mrs. Jones was smoking a cigarette and a hot ash accidentally fell on the coat while she was wearing it. The ash melted a hole in the coat. Mrs. Jones knew that fur burns, but acrylic melts. The attorney wants you to use federal law.

## 1. How to Phrase the Issue If You Are Researching the Fur Labeling Problem

ISSUE

Whether a furrier is liable to a consumer for mislabeling a product.

## 2. First Steps

First, perform **background research** using secondary sources to educate yourself about the area of law. This helps you become familiar with the

types of legal materials controlling the issue. The background research provides information indicating whether the topic (in our problem, fur labeling) is controlled by statutes, cases, or regulations and whether federal or state law controls. You should develop a research vocabulary from your readings that helps you use the index volumes more effectively.

Start with the descriptive word index of the relevant state statute and the descriptive word index of the *United States Code Annotated* (U.S.C.A.) or the *United States Code Service* (U.S.C.S.) to see if any federal statutes have been violated. The words to check are: **label, fur**, and **product mislabeling.** You can also start your research at www.gpo .gov/fdsys/ to see if there are any relevant U.S. Code provisions by searching: label fur product misleading. After retrieving the relevant code section(s), check the annotated statutes to see if any relevant cases are cited discussing or analyzing the issue. You should validate any relevant case or statute with *Shepard's* or KeyCite. You may also check if there are any federal regulations in the *Code of Federal Regulations* (C.F.R.) concerning fur labeling. If you find a relevant regulation, you will have to make sure it is up to date and you will have to validate the cite. Validation also leads you to any newer cases discussing the issue.

After determining that the relevant cases and statutes are valid, a thorough reading of the decisions is necessary. You should make a list of all of the cites checked at this point and place a check next to the cites that are valid. Add a check next to the cite after you have read the full text of the opinion or statute. This will save you time later if you expand your research. You can merely review your list of cites to see if it is valid and to see if you read the full text of the authority.

## 3. What Sources to Consult and Why

Explore virtualchase.justia.com/legal-research for valuable research tips.

1. Consult the U.S.C.A. or the U.S.C.S. because fur labeling is regulated by the Federal Trade Commission. You can search the U.S. Code online via Lexis, Westlaw, or www.gpo.gov/fdsys/ or use one of the hard-copy annotated sets. An annotated code provides recent case references as well as references to administrative material (particularly the U.S.C.S., which provides references to administrative materials; see Chapter 7 for a discussion of statutes). Also, consumer fraud issues could be researched. Use the index to the U.S.C.A. and

look up the applicable research terms that you derived from the secondary sources.

2. Consult the C.F.R. to see the particular agency rules pertaining to fur labeling and intentional mislabeling. If you found a C.F.R. cite when using the U.S.C.S., look up the provision in the C.F.R. Otherwise, search the C.F.R. online for free at www.gpo.gov/fdsys/ or use the index to the C.F.R. to find the appropriate titles that discuss furs, fur labeling, labeling, and labeling requirements. The research vocabulary that you generate are the words you look up in the index. Note the administrative agency Internet address in case you need to contact the agency. (See Chapter 9 for C.F.R. use.)

3. Consult the *American Law Reports* (A.L.R.) because this is a narrow, well-defined issue and the A.L.R. may have explored this issue thoroughly. A.L.R. is easy to search on Lexis or Westlaw. The Federal Trade Commission might regulate fur labeling. (See Chapter 6 for a discussion on using the A.L.R.)

## 4. What to Do After Completing Your Research

Create a body of information on which to base your memo. Detailed note taking and careful citation to references on sheets of paper for each source are performed here. Also, keep a complete list of all sources consulted, whether a statute, case, regulation, periodical article, or other source. Your list of sources consulted helps later on when you may have to expand your research. You can then check the list to see if you already reviewed a source and to see if it was pertinent.

Remember to Shepardize or KeyCite any primary authority that you use in your memo, for this ensures that the authority, whether it is a case, statute, or regulation, is still good or valid law.

Outline the issues that you discuss in your memo or letter. Insert the applicable legal authority under the outline entry.

Review your outline and evaluate whether you have sufficient legal authority to support and to resolve the issues raised by the problem. If you have sufficient authority, begin to write. If you do not have sufficient authority, expand your research. Check your notes and the list of materials found to help you avoid duplicating your efforts and wasting time.

Cost-effective legal research tips and links are available at www.law
.georgetown.edu/library/research/guides/freelowcost.cfm.

# 5. Combining Computerized Research Methods with Hard-Copy Method

It is most efficient to combine hard-copy and computerized resources. Always ask, when working, about the budget for the project. You will have to determine the most cost-effective route. The principal difference between the hard-copy method and the combination computerized and hard-copy method is that instead of using indexes to the statutes, C.F.R., and the A.L.R., you construct a search query and search the materials online. You also search legal periodicals online with search queries. The validation, Shepardizing or KeyCiting, is performed online as well.

Performing background research using secondary sources is very important for educating yourself in the area of law and for generating a research vocabulary to use later when constructing the research queries for Lexis or Westlaw. Secondary source research is still most efficiently and cost-effectively done with hard-copy sources. You can start your secondary source research with Google Scholar, at scholar.google.com, to find citations to relevant articles.

It is also cost effective to view a statute in the book so you can browse related provisions quickly.

Computerized legal research requires you to select precise words to retrieve documents that contain those words and that are on point. Using Lexis Advance and Westlaw is most productive after you are versed in the subject and are aware of the words that judges, legislatures, and agencies use when writing about a legal topic.

# 6. Using Online Services in the Fur Labeling Problem

1. Using Lexis Advance, first click the "statutes and legislation" tab to find any statutes addressing fur labeling. (This can also be performed using Westlaw in the U.S.C.A. database.) The query constructed and entered is **fur w/s label!**. *Fur* is an essential factual term. The connector *w/s* (the group of letters indicating to Lexis Advance the relationship between fur and label!) indicates that *fur* must be within the same sentence as *label*. This connector parallels written English and ensures that the terms keep their significance in the context of the document. For instance, using the connector *and* instead of *w/s* would require Lexis Advance to search for the appearance of the words fur and label anywhere in the document regardless of their proximity to one another. The exclamation point (!) after *label* indicates to Lexis Advance to search for all possible endings for the word *label*, so that *labeling* would be picked up as well as *labeled* and *labels*. You are using Lexis Advance instead of the index to the U.S.C.S. You will get many hits. A few hits are cites to pending legislation that you may be interested in. You will have to scroll through the search results to see the cites to the U.S.C.S.

2. Use the same search again to see if any federal administrative regulations are relevant. Search the C.F.R online with the query **fur w/s label!**. Start on Lexis Advance and click: "U.S. Federal" to search federal primary sources. Enter your search: "fur w/s label!". You will have many hits. To narrow the material retrieved and to view only federal administrative regulations, at the top of the screen, click: "Admin Codes". Review the sections of the C.F.R. retrieved to see if any are on point. You are using Lexis instead of the C.F.R. index. Remember that you can update C.F.R. citations on Lexis. (See Chapter 9 for a discussion on updating C.F.R. provisions.)

3. Use the same search a third time to find secondary source citations, using the query **fur w/s label! On Lexis Advance, click on "US Federal" and enter the search. Then click, at the top of the screen, "second"**. Once again, your query is a substitute for using the index to the secondary sources such as encyclopedias, the A.L.R, and legal periodicals. You will find citations discussing fur labeling and references to primary authority.

4. Use Google Scholar to see if any other resources are relevant. Be sure to just look at the first page of hits. Search: regulations fur labeling. Any statutory or regulatory information obtained by searching Google must be updated and validated.

5. Read the text of any material that you found on Lexis Advance. It is most cost-effective to use the citations to the materials found on Lexis Advance and read the full text source in hard-copy format, if the hard copy is available. Take detailed notes. List all of the sources that you consult. Write the correct citation for each source. Update and Shepardize or KeyCite any primary authority on which you will rely. Use www.gpo.gov/fdsys/ to see the most recent version of the C.F.R. or if the budget permits, use either Lexis or Westlaw to obtain the C.F.R. section and to make sure that the C.F.R. provision is current. (See Chapter 10 for information on computer-assisted legal research.)

6. At this point, you must create an outline of the issues and subissues to be addressed. Insert the appropriate legal authority under each outline category. Expand your research if you do not have sufficient authority.

## SUMMARY CHECKLIST

1. When you receive the problem:
   a. Clarify legal issues being researched.
   b. Determine relevant jurisdiction.
   c. Determine area of the law.
   d. Gather all of the facts.
   e. Draft a statement of the issue or question that you are researching.

2. Introductory research
   a. Educate yourself in the area of law.
   b. Scan a hornbook or textbook on the subject.
   c. Learn the relevant vocabulary.
   d. Note the major cases.
   e. Make an outline of the issues and subissues of your problem.
3. Targeted research
   a. Use a legal encyclopedia or an annotated statute (use descriptive word index), particularly helpful for matters involving state law, to find discussion of legal issue and relevant case and statute citations.
   b. Go to the digest for the relevant jurisdiction, and use the one good case method to find other cases.
   c. Shepardize or KeyCite to find other cites and to validate your citations before relying on them as authority.
   d. Brief cases and relate them to one another (see Chapter 23 on Synthesis).
   e. Review the outline of the issues and subissues that you drafted. Revise the outline to reflect your increased knowledge of the subject.
4. Computerized research
   a. Particularly helpful when the facts are unique and the legal issue is narrow (for instance, whether malpractice occurred during the insertion of a chin implant), not broad (for instance, whether a breach of contract occurred).
   b. Best to be thorough and combine computerized and hard-copy methods.
   c. Using Google Scholar, Google the search terms to see if any other information comes up in the first page of hits and update any citations to primary authority. Always read any authority that you will rely on.
5. Create an audit trail of your research
   a. Take notes of sources and location, including page number, in *Bluebook* format.
   b. Note whether Shepardizing or KeyCiting has been completed and date completed.
6. Organizing your research findings
   a. Review the outline of the issues and the subissues that you created and revise it to reflect any new knowledge.
   b. Insert the applicable authority discussing the relevant subissue under the appropriate outline heading.
   c. Review the filled-in outline to make sure that you have found adequate authority to address each subissue listed.
   d. If you have sufficient legal authority, begin to write. If you do not have sufficient legal authority, expand your research. Always check your list of sources consulted when you are expanding your research to make sure that you do not waste precious time with sources that you have already consulted.

> ### *PRACTICE POINTER*
>
> Take advantage of any training offered at your firm or through legal publishers. Publishers and online database vendors offer training, very often for free, that will enhance your research skills and help you become familiar with new products. Sometimes existing products are very complex, and training will help you use the resources efficiently.

## CHAPTER SUMMARY

This chapter led you through the entire research process from initially receiving the project to completing research. Refining the issue at the beginning and focusing on your important sources are as essential as knowing when to stop researching. This chapter and your own experience will guide you through this process. Keep records of all sources consulted and make sure that your citations are accurate; these help when you are ready to write. Also, do not forget to validate all necessary documents and to update all resources. Now you are equipped to write.

## KEY TERMS

background research                 record keeping
facts                              research vocabulary
note taking                        *West's Law Finder*

## EXERCISES

### RESEARCHING IN GENERAL

1. Before you begin a research project, what general questions should you resolve with the assigning attorney?
2. What is the benefit of record keeping when researching?

### HARD-COPY RESEARCH

3. You have just received a research project. Outline your research plan using hard-copy resources.
4. Read the following fact pattern and answer the questions.

**Facts**
John Clark comes to your firm with a question regarding the tax status of his residence. John Clark was just ordained as a Methodist minister.

He will be receiving a housing allowance from First Methodist Church, where he will be an assistant pastor. He wants to know if this housing allowance can be excluded from income on his tax return even though the residence is his own.

**a.** How would you phrase this issue if you were researching this problem using hard-copy resources?

**b.** What would be your research strategy using hard-copy resources?

**c.** List three sources that you would consult. Why would you consult them?

## HARD-COPY AND ONLINE RESEARCH COMBINED

5. Draw a flow chart of your research strategy using a combination of hard copy and computerized resources.

6. Read the following fact pattern and answer the questions.

**Facts**

On November 29, 2013, Michael Jones purchased a used truck from Grimy's Auto and Truck Service. At the time of purchase, Grimy's stated that the engine was completely overhauled and consisted of rebuilt and reconditioned parts, all parts were guaranteed, and invoices for all new parts would be provided. On November 13, 2014, after using the truck for almost one year, Jones discovered that several engine parts were not rebuilt or reconditioned and other engine parts were defective, which caused the truck to break down. This resulted in lost wages and lost profits for Jones. Jones made repairs to the truck on November 13, 2014, December 13, 2014, and December 16, 2014. Jones did not attempt to return the truck and did not notify Grimy's that the truck was defective. The truck is currently disabled in Columbus, Ohio. Jones came to your firm because he wants to sue Grimy's for damages for breach of contract.

**Issue**

Is Jones entitled to receive damages for breach of contract because the truck does not conform to the terms of the agreement? Remember that Grimy's will assert that Jones continued to use the truck for more than a reasonable time and failed to return the truck or to notify Grimy's of its defects in a timely manner.

**a.** What would be your research strategy if you were using a combination of hard copy and computerized resources?

**b.** How would you educate yourself on the relevant topic so that you could find primary sources?

**c.** List one secondary source and two primary sources that you would consult. Why would you consult these sources?

**d.** Use either Lexis Advance or Westlaw and formulate a search query that you could use to find primary authority.

# PART 2

# LEGAL WRITING

# GETTING READY TO WRITE

| | | |
|---|---|---:|
| **A.** | **WRITING GOALS AND HOW TO ACHIEVE THEM** | 346 |
| **B.** | **THE WRITING PROCESS** | 346 |
| | 1. Preparing to Write: Purpose and Audience | 346 |
| | 2. Drafting a Detailed Outline | 348 |
| | 3. Revision: The Final Part of the Process | 349 |
| | 4. Example of Process Writing Techniques | 350 |

## CHAPTER OVERVIEW

Writing involves planning—the more planning, the more effective the written document. Legal writing has three components: prewriting (which includes researching and planning your written document), drafting, and revising. This chapter explains how to draft documents and how to revise your work so that it is written clearly and concisely. This chapter provides step-by-step techniques to use when preparing to write. To systematically prepare to write, first determine the purpose, audience, and organization of the document. Then, you must carefully revise your work product to tailor it precisely to the assignment, the client, and the facts. The focus of this chapter is the fundamentals of good writing. Specific tips are provided to improve your drafts.

# A. WRITING GOALS AND HOW TO ACHIEVE THEM

The keys to writing well are **clarity** and **organization.** Your readers must understand what you are trying to convey to them. Whether you are writing a letter or a memorandum, your communication must be clear so that it can be understood. Often several proper formats, used at different times, will make your writing easier to read and understand.

### ▼ How Do You Plan Your Communication and Revise It?

You must think about what you want to say. Outline the communication. Next, write it using correct grammar and spelling, and most important, rewrite it several times. As you rewrite your letters and memos, you will always find that you can eliminate unnecessary words and legalese. Use simple words even though you know more elaborate ones. Doing so makes your writing inviting rather than pompous.

# B. THE WRITING PROCESS

Follow a method or format when preparing to write to make the actual drafting process easier. Focus on the mechanics and components of the writing process rather than the finished product. The method that follows is a checklist to ensure thoroughness and to give you confidence in your newly acquired skills. The fundamental components of process writing are assessing the document's purpose and intended audience, drafting a detailed outline before writing, revising your findings into the categories of purpose and audience, and outlining and revising your work.

## 1. Preparing to Write: Purpose and Audience

### ▼ How Do You Complete the Research Process and Make the Transition to Writing?

Remember that what we plan as we prepare to write is as important as the final product. The more time you can put into the process, the better is the product. Spend at least 50 percent of the time budgeted for writing in the **prewriting stage.** However, time management is crucial with any assignment because time is money and knowing when to stop researching and when to begin writing is important. Therefore, when the project is assigned ask how much time you should spend on the project. What is the budget? A good clue as to when you have completed your research is when you do not retrieve any new information; the same sources keep appearing. Ask your law librarian or

another paralegal to briefly review your research strategy and ask if there are any other avenues that he or she would have taken.

Take detailed notes and make careful citations to references for each source. Also, keep a complete list of all sources consulted, whether a statute, case, regulation, periodical article, or other source. Your list of sources consulted helps later on, when you may have to expand your research. You can then check the list to see if you already reviewed a source and to see if it was pertinent.

Shepardize or KeyCite any primary authority that you use in your memo to ensure that the authority, whether it is a case, statute, or regulation, is still good or valid law. Never start to write using a source of authority without Shepardizing or KeyCiting it first.

For tips on word selection in legal writing, visit www.llrx.com/columns/ grammar10.htm.

## a. Purpose

### ▼ What Is the Purpose of the Document?

When you sit down to write, begin by asking yourself: What is the **purpose** of the document that I am preparing? Because a legal document has a variety of goals (to inform, persuade, or advise), you must determine the document's intent before writing. The purpose determines the posture and the format of your work product. If the document is to inform the attorney as to all available law on a particular issue, it is neutral in tone and takes the form of an objective memo. If your goal is to convince another party that your position is correct, then the document may be in the form of a memo for the assigning attorney, a memo for the court, a trial or an appellate brief, and the tone will be persuasive. Sometimes a persuasive document takes the form of a letter that requests an individual or entity to act in a certain way. Examples of persuasive letters are demand letters requesting payment owed, or eviction letters demanding that a tenant vacate the premises. Sometimes you must convey an attorney's advice to a client. The document may then be in the form of a letter giving counsel, written as simply as possible, to be signed by the supervising attorney. Simplicity is best for a client who may not have a legal education. The purpose of the document determines its format and the rhetorical stance: objective, persuasive, or instructive.

**NET NOTE**

Cornell's Legal Information Institute provides a brief overview of the types of legal writing at www.law.cornell.edu/wex/legal_writing.

## b. Audience

### ▼ To Whom Are You Speaking?

As you prepare to write, determine carefully who the **audience**, or reader, is. Is the reader the assigning attorney? This is often the case when the project is the preparation of an office memo. The memo should be easy for the intended reader to understand; you should insert headings, if necessary, to guide the reader. If the document is intended for a court, then the reader will be a judge and opposing counsel, and your tone will be formal yet persuasive. The assertions or points that you want to prove should be clear and straightforward. The document should always be prepared using language that the reader can comprehend; this is also required when drafting client letters and demand letters.

*PRACTICE POINTER*

After you receive the assignment and understand what you are asked to do, inquire as to the number of hours that is budgeted for the project. Also, ask the assigning attorney questions after you have reviewed the assignment, but before you begin to write, to make sure that the purpose and audience are agreed upon so that you stay focused on the attorney's objectives.

## 2. Drafting a Detailed Outline

### ▼ How Do You Organize Your Ideas?

The next stage is to prepare an **outline** of whatever document you are writing. If it is an office memo, outline the issues and subissues of points that you want to articulate. Make sure that the outline flows logically. See if there are any gaps by reviewing your outline carefully. Organization is crucial to effective legal writing to ensure completeness. Having a complete outline also helps when you have to put your project down for a considerable period of time, or when you

must work on more than one matter at a time and want to easily pick up where you left off.

Organize your research findings according to where they are pertinent in your outline. It is best to let your issues or assertions determine where the research should be placed rather than letting the sources determine the placement in the document. Never use your sources as your outline; rely on the issues.

## 3. Revision: The Final Part of the Process

*PRACTICE POINTER*

When revising, consult a dictionary to ensure that all of the words are properly spelled and used. Check a thesaurus to vary your terms.

**Rewriting** is a continuous part of the writing process and a vital final step. Reread the material after you have reviewed your word choices and eliminated unnecessary words. Rewriting may seem like a tedious waste of time, but it is of the most important steps in preparing a well-written document.

Review all the steps you have taken in the prewriting stage. Ask yourself: Is the purpose of the document being prepared according to the assignment, and is it meeting the client's needs? Does the document clearly fulfill its goal of either informing, persuading, or advising? Do the language and format reflect the purpose?

Examine your intended audience. What language is appropriate for the intended reader? What level of sophistication is required? Ask yourself about voice (how it will sound), diction (word choice), and rhetoric (the way you use speech).

Review your outline. Check to see if the outline is well organized, logical, and flows smoothly. At this point, reexamine the issues or assertions that you want to include and make sure that the points are clearly discernible. Insert the appropriate research findings in the relevant place in the outline, as well as the necessary facts and the conclusions that you want to draw. Now you are ready to write. After you write the first draft, revise and pay attention to these details.

*PRACTICE POINTER*

Review documents in files to see the firm's writing style.

## 4. Example of Process Writing Techniques

Ms. Partner calls you into her office and asks you to prepare a client letter to Mrs. Jones advising her as to a course of action that she can take to rectify the problem of her mislabeled fur coat. The facts of the problem are as follows: Mrs. Jones bought a fur coat from John J. Furriers. The coat was labeled 100 percent raccoon. One day Mrs. Jones was smoking a cigarette and a hot ash fell on the coat while she was wearing it. The ash melted a hole in the coat. Mrs. Jones knew that fur burns, but acrylic melts.

First, what is the purpose of the document? The document's goal is to advise Mrs. Jones as to a course of action against the seller, John J. Furriers. The partner specified the document's form, a letter.

Next, you must examine your audience. Who is your reader? Is Mrs. Jones an attorney? Probably not. You can ask the attorney making the assignment for some background information about the client. This will help you tailor a document to the reader's precise needs. Mrs. Jones is a stock analyst. She is a sophisticated individual but she does not possess a legal education. The language used in the letter must be understandable to Mrs. Jones. The voice—how the letter sounds—should be instructive and advisory without being condescending. The diction, or word choice, should be simple; avoid legalese.

Now outline the points that you want to address in the letter. Begin by restating the facts as you know them. List the points.

1. The fur coat was mislabeled.
2. The seller misrepresented his product.
3. If the misrepresentation was intentional, there is the possibility of fraud.
4. Mrs. Jones would like to obtain a full refund for the coat that she purchased.
5. If a refund is not given in seven days, court action will proceed.

Insert your research findings, in general language, in the appropriate spot in the outline. In a client letter of this nature there is no need to cite to authority. Use the facts to draft a letter for the attorney to advise Mrs. Jones as to how she should proceed with the matter. Remember that an attorney must always review and sign any letter that you prepare that gives legal advice. Only an attorney may sign such a letter.

Revise all your prewriting steps by checking your purpose, audience, and outline once again. Now you are ready to write.

---

### PRACTICE POINTER

Prewriting preparation is time well spent. Thoroughness and accuracy are so important, and attorneys have little patience for anything besides perfection. Careful note taking, outlining, and citing will provide not only an excellent start to a writing project but ample material if you are called on to discuss a project prior to its completion. Knowing the key points will also help you to draft an e-mail concerning the matter.

*CHECKLIST*

1. When you receive the problem
   a. Clarify the legal issues being researched.
   b. Determine the relevant jurisdiction.
   c. Determine the area of the law.
   d. Gather all the facts.
   e. Draft a statement of the issue or question that you are researching.
2. Introductory research
   a. Educate yourself in the area of the law.
   b. Consult a legal encyclopedia for a general overview to find major cases on point.
   c. Learn the relevant vocabulary.
   d. Note the major cases.
   e. Make an outline of the issues and subissues in your problem.
3. Process writing
   a. Purpose: Determine the purpose of the document. The document's goal is either to inform, to persuade, or to advise. Select the appropriate rhetorical stance and determine the format (office memo, court memo, brief, or letter).
   b. Audience: Find out who the reader or readers will be. Determine the language that is most comprehensible to the particular reader. Select an appropriate voice for the purpose, format, and reader. Note your diction.
   c. Outline: Outline the issues, assertions, or points that you want to include. Organize research findings according to the outline. Place facts in the appropriate spot and state conclusion.
   d. Revise: Review the purpose and the audience of the intended document and check your outline for appropriateness. Revise your outline to reflect any new knowledge, legal or factual. Reread the outline to ensure that it is complete and flows logically.

NET NOTE

A list of resources for legal writers is available at lib.law.washington.edu/ref/writing.html.

## CHAPTER SUMMARY

This chapter led you through the writing process. This will ensure thoroughness when planning and starting a writing project. Before writing, determine

the purpose of your assignment. This will guide your writing. Also, determine the audience for your work. This will determine the style of your writing. Carefully outline the document before writing and then revise the document by preparing an outline of the material that you prepared, an after-the-fact outline. Review the after-the-fact outline to make sure that it is logically organized and includes all points that the issues require to be addressed.

The time that you spend in the prewriting stage ensures a better work product that is produced more efficiently than one created by lunging into the writing process. Think about what you want to say, outline it, and write it using good grammar and correct spelling. Then rewrite and edit your work. Use these tips even when drafting a short memo to e-mail to an attorney. Prewriting takes planning, but with the methodology outlined in this chapter you will be equipped to write in any format.

## KEY TERMS

audience
clarity
organization
outline

prewriting stage
purpose
rewriting

## EXERCISES

### PREPARING TO WRITE

1. Why would you use a process method for legal writing?
2. Why would you outline before you write as well as create an outline of your finished document?
3. Why is it important to determine the audience and purpose before writing?

### PROCESS-WRITING EXERCISE

4. Read the following fact pattern and answer the questions.

**Facts**

John Clark comes to your firm with a question regarding the tax status of his residence. He has just been ordained as a United Methodist minister and will be receiving a housing allowance from First United Methodist Church, where he will be an assistant pastor. He wants to know if this housing allowance can be excluded from income on his tax return even though the residence is his own.

    a. How would you phrase this issue if you were researching this problem?
    b. What would be your research strategy?
    c. Construct an outline of this problem.
5. The assignment partner requests that you draft a letter of your findings to Rev. Clark. List, in detail, the purpose, audience, and resulting outline of the letter.

6. How would the purpose, audience, and outline change if the assignment partner requests a memo concerning your research findings? Once again, how would the purpose, audience, and outline change if you are requested to prepare a court brief?

## IN-CLASS EXERCISES

1. For this exercise, use a paper that you have already written.
   a. Examine the paper. What is the purpose and the audience?
   b. Extract an outline from the paper. Outline the ideas explained in the paper.
   c. Revise your outline to clarify your ideas.
2. Write a letter to a neighbor discussing the highlights of the past season.
   a. What is the audience and, consequently, the tone?
   b. Rewrite the letter to a government official. In the rewritten letter, express dissatisfaction with a service that is supposed to be provided by the local government and was not provided adequately during the past season. For example, in the letter to your neighbor, you write about the great snowfall during the winter. In the rewritten letter to a government official, you also write about the great snowfall, but also include how the locality failed to plow sufficiently. What is the purpose and audience of the letter to the government official?

# 16

# CLEAR WRITING AND EDITING

| | | |
|---|---|---|
| **A.** | **PURPOSE OF EDITING** | 355 |
| **B.** | **PROCESS OF EDITING** | 356 |
| **C.** | **SPECIFIC ITEMS TO REVIEW WHILE EDITING** | 357 |
| | 1. Diction | 357 |
| | 2. Voice | 359 |
| | 3. Paragraphs | 360 |
| | 4. Sentences | 360 |
| | 5. Other Key Rules | 361 |

## *CHAPTER OVERVIEW*

The key to effective writing is clarity. Preparing a first draft of a document can be quite an undertaking, but that is only a start. Until you have carefully edited and revised your drafts at least once, you have not completed your project. This chapter provides you with guidance in editing and revising your documents and preparing them for clients, courts, and attorneys.

## A. PURPOSE OF EDITING

Editing and revising are essential if you want to have well-drafted and organized documents. A well-drafted document is one in which your

readers understand what you are trying to convey. Be clear and make it easy to read. Few documents are written well after one draft. Good writing entails rewriting. Each time you review your document and revise it, you improve its content and make it more understandable. **Editing** allows you to review your word choices, your grammar, your spelling, and your outline and organization of each sentence and paragraph, as well as the outline and organization of the entire document. It enables you to determine whether the document you wrote is clear and will be understood by your audience. Editing also provides you with the opportunity to enhance your work with additional thoughts and clarify your document by eliminating unnecessary words, ideas, and legalese.

## B. PROCESS OF EDITING

The process of editing starts with a first draft and often ends after many more drafts. After you complete your first draft, you must proofread and edit your work. Consider each word you select. Review your overall outline and organization. Then review the outline and organization of each sentence and paragraph.

When you review your draft, you should read it as if you were reading it for the first time. Pretend that you are a stranger to the project and that you don't know anything about it. Ensure that it is understandable. If you have time, put the first draft aside for a day or two and then review it again. It will give you a fresh perspective.

Next, consider whether each part follows the next. The work should flow in a logical order. Consider whether the organization of the document or of any paragraphs or sentences should be revised. Question the structure and organization of each sentence and paragraph. Change passive voice sentences to active voice. For more discussion of passive and action voice, review this chapter's Section C-2, Voice.

Read your writing aloud. Do you notice anything is missing? Sometimes when you read your work aloud, you find that it is missing something needed to get you from point A to point B in the discussion. Add any such missing elements.

Note whether your writing contains transitions and easily flows from one section to the next. If it doesn't, revise it. Add transitional words, phrases, or sentences where necessary. **Transitions** help move readers from one sentence to the next and from one paragraph to the next.

Next, think about whether you can eliminate unnecessary words, a process called tightening or editing. Focus on your words. Change elaborate or unfamiliar words to simpler words—often those you used in grade school. Doing so makes your writing inviting rather than pompous. Make certain that your words provide the reader with a visual image of what you mean. Ensure that your words accurately convey your ideas. For additional information about word choice, see this chapter's Section C-1, Diction.

Review your grammar. Ensure that your punctuation is correct and that the elements of each sentence and paragraph are correct. Check your citation for errors as well.

# C. SPECIFIC ITEMS TO REVIEW WHILE EDITING

## 1. Diction

### ▼ What Is Diction?

**Diction** means choice of words when writing. Selecting the appropriate words to express your idea precisely is a skill that is developed over time. When you are revising a document, consider whether your words convey your ideas precisely. Sometimes you must use a dictionary or thesaurus to assist you in selecting the best word.

Select concrete words that allow the readers to visualize what you are saying. Read the following example:

He harmed one of his body parts in the device at issue in the case.

It is better to say:

His arm was severed when the threshing machine stalled and he fell forward in front of the machine.

The second example is clearer because the reader knows what happened and to which body part it happened: The arm was severed. The second sentence also conveys that the device was a threshing machine and that it stalled, throwing the man forward.

### ▼ What Are Concrete Verbs?

Use **concrete verbs** that exactly describe the action taken. Read the following examples:

The parties entered into an agreement on July 8, 2013.
There was an agreement entered into on July 8, 2013.
The parties agreed to the terms on July 8, 2013.

The last example is the best because it is the simplest and uses the word *agreed* as a verb rather than as a noun. It is the easiest sentence of the three to understand and to visualize.

The first two examples turn the verb *agree* into a noun, a process called **nominalization.** The following illustrates a second example:

The parties entered into an agreement on November 15, 2013, to make a change in the purchase price of the original contract from $1,500 to $2,000.

It is better to say:

> The parties agreed to increase the original contract purchase price from $1,500 to $2,000.

In the second sentence, *entered into an agreement* becomes *agreed* and *to make a change* becomes *increase*. These changes eliminate the use of verbs as nouns.

Another example is as follows:

> The plaintiff made a statement to police that the defendant ran a red light before the crash.

It is better to say:

> The plaintiff told police that the defendant ran the red light before the crash.

> or

> The plaintiff stated to police that the defendant ran the red light before the crash.

Select simpler words and make sentences short. Review the following example.

> Prior to 9/11, airport security was incomplete.

It is better to say:

> Before 9/11, airport security was lax.

*Before* is a simpler word than *prior to* and *lax* is more descriptive than *incomplete*.

Review these statements and determine which is clearer:

> The state driver's license bureau now requires a social security card as **verification** of a person's identity.

> or

> The state driver's license bureau now requires a social security card as **proof** of a person's identity.

The second sentence is clearer. The use of the simple word *proof* rather than the pompous word *verification* makes the sentence easier to understand.

## ▼ How Do You Avoid Legalese or Legal Speak?

Avoid **legalese** or **legal speak.** What does this mean? Use plain English that your nonattorney clients would use. Consider your audience.

Clear writing avoids using unnecessary legal words. For example, do not use the word *scienter* for *intent*. At the end of an affidavit, you often see the phrase *Further affiant sayeth not*, which means that the person signing the affidavit has nothing further to say. Because that should be clear without the legalistic phrase, skip it (and others like it that add nothing to your writing).

## 2. Voice

**Voice** is the tone of your document. In professional writing, the document's tone is formal. Selecting language that is not colloquial and avoiding slang are ways to ensure that the tone of the document is correct for the law firm or corporate legal department environment. Avoid anything that personalizes the contents. Never use the first person. Conjunctions like *can't* are more casual than *cannot*. When revising, be sensitive to the tone of your document; it should have the requisite formal voice.

### ▼ What Is the Difference Between Active Voice and Passive Voice?

**Active voice** is when the subject of the sentence is doing the action of the verb. Active voice emphasizes the actor. Active voice is the preferred voice because it is clearer, more concise, and more lively.

| | |
|---|---|
| **Active voice:** | Ben hit a home run. |
| | Sarah danced the tango. |

**Passive voice** is when the subject of the sentence is being acted on. Although passive voice has its uses, it is generally wordier and not as strong as active voice.

| | |
|---|---|
| **Passive voice:** | The home run was hit by Ben. |
| | The tango was danced by Sarah. |

Often the word *by* is used in a passive voice sentence. When you see the word *by*, consider rewriting the sentence.

| | |
|---|---|
| **Passive example:** | Their initial quote for heat stamping equipment was rejected by Abbey. |
| **Rewritten example:** | Abbey rejected their initial quote for heat stamping equipment. |

The second example is clearer and more concise.

Passive voice, however, is sometimes acceptable. In some cases, the person or thing performing the action is unknown. For example:

Taxes were not deducted from her paychecks.

Jenna received health and life insurance benefits.

In other cases, the actor does not need to be mentioned because he or she is less important than the action. If you believe it advantageous to change the emphasis of the sentence from the person doing the action to the action, use passive voice. For example, if your client is the defendant in a proceeding and you do not want to emphasize her action, you would write a sentence in passive voice, as follows:

The action stems from a contract dispute in which goods were rejected by the defendant.

This sentence in active voice would emphasize the defendant, as follows:

The defendant rejected the goods, resulting in a contract dispute.

## 3. Paragraphs

A **paragraph** is a collection of statements that focus on the same general subject. Effective paragraphs have a unified purpose, a thesis or topic sentence, and transitions between sentences.

The **topic sentence** is generally the first sentence of a paragraph; it tells the reader the subject of the paragraph. This sentence also indicates that a new topic will be discussed. In legal writing, this sentence often introduces the issue or subissues that will be discussed within the paragraph.

You should use transitions to guide your reader from one paragraph to the next. Transitions tell the reader that the ideas follow from each other and are related. A transitional sentence ties two paragraphs together. Think of this sentence as a bridge. Whenever you start your new paragraph, think about how you will relate it to the previous paragraph.

## 4. Sentences

A **sentence** is a statement that conveys a single idea. It generally should be written in active voice and must include a subject and predicate. To avoid confusing your reader, do not place the subject too far from the verb. The focus of your sentence should be the idea you wish to convey. Do not make your readers work too hard to understand your sentence. Be direct and to the point. Keep your sentences short,

generally not more than 25 words. As with any rule, you may break this rule about sentence length, but be careful not to make your sentences too complex.

One common mistake in writing sentences is to use a sentence fragment or incomplete sentence.

|  |  |
| --- | --- |
| **Incomplete sentence:** | The extent of the employer's control and supervision over the worker. |
| **Complete sentence:** | The court will consider the extent of the employer's control and supervision over the worker. |

The first example is a sentence fragment. It is incomplete and is missing a verb. The second sentence is a complete thought. It contains both a subject and a verb.

## 5. Other Key Rules

Do not start your paragraph or sentence with a citation. Instead, start with the rule summarizing the cited authority.

Use quotations sparingly. Most often, you can paraphrase what a court decision or other authority states. Your words convey the concept more clearly to the reader. Direct quotations that are used to convey an idea often are cluttered with unnecessary words or do not effectively explain a concept in the context of your use of the quotation. An added bonus for you when you paraphrase a court decision or other authority is that you are forced to analyze carefully the language of the authority. This ensures that you understand the concepts presented.

Review the following paragraph. Note that unnecessary words are located in parentheses.

> The plaintiff (made a statement) that in his (own) opinion, during (the course of) (a period of) a year, the defendant (completely) destroyed the furniture the plaintiff hired the defendant to restore. The defendant failed to warn the plaintiff (in advance) that he couldn't restore the piece (properly) and that the price of the work originally estimated (roughly) at $600 would now cost her $2,200.

None of the words in parentheses add anything to the reader's understanding of the sentences or paragraph. The phrase *made a statement* should be shortened to *stated.* When you read your paragraphs, review each word and determine whether it adds to the sentence. If not, delete it.

REVISION CHECKLIST
 1. Does the material make sense?
 2. Do the words accurately convey what happened?
 3. Would another word more accurately convey your intended meaning?
 4. Can the reader visualize what occurred?
 5. Is it logical?
 6. Should the organization of the piece be changed?
 7. Does one paragraph flow into the other?
 8. Should the paragraphs be rearranged?
 9. Does one sentence follow from the next?
10. Should the organization of any sentence be changed?
11. Are there any gaps in the sentence?
12. Review your voice.
13. Is the voice consistent?
14. Is the voice used the intended voice?
15. Can you eliminate passive voice?
16. Be certain the verbs are concrete.
17. Check for nominalizations.
18. Are there any punctuation errors?
19. Are any words misspelled?
20. Are there any typographical errors?
21. Are there any citation errors?
22. Eliminate any legalese.

## CHAPTER SUMMARY

This chapter led you through the editing process generally and then more specifically. It outlined essential items to check during your editing process.

Choose your words carefully. Select concrete verbs and avoid legalese. Most often, use active voice in which the subject of the sentence is doing the action of the verb.

Make sure your paragraphs focus on a single subject or aspect of a subject and use topic and transition sentences. Use full sentences that are direct and convey the idea you intend.

Use quotations sparingly to effectively convey your messages.

## KEY TERMS

active voice
concrete verbs
diction
editing
legal speak
legalese
nominalization

paragraph
passive voice
sentence
topic sentence
transitions
voice

# EXERCISES

1. Eliminate the unnecessary words from the following statements:

   At the time when the parties entered into the agreement of purchase and sale it is important to note that neither of them had knowledge of contents of the dresser drawer. Because of the fact that previous to the contract the seller did not own the dresser and the seller's mother had not had many valuable pieces of jewelry despite having a large income, the seller had made the assumption that the dresser did not contain anything. Due to the fact that the seller had made a statement to the buyer of the fact that his mother did not own any jewelry in the buyer's thinking, he had no purpose to make any further investigation or inspection of the drawers as he might otherwise have considered making. For these reasons, there was no provision in the contract for an upward modification in the payment to be made by the buyer to the seller in the event that the dresser drawer later proved to be filled with jewels.

2. The police report said that Mr. Harris had a blood alcohol level of 1.7 based on an on-site blood alcohol test and states further that there were swerve marks on the street. The report also stated that there were no brake marks and that the driver was cited by the officer for drunk driving.

3. The personnel manager did all of the hiring and firing of the restaurant and golf course and the part-time accountant manages all bookkeeping and tax work for the restaurant and golf course.

4. Candy Graham who did not have an employment contract was, despite her freedom to set her own hours and work from her own home, also an employee.

5. Which is the best sentence? Why?
   a. A modification to the contract occurred on January 28, 2014.
   b. There was a modification of the contract January 28, 2014.
   c. Harry and Morgan modified their contract on January 28, 2014.

## TIGHTENING

6. At approximately 7:30 P.M. on May 4, 2013, the plaintiff, Lidia Gregory, was weeding the front garden at her home at 2088 Vista Drive in Phoenix. She was about five feet from the street. The children also were playing in the front yard which was near the street.

7. Based on a blood alcohol test done at the scene of the accident, it was determined that Ronnie Walden was intoxicated.

8. The day the accident occurred it was very clear and had not rained to make the road slick.

9. The issue is whether or not it is a nuisance.

## SCREENING FOR LEGALESE—SAY IT IN ENGLISH, PLEASE

10. In the aforementioned case, the funeral home was not found to be a nuisance because the court held that the funeral home in question was "reasonably located on the outskirts of the city."

11. Now comes the plaintiff, by and through her attorney, causes this complaint to be filed with the court.
12. Further affiant sayest not.
13. The party of the first part claims that the party of the second part said that he wanted to cause her to go out of business.

## ACTIVE AND PASSIVE EXERCISES

14. Two businesses are owned by Max and Sam Maine and they are being sued in federal court by two former workers for sex discrimination.
15. Ricki Ashton's office supplies and office were provided by Whole In One.
16. The funeral home was controlled by William Halsey and owned jointly by Halsey and Ivy Courier.

## CHAPTER 17

# WRITING BASICS

| | | |
|---|---|---|
| **A. PUNCTUATION** | | 366 |
| 1. Commas | | 366 |
| 2. Special Comma Rules | | 367 |
| 3. Semicolons | | 368 |
| 4. Colons | | 368 |
| 5. Parentheses | | 369 |
| 6. Double Quotation Marks | | 369 |
| 7. Single Quotation Marks | | 369 |
| **B. MODIFIERS** | | 369 |
| **C. PARALLEL CONSTRUCTION** | | 370 |
| **D. SUBJECT AND VERB AGREEMENT** | | 370 |
| **E. RUN-ON SENTENCES** | | 372 |
| **F. SENTENCE FRAGMENTS** | | 373 |
| **G. THAT AND WHICH** | | 373 |

## *CHAPTER OVERVIEW*

This chapter reinforces grammar concepts and focuses on problem areas. It provides concrete examples of grammatically correct and incorrect sentences and explains the difference. Because it cannot address all points of grammar that students need to know, you should consult other grammar resources.

# A. PUNCTUATION

The punctuation of a sentence, especially the placement of a comma, can change the meaning of that sentence. Therefore, you must carefully place each punctuation mark. The following provides you with some basic rules for checking your punctuation placement.

## 1. Commas

**Commas** tell a reader to pause. Use commas to separate a series of items. For example:

Wally ran to the school, the store, the baseball field, and then home.

Be careful not to use commas to divide run-on sentences. The first example below should be two separate sentences.

**Incorrect:**   Tildy's role is merely advisory, although she might be asked to supply facts about the spill, her opinion probably would not form the basis of any final decision.

**Correct:**   Tildy's role is merely advisory. Although she might be asked to supply facts about the spill, her opinion probably would not form the basis of any final decision.

In the second example, the two sentences are correctly separated with a period. You also could use a semicolon. For some run-on sentences, you could divide the sentences with a comma and a conjunction. In the above example, that solution would not cure the problem completely because the second sentence is too long.

Commas also are used to set apart parenthetical phrases. In such a situation, commas should be used in pairs.

The defendant, George K. Dwyer, filed an answer to the complaint.

The name *George K. Dwyer* is parenthetical because the meaning of the sentence would not be changed if the name was omitted. In contrast, read the following examples:

Judges who take bribes should be indicted.

Judges, who take bribes, should be indicted.

In these examples, the phrase *who take bribes* is not parenthetical. If it was omitted, the sentence would say, "judges should be indicted." The phrase *who take bribes* must be part of the sentence to convey the

correct meaning. Therefore, it is not parenthetical, and the commas should be omitted.

Place commas around unnecessary words or phrases. For example, a client has one child, William, and wants to name him as the executor of her estate. In a document to name him as executor, you could use either of the following sentences and the meaning would not be altered.

> I name my son, William, as the executor of my estate.

> I name my son as the executor of my estate.

Do not place commas around words or phrases that are necessary in order to understand a sentence.

In the next example, your client has two sons, William and Randall. She wants William to be the executor of the estate. The document should read as follows:

> I name my son William as the executor of my estate.

The following sentence would be incorrect:

> I name my son, William, as the executor of my estate.

## 2. Special Comma Rules

Commas separate a year from the date.

> The plaintiff and the defendant agreed to the settlement on November 15, 2013.

Commas also set off the date from a specific reference to a day of the week.

> The judge decided the summary judgment motion on Monday, November 7, 2013.

Commas separate a proper name from a title that follows it.

> The plaintiff sued RAM Enterprises and Samuel Harris, company president.

Commas and periods should always appear inside quotation marks. This rule is often mistakenly broken.

> "But I wasn't in Toledo on the night of the murder," the defendant protested. "I was in Scottsdale with my elderly mother."

## 3. Semicolons

**Semicolons** are similar to commas because they tell a reader to pause and they break apart thoughts. Semicolons are used to separate two independent sentences.

| | |
|---|---|
| **Two sentences:** | The paralegal's responsibilities are broad. They include summarization of depositions. |
| **One sentence:** | The paralegal's responsibilities are broad; they include summarization of depositions. |

Semicolons separate clauses of a compound sentence when an adverbial conjunction joins the two.

> The defendants presented a good case; however, they lost.

Semicolons are used to separate phrases in a list.

> The committee members were Robert Harris, vice president of Harris Enterprises; Edna Williams, owner of Walworth Products; Barbara Halley, an attorney; and Benjamin Marcus, an accountant.

## 4. Colons

**Colons** are marks of introduction: what follow are explanations, conclusions, amplifications, lists or series, or quotations. A colon is always preceded by a main clause, one that can stand alone as a sentence. A main clause may or may not follow a colon.

> Help was on the way: Someone had called the police.

> Sandra had two assignments: a five-page paper and a book report.

> The mayor stepped to the podium: "I regretfully must submit my resignation."

Colons should appear only at the end of a main clause. They should never directly follow a verb or a preposition.

| | |
|---|---|
| **Incorrect:** | The hours of the museum are: 10:00 A.M. to 6:00 P.M. |
| **Correct:** | The hours of the museum are 10:00 A.M. to 6:00 P.M. |
| **Incorrect:** | Marc loved many sports, such as: soccer, tennis, and softball. |
| **Correct:** | Marc loved many sports, such as soccer, tennis, and softball. |

As with any punctuation mark, use colons only when they best serve your writing purpose. Do not overuse them.

## 5. Parentheses

**Parentheses** tell the reader that the idea is an afterthought or is outside the main idea of a sentence.

> The tort involved a banana peel (the classic culprit) and a crowded grocery store.

Use parentheses infrequently because they tend to break the flow of the sentence.

## 6. Double Quotation Marks

These marks enclose direct quotations.

> The judge said, "The trial date will not be continued."

Note that the first word of the quotation should be capitalized if it is a complete sentence.

## 7. Single Quotation Marks

These marks are used to define a quotation within a quotation.

> The client told the lawyer, "My boss said, 'You cannot be a good accountant and be a good mother,' and then he fired me."

If you end a quotation with quoted words, you place a single quotation mark and follow it with a double quotation mark.

> The witness testified, "The robber said, 'Give me all your money.'"

# B. MODIFIERS

**Modifiers** provide a description about a subject, a verb, or an object in your sentence. If you misplace a modifier, you might confuse your reader or convey an incorrect message. A modifier should be placed in proximity to the subject, verb, or object it modifies.

**Incorrect:** Deadlocked for more than two days, the judge asked the jury to continue to deliberate.

**Correct:** The jury had been deadlocked for two days. Nonetheless, the judge asked the jury to continue to deliberate.

In the first example, the phrase *deadlocked for more than two days* incorrectly modifies the judge rather than the jury. This is a dangling modifier.

# C. PARALLEL CONSTRUCTION

**Parallel construction** is when you make each of the phrases within your sentence follow the same grammatical pattern or number. A plural subject must have a plural verb. A singular subject must have a singular verb. You also must use parallel tenses when you are listing a series of activities. A parallel grammatical pattern makes your writing balanced.

**Incorrect:** The paralegal association set the following goals: recruitment of new members, educating the community, and improvement of paralegal work conditions.

**Correct:** The paralegal association set the following goals: recruitment of new members, education of the community, and improvement of paralegal work conditions.

In the correct example, the words *recruitment, education,* and *improvement* are parallel.

# D. SUBJECT AND VERB AGREEMENT

Subject and verb agreement, so essential to proper sentence construction, causes great confusion for many writers. The following are sample situations in which errors are most often made. You must use plural pronouns and verbs when the subjects are plural.

**Incorrect:** Software Developments Inc. sent Cheryl Faith, a company sales representative, and Nicholas Tallis, their plant manager, to Bailey's plant.

**Correct:** Software Developments Inc. sent Cheryl Faith, a company sales representative, and Nicholas Tallis, its plant manager, to Bailey's plant.

The second example is correct because *Software Developments Inc.* is a singular subject; therefore, the pronoun before *plant manager* should be the singular possessive *its* rather than *their*.

**Incorrect:** To assert the attorney-client privilege, the claimant must show that the statements were made in confidence and was made to an attorney for the purpose of obtaining legal advice.

**Correct:** To assert the attorney-client privilege, the claimant must show that the statements were made in confidence and were made to an attorney for the purpose of obtaining legal advice.

The second example is correct because the verbs must be plural when they have a plural noun. In this example, the word *statements* should have a plural verb.

If you have a singular subject, then each of the pronouns in the sentence that describes that subject should be singular.

**Incorrect:** To receive this protection in the corporate setting, an individual must show that they were a decision-making employee.

**Correct:** To receive this protection in the corporate setting, an individual must show that he or she was a decision-making employee.

**Collective nouns** such as *jury, court, committee,* and *group* often pose a problem for writers. They take a singular verb because they are considered one unit. For example, *jury* is considered one unit; it refers to the group, not to individual jurors.

**Incorrect:** The jury were to eat lunch at noon.
**Correct:** The jury was to eat lunch at noon.

**Compound subjects** also cause confusion. Subjects joined by the word *and* usually use a plural verb, regardless of whether any or all of the individual subject are singular.

**Incorrect:** The attorney and the paralegal was available for the client.
**Correct:** The attorney and the paralegal were available for the client.

When a compound subject is preceded by *each* or *every*, the verb is usually singular.

**Incorrect:** Each attorney and paralegal in the room have access to the library.
**Correct:** Each attorney and paralegal in the room has access to the library.

When a compound subject is joined by *or* or *nor*, it takes a singular verb if each subject is singular. It takes a plural verb if each subject is plural. If one subject is singular and the other is plural, the verb follows the closest subject.

**Subjects singular:** An apple or an orange is my favorite snack.
**Subjects plural:** Apples or oranges are my favorite snacks.

**Subjects singular and plural:** Neither the mother nor the children were happy.

To avoid awkwardness, place the plural noun closest to the verb so that the verb is plural.

**Awkward:** Neither the dogs nor the cat was anywhere in sight.
**Revised:** Neither the cat nor the dogs were anywhere in sight.

**Indefinite pronouns** may also throw up roadblocks for writers. Indefinite pronouns are those that do not refer to a specific person or thing. Some common indefinite pronouns are

| | |
|---|---|
| all | nobody |
| any | none |
| anyone | nothing |
| each | one |
| either | some |
| everyone | something |

Most indefinite pronouns refer to singular subjects and therefore take a singular verb.

**Incorrect:** Everyone are free to go. Each of the stores were open on Sunday.
**Correct:** Everyone is free to go. Each of the stores was open on Sunday.

Some indefinite pronouns (all, any, none, some) may take either a singular or plural verb depending on the meaning of the word they refer to.

**Singular:** All of the library was quiet. (The library was quiet.)
**Plural:** All of the paralegals were researching the case. (The paralegals were researching the case.)

## E. RUN-ON SENTENCES

A run-on sentence is one in which two separate sentences are connected by using a comma or are sentences without punctuation. Be careful not to use commas to divide run-on sentences. The first example below should be two separate sentences.

**Incorrect:** Tildy's role is merely advisory, although she might be asked to supply facts about the spill, her opinion probably would not form the basis of any final decision.

**Correct:** Tildy's role is merely advisory. Although she might be asked to supply facts about the spill, her opinion probably would not form the basis of any final decision.

In the second example, the two sentences are correctly separated with a period. You also could use a semicolon to fix the sentence. For some run-on sentences, you could divide the sentences with a comma and a conjunction such as **and**. In the above example, that solution would not cure the problem because the second sentence is too long.

# F. SENTENCE FRAGMENTS

A sentence fragment is a piece of a sentence. It is an incomplete statement as it lacks either a subject or a verb.

**Incorrect:** The judge presiding over the case.
**Correct:** The judge was presiding over the case.

Check to see if a sentence has a verb and a subject. If one is missing, add it.

**Incorrect:** A case on point.
**Correct:** The attorney cited a case on point.

# G. THAT AND WHICH

Whether to use that or which depends on whether the clause that follows is essential to convey the meaning of the sentences. If the clause cannot be omitted, use **that**. If the clause can be omitted and the sentence meaning will not change, then use **which**. As stated earlier, a clause that can be omitted or that contains superfluous information is set off with commas. A clause that is essential should not be surrounded by commas.

## CHAPTER SUMMARY

This chapter reviewed basic grammar rules concerning punctuation, modifiers, parallel construction, and subject-verb agreement. It emphasized the importance correct grammar plays in legal writing by demonstrating how errors like incorrect punctuation, misplaced modifiers, and faulty subject-verb agreement can affect meaning.

## KEY TERMS

collective nouns

colons

commas

compound subjects

indefinite pronouns

modifiers

parallel construction

parentheses

semicolons

## EXERCISES

Edit the following sentences. Name the grammar mistake in each sentence (e.g., misplaced modifier, faulty parallelism, and so forth). Then correct the error by rewriting the sentence.

1. At a time when many law firms and corporations are eliminating jobs for the purpose of elimination from the budget excess expenditures, paralegals may become more of an asset.
2. Because of the fact that paralegals' time is charged at lower rates, paralegals may be employed by law firms and corporations to perform tasks previously performed by lawyers.
3. With specificity, paralegals may be asked to perform legal research of case and statutory materials in the event that a client requests an answer to a problem of a legal nature and is concerned about saving money.
4. In the situation where a paralegal is well trained, that paralegal can be asked by an attorney to perform legal research for the purpose of determining a response to the client's question.
5. With regard to ethical considerations, paralegals can perform legal research under the supervision of an attorney.
6. Subsequent to the research, however, the attorney must be the person who renders the legal opinions that need to be made, the reason being that a paralegal cannot provide legal advice.
7. It is important to note that some states are considering allowing paralegals to practice independently.
8. Try this schedule; shower, eat breakfast, drive to the train, go to work, and come home.
9. There are only one hour and thirty-five minutes left to voir dire, the judge stated.
10. Among the defendants was Max Craig, Sam Harris, and Ricki Anya.
11. The prosecutor will attempt to within the course of the trial persuade you that the defendant committed the crime.
12. The foreman, as well as half of the jury, were late for the afternoon court session.
13. Every one of the councilmen we have named to the commission want to serve.
14. The heart of a trial are the witnesses.
15. None of the players were willing to sign contracts.
16. The substance of Walter Mondale's speeches is more similar to Jimmy Carter.

17. The house was vacated by the tenants.
18. The judge said to the jurors, "please refrain from discussing the case."
19. Four of the five jurors were men (These were Steer, Halsey, Grodsky, and Molitor.).
20. In her testimony, the witness said she remembered that the defendant asked her "Do you have an aspirin"?
21. These modems are shared with the other subscribers, so the more people on the connection the slower.
22. Working at a law firm from 8:30 A.M. to 5 P.M. handling high-level paralegal work may seem ideal, especially if you rarely work weekends.
23. The National Association of Paralegals said 12 percent of the law firms responded to their survey.
24. Mrs. Newman, at first thought her son, Patrick, was dead because of the amount of blood and broken bones that surrounded the car.
25. The extent of the employer's control and supervision over the worker, including directions on scheduling and performance of work.
26. In the line up the man which was wearing a red shirt committed the crime.
27. The judge based her decision on the case which had a similar set of facts.
28. The juror in green.
29. The judge's clerks draft opinions.
30. Law clerks Robert and Karen each wrote a motion. Robert and Karen's motions were excellent.

## CHAPTER 18

# CASE BRIEFING AND ANALYSIS

| | |
|---|---|
| **A. PURPOSE OF A CASE BRIEF** | 378 |
| **B. DIAGRAM OF A DECISION** | 378 |
| **C. ANATOMY OF A CASE BRIEF** | 381 |
|   1. Citation | 381 |
|   2. Procedural History | 384 |
|   3. Issues | 386 |
|   4. Holding | 388 |
|   5. Facts | 389 |
|   6. Reasoning | 392 |
|   7. Dicta | 394 |
|   8. Disposition | 394 |
| **D. CASE ANALYSIS** | 405 |
|   1. Sample Single Case Analysis | 405 |
|   2. Sample Analysis Using Two Cases | 412 |

## CHAPTER OVERVIEW

This chapter teaches you how to brief a case and how to apply a case to a specific fact pattern. Applying a case to a specific fact pattern is case analysis and is used to predict how a court may resolve an issue. The chapter discusses the components of a case brief: the issue, the holding, the facts, the rationale or reasoning, and the disposition. You will learn what to include in each section of the brief and how to skillfully draft the brief.

This chapter also teaches you how to use cases to perform legal analysis.

## CASE BRIEFING, IN GENERAL

Case briefing is a skill that you must master to effectively record your research results and analyze a case. Often attorneys will ask you to summarize a case in the form of a case brief. The key to a good brief is that it must be usable. You must be able to return to the brief months after you have prepared it and still be able to quickly understand the facts, the issues, the holdings, and the reasoning of the court.

A good case brief can be done in a variety of ways. Always ask an attorney if he or she has a preference. If not, you should consider the method discussed in this chapter.

# A. PURPOSE OF A CASE BRIEF

The goal in writing a **case brief** is to summarize a court decision. A well-drafted brief saves you time because you do not have to reread the original decision to understand its significance. You are able to review the brief to obtain any necessary information. The next goal in briefing a case is to put the components of a decision in a uniform format. This is why we have specified eight set categories for a brief: citation, procedural facts, issues, holding, facts, rationale, dicta, and disposition. The rationale contains the basis for the judge's opinion. The judge relies on the relevant legal rule to support her holding. The legal rule is the test, principle, or standard set down in prior opinions. However, many attorneys use their own uniform format, and sometimes that format will depend on why you are briefing a case.

Sometimes you must brief cases in response to a particular legal issue that you are researching. Sometimes you must brief cases just to summarize decisions.

Remember that a brief is a case summary in a uniform format with established categories of information. The set categories make it easier to compare and contrast decisions. Also, this enables you to see how a case supports a client's problem.

# B. DIAGRAM OF A DECISION

Before you begin to write your brief, read the case thoroughly several times. See Illustration 18-1. Consider the questions the court was asked to decide. Determine the parties in the action and what each party is seeking. Sometimes this is complicated, and it helps to draw a diagram of the parties. For example, when the parties are involved in a three-way dispute such as a cross-claim, it might take some time to determine what each party is seeking. Make a column for each party in which you list an

issue raised and a remedy sought. After you have read the case, you are ready to write the case brief.

## ILLUSTRATION 18-1.  Sample Case, *Seymour v. Armstrong*

---

612                                64 PACIFIC REPORTER.                                (Kan.

**(1)** (62 Kan. 720)

**(2)**  SEYMOUR v. ARMSTRONG et al. **(3)**

(Supreme Court of Kansas.  April 6, 1901.)

CONTRACT—VALIDITY—CONSTRUCTION—
EVIDENCE.

**(4)** 1. A contract may originate in an advertisement or offer addressed to the public generally, and, if the offer be accepted by any one in good faith, without qualifications or conditions, it will be sufficient to convert the offer into a binding obligation.

2. If the acceptor affixes conditions to his acceptance not comprehended in the proposal, there can be no agreement without the assent of the proposer to such conditions.

3. If persons carrying on a trade or business give to words and phrases a technical or peculiar meaning, they will be presumed to have contracted with reference to such meaning or usage, unless the contrary appears.

4. Where a term employed in a written contract has a meaning different from the ordinary meaning when used in connection with a trade or business, evidence is admissible to show such meaning, and the sense in which it was used by the parties.

(Syllabus by the Court.)

Error from court of appeals, Northern department, Eastern division.

Action by T. F. Seymour against Armstrong & Kassebaum. Judgment for defendants was affirmed by the court of appeals (61 Pac. 675), and plaintiff brings error. Affirmed.

J. A. Rosen and David Martin, for plaintiff in error. Isenhart & Alexander, for defendants in error.

**(5)**  JOHNSTON, J.  This was an action to recover damages for the breach of an alleged
**(6)** contract. On February 15, 1896, Armstrong & Kassebaum, commission merchants of Topeka,
**(7)** inserted an advertisement in a weekly newspaper, which, among other things, contained the following proposition: "We will pay 10½c., net Topeka, for all fresh eggs shipped us to arrive here by February 22. Acceptance of our bid with number of cases stated to be sent by February 20th." On February 20, 1896, T. F. Seymour, a rival commission merchant of Topeka, sent the following note to Armstrong & Kassebaum in response to their proposition: "I accept your offer in Merchants' Journal, 10½ cents, Topeka, for fresh eggs, and will ship you on C., R. I. & P. R. R. 450 cases fresh eggs, to arrive on or before February 22d. The eggs are all packed in new No. 2 white wood cases, and I will accept 15 cents each for them, or you can return them, or new ones in place of them." On receipt of this note, Armstrong & Kassebaum at once notified Seymour that they would not accept the eggs on the terms proposed by him. Notwithstanding the refusal, Seymour pro-

cured a car, and loaded it with eggs. Not having a sufficient number of eggs to fill the car, Seymour found two other commission merchants who were willing to co-operate with him, and who furnished 190 of the 450 cases, which were loaded in Topeka, only a few hundred feet away from the place of business of Armstrong & Kassebaum, sealed up, and then pushed a short distance over to their business house. They refused to receive the eggs, and Seymour shipped them to Philadelphia, where they were sold for $391.83 less than they would have brought at the price named in Seymour's note of acceptance. For this amount the present action was brought, and the plaintiff is entitled to recover if the defendants' offer on eggs was unconditionally accepted. At the trial a verdict was returned **(8)** in favor of the defendants, and the result of the general finding is that the pretended acceptance of Seymour was not unconditional, and that no contract was, in fact, made **(10A)** between him and the defendants.

Did the negotiations between the parties result in a contract? A contract may originate in an advertisement addressed to the public generally, and, if the proposal be accepted by any one in good faith, without qualifications or conditions, the contract is complete. The fact that there was no limit as to number or quantity of eggs in the **(9)** offer did not prevent an acceptance. The number or quantity was left to the determination of the acceptor, and an unconditional acceptance naming any reasonable number or quantity is sufficient to convert **(11A)** the offer into a binding obligation. It is essential, however, that the minds of the contracting parties should come to the point of agreement,—that the offer and acceptance should coincide; and, if they do not correspond in every material respect, there is no acceptance or completed contract. In our view, the so-called "acceptance" of the plaintiff is not absolute and unconditional. It affixed conditions not comprehended in the proposal, and there could be no agreement without the assent of the proposer to such **(9)** conditions. It is true, the plaintiff agreed to furnish eggs at 10½ cents per dozen, but his acceptance required the defendant to pay 15 cents each for the cases in which the eggs were packed, or to return the cases, or new ones in place of them. It appears from the record that according to the usages of the business the cases go with the eggs, as was done in this case.

One of the grounds of complaint is that **(10B)** the court erred in admitting testimony as to the sense in which the word "net" was used in the negotiations between the parties, and in submitting to the jury the question of whether the offer of the defendants was accepted. The plaintiff is hardly in a position to question the propriety of receiving evidence as to the meaning of the word "net," used in the offer and acceptance.

## ILLUSTRATION 18-1. *Continued*

Kan.) CITY OF KANSAS CITY v. SMILEY. 613

He was the first to open an inquiry, and to bring out testimony as to what was meant by the term when used in connection with a sale of eggs. Aside from that consideration, the term appears to have a meaning in connection with the business different from the ordinary meaning, and in such case evidence of the meaning given by usage of the trade or business is admissible. If persons carrying on a particular trade or business give to words or phrases a technical or peculiar meaning, they will be presumed to contract with reference to the usage, unless the contrary appears. There was abundant evidence to show that the use of the word "net," according to the usage of the business, includes the cases of eggs like the one in question. The witnesses stated that it was a price clear to the purchaser without commissions, cartage, or any charge for cases. The finding of the jury, in effect, that it was understood and agreed that the cases went with and were included in the price quoted for the eggs, and the acceptance, therefore, did not correspond with the offer, nor complete the contract. We think that under the circumstances parol testimony of the sense in which the terms were used, and as to what the parties intended by them, was properly received, and that the court properly charged the jury as to the elements entering into a contract. Cosper v. Nesbit, 45 Kan. 457, 25 Pac. 866. Others of the instructions are criticised, but we find nothing substantial in any of the objections made nor in any of the grounds assigned for reversal. The judgment of the court of appeals and the district court will be affirmed. All the justices concurring.

| | |
|---|---|
| 1 | Citation |
| 2 | Case name |
| 3 | Date of decision |
| 4 | Syllabus by court |
| 5 | Judge's name authoring the opinion |
| 6 | Opinion |
| 7 | Facts |
| 8 | Procedure |
| 9 | Rationale or reasoning |
| 10A | Issue 1 |
| 10B | Issue 2 |
| 11A | Holding 1 |
| 11B | Holding 2 |
| 12 | Disposition |

Reprinted with permission of Thomson Reuters.

Write the brief in your own words and paraphrase rather than quote a court's statements unless the statements are well phrased, concise, and understandable. Paraphrasing the information from the cases helps you analyze a case and allows you to understand the brief quickly when you return to it later. Also, paraphrasing cases helps when you are writing about an opinion in a memo. The memo will read more smoothly if you use your own voice when you import the information from case brief rather than using quoted language from the opinion.

## IN-CLASS EXERCISE

Compare the writing styles in the *Molitor* and the *Morganroth* decisions in this chapter. You will notice that the writing styles differ. If you paraphrase the points from the cases, your writing will be smoother. Use your own language but always provide citations to authority.

# C. ANATOMY OF A CASE BRIEF

Because a brief is a summary of a decision in a uniform format, there are set categories. You should label the remaining sections of the brief: citation, procedural history or procedure, issue, holding, rationale (which includes the legal rule or standard), dicta (if it exists in the case), and disposition.

## 1. Citation

The case brief starts with a **case citation**, which allows you to find the case at a later date. First, note the name of the case, which is generally found at the top of the page. Then add the case citation or docket number of the case. See Illustration 18-2. Be sure to include the date of the decision and the name of the deciding court. Next, you might want to make a note concerning whether the decision is primary binding or primary persuasive authority. (For more information about binding and persuasive authority, see Chapter 2.) Follow either *Bluebook* or *ALWD* rules for case citation format.

*NET NOTE*

Important tips for briefing cases can be found at cjed.com/brief.htm.

*PRACTICE POINTER*

Obtain all of the citation information when you are using the reporter or have accessed the case online. Once you record all of the citation information in the brief, you will not have to revisit the decision later to get the cite information.

**ILLUSTRATION 18-2.  Sample Case,** *King v. Miller*

### *KING v. MILLER*

1000 E.R. 108 (Karen Ct. App. 2011)

Evelyn King, an insurance agent who worked for the defendant, Miller Company, filed a lawsuit claiming that the defendant discriminated against her on the basis of her sex in violation of Title VII, 42 U.S.C. § 2000e et seq. Upon a motion for summary judgment, the district court granted the motion in favor of Miller. The district court found that King

## ILLUSTRATION 18-2. *Continued*

was not an employee of the defendant. She did not work in a manner consistent with an employee. The court said that King was an independent contractor. As an independent contractor, her discrimination claim was outside the protection of the federal law. King appealed the trial court's decision.

In 2009, King was hired by Miller to work as an "employee agent." As such, she was paid a salary. Income taxes and Social Security were withheld by Miller. She was promoted to "independent contract agent." King could not remain an employee agent for more than one year. When she was promoted she had to sign an agreement that stated that she was an independent contractor.

As an independent contract agent, King earned a commission on her sales and some bonuses. She did not receive any paid holidays, sick days, or vacation days. She paid for her own health, life, and disability insurance.

Miller, however, provided office space, furniture, file cabinets, rate books, forms, shared secretarial services, stamps, computers, and Miller's stationery. King purchased her own personalized stationery, pens, and business cards. Miller paid King's tuition for required special insurance seminars, provided lunch at such programs, and rented the space for the sessions.

King had wanted to work for Miller because Miller had a good reputation. Before coming to Miller's office, King worked for three other insurance companies. King was a single, 30-year-old mother of two children. Before her experience in the insurance industry, she worked as a sales clerk at a local boutique.

While working as an independent contract agent for Miller, King could not sell insurance for any other company. She also could only sell insurance in the county designated by the company manager. She had to work at the Miller office three and one-half days a week and every third Saturday, attend two hour-long meetings each week, and retrieve mail every day.

King was responsible for finding her own customers and deciding which products to offer. She could set the hours she worked and she worked without direct supervision. Miller did not regularly review her work. King was fired in 2010, and a man was hired to take her place.

The district court found that based upon these facts, King was an independent contractor, not an employee. The court focused on the economic realities test. One of the factors it considered as part of its test for determining whether King was an employee or an independent contractor was Miller's right to control King. *Spirides v. Reinhardt,* 613 F.2d 826, 831 (D.C. Cir. 1979), is the leading case regarding the question of whether an individual is an employee, or an independent contractor, under the federal discrimination laws. The *Spirides* court adopted an 11-part test. These factors are:

> 1) the kind of occupation, whether the work is usually done under the direction of a supervisor or without a supervisor; 2) the skill required;

**ILLUSTRATION 18-2.** *Continued*

3) whether the "employer" provides the equipment used and the work-place; 4) how long the individual has worked; 5) how the individual is paid, whether by assignment, piece, or time; 6) how the work relationship is to be terminated, i.e., was notice required; 7) whether vacation is provided; 8) whether retirement benefits are provided; 9) whether the employer deducts social security and income tax payments; 10) whether the work is an integral part of the employer's business; and 11) the intention of the parties.

*Id.*

The Karen district court focused on five of those factors: 1) the extent of Miller's control and supervision of King concerning scheduling and performance of work; 2) the kind of occupation and the nature of the skill required; 3) the division of the costs of the operation, equipment, supplies, and fees; 4) the method and form of payment and benefits; 5) length of job commitment. Central to its decision was the lack of control Miller exercised over King. The court found that King had a great deal of freedom to select her hours, her clients, and the insurance products she sold.

King must prove that an employment relationship existed between herself and Miller in order to maintain a Title VII action against Miller. Independent contractors are not protected by Title VII. *Spirides*, 613 F.2d at 831. Title VII defines employee "as an individual employed by an employer." 42 U.S.C § 2000E(f). "In determining whether the relationship is one of employee-employer, courts look to the 'economic realities' of the relationship and the degree of control the employer exercises over the alleged employee." See *Unger v. Consolidated Foods Corp.*, 657 F.2d 909, 915-916 n.8 (7th Cir. 1981).

On appeal, King contends that the district court placed too much weight on the "control factor" and the fact the Miller did not supervise King's work and did not dictate King's hours, products or customers. Based upon this emphasis, King argues that the district court's decision was erroneous.

However, this court finds that the district court correctly considered other facts such as that King was paid on commission, did not receive benefits, and provided many of her own supplies, including stationery and business cards.

Although this court was not asked to determine whether the district court should have considered all of the facts that were relevant to each of the 11 factors stated in the *Spirides'* economic realities test, this court finds that the district court should have done so.

Although we think that the district court should have focused its analysis on all 11 factors, we do not think that its decision is clearly erroneous; therefore, we affirm the decision of the district court in granting summary judgment for the defendant, Miller.

## 2. Procedural History

This section of the case brief should be labeled **procedural history** or simply procedure. These facts explain the status of the case. You will summarize how this case traveled through the court system to reach this point. See Illustration 18-3. In this section, you note the action of the prior courts. For example, if the decision concerns an appeal to a federal appellate court, note that. Also, state whether the court reversed or affirmed the lower court's decision and whether the case was remanded.

---

### *PRACTICE POINTER*

Always validate any case that you brief by using *Shepard's* or KeyCite. Note the date validated at the top of the brief so that you know to update if necessary.

---

**ILLUSTRATION 18-3.   Sample Case Brief, *King v. Miller***

### *KING v. MILLER*

1000 E.R. 108 (Karen Ct. App. 2011)

PROCEDURAL HISTORY
    The case was on appeal from the District Court's grant of summary judgment for the defendant Miller.

ISSUE
    Is King, a worker subject to only minimal company control and who was paid commissions rather than a salary and benefits, an employee protected by Title VII or an independent contractor who is outside the protection of the federal law?

HOLDING
    King, a worker subject to only minimal company control and who was paid commissions rather than a salary and benefits, was an independent contractor rather than an employee protected by Title VII.

FACTS
    King first worked for Miller as an employee agent. During that time, she received a salary and the company withheld income tax and social security payments. King later was promoted to independent contract agent.
    As an independent contract agent, King earned a commission and bonuses but did not receive a salary. She signed an agreement that stated that she was an independent contractor. As a contract agent, she did not receive paid holidays, sick days, or vacation days, and she

**ILLUSTRATION 18-3.** *Continued*

paid for her own health, life, and disability insurance. King supplied her own personalized stationery, business cards, and pens. She found her own customers, decided which products to sell, and set her own hours.

For its contract agents, Miller supplied office space, furniture, file cabinets, forms, shared secretarial services, stamps, computers, and stationery. Miller also paid for required insurance seminars. Miller required that contract agents, such as King, attend weekly meetings, work in the office three and one-half days per week and every third Saturday, check their mail and retrieve messages daily, and sell only Miller insurance. Miller also restricted King's sales area. Miller did not regularly review King's work.

REASONING

In order to determine whether an individual is an employee or an independent contractor, the employment relationship between the parties needs to be evaluated based upon the economic realities and circumstances of the relationship. The court considered the control exercised by the "employer" over the worker; the method of payment; who paid for the individual's benefits, such as life and health insurance; and who paid for the operation. In this case, the court found that King was an independent contractor because she was paid on commission, she paid for her own benefits, she supplied her own supplies, and she controlled her work. The court found that she set her own hours, selected the product she sold, and generated her own clients. Based upon these facts, the appellate court found that King should be considered an independent contractor rather than an employee.

DICTA

The 11-part test set by the *Spirides* court should be applied to determine whether an individual is an employee or an independent contractor.

DISPOSITION

The Court of Appeals affirmed the district court's judgment in granting summary judgment for the defendant.

---

*PRACTICE POINTER*

Obtain all of the citation information when you are using the reporter or accessing the case online. Record all of the citation information in the brief, including the precise pages where you obtained the information, the pin cites. Write the cites in *Bluebook* or *ALWD* format. Later, when writing, you will not have to revisit the decision to get the cite information.

## 3. Issues

Next, list the **issue** or issues presented in the case. See Illustration 18-3. Although determining the issues in a case is a difficult process at first, it does get easier with practice.

The issues are the questions the parties asked the court to decide. In most cases, multiple issues are presented. To determine the issues, you must understand the legal rules that govern a particular case. If you are briefing a case and you have not been assigned an issue to research, list all the issues presented in the case. If you have been given a research assignment, you need only brief the issues that are relevant to your research, listing each one separately.

### ▼ How Do You Determine the Legal Issue or Issues Presented When Examining a Client's Problem?

To understand this process, assume you have been asked to research whether your firm's client, Whole In One, will be subject to the federal antidiscrimination laws. Whole In One is a seasonal restaurant and golf course in Glenview, Illinois. Two women, Victoria Radiant and Karen Walker, brought suit against Whole In One for sex discrimination. Their claims are based on a federal antidiscrimination statute commonly known as Title VII. You have been asked to research whether Whole In One is an employer and whether the women are employees under the definitions included in the federal law. During your research, you find the case of *King v. Miller*. Review Illustration 18-2.

To determine the issue, read the case. Ask yourself, "What did the parties ask the court to determine?" Sometimes the court will note the issue directly in its opinion. Other times, you must search through the opinion to determine the issue. After you have read the *King* case, you should note that it involves a question of sex discrimination. However, your research is limited to the issues that concern the definitions of *employer* and *employee*. Therefore, the case brief should focus on issues that relate to your research problem.

Once you have read the *King* case, you will find that it addresses the question of whether an individual is an employee protected by Title VII. Now you are ready to draft the issue.

### ▼ How Do You Draft a Statement of the Issue or Issues?

For the *King* case, you might start with this brief issue:

> Is King an employee protected by Title VII or an independent contractor who is outside the protection of the federal law?

Now that the issue is presented in question format, you could leave the issue section here. However, the issue would be more meaningful for your research if you included more information about the legal

issue the court focused on in making its determination. In its discussion, the *King* court focused on the amount of control that an employer must exercise before an individual is viewed as an employee rather than an independent contractor. You could incorporate the court's focus on control into the issue as follows:

> Is King, a worker subject to only minimal company control, an employee protected by Title VII, or an independent contractor who is outside the protection of the federal law?

You also should include relevant facts in your issue statement. Again, this will make the issue more meaningful for your research. In this case, for example, you might add some facts about the company's method of payment and its lack of provisions for benefits:

> Is King, a worker subject to only minimal company control who was paid commissions rather than salary and benefits, an employee protected by Title VII or an independent contractor who is outside the protection of the federal law?

The final issue statement is the best because it incorporates the relevant facts that affect a court's decision concerning this issue and the **rule of law** that will be applied.

You might wonder why the issue did not focus on the appellate court's consideration of the district court's action in granting the motion for summary judgment in favor of the defendant. Students often phrase such an issue as follows:

> Did the district court err in granting summary judgment in favor of the defendant?

However, this issue focuses too heavily on the procedural question posed in the *King* case and does not include the applicable law or any of the legally significant facts. Your issue should concern the legal, not the procedural, questions a court was asked to decide. As you learned above, the *King* case involved a motion for summary judgment.

To find the substantive legal issue, determine the legal question the parties asked the court to answer in the motion for summary judgment. In the *King* case, the parties asked the court to determine whether, as a matter of law, King was an independent contractor rather than an employee. This is the central legal issue. By focusing on this substantive issue rather than the procedural issue, your brief will be more useful to you in your research of the *Whole In One* case.

Some of you might wonder why you do not focus on the question of discrimination in your issue section. Remember the issue you were asked to answer with your research. You were asked to deal with the issues of the definitions of *employee* and *employer*. You should tailor your brief to address only these issues.

## 4. Holding

The next section should be your **holding.** Essentially a holding is the court's answer to the issue or question presented. However, it is not a yes, no, or maybe answer to the issue. The holding should be a full sentence that responds directly to the issue posed and that incorporates both the legal standards and the most significant legal facts on which the answer is based. A holding differs from a legal rule in that a legal rule is the standard, test, or principle that the court uses in its rationale, or reasoning, to explain its holding. The holding addresses the specific question before the court.

### ▼ How Do You Draft a Holding?

The process for drafting the holding is similar to the process for writing your issue statement. First, your holding should be a statement that answers the issue. Assume you selected the first issue statement considered in this discussion:

> Is King an employee protected by Title VII or an independent contractor who is outside the protection of the federal law?

You might consider answering it as follows:

> King is an independent contractor rather than an employee and therefore is outside the protection of Title VII.

While this statement is simple and direct, similar to the first issue statement, it does not contain any relevant facts or incorporate any legal standards. This holding should be rewritten, incorporating the elements or legal standards that would be considered. Such a change would make the holding more meaningful in the context of this research.

The rewritten issue, for which we will draft a holding, could read:

> Is King, a worker subject to only minimal company control, an independent contractor or is she an employee protected by Title VII?

Again, you might want to include additional facts the court considered in determining that King was an independent contractor. For the holding, rewrite the final issue statement drafted above in the form of a statement.

> King, a worker subject to only minimal company control who was paid commissions rather than salary and benefits, was an independent contractor rather than an employee protected by Title VII.

The key to drafting a clear issue statement, holding, or any other component of the brief, is rewriting and editing. You must make your holding broad enough so that it could be useful for various research projects involving different fact patterns. However, a clear holding

incorporates facts from the case at hand that make it unique and that limit the holding so that you can understand the facts that form the basis for the court's decision. These facts are the **legally significant facts.** Also, try to make the statement of the holding narrow enough so that it reflects the unique legal issue in the case. Refine your statements and assess whether they are helpful in your research summary.

Also, be careful to incorporate the facts and the underlying law into your holding statement, as you did in your issue statement. A holding such as:

> The district court did not err in granting summary judgment in favor of the defendant.

is not valuable for your research. It does not explain why the court found that the district court's decision was correct.

## 5. Facts

The next section of the brief should be the **facts.** Be certain to include the names of the parties, a notation concerning whether the party is a plaintiff, a defendant, an appellant, or appellee, and some details about the party, such as whether it is a corporation or an individual. State the relevant rather than procedural facts in this section. Also, explain why a party sought legal assistance.

### ▼ What Are the Relevant Facts?

**Relevant facts** are those facts that may have an effect on the legal issues decided in a particular action. To write this section, you must clearly understand the issues decided by the court. Decide which facts the court relied on to make its decision. Those are the facts that you should include in this section. The facts should be presented in a paragraph form rather than in a list or in bullet points. Also, mention any facts that will assist you in understanding the relationship between the parties and the nature of the dispute.

In the *King* case, the court relied on facts that explained the relationship between King and the Miller Co. For example, the court considered that King earned commissions and bonuses rather than a salary. That fact should be listed. Before you write your facts statement in paragraph format, make a rough outline of all the facts that the court considered in making its decision. Sometimes a chronological timeline helps when organizing the facts. For the *King* case, your outline might look like this:

> King first worked as an "employee" agent
>> As an employee agent, King was paid salary, and the company withheld taxes
>
> King later was designated an "independent contract" agent, earned commission and bonuses but no salary

King signed an agreement that she was an independent contractor

Did not receive paid holidays, sick days, or vacation

Paid for her own health, life, and disability insurance

Miller supplied office space, furniture, file cabinets, forms, shared secretarial services, stamps, computers, and Miller stationery

Miller paid for insurance seminars and lunches at the seminars

Miller required that King attend weekly meetings, work in the office three and one-half days per week and every third Saturday, check her mail and retrieve messages daily, and sell only

Miller insurance

Miller restricted King's sales area

Miller did not regularly review King's work

King supplied her own personalized stationery, business cards, pens

King found her own customers, decided which products to sell, and set her own hours

The court listed additional facts, such as:

King had wanted to work for Miller because Miller had a good reputation

Before coming to Miller's office, King worked for three other insurance companies

King was a single, 30-year-old mother of two children

Before her experience in the insurance industry, she worked as a sales clerk at a local boutique

Note that for its decision the court did not consider any of the facts contained in the outline under additional facts. Therefore, they are not relevant, or legally significant, facts and should not be included in your brief. After you have made your outline and determined which facts are relevant, you should draft your facts statement in a paragraph format. A list is not as helpful as a paragraph when you want to review the brief at a later date.

### ▼ How Do You Organize Your Facts Statements?

Your facts statement could be written in chronological order, in topical order, or using a combination of the two methods. Chronological order often works best when the case involves facts that need to be placed in order according to when they occurred. For example, in a personal injury action that results from a car accident, a chronological set of facts is best. Start with the first fact that occurred and work forward.

A chronological organization for the facts in the *King* case would read as follows:

In 2009, King started to work for Miller. King first worked for Miller as an employee agent. During that time, she received a salary and the company withheld income tax and social security payments. King later was promoted to contract agent. King was fired in 2010, and a man was hired to take her place.

A topical organization is the best choice for facts that have no temporal relationship. Instead, these facts are grouped by topic or legal claim. In this case, the topic is the legal question of whether King was an independent contractor. Therefore, you would group together all the facts that relate to this question.

As an independent contract agent, King earned a commission and bonuses but did not receive a salary. She signed an agreement that stated that she was an independent contractor. As a contract agent, she did not receive paid holidays, sick days, or vacation days, and she paid for her own health, life, and disability insurance. King supplied her own personalized stationery, business cards, and pens. She found her own customers, decided which products to sell, and set her own hours.

For its independent contract agents, Miller supplied office space, furniture, file cabinets, forms, shared secretarial services, stamps, computers, and Miller stationery. Miller also paid for required insurance seminars. Miller required that contract agents, such as King, attend weekly meetings, work in the office three and one-half days per week and every third Saturday, check their mail and retrieve messages daily, and sell only Miller insurance. Miller also restricted King's sales area. Miller did not regularly review King's work.

In the *King* case, a combination of a chronological and topical organization works best. The *King* brief facts statement might read as follows:

King first worked for Miller as an employee agent. During that time she received a salary and the company withheld income tax and social security payments. King later was promoted to independent contract agent.

As an independent contract agent, King earned a commission and bonuses but did not receive a salary. She signed an agreement that stated that she was an independent contractor. As a contract agent, she did not receive paid holidays, sick days, or vacation days, and she paid for her own health, life, and disability insurance. King supplied her own personalized stationery, business cards, and pens. She found her own customers, decided which products to sell, and set her own hours.

For its contract agents, Miller supplied office space, furniture, file cabinets, forms, shared secretarial services, stamps, computers, and Miller stationery. Miller also paid for required insurance seminars. Miller required that contract agents, such as King, attend weekly meetings, work in the office three and one-half days per week and every third Saturday, check their mail and retrieve messages daily, and sell only Miller insurance. Miller also restricted King's sales area. Miller did not regularly review King's work.

The above facts statement begins with a chronological organization. It explains the beginning of the relationship between King and Miller. Next, it states all the facts that pertain to King's benefits and her control of her work. The next paragraph explains what Miller provided for the independent contract agents and what Miller required of them. Following this facts section, you should include a reasoning or rationale section in a brief.

## 6. Reasoning

In the **reasoning** or **rationale** section, you should explain the court's thought process and relevant cases or statutes, then apply the law to the facts of the case you are briefing. Essentially, you will explain the law the court relied on in making a decision and why the court reached its decision. The court will base its opinion on the relevant legal rule. The legal rule is the principle, test, or standard. Sometimes the court uses more than one rule. For example, the *King* court reviewed the definition of *employee* contained in Title VII and past case precedent, such as *Spirides v. Reinhardt,* 613 F.2d 826, 831 (D.C. Cir. 1979), and *Unger v. Consolidated Foods Corp.,* 657 F.2d 909, 915-916 n.8 (7th Cir. 1981), to determine that independent contractors are not protected by Title VII. Both of these cases are from different jurisdictions. The *Spirides* case is primary binding authority only in the District of Columbia Circuit and *Unger* is primary binding authority only within the Seventh Circuit. However, both are persuasive authorities in other circuits. Explain in this section whether the court relied on binding or persuasive authority.

You also must review a decision for any tests a court considered in making its decision. In *King,* the court considered the economic realities test. Finally, note how the court applied the law to the facts of the particular case.

For the *King* case, you might include the following reasoning section in your brief:

> To determine whether an individual is an employee or an independent contractor, the employment relationship between the parties needs to be evaluated based on the economic realities and circumstances of the relationship. The court reviewed several of the factors set forth by the District of Columbia Circuit Court in *Spirides v. Reinhardt,* 613 F.2d 826, 831 (D.C. Cir. 1979), a persuasive authority, and the economic realities of the situation as defined by the Seventh Circuit court in *Unger v. Consolidated Foods Corp.,* 657 F.2d 909, 915-916 n.8 (7th Cir. 1981), another persuasive decision. Based upon these factors, the King court considered the control exercised by the "employer" over the worker; the method of payment; who paid for the individual's benefits, such as life and health insurance; and who paid for the operation. In this case, the court found that King was an independent contractor because she was paid on commission, she paid for her own benefits, she provided her own supplies, and she controlled her work. The court found that she set her own hours, selected the

products she sold, and generated her own clients. Based on these facts, the appellate court found that King should be considered an independent contractor rather than an employee.

Or you could prepare the reasoning section without any reference to the underlying, or embedded, case law.

To determine whether an individual is an employee or an independent contractor, the employment relationship between the parties needs to be evaluated based on the economic realities and circumstances of the relationship. The *King* court considered the control exercised by the "employer" over the worker; the method of payment; who paid for the individual's benefits, such as life and health insurance; and who paid for the operation. In this case, the court found that King was an independent contractor because she was paid on commission, she paid for her own benefits, she provided her own supplies, and she controlled her work. The court found that she set her own hours, selected the products she sold, and generated her own clients. Based on these facts, the appellate court found that King should be considered an independent contractor rather than an employee.

In the reasoning section, you should include an application of the law to the facts of the case and a mini-conclusion that summarizes the court's decision. In the above example, the following section is the application of the court's reasoning to the facts of the case.

In this case, the court found that King was an independent contractor because she was paid on commission, she paid for her own benefits, she provided her own supplies, and she controlled her work. The court found that she set her own hours, selected the products she sold, and generated her own clients.

This also provides insight into the legally significant facts, so that when you examine your problem, you will look at parallel facts to determine if the client was an employee.

In the above example, the following statement is the mini-conclusion:

Based on these facts, the appellate court found that King should be considered an independent contractor rather than an employee.

In some cases, you will find that a court bases its decision on reasons other than statutes or past cases. For example, a court might consider whether its decision would be fair under the circumstances. This type of analysis is called the court's consideration of policy, which sometimes is a question of what would benefit society, such as equal rights in an educational setting. Incorporate this policy into your reasoning section whenever it is useful for your research. After the reasoning or rationale, discuss any dicta contained in the court's decision.

## 7. Dicta

If a court makes a statement concerning a question that it was not asked to answer, this statement is called **dicta.** Although dicta does not have any binding effect, it is often useful to predict how a court might decide a particular issue in the future. Therefore, you want to include any dicta that might affect your case.

In the *King* case, the court stated that it was not asked to decide whether the district court should have considered all 11 factors before it rendered its decision. However, the court stated that the district court should have based its decision on all 11 factors. This statement by the court was dicta. It is helpful for your research problem because it states the factors that this circuit court might consider in determining whether an individual is an independent contractor rather than an employee.

The dicta section for the *King* case might read as follows:

> The 11-part test set by the *Spirides* court should be applied to determine whether an individual is an employee or an independent contractor.

## 8. Disposition

The final section of your brief is the **disposition.** The disposition of a case is essentially the procedural result of the court's decision. For example, in the *King* case, the court found that the district court's decision to grant summary judgment for the defendant was correct. Therefore, the disposition section would state:

> The court of appeals affirmed the district court's judgment in granting summary judgment for the defendant.

Finally, remember to rewrite your brief, but do not spend too much time rewriting it. Use your own words rather than many quotes from the court opinions. Paraphrasing in your own words helps you analyze the case and better understand it when you review your brief in the future. Also, paraphrasing allows you to import the information from the brief into a document that you draft later. You may even cut and paste portions of a well-drafted brief into a memo. See Illustration 18-4 for an overview of the case briefing process.

---

*PRACTICE POINTER*

Reread your brief as if you were unfamiliar with the case. If you cannot understand what happened, rewrite your brief.

---

**ILLUSTRATION 18-4.   Case Briefing Process**

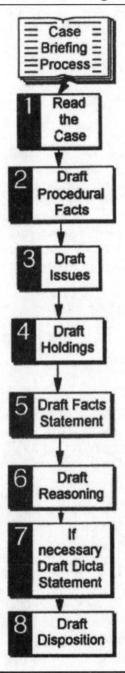

A basic overview of how to brief a case is found at www.lib.jjay.cuny.edu/ research/brief.html.

## *IN-CLASS EXERCISE*

Sometimes learning to brief can seem like an abstract exercise. The following exercise is designed to hone your brief drafting skills. It is best for students to read the illustrations for this exercise before class. Read the abridged *Molitor* case found in Illustration 18-5. Then read the case brief in Illustration 18-6. After reading the case and the brief, go back to the case and try to find where the issue, facts, holding, and reasoning were obtained. This will give you insight into the information that must be pulled from a case to write a brief.

**ILLUSTRATION 18-5.**    *Molitor v. Chicago Title & Trust Co.*

### *MOLITOR v. CHICAGO TITLE & TRUST CO.*

325 Ill. App. 124, 59 N.E.2d 695 (1945)

SCANLAN, Justice.

Robert H. Molitor, plaintiff, sued Chicago Title & Trust Company, a corporation, for breach of an employment contract, and also sued Justin M. Dall for damages resulting from the breach of the said contract because of his want of authority, if the evidence should show a want of authority. A jury returned a verdict finding the issues in favor of plaintiff and against Chicago Title & Trust Company and assessing plaintiff's damages at $15,480, and also a verdict finding the issues in favor of defendant Dall. The trial court reserved rulings on motions of defendants for directed verdicts and after verdicts sustained a motion of Chicago Title & Trust Company for judgment in its favor notwithstanding the verdict against it. Plaintiff appeals from that judgment. Judgment was entered upon the verdict in favor of defendant Dall after plaintiff's motion for a new trial had been denied. Plaintiff has not appealed from that judgment. Some days after the entry of the judgment against Chicago Title & Trust Company it entered a motion for a new trial and the trial court entered an order granting the motion, but providing that "this ruling shall not become effective unless and until the order granting the motion for judgment notwithstanding the verdict shall hereafter be reversed, vacated or set aside in the manner provided by law." Plaintiff also appeals from that judgment. . . .

. . . The complaint alleges that Chicago Title & Trust Company, on or about March 20, 1936, "desiring to continue the service of plaintiff permanently, promised and agreed that in consideration of the plaintiff

## ILLUSTRATION 18-5. *Continued*

giving up his residence in the State of New York, and giving up and forgoing all his other engagements and professional connections as aforesaid by moving his family to Cook County, State of Illinois, and thereafter devoting all his time exclusively to the service of the Company, that it would give plaintiff steady, continuous and permanent employment as an examiner of titles; that is to say, for and during the period of his natural life, or so long as said Company required the services of an examiner of titles and plaintiff was willing and able to do such work." Said defendant, in its answer, denies the aforesaid allegations. We may assume from the briefs filed by both parties that the trial court based his ruling upon the assumption that there was no evidence offered by plaintiff that tended to prove an enforceable agreement that plaintiff was to have permanent employment. . . .

. . . Observing these rules we find the following evidence: The Chicago Title & Trust Company is engaged, inter alia, in the business of insuring titles to and interests in real estate in Cook County and elsewhere. It employs a large number of men known as title examiners, who are especially trained and experienced in the law of real property and the validity of real estate titles. It depends upon the ability and integrity of these title examiners to discover defects, it there be any, in real estate titles. In the selection of title examiners it exercises great caution, and applicants for such position go through a long probationary period before they are given "continuous employment." In 1920 plaintiff applied for a position as title examiner and was employed on probation. He had theretofore been engaged in the practice of law in South Dakota. After a number of years of service as a probationer, he was made a regular examiner at a salary of $85 per week. In August, 1927, he quit the services of the defendant company and moved, with his family, to New York to take employment in the office of a former client, the new position paying him twice the salary he was getting as a title examiner. Because of the economic depression, he lost the New York position on February 1, 1933, and he then started to practice his profession in New York—having been admitted to the bar in New York—and by June, 1934, he was commencing to build up a paying practice. About that time one of the departments of defendant company, that was managed by Mr. Dall, was swamped with thousands of HOLC orders for title insurance, and speedy service was demanded. Mr. Dall, in letters and telegrams to plaintiff, asked him to reenter the employ of defendant company. Dall stated that the company was very busy with rush orders from the HOLC but that there was no profit in the business and that the work would probably last about six months. Plaintiff told Mr. Dall that since 1933 conditions had changed for the better for him and his family and that they now had an income; that from time to time he was getting law business which paid substantial fees; that his wife had a music class in New York from which she derived a substantial income every month and that he might have trouble inducing her to

## ILLUSTRATION 18-5.   *Continued*

give up her work unless plaintiff would have better prospects in Chicago than in New York. Further correspondence followed, and plaintiff finally accepted the offer of employment with the understanding that when the HOLC work gave out that Mr. Dall might be free to dispense with his services. In view of the temporary character of the agreement plaintiff decided not to move his family to Chicago. He came to Chicago on July 23, 1934, and told Mr. Dall, in a conference, that he desired to preserve his business connections in New York and to have his wife retain her music classes there, and that it would be necessary for him to be absent from his work with the defendant company when matters came up in New York that required his presence there. Mr. Dall agreed to this arrangement. Immediately following this conference plaintiff went to work for defendant company and for three or four months thereafter the title examiners were obliged to work four hours overtime every day, all day Saturdays, and some Sundays. Plaintiff spent five days in New York in the following September to attend to a legal matter in which he had been appointed referee. He was also absent from his work during the month of June, 1935, when he was conducting legal business for clients in New York and Philadelphia, and was absent again, upon like work, between December 14, 1935, and February 17, 1936. All of the absences were with the knowledge and consent of Mr. Dall. The HOLC work was tapering off in 1935, and it ended on June 12, 1936. About this time Mr. Dall was preparing for an anticipated improvement in the regular business of defendant company and he became dissatisfied with the arrangement that allowed plaintiff to be absent from his work on trips to New York, and in a conference with plaintiff it was agreed that the trips to New York caused undesirable breaks in plaintiff's work and a new arrangement as to plaintiff's employment was made. The following is plaintiff's evidence as to the agreement: Dall stated to him that the HOLC work would soon be played out but that they were looking for a big boom in regular real estate business, and he asked plaintiff to abandon his New York connections and move his family to Chicago so that he could give the company his continuous service from then on. Plaintiff replied that he would not give up his New York connections so long as there was any uncertainty about his employment in Chicago being continuous. Mr. Dall stated that two of the examiners had died, that there was now a place for plaintiff and that he could depend on the position being permanent. Plaintiff asked him what he meant by that, to which Dall replied, "You can consider yourself employed from now on—the custom here is to retain examiners as long as we can. We have men that have been here all their lives, and there is no reason why you couldn't have a job here the rest of your life." Plaintiff replied that if he could rely on that promise he would buy a house in Chicago and move his family here, that his wife had a big music class in New York and that she would refuse to move unless he had a permanent position in Chicago,

## ILLUSTRATION 18-5. *Continued*

to which Mr. Dall replied, "You can rely on it being permanent." Plaintiff then accepted the position and told Mr. Dall that he would abandon his New York connections, buy a house here, and move his family to Chicago. His salary was fixed at $70 per week. Plaintiff thereupon continued in his work with defendant company and began preparations for carrying out his part of the agreement. He abandoned all his business in New York and his wife abandoned her music classes. He bought a home at 7219 Vernon Avenue and the family moved to Chicago. The defendant company loaned plaintiff $200 to enable him to move. Plaintiff thereafter continued in the employ of defendant company under the arrangements made with Mr. Dall until March 15, 1938, when he was discharged by defendant company upon the ground that business had fallen off to such an extent that the company could not afford to hold plaintiff any longer. There was evidence tending to show that defendant company about two years prior to plaintiff's discharge employed thirteen new title examiners whose salaries averaged less than $40 per week, and that only one of the thirteen was discharged at the time of plaintiff's discharge.

In passing upon plaintiff's instant contention we must assume that defendant company promised plaintiff "permanent employment" and that plaintiff accepted employment because of that promise, and the question is, What did the parties intend by "permanent employment"?...

... "The rule is that a contract for lifetime employment will be given effect, according to its terms, if the intention of the parties to make such an agreement is clear, even though the only consideration for it, so far as the employer is concerned, is the promise of the employee to render the service called for the contract."

But the defendant contends (a): "There was no evidence that Dall had authority to enter into the alleged contract to employ plaintiff for life or that defendant company ratified the alleged contract;" and (b) "There was no evidence that defendant company acted in bad faith in discharging plaintiff." All of these contentions involve disputed questions of fact and therefore they cannot be considered in determining the instant contention of plaintiff. After a careful consideration of the question before us we have reached the conclusion that the trial court erred in entering judgment for the defendant company not withstanding the verdict for plaintiff . . .

The judgment order of the Superior Court of Cook County entered May 13, 1943, entering judgment in favor of the defendant Chicago Title & Trust Company non obstante veredicto is reversed. The judgment order of the Superior Court of Cook County entered June 3, 1943, setting aside the verdict of the jury and granting the defendant Chicago Title & Trust Company a new trial is affirmed. The cause is remanded for a new trial.

SULLIVAN, P.J., and FRIEND, J., concur.

**ILLUSTRATION 18-6.  Case Brief for *Molitor v. Chicago Title & Trust Co.***

## *MOLITOR v. CHICAGO TITLE & TRUST CO.*

325 Ill. App. 124, 59 N.E.2d 695 (1945)

PROCEDURE

Plaintiff, Molitor, appeals judgment in favor of the defendant, Chicago Title, notwithstanding the verdict and judgment granting a new trial.

ISSUE

Was there a breach of an oral contract for permanent employment when the plaintiff moved to Chicago in consideration of the defendant's promise to employ him, and when the defendant promised to employ the plaintiff for as long as he was willing and able to do the work?

HOLDING

A contract for lifetime employment is in effect if the intention of the parties is clear even if the only consideration for the contract is the promise of the employee to render the service called for by the contract.

FACTS

The plaintiff, Robert Molitor, was employed by Chicago Title & Trust as a probationary examiner for seven years before leaving and moving his family to New York to work for a former client. After losing that job, he began to practice law in New York. In June 1934, Mr. Dall of CT&T contacted the plaintiff and asked him to reenter CT&T's company temporarily. The plaintiff and Mr. Dall arranged for the plaintiff to work for a period for CT&T while retaining his law practice. He was absent from his work for CT&T to attend to his practice on several occasions with the knowledge of Mr. Dall. In June 1936, Mr. Dall offered the plaintiff a new agreement, asking him to leave his law practice and move his family to Chicago for permanent employment with CT&T. The plaintiff replied that if he could rely on that promise of permanent employment, he would buy a house in Chicago and move his family there. Mr. Dall replied that the position was permanent. Then the plaintiff severed his New York connections and moved his family. On March 15, 1938, Mr. Dall discharged him.

REASONING

To decide what was meant by "permanent employment," the situation, and the relationship of the parties, and the common understanding of the meaning of the words used must be considered. The surrounding circumstances in the making of a contract must also

## ILLUSTRATION 18-6.   *Continued*

be considered to ascertain what the parties intended by "permanent employment."

DISPOSITION
   Reversed in part and remanded.

After reading *Molitor* and its brief, read the *Heuvelman* decision found in Illustration 18-7. Although it is also decided by the Illinois Appellate Court and deals with the issue of permanent employment, it was decided 14 years after *Molitor*. Read the brief following the decision found in Illustration 18-8. You will notice that *Heuvelman* cites *Molitor;* this is an example of how legal precedent is used. This also illustrates that we perform case law research to predict how a court will view our issue. Now compare the briefs for the two cases. Since both sets of briefs are drafted with the same categories (citation, procedure, issue, facts, holding, rationale, and disposition), you can compare and contrast cases easily and quickly. Compare the issues and you will see that they are similar. Now compare the facts and the holdings and you will notice that they differ.

## ILLUSTRATION 18-7.   *Heuvelman v. Triplett Elec. Instrument Co.*

### *HEUVELMAN v. TRIPLETT ELEC. INSTRUMENT CO.*

23 Ill. App. 2d 231, 161 N.E.2d 875 (1959)

SCHWARTZ, Justice.
   The trial court sustained both defendant's motion for a summary judgment and its motion to strike the amended complaint, and thereupon dismissed the suit with prejudice. From these orders plaintiff has appealed. The principal issue involved turns on an alleged oral agreement for permanent employment.
   The amended complaint consists of three counts. Count 1 seeks a declaratory judgment finding that plaintiff and defendant entered into a contract for the permanent employment of plaintiff as a sales representative for the sale of electrical and radio equipment; that the contract was breached; and that plaintiff suffered damages in the sum of $250,000. . . .
   . . . The pertinent facts extracted from these documents follow. From 1925 to January 1933 plaintiff was employed by an agency which served as defendant's sales representative in the Midwest. In January 1933 defendant hired plaintiff as its sole sales representative for the territory previously covered by the agency. The agreement specified no definite time of employment. In April 1933 defendant desired to secure the services of another sales representative, Jerome T. Keeney,

## ILLUSTRATION 18-7. *Continued*

employed by competitor of defendant, and defendant brought plaintiff and Keeney together for the purpose of having them become associated as joint representatives for the sale of defendant's products. At that meeting, as plaintiff alleges, defendant agreed that plaintiff's employment would continue as long as defendant manufactured and sold electrical equipment and as long as plaintiff acted as sales representative in that field. Plaintiff charges that it was on the basis of that agreement that he consented to enter into a partnership with Keeney. Instead of a partnership, however, a corporation was formed, the Instrument Sales Corporation, in which plaintiff and Keeney owned stock.

The business association between plaintiff and Keeney continued until 1940, when Keeney left plaintiff to join the Simpson Electric Company, a competitor of defendant. At that time Simpson also made plaintiff an offer. Plaintiff orally discussed with defendant the matter of his leaving and, as stated by plaintiff but denied by defendant, Triplett, president of defendant company, told plaintiff as they walked down State Street in Chicago, that their arrangement was a permanent one. It continued until October 1955, when defendant notified plaintiff that it terminated the relationship effective November 30, 1955.

We will first consider the motion for summary judgment as it applies to Count I. Oral contracts for "permanent employment" (meaning that as long as defendant was engaged in the prescribed work and as long as plaintiff was able to do his work satisfactorily, defendant would employ him) have been sustained, provided such contracts are supported by a consideration other than the obligation of services to be performed on the one hand and wages to be paid on the other. *Molitor v. Chicago Title & Trust Co.*, 1845, 325 Ill. App. 124, 132-133, 59 N.E.2d 695-698; *Carnig v. Carr*, 1897, 167 Mass. 544, 46 N.E 117, 35 L.R.A. 512; *Riefkin v. E. I. Du Pont, etc., & Co.*, 1923, 53 App. D.C. 311, 290 F. 286; *Eggers v. Armour & Co.*, 8 Cir., 1942, 129 F.2d 729; *Roxana Petroleum Co. of Oklahoma v. Rice.*, 1924, 109 Okl. 161, 235 P. 502. In the *Molitor* case the consideration was the giving up by the employee of a profitable law practice in New York in order to move to Chicago in reliance on a promise of permanent employment. The *Molitor* case was supported and approved, but distinguished, in *Goodman v. Motor Products Corp.*, 1950, 9 Ill. App. 2d 57, 77 132 N.E.2d 356, 366. In *Carnig v. Carr*, supra, the plaintiff gave up a going and competitive venture to go with his employer. In *Riefkin v. E. I. Du Pont, etc., a & Co.*, supra, the employee gave up his position in government, a position of security and prestige. The case of *Roxana Petroleum Co. v. Rice*, supra, concerned a firm's giving up its whole law practice in order to represent a single client. Where there is no particular detriment to the employee, the act of terminating other employment is not a sufficient consideration to make the new contract

## ILLUSTRATION 18-7. *Continued*

binding. *Edwards v. Kentucky Utilities Co.*, 1941, 286 Ky. 341, 150 S.W.2d 916, 135 A.L.R. 642.

In the instant case the time of the first alleged conversation on which permanent employment is based is April 1933. At that time plaintiff was already employed by defendant and the formation of a partnership with Keeney, terminable at will, so far as appears from anything in the record, cannot be considered a detriment but an advantage, Keeney being a man of considerable experience and competence, as was plaintiff in this business. The alleged renewal of the offer in 1940, when plaintiff was being solicited to join Simpson, is presented in such a vague, indefinite way that it is impossible to consider it as an obligation. Plaintiff says Simpson offered him a 25% interest in a new business venture. It does not appear whether this was a gift or a capital contribution. It is not sufficient consideration for a contract of permanent employment to forgo another employment opportunity. *Lewis v. Minnesota Mutual Life Insurance Co.*, 1949, 240 Iowa 1249, 37 N.W.2d 316; *Skagerberg v. Blandin Paper Co.*, 1936, 197 Minn. 291, 266 N.W. 872.

It is our further conclusion that . . . , no contract for permanent employment was made, nor was any adequate consideration to support one shown. Such contracts extending for a long duration and resting entirely on parole should have for their basis definite and certain mutual promises. The words and the manner of their utterance should not be of that informal character which expresses only long continuing good will and hopes for eternal association. . . .

. . . The order insofar as it sustains the motion to strike Count I and enters summary judgment thereon is affirmed. . . .

. . . Affirmed in part and reversed in part, and cause remanded for further proceedings.

DEMPSEY, P.J., and McCORMICK, J., concur.

## ILLUSTRATION 18-8. Case Brief for *Heuvelman v. Triplett Elec. Instrument Co.*

### *HEUVELMAN v. TRIPLETT ELEC. INSTRUMENT CO.*

23 Ill. App. 2d 231, 161 N.E.2d 875 (1959)

### PROCEDURE

The plaintiff appeals summary judgment for the defendant, dismissing his suit for breach of oral contract for permanent employment.

### ISSUE

Whether there an oral contract for permanent employment between plaintiff and defendant?

## ILLUSTRATION 18-8. *Continued*

### HOLDING

No oral contract for permanent employment was made, nor was adequate consideration to support one shown by the employee forsaking another offer. . . . Instead the employer verbally extended a gesture of goodwill.

### FACTS

The plaintiff was hired by the defendant as a sales representative in January 1933. The agreement specified no definite time of employment. The defendant hired another sales representative in April 1933 to work with the plaintiff. Plaintiff consented to enter into a sales partnership with the new representative on the basis of defendant's promise of permanent employment. A competitor offered plaintiff a job in 1940, which he refused after discussing it with defendant. After the other sales representative resigned, plaintiff received an offer from another employer and mentioned it to Triplett, his current employer. Plaintiff claims the defendant told him, orally, that the employment arrangement was permanent as they walked together down State Street. The defendant denies the claim. In October 1955, the defendant terminated plaintiff's employment as of November 30, 1955.

### REASONING

The act of terminating other employment is not sufficient consideration to make a new contract binding if there is no detriment to the employee. Oral contracts for permanent employment are valid as long as they are supported by consideration other than the obligation of services to be performed on the one hand and wages to be paid on the other. Where there is no particular detriment to the employee, the act of terminating other employment is not a sufficient consideration to make the new contract binding. When plaintiff was being solicited to join the competitor, the renewal with Triplett Electrical was presented in a vague and indefinite way and cannot be considered as an obligation. Contracts extending for long duration resting entirely on oral statements, parole, should have basis on definite and mutual promises. Words should not be of informal character expressing goodwill and hope for eternal association.

### DISPOSITION

Affirmed Count I granting defendant summary judgment on claim of breach of contract, reversed in part, and remanded.

# D. CASE ANALYSIS

**Case analysis** requires you to compare and contrast decisions to assess the outcome of an issue posed by a factual scenario. Case analysis is particularly important when you want to evaluate a client's situation and get an idea of how the law will determine the outcome. We look to prior cases to anticipate how a court will rule on the issue we are researching. You must determine if the question before the court, the issue, is the same as or different than the question the client's problem raises. You must examine the facts of the case and the facts of the client's problem to ascertain the similarities and differences. Sometimes only one component of the decision addresses one part of a client's problem. Last, you must use the relevant cases from the appropriate jurisdiction.

## 1. Sample Single Case Analysis

Read the following abridged case and then read the fact pattern from the client's situation.

**ILLUSTRATION 18-9.** *Shila Morganroth, Plaintiff-Appellant v. Susan Whitall and The Evening News Association, Inc.*

---

### SHILA MORGANROTH, PLAINTIFF-APPELLANT v. SUSAN WHITALL AND THE EVENING NEWS ASSOCIATION, INC., A CORPORATION, DEFENDANTS-APPELLEES

Docket No. 91215
COURT OF APPEALS OF MICHIGAN
161 Mich. App. 785; 411 N.W.2d 859; 1987 Mich. App.
LEXIS 2608; 14 Media L. Rep. 1411
April 14, 1987, Submitted
July 21, 1987, Decided

"Truth is a torch that gleams through the fog without dispelling it."
—Claude Helvetius, *De l'Esprit.*

In this heated dispute, the trial court granted summary disposition in favor of defendants on plaintiff's claims of libel and invasion of privacy by false light. Plaintiff now appeals and we affirm.

Plaintiff alleges that she was libeled and cast in a false light by an article written by defendant Whitall which appeared in the Sunday supplement of the *Detroit News* on November 11, 1984. The article was entitled "Hot Locks: Let Shila burn you a new 'do." The article was accompanied by two photographs, one depicting plaintiff performing her craft on a customer identified as "Barbara X" and the second showing Barbara X and her dog, identified as "Harry X," following completion of the hairdressing. Central to the article was the fact that plaintiff used a blowtorch in her hairdressing endeavors. According to the article,

## ILLUSTRATION 18-9.   *Continued*

plaintiff's blowtorch technique was dubbed "Shi-lit" and was copyrighted.[1] The article also described two dogs, Harry and Snowball, the latter belonging to plaintiff, noting that the canines have had their respective coats colored at least in part. The article also indicated that the blowtorch technique had been applied to both dogs. Additionally, the article described plaintiff's somewhat unusual style of dress, including a silver holster for her blowtorch and a barrette in her hair fashioned out of a $100 bill. Much of the article devoted itself to plaintiff's comments concerning her hairdressing and the trend of what, at least in the past, had been deemed unusual in the area of hair styles. . . . [Editor's note: Text removed from original opinion.]

Plaintiff's rather brief complaint alleges that the article, when read as a whole, is false, misleading and constitutes libel. More specifically, the complaint alleges that the article used the terms "blowtorch lady," "blowtorch technique" and the statement that plaintiff "is dressed for blowtorching duty in a slashed-to-there white jumpsuit" without any factual basis and as the result of defendants' intentional conduct to distort and sensationalize the facts obtained in the interview. The complaint further alleges that the article falsely portrayed plaintiff as an animal hairdresser, again as part of a deliberate action by defendants to distort and sensationalize the facts. In her brief on appeal, plaintiff also takes exception to her being cast as an animal hairdresser and claims as inaccurate the portrayal in the article that she does "mutt Mohawks for dogs" and the reference to "two canines who have been blowtorched." . . . [Editor's note: Text removed from original opinion.]

. . . [Editor's note: Text removed from original opinion.] The elements of defamation were stated by this Court in *Sawabini v Desenberg,* 143 Mich App 373, 379; 372 NW2d 559 (1985):

> The elements of a cause of action for defamation are: "(a) a false and defamatory statement concerning plaintiff; (b) an unprivileged publication to a third party; (c) fault amounting at least to negligence on the part of the publisher; and (d) either actionability of the statement irrespective of special harm (defamation per se) or the existence of special harm caused by the publication (defamation *per quod*)." *Postill v Booth Newspapers, Inc,* 118 Mich App 608, 618; 315 NW2d 511 (1982), lv den 417 Mich 1050 (1983), citing Restatement Torts, 2d, β 558; *Curtis v Evening News Association,* 135 Mich App 101, 103; 352 NW2d 355 (1984); *Ledl v Quik Pik Food Stores, Inc,* 133 Mich App 583; 349 NW2d 529 (1984).

See also *Rouch v Enquirer & News of Battle Creek,* 427 Mich 157, 173-174; 398 NW2d 245 (1986).

The *Sawabini* Court further commented on the appropriateness of dismissing a defamation claim by summary disposition:

> The court may determine, as a matter of law, whether the words in question, alleged by plaintiff to be defamatory, are capable of defamatory

# ILLUSTRATION 18-9.  *Continued*

meaning. See, *e.g., Ledsinger v Burmeister,* 114 Mich App 12, 21; 318 NW2d 558 (1982). Where the words are, as a matter of law, not capable of carrying a defamatory meaning, summary judgment under GCR 1963, 117.2(1) is appropriate. See *Lins v Evening News Association,* 129 Mich App 419, 422; 342 NW2d 573 (1983).

"A communication is defamatory if it tends so to harm the reputation of another as to lower him in the estimation of the community or to deter third persons from associating or dealing with him. *Nuyen v Slater,* 372 Mich 654, 662, fn; 127 NW2d 369 (1964); *Ledsinger v Burmeister,* 114 Mich App 12, 21; 318 NW2d 558 (1982)." *Swenson-Davis v Martel,* 135 Mich App 632, 635-636; 354 NWd 288 (1984), *lv den* 419 Mich 946 (1984). In assessing whether language is defamatory, the circumstances should be considered. *Ledsinger v Burmeister, supra.* [143 Mich App 379-380.]

In determining whether an article is libelous, it is necessary to read the article as a whole and fairly and reasonably construe it in determining whether a portion of the article is libelous in character. *Sanders v Evening News Ass'n,* 313 Mich 334, 340; 21 NW2d 152 (1946); *Croton v Gillis,* 104 Mich App 104, 108; 304 NW2d 820 (1981).

Reading the article as a whole, we believe that it is substantially true; therefore plaintiff's complaint lacks an essential element of her defamation claim, namely falsity. In looking at plaintiff's specific allegations of falsity, for the most part we find no falsehood. Considering as a group the various references to plaintiff's using a "blowtorch" in hairstyling, we note that *The Random House College Dictionary, Revised Edition* (1984), defines "blowtorch" as follows:

[A] small portable apparatus that gives an extremely hot gasoline flame intensified by air under pressure, used esp. in metalworking.

In looking at the photographic exhibits filed by defendants, we believe that the instrument used by plaintiff in her profession can accurately be described as a blowtorch.[2] Accordingly, while the use of the term "blowtorch" as an adjective in connection with references to plaintiff or her hairdressing technique may have been colorful, it was not necessarily inaccurate and certainly not libelous. As for the reference that plaintiff was "dressed for blowtorching duty in a slashed-to-there white jumpsuit," we have examined the photographic exhibits submitted by defendant at the motion hearing and we conclude that reasonable minds could not differ in reaching the conclusion that plaintiff did, in fact, wear a jumpsuit "slashed-to-there."

---

[2] We acknowledge that *The Random House Dictionary's* definition did not list hairdressing as an example. However, we are not persuaded that the dictionary's editors intended their examples to be exclusive. See also "blowtorch," *Webster's New World Dictionary, 2d College Edition* (1976).

## ILLUSTRATION 18-9. *Continued*

Finally, while having disposed of the allegedly libelous claims contained in the complaint, we briefly turn to the additional allegations of false statement listed in plaintiff's brief on appeal. In her brief, plaintiff claims that defendants inaccurately described her as being a hairdresser for dogs, giving dogs a Mohawk cut, and using a blowtorch on the dogs. While it appears that plaintiff did do hairdressing on dogs, it is not necessarily certain at this point that she did, in fact, use the blowtorch on the dogs. However, as noted above, plaintiff filed no response to the motion for summary disposition in the trial court and, thus, presented no affidavits or other evidentiary showings that the statements in the article were false. Thus, there has been no showing by plaintiff that the statements relating to the dogs were false.

Moreover, inasmuch as it appears undisputed that plaintiff at least dyed the fur of the dogs, which would constitute hairdressing of dogs, we are not persuaded that the article, when read as a whole, becomes libelous because of an inaccurate reference to using the blowtorch on the dogs. This is particularly true since, by plaintiff's conduct, she asserts that blowtorching is a safe practice when performed on humans. Therefore, it would appear that, from plaintiff's perspective, blowtorching would also be safe on dogs, even if she did not engage in such a practice. Furthermore, her claim that she was libeled by labeling her as both a dog hairdresser and a human hairdresser is unsupported in light of the tinting of the dogs' hair. Since the undisputed factual showing indicates that plaintiff did blowtorch her human clientele and style her pooch's fur, we will not split hairs at this point to conclude that the statement that she used her blowtorch on dogs, even if inaccurate, is libelous.

For the above-stated reasons, we conclude that, when reviewing the article and accompanying photographs as a whole, the article was not libelous.

On appeal, plaintiff also argues that the article invaded her privacy by casting her in a false light. . . . [Editor's note: Text removed from original opinion.]

See Restatement Torts, 2d, β 652 E, comment a. Furthermore, comment b to β 652 E, p 395, explains that:

> "The interest protected by this section is the interest of the individual in not being made to appear before the public in an objectionable false light or false position, or in other words, otherwise than as he is. In many cases to which the rule stated here applies, the publicity given to the plaintiff is defamatory, so that he would have an action for libel or slander. . . . In such a case the action for invasion of privacy will afford an alternative or additional remedy, and the plaintiff can proceed upon either theory, or both, although he can have but one recovery for a single instance of publicity.

# ILLUSTRATION 18-9. *Continued*

"It is not, however, necessary to the action for invasion of privacy that the plaintiff be defamed. It is enough that he is given unreasonable and highly objectionable publicity that attributes to him characteristics, conduct or beliefs that are false, and so is placed before the public in a false position. When this is the case and the matter attributed to the plaintiff is not defamatory, the rule here stated affords a different remedy, not available in an action for defamation."

As indicated in the above discussion under the theory of defamation, with the exception of certain references to hairdressing dogs, none of the conduct attributed to plaintiff in the article was false. Therefore, it could not place plaintiff in a false light. With reference to the assertions concerning her hairdressing of dogs, we do not believe that a rational trier of fact could conclude that, even if inaccurate, those references are unreasonable or put plaintiff in a position of receiving highly objectionable publicity. The article did not indicate that plaintiff harmed, injured or inflicted pain upon the dogs. Rather, at most, the article inaccurately stated that plaintiff used techniques on the dogs, such as blowtorching, which she also used on humans. While the article may have overstated the techniques that she uses on dogs, inasmuch as she advocates those techniques for use on humans, we cannot conclude that plaintiff would believe it highly objectionable that those techniques also be performed on dogs. Similarly, she cannot have been placed in false light as being both the hairdresser of dogs and humans inasmuch as the tinting of the canines' fur would constitute hairdressing. Thus, it would not be placing plaintiff in a false light to indicate that she served both dog and man. Accordingly, we believe that summary disposition was also properly granted on the false light claim.

In summary, although the manner in which the present article was written may have singed plaintiff's desire for obtaining favorable coverage of her unique hairdressing methods, we cannot subscribe to the view that it was libelous. We believe that the trial court aptly summarized this case when it stated that "this Court is of the Opinion that the Plaintiff sought publicity and got it." Indeed, it would appear that the root of plaintiff's dissatisfaction with defendants' article is that the publicity plaintiff received was not exactly the publicity she had in mind. While the publicity may have been inflammatory from plaintiff's vantage point, we do not believe it was libelous. At most, defendants treated the article more lightheartedly than plaintiff either anticipated or hoped. While this may give plaintiff cause to cancel her subscription to the *Detroit News*, it does not give her cause to complain in court.

Affirmed. Costs to defendants.

---

## CLIENT'S FACTUAL SCENARIO

The partner asked you to apply the Morganroth case to the client's facts. Mrs. Smith came to your firm because she was concerned that an article published in the local newspaper, *The Star News*, was defamatory. *The Star News* reported that Mrs. Smith is a professional pancake flipper and cheerleader for she dresses in a cheerleader's outfit and performs cheers when she delivers the platters of pancakes. Mrs. Smith claims that the article's depiction is untrue. Mrs. Smith asserted that she is a business owner and a professional chef. Mrs. Smith hoped that the article would provide a restaurant review highlighting the culinary integrity of her cuisine. Additionally, the article had a picture of Mrs. Smith in a cheerleader's skirt and a letter sweater. Also, there was a picture of Mrs. Smith jumping in the air after she delivered a platter of pancakes to a table. Mrs. Smith claims that she is merely energetic and enthusiastic. Mrs. Smith also claims that the outfit fits in with the restaurant's theme as it is called "Collegiate Cakes." Mrs. Smith claims that the article is libelous because portraying her as a cheerleader is inaccurate.

The first task is to brief the case focusing solely on the issue that Mrs. Smith raised. Mrs. Smith's sole issue is whether the newspaper article portraying her as a cheerleader was libelous. The case also analyzes the issue of false light but since this is not relevant for our analysis it will not be included in the brief.

## ILLUSTRATION 18-10. Brief of *Morganroth v. Whitall*

### MORGANROTH v. WHITALL

411 N.W.2d 859 (Mich. Ct. App. 1987)

PROCEDURE

Plaintiff, Shila Morganroth appeals the trial court's decision granting summary disposition to the defendants on the libel claim.

ISSUE

Whether the plaintiff was libeled in an article, written by Whitall a reporter for *The Evening News*, entitled: "Hot Locks: Let Shila burn you a new do" indicated that the plaintiff used a blowtorch to style hair, that she also styled dogs' hair and that she wore a jumpsuit "slashed-to-there" that when read as a whole, can be fairly and reasonably construed as true.

HOLDING

The article was not libelous because as a whole it was true as the instrument the plaintiff used to style hair could be considered similar to a blowtorch, she did color dogs' hair and her jumpsuit, as shown in photos, was revealing.

# ILLUSTRATION 18-10. *Continued*

FACTS
The plaintiff, Ms. Morganroth, was a hairdresser. The article about Ms. Morganroth and her hair styling techniques was in the Sunday supplement of the *Detroit News* on November 11, 1984. The article stated that Ms. Morganroth used a blowtorch to style hair and that she styled the hair of both humans and dogs. Additionally, the article stated that Ms. Morganroth dressed in an unusual manner and wore a holster to hold her blow torch. The article also had pictures of Ms. Morganroth in a jumpsuit with a deep slash in the front. The plaintiff alleged that the defendant 's article was libelous as it did not contain any factual basis when it used the terms "blowtorch lady," "blowtorch technique," and "is dressed for blowtorching duty in a slashed-to-there white jumpsuit."

REASONING
The court determined that the motion for summary disposition should be affirmed because the plaintiff did not file a response indicating that there was a genuine issue of material fact. The court examined the rule of defamation. The court noted that the first element, of defamation, requires that for a statement to be defamatory, it must be false. The court also noted that the words may be examined to determine if they alone have defamatory meaning. The article must be read as a whole to evaluate its meaning to see whether it is libelous completely or whether a part of it is. An article read as a whole will not be capable of defamatory meaning when it is substantially true. The words alone must be false. The court stated that the article, when read in totality, was substantially true. The court construed the dictionary definition of "blowtorch" and determined that the photographs of the plaintiff showed that the instrument she used matched the dictionary definition of "blowtorch." Also the photographs showed the plaintiff wearing a revealing jumpsuit. Consequently, because the article as a whole was true, it was not libelous.

DISPOSITION
Affirmed.

## PROCESS FOR CASE ANALYSIS

The second task is to look at the parallels between the case and the client's situation.

Both the case and the client's facts concern a person alleging that she was libeled by a newspaper article. In both instances the articles were substantially true. In our facts, Mrs. Smith does dress in a cheerleading skirt and letter sweater when waiting on tables. Mrs. Smith also

jumps in the air at the restaurant. Although jumping in the air may not be a "cheer," it is pretty similar to cheerleading.

The court, in *Morganroth*, stated that if the article read as a whole is false and misleading then it constitutes libel. Here, Mrs. Smith actually dresses in a cheerleading skirt and letter sweater when she waits on tables. The article in *The Star News* depicted Mrs. Smith, both in text and in photos, as she actually dressed at work and therefore the article is substantially true. Because the article in *The Star News* is substantially true, the article did not convey any false information, it lacked an essential element of the claim for defamation. Defamation requires the statement concerning the plaintiff to be false. Therefore, based on *Morganroth*, the article in *The Star News* is most probably not libelous.

## 2. Sample Analysis Using Two Cases

Compare the briefs in Illustrations 18-6 and 18-8. The holding for *Molitor* is:

> A contract for lifetime employment is created if the intention of the parties is clear even if the only consideration for the contract is the promise of the employee to render the service called for by the contract.

The holding for *Heuvelman* is:

> No oral contract for permanent employment was made, nor was adequate consideration to support one shown when an employee only declines another offer, instead the employer made a verbal gesture of goodwill.

Note the differences in the holdings. *Molitor* states that the only consideration required to support the permanent employment contract is for the employee to perform the services required by the contract. *Heuvelman* states that a contract for permanent employment requires additional consideration beyond forgoing another employment opportunity. *Molitor* is from 1945 and *Heuvelman* is from 1959.

Now let's examine the following fact pattern:

> Howard Frist contacted Mary Dole, the senior partner of Dole, Dole & Dole regarding the situation described below.

> Howard Frist is a well-regarded college administrator. For the past ten years he has been vice president for development at State University, located in Springtown, Illinois. He gained a national reputation for successful fundraising. He also held the faculty rank of full professor with tenure.

> In the spring of 2012, Prestige University of Urban, Illinois, a private university 200 miles north of Springtown, was looking for a new vice

president for development. Frist's friend at Prestige encouraged him to apply for the position. Frist submitted an application to Mark Clark, Prestige's president.

Clark knew of Frist's fine reputation, and immediately scheduled interviews with Prestige's search committee. The interviews went extremely well, and at the end of the day Clark offered the job to Frist.

Frist responded, "Well, I'm very flattered. But frankly, it would have to be a major deal. I'd be giving up a happy situation and a very secure position with tenure and all."

Clark replied, "I think we can make you even happier. We will offer you $200,000 a year to start, plus a new car. And I look forward to having you at Prestige University for the rest of your life."

Frist responded, "The money is great, but I am concerned about the job security and moving 200 miles."

Clark replied, "Like I said, I look forward to your presence at Prestige for the rest of your life."

Frist immediately accepted the position at Prestige. No written document was signed. The men did shake hands immediately after Clark stated his acceptance.

Frist soon resigned his position at State, moved to Urban, purchased a home for $500,000, and started his new position as Vice President for Development at Prestige University. However, within five months, Frist and Clark had several disagreements over fundraising strategies. When the disagreements continued, Clark fired Frist, less than ten months after the agreement was reached.

Frist wants to file suit against Prestige University for the breach of an oral contract for permanent employment. Please assess whether a valid oral contract for permanent employment existed between Frist and Prestige University or whether the contract was terminable at will.

Examine the *Molitor* brief and the *Heuvelman* brief, particularly the holdings and the reasoning, as applied to the Frist problem set out above. Look for parallels and distinctions from the cases when compared to the Frist fact scenario. *Molitor* holds that the only consideration required to support an oral contract for permanent employment is for the employee to perform the services required by the contract. In our problem, Frist and Clark had disagreements over how Frist was performing his job. The facts did not contain a specific job description for the Vice President for Development at Prestige. However, because of the battles between Frist and Clark over fundraising strategies, it seems that Frist was not performing his job as Clark expected. Therefore, since Frist did not perform the services implied by their

agreement, Frist did not render adequate consideration to support the permanent employment contract.

However, *Heuvelman* holds that a contract for permanent employment requires additional consideration beyond forgoing another employment opportunity. Aside from relinquishing his position at State, Frist purchased a home for $500,000 and moved 200 miles. Additional consideration, aside from forgoing another employment opportunity, exists to support a contract for permanent employment between Frist and Prestige University.

Notice how the facts are examined in our client's situation and applied to the holdings from the cases. We also try to parallel the courts' reasoning when we insert our facts into the tests that the courts used. These are essential parts of legal analysis. Also, compare and contrast the decisions. Briefing cases on a single page, in uniform categories, helps us compare and contrast decisions easily. Look carefully at the facts that the judge uses to apply the law to the issue raised in the case—this provides crucial insight into legally significant facts.

---

## *PRACTICE POINTER*

When evaluating which case or cases to use, remember that cases from the appropriate jurisdiction are essential for binding precedent. Also, newer cases are stronger than older cases. Cases from higher courts are stronger than those from lower courts.

---

## CHAPTER SUMMARY

A case brief has several components, including a citation, the procedural history, an issue, a holding, the relevant facts, the reasoning, and the case disposition. These briefs are designed to assist you and sometimes an attorney in understanding a case.

The brief's procedural facts statement should explain briefly how a case came before a court.

The issue statement presents the questions posed by the parties. The holding is the rule of law established by the court. The facts statement should include any relevant facts that affected the court's decision in the case. The reasoning explains how the court developed the rule of law and how it relates to the facts of the case. The disposition is the procedural result of the case.

Dicta often is included in a court decision. It is a statement made by a court concerning an issue other than one the court was asked to decide.

This chapter also provides you with your first exposure to legal analysis. You learned the step-by-step process of drafting a case brief as well as how to compare cases with one another and a legal problem.

# KEY TERMS

| | |
|---|---|
| case analysis | issue legally significant fact |
| case brief | procedural history |
| case citation | rationale |
| dicta | reasoning |
| disposition | relevant facts |
| facts | rule of law |
| holding | |

# EXERCISES

## IN-CLASS

### Issues

1. Review the following issues prepared for a case brief of the *King* case. List any problems you find. Which issue of the following five is best, and why?

   Issue 1. Was the district court's decision that King was an independent contractor rather than an employee of the Miller Co. erroneous?

   Issue 2. Whether King was an employee of Miller or an independent contractor for these reasons:

   a. The control factor, in which agents are restricted in the selling of insurance as to whom or where. Agents also have mandatory requirements for working at designated times and dates. In addition, they are expected to attend weekly meetings and engage in daily office tasks.

   b. The economic factor, in which agents are not allowed to sell products for anyone but Miller and that agents are "integral" to Miller's business.

   c. As with employees, services, supplies, and education expenses are provided. Compensation is made in the form of commissions.

   d. Work hours are based on flexibility for prime selling.

   e. Performance evaluations and documents of rules of conduct are customary requirements of an employer-employee relationship.

   Issue 3. Whether, in finding the plaintiff was not an employee under the Title VII definition, the trial court erred by:

   f. failing to properly evaluate the nature of insurance sales;

   g. failing to evaluate and weigh the integral economic relationship between the defendant and the plaintiff; and

   h. failing to discuss other evidence regarding the "control" criterion used to judge eligibility.

   Issue 4. Whether the district court was clearly erroneous in determining that an insurance agent is an independent contractor rather than an employee when the individual is paid commissions and bonuses rather than a salary and her work is not supervised by the company.

   Issue 5. Does an employer have to exercise control over a worker before that individual is considered an employee under Title VII?

**Holdings**

2. Review the holdings below that were drafted for a brief in the *King* case, list any problems you see with each, and note which is the best.

Holding 1. The court of appeals affirmed the lower court's decision that King is an independent contractor rather than an employee of the Miller Co.

Holding 2. Because the trial court did understand the law and its factual findings are not clearly erroneous, its decision is affirmed.

Holding 3. The district court's underlying factual findings are not clearly erroneous; therefore, the decision of the district court was affirmed.

Holding 4. Yes. An employer must exercise control over a worker before that individual is considered an employee under Title VII.

## HOMEWORK

**Briefing**

3. Brief *Kalal v. Goldblatt Bros.*, 368 N.E.2d 671 (Ill. App. Ct. 1977).
4. Brief the following case:

<u>*KREIGER v. KREIGER*</u>
No. 371
SUPREME COURT OF THE UNITED STATES
334 U.S. 555
February 2-3, 1948, Argued
June 7, 1948, Decided

... The parties were married in New York in 1933 and lived there together until their separation in 1935. In 1940 respondent obtained a decree of separation in New York on grounds of abandonment. Petitioner appeared in the action; and respondent was awarded $60 a week alimony for the support of herself and their only child, whose custody she was given.

Petitioner thereafter went to Nevada where he continues to reside. He instituted divorce proceedings in that state in the fall of 1944. Constructive service was made on respondent who made no appearance in the Nevada proceedings. While they were pending, respondent obtained an order in New York purporting to enjoin petitioner from seeking a divorce and from remarrying. Petitioner was neither served with process in New York nor entered an appearance in the latter proceeding. The Nevada court, with knowledge of the injunction and the New York judgment for alimony, awarded petitioner an absolute divorce on grounds of three consecutive years of separation without cohabitation. The judgment made no provision for alimony. It did provide that petitioner was to support, maintain, and educate the child, whose custody it purported to grant him, and as to which jurisdiction was reserved. Petitioner thereafter tendered $50 a month for the support of the child but ceased making payments under the New York decree.

Respondent thereupon brought suit on the New York judgment in a federal district court in Nevada. Without waiting the outcome of that litigation she obtained a judgment in New York for the amount of the

arrears, petitioner appearing and unsuccessfully pleading his Nevada divorce as a defense. The judgment was affirmed by the Appellate Division, two judges dissenting. 271 N.Y. App. Div. 872, 66 N.Y.S.2d 798. The Court of Appeals affirmed without opinion, 297 N.Y. 530, 74 N.E.2d 468,. . . . Respondent does not attack the bona fides of petitioner's Nevada domicile.

. . . [W]e hold that Nevada had no power to adjudicate respondent's rights in the New York judgment and thus New York was not required to bow to that provision of the Nevada decree. It is therefore unnecessary to pass upon New York's attempt to enjoin petitioner from securing a divorce or to reach the question whether the New York judgment was entitled to full faith and credit in the Nevada proceedings. No issue as to the custody of the child was raised either in the court below or in this Court. The judgment is

Affirmed.

MR. JUSTICE FRANKFURTER dissents . . .
MR. JUSTICE JACKSON dissents . . .

5. Brief *Talford v. Columbia Med. Ctr. at Lancaster Sub., L.P.*, 198 S.W.3d 462 (Tex. App. 2006).
6. Brief *DeMercado v. McClung*, 55 Cal. Rptr. 3d 889 (Ct. App. 2007).

## Analysis Exercises

7. Review *Seymour v. Armstrong* in Illustration 18-1. An attorney asked you to apply the holdings of *Seymour* to the following fact pattern.

    Mrs. Johnson, the owner of Frocks, Etc., ordered 50 dresses at the price of $35 per dress to be delivered in one week. Mrs. Johnson ordered the dresses from ABC Dress Company and sent a contract stating that she requests 50 dresses at $35 per dress, totaling $1750 payable upon receipt of the dresses. Mrs. Johnson assumes that when ABC ships the dresses this indicates that they are assenting to the contract by their action. However, ABC sends an invoice with the dresses for $1750 plus shipping of $106. The attorney wants to know, in light of the holding in *Seymour*, if ABC is imposing a new condition in the contract, with no agreement existing between ABC and Frocks, Etc.?

8. Reread *Seymour v. Armstrong* in Illustration 18-1. Now find and read *Steele v. Harrison*, 522 P.2d 957 (Kan. 1976).
    a. Was there a meeting of the minds in the contract in *Steele?*
    b. Was there a meeting of the minds in the contract in *Seymour?*
    c. How is *Steele* similar to *Seymour?*
    d. How does *Steele* differ factually from *Seymour?*
    e. Does *Steele* apply the holding from *Seymour?*

9. Read *Farone v. Bag'n Baggage, Ltd.*, 165 S.W.3d 795 (Tex. App. 2005). How is *Farone* factually similar to the Frist/Prestige University fact pattern in section D of this chapter? Which facts differ?

## CHAPTER 19

# THE LEGAL MEMORANDUM

| | | |
|---|---|---|
| **A.** | **THE LEGAL MEMORANDUM** | 420 |
| **B.** | **AUDIENCE** | 420 |
| **C.** | **COMPONENTS OF A MEMORANDUM** | 421 |
| | 1. Heading | 423 |
| | 2. Questions Presented or Issues | 425 |
| | 3. Conclusion or Brief Answer | 425 |
| | 4. Facts | 426 |
| | 5. Discussion | 427 |
| **D.** | **STEPS IN DRAFTING A MEMORANDUM** | 427 |
| | 1. Memo Drafting Tips | 429 |

## *CHAPTER OVERVIEW*

This chapter introduces you to the legal memorandum. You learn about your audience and how to write objectively. You are introduced to the components of the memorandum, such as the issues, conclusion or brief answer, facts, and discussion sections. The chapter concludes with a brief overview of the process of writing a memorandum.

# A. THE LEGAL MEMORANDUM

## ▼ What Is an Objective Legal Memorandum and Why Is It Written?

An **office memorandum**, often called a memo, explains in an objective rather than a persuasive or argumentative manner the current state of the law regarding an issue. It clarifies how that law applies to a client's transaction or legal dilemma. A memo should explain the current law—both favorable and unfavorable—and any legal theories pertaining to the issues.

The balanced approach of a legal memo helps an attorney see the strengths and weaknesses of a transaction or dispute. Only when an attorney can see all sides of an issue can the attorney determine how best to represent a client. Sometimes your research will determine whether the client has a case or not. If in writing a memo you advocate a single position or attempt to persuade an attorney, the attorney cannot make an informed decision about a dispute or transaction. This can be a very costly error in terms of money, time, client loyalty, and court favor.

A memo also assists an attorney in predicting how a court might decide a particular issue. A memo could be drafted to address an issue raised as a case progresses in court. As a paralegal, you might research whether the law provides for the dismissal of an action; your research and memorandum might form the basis for such a motion to dismiss or for subsequent court documents. You might also write a memo to assist an attorney in drafting an appellate brief, a document used to appeal a trial court's decision.

# B. AUDIENCE

## ▼ Who Reads a Memorandum?

You will usually research a legal question to determine whether a client has a claim or should proceed with a case. Following your research, you generally prepare a memo for an attorney. Your memo also might be sent to the client. Your primary audience, then, is the attorney, and the secondary audience is the client.

Often memoranda are saved in **memo banks** accessible to all firm or corporation attorneys and paralegals, so other attorneys and paralegals might review your memo.

ETHICS ALERT

Do not send a research memo to a client unless an attorney has reviewed and approved the document.

# C. COMPONENTS OF A MEMORANDUM

▼ What Is Included in a Memorandum?

A memorandum can have a variety of components arranged in different orders. The components and their order often vary from attorney to attorney. Ask the assigning attorney if your firm or corporation has a particular style. Request a sample memo so that you can review the style he or she prefers, or go to the memo bank to review a sample. The format discussed in this chapter is one commonly accepted style. See the sample memo in Illustration 19-1. Additional sample memos may be found in Appendix C.

## ILLUSTRATION 19-1.    Sample Memorandum

### MEMORANDUM

To: Benjamin Joyce
From: William Randall
Date: January 28, 2014
Re: *Harris v. Sack and Shop*

**QUESTION PRESENTED**

Is Sack and Shop, a grocery store, liable for injuries sustained by Harris, a store patron who slipped on a banana peel that had been left on the grocery store floor for two days?

**BRIEF ANSWER**

Probably yes. Sack and Shop, a grocery store, probably will be liable based on negligence for injuries sustained by Harris, a store patron who slipped on a banana peel that had been on the grocery store floor for two days.

**FACTS**

Our client, Sack and Shop Grocery Store, is being sued for negligence by Rebecca Harris.

Harris went to the store to purchase groceries on July 8, 2013. While she was in the produce section, she slipped on a banana that a grocery store employee left on the floor. The employee had dropped it on the floor two days earlier and had failed to clean it up after a patron asked him to do so.

Harris sustained a broken arm and head injuries as a result of the slip and fall.

**DISCUSSION**

The issue presented in this case is whether Sack and Shop Grocery Store was negligent when Rebecca Harris slipped in the store's produce

## ILLUSTRATION 19-1.   *Continued*

section. A grocer will be found negligent if a store employee breached the store's duty of reasonable care to its patrons and, as a result of that breach, the patron was injured. *Ward v. K Mart Corp.*, 554 N.E.2d. 223 (Ill. 1990). In *Ward*, the grocery store employee failed to clean up a banana peel for two days and that peel caused a patron to be injured. Similarly in our case Sack and Shop failed to remove the banana peel for two days. Therefore, Sack and Shop is likely to be found liable for the injuries Harris sustained.

The first element to consider is whether Sack and Shop owed a duty of reasonable care to Harris. A grocery store owes a duty of care to any patron. *Ward*, 554 N.E.2d at 226. Harris was a customer in the store. Therefore, Sack and Shop owed her a duty of care.

The next question to consider is whether Sack and Shop breached its duty of reasonable care to Harris. A store will be found to have breached its duty of reasonable care to a patron if a store employee fails to properly and regularly clean the floor of the store. *Olinger v. Great Atl.& Pac. Tea Co.*, 173 N.E.2d 443 (Ill. 1961). In *Olinger*, the store was found liable because a store employee failed to clean the floor for one day and a patron slipped on a substance on the floor. 173 N.E.2d at 447. No one had told any store employee about the slippery substance. *Id.* at 447. Nonetheless, the Illinois Supreme Court found the store liable, saying that the store employees had sufficient time to notice the substance if they had used ordinary care. *Id.* In our case, Sack and Shop's employee had two days to clean the floor before Harris fell. In addition, a customer had placed the store employee on notice of the banana. Therefore, Sack and Shop breached its duty of care to Harris.

The plaintiff, however, still must establish proximate cause, that is, that the injury resulted as a natural consequence of Sack and Shop's breach of its duty. A store owner's failure to clear debris from a store floor, resulting in injury to a patron who slipped on the floor, was found to be the proximate cause of the patron's injuries. *Id.* at 449. In this case, Sack and Shop's failure to clean the peel from the floor was a breach of its duty of care to Harris. This breach resulted in injury to Harris. Sack and Shop's breach will be found to be the proximate cause of Harris's injuries.

The final element that must be established is that the plaintiff, Harris, suffered injuries. Harris sustained a broken arm and head injuries as a result of the slip and fall. Therefore, she will be able to show that she was injured.

### CONCLUSION

Sack and Shop owed Harris a duty of reasonable care. The store is likely to be found to have breached that duty of reasonable care because an employee failed to remove a banana peel from the grocery store floor during the preceding two days. The injuries Harris sustained were directly caused by a slip on a banana peel. Therefore, Sack and Shop is likely to be found liable to Harris.

# 1. Heading

In Illustrations 19-1 and 19-2, the first part of the memo is the **heading.** A sample heading also is shown in Illustration 19-3. The first notation in the heading of either illustration is the word "MEMORANDUM," placed in all capital letters at the top of the page. The next notations in Illustrations 19-1, 19-2, and 19-3 tell the reader who the memorandum is written to and from, the date, and the subject. The regarding line, indicated by the "Re:," varies depending on the firm's style. For example, some insurance clients ask that you include claim numbers in the regarding line. Some attorneys prefer court case numbers, and still others prefer clients' billing numbers and file numbers.

**ILLUSTRATION 19-2.   Sample Memorandum: McMillan Battery Action**

---

**MEMORANDUM**

To: William Houck
From: Ivy Courier
Date: November 7, 2013
Re: McMillan Battery Action

**QUESTION PRESENTED**

Did an actionable battery occur when Mann intentionally struck McMillan with a bucket, without McMillan's consent, causing McMillan to suffer physical and monetary injuries?

**CONCLUSION**

Mann's intentional striking of McMillan with a bucket and sand was an actionable battery.

**FACTS**

Our client, Mary McMillan, a 36-year-old bank teller, wants to bring an action for battery against Carol Mann, a 36-year-old mother, who threw a metal bucket filled with sand at McMillan at a local park. While McMillan sat on a park bench, she teased Mann's seven-year-old son. Mann did not like this teasing and threw a bucket filled with sand at Mary. Sand landed in McMillan's eyes while she was wearing soft contact lenses. As a result, McMillan's contacts had to be replaced. The bucket also cut McMillan's eye and cheek. She had stitches in both places. McMillan asked Mann to pay for her doctor bills and for the new contacts. Mann refused and added, "I'm not sorry. I meant to hurt you."

**DISCUSSION**

The issue presented is whether Mann's intentional touching of McMillan with a bucket rather than her person is an actionable battery. A battery is the intentional touching of another without consent, which causes injury. *Anderson v. St. Francis-St. George Hosp., Inc.*, 77 Ohio St. 3d

## ILLUSTRATION 19-2. *Continued*

82, 671 N.E.2d 225 (1996). A touching can occur when an object rather than an individual's body contacts the other party. *Leichtman v. WLW Jacoc Communications, Inc.*, 92 Ohio App. 3d 232, 634 N.E.2d 697 (1994); *Smith v. John Deere Co.*, 83 Ohio App. 3d 398, 614 N.E.2d 1148 (1993). In this case, Mann intentionally struck McMillan with a bucket without McMillan's consent and that touching resulted in injuries. Therefore, a battery occurred.

The threshold issue is whether a touching occurred when the bucket struck McMillan. A contact between a nonconsenting party and object rather than the actor's body can be a battery. *Leichtman v. WLW Jacoc Communications, Inc.*, 92 Ohio App. 3d 232, 634 N.E.2d 697 (1994); *Smith v. John Deere Co.*, 83 Ohio App. 3d at 398, 614 N.E.2d at 1148. In *Leichtman*, one person blew cigar smoke at another person, resulting in injuries. The court found that the cigar smoke was an extension of the person and that a contact between the smoke and the nonconsenting person met the requirement of a touching for civil battery. In this case, Mann threw the bucket at McMillan, and the bucket contacted her face. Following the reasoning in the *Leichtman* case, the bucket would be an extension of Mann's body, and the contact between McMillan and the bucket would be considered a touching under the theory of civil battery.

Next, the question to consider is whether under the statute Mann intended to touch McMillan when she struck her with the bucket. A person intends his or her conduct when he or she undertakes an action with a knowing mind. *Smith v. John Deere Co.*, 83 Ohio App. 3d 398, 614 N.E.2d 1148 (1993). In *Smith*, a police officer handcuffed the plaintiff. The court found that the officer must have intended his actions because you could not accidentally handcuff a person. *Smith*, 83 Ohio App. 3d at 399, 614 N.E.2d at 1149. In McMillan's case, Mann aimed the bucket at McMillan purposefully trying to strike her, Mann later told McMillan that she deliberately threw the bucket at her. McMillan probably will be able to establish that Mann had the statutory intent.

The next factor to consider is whether McMillan consented to the contact. If a person consents to the touching, a battery has not occurred. *Love v. Port Clinton*, 37 Ohio St. 3d 98, 524 N.E.2d 166 (1988). In our case, McMillan did not consent to Mann's throwing of the bucket at her face. Therefore, McMillan did not consent to any contact. Finally, the question is whether McMillan suffered physical injuries. A battery occurs only if a plaintiff sustains physical injuries as a result of the touching. *Anderson v. St. Francis-St. George Hosp., Inc.*, 77 Ohio St. 3d 82, 671 N.E.2d 225 (1996). McMillan sustained cuts on her face and the sand flying out of the bucket into her eyes. McMillan will be able to show that she sustained physical injuries as a result of the contact with the bucket.

## ILLUSTRATION 19-3.   Sample Memorandum Heading

**MEMORANDUM**

To: Sarah E. Lillian
From: Kelsey Barrington
Date: July 8, 2013
Re: Negligence Action between Sack and Shop Grocery Store and Rebecca Harris

## 2. Questions Presented or Issues

The next portion of the memo seen in Illustrations 19-1 and 19-2 is the questions presented section, which is sometimes called the issues section.

The terms **issues** or **questions presented** are synonymous. For our purposes, we will use the terms *question presented* or *questions presented.* The questions presented are the specific legal questions an attorney has asked you to research. The question presented is phrased in the form of a question concerning the legal issue posed, and it includes a reference to the applicable law and some **legally significant facts.** See Illustration 19-4. The legal issue in Illustration 19-4 is whether the grocery store owner was negligent and whether he owed a duty to the patron. The legally significant facts are that the patron slipped on a banana peel that had been on the grocery store floor for two days. (A detailed explanation of how to draft the questions presented is provided in Chapter 21.) Note the facts included in the questions presented section of Illustration 19-2. These facts are the legally significant facts. They are interwoven with the standard of law applicable to this case.

## ILLUSTRATION 19-4.   Question Presented

Is a grocery store owner liable for injuries sustained by a store patron who slipped on a banana peel that had been on the grocery store floor for two days?

## 3. Conclusion or Brief Answer

You should follow the questions presented section with a **brief answer** or a **conclusion.** Brief answers and conclusions differ in format, although their purposes are similar. A brief answer is a short statement that directly answers the question or questions presented. See Illustration 19-5. A conclusion is similar, but it is usually longer. In Illustration 19-2, you will find an example of a conclusion. If there were two issues presented, you would include two conclusions, placed in the same order as the issues that they answer.

## ILLUSTRATION 19-5.   Brief Answer

Probably yes. A grocery store owner probably will be liable based upon negligence for injuries sustained by a store patron who slipped on a banana peel that a store employee left on the grocery store floor for two days.

▼ What Is the Difference Between a Conclusion and a Brief Answer?

Some attorneys prefer a brief answer immediately following the question or questions presented and a formal conclusion at the end of the memo. The brief answer should be presented in the same order as the questions they answer.

For other attorneys, a conclusion without a brief answer is sufficient. A conclusion is an in-depth answer to the question presented. There is no set length for a conclusion; it should be a succinct statement that summarizes the substance of the memo. See Illustration 19-6. As you can see in Illustration 19-6, the conclusion is more in-depth than the brief answer. However, note that both the conclusion and the brief answer include references to the legally significant facts: the failure to remove the banana peel from the grocery store floor. In the conclusion, you provide your opinion concerning the case. However, a paralegal should refrain from telling an attorney how to proceed. For example, do not say "I think that we will lose this case, so we should settle it." Instead, say "This case is not likely to be won." Allow the attorney to determine whether the case should be settled. (Drafting conclusions and brief answers is explained in detail in Chapter 20.)

## ILLUSTRATION 19-6.   Conclusion

A grocery store owner owes a patron a duty of reasonable care. The store owner is likely to be found to have breached that duty of reasonable care because he failed to remove a banana peel from the grocery store floor during the preceding two days. The injuries the patron sustained were directly caused by a slip on a banana peel. Therefore, the grocery store owner is likely to be found liable to the patron.

## 4. Facts

Following the conclusion or brief answer, you should include a **facts statement** that explains the status of the case and all the facts that might have a bearing on the outcome of a client's case. These facts are called legally significant facts. You should include facts that cast your client's dispute or transaction in a good light and those that shade it in a negative light. See Illustration 19-7. The presentation of facts should be balanced rather than slanted.

**ILLUSTRATION 19-7.   Facts Statement**

Our client, Sack and Shop Grocery Store, is being sued for negligence by Rebecca Harris.

Harris went to the store to purchase groceries on July 8, 2013. While she was in the produce section, she slipped on a banana peel that had been left on the floor by a grocery store employee. The employee had dropped it on the floor two days earlier and had failed to clean it up after a patron asked him to do so. Harris sustained a broken arm and head injuries as a result of the slip and fall.

## 5. Discussion

Following the facts, you will include your **discussion** in which you will explain the current state of the applicable law, analyze the law, and apply the law to the legally significant facts noted in the facts statement. Any problems posed in the client's case and counterarguments should be presented here. This should not be an exhaustive review of the history of the law but should be focused analysis of the current state of the law. The law should be applied to each of the legally significant facts. Note if the law is primary binding or merely persuasive authority. Use only highly persuasive secondary authorities if primary authorities are not available.

Finally, following the discussion, you should include a conclusion if a brief answer rather than a conclusion has been used earlier. Review the discussion sections in Illustrations 19-1 and 19-2. Note that Illustration 19-2 contains multiple issues, and they are discussed separately within the memo.

*PRACTICE POINTER*

Review memos prepared previously for the attorney who assigned the memorandum. Follow that format or ask the assigning attorney what format he or she prefers.

# D. STEPS IN DRAFTING A MEMORANDUM

▼ What Steps Should You Take in Drafting a Memo?

1. An attorney will assign a research problem to you. Discuss the problem thoroughly with the attorney. Be certain to ask the attorney questions to clarify the legal issues and the facts of a dispute or transaction. Ask for guidance concerning possible topics to research and resources to consult.

2. Immediately following your meeting, draft a preliminary statement of the legal issues and the relevant facts.

3. Begin your research. To develop an understanding of the issues and the general legal rules applicable to your problem, and to provide you with some search terms, read secondary authorities such as encyclopedias and *American Law Reports.* During your research, you often will discover other issues that may be relevant, and you will find additional facts that are important. If you are uncertain whether to pursue these additional issues, ask the attorney who assigned the case whether the issues are relevant.

4. If you have additional questions about the facts of a case, ask the attorney or the client for additional facts to assist you in determining what authorities are relevant to your research.

5. Find primary binding authorities. If you are unable to find those, locate persuasive primary or secondary authorities.

6. After you find relevant authorities, validate the authorities and review the citators for more current, valuable authorities. If necessary, review these additional authorities.

7. Prepare case briefs of the relevant cases. (See Chapter 18 for a detailed discussion of case briefing.)

8. After you have completed your research, rewrite the questions presented.

9. Rewrite the facts and then draft the brief answers or conclusions (or both).

10. Next, outline the discussion section. (See Chapter 24 for a discussion of outlining and organizing the memorandum.) While you are preparing your outline, you should synthesize the legal authorities. (This process is explained in Chapter 23.) You should formulate your discussion and paragraphs in a special format called IRAC, which is an abbreviation for the formula Issue, Rule, Application, and Conclusion. (This format is discussed thoroughly in Chapter 22.) You can now begin to write your memorandum.

## CHECKLIST FOR DRAFTING A MEMORANDUM

1. Discuss the case with the attorney
   a. Discuss the legal issues presented
   b. Discuss the known facts
   c. Determine whether additional facts should be investigated
   d. Determine what law governs
   e. Check the memo bank to determine firm's style and to learn whether the issue has been researched previously
2. Draft a preliminary statement of the facts
3. Draft a preliminary statement of the legal issues or questions presented
4. Research the legal issue or issues

a. If you find additional relevant issues, discuss them with the attorney

b. Determine whether additional facts should be considered in light of the new issues; ask the attorney or client about additional facts

c. Research the new issues, if necessary

5. Rewrite the issues or questions presented after your research has allowed you to focus them better

6. Draft a brief answer or a conclusion (or both)

7. Rewrite the facts statement of the memo

8. Draft an outline of the discussion section of the memo; organize the discussion

9. Draft the discussion section

10. Reevaluate the facts and rewrite the facts statement to include only legally significant facts

11. Rewrite the conclusion

## 1. Memo Drafting Tips

You should be careful to guide your reader through each section of your memo and from issue to issue. To do this, introduce the legal issues in the facts section and again in the discussion section. Also, use headings and transitions to guide your reader into the new sections. Your memo should be clearly written, accurate, concise, and thorough. Use everyday language rather than legalese. Write the memo as if the reader is unfamiliar with the law, but do not be condescending.

Your memo should not trace the legal history of the law. Instead, it should be a statement of the current state of the law.

When you approach a legal rule, start with the rule rather than the citation for the authority. Doing so makes your discussion stronger.

Be certain that your discussion supports your conclusions. Incorporate the relevant facts into your discussion.

## CHAPTER SUMMARY

The legal memorandum is composed of issues, conclusions and brief answers, facts, and a discussion section. These are written for attorneys and clients. Memoranda are designed to assist them in determining the current state of the law regarding a legal issue and how that law applies to the facts presented in a particular case.

In the next few chapters, you will learn about each one of the components of a memorandum, the questions presented, the facts, the conclusions, the brief answers, and the discussion.

## KEY TERMS

| | |
|---|---|
| brief answer | discussion |
| conclusion | facts statement |

heading                               memo banks
issues                                office memorandum
legally significant facts             questions presented


## EXERCISES
### TRUE OR FALSE

1. A memorandum should be persuasive in its style.
2. A memorandum should present only facts that are favorable to your client's position.
3. A memorandum should inform the attorney and the client about the favorable authorities and known facts as well as the authorities and facts that pose problems for a client's case.
4. Your memorandum will never be read by a client.
5. You should include descriptive words in the facts section that slant the facts in favor of your client's position.
6. What are the components of a memorandum?

## CHAPTER 20

# QUESTIONS PRESENTED AND CONCLUSIONS OR BRIEF ANSWERS

| | | |
|---|---|---|
| **A.** | **QUESTIONS PRESENTED OR ISSUES** | 431 |
| | 1. First Draft | 432 |
| | 2. Research the Issue and Revise It | 433 |
| | 3. Specificity and Precision | 434 |
| **B.** | **BRIEF ANSWERS AND CONCLUSIONS** | 435 |
| | 1. Brief Answers | 435 |
| | 2. Conclusions | 436 |
| | 3. Drafting Conclusions | 436 |

## *CHAPTER OVERVIEW*

Chapter 19 introduced you to the legal memorandum and its components. This chapter explains the reasons for drafting questions presented, issues, brief answers, and conclusions and teaches you how to draft these items.

## A. QUESTIONS PRESENTED OR ISSUES

The **questions presented** or **issues** are the problems you must research to answer the attorney's or client's questions. These questions provide a preview to the reader about the applicable legal standards and the relevant facts. They are always posed in the form of a question.

▼ Who Reads the Questions Presented Statement?

The questions presented statement often is the first portion of a memorandum an attorney reviews. Many attorneys focus on these questions and the **conclusions** or **brief answers.** Some attorneys read these questions and answers without reading the entire memorandum. Therefore, your questions presented statement must be easy to understand and allow the reader to quickly grasp the legal questions that the memo will address.

## 1. First Draft

The first draft of the questions presented should be done following the receipt of the initial research assignment from the attorney. Draft a simple statement that explains the questions you were asked to research. For example, suppose an attorney provides you with the following facts:

> While driving a car Ronnie Randall struck Janice Kahn's son at 5:00 P.M. on August 29, 2013. It was bright and clear. No skid marks appeared on the dry street following the accident.
>
> Janice Kahn was working in her garden about five feet from the accident scene at the time of the accident. Her son was playing a game in the street before Randall's car struck him. Kahn saw the car strike her son. When she first looked up from her garden, she thought her 11-year-old son was dead. He was covered with blood and had several broken bones. However, Kahn's son was conscious after the accident.
>
> Immediately after the accident, police tested Randall's blood alcohol level and found that it was .11. Police cited Randall for drunk driving and driving with a suspended driver's license. Police had charged him with drunk driving and had suspended his license two weeks earlier after the car he was driving struck another child at the same spot. Randall had a drinking history.
>
> Following the accident, several witnesses said Randall was upset and wobbled as he walked. One witness said that Randall intentionally turned the steering wheel to hit Kahn's son. Kahn stated that Randall often swerved down her street to get her attention.
>
> Rhonda Albert, Kahn's neighbor, said she heard Randall say he would get even with Kahn after Kahn broke off a ten-year relationship with him. During Kahn and Randall's ten-year relationship, Randall was close to Kahn's son. He took him to ball games, including one in April, and attended the son's baseball games. Randall knew that Kahn's son was the most important person in her life.

Since the accident, Janice Kahn vomits daily and suffers from anxiety and headaches. Dr. Susan Faigen, Kahn's internist, states that the vomiting, anxiety, and headaches are the result of the accident.

The attorney wants you to research whether Janice Kahn has a claim against Ronnie Randall for intentional infliction of emotional distress. Your first draft of the question presented might be:

> Does Janice Kahn have a valid claim for intentional infliction of emotional distress against Ronnie Randall?

This statement is devoid of legally significant facts.

### ▼ What Are Legally Significant Facts?

These are facts that will have an impact on a jury's or judge's decisions concerning Kahn's claim. This question as presented is too vague. To make your question more understandable in the context of Kahn's case, you must incorporate **legally significant facts.**

---

**Legally Significant Facts**

Kahn saw Randall strike her 11-year-old son
Randall struck the boy with his car
Kahn now suffers from anxiety, headaches, and vomiting

---

You might rewrite the question presented with the fact that Kahn saw Randall strike her 11-year-old son with his car. That fact is legally significant. The rewrite might read as follows:

> Does Janice Kahn have a valid claim for intentional infliction of emotional distress against Ronnie Randall when Kahn **saw** Randall strike her 11-year-old child with his car?

By incorporating some legally significant facts, you have drafted a question presented that places the issue in perspective for the reader and that clearly identifies the parties in the action. This question presented allows the reader to understand the legal issue in the context of the factual circumstances surrounding the claim.

## 2. Research the Issue and Revise It

Now you are ready to research the issue. After you complete your research, you determine what law applies to a claim for intentional infliction of emotional distress. Once you determine the legal standard, you rewrite the question presented to incorporate that standard and only the legally significant facts. Your rewrite should frame the questions presented around the applicable legal standard and should present the applicable legal standard in the context of the facts that will affect the determination of a claim.

In the case of Janice Kahn, you learn from a decision of the highest court in your state that intentional infliction of emotional distress is "an act done by a person which is extreme and outrageous, done with intent to cause another to suffer severe emotional distress, and which results in distress and emotional injury to another. The emotional injury must manifest itself with a physical problem." If you rewrite the question presented above to incorporate the legal standard and legally significant facts, it might read as follows:

> Does Janice Kahn have a valid claim for intentional infliction of emotional distress against Ronnie Randall after Kahn saw Randall turn his car to strike Kahn's 11-year-old child in front of her, causing her to suffer from anxiety, headaches, and vomiting?

This question presented incorporates legally significant facts and provides these facts in the context of the legal standard. Randall's intention is one of the legal factors or elements in determining whether Kahn has a claim for intentional infliction of emotional distress. The question presented notes the legally significant fact that Randall turned his car to strike the child. The fact that Kahn now suffers from anxiety, headaches, and vomiting also is legally significant and relates to the legal standard because it may show that Kahn suffers from severe emotional distress. Although you should mention legally significant facts and the legal standard, keep the issue short enough for the reader to understand.

When you have multiple questions presented, the conclusion section should answer the questions in the same order as they were presented.

Review the question presented in Illustration 20-1. Determine what legal issue is presented. Then find the legally significant facts that are included in the question presented.

## ILLUSTRATION 20-1.   Question Presented

Is the grocery store owner liable for injuries sustained by a store patron who slipped on a banana peel that had been on the grocery store floor for two days?

## 3. Specificity and Precision

The facts should be **specific** and your characterization of the parties and the issues should be **precise**. For example, consider a case that concerns whether an individual, Walker, is an independent contractor or an employee of the Whole in One company. Walker did not work for any other companies. She paid her own taxes quarterly rather than through payroll deductions. She worked with limited company supervision. Title VII of a federal law applies. You could pose the question presented as follows:

Under Title VII, was Walker an employee when she worked exclusively for Whole In One, paid her own taxes quarterly rather than through deductions, and worked with limited company supervision?

The facts in this case are specific: Walker paid her taxes quarterly rather than through payroll deductions. However, the question presented is not precise because it does not characterize the legal issue presented completely. The legal issue is whether Walker is an independent contractor rather than an employee. Therefore, the question presented could be refined as follows:

Under Title VII, was Walker an independent contractor rather than an employee when she worked exclusively for Whole In One, paid her own taxes quarterly rather than through deductions, and worked with limited company supervision?

You must only ask a question in the questions presented statement, not provide an answer. You will answer the question presented in the brief answer or conclusion section.

If you have more than one issue or question presented, place them in a logical order and make that order consistent throughout the memo. The first question presented, then, should be answered first in the conclusion or brief answer statement and should be the first issue addressed in the discussion. See Illustration 19-1 in Chapter 19.

# B. BRIEF ANSWERS AND CONCLUSIONS

## 1. Brief Answers

Brief answers are the quick answers to the question or questions presented. A brief answer is a short statement. Some attorneys prefer a brief answer that is later accompanied by a formal conclusion at the end of the memorandum. The brief answer allows an attorney to read a memo in a hurry and determine the legal issues. See Illustration 20-2.

### ILLUSTRATION 20-2.   Question Presented and Brief Answer

---

Question Presented: Does Janice Kahn have a valid claim for intentional infliction of emotional distress against Ronnie Randall after Kahn saw Randall turn his car to strike Kahn's 11-year-old child in front of her, causing her to suffer from anxiety, headaches, and vomiting?

Brief Answer: Yes. Kahn can bring a successful action for intentional infliction of emotional distress against Ronnie Randall because she saw Randall turn his car to strike her 11-year-old son, causing her to suffer severe anxiety, headaches, and vomiting.

---

The brief answer should include a brief statement of the applicable law and some relevant facts. A brief answer for the question presented above in Illustration 20-1 could be presented as follows in Illustration 20-3.

## ILLUSTRATION 20-3.  Brief Answer

Probably yes. A grocery store owner probably will be liable based upon negligence for injuries sustained by a store patron who slipped on a banana peel that had been on the grocery store floor for two days.

In the memorandum, it would appear as follows:

**Question Presented:** Is the grocery store owner liable for injuries sustained by a store patron who slipped on a banana peel that had been on the grocery store floor for two days?
**Brief Answer:** Probably yes. A grocery store owner probably will be liable based upon negligence for injuries sustained by a store patron who slipped on a banana peel that had been on the grocery store floor for two days.

The legal standard of conduct applicable to this case, negligence, is mentioned in the brief answer along with legally significant facts.

## 2. Conclusions

A conclusion also is an answer to the question presented and a summary of the discussion section. For some attorneys, a conclusion without a brief answer is sufficient. However, other attorneys prefer both a brief answer and a conclusion.

### ▼ How Is a Conclusion Different from a Brief Answer?

A conclusion does not have a set length, but it is generally longer than a brief answer. It is not a detailed or in-depth discussion of the legal issue presented in the case. It is a succinct summary of the substance of the memo. The conclusion should include legally significant facts and the applicable legal standard. In the conclusion, you must answer the question presented and provide your best prediction concerning the outcome of the case. It is acceptable to use terms such as *likely* or *probably* when you think that the outcome of an action is uncertain.

## 3. Drafting Conclusions

Before you draft your conclusion, review the questions presented and your preliminary facts statement. (A detailed explanation of the facts statement is presented in Chapter 21.)

Next, write the conclusion as an answer to the question presented and incorporate some of the relevant facts contained in the facts section of the memo. Refine the conclusion so that the reader understands the legal standard and the applicable facts. Conclusions often work well when drafted in an IRAC formula: Issue, Rule, Application, and Conclusion. (For a thorough discussion of the IRAC formula, see Chapter 22.)

For the facts and the question presented in the *Kahn* case, the following conclusion might be prepared:

> The central question is whether Janice Kahn has a valid claim for intentional infliction of emotional distress against Ronnie Randall. To successfully prove a claim for intentional infliction of emotional distress, Khan must show that the act that caused the distress was extreme and outrageous and done with intent. In the case, Kahn saw Randall turn his car to strike her 11-year-old child, Bill. Seeing this accident caused Kahn to suffer from anxiety, headaches, and vomiting daily. Several witnesses can testify that Randall said that he intended to harm Kahn, and Kahn states that Randall turned the car to strike her son. Two factors, however, might show that Randall lacked intent: the statement that he made to the police that he did not intend to hit the child and the fact that his blood alcohol level was .11, possibly preventing him from formulating the needed intent. Kahn probably has a claim for intentional emotional distress.

This conclusion provides a summary of the writer's prediction of the outcome of the case after the legal standards are applied to the legally significant facts:

> Janice Kahn probably has a valid claim for intentional infliction of emotional distress against Ronnie Randall.

Facts such as that Kahn saw Randall turn the car to strike her son and that witnesses can testify concerning what Randall said he intended to do are relevant to the question of whether the act was extreme and outrageous. The legal standard provides that the act must be extreme and outrageous before an individual can be liable for intentional infliction of emotional distress. In addition, the extreme and outrageous act must be done with intent. Randall's intent also is discussed in the conclusion.

Many students include an authority, such as a statute or case, in the conclusion. Most often, however, your analysis of a claim requires that you synthesize a number of authorities to determine the applicable law. It would be misleading, therefore, to include only one authority in your conclusion. You might include an authority if it is the sole authority governing a claim.

When two or more questions presented are noted in the memorandum, a conclusion or a brief answer and then a conclusion for each question should be noted in the same order as the question presented. See Illustration 20-4.

## ILLUSTRATION 20-4. Questions Presented and Conclusion

### QUESTIONS PRESENTED

1. Does Janice Kahn have a valid claim for intentional infliction of emotional distress against Ronnie Randall after Kahn saw Randall turn his car to strike Kahn's 11-year-old child in front of her, causing her to suffer from anxiety, headaches, and vomiting?

2. Does Janice Kahn's 11-year-old child, Bill, have a claim against Randall for battery after Randall turned his car to strike Bill, and did strike him, breaking Bill's bones?

### CONCLUSIONS

1. The central question is whether Janice Kahn has a valid claim for intentional infliction of emotional distress against Ronnie Randall. To successfully prove a claim for intentional infliction of emotional distress, Kahn must show that the act that caused the distress was extreme and outrageous and done with intent. In the case, Kahn saw Randall turn his car to strike her 11-year-old child. Seeing this accident caused Kahn to suffer from anxiety, headaches, and vomiting daily. Several witnesses can testify that Randall said that he intended to harm Kahn, and Kahn states that Randall turned the car to strike her son. Two factors, however, might show that Randall lacked intent: the statement that he made to the police that he did not intend to hit the child and the fact that his blood alcohol level was .11, possibly preventing him from formulating the needed intent. Kahn probably has a claim for intentional emotional distress.

2. Bill Kahn is likely to make a successful claim for battery against Randall. A battery is the intentional touching of another without consent, which causes injury. A touching can occur when an object rather than an individual's body contacts the other party. In this case, Randall struck Bill Kahn with his car without Bill Kahn's consent and that touching resulted in injuries. Intent may be an issue because Randall said he did not intend to hit the child and his blood alcohol level was .11, possible preventing him from formulating the needed intent. However, the fact that he turned the wheel to strike Bill Kahn is likely to show intent.

---

*PRACTICE POINTER*

When you have multiple questions presented, the conclusion section should answer the questions in the same order as they were presented.

# CHAPTER SUMMARY

In this chapter, you learned how to draft questions presented, issues, brief answers, and conclusions. Questions presented or issues should incorporate legally significant facts and the rule of law. Legally significant facts are facts that will affect a decision concerning an issue of law.

Legally significant facts and the current rule of law also should be included in the conclusions or brief answers that answer the questions presented or issues.

Some attorneys prefer both a brief answer and a conclusion, while others require only a conclusion.

The process of writing the questions presented, issues, brief answers, and conclusions requires that you rewrite these components of a memorandum several times. The questions presented or issues should be drafted before you perform your research. The conclusions or brief answers also should be rewritten in light of the facts presented in a case.

In the next chapter, you learn how to draft facts statements for your memoranda.

# KEY TERMS

brief answers
conclusion
issues
legally significant facts

precise
questions presented
specific

# EXERCISES
## SHORT ANSWER

1. What is a brief answer?
2. How does a brief answer differ from a conclusion?
3. Is an issue or question presented written as a statement or a question?
4. If you have four questions presented, how many conclusions or brief answers should you have?
5. What is the purpose of a question presented?
6. What is the purpose of a conclusion?

## QUESTIONS PRESENTED
Draft questions presented for memos in the following cases.

7. You work as a paralegal for the country prosecutor's office in Houcktown County. One of the assistant prosecutors asks you to research whether Bonnie Bill has committed aggravated burglary under the Houcktown Rev. Code § 2911. The attorney has provided you with the following facts:

Merriweather Halsey and Bonnie Bill were at the Masonic Temple for a fundraiser to fight AIDS. During the fundraiser Bill told a drunken Halsey that she intended to steal the $8,000 fundraiser proceeds from the Masonic Temple after the fundraiser and that she intended to steal a pearl necklace from Alice McKinley.

Bill, who had helped organize the fundraiser, watched as the chairperson of the fundraiser opened the safe and placed the money in it. She memorized the combination and decided that she would use it later to steal the money.

After the fundraiser, Bill walked home to get a credit card and a crowbar to open the door if she needed it. Bill went to the Masonic Temple after the fundraiser, wearing a disguise, showed the guard her invitation, and told him that she lost her mother's diamond brooch inside. Although the guard did not remember her, he allowed her to go into the temple. She wandered around the building for about an hour with the brooch inside her purse.

When the guard decided to eat his supper and call home, Bill went to the safe. She opened it and pulled out all the money, except for $1,000.

Bill told the guard she found the brooch and then left. She went to Alice McKinley's home, entered the house through an open ground-floor window, took the pearl necklace she had seen Alice wearing earlier, and then left.

The relevant statute is as follows:

## § 2911 Aggravated Burglary

(A) A person is guilty of aggravated burglary when the person, by force or deception, trespasses in any house, building, outbuilding, watercraft, aircraft, railroad car, truck, trailer, tent vehicle or shelter with the purpose of committing a theft; and

(1) inflicts or attempts or threatens to inflict physical harm to another; or
(2) the person has a deadly weapon, which is any instrument, device, or thing capable of inflicting death or designed or specially adapted for use as a weapon; or
(3) the person has a dangerous ordnance such as any automatic or sawed off firearm, zip gun or ballistic knife, explosive or incendiary device; or
(4) the structure is the permanent or temporary dwelling of a person.

8. An assistant county prosecutor wants you to research whether Merriweather Halsey committed aggravated burglary based on the following facts:

Merriweather Halsey considered borrowing money from a friend who worked at the local bulb factory. She wandered into the factory around 4:00 A.M., after an AIDS fundraiser. The guard had stepped away from the door for a break. She headed toward her friend's workstation, but she stumbled into an open office where the petty cash was kept. She fell over a secretary's desk. Her leg caught the desk and pulled open a drawer

that contained $500. She thought about taking the money, but she passed out before she took it. She woke up at about 6:00 A.M., when a secretary found her and summoned the security guard.

Halsey then fell onto the security guard, causing him to crash his head into a planter. The guard cut his head and later required six stitches. Halsey thought the security guard was a robber, so she grabbed a letter opener from a nearby desk and told the security guard to back off. The security guard took the letter opener. Halsey's mind was still fuzzy from the alcohol, but she decided to pull a squirt gun out of her pocket to scare the robber.

Draft a question presented for this problem based on the aggravated burglary statute noted in exercise 7 above.

## CONCLUSIONS

9. Draft a conclusion for the problem discussed in exercise 7.
10. Draft a conclusion for the problem discussed in exercise 8.
11. Review the following facts. Make a list of the legally significant facts. Then prepare an issue statement and a conclusion for this problem.

Your client, Hospitality Resorts International, Inc., which does business in your state, is defending an action against James Panhandle, a 70-year-old doctor from Akron, Ohio, who slipped and fell at a London hotel bearing the name Hospitality Resorts of London on January 28, 2014. Panhandle, a semi-retired general practice physician, smashed his head on some wet marble flooring next to the pool. A sign saying "slippery when wet" was set up next to the pool, but Panhandle didn't see the sign. He sustained severe and permanent injuries and was unable to practice medicine for two years.

Panhandle often stayed at the Hospitality Resorts. The resorts were known for cleanliness and hospitality. The staff was friendly and always helpful. The advertising for the resorts claimed that it was the "cleanest in the world. We stay on top of our hotels." Most advertisements stated that the hotels were independently owned and operated. Some ads, such as the one that appeared in the Doctor's Weekly, which Panhandle read, did not state that independent owners owned the London hotel. That ad boasted about the resort, "We care about you. We take care of you. We take care of your home—our resort."

Hospitality Resorts was a trade name. The company that licensed the name Hospitality Resorts to other hotels was called Hospitality Resorts International, Inc. (HRII), your client. Hospitality Resorts licensed its trade name to Fred and Ethel Carrigan of London, England, for use in a hotel there. The Carrigans called the hotel Hospitality Resorts of London. As part of the license agreement, Hospitality Resorts provided training to the staff. The Carrigans hired and fired the staff. HRII had no authority to hire and fire staff.

Panhandle did not know anything about the training or the connection between the London hotel and HRII.

HRII provided operations manuals and suggested procedures and menus. Personnel from HRII regularly traveled to London to advise the hotel employees about their jobs. HRII had no ownership interest in the London hotel. HRII was not authorized to act on behalf of the hotel nor was the hotel authorized to act on behalf of HRII.

The license agreement between HRII and Hospitality Resort of London only provided for HRII to provide its name Hospitality Resort to the London hotel as well as some manuals and technical assistance. It did not authorize the London hotel to act as its agent and HRII was not an agent of the London hotel. HRII did include the Hospitality Resort of London in its list of Hospitality Resorts. That list appeared in many ads as well as in a brochure.

Plaintiff filed suit against the Hospitality Resort in London and Hospitality Resorts, and Hospitality Resorts International, Inc., alleging that HRII is in an agency relationship or apparent or ostensible agency relationship with the London Hospitality Resort. Thus, plaintiff claims that HRII and the London hotel are both responsible for his injuries. This suit was filed in the United States District Court for your area. All the rules of that court and the Federal Rules of Civil Procedures apply.

Does our client have a good defense to the plaintiff's claim that it was in an agency relationship with the London hotel?

Assume that the highest court in your state has held that a hotel owner can be liable based upon the theory of apparent agency. Under that theory, if a business allows another to hold itself out as its representative or the individual or entity holds itself as acting on behalf of the business, the business may be liable for the acts of the individual or entity. Also assume that a decision of the federal appellate court in your area follows your high court's decision.

12. Review this question presented and this conclusion. What legally significant facts are included in the question presented? What legally significant facts are included in the conclusion?

### Question Presented

Did an actionable battery occur when Mann intentionally struck McMillan with a bucket, without McMillan's consent, causing McMillan to suffer physical and monetary injuries?

### Conclusion

Mann's intentional striking of McMillan with a bucket and sand was an actionable battery.

## CHAPTER 21

# FACTS

A.  **FACTS STATEMENT**                                                  444
    1.  Defining *Fact*                                                  444
    2.  Legally Significant Facts                                        444
    3.  Fact Versus a Legal Conclusion                                   446
    4.  Source of Information for a Facts Statement                      447
B.  **ORGANIZING THE FACTS STATEMENT**                                   447
    1.  Chronological Organization                                       447
    2.  Organization by Claim or Defense                                 448
    3.  Organization by Party                                            449
    4.  Combination of Chronological and Claim or Party                  450
        Organization
C.  **WRITING THE FACTS STATEMENT**                                      453
    1.  Prepare a List of Facts and Preliminary Statement                453
    2.  Research the Issue                                               454
    3.  Revise to Include Only Legally Significant Facts                 455
    4.  Organize the Facts                                               455
    5.  Rewrite the Facts Statement                                      456

## CHAPTER OVERVIEW

This chapter explains the purpose of a facts statement and how to draft one. To do this, you need to learn how to determine which facts are legally significant. The chapter discusses the difference between a fact

and a legal conclusion and demonstrates the different organizational structures for the facts section.

# A. FACTS STATEMENT

The **facts statement** is a summary of the information that is relevant to the determination of whether a legal claim exists or whether a defense to such a claim can be made. It is also a summary of the status of a pending case.

A fact statement is an integral part of the office memorandum. Often, an attorney reads this statement to refresh his or her memory about the facts of the case before meeting with a client or a judge. The facts detailed in a memorandum also provide a reference point for your research and the framework for the application of the law.

## 1. Defining *Fact*

A **fact** may be something that is known with certainty. It can be an event. It can be an observation. The answer is not clear-cut. Some facts are pure facts, which means there is no dispute about them. For example, an individual's birth is a **pure fact.** Facts in the court document, such as a complaint or an answer, are **asserted facts**, which means the individual is claiming they occurred. Some information can be objectively tested. That is a fact. For the purpose of the facts statement, note all of this information as facts.

## 2. Legally Significant Facts

▼ What Facts Should Be Included in the Facts Statement?

All facts that might have an impact on the issues presented in a particular case must be included in the memo. These facts are called **legally significant facts.** A good rule is that if you plan to include a fact in your discussion of the law, it should be mentioned in the facts statement.

Legally significant facts are those facts that may affect how a court would decide a particular legal issue. To determine which facts are legally significant, you must understand the legal issue or issues presented in your case. A **legal claim** is comprised of components called **elements** that must be proven before a claim is successful. Legally significant facts are those facts that might prove or disprove any of those elements.

For example, you are asked to research the factors a court will consider when it decides whether Sack and Shop Grocery Store was liable to Rebecca Harris, a patron, for a slip-and-fall accident that occurred in the store. Ms. Harris was injured when she slipped on a

banana peel that a store employee failed to remove from the store floor for two days. Ms. Harris's shopping list included bananas, cherries, and strawberries. You determine that the action or legal claim is based on negligence. You learn that negligence is the breach of a duty of reasonable care that results in an injury to another person. The legal elements of negligence are as follows:

* Existence of a duty
* Breach of that duty
* Injury caused by the breach of the duty

Legally significant facts are those facts that might prove or disprove any of those elements. In this case, the legally significant facts and the legal element that they might prove or disprove would include:

* The slip and fall occurred in the store. (injury, breach)
* Rebecca Harris slipped on a banana peel that a store employee left on the store floor for two days. (injury, caused by breach)
* Rebecca Harris suffered injuries as a result of the fall. (injury)
* Rebecca Harris shopped daily at the store. (duty)
* Rebecca Harris went to the store to make a purchase. (duty)

A fact that is not necessarily legally significant is:

* Rebecca Harris's shopping list included bananas, cherries, and strawberries.

This fact does not prove or disprove any of the elements.

Do not omit any legally significant facts even if you think that an attorney should remember them from client meetings. Attorneys are responsible for multiple cases, and these statements often are used to refresh their recollection. If a fact is not legally significant, you generally would exclude it. However, if the fact explains how a dispute or transaction arose or explains the relationship between the parties, then that fact should be noted. Such a **procedural fact** would assist the reader in understanding the status of a case.

Facts statements provide facts that are advantageous for your clients and those facts that are unfavorable to them. Remember that this is an objective memo. The facts should be presented in a neutral manner, devoid of emotion. Compare the following two examples.

### *EXAMPLE ONE*

Our client, Janice Kahn, seeks to sue Ronnie Randall for intentional infliction of emotional distress following a car accident in which Randall brutally struck Kahn's only child while the precious child was playing T-ball in the street with his friends. This brutal act was done in the presence of Ms. Kahn, a caring mother, who was gardening while

watching her child play. As a result of the incident, Kahn was devastated and emotionally distraught.

### EXAMPLE TWO

Our client, Janice Kahn, seeks to sue Ronnie Randall for intentional infliction of emotional distress following a car accident in which Randall struck Kahn's child while the child was playing T-ball in the street with his friends. After Randall struck the child, he backed up and struck the boy again, running over his head with the rear tire. Ms. Kahn was gardening nearby while watching her child play.

The first example contains several adjectives that slant the statement in favor of Kahn. The statement "Randall brutally struck Kahn's only child" characterizes the action as brutal. This is not a statement of fact. The adjective *brutal* should not be included in a facts statement. The second example is devoid of these **emotional adjectives.** Instead of using the word *brutal,* the example two details the underlying acts that constitute a brutal strike:

> After Randall struck the child, he backed up and struck the boy again, running over his head with the rear tire.

Example two allows readers to draw their own conclusions. The facts statement should not be slanted. Facts such as that Kahn was "a caring mother" or that the child was "precious" should not be incorporated into a facts statement. You should mention only facts, not legal conclusions or definitions of the law.

## 3. Fact Versus a Legal Conclusion

A fact is a piece of information that might explain to the reader what occurred in a particular case. In contrast, a **legal conclusion** is an opinion about the legal significance of a fact. Read the following facts statement:

> Our client, Janice Kahn, seeks to sue Ronnie Randall for intentional infliction of emotional distress following a car accident in which Randall maliciously struck Kahn's only child while the child was playing T-ball in the street with his friends. This malicious and intentional act was done in the presence of Ms. Kahn, a caring mother, who was gardening while watching her child play.

The statements that the act was *malicious* and *intentional* are legal conclusions because the writer makes assumptions about the state of mind of the actor. The term *malicious* is a legal element of many claims; it describes a wicked state of mind. *Intentional* also describes a legal element. You should exclude such characterizations from your facts statements. Instead, describe the acts a person committed that could

be considered malicious, or statements that could indicate that an act was intentional. For example:

> Randall struck Kahn's only child after he told a neighbor that he intended to hit the child with his car while the child was playing T-ball. Randall struck the child with his car while the car was traveling at 25 miles an hour.

The information about Randall's comments to the neighbor, coupled with the speed at which he struck the child, could indicate that Randall struck the child maliciously and intentionally. The proper place to discuss whether an act is either malicious or intentional is in the discussion section of the memo. A definition of the law also is not a statement of fact and should be noted only in the memo discussion.

## 4. Source of Information for a Facts Statement

Most often, information from a client interview is the basis for your facts statement. See the example in Illustration 21-7 later in this chapter. During a court dispute, information for the facts statement also can be found in witness statements, complaints, answers, or discovery materials, such as depositions and interrogatories. For these facts, note the source of the information. For transactions, information might be contained in various business records or contracts.

# B. ORGANIZING THE FACTS STATEMENT

A facts statement can be organized in several ways: chronologically, by claim or defense, by party, or according to a combination of these three methods.

▼ What Are the Different Methods of Organizing a Facts Statement?

## 1. Chronological Organization

A **chronological organization** is based on the order of events. You start with the event that occurred first and end with the event that occurred last. You also can write the statement in **reverse chronological order**, beginning with the last event and ending with the first. For some claims, such as those stemming from an accident, a contract dispute, or a criminal case, chronological organization works well because these concerns often are ordered by time. See Illustration 21-1.

The statement in Illustration 21-1 first introduces the claim. In the succeeding paragraphs, the events are detailed in chronological order from start to finish. Illustration 21-2 starts with the last event and ends with the information about the beginning of the day.

## ILLUSTRATION 21-1.   Chronological Organization

Dr. James Panhandle is suing our client, Hospitality Resorts International, Inc., for negligence stemming from injuries he sustained when he slipped and fell on January 28, 2014, at the Hospitality Resort of London. The doctor seeks $8 million in damages.

On the day of the accident, children were playing in the pool at 8:00 A.M. The children splashed water out of the pool and onto the marble floor near the pool. The floor had not been mopped at any time during the day.

At 8:00 P.M., Dr. Panhandle was walking slowly out of the hotel coffee shop that was adjacent to the pool. He slipped on the wet marble floor next to the pool.

The doctor hit his head on the marble floor, causing him to crack his skull and to bleed.

## ILLUSTRATION 21-2.   Reverse Chronological Order

Dr. James Panhandle is suing our client, Hospitality Resorts International, Inc., for negligence stemming from injuries he sustained when he slipped and fell on January 28, 2014, at the Hospitality Resort of London. The doctor seeks $8 million in damages.

The doctor hit his head on the marble floor, causing him to crack his skull and to bleed.

At 8:00 P.M., Dr. Panhandle was walking slowly out of the hotel coffee shop that was adjacent to the pool. He slipped on the wet marble floor next to the pool.

On the day of the accident, children were playing in the pool at 8:00 A.M. The children splashed water out of the pool and onto the marble floor near the pool. The floor had not been mopped at any time during the day.

## 2. Organization by Claim or Defense

Facts statements also can be **organized by claim or defense.** In statements of this kind, legally significant facts that relate to a claim or a defense are grouped together. See Illustration 21-3. This method is useful when the issue does not concern events that can be organized by time sequence and the information involves individuals who are not parties to the action.

**ILLUSTRATION 21-3.   Organization by Claim or Defense**

Our clients, the Black Hawks, want to know whether the attorney-client privilege can be asserted by a former company president, Debbie Irl, and a current employee, Meredith Tildy, head of the cleaning staff. These questions arose while the plaintiff's attorney was deposing these individuals on July 8, 2013, as part of the discovery in a personal injury lawsuit stemming from a slip and fall at the stadium.

Irl, president of the Hawks at the time of the accident, left the organization in June 2010. During her tenure with the organization, she was a decision maker and she drafted the cleaning policy for the stadium. Irl had spoken with the Hawks' attorney, Ace Rudd, about the accident on July 10, 2012. Irl is not named as a party in the lawsuit and is merely a witness. During the deposition, the plaintiff's attorney asked Irl about her conversation with Rudd. Irl asserted the attorney-client privilege.

Meredith Tildy, the current head of the Hawks' cleaning staff, knew about the accident. Beer had been spilled the night before the accident. A patron told the staff to mop up the beer when it happened. Tildy knew that the cleaning staff had failed to clean up the beer. In her position, Tildy schedules the staff and decides whether the stadium should be cleaned completely each night. On July 10, 2012, Tildy spoke with Rudd, the company attorney, about the accident. The plaintiff's attorney asked Tildy about her conversation with Rudd. Based upon Rudd's advice, Tildy asserted the attorney-client privilege.

In Illustration 21-3's sample facts statement, the details are organized by claim. The first paragraph introduces the claims—the assertion of attorney-client privilege by Irl and Tildy. The next paragraph includes the facts that are legally significant to Irl's claim of attorney-client privilege. The final paragraph focuses on the facts that are legally significant to Tildy and Tildy's assertion of the attorney-client privilege. Because neither Irl nor Tildy is a party, this organization works well.

## 3. Organization by Party

Another way to organize the facts is to **organize by party**, grouping the facts according to the party the facts describe. This method is useful when multiple parties are involved in a dispute. See Illustration 21-4, which involves a dispute between three parties: a company and two individuals. The memo focuses on whether Whole In One is an employer under Title VII and whether two individuals are employees or independent contractors.

The first paragraph in Illustration 21-4 introduces the claim. The next paragraph describes one of the parties, Whole In One. The next paragraph describes another party, Walker. The final paragraph tells the reader about Radiant, the third party in the action.

## ILLUSTRATION 21-4.   Organization by Party

Victoria Radiant and Karen Walker, two former Whole In One Enterprises workers, brought a federal sex discrimination lawsuit, based upon Title VII, against our client, Whole In One Enterprises, owned by Nancy and Craig Black. The lawsuit, filed in the U.S. District Court for the Northern District of Illinois, stems from the dismissal of the two women by the Blacks during 2012.

The Blacks own Whole In One Enterprises, which operates a miniature golf course and restaurant in Glenview, Illinois. During the 24-week 2012 restaurant season, 10 people worked full-time and 14 people worked part-time for Whole In One. However, no more than 14 people worked on any one day. Of those 14 people, only 3 were full-time employees. The other full-time employees regularly took days off during the summer restaurant and golf season. Among the full-time workers was Karen Walker, who worked as a public relations director for Whole In One. Walker responded to an ad that said that "an employer" sought an individual to perform public relations work. Whole In One hired Walker without a contract and told her she was prohibited from working for other firms. However, Walker worked from home and set her own hours. Whole In One required Walker to attend weekly staff meetings at the company offices, where Whole In One would review and revise Walker's work. The company supplied Walker with paper, pencils, stamps, and telephone service and paid for her life and health insurance. Whole In One did not withhold taxes from Walker's commissions.Victoria Radiant, who had a two-year employment contract with the company, provided marketing services to Whole In One from October of 2010 until she was fired in 2012. Although Radiant worked in the company office, Whole In One management rarely supervised her work. The company paid for her continued education, provided her with bonuses, and deducted taxes from her weekly salary.

## 4. Combination of Chronological and Claim or Party Organization

Some facts statements do not lend themselves to one type of organization. Some facts should be arranged by the order of the events, and others do not fit neatly into this arrangement. Therefore, you might group facts in chronological order and by party or claim. See Illustration 21-5.

The facts statement in Illustration 21-5 concerns the question of whether Janice Kahn can successfully pursue a claim against Ronnie Randall for intentional infliction of emotional distress after Randall struck Kahn's 11-year-old son with Randall's car. The accident itself is best described in a chronological manner because the events can be explained in a sequential order. However, the witness statements and other "facts" that relate to whether Randall intentionally struck the child and whether Randall intended to cause emotional distress when he struck the child should be organized by issue or claim.

In some instances, your organization should be structured by the sequence of the events and by the parties. See Illustration 21-6.

## ILLUSTRATION 21-5.  Chronological and Claim Organization

While driving a car, Ronnie Randall struck Janice Kahn's son at 5:00 P.M. on August 29, 2013. It was bright and clear. No skid marks appeared on the dry street following the accident. Janice Kahn was working in her garden about five feet from the accident scene at the time of the accident. Her son was playing a game in the street before Randall's car struck him. Kahn did not see the car strike her 11-year-old son. When she first looked up from her garden, she thought her son was dead. He was covered with blood and had several broken bones. However, Kahn's son was conscious after the accident.

Immediately after the accident, Randall, who had a blood alcohol level of .11, was cited for drunk driving and driving with a suspended driver's license. Police had charged him with drunk driving and suspended his license two weeks earlier after the car he was driving struck another child at the same spot. Randall has a history of alcohol abuse.

Following the accident, several witnesses said Randall was upset and wobbled as he walked. One witness said that Randall intentionally turned the steering wheel to hit Kahn's son. Kahn stated that Randall often swerved down her street to get her attention.

Rhonda Albert, Kahn's neighbor, said she heard Randall say he would get even with Kahn after Kahn broke off a ten-year relationship with him.

During Kahn and Randall's ten-year relationship, Randall was close to Kahn's son. He took him to ball games, including one in April, and attended the son's baseball games. Randall knew that Kahn's son was the most important person in her life.

Since the accident, Kahn vomits daily and suffers from anxiety and headaches. Dr. Susan Faigen, Kahn's internist, states that the vomiting, anxiety, and headaches are the result of the accident.

### ILLUSTRATION 21-6.    Chronological and Party Organization

Merriweather Halsey and Bonnie Bill were at the Masonic Temple for a fundraiser to fight AIDS. During the fundraiser Bill told a drunken Halsey that she intended to steal the $8,000 proceeds from the Masonic Temple and a pearl necklace from Alice McKinley after the fundraiser. Bill, who had helped organize the fundraiser, watched as the chairperson of the fundraiser opened the safe and placed the money in it. She memorized the combination and decided that she would use it later to steal the money.

After the fundraiser, Bill walked home to get a credit card and a crowbar to open the door if she needed it. Bill went to the Masonic Temple after the fundraiser, wearing a disguise, showed the guard her invitation, and told him that she had lost her mother's diamond brooch inside. Although the guard did not remember her, he allowed her to go into the temple. She wandered around the building for about an hour with the brooch inside her purse.

When the guard decided to eat his supper, Bill went to the safe. She opened it and pulled out all the money, except for $1,000.

Bill told the guard she had found the brooch and then left. She went to Alice McKinley's home, entered the house through an open ground-floor window, and took the pearl necklace she had seen Alice wearing earlier, and then left.

Merriweather Halsey considered borrowing money from a friend who worked at a local bulb factory. She wandered into the factory around 4:00 A.M., after the fundraiser. The guard had stepped away from the door for a break. She headed toward her friend's workstation, but she stumbled into an open office where the petty cash was kept. She fell over a secretary's desk. Her leg caught the desk and pulled open a drawer that contained $500. She thought about taking the money, but she passed out before she took it. She woke up about 6:00 A.M., when a secretary found her and summoned the security guard.

Halsey then fell into the security guard, causing him to crash his head into a planter. The guard cut his head and later required six stitches. Halsey thought the security guard was a robber, so she grabbed a letter opener from a nearby desk and told the security guard to back off. The security guard took the letter opener. Halsey's mind was still fuzzy from the alcohol, but she decided to pull a squirt gun out of her pocket to scare the robber.

The question is whether Bill or Halsey can be convicted of aggravated burglary under Houcktown County law.

---

In Illustration 21-6, the first paragraph introduces both parties, Bonnie Bill and Merriweather Halsey. The facts statement details most of the night's events in chronological order. However, the parties, Bill and Halsey, leave the fundraiser separately. At this point, the organization changes from chronological to one focusing on each party. First, facts that are legally significant to Bill's escapades are explained. These are noted in chronological order from start to finish.

After the facts concerning Bill's adventure, the facts related to Halsey's acts at the bulb factory are detailed. These facts also are explained in chronological order. The final paragraph tells the reader the issues that will be considered in the memo.

# C. WRITING THE FACTS STATEMENT

## 1. Prepare a List of Facts and Preliminary Statement

After you meet with an attorney to discuss your research assignment, make a list of the facts and draft a preliminary facts statement. Illustration 21-7 shows an excerpt from a client interview. Following the interview is a list of the facts and a preliminary facts statement, Illustration 21-8, that includes all the facts provided in the interview.

### ILLUSTRATION 21-7.   Excerpt from a Client Interview

*Attorney:* What can I do for you today, Mr. Grocer of Sack and Shop?

*Grocer:* Rebecca Harris, one of my regular customers, is suing me for $1 million.

*Attorney:* What happened?

*Grocer:* Ms. Harris came to the store to purchase cherries, strawberries, and bananas. When she was turning the corner in the produce section, she slipped on a banana peel.

*Attorney:* How long had the banana peel been on the floor?

*Grocer:* Two days.

*Attorney:* Did you or any of your employees know about the banana peel on the floor?

*Grocer:* Yes. One of the patrons told the head of the produce department to clean up the banana peel two days before Ms. Harris fell.

*Attorney:* Why wasn't it picked up?

*Grocer:* The produce department head was in a hurry to leave and forgot to do it. The next day, he was very busy and he kicked the banana peel into a corner. Apparently it somehow was knocked out of the corner and to the middle of the floor where Ms. Harris slipped on it.

*Attorney:* Were there any witnesses?

*Grocer:* I saw her slip.

*Attorney:* What was Ms. Harris doing when she slipped?

*Grocer:* She was walking toward the green peppers.

*Attorney:* What day did the incident occur?

*Grocer:* July 8, 2013. The same day another accident occurred in the produce section that involved a piece of cut cantaloupe.

*Attorney:* Was Ms. Harris injured?

*Grocer:* She hurt her head and broke her arm At least, I think she broke her arm because the bones didn't seem to be connected properly. It looked like part of the bone was dangling.

*Attorney:* Was anyone injured in the second accident?

*Grocer:* Yes. A man slipped on the cantaloupe and broke his finger.

## ILLUSTRATION 21-8. Sample Preliminary Facts Statement Based on the Client Interview

BRIEF LIST OF FACTS:
Client: Sack and Shop Grocery Store
Plaintiff: Rebecca Harris

Slip and fall at grocery store on July 8, 2013.

Plaintiff slipped on a banana peel, which had been left on the store floor for two days.

Harris was walking to the green peppers.

Another accident happened in the same section when a man slipped on a cantaloupe and broke his finger.

A patron told the store employee to clean up the banana peel two days earlier.

The employee kicked it into a corner.

Somehow the peel got to the middle of the floor again.

Harris came to the store to purchase cherries, strawberries, and bananas.

### Preliminary Facts Statement

Our client, Sack and Shop Grocery Store, is being sued for negligence by Rebecca Harris.

Harris went to the store to purchase cherries, strawberries, and bananas on July 8, 2013.

While Harris was in the produce section, she slipped on a banana peel that had been left on the floor by a grocery store employee. The employee dropped it on the floor two days earlier and had failed to clean it up after a patron asked him to do so. The employee had kicked the peel into the corner two days before the accident. Somehow the peel found its way to the middle of the floor on the date of the accident.

Harris sustained a broken arm and head injuries as a result of the slip and fall. Another man was injured in the produce department that same day when he slipped and fell on some cantaloupe.

## 2. Research the Issue

After you prepare your list and preliminary facts statement, the next step is to research the legal issue or issues and to determine the applicable law.

## 3. Revise to Include Only Legally Significant Facts

Revise your list so that it includes only the legally significant facts, the facts that will have a bearing on the applicable law. See Illustration 21-9. To draft this list, you must determine the legal elements necessary to establish a claim. In the case of negligence, you would learn that negligence is the breach of a duty of reasonable care that results in injuries to another person. The elements then would be:

- duty of reasonable care
- breach of the duty
- a link between the breach of the duty and the resulting injuries
- injuries

You should review the facts and determine which facts may affect whether the plaintiff can establish one of these elements or whether the defendant would be able to disprove one of the elements—in other words, the legally significant facts. In this case, you should include all of the facts listed in Illustration 21-9. In that illustration, the element of the legal theory is noted in parentheses next to the legally significant fact. The fact that Harris was purchasing cherries, strawberries, and bananas is not legally significant. Similarly, the fact that another patron was injured in the produce section that day did not affect whether Harris was injured and therefore is not legally significant.

### ILLUSTRATION 21-9. List of Legally Significant Facts

- The slip and fall occurred in the store on July 8, 2008. (breach and duty)
- Rebecca Harris slipped on a banana peel that had been left on the store floor for two days. (breach and duty)
- The store employee dropped the banana peel on the floor two days earlier. (breach and duty)
- A store employee knew about the banana peel on the floor two days before the accident. (breach and duty)
- The employee kicked the peel into the corner after a patron told him to clean it up. (breach and duty)
- Rebecca Harris suffered injuries as a result of the fall. (link and injuries)

## 4. Organize the Facts

After you have made your list of facts, decide how to organize them. After you select your organizational method, group the legally significant facts together in the organizational style you have selected.

---

*PRACTICE POINTER*

Sometimes you will use multiple organization methods.

---

## 5. Rewrite the Facts Statement

The facts contained in Illustration 21-9 lend themselves to a chronological organization because they can be ordered by time. Illustration 21-10 is a rewritten facts statement that includes only the legally significant facts. Finally, remember to introduce the legal issue or issues presented in the facts statement, as shown in the first paragraph of Illustration 21-10.

### ILLUSTRATION 21-10.  Sample Facts Statement for Slip-and-Fall Case

---

Rebecca Harris, a store patron, is suing our client, Sack and Shop Grocery Store, for negligence.

While Harris was in the produce department, on July 8, 2013, she slipped on a banana peel that had been left on the floor by a grocery store employee. The employee dropped it on the floor two days earlier and had failed to clean it up after a patron asked him to do so. When he was told to pick up the peel, the employee kicked the peel into the corner.

Harris sustained a broken arm and head injuries as a result of the slip and fall.

---

## CHAPTER SUMMARY

A facts statement is designed to refresh an attorney's memory about a case or to educate a new attorney about the case. It is a statement of all facts that are legally significant (facts that might affect the outcome of a legal issue). Facts that are not legally significant should be omitted from a facts statement.

Facts statements can be organized in chronological or reverse chronological order, by claim or defense, by party, or any combination of these three.

To draft your statement, make a list of the facts, plan your organization, then write the statement. Next, research the legal issue, then rewrite your facts statement because the legally significant facts may have changed based on your research.

In the next chapter, you will learn how to organize using the IRAC methodology.

## KEY TERMS

| | |
|---|---|
| asserted facts | legal conclusion |
| chronological organization | legally significant facts |
| elements | organization by claim or defense |
| emotional adjectives | organization by party |
| fact | procedural fact |
| facts statement | pure fact |
| legal claim | reverse chronological order |

## EXERCISES

### SHORT ANSWER

1. What is a facts statement?
2. What are legally significant facts?
3. What are pure facts?
4. What are asserted facts?
5. What are procedural facts?
6. What facts should be included in the facts statement?
7. What is the difference between a fact and a legal conclusion?
8. Where do you find the information to include in the facts statement?
9. List several methods for organizing a facts statement.
10. Explain two methods of organization.

### DRAFTING A LIST OF RELEVANT FACTS

11. Review the following Uniform Commercial Code section and read the list of facts that follows. Make a list of the legally significant facts based on the statute. Next to each fact, list the relevant portion of the statute.

### § 2-315 Implied Warranty of Fitness for a Particular Purpose

Where the seller at the time of contracting has reason to know any particular purpose for which the goods are required and that buyer is relying on the seller's skill or judgment to select or furnish suitable goods, there is unless excluded or modified under the next section an implied warranty that the goods be fit for such purpose.

### Facts

Your client is Sue A. Buyer. She lives at 3225 Wilmette Avenue, Glenview, Illinois. The defendants are Lee R. Merchant, owner of Mowers R Us, in Glenview, Illinois, and Manny U. Facture, the owner of a manufacturing concern that is not incorporated called Mowers, of Rosemont, Illinois. Ms. Buyer went to the defendant's store, Mowers R Us, to purchase a lawn mower for her new home. She was a first-time homeowner and was unfamiliar with lawn mowers. She had never operated a lawn mower because her brothers had always mowed the lawn when she was a child.

When she went to Mowers R Us, she asked to speak with the owner. She told Mr. Merchant: "I don't know anything about these mowers, and I need to talk with an expert." Mr. Merchant said, "I'm the owner, and you couldn't find a better expert anywhere in the Chicagoland area. I have been in the business of selling mowers for more than 40 years. I only sell mowers and the equipment to clean and repair them. Are you familiar with the type of lawn mower you would like?"

"No, I don't know anything about lawn mowers. I just know that I have to have a lawn mower that will mulch my grass clippings, because I cannot bag the clippings. The village of Glenview does not permit me to bag the clippings, so the clippings must remain on my lawn."

"You're absolutely correct. You must have a mulching mower," Mr. Merchant said. "That type of mower will grind the grass clippings, and you will not notice them on your grass. I have the perfect mower for you. It is a used model that will fit into your price range, only $200. It's a good brand, a Roro, and will mulch the grass as well as any of the new mowers. This one is true blue. You can purchase a separate mulching blade, which will easily attach to it for an additional $50," he added.

"Do you think that I need the mulching blade?" Ms. Buyer asked, "I've never used a lawn mower, so I don't know what to expect, and you appear to be the expert."

"I think that you could do without the mulching blade unless you want the grass ground up very fine."

"I think that I would like it ground up fine. I'll defer to your judgment. If you think a mulching blade is necessary, then I'll buy that with the mower. Do you think that this is the best mower for mulching, or should I go with a new one?"

"Absolutely the used one is best; I told you: it's a true value. It will mulch with the best of them."

"If you think it can do the job, I'll trust your judgment," said Ms. Buyer, "I'll take the mower and the mulching blade. Can you install the mulching blade? I don't know anything about the installation.

"Sure, we can install any blade for another $30."

Ms. Buyer purchased the mower and the blade. She used the mower after Mr. Merchant installed the new mulching blade. It barely cut the grass and certainly didn't mulch the clippings into fine pieces as Mr. Merchant had claimed.

She brought the mower back to Mr. Merchant. He said that he had made no warranties about the mower. He showed her the language on the receipt that said that he did not expressly warrant anything.

Ms. Buyer brought the mower to a Roro dealer. The owners of the Roro dealership, Abe Saul and Lou T. Wright, said that the mower Ms. Buyer had purchased from Mowers R Us was not a mulching mower. It was a mower built before mulching was popular. Therefore, it would not perform the mulching task. It was designed merely to cut the grass. "Any merchant who has been in business even for one year should have known that mowers built before 2000 were not designed for mulching," Mr. Wright said. He showed Ms. Buyer where the manufacturing date appeared on the mower. "Manufactured in

August 1999," it said on the plate with the serial number. "Also, mulching blades cannot be placed on these old mowers. Any mower dealer should know that too," Mr. Wright added. "However, this mower isn't bad. It can cut the grass without mulching it."

Ms. Buyer brought an action against Mr. Merchant and Mr. Facture in the Cook County Circuit Court, Skokie, IL.

## OBJECTIVE WRITING

12. Write three different discussions about your high school career. One discussion should present the experience in a negative manner. The second should attempt to persuade the reader that the experience was positive. Finally, write about your experience in a neutral manner, without any emotion. Compare the three discussions.

## DRAFTING A FACTS STATEMENT

13. Draft a facts statement for our client, Ronnie Randall. Janice Kahn, the plaintiff, brought an action against Randall for intentional infliction of emotional distress. You should prepare your facts statement based on this excerpt from a deposition transcript, witness statements, and a police report. The facts statement will be included in a memo that discusses the issue of intentional infliction of emotional distress. For the purpose of this memo, intentional infliction of emotional distress is defined as follows:

An act by a person that is extreme and outrageous conduct, done with intent to cause another to suffer severe emotional distress, and which results in distress and emotional injury to another. The emotional injury must manifest itself with a physical problem.

Below is a portion of Janice Kahn's deposition transcript.

*Q.* What were you doing when the accident occurred?
*A.* Working in my garden. I planted tomatoes, green peppers, carrots, and broccoli.
*Q.* Where is your garden located on your property?
*A.* In the front, near the street. It is next to a brick wall. I can't see the garden from my house.
*Q.* What direction were you facing in your garden?
*A.* North.
*Q.* Does that direction face the street?
*A.* No.
*Q.* What do you usually do in your garden when you work?
*A.* Weed it.
*Q.* What were you doing in your garden when the accident occurred?
*A.* Weeding it.
*Q.* Where is the street in relation to your garden?

*A.*   About five feet.

*Q.*   Where do the children generally play?

*A.*   In the backyard.

*Q.*   Where were the children playing on the day of the accident?

*A.*   They were playing T-ball in the front yard.

*Q.*   Were you watching the children at the time of the accident?

*A.*   Yes I could see them.

*Q.*   Did you see the accident occur?

*A.*   Sort of.

*Q.*   Did you or did you not see the accident?

*A.*   I saw my son, who is 11 years old, on the ground covered with blood, and blood all over the front of the Cadillac.

*Q.*   Did you actually see the driver strike your son?

*A.*   No. But I know Ronnie hit him. I saw my son next to Ronnie's car. I heard him swerve.

*Q.*   Did you know the driver?

*A.*   Yes.

*Q.*   How did you know him?

*A.*   We met at a state fair. We dated for ten years. I broke up with him two weeks before the accident.

*Q.*   Did he know your son?

*A.*   He knew my son was the most important person to me, and he tried to kill him to pay me back for dumping him.

*Q.*   Are you accusing the driver of intentionally striking your son?

*A.*   Yes. He wanted to get back at me, so he hit my boy.

*Q.*   What happened to your son on the day of the accident?

*A.*   He sustained head injuries and several broken bones. He can't play T-ball for the rest of the season, and we had to cancel our vacation to the Dells because he's been hurting so much.

*Q.*   Was he conscious when you first saw him after the accident?

*A.*   He was awake, but I thought he was dead at first. He had blood everywhere. I knew the driver, Ronnie, was drunk when he hit him. He wasn't even looking where he was going. He always swerves down our street to get my attention.

*Q.*   Did your son speak to you right after the accident?

*A.*   Barely. I told him that Ronnie was speeding and trying to run him down on purpose. I was horrified to see the blood and the broken bones. I couldn't move and I was so angry at Ronnie because I knew he did this on purpose.

*Q.*   Did you go to the doctor after this accident?

*A.*   I went by ambulance with my son to the doctor. His doctor looked me over and said I was suffering from shock. Since then, I suffered from anxiety and headaches. I throw up every day.

*Q.*   Have you seen a doctor for your complaints?

*A.*   Yes. She said that they are related to the accident. I just keep thinking back to that day when the neighbor told me that Ronnie intentionally turned the wheel to hit my boy.

*Q.* Was your son able to move after the accident?

*A.* Slightly. He looked just like our neighbor's son did after Ronnie hit him with his car two weeks before at the same curve.

### Police Report, State of Illinois

Ronnie Randall, the driver of a 2013 Cadillac, was cited for driving while under the influence of alcohol and/or drugs, reckless driving, and driving with a suspended license. I will ask the prosecutor to consider either reckless assault charges or vehicular homicide, depending upon the condition of the boy. I tested Randall for alcohol intoxication. His blood alcohol level was .11. Randall struck another boy, Tommy Albert, at the same site two weeks earlier. He was cited for reckless driving for that accident and drunk driving. As I arrested Randall, he said that he was daydreaming during the accident and that he did not mean to hit the child. There were no skid marks. The street was dry.

The boy's mother, Janice Kahn, was working in her garden about five feet from the accident scene at the time of the accident. Her son, Billy Kahn, was playing a game in the street.

### Witness Statement

Two days before the accident, Rhonda Albert, a neighbor of Janice Kahn, heard Randall say that he planned to get even with Kahn after Kahn broke off her ten-year relationship with Randall. Albert saw the car strike Kahn's son. According to Albert, after the car struck the boy, Randall got out of his car and said, "Oh, my God. I didn't mean to hit him. Is he okay?" Albert could smell alcohol on Randall's breath.

### Witness Statement

Rebecca Mark saw the driver, Ronnie Randall, turn the car toward Kahn's son.

## REVIEW OF FACTS STATEMENTS

14. Now that you have reviewed the facts for the *Janice Kahn* case and have drafted a statement of your own, read the following statements of facts. Determine which facts statement is best. List any errors you find in any of the statements.

    A. The plaintiff, a single mother, and the defendant, her ex-boyfriend, are involved in a lawsuit. The plaintiff alleges in her deposition that the defendant was driving recklessly and intentionally struck her son with his car. The defendant's motive was to pay her back for ending their relationship. He tried to kill her son for this reason. As a result of the accident, the plaintiff went into shock and suffers from anxiety, headaches, and vomiting.

    B. The plaintiff was working in her tomato garden located in the front of the property about five feet from the street. She could see the children playing in the front yard. She did not see the driver, Ronnie Randall, hit her son with his Cadillac but did see blood on the front of the Cadillac and on her son, who was on the ground.

The plaintiff dated Randall for ten years and had just ended their relationship. She states that Ronnie hit her son to pay her back for ending their relationship. Two weeks before, Ronnie had hit a neighbor's son at the same curve.

The plaintiff states that her son was covered with blood, able to move slightly. He suffered head trauma and broken bones.

The plaintiff is suffering from shock after seeing her son. She remembers a neighbor telling her that Ronnie intentionally turned the wheel to hit her son.

The plaintiff suffers from anxiety and headaches and vomits daily.

C. Janice Kahn is bringing an action against Ronnie Randall for the intentional infliction of emotional distress. Her son was recently hit by Ronnie Randall's car on the street in front of the Kahn home. At the time of the injury, Kahn was working in the front yard near her son. Her son went into the street and Randall hit him. At the time of the accident, Randall was legally drunk and driving with a suspended license.

Randall had previously told Kahn's neighbor, a Ms. Albert, that he was going to get even with Ms. Kahn over the breakup of their ten-year relationship. He also told Ms. Albert that he knew that Ms. Kahn's son was very important to her.

Since the accident, Kahn vomits daily and suffers from anxiety and headaches. She has stated that Mr. Randall often drives by her home in an erratic fashion and on another occasion hit a neighbor's child. Kahn feels that Randall hit her son intentionally. Kahn did not see the injury take place but was at her son's side immediately after the injury. Kahn also says that Randall never slowed down until after he hit her son.

D. On August 12, 2013, Janice Kahn filed a lawsuit against Ronnie Randall for intentional infliction of emotional distress stemming from an accident involving Kahn's 11-year-old son.

On July 8, 2013, Janice Kahn was weeding her tomato garden while her children played T-ball a few feet away from her in the street. As she worked, Kahn heard a car swerve. She looked up to see her son, covered in blood, lying on the ground in front of a Cadillac, driven by Ronnie Randall.

Two neighbors witnessed the accident. Rebecca Mark saw the driver, Ronnie Randall, turn the car toward Kahn's son. Rhonda Albert also saw the car strike Kahn's son. According to Albert, after the car struck the boy, Randall got out of his car and said, "Oh, my God. I didn't mean to hit him. Is he okay?"

Albert could smell alcohol on Randall's breath. Police tested his blood alcohol level and found that it was .11. Police cited Randall for drunk driving, speeding, and reckless driving.

After police arrived, an ambulance took Kahn and her son to the hospital, where he was treated for head injuries and broken bones. The doctor who treated Kahn's son told Kahn that she should be treated for shock. Since the accident, Kahn has suffered from anxiety and headaches and vomits daily. Her doctor said that the anxiety, headaches, and vomiting are the result of the accident.

The driver of the car involved in the accident was Kahn's former boyfriend. They had dated for ten years; however, Kahn broke off the relationship about two weeks before the accident. Kahn stated in her deposition that she believes Randall intentionally struck her son to pay her back for ending the relationship.

Also, two days before the accident Albert heard Randall say that he planned to get even with Kahn after Kahn broke off their ten-year relationship. However, the police report stated that Randall said that he was daydreaming during the accident and that he did not mean to hit the child. Since the breakup, Kahn has seen Randall often swerve down the street in front of her home. Two weeks before the accident, Randall hit Rhonda Albert's son with his Cadillac at the same curve.

## CHAPTER 22

# THE IRAC METHOD

| | | |
|---|---|---|
| **A.** | **PURPOSES OF IRAC** | 466 |
| **B.** | **IRAC COMPONENTS** | 466 |
| | 1. Issues | 468 |
| | 2. Rules of Law | 469 |
| | 3. Application of the Law to the Problem's Facts | 471 |
| | 4. Conclusion | 472 |

## *CHAPTER OVERVIEW*

The IRAC chapter focuses on the writing style used for the discussion portion of the memo. IRAC is an acronym for Issue, Rule, Application, Conclusion. These are the building blocks of a memo's discussion. IRAC is used most frequently in objective writing. You will learn to identify issues and applicable legal authority. You will also learn how to extract the legally significant facts and apply them to the relevant law to draw substantiated conclusions. You will learn to identify effective IRAC use by dissecting discussions and labeling the IRAC components, and you will learn to draft IRAC sequences as well.

# A. PURPOSES OF IRAC

### ▼ What Is IRAC?

**IRAC** stands for Issue, Rule, Application, Conclusion. IRAC is the architectural blueprint for the discussion portion of a legal memo. It gives legal writing continuity and clarity and organizes the contents of the discussion. The IRAC format provides an organizational structure for your document. IRAC provides legal support and analysis for the issues posed by the problem and guides the writer toward a well-supported conclusion.

IRAC benefits both the writer and the reader because the components are essentially a checklist designed to ensure that the discussion is analytically well thought-out and that it contains the necessary legal authority. IRAC is very important because it lets the reader see the particular legal point being addressed, the relevant legal rule, the application of the law to the facts, and the conclusion. It is formula writing in the same way that formula movie romances, westerns, and thrillers are. The predictability of the IRAC format enables the reader to obtain the information quickly.

The CUNY Law School Writing Center website has information on using the IRAC format at www.law.cuny.edu/legal-writing/students/irac-crracc/irac-crracc-1.html.

# B. IRAC COMPONENTS

Each IRAC sequence is composed of an issue, which is really a legal element or component; the **legal rule** or holding from a case or statutory authority; the application, which is a demonstration of how the legal authority applies to the problem that you are writing about; and the conclusion, the final assessment of how the rule applies to the facts of your problem.

### ▼ What Does an IRAC Paragraph Look Like?

This fact pattern forms the basis of the IRAC paragraph example.

On August 7, 2013, Ms. Howard went to Rough & Tough Pawn Shop in Chicago to obtain a loan using a diamond ring as collateral. Rough & Tough loaned Ms. Howard $800, and she agreed to pay $75 per month

for a total of 13-1/2 months. Ms. Howard knew that she would have to pay off the balance of $1,025 in 12 months because at that time Rough & Tough would have the right to sell the ring. On September 11, 2013, Ms. Howard received a postcard from Rough & Tough stating that it was selling the shop and all of its assets to Able Pawn. Mr. Sam Able would assume the business of Rough & Tough, including all pawned items and outstanding loans. On the bottom of the postcard was a notice stating; "If you want your item, please pick it up by September 29, 2013, and pay off your note by September 29, 2013." Because Ms. Howard did not have the money to pay off the note, she decided to pay Able Pawn the $75 per month once the loan was transferred in the sale. In October 2013, Able Pawn was robbed and all the jewelry, including Ms. Howard's ring, was stolen. Able Pawn had a security alarm system and a guard dog to protect the property, but the robbers were able to circumvent these obstacles.

We will work through the following sample IRAC paragraph, based on the Howard fact pattern, and its components to illustrate how to draft an IRAC paragraph.

(**I**) Whether a bailment for the mutual benefit of Rough & Tough and Howard existed. (**R**) A pawn is a form of bailment, made for the mutual benefit of bailee and bailor, arising when goods are delivered to another as a pawn for security to him on money borrowed by the bailor. *Jacobs v. Grossman,* 141 N.E. 714, 715 (Ill. App. Ct. 1923). In *Jacobs,* the court found that a bailment for mutual benefit arose because the plaintiff pawned a ring as collateral for a $70 loan given to him by the defendant. *Id.* (**A**) Similarly in our problem, Howard pawned her ring as collateral to secure an $800 loan given to her by Rough & Tough, the pawnbroker. (**C**) Therefore, Howard and Rough & Tough probably created a bailment for mutual benefit.

Note that the first sentence of the IRAC paragraph is a statement of the issue that will be examined in the paragraph. The issue is narrowly defined and focused on one of the analytical elements of the problem. The rule of law, the next component of the paragraph, provides the legal basis for the analysis of the issue. Then, it is appropriate to discuss some of the facts of the cited case if these facts help explain how the legal rule can be applied to your facts. Notice that everything that comes from an opinion is given citation credit.

The most important component of the IRAC paragraph is the application portion. The application is where you use the facts of your problem to demonstrate, but not to conclude, why the legal rule should apply to the issue posed. This is the legal analysis. (See Chapter 18 for more discussion.) The facts speak for themselves when you demonstrate how the legal rule applies to the scenario at hand by contrasting or paralleling the facts of the case and the problem. After laying out this relationship, you will then draw a conclusion. The conclusion answers the issue posed. The issue is the question being examined in the discussion, and the conclusion is the answer.

This example illustrates how the conclusion responds directly to the issue:

**Issue:** Whether a bailment for the mutual benefit of Rough & Tough and Howard existed.

**Conclusion:** Therefore, Howard and Rough & Tough probably created a bailment, for it was for their mutual benefit because a loan was given upon the receipt of valuable collateral.

## 1. Issues

The question presented is the overall legal **issue** that will be resolved in the memo. A **subissue** in the IRAC paragraph is a point or query that must be addressed to substantiate one legal element of the problem. When analyzing and writing about a legal problem objectively, it is often important to address subissues in the order that they must be resolved to support legal analysis. For example, the general rule for arson in Illinois is the malicious burning of the dwelling house of another. The question presented for a memo on arson would be:

Whether Mr. Smith committed arson by intentionally burning down his brother's factory.

The subissues addressed in the IRAC paragraphs would be:

Whether there was a malicious burning

Whether the factory is a dwelling house

Whether the factory of Mr. Smith's brother constitutes the property of another person

The subissues form the **topic sentences** of the IRAC paragraphs. They provide the analytical steps that you must take in your thought process and your legal reasoning to resolve the overall issue the problem poses; the overall question is the question presented for the entire memo. The topic sentences in the IRAC paragraph introduce the legal element in question that needs to be resolved to complete the steps necessary to thoroughly examine the problem and to determine a response to the question presented.

### ▼ What Is the Difference Between the Question Presented and the Issues in IRAC Paragraphs?

The question presented is the overall problem that must be resolved in the objective memo. The question presented for the Howard fact pattern is:

Whether Ms. Howard has a claim against Rough & Tough or against Able Pawn Shop for the value of her ring.

The subissues are determined by the legal elements or tests involved in the problem. The elements are discussed individually along with the relevant legal rule. There is a certain logical order when presenting the elements. Let the legal rules guide you in establishing the order of the subissues. Notice that each issue centers on a single step of the legal analysis necessary to fully examine the question presented.

The subissues that form the topic sentences of the IRAC paragraphs in a memo addressing Ms. Howard's problem would be as follows:

> The first issue is what type of relationship does a pawner and a pawnee have?
>
> What property rights do Ms. Howard and Rough & Tough Pawn have when they enter into a mutual bailment?
>
> Can Rough & Tough Pawn transfer its interest in Ms. Howard's property to Able Pawn?
>
> Did Rough & Tough Pawn receive the proper consent for the transfer of the ring from Ms. Howard?
>
> Is Rough & Tough liable for the loss of Ms. Howard's property after transferring its interest to Able Pawn?
>
> Is Able Pawn liable for the theft of Ms. Howard's property while it was in its possession?

All of these queries are really elements that must be addressed, step by step, to resolve the question presented.

Each of the subissues will be a topic sentence of the IRAC paragraph highlighting the analytical focus of the legal discussion in that paragraph. Each issue is a step in the thought process required to thoroughly prove all of the underlying elements necessary to address the question presented.

Notice how one issue statement logically leads into the next. A good test to see if your discussion is well organized is to write down all your issue statements from your IRAC paragraphs. If the issue statements flow logically, one to the next, then the organization of your discussion will be logical.

To analyze the problem thoroughly, a number of issues must be examined in the discussion. To make the analysis logical, the issues must be examined in a certain order.

## 2. Rules of Law

The **legal rule**, or synthesized compilation of the pertinent legal rules, follows the issue at the beginning of the IRAC paragraph. (For an in-depth discussion of the process of synthesizing authority, see Chapter 23)

A rule of law is the court's test, standard, or principle on the point. A rule also can be a statute and the legal elements laid out by the statute. A synthesis of a statute and a case applying or interpreting the statute also constitutes a rule.

In our IRAC example, note that the first sentence is the issue, and the second sentence is the legal rule.

| | |
|---|---|
| **Issue:** | Whether a bailment for the mutual benefit of Rough & Tough and Howard existed. |
| **Rule, followed by pinpoint citation:** | A pawn is a form of bailment, made for the mutual benefit of the bailee and the bailor, arising when goods are delivered to another as a pawn for security to him on money borrowed by the bailor. *Jacobs v. Grossman*, 141 N.E. 714, 715 (Ill. App. Ct. 1923). |

When organizing the discussion, first discern what issues are to be addressed, then find the pertinent mandatory authority that addresses the issues raised. Do not write the discussion around the authority but make the authority address the issues. To demonstrate clearly how the authority supports or addresses the issues raised, discuss the pertinent facts of the cited case after you state the case's legal rule. This is particularly helpful when the rule is very broad. You must demonstrate that the cited case truly supports the premise discussed in the IRAC paragraph. Your reader will want to see why the case is relevant and will want to understand what happened in the case factually.

## ▼ Why Is Citation Important?

**Citation** is an essential component of the rule portion of the IRAC paragraph. (See Appendix B.) You must always give proper credit in *Bluebook* or *ALWD* format to any statement made that is not wholly your own. Any legal principle or authority must be attributed to its source. Proper attribution of authority tells the reader where you obtained the legal principle that supports the discussion. The cite allows the reader to find the source too. Most important, the cite tells the reader whether the authority is primary mandatory authority, primary persuasive, or secondary authority. A cite also provides information without including the information in the discussion's text. For example, you could write a rule as follows:

> The state of Kimberly Supreme Court held in 1983 that individuals have a right to privacy. *Jones v. City of Moose*, 121 Kim. 12, 13 (1983).

A more effective version of the same rule, to include in the rule portion of the IRAC paragraph, is:

> Individuals have a right to privacy. *Jones v. City of Moose*, 121 Kim. 12, 13 (1983).

The citation itself provides the information about the court, its jurisdiction and level, and the year. The text need not repeat this

information. Citations are valuable sources of information about the legal authority presented in the rule component of the IRAC paragraph.

## 3. Application of the Law to the Problem's Facts

▼ How Do You Use the Legally Significant Facts?

Think of the legal rule as a test or a series of elements requiring certain facts to be used to support the outcome of the test. The facts used are **legally significant facts** because they bear legal significance as to the outcome of an issue. Our arson example mentioned at the beginning of the chapter illustrates this point.

### THE ARSON HYPOTHETICAL

John Smith lived in Arkville. John Smith's brother, Richard Smith, lived in Barkville Estates. Richard Smith owned a factory in downtown Barkville. John Smith was consumed by a jealous rage over his brother Richard's success and intentionally and maliciously burned down the factory in Barkville. The question to be examined is whether John Smith committed arson by intentionally and maliciously burning down his brother's factory.

The general rule for arson is the malicious burning of a dwelling house of another. This general rule would be the legal authority used in the rule portion of the IRAC paragraph.

An IRAC paragraph on this topic would be as follows:

**Issue:** Whether John Smith committed arson when he burned down his brother's factory.

**Rule:** Arson is the malicious burning of a dwelling house of another. 9 Stat. §§ 21, 23 (2013).

**Application:** John Smith burned down the factory of his brother, Richard Smith. John Smith's actions were intentional and malicious. Richard resides in Barkville Estates.

**Conclusion:** John Smith did not commit arson because he burned down his brother's factory, not his brother's residence or dwelling house.

The **application** lays a factual foundation on which the conclusion can be based. The facts are selected because each fact illustrates a legal point related to your rule of law: the malicious act, the intentional burning down of a building, the use of the building—whether it serves as a residence or dwelling house or whether it serves another purpose. The rule indicates which facts you should examine. After you lay the factual foundation by using the problem's facts to illustrate how the law should apply, you can draw a conclusion.

## 4. Conclusion

The **conclusion** resolves the issue posed at the beginning of the IRAC sequence. The conclusion should reflect directly the issue posed. If you remove the rule and the application portions of the IRAC paragraph, the issue and the conclusion should read as if they are a question and an answer. The conclusion generally restates the issue and includes the basis for the answer. The arson example with John Smith illustrates the role of the conclusion.

> **Issues:**      Whether John Smith committed arson when he
>                  burned down his brother's factory.
> **Conclusion:**  John Smith did not commit arson because he
>                  burned down his brother's factory, not his
>                  residence or dwelling house.

Notice how the conclusion responds directly to the issue posed. The conclusion focuses directly on the question raised at the beginning of the IRAC sequence. Each element of the discussion is resolved before addressing the next element or issue.

---

*PRACTICE POINTER*

To test if your conclusion is focused on the issue raised, read the issue at the beginning of the IRAC sequence, then read the conclusion. If the issue and the conclusion read like a question and a reasoned answer that responds directly to the question raised, then you have stayed focused and adequately addressed the issue.

---

## CHAPTER SUMMARY

IRAC—standing for Issue, Rule, Application, Conclusion—provides the structure for the legal discussion. The IRAC structure provides a checklist for you to make sure that you have included all the necessary components in the discussion and supported every premise with legal authority. Because it follows a predictable pattern, IRAC permits the reader to obtain information quickly. Mastering the IRAC format requires practice, which involves rereading and revising your work. Once you feel comfortable with the IRAC format, you should be confident that the discussion portions of your memos are logically ordered and analytically complete.

# KEY TERMS

application
citation
conclusion
IRAC
issue

legal holding
legal rule
legally significant facts
subissue
topic sentence

# EXERCISES
## SHORT ANSWER

1. What does "IRAC" stand for? Define each component.
2. Why do we use the IRAC format?
3. What is a legally significant fact?

## DIAGRAMMING IRAC COMPONENTS

4. Diagram the IRAC components of each paragraph in the discussion section. Note where the writing digresses from the IRAC format.

**Discussion**

To be successful in a claim against Rough & Tough or Able Pawn, Ms. Howard would have to prove that Rough & Tough was liable for the loss of her ring. First, for an action against Rough & Tough, she would have to show that the company had no right to transfer her pawned property without her written consent. Illinois Pawnbrokers Act, 205 Ill. Comp. Stat. 510/7 (2013). If pledged property was transferred without written consent of the property owner, the pawnbroker can be held responsible for loss or theft of pawned property because the property was in his safekeeping and was transferred illegally. *Jacobs v. Grossman*, 141 N.E. 714, 716 (Ill. App. Ct. 1923). Rough & Tough did not get a written consent for the transfer of Ms. Howard's property. In its defense the company could claim that written correspondence without the written consent would be enough to inform the pawner of the transfer of her property. Second, for an action against Able Pawn, Ms. Howard would have to show negligence in its care of her pawned ring. Illinois courts have ruled that in bailment for mutual benefit, the ordinary care or diligence that one would give to one's own property would be adequate to avoid negligence. *Id.* at 715; *Bielunski v. Tousignant*, 149 N.E.2d 801, 803 (Ill. App. Ct. 1958). Mrs. Howard would have to prove that a security system and a guard dog would not be ordinary care and diligence. In his defense Mr. Able could argue that these were sufficient to be considered ordinary care and diligence. For a claim against Village Jewelers to be successful, Ms. Howard would have to establish that she held good title to her property because a thief cannot convey good title to stolen property. *Hobson's Truck Sales v. Carroll Trucking*, 276 N.E. 89, 92 (Ill. App. Ct. 1971). Village Jewelers, which purchased the ring from the robbers, could not have good title to Ms. Howard's ring. Ms. Howard probably

could have a successful claim against Rough & Tough and Village Jewelers. She probably would not be able to prove Able Pawn negligent in the care of her ring.

Does a pawnbroker have the right to transfer pawned property or interest in that property without written consent of the pawner? Pawned property cannot be transferred within a year from the pawner's default without written consent of the pawner. Illinois Pawnbrokers Act, 205 Ill. Comp. Stat. 510/7. One Illinois court ruled that a pawnbroker had no right to transfer the plaintiff's pledged diamond ring to another pawnbroker within a year of the plaintiff's default of her loan, without written consent of the pawner. *Jacobs*, 141 N.E. at 716. In our situation, Rough & Tough sold its shop and assets to Sam Able within two months of Ms. Howard's pawning her grandmother's engagement ring. Because the sale occurred within a year of Ms. Howard's transaction with Rough & Tough, the company had a legal obligation under the Illinois statute to require a written consent for the transfer of her property. Also, the statute states that the time period for requirement of written consent for transfer of pledged property is established from the time of the pawner's default. 205 Ill. Comp. Stat. 510/7. Our client has not defaulted, and she deserves at least all the rights offered by the statute to a pawner who is in default. Rough & Tough did send Ms. Howard a postcard notifying her that it had sold all the pawned items and outstanding loans, including her ring, but it did not get her written consent for the sale of her property. Rough & Tough did not have the right to transfer Ms. Howard's ring without her written consent, and the sale of her property was probably not a legal sale.

Is a postcard sent to a pawner by a pawnbroker sufficient notice for the transfer of pawned property? Personal pawned property cannot be sold by a pawnee within one year from the time the pawner has defaulted in the interest payment unless the pawner has given written consent. Illinois Pawnbrokers Act, 205 Ill. Comp. Stat. 510/7. The statute uses a definite and clear term: "written consent." Ms. Howard did not default, and she would have at least all the rights of a pawner that did default. Therefore, the pawnbroker was required to receive her written consent before transferring her property. A postcard with written notice of a sale of pawned property is not a written consent by the pawner and would probably not be sufficient notice to constitute a legal sale.

5. Diagram the IRAC components of each paragraph in the discussion section. Note where the writing digresses from the IRAC format.

### Facts

The Blacks came to us with the following problem and want to know what type of damages they are entitled to.

Mr. and Mrs. Black wanted to have a chair and a loveseat made to match the living room in their new home. The Blacks searched for weeks at various local furniture retailers for a furniture style and fabric that they liked but were unsuccessful. Finally, the Blacks went to a fabric sale at Fabric Retailers and found the upholstery fabric of their dreams. The Blacks purchased 50 yards of the fabric to make sure that they would have enough for any project. Mr. Black

called all the furniture retailers in the area to inquire whether customers can have furniture covered in their own material. Finally, Comfy Furniture said that they permit customers to bring in their own material to cover upholstered furniture ordered from Comfy. The Blacks hurried over to Comfy with the 50 yards of fabric and placed an order for a chair and a loveseat using their own fabric. The price agreed on was the base price of $500 for the chair and $800 for the loveseat. Mr. Blaine, of Comfy Furniture, was their salesperson. Mr. Blaine said that the fabric was ideal for the styles selected because it required no matching. He added that there was plenty of yardage because 30 yards is adequate for jobs of this nature. The fabric was a small paisley print, with the right side having a lovely sheen and vibrant coloration. The Blacks placed the order on July 7, 2013, because they were planning a family reunion for Thanksgiving and felt that that date would give them plenty of time to completely decorate their living room. The new pieces would provide plenty of seating for the family reunion. The Blacks indicated to Mr. Blaine that they needed the furniture for the reunion. Mr. Blaine asserted that the furniture would be ready by September 15. The Blacks gave Comfy Furniture a deposit of $1,000. The loveseat and the chair were delivered to the Black home on September 10, but the furniture was upholstered with the fabric's reverse side showing. The Blacks were devastated.

## Issues

Whether the Blacks are entitled to damages from Comfy Furniture for incorrectly upholstering their furniture.

Whether the Blacks are entitled to damages from Comfy Furniture for the expense of decorating their living room to match the furniture they did not receive in the agreed-on condition.

## Discussion

Are the Blacks entitled to special damages from Comfy Furniture for the cost of the redecoration of their living room? An Illinois Appellate Court decided that the nonbreaching party should be put back in the position that it was in when the contract was formed. *Kalal v. Goldblatt Bros.*, 368 N.E.2d 671, 673 (Ill. App. Ct. 1977). The Blacks stated their intention at the beginning concerning the fabric, the redecoration of the living room, and the family reunion. This fact was a part of their original position. The living room was redecorated. The furniture was delivered; however, the fabric was incorrect. Therefore, the Blacks have a right to recover consequential damages for the cost of the redecoration of their living room because the end result was not achieved: correctly upholstered furniture, newly redecorated living room to match, and sufficient seating for the reunion. The conditions of the original contract were not met, and there was a breach of contract as embodied by the incorrectly upholstered furniture.

Under contract law, what damages are the Blacks entitled to pursue? Damages for breach of contract should place the plaintiff in a position he would have been in had the contract been performed. *Kalal*, 368 N.E.2d at 671. The plaintiffs in *Kalal* received a sofa that had been reupholstered in the wrong fabric after numerous delays, during which they had chosen three

different fabrics in succession. *Id.* The court held that the defect could be remedied by the cost of reupholstering the sofa in the proper fabric. *Id.* at 674. The Blacks' sofa and loveseat were improperly upholstered. Comfy Furniture upholstered their furniture with the reverse side of the fabric showing. Therefore, they were entitled to damages equal to the cost of upholstering their furniture correctly. However, the Blacks' situation is distinguished from *Kalal* in that their furniture was delivered before the date set in the contract, and it can be argued by Comfy that there was time to remedy the defect before their target date of Thanksgiving.

Are the Blacks entitled to compensation for the loss of use of their furniture? The question of compensation for loss of use of the furniture was considered by both parties in *Kalal* to be appropriate since the plaintiffs in the case were without their furniture for several months while waiting for it to be reupholstered. *Id.* The Blacks have been similarly inconvenienced in that they, too, have been without the use of their new furniture. Thus, they are entitled to compensation for the loss of use of the furniture. However, it can be argued by Comfy Furniture that the furniture in the *Kalal* case was used and had been removed from the home for the purpose of reupholstering it. *Id.* In the present case, the furniture was new and had never been in the Blacks' home, and Comfy may argue that the Blacks did not actually suffer loss of use of the new furniture.

Are the Blacks entitled to damages for the expense of decorating their living room to match the furniture they did not receive in the agreed-on condition? The redecorating of the living room in *Kalal* was not in the contemplation of either party at the time the contract was executed. *Kalal,* 368 N.E.2d at 671. Subsequently, the court held that the only damages that were recoverable for breach of contract are limited to those that were reasonably foreseeable and were within the contemplation of the parties at the time the contract was executed. *Id.* at 674. By the express terms of the Uniform Commercial Code, the court cannot follow tort theories to award damages. The legislative history of the U.C.C. indicates that contractual disputes should apply to the findings of the court. *Moorman Mfg. Co. v. National Tank Co.,* 435 N.E.2d 443, 453 (Ill. 1982). The Blacks only told Mr. Blaine that they needed the furniture to be completed in time for a family reunion. Comfy knew that the Blacks were under a time constraint for the delivery, but apparently there was no communication regarding the redecorating of the living room. With regard to Comfy Furniture, the redecorating of the Blacks' living room was an unforeseeable event, and consequently they would not be held responsible for the expense. Because the fact that the redecorating of the living room was unforeseeable, it was not included within the terms of the contract. Therefore, Comfy only breached the express terms of the contract. The Blacks probably will not be awarded compensatory damages.

## APPLICATION EXERCISES

6. Write an IRAC paragraph using the following information. You need not include all the information. The issue is whether the plaintiff can show that his attorney's failure to attend hearings was excusable neglect.

A number of the text blocks below contain statements of rules. Other text blocks include legally significant facts. In some paragraphs, conclusions have been drawn for you. Combine the rules where necessary and form an IRAC paragraph for the issue.

Fed. R. Civ. P. 60(b) provides for relief from judgment if plaintiffs can show that a mistake was made or that there was excusable neglect on the part of their attorney.

Rule 60(b) is an extraordinary remedy, granted in only exceptional cases. *Harold Washington Party v. Cook City. Illinois Democratic Party*, 984 F.2d 875 (7th Cir. 1993).

In this case, the plaintiff's attorney, Mark Adly, missed four court-set status hearings. He failed to appear. He failed to answer motions. Court status hearings are routinely held every three months.

Adly claims he did not have any notice of the hearings. Adly knew status proceedings normally were held. He attended depositions in this matter. Court records show that he was sent notices of the hearings to the address Adly says is correct.

"Excusable neglect may warrant relief under Rule 60(b)." *Zuelzke Tool & Eng'g v. Anderson Die Casting*, 925 F.2d 226 (7th Cir. 1991). In this case, the defendant relied on a third party who told them to refrain from further action because efforts were being made to have the defendant removed as defendant. *Id.* at 228. Anderson did not answer any complaints or file any pleadings. *Id.* The lack of response led the court to enter a default judgment against the company. *Id.* at 229. The district court refused the motion to vacate, saying that the defendant had voluntarily chosen not to control its fate in the litigation. *Id.*

7. Review the following paragraph. Note the issue, the rule, the application of law to facts, and the conclusion.

An important factor in determining whether a funeral home is a nuisance is the suitability of its location. "Funeral homes are generally located on the edge of purely residential but not predominantly residential areas." *Bauman v. Piser Undertakers Co.*, 34 Ill. App. 2d 145, 148, 180 N.E.2d 705, 708 (App. Ct. 1962). A carefully run funeral home may be located on a property zoned for business at the edge of a residential neighborhood. *Id.* The funeral home in this case is located in a predominantly rural area. It is outside the boundary lines of the Up and Coming Acres subdivision. It is a lawful business located on a parcel zoned for business. The funeral home is in a suitable location.

8. Read the following facts carefully.

Mr. and Mrs. Mortimer reserved the party room at Harvey's Restaurant and gave Harvey's a $500 deposit. Their party was scheduled for

November 3, 2013. Mrs. Mortimer sent the invitations out on October 1, 2013. The Mortimers agreed to the quoted price of $62.50 per person. The purpose of the event was for Mr. Mortimer to establish relationships with current and prospective legal clients.

On October 20, 2013, Mrs. Mortimer called Harvey's to confirm party details. She was informed that the party room was under demolition and could not be used for the party. Mrs. Harvey offered to lower the price to $57.50 per person and reserve a portion of the dining room. Although she believed these arrangements were not suitable, Mrs. Mortimer agreed to use the dining room since the invitations were sent and many people accepted.

Mrs. Mortimer ordered lump crab meat as an appetizer for the party. A waitress told Mrs. Mortimer that imitation crab meat was used when Mrs. Mortimer inquired about the crab's unusual crunchiness.

The Mortimers want to sue Harvey's for breach of contract and believe that they relied to their detriment on this contract. They assert that Harvey's failed to notify them of the changes in a timely manner, consequently preventing them from making other arrangements. Additionally, the Mortimers want to know if they have a cause of action for the substitution of imitation crab meat for genuine.

The following is a portion of a memo relating to one of the issues raised by the Mortimers. Read the paragraphs carefully and revise in IRAC format. Remember that each IRAC sequence can span more than one paragraph (for example, paragraph 1—issue and rule; paragraph 2—application and conclusion).

Did the Mortimers suffer a loss of business because of Harvey's Restaurant's promise of the entire party room? The Mortimers can argue that a false representation surrenders the restaurant's interest. "When parties enter into a contract for the performance of the same act in the future they impliedly promise that in the meantime neither will do anything to harm or prejudice the other inconsistent with the contractual relationship they have assumed. . . . If one party to the contract renounces it, the other may treat the renunciation as a breach and sue for damages at once." The restaurant can argue that the contract did not cover the entire performance but was modified; therefore, no harm was done to the contractual relationship. *Pappas v. Crist*, 233 N.C. 265, 25 S.E.2d 850 (1943).

The Mortimers can argue that "damages are not speculative merely because they cannot be computed with mathematical exactness, if, under evidence they are capable of reasonable approximation." *Hawkinson v. Johnston*, 122 F.2d 724 (8th Cir. 1941). The "rainmaking" potential was minimized because of the restaurant's failure to supply the room contracted for.

The restaurant would argue that the "period for which the damages can be reasonably forecast or soundly predicted in such a situation must depend on the circumstances and evidence of the particular case." *Id.* at 727. Therefore, the Mortimers can only quantify the number of RSVPs, not the number of rejects due to the smaller room.

9. This exercise will highlight organizational problems in the discussion and help you to write more logically.

Review the discussion section of a previously drafted memo. Label, in the margin, the issues, the rules, the application portions, and the conclusions. Examine each component to see where you digress from the IRAC format in the discussion. Revise the discussion to conform more closely with the IRAC format.

## CHAPTER 23

# SYNTHESIZING CASES AND AUTHORITIES

| | | |
|---|---|---|
| A. | SYNTHESIS | 482 |
| B. | TYPES OF SYNTHESIS | 483 |
| C. | STEP-BY-STEP PROCESS TO SYNTHESIZING LEGAL RULES | 483 |
| D. | EXAMPLES OF CASE SYNTHESIS | 485 |

## CHAPTER OVERVIEW

You will learn about the methods of synthesis used when writing a memo. Synthesizing authority requires finding a common theme from two or more sources that ties together the legal rule. Cases are synthesized because it is hard to find a single decision that articulates the precise rule of law to support a point in a memo or brief. Often one case rule will expand another, so the two rules can be combined, or synthesized, to reflect an accurate statement of the law.

You will also become adept at synthesizing statutory authority as well as combining case law and statutes. Constitutions should be given the highest regard in the hierarchy of authority, then statutes. You will probably not use many constitutional provisions in your writing, but statutes play a very large role in legal research and writing. If you find case law that applies or interprets a statute, synthesize the statute and the rule from the case.

# A. SYNTHESIS

Synthesis is the bringing together of various legal authorities into a unified cohesive statement of the law. The process of synthesizing authority requires finding a common theme or thread that relates to the various legal rules and tying the rules to that unified theme. Discussing related decisions and statutes separately in a memo makes your points sound more like a list than an integrated, well-thought-out whole. Synthesis adds analytical insight to your legal documents and makes reading them easier.

### ▼ What Is the Process of Synthesizing Legal Rules?

We synthesize cases and enacted law because memos and opinion letters are organized by legal issue and not by cited references. Frequently, more than one source of primary authority addresses a particular legal issue. The synthesis of related legal principles enables you to compare and to contrast the legal rules easily as well as to demonstrate how factual applications differ and to show how legal rules expand or contract. Often enacted law and case law are synthesized because the case law applies the statute or interprets the extent to which the statute can be applied. Sometimes the rules that are on point are derived from relevant statutes only. Enacted law that comes from more than one statute section also must be synthesized under a common legal principle to promote cohesiveness and to add your analytical viewpoint to the memo.

### ▼ Why Do We Synthesize Legal Authority?

The legal issues form the framework for the discussion. The synthesized authority groups the legal rules together to address the issues raised.

The following example demonstrates how one case defines an easement in gross and then another case explains how an easement in gross is retained. Both cases discuss easements in gross, yet one expands on the other. The facts on which the example is based are as follows:

> Robert and Jan Murray live in Evanston and are building an addition to their house on Ashland Avenue. There is eight feet between their house and their neighbor's, Mrs. Brown's, house. The properties are adjoining. A driveway does not separate the houses. Also, there is no alley that would provide access to either property. The Murrays' contractors and construction workers must enter Mrs. Brown's property to work on the addition. Mrs. Brown is not very pleased that workers are entering her property. The Murrays came to our office wondering whether they should purchase an easement from Mrs. Brown, their neighbor.

### *EXAMPLE*

Should the Murrays purchase an easement in gross from Mrs. Brown? An easement in gross, sometimes called a personal easement, is a right in the land of another that is not permanently part of the title of the

property. An easement in gross allows for use of the land of another for a limited purpose. *Willoughby v. Lawrence*, 4 N.E. 356 (Ill. 1886). It belongs to the easement holder independent of his ownership or possession of any tract of land and does not benefit the possessor of any tract of land in his use of it. *Schnabel v. County of DuPage*, 428 N.E.2d 671 (Ill. App. Ct. 1981). The Murrays are building an addition to their house. They want to have a right to use the adjoining land only to perform the construction of their addition. They do not need an easement that would be a permanent part of the property's title. The interest that the Murrays have in Mrs. Brown's land is personal and would not benefit either tract of land. Therefore, the Murrays can purchase an easement in gross from Mrs. Brown that would permit the workers to enter the Brown property for the limited purpose to complete the construction project.

# B. TYPES OF SYNTHESIS

▼ What Are the Four Methods of Synthesizing Authority?

As we discussed previously, synthesizing primary authority requires finding a common theme that is used to unify all of the various rules related to the issue. The common legal theme can be developed by classifying the applicable precedent into categories. There are four basic ways to combine and to analyze legal rules to render a coherent distillation of the law:

1. **Primary authority** can be grouped by related rules of law found in the text of the decision or in the statute or constitution.
2. Synthesis can be focused around the **reasoning** that the judges use as the basis for the holdings
3. The various **facts** from different cases can form the foundation of the synthesis.
4. The **causes of action** are the last category of case synthesis.

To synthesize primary authority, you will group related legal rules. All the examples focus on this method of synthesis. Detailed instruction as to how to synthesize various sources of case law, case law combined with statutory authority, as well as two sources of statutory authority follow.

# C. STEP-BY-STEP PROCESS TO SYNTHESIZING LEGAL RULES

The most effective synthesis of legal rules follows conscientious case briefing and careful reading of enacted law. Case briefing requires summarizing a decision in set categories: citation, procedure, issue, facts, holding, legal rule (the test or standard the court used to arrive at its decision), rationale (the court's reason for its holding), and

disposition. (See Chapter 18.) The following steps take you through the synthesizing process.

1. *Summarize enacted law. Brief relevant decisions.* Once you have summarized enacted law, constitutional provisions, and statutes, after reading for their plain meaning, and carefully and meticulously briefed all the decisions that you plan to use in your memo, you can establish categories of legal rules to make comparing and contrasting authorities easier. It is far simpler to compare and to contrast seven rules from briefed decisions than to flip through printouts of authority.

2. *Outline the problem.* The next step is to formulate the analytical outline of your letter or memo and to pinpoint the issues and subissues that must be addressed to fully explore the memo topic.

3. *Relate research to legal issues raised.* To organize the primary authority, relate the research findings to the issues the problem raises. Remember: Legal writing is never organized around your sources of authority but around the issues the problem poses. After pinpointing the legal issues that will be explored, decide on the general rule relating to that point of law.

4. *Under each issue, organize your primary sources by hierarchy of authority.* Enacted law comes before common law, constitutions come before statutes, newer case decisions interpreting statutes come before common law cases, higher court holdings come before lower court holdings, and newer case holdings are more relevant than older holdings on the same point of law from the same court.

5. *Compare and contrast legal rules and statutes.* Using the case briefs that you prepared and the notes you made from the plain reading of the enacted law, compare and contrast the holdings and statutory texts.

6. *Formulate a statement of the law.* Your statement should incorporate all the primary sources that will be used under the subissue heading. Ask yourself: What are the similarities and differences between the various cases and statutes? In the cases, how do the legal rules or tests the court used differ from or expand on one another? How do the facts differ? What do the documents have in common?

7. *Correct citation.* Remember that you must attribute the authority for any legal statement, even if it is a clause, using the proper *Bluebook* or *ALWD* citation.

NET NOTE

The CUNY Law School Writing Center has information on rule synthesis at www.law.cuny.edu/legal-writing/students/irac-crracc/irac-crracc-3.html. The site also has an example of rule synthesis.

# D. EXAMPLES OF CASE SYNTHESIS

This example demonstrates synthesizing the holdings from two legal decisions. A problem and two fictitious legal decisions are provided below on which case synthesis is performed.

### *PROBLEM*

Mr. and Mrs. Black wanted to have a chair and a loveseat made to match the living room in their new home. The Blacks searched for weeks at various local furniture retailers for a furniture style and fabric that they liked but were unsuccessful. Finally, the Blacks went to a fabric sale at Fabric Retailers and found the upholstery fabric of their dreams. The Blacks purchased 50 yards of the fabric of their dreams to make sure that they would have enough for any project. Mr. Black called all the furniture retailers in the area to inquire whether customers can have furniture covered in their own material. Finally, Comfy Furniture said that they permit customers to bring in their own material to cover upholstered furniture ordered from Comfy. The Blacks hurried over to Comfy with the 50 yards of fabric and placed an order for a chair and a loveseat using their own fabric. The price agreed on was the base price of $500 for the chair and $800 for the loveseat. Mr. Blaine, of Comfy Furniture, was their salesperson.

Mr. Blaine said that the fabric was ideal for the styles selected because it required no matching. He also offered that there was plenty of material, that 30 yards was adequate for a job of this nature. The fabric was a small paisley print, with the right side having a lovely sheen and vibrant coloration. The Blacks placed the order on July 7, 2014. They were planning a family reunion for Thanksgiving and felt that ordering in July would give them plenty of time to completely decorate their living room. The new pieces would provide plenty of seating for the family reunion. The Blacks indicated to Mr. Blaine that they needed the furniture for the reunion. Mr. Blaine asserted that the furniture would be ready by September 15. The Blacks gave Comfy Furniture a deposit of $1,000. The loveseat and the chair were delivered to the Black home on September 10, but the furniture was upholstered with the fabric's reverse side showing. The Blacks were devastated.

The legal issue is whether the Blacks are entitled to damages for the breach of the contract to upholster the furniture.

The legal principle surrounding this problem is the expectation interest in a contract. The expectation interest is the expectation of gain from the performance of the contract. The damages are assessed to give the nonbreaching party the measure of gain that he or she would have received if the contract was performed as agreed. Sometimes special or consequential damages are awarded in addition to the expectancy interest.

## CASE A

The Cahill family ordered a sofa from the Acme Furniture Company in red tapestry, on June 1, 2013, due to be delivered in six weeks, on July 15, 2013. The Cahills paid $600 for the sofa at the time of the order. After 10 weeks, Acme delivered a gold sofa to the Cahill home. The Cahills called Acme to complain, and Acme picked up the sofa with the promise that it would be reupholstered in red. The sofa was delivered in green six weeks later. In the meanwhile, the Cahills decorated their living room to match the red sofa. After the sofa was delivered in green, 16 weeks after the initial order, the Cahills sued Acme for breach of contract and for damages resulting from the breach, which included the cost of redecorating their living room to match the red sofa. The legal rule is that the nonbreaching party can only collect damages to recoup the expected gain from the contract if performed as agreed. The nonbreaching party cannot receive damages for expenses incurred that were not in contemplation at the time the contract was formed. The Cahills are entitled to damages for the upholstering of the sofa in the incorrect color and are entitled to compensation for the loss of the use of their sofa for 16 weeks as well as the cost of a new red sofa.

## CASE B

Jane Smith ordered a new car from Lunar Motors on June 1, 2013. The Lunar coupe in black was ordered, but the salesperson suggested that the gray floor model, which was used only for demo drives, would represent a $300 savings off the sticker price of the Lunar coupe. Ms. Smith agreed to purchase the floor model for $15,700 rather than pay $16,000 for the special-order car. The salesperson once again asserted that the floor model was new, was used only for demo drives, and had only 5 miles on the odometer. Ms. Smith returned to Lunar Motors on June 3, 2013, paid the $15,700 for the gray floor model Lunar coupe, and drove home. While driving home, Ms. Smith noticed that the car veered dramatically to the left. Ms. Smith took the car to her mechanic, who reported that the car was in an accident previously and had been repaired, but the frame was bent in such a manner as to distort the alignment. Ms. Smith contracted to and expected to receive a new, undamaged car with mileage and wear and tear due to demo drives. Ms. Smith did not contract to receive a damaged car. The salesperson asserted the car was like new. The holding of the court is that the nonbreaching party is entitled to the gain expected from the performance of the contract as agreed, and if the contract is not performed as agreed, the nonbreaching party is entitled to receive the benefit that she would have received if the contract had been performed as agreed. Ms. Smith is entitled to a complete refund of the $15,700 she paid for the car plus the daily cost of the loss of the use of the automobile to be tabulated by the fair market rental value per day of a Lunar coupe.

To synthesize the rule, or tests, from the fictitious cases, you would find a common theme that ties together the rules of law from both decisions. Basically, both cases state that the nonbreaching party in a contract is entitled to receive the benefit of the deal that would have been received if the contract had been performed as agreed. First, write a general statement of the law. Then, mention the legal rules from Case A and Case B as they pertain to the general statement of the law.

### EXAMPLE

Are the Blacks entitled to damages compensating them for the breach of the contract to reupholster the loveseat and the chair? Damages are assessed in a breach of contract action (to give the non-breaching party the measure of gain that he would have received if the contract had been performed as agreed) in a very specific manner. The nonbreaching party can collect damages to recoup the gain expected from the contract if the contract had been performed as agreed. Case A; Case B. If the contract is not performed as agreed, the nonbreaching party is entitled to the benefit he would have received if the contract had been performed as agreed. Case B. The nonbreaching party cannot be compensated for expenses incurred that were not in contemplation at the time the contract was formed. Case A. In the alternative, the nonbreaching party can be compensated for expenses incurred that were in contemplation at the time the contract was formed. Case A. In our problem, the Blacks contracted to have the chair and loveseat upholstered in paisley fabric with the correct side showing. The furniture was upholstered with the wrong side of the fabric showing. When ordering the furniture, the Blacks stipulated that they needed the pieces for a family reunion and that the pieces would provide the necessary seating. The Blacks were without their furniture because of Comfy Furniture's error. The Blacks communicated the need for the seating at the time of the contract formation. The Blacks should receive the gain they expected from the performance of the contract as agreed as well as compensation for the expense of providing alternative seating for the family reunion based on the rental cost of chairs.

An ineffective case synthesis based on our hypothetical problem would be as follows.

> Are the Blacks entitled to damages from Comfy Furniture for breach of contract? "The nonbreaching party is entitled to the gain expected from the performance of the contract as agreed and if the contract is not performed as agreed, the nonbreaching party is entitled to receive the benefit that she would have received if the contract had been performed as agreed." (Rule from) *Case B.* The Blacks were the nonbreaching party and anticipated a loveseat and a chair to be upholstered in paisley with the correct side showing. Therefore, the Blacks are entitled to be compensated by a damage award to put them in a position as if the contract

had been performed as agreed. Are the Blacks entitled to be compensated for not having adequate seating for the family reunion? The non-breaching party cannot receive damages for expenses incurred that were not in contemplation at the time the contract was formed. (Rule from) *Case A*. The Blacks alerted Mr. Blaine, the salesperson, that the couches were needed for a family reunion at Thanksgiving. The Blacks indicated that the additional seating provided by the chair and the loveseat would be necessary at the reunion when ordering the furniture. Since the need for the seating, that the furniture would provide, was in contemplation at the time the order was placed, the Blacks should be compensated for not having adequate seating at the time of the reunion. The damages should be measured by the cost of providing alternative seating.

This example, although clear and coherent, does not synthesize the decisions and unify the concepts articulated in the cases. Each rule is addressed separately, although one rule relates to the other. Also, the rules are presented in the form of holdings because they read as answers to the question before the court rather than as a test or principle. The authority is presented more as a list than as a cohesive unit.

When you have found a relevant statute for a problem, give it the highest regard, because statutes on point govern before case law. (See Chapters 1 and 2.) Generally, synthesize statutes separately from case law holdings. However, if you find cases that interpret and apply the relevant statutes, synthesize the statute text with the application found in case law. Always apply the plain meaning rule to statutes. The plain meaning of the statute text is derived from a reading of each word at its face value.

The problem below illustrates the synthesis of a statute and a case.

## *PROBLEM*

### FACT PATTERN

On August 7, 2014, our client, Jane Howard, obtained an $800 loan from Rough & Tough Pawn Shop, using her grandmother's engagement ring as collateral. Howard agreed to make monthly payments on the loan for a minimum of 13 months. After 12 months, Rough & Tough had the right to sell the ring and to refund Howard the difference between her outstanding debt and the price received for the ring.

On September 7, 2014, Howard received a postcard from Rough & Tough stating that its shop and its assets will be sold to Able Pawn. The postcard also stated that Able would assume the business of Rough & Tough, including the items pawned and the loans outstanding. The postcard alerted Howard to pick up the ring and to pay off her note by September 29, 2014, if Howard wanted to reclaim her property.

Howard decided to continue to make her monthly payments to Able Pawn, where her loan would be transferred.

On October 1, 2014, Able Pawn was robbed and all the jewelry was stolen, including Howard's ring. The premises were protected by a security alarm system and a guard dog.

## ISSUE

The issue to be examined is whether Rough & Tough had authority to sell its interest in Howard's ring.

## STATUTORY AUTHORITY

The applicable statute is from the Pawnbrokers Regulation Act, 205 Ill. Comp. Stat. 510/10 (2012).

> *Sale of Property.* No personal property received on deposit or pledge or purchased by any such pawnbroker shall be sold or permitted to be redeemed or removed from the place of business of such pawnbroker for the space of 48 hours after the delivery of the copy and statement required by Section 7 of this Act required to be delivered to the officer or officers named therein. If the pawner or pledger fails to repay the loan during the period specified on the pawn ticket, the pawnbroker shall automatically extend a grace period of 30 days from the default date on the loan during which the pawnbroker shall not dispose of or sell the property pledged. The parties may agree to extend or renew a loan upon the terms agreed upon by the parties, provided the terms comply with the requirements of this Act.

## RELEVANT CASE LAW

This decision interprets and applies the relevant statute, so the statute and the decision should be synthesized.

### *JACOBS v. GROSSMAN*
310 Ill. 247, 141 N.E.2d 714 (1923)

DUNCAN, J.

This case is brought to this court on a certificate of importance and appeal from a judgment of the Appellate Court for the First District, affirming a judgment of the municipal court of Chicago in favor of the appellee and against appellant in the sum of $330. Appellee, Minnie Jacobs, on April 8, 1921, began an action of replevin (replevin is an action where the owner of property attempts to recover the property from someone who wrongfully took or held the property) in the municipal court of Chicago against appellant, Harry Grossman, a licensed pawnbroker, to recover possession of a diamond ring delivered by herself to appellant to secure the payment of $70 borrowed from him. . . . The case was heard before the court without a jury.

On June 3, 1919, appellee placed in pawn with appellant, a licensed pawnbroker doing business at 426 South Halsted Street, Chicago, the

ring, and received thereon the sum of $70. Interest on the loan was paid to June 7, 1920. The pawn ticket issued to appellee contained this statement, "This office protected by the Chicago Electric Protective Company," and described the location and name of the pawnbroker as "Metropolitan Loan Bank, 426 South Halsted St." The ticket further described the goods pawned, the amount loaned, and the time of redemption. Between October 7 and 10, 1920, appellant sold all his interest in whatever pledges he had to Jacob Klein, another duly licensed pawnbroker at 502 South Halsted Street, for the sum of $16,000 or $17,000, which represented the principal sums loaned on said pledges with interest thereon. The pledges were sold by appellant to Klein upon the express understanding that the pledgors might redeem from Klein in the same manner as they could from appellant, had he not sold his interest in the pawns. It was admitted that Klein is a reputable business man, and it was also conceded by appellant that no notice was given by him, either expressly or impliedly, to the appellee of the transfer of her property. On January 8, 1921, the pawnshop of Klein was entered by four armed robbers. The robbers ordered the clerks employed there to hold up their hands, and they forcibly took from a safe a large number of articles, including the diamond ring in question of appellee, which has never been recovered. . . .

Counsel for appellant relies for a reversal of the judgment on two propositions: First, that a pawnbroker is bound only to use ordinary care for the safety of the pawner's property, and, if the property is lost or destroyed without the negligence of the pawnee, then he is not liable; second, that a pawnbroker has the right to assign or sell to another his interest in an article pledged to him.

A pawn is a species of bailment which arises when goods or chattels are delivered to another as a pawn for security to him on money borrowed of him by the bailor. It is the pignari acceptum of the civil law, according to which the possession of the pledge passes to the creditor, therein differing from a hypotheca. It is a class of bailment which is made for the mutual benefit of the bailor and bailee. All that is required by the common law on the part of a pawnee in the protection of the property thus entrusted to him is ordinary care and diligence. Consequently, unless a failure to exercise such care and diligence is shown, a pawnee is not answerable for the loss of the article pledged. 30 Cyc. 1169; *Standard Brewery v. Malting Co.*, 171 Ill. 602, 49 N.E. 507. This is an elementary principle, and there can be no question as to the accuracy and correctness of appellant's first proposition.

But the question arises as to whether or not appellant was guilty of negligence in transferring the interest of the pawner without giving her any notice of such transfer. Appellant's duty to her was to safely keep and protect the property pledged. It was a legal obligation on his part to appellee, from which he could not relieve himself by transferring the pledge to another without her consent. Appellee relied upon him to keep and protect her property where it would be reasonably safe, and he had in substance assured her by the language on the ticket that her

property was insured or safeguarded. He violated this duty or obligation to her by transferring the possession of her property to another, to be kept at another place, which the evidence does not show to be protected by a protective company, and without giving her notice of such custody and transfer.

Whatever may be the right of the parties in a bailment for the mutual benefit of the bailor and the bailee, it is unquestionably the law that the parties may increase or diminish these rights by stipulations contained in the contract of bailment. 30 Cyc. 1167; *St. Losky v. Davidson*, 6 Cal. 643. The sum and substance of appellant's contract was that he would keep appellee's property at his office or shop described as aforesaid, and which was protected as aforesaid. The pawning of the ring by appellee under the circumstances imposed a personal trust upon appellant to personally keep the property at his shop and under the assurance of protection as aforesaid, and he could not at his will, without the consent of appellee, transfer the possession and custody thereof to another without such consent. The rule is stated in 3 R.C.L. 112, that any attempt on the part of the bailee in an ordinary simple bailment of a pawn to sell, lease, pledge, or otherwise part with the title or possession of the bailment, constitutes a conversion in every case where the bailment can be properly regarded as a personal trust in the bailee.

There is another controlling reason for holding that appellant is liable for the loss of the ring, and for holding that he could not transfer the possession of the article pawned to him to another and escape liability for a conversion. Section 10 of the Pawnbroker's Act (Smith-Hurd Rev. St. 1923, c. 107 1/2) provides, in part, as follows:

> No personal property pawned or pledged shall be sold or disposed by any such pawnbroker within one year from the time when the pawner or pledger shall make default in the payment of interest on the money so advanced by such pawnbroker, unless by the written consent of such pawner or pledger.

Appellant claims that the proper interpretation of this statute is that it prohibits the sale of an article, including the interest of the pledger or pawner as well as his own, and does not refer to a sale of only the interest of the pawnbroker or pledgee. The statute is not subject to such construction. It should be construed to mean what it says: That the property must not be sold or disposed of by the pawnbroker without the written consent of the pledgor. The statute does not confine itself to a sale, but also forbids any disposition of the same without consent as aforesaid. It cannot be seriously disputed that appellant did dispose of the property without the consent of appellee, within the meaning of the foregoing section of the statute.

The judgment of the Appellate Court is affirmed.

Judgment affirmed.

**SAMPLE SYNTHESIS**

Does Rough & Tough have the authority to sell its interest in Howard's ring? Unless the pawner and pawnbroker agree, pawned property may be sold or disposed of by any pawnbroker only after 30 days from the time the pawner defaults in the payment of interest on the money advanced by the pawnbroker. 205 Ill. Comp. Stat. 510/10 (2012). Where a pawnbroker neglected to give notice of the intent to sell his interest in a particular property and neglected to receive written consent for such sale, the pawnbroker lacked authority to transfer his interest in the property, the ring, to another. *Jacobs v. Grossman*, 141 N.E. 714, 715 (Ill. App. Ct. 1923). Although Rough & Tough gave Howard notice of its intent to sell the shop and its assets, R&T failed to obtain Howard's written consent to sell her ring. Additionally Jane Howard continued to make the payments on the loan so default is not an issue. Rough & Tough's transfer of the ring, the property, occurred during the term of the loan. Therefore, a court will probably find that Rough & Tough lacked the authority to sell its interest in Howard's ring to another pawnbroker.

The above example synthesizes the statute and the *Jacobs* case as they relate to the issue of a pawnbroker's authority to sell its interest in a pawned item without the consent of the pawner. Notice how the statute is mentioned first because its authority ranks higher than the case. The *Jacobs* case follows the statute because the rule is more detailed on the issue of a pawnbroker's duty to give notice before selling his interest in the pawner's property, a ring, and the facts are similar to Jane Howard's situation. Two sources of primary authority, a statute and a case, are used together in this sample synthesis because both sources relate to a single legal issue.

### ▼ How Do You Synthesize Two Sources of Statutory Authority?

Often you must use two or more sections of a statute in conjunction to explain the legal rule completely. Sometimes definitional provisions are located in one section and the applicable code section is located in another.

**Facts:** Mr. Thomas was arrested on charges of domestic battery. He punched his wife in the face three times and broke her nose. Mr. and Mrs. Thomas live in Illinois, but they are living apart.

**Issue:** Whether the Illinois domestic battery statute applies to an estranged husband and whether punching is considered battery.

This problem requires you to use two statutory provisions. One section defines the relevant terms, and the other section details actions that constitute domestic battery. The statutory definition of family and household members as pertaining to domestic battery follows.

### 725 Ill. Comp. Stat. 5/112A-3(3) (2012):

"Family or household members" include spouses, former spouses, parents, children, stepchildren and other persons related by blood or by present or prior marriage, persons who share or formerly shared a common dwelling, persons who have or allegedly have a child in common, persons who share or allegedly share a blood relationship through a child, persons who have or have had a dating or engagement relationship, persons with disabilities and their personal assistants, and caregivers. . . . For purposes of this paragraph, neither a casual acquaintanceship nor ordinary fraternization between 2 individuals in business or social contexts be deemed to constitute a dating relationship.

### The Domestic Battery Statute at 720 Ill. Comp. Stat. 5/12-3.2 (2012):

(a) A person commits domestic battery if he intentionally or knowingly without legal justification by any means:

(1) Causes bodily harm to any family or household member;
(2) Makes physical contact of an insulting or provoking nature with any family or household member.

Sample synthesis using two statutory provisions:

We must determine whether the domestic battery statute, 720 Ill. Comp. Stat. 5/12-3.2 (2012), applies to married couples living apart and if so, whether Mr. Thomas, an estranged husband, committed domestic battery by punching his wife. The domestic battery statute applies to family members. "Family members" is defined to include "spouses formerly sharing a common dwelling." 725 Ill. Comp. Stat. 5/112A-3(3) (2012). "A person commits domestic battery if he intentionally or knowingly without legal justification by any means:
(1) Causes bodily harm to any family or household member. . . ." 720 Ill. Comp. Stat. 5/12-3.2 (2012). Since Mr. Thomas is a spouse who formerly shared a common residence with his wife, he is a family or household member, and the domestic battery statute is applicable. Mr. Thomas punched his wife in the face three times, which caused her nose to break. The facts do not state that his mental capacity was altered by inebriation or severe mental illness, so his actions can be deduced to be intentional. The facts also do not indicate if Mr. Thomas was provoked to commit battery by extreme jealousy. It appears that there was no legal justification for the bodily harm inflicted on Mrs. Thomas by Mr. Thomas. Although Mr. Thomas is a spouse formerly sharing a common dwelling with Mrs. Thomas, he is a family member and is governed by the domestic battery statute. By punching his wife, breaking her nose, and causing her bodily harm, Mr. Thomas committed domestic battery.

### CHECKLIST

1. Summarize the relevant statutes and brief the relevant cases.
2. Outline the problem.
3. Organize the primary authority.

4. Under each issue, organize your primary sources by hierarchy of authority.
5. Compare and contrast the case holdings and statutory text.
6. Formulate a statement of the law that incorporates all the primary sources that will be used under the subissue.
7. Attribute the authority for any legal statement by using the proper *Bluebook* or *ALWD* citation.

---

### PRACTICE POINTER

When synthesizing authorities, always cite to every source that you use. Often the information gathered from the authority is not from the first page of the decision. You must use pinpoint cites to indicate from exactly where within the decision the information is obtained. Also, often you will use authorities more than once. This calls for subsequent citation format. Use *Bluebook* **Rule 10.9** or *ALWD* **Rule 12.19** for guidance on short citation when citing cases subsequently.

---

## CHAPTER SUMMARY

Learning to synthesize authority is a mechanical process at first. Brief the cases and summarize the statutory authority. Insert the applicable authority in your outline by grouping together related statements of the law. Draft cohesive statements of the legal authority that you grouped together. Cite all authority accurately even if string citations are needed or if two separate clauses in a single sentence are each supported by a different authority.

As you become more adept at synthesis, you will see that your writing is smoother and less redundant. Synthesizing authority lets you write in one voice rather than awkwardly switching back and forth between your words and the words of the court.

## KEY TERMS

causes of action                      reasoning
facts                                 synthesis
primary authority

## EXERCISES
### SHORT ANSWER
1. Why do we synthesize authority?
2. What are the four basic types of synthesis?
3. What are the steps required to synthesize legal rules?

## APPLICATION

4. Read the following fact pattern and cases carefully. Draft a paragraph in which you synthesize the holdings of the cases. The issue that you will address is provided as well. Remember that proper synthesis requires you to relate the authority to a common legal theme. The problem's issue will guide you in synthesizing the authority.

### Facts

On November 29, 2013, Michael Jones purchased a used truck from Grimy's Auto and Truck Service. At the time of the purchase, Grimy's stated that the engine was completely overhauled and consisted of rebuilt and reconditioned parts, that all parts were guaranteed, and that invoices for all new parts would be provided. On December 13, 2014, after using the truck for over one year, Jones discovered that several engine parts were not rebuilt or reconditioned and that other engine parts were defective. These defects caused the truck to break down, resulting in lost wages and lost profits for Jones. Jones made repairs to the truck on December 13, 2014, December 16, 2014, and December 31, 2014. Jones did not attempt to return the truck and did not notify Grimy's that the truck was defective. The truck is currently disabled in Columbus, Ohio. Jones wants to sue Grimy's for damages for breach of contract.

### Issue

Whether Jones continued to use the truck for more than a reasonable time after noticing the defects and failed to properly reject the truck and to notify Grimy's as to the defects.

### Case A

A buyer of goods must alert the seller as soon as he discovers that the goods are not as agreed on. A buyer must rescind a sales contract as soon as he discovers the breach or after he has had a reasonable time for examination. The buyer waives the right to rescind a contract for the sale of goods by continuing to use allegedly defective goods for more than a reasonable time.

### Case B

To meet the requirements of an effective rejection, the buyer must reject the goods within a reasonable time and reasonably notify the seller.

5. Read the following fact pattern and cases carefully. Draft a paragraph in which you synthesize the holdings of the cases. The issue that you will address is provided as well.

### Facts

Robert and Jane Moore live in Evanston and have to repair the gutters on their house. There is eight feet between their house and their neighbor's. The properties are adjoining; the neighboring Kandler house is north of the Moore house. The Moore's contractors and carpenters must enter the Kandler property to work on the gutters on the north side of the house.

Mrs. Kandler is not very pleased that workers are entering her property. The Moores came to our office to find out what they should do. The Moores specifically asked if they should obtain an easement to grant them a right of way on Mrs. Kandler's property to make the repairs.

### Issue

What legal access would allow the contractors and carpenters, repairing the gutters on the Moore house, to enter the adjoining property belonging to Mrs. Kandler?

### Statutory Authority

Ch. 12 § 99: If the repair and maintenance of an existing single-family residence cannot reasonably be accomplished without entering onto the adjoining land, and if the owner of the adjoining land refuses to permit entry onto that adjoining land for the purpose of repair and maintenance of the single-family residence, then the owner of the single-family residence may bring an action in court to compel the owner of the adjoining land to permit entry for the purpose of repair and maintenance where entry will be granted solely for the purposes of repair and maintenance.

### Case Y

The need to enter the land of an adjoining property for the purpose of making repairs to one's own property should not mandate that an easement be acquired. An easement grants a right of way, but only the landowner can create an easement. The adjoining landowner may view the repairs as a nuisance and would not grant the easement. Sometimes repairs must be performed on a single-family residence that requires entering the adjoining land. Statute Ch. 12 § 99 was created to avoid the need to obtain an easement to enter adjoining land when the sole reason for the right of way is to make repairs on a single-family residence.

## REINFORCEMENT EXERCISE

6. Review a memo that you have recently completed. Examine the body of the discussion carefully. Highlight a paragraph that states the rule, its application, and conclusion. Examine a subsequent paragraph that expands on the initial rule by citing a separate opinion. Reformulate the rules statement to incorporate the initial rule and the subsequent rule to create a comprehensive statement of the law on that particular point.

## CHAPTER 24

# OUTLINING AND ORGANIZING A MEMORANDUM

| | | |
|---|---|---|
| **A.** | **PURPOSE OF OUTLINING** | 498 |
| **B.** | **STEPS TO OUTLINING** | 498 |
| | 1. Steps in Compiling a List of Legal Authorities | 498 |
| | 2. Organize Issues | 501 |
| | 3. Draft a Thesis Paragraph | 502 |
| | 4. Determine Which Element to Discuss First | 503 |
| | 5. List Elements or Subissues | 503 |
| | 6. Add Authority | 504 |
| | 7. Refine Issues | 504 |
| | 8. Arrange the Order of Elements | 504 |
| | 9. Organize into IRAC Paragraph | 504 |
| **C.** | **MULTI-ISSUE MEMORANDUM** | 505 |

## CHAPTER OVERVIEW

In Chapters 19 to 23, you learned about the components of a legal memorandum as well as some drafting pointers. This chapter teaches you how to organize the discussion section of your memorandum. You are shown some outlining techniques. These are suggested techniques only. You may have a technique of your own that works well. Feel free to use it. In this chapter, you also learn how to draft thesis paragraphs for your discussion.

# A. PURPOSE OF OUTLINING

The key to a well-organized memo is a well-drafted outline. **Outlining** allows you to organize your discussion easily so that it is smooth and cogent. An outline ensures that you cover all the legal rules and apply all the legally significant facts to those rules. An outline also simplifies your discussion drafting.

# B. STEPS TO OUTLINING

The outline should be done in two stages, each of which consists of a number of steps. In the first stage, you compile a **list of legal authorities**, which includes the names of and the citations to authorities, a note about the legally significant facts presented in any case, and a statement that summarizes each authority's significance to the issues presented in your research problem. See Illustration 24-1. In the second stage, you arrange the discussion sections concerning each issue and, in some cases, arrange each paragraph. See Illustration 24-2.

## 1. Steps in Compiling a List of Legal Authorities

1. Draft the statement of the facts, the questions presented, and the conclusions.
2. Research your issues.
3. Read the cases.
4. Brief the authorities as discussed in Chapter 18. Once you have briefed the authorities, you will write a holding for each case. These holdings should be used in your list of authorities. These holdings will summarize the significance of the authorities. If the holdings are well written, they will incorporate important facts derived from the authorities.
5. Write a summary statement for each statute or other noncase authority you plan to cite.
6. Prepare a list of each of the relevant authorities. Note that not all authorities will be relevant. Include only those that help you to determine the law involved in your case. For your list, include the name of the authority. If the authority is a case, list the holding or summary statement of the significance of the authority. Note the complete citation. It is also helpful to list whether the authority is a primary binding, primary persuasive, or secondary authority.

Now review Illustrations 24-1 and 24-3. Illustration 24-1 is a list of the significant authorities for the memo in Illustration 24-3.

## ILLUSTRATION 24-1.   List of Authorities

1. *Anderson v. St. Francis-St. George Hosp., Inc.*, 77 Ohio St. 3d 82, 671 N.E.2d 225 (1996): A civil battery occurs when one individual touches another individual without his or her consent and a physical injury occurs. (primary binding)

2. *Leichtman v. WLW Jacoc Communications, Inc.*, 92 Ohio App. 3d 232, 634 N.E.2d 697 (1994): A contact between a nonconsenting individual and a substance or an object such as cigar smoke is sufficient to be a touching within the context of the tort of civil battery because the substance or object would be an extension of the offender's body. (primary binding)

3. *Smith v. John Deere Co.*, 83 Ohio App. 3d 398, 614 N.E.2d 1148 (1993): A person intends his or her conduct when he or she undertakes an action with a knowing mind. (primary persuasive)

4. *Love v. Port Clinton*, 37 Ohio St. 3d 98, 524 N.E.2d 166 (1988): If a person consents to the touching, a battery has not occurred. (primary binding)

## ILLUSTRATION 24-2.   Outline of Battery Discussion

**Element or Subissue 1**

Issue: Did a touching occur?

Rule: Objects are extensions of body parts. Contact with a substance or an object can be touching (*Leichtman*)

Application of law to facts: Bucket contacted McMillan

Conclusion: A touching occurred

**Element or Subissue 2**

Issue: Did Mann intend to hit McMillan?

Rule: A person intends an act when it is done purposefully (*Smith*)

Application of law to facts: Mann purposefully threw the bucket at McMillan and said she intended to strike her

Conclusion: Mann had intent

**Element or Subissue 3**

Issue: Did McMillan consent to touching?

Rules: If a party consented to the touching, no battery occurred. (*Love*)

Application of law to facts: McMillan did not consent

Conclusion: A touching without consent as in this case can be a battery

**Element or Subissue 4**

Issue: Did McMillan suffer the requisite physical injuries as a result of the contact?

Rule: Physical injuries must result from contact for battery (*Anderson*)

Application of law to facts: McMillan sustained cuts and eye irritation from bucket and sand contact

Conclusion: McMillan had requisite physical injuries

## ILLUSTRATION 24-3. Memorandum: McMillan Battery Action

### MEMORANDUM

To: William Mark
From: Ivy Courier
Date: November 7, 2013
Re: McMillan Battery Action

### QUESTION PRESENTED

Did an actionable battery occur when Mann intentionally struck McMillan with a bucket, without McMillan's consent, causing McMillan to suffer physical and monetary injuries?

### CONCLUSION

Mann's intentional striking of McMillan with a bucket and sand without McMillan's consent was a battery.

### FACTS

Our client, Mary McMillan, a 36-year-old bank teller, wants to bring an action for battery against Carol Mann, a 36-year-old mother, who threw a metal bucket filled with sand at McMillan at a local park. While McMillan sat on a park bench, she teased Mann's seven-year-old son. Mann did not like this teasing and threw a bucket filled with sand at McMillan. Sand landed in McMillan's eyes while she was wearing soft contact lenses. As a result, McMillan's contacts had to be replaced. The bucket also cut McMillan's eye and cheek. She required stitches in both places. McMillan asked Mann to pay for her doctor bills and for the new contacts. Mann refused and added, "I'm not sorry. I meant to hurt you."

### DISCUSSION

The issue presented is whether Mann's intentional touching of McMillan with a bucket rather than her person is a battery. A battery is the intentional touching of another without consent, which causes injury. *Anderson v. St. Francis-St. George Hosp., Inc.*, 77 Ohio St. 3d 82, 671 N.E.2d 225 (1996). A touching can occur when an object rather than an individual's body contacts another person. *Leichtman v. WLW Jacoc Communications, Inc.*, 92 Ohio App. 3d 232, 634 N.E.2d 697 (1994); *Smith v. John Deere Co.*, 83 Ohio App. 3d 398, 614 N.E.2d 1148 (1993). In this case, Mann intentionally struck McMillan with a bucket without McMillan's consent and that touching resulted in injuries. Therefore, a battery occurred.

The **threshold issue** is whether a touching occurred when the bucket struck McMillan. A contact between a nonconsenting party and object rather than the actor's body can be a battery. *Leichtman v. WLW Jacoc Communications, Inc.*, 92 Ohio App. 3d 232, 634 N.E.2d 697 (1994); *Smith v. John Deere Co.*, 83 Ohio App. 3d at 398, 614 N.E.2d at 1148. In *Leichtman*, one person blew cigar smoke at another person,

## ILLUSTRATION 24-3. *Continued*

resulting in injuries. The court found that the cigar smoke was an extension of the person and that a contact between the smoke and the nonconsenting person met the requirement of a touching for civil battery. In this case, Mann threw the bucket at McMillan, and the bucket contacted her face. Following the reasoning in the *Leichtman* case, the bucket would be an extension of Mann's body, and the contact between McMillan and the bucket would be considered a touching under the theory of civil battery.

Next, the question to consider is whether under the statute Mann intended to touch McMillan when she struck her with the bucket. A person intends his or her conduct when he or she undertakes an action with a knowing mind. *Smith v. John Deere Co.*, 83 Ohio App. 3d 398, 614 N.E.2d 1148 (1993). In *Smith*, a police officer handcuffed the plaintiff. The court found that the officer must have intended his actions because you could not accidentally handcuff a person. *Smith*, 83 Ohio App. 3d at 399, 614 N.E.2d at 1149. In McMillan's case, Mann aimed the bucket at McMillan purposefully trying to strike her, Mann later told McMillan that she deliberately threw the bucket at her. McMillan probably will be able to establish that Mann had intent.

The next factor to consider is whether McMillan consented to the contact. If a person consents to the touching, a battery has not occurred. *Love v. Port Clinton*, 37 Ohio St. 3d 98, 524 N.E.2d 166 (1988). In our case, McMillan did not consent to Mann's throwing of the bucket at her face. Therefore, McMillan did not consent to any contact. Finally, the question is whether McMillan suffered physical injuries. A battery occurs only if a plaintiff sustains physical injuries as a result of the touching. *Anderson v. St. Francis-St. George Hosp., Inc.*, 77 Ohio St. 3d 82, 671 N.E.2d 225 (1996). McMillan sustained cuts on her face and the sand flying out of the bucket into her eyes. McMillan will be able to show that she sustained physical injuries as a result of the contact with the bucket.

## 2. Organize Issues

After you have prepared a detailed list of authorities, you are ready to organize your issues and to determine each of the legal elements that your memo should address. Each legal theory is defined as several factors called **elements.** You can think of the elements as pieces of a puzzle. You must consider each element before you complete your discussion. You can think of your discussion of these elements as a discussion of the subissues of the questions presented. Your discussion of some of these subissues will be cursory; some elements can be discussed in a single sentence. Most subissues, however, will be discussed in one or more paragraphs, generally organized in the IRAC (Issues, Rules, Application, Conclusion) format discussed in Chapter 22.

▼ What Steps Should You Follow in Preparing Your Outline
of Each of the Issues?

The first step in organizing your outline is to write a **thesis paragraph.**
This is the first paragraph of your discussion. It usually is a summary
of the legal issue you plan to discuss. In the thesis paragraph you introduce the issue, define the applicable rule of law, introduce each legal
element, apply the legally significant facts to the rule of law, and provide a short conclusion, usually one sentence long. When you have
multiple issues, the thesis paragraph will introduce all the issues presented and give readers a road map of what will be discussed. Then,
each issue will begin with a separate thesis paragraph.

## 3. Draft a Thesis Paragraph

The best and most typical format for the thesis paragraph is the IRAC
format. (For a full discussion of this format, see Chapter 22.) The first
sentence of a thesis paragraph introduces the overall issue presented in
the memo. The second sentence explains the rule of law. The next
sentence applies the rule of law to the facts of your case, and the
final sentence states a conclusion. A general outline for a thesis
paragraph, then, is:

1. Introduce the legal issue or question presented.
2. Summarize the legal rule for the question presented and each legal
   element to be discussed.
3. Apply the legally significant facts to the legal rule.
4. Conclude.

Review the thesis paragraph in Illustration 24-4. It is the first
paragraph of the discussion section of the memo in Illustration 24-3.
The first sentence introduces the issue: whether a battery occurred
when Mann struck McMillan with the bucket. This sentence mirrors
the question presented. See Illustration 24-3. The second sentence is
the rule of law. In this sentence you introduce each of the legal
elements or factors that will be discussed. In the *McMillan* case, the
elements are touching, intent, lack of consent, and resulting physical
injury. Each of these elements is discussed separately in the succeeding
memo paragraphs. A thesis paragraph should introduce the reader to
as many legal elements as possible in the thesis paragraph. The third
sentence of this thesis paragraph is the application of the law to the
facts. In this sentence, you explain to the reader the relationship
between the relevant law and the facts of your case. In Illustration
24-4, the fact that Mann struck McMillan with the bucket without
McMillan's consent was applied to the rule of law stated in the second
sentence. The final sentence is a conclusion. This sentence explains to
your readers your view of how the law and facts relate to each other.
In the *McMillan* case, the writer concluded that a battery occurred.

## ILLUSTRATION 24-4. Thesis Paragraph

The issue presented is whether Mann's intentional touching of McMillan with a bucket rather than her person is a battery. A battery is the intentional touching of another without consent which causes injury. *Anderson v. St. Francis-St. George Hosp., Inc.*, 77 Ohio St. 3d 82, 671 N.E.2d 225 (1996). A touching can occur when an object rather than an individual's body contacts another person. *Leichtman v. WLW Jacoc Communications, Inc.*, 92 Ohio App. 3d 232, 634 N.E.2d 697 (1994); *Smith v. John Deere Co.*, 83 Ohio App. 3d 398, 614 N.E.2d 1148 (1993). In this case, Mann intentionally struck McMillan with a bucket without McMillan's consent and that touching resulted in injuries. Therefore, a battery occurred.

### *OUTLINE OF THESIS PARAGRAPH FOR McMILLAN CASE*

1. Introduce the battery issue or question presented.
2. Summarize the legal rule: Battery is the intentional touching of another without consent that results in physical injury; touching can be done with an object.
3. Apply the legally significant facts to the legal rule: touching occurred when bucket struck McMillan.
4. Conclusion: battery occurred.

## 4. Determine Which Element to Discuss First

The next step is to determine which element to discuss first. If a legal claim has a threshold issue or element, it should be discussed first. A threshold issue is an issue that, if decided one way, would eliminate any further consideration of the legal claim. For example, in a breach of contract case, you must decide first whether a contract was formed before determining whether a breach occurred. Because courts sometimes change current law or approach legal claims differently than expected or than the law provides, you should fully discuss all subissues or elements, even if your threshold issue would dispose of the legal claim. For the memo in Illustration 24-3, the touching is the threshold issue. If Mann did not touch McMillan, then McMillan could not bring an action for battery. Therefore, this issue must be considered first.

## 5. List Elements or Subissues

Next, make a list of the elements or subissues to discuss. In the *McMillan* case, the elements list might be as follows:

touching
intent
lack of consent
physical injury

## 6. Add Authority

Now add the authority or authorities that relate to each element:

touching (*Leichtman, Smith*)
intent (*Smith*)
lack of consent (*Anderson*)
physical injury (*Anderson*)

## 7. Refine Issues

You might refine the issues so that they include facts from your case or incorporate further questions that are raised by the issues. For example, the issue of touching involves a secondary question of whether contact with an object rather than a person is a touching sufficient to constitute a battery. Your new list might be as follows:

touching (*Leichtman, Smith*)>
object rather than person (*Leichtman*)>
intent (*Smith*)>
lack of consent (*Anderson, Love*)>
physical injury (*Anderson*)

## 8. Arrange the Order of Elements

Now arrange the order of the elements. Touching is the threshold element or subissue, so you should discuss it first. The order of the other issues is a value judgment. If one or more elements can be easily discussed in a single sentence, often it is best to consider them after the threshold issue. If none of the elements is a threshold issue, then consider those elements that can be discussed easily first.

## 9. Organize into IRAC Paragraph

After you have determined the order of the elements, organize each element or subissue into an IRAC paragraph. Introduce the issue, present the rule, apply the law to the facts of your case, and conclude. For the *McMillan* memo, the discussion outline for each element might be as shown in Illustration 24-2. Review Illustration 24-2 and compare it to the text of the memo in Illustration 24-3. The discussion is derived entirely from the outline and follows it closely in IRAC format.

# C. MULTI-ISSUE MEMORANDUM

If you have a multi-issue memorandum, you will use many of the same techniques discussed above.

### ▼ How Do You Organize a Multi-Issue Memorandum?

1. Determine how many issues you will discuss. Often an attorney will help you make this determination. Decide which issue should be discussed first. Again, consider whether there is a threshold issue. In the memo above, the first issue is whether Mann committed a battery. If a touching did not occur when the bucket struck McMillan, then the later issues do not need to be addressed. Therefore, this issue is the threshold issue and should be placed first. However, you should still discuss the later issues even if you determine that the first issue would be decided in a manner that would dispose of a case. Courts are unpredictable and might decide the issue differently than you did.
2. Determine the legal elements you will discuss and a logical order for this discussion.
3. Prepare a detailed outline of the discussion. For each issue, note each legal element you will address, the authority related to that element, and the legally significant facts applicable to that element.
4. Write a thesis paragraph. For a multi-issue memo, such as the one in Illustration 24-5, introduce the issues and explain the rules of law in the thesis paragraphs that introduce each issue. Your organization for a multi-issue memo might be as follows:

Thesis Paragraph
    Introduce all legal issues or questions presented
    Conclusions

Thesis Paragraph for Issue or Question Presented #1
    Introduce the legal issue or question presented
    Summarize the legal rule for the question presented #1 and
        each legal element to be discussed
    Apply the legally significant facts to the legal rule
    Conclusion

First Legal Element or Subissue
    Introduce the legal element
    Summarize the legal rule
    Apply the legally significant facts to the legal rule
    Conclusion

Second Legal Element or Subissue
    Introduce the legal element
    Summarize the legal rule
    Apply the legally significant facts to the legal rule
    Conclusion

Thesis Paragraph for Issue or Question Presented #2
    Introduce the legal issue or question presented
    Summarize the legal rule for the question presented #2 and
        each legal element to be discussed
    Apply the legally significant facts to the legal rule
    Conclusion

First Legal Element or Subissue
    Introduce the legal element
    Summarize the legal rule
    Apply the legally significant facts to the legal rule
    Conclusion

Second Legal Element or Subissue
    Introduce the legal element
    Summarize the legal rule
    Apply the legally significant facts to the legal rule
    Conclusion

5. Use headings to introduce new issues. Use transitions to guide the reader from one issue to another and one paragraph to another.

Illustration 24-6 is an outline of the memo shown in Illustration 24-5.

Once you complete your outline, you are ready to begin writing your discussion. Follow your outline and use the applicable law and the facts from cases when they are useful. Once you have completed your draft, compare the draft to the outline to ensure that you have incorporated all the components in your outline and that your text matches your outline organization.

Review Illustration 24-7 and compare the outline provided to the discussion section that follows. Now compare this to the discussion section to the discussion sections that concern this point of law found in Illustrations 24-3 and 24-5.

**ILLUSTRATION 24-5.   Multi-Issue Memorandum: McMillan Battery Action**

---

### MEMORANDUM

To: William Mark
From: Ivy Courier
Date: November 7, 2013
Re: McMillan Battery Action

### QUESTIONS PRESENTED

1. Did a battery occur when Carol Mann intentionally struck Mary McMillan with a bucket, without McMillan's consent, causing McMillan to suffer physical and monetary injuries?

2. Does eight-year-old Rachel McMillan have a valid claim for intentional infliction of emotional distress against Carol Mann after the child saw Mann throw a rusty metal bucket of sand at her mother's face and head, causing physical injuries to the elder McMillan and resulting in the child suffering from anxiety, headaches, and vomiting?

3. Was Camp Cougar vicariously liable for the intentional torts of Mann, a volunteer whom camp officials asked to supervise children in the sandbox?

### CONCLUSIONS

1. When Mann intentionally struck McMillan on the head and in the face with a rusty, metal bucket and sand without McMillan's consent and McMillan was injured, a battery occurred.

2. Eight-year-old Rachel McMillan has a claim for intentional infliction of emotional distress against Carol Mann because the child can show that she suffered emotional distress as a result of Mann's extreme and outrageous act of intentionally throwing a rusty, metal bucket at the child's mother, causing the older McMillan to suffer physical injuries and the child to suffer from anxiety and post-traumatic stress syndrome—mental anguish no child should be expected to endure.

3. Camp Cougar will not be found vicariously liable for an intentional act of its agent, Mann, because it did not benefit from that act nor did the camp control Mann's actions.

### FACTS

Our client, Mary McMillan, a 36-year-old bank teller, seeks to bring an action for battery against Carol Mann, a 36-year-old mother, who threw a rusty, metal bucket filled with sand at her at a local camp. She also wants to bring an action against Camp Cougar for vicarious liability for the intentional torts of camp volunteer Carol Mann. Camp Cougar enlisted Carol Mann, a camper's parent, to act as volunteer supervisor of the sandbox during Parent Visitor Day at Camp Cougar. Camp Cougar officials told Mann to ensure that no one was injured while playing in the sandbox. Mann had handled this responsibility during Parent Visitor Day in the past. Mary McMillan came to see her

## ILLUSTRATION 24-5. *Continued*

eight-year-old daughter, Rachel, during Camp Cougar Parent Visitor Day. While McMillan sat on a camp bench, she teased Mann's seven-year-old son. Mann did not like this teasing and threw a rusty, metal bucket filled with sand at McMillan's head and face. Sand landed in McMillan's eyes while she was wearing soft contact lenses. As a result, McMillan's contacts had to be replaced. The bucket also cut McMillan's head, eye, and cheek. She lost a lot of blood from her head, requiring a transfusion of one pint of blood. She had stitches on her eyelid and cheek. After the bucket struck McMillan, Mann told McMillan in front of three witnesses, "I'm not sorry. I meant to hurt you."

Immediately after Rachel McMillan saw her mother bleeding, she began to cry and vomit. She told the camp counselors that her head hurt and she would not go with the camp director to the hospital. She said she was afraid the director would throw a bucket of sand at her if she didn't like what she said. The child missed the remainder of camp because she suffered from daily headaches and vomiting and she was afraid of the adults at the camp. A child psychologist examined the child and said she was suffering headaches, vomiting, and anxiety as a result of seeing a bucket thrown by an adult at her mother. He said she was experiencing post-traumatic stress syndrome.

### DISCUSSION

This memo first will address whether Carol Mann can be held liable for battery when she intentionally struck McMillan with a rusty, metal bucket, without McMillan's consent, causing McMillan to suffer physical and monetary injuries. Next, the discussion will consider whether eight-year-old Rachel McMillan has a claim for intentional infliction of emotional distress against Mann after the child saw Mann throw a rusty, metal bucket of sand at her mother's head and face, resulting in injury to her mother and causing the young girl to suffer from anxiety, headaches, and vomiting. Finally, the memo will explore whether McMillan can establish that Camp Cougar was vicariously liable for the intentional actions of one of its volunteers, Carol Mann, that resulted in injury to McMillan.

### 1. WAS MANN'S INTENTIONAL TOUCHING OF McMILLAN WITH A BUCKET BATTERY?

The issue presented is whether Mann's intentional touching of McMillan with a bucket rather than her person is a battery. A battery is the intentional touching of another without consent, which causes injury. *Anderson v. St. Francis-St. George Hosp., Inc.*, 77 Ohio St. 3d 82, 671 N.E.2d 225 (1996). A touching can occur when an object rather than an individual's body contacts another person. *Leichtman v. WLW Jacoc Communications, Inc.*, 92 Ohio App. 3d 232, 634 N.E.2d 697 (1994); *Smith v. John Deere Co.*, 83 Ohio App. 3d 398, 614 N.E.2d 1148 (1993). A person intends his or her conduct when he or she undertakes an

**ILLUSTRATION 24-5.** *Continued*

action with a knowing mind. If a person consents to the touching, a battery has not occurred. *Love v. Port Clinton*, 37 Ohio St. 3d 98, 524 N.E.2d 166 (1988). A battery occurs only if a plaintiff sustains physical injuries as a result of the touching. *Anderson v. St. Francis-St. George Hosp., Inc.*, 77 Ohio St. 3d 82, 671 N.E.2d 225 (1996). In this case, Mann intentionally struck McMillan with a bucket without McMillan's consent and that touching resulted in injuries. Therefore, a battery occurred.

The threshold issue is whether an intentional touching occurred when a bucket Mann threw struck McMillan. A touching can occur when an object rather than an individual's body contacts another person. *Leichtman v. WLW Jacoc Communications, Inc.*, 92 Ohio App. 3d 232, 634 N.E.2d 697 (1994); *Smith v. John Deere Co.*, 83 Ohio App. 3d at 398, 614 N.E.2d at 1148. In *Leichtman*, one person blew cigar smoke at another person, resulting in injuries. The court found that the cigar smoke was an extension of the person and that a contact between the smoke and the nonconsenting person met the requirement of a touching for civil battery. In this case, Mann threw the bucket at McMillan, and the bucket contacted her face and head. Following the reasoning in the *Leichtman* case, the bucket would be an extension of Mann's body, and the contact between McMillan and the bucket would be considered a touching under the theory of civil battery.

Next, the question to consider is whether under the statute Mann intended to touch McMillan when she struck her with the bucket. A person intends his or her conduct when he or she undertakes an action with a knowing mind. *Smith v. John Deere Co.*, 83 Ohio App. 3d 398, 614 N.E.2d 1148 (1993). In *Smith*, a police officer handcuffed the plaintiff. The court found that the officer must have intended his actions because you could not accidentally handcuff a person. *Smith*, 83 Ohio App. 3d at 399, 614 N.E.2d at 1149. In McMillan's case, Mann aimed the bucket at McMillan, purposefully trying to strike her. Mann later told McMillan that she deliberately threw the bucket at her. McMillan probably will be able to establish that Mann had the statutory intent.

The next factor to consider is whether McMillan consented to the contact. If a person consents to the touching, a battery has not occurred. *Love v. Port Clinton*, 37 Ohio St. 3d 98, 524 N.E.2d 166 (1988). In our case, McMillan did not consent to Mann's throwing of the bucket at her face. Therefore, McMillan did not consent to any contact. Finally, the question is whether McMillan suffered physical injuries. A battery occurs only if a plaintiff sustains physical injuries as a result of the touching. *Anderson v. St. Francis-St. George Hosp., Inc.*, 77 Ohio St. 3d 82, 671 N.E.2d 225 (1996). McMillan sustained cuts on her face and the sand flying out of the bucket into her eyes. McMillan will be able to show that she sustained physical injuries as a result of the contact with the bucket.

## ILLUSTRATION 24-5. *Continued*

### 2. IS MANN LIABLE FOR INTENTIONAL INFLICTION OF EMOTIONAL DISTRESS?

The next issue to consider is whether eight-year-old Rachel McMillan has a claim for intentional infliction of emotional distress against Carol Mann. To successfully prove intentional infliction of emotional distress, McMillan must show that Mann intentionally committed an extreme and outrageous that caused emotional distress that no reasonable person could be expected to endure. *Yeager v. Local Union 20*, 6 Ohio St. 3d 369, 453 N.E.2d 666 (1983). *Pyle v. Pyle*, 11 Ohio App.3d 31, 34, 463 N.E.2d 98, 101 (1983). In the case, Rachel McMillan, a child, saw Mann, an adult, throw the rusty, metal bucket filled with sand at her mother's head and face, causing her mother to bleed. Seeing this act caused the child to suffer from anxiety, headaches, and vomiting daily. Several witnesses can testify that Mann said that she intended to harm McMillan. A child should not be expected to endure the pain of seeing her mother injured. Therefore, Rachel McMillan has a claim for intentional emotional distress

The threshold issue is whether Mann's act of throwing a rusty, metal bucket at the head and face of another adult in front of children was an extreme and outrageous act. An act is extreme and outrageous if it goes "beyond all possible bounds of decency," *Yeager* 6 Ohio. St. 3d at 375, 453 N.E.2d at 672, and is regarded as "atrocious, and utterly intolerable in a civilized community." *Id.* In this case, Mann, an adult who was asked to supervise the sandbox and ensure the safety of others, threw a rusty, metal bucket filled with sand at another adult in front of young children, including her child and Rachel McMillan. The bucket struck the older McMillan, causing her to bleed. That act went beyond all possible bounds of decency and was atrocious and utterly intolerable in a civilized community. This is especially true since Mann was charged with ensuring the safety of people in the sandbox area. Therefore, Mann's act would be found to be an extreme and outrageous act.

Next, the young McMillan must show that the act was done with intent. A person intends his or her conduct when he or she undertakes an action with a knowing mind. *Smith v. John Deere Co.*, 83 Ohio App. 3d 398, 614 N.E.2d 1148 (1993). If an actor knew or should have known that his or her actions would cause serious emotional distress, intent is established. *Phung v. Waste Mgt., Inc.*, 71 Ohio St. 3d 408, 410, 644 N.E.2d 286, 288 (1994). In this case, Mann not only knew or should have known that throwing a rusty, metal bucket filled with sand at the head and face of another adult in front of the other adult's child resulting in the adult bleeding would cause an eight-year-old child to suffer serious emotional distress. For those reasons, the young McMillan should be able to show intent.

The third element McMillan must establish is that the extreme and outrageous act was the proximate cause of her emotional and physical distress. Proximate cause exists when an act precedes and produces an

## ILLUSTRATION 24-5. *Continued*

injury that is likely to have occurred as a result of the act or which might have been anticipated. *Jeffers v. Olexo*, 43 Ohio St. 3d 140, 143, 539 N.E.2d 614, 617 (1989). In this case, the young McMillan can show that a child likely would experience emotional distress when she saw her mother injured and bleeding. Therefore, the child will be able to establish that the extreme and outrageous act was the proximate cause of her emotional distress.

Finally, the child must show that she suffered from serious emotional distress. To establish serious emotional distress, the mental anguish she suffered must be serious and of a nature that "no reasonable man could be expected to endure it." Id. Serious emotional distress goes "beyond trifling mental disturbance, mere upset or hurt feelings" and "may be found where a reasonable person, normally constituted, would be unable to cope adequately with the mental distress engendered by the circumstances of the case." *Paugh v. Hanks*, 6 Ohio St. 3d 72, 78, 451 N.E.2d 759, 765 (1983). It is not necessary to prove any physical harm. *Pyle v. Pyle*, 11 Ohio App.3d 31, 34, 463 N.E.2d 98, 101 (1983). Various neurosis, psychosis and phobias are examples of serious emotional distress. *Paugh v. Hanks*, 6 Ohio St. 3d 72, 78, 451 N.E.2d 759, 765 (1983). In this case, a psychologist examined the child and found that she suffered from post-traumatic stress syndrome and as well as physical symptoms such as headaches and vomiting after she saw an adult throw a bucket at her mother. Post-traumatic stress and anxiety coupled with these physical manifestations should be sufficient for young McMillan to establish serious emotion distress that is beyond mere upset or hurt feelings and that a reasonable person would be unable to cope.

### 3. WAS CAMP COUGAR VICARIOUSLY LIABLE FOR MANN'S INTENTIONAL TORTS?

The final claim to consider is whether Camp Cougar will be vicariously liable to both McMillans for Mann's intentional torts. An entity can be held vicariously liable for the actions of its agent. *Byrd v. Faber*, 57 Ohio St. 3d 56, 58-59, 565 N.E.2d 584-586 (1991). A principal-agent relationship is established when one party exercises control over the actions of another and those actions are done for the benefit of the party exercising control. See *Hanson v. Kynast*, 24 Ohio St. 3d 171, 173, 494 N.E.2d 1091 (1986). However, a master can be vicariously liable for its agent's intentional tort only if the entity controlled the agent's conduct and the agent's acts benefited the entity. *Id.* In this case, Camp Cougar directed Mann to supervise a camp activity. Therefore, Mann may be found to be Camp Cougar's agent. However, Mann's actions did not benefit the camp, nor did the camp exercise control over her actions. In fact, these actions may have harmed the camp. Therefore, it is unlikely that Camp Cougar would be found liable for Mann's torts.

The threshold issue is whether Mann is Camp Cougar's agent. A principal-agent relationship is established when one party exercises

## ILLUSTRATION 24-5. *Continued*

control over the actions of another and those actions are for the benefit of the party exercising control. See *Hanson v. Kynast*, 24 Ohio St. 3d 171, 173, 494 N.E.2d 1091 (1986). In this case, Camp Cougar directed Mann to act as the sandbox supervisor and specifically directed her to keep people safe. Therefore, Mann is likely to be found to be an agent of Camp Cougar.

The next issue to consider is whether a master can be vicariously liable for its agent's intentional torts. A master can be vicariously liable for its agent's intentional tort only if the master controlled the agent's conduct and the agent's acts benefited the master. See *Hanson v. Kynast*, 24 Ohio St. 3d 171, 173, 494 N.E.2d 1091 (1986). The camp did not direct Mann to injure McMillan, nor did the camp benefit from Mann's actions. Therefore, Camp Cougar would not be vicariously liable for Mann's act of throwing the bucket of sand at McMillan or causing young McMillan's serious emotional distress because it did not control Mann's actions, nor did the camp benefit from Mann's actions.

## ILLUSTRATION 24-6. Multi-Issue Outline

Thesis Paragraph
Introduce issues
Whether Carol Mann's touching of McMillan was battery
Whether Carol Mann committed the tort of intentional infliction of emotional distress
Whether Camp Cougar can be vicariously liable for Carol Mann's acts

Heading: Issue 1 or Question Presented 1
Introductory issue: Did Carol Mann commit the tort of battery?
Rules: (1A) A battery is the intentional touching of another without the consent of the person touched that results in injury. (*Anderson*) (primary binding) (first element or subissue)
(B) A contact between a nonconsenting party and object rather than the actor's body can be a battery. (*Leichtman*) (primary binding) (first element or subissue)
Rule (2) A person intends his or her conduct when he or she undertakes an action with a knowing mind. (*Smith*) (primary binding) (second element or subissue)
Rule (3) If a person consents to the touching, a battery has not occurred. (*Love*) (primary binding) (third element or subissue).
Rule (4) A battery occurs only if a plaintiff sustains physical injuries as a result of the touching. (*Anderson*) (primary binding) (fourth element or subissue).

**ILLUSTRATION 24-6.** *Continued*

Application of law to facts: In McMillan's case, Mann not only aimed the bucket at McMillan purposefully to strike her, she struck Mann with it and the sand. The bucket and the sand striking McMillan would be sufficient to establish that a "touching" occurred. Mann later told McMillan that she deliberately threw the bucket at her. McMillan's did not consent to being hit by the bucket and that touching resulted in injuries.

Conclusion: The touching was a battery.

First Legal Element or Subissue 1

Issue: Did a touching occur?

Rule: Objects are extensions of body parts. Contact with a substance or an object can be touching. (*Leichtman*)

Application of law to facts: Bucket contacted McMillan.

Conclusion: A touching occurred.

Second Legal Element or Subissue 2

Issue: Did Mann intend to hit McMillan?

Rule: A person intends an act when it is done purposefully. (*Smith*)

Application of law to facts: Mann purposefully threw the bucket at McMillan and said she intended to strike her.

Conclusion: Mann had intent.

Third Legal Element or Subissue 3

Issue: Did McMillan consent to touching?

Rule: If a party consented to the touching, no battery occurred. (*Love*)

Application of law to facts: McMillan did not consent.

Conclusion: A touching without consent as in this case can be a battery.

Fourth Element or Subissue 4

Issue: Did McMillan suffer the requisite physical injuries as a result of the contact?

Rule: Physical injuries must result from contact for battery. (*Anderson*)

Application of law to facts: McMillan sustained cuts and eye irritation from bucket and sand contact.

Conclusion: McMillan had requisite physical injuries.

Thesis Paragraph to Introduce Issue 2

Issue: Does eight-year-old Rachel McMillan have a claim for intentional infliction of emotional distress against Carol Mann?

Rule: Intentional infliction of emotional distress occurs when an individual intentionally commits an extreme and outrageous

## ILLUSTRATION 24-6. *Continued*

act that causes emotional distress that no reasonable person can be expected to endure. (*Yeager*) (primary binding).

Application: Rachel McMillan, a child, saw Mann, an adult who was asked to supervise the sandbox and ensure the safety of others, throw the rusty, metal bucket filled with sand at her mother's head and face, causing her mother to bleed. Seeing this act that was "beyond all possible bounds of decency" and therefore extreme and outrageous caused the child to suffer from anxiety, headaches, and vomiting daily—symptoms no reasonable child should be expected to endure. Several witnesses can testify that Mann said that she intended to harm McMillan.

Conclusion: Rachel McMillan has a claim for intentional emotional distress.

Issue 2 First Element or Subissue 1

Issue: Did Mann commit an extreme and outrageous act?

Rule 1: An extreme and outrageous act is one that no reasonable person can be expected to endure (*Yeager*) (primary binding) (*Pyle*) (primary persuasive).

Rule 2: An act is extreme and outrageous if it goes beyond all possible bounds of decency and is intolerable in a civilized community. (*Yeager*) (primary binding).

Application of law to facts: Mann, an adult who was asked to ensure safety in the sandbox, threw a rusty, metal bucket filled with sand at another adult in front of young children, including her child and Rachel McMillan, the injured party's daughter. That act goes beyond all possible bounds of decency and would be intolerable in a civilized community.

Conclusion: Mann's act would be found to be an extreme and outrageous act.

Issue 2 Second Element or Subissue 2

Issue: Was the extreme and outrageous act done with intent?

Rule 1: A person intends his or her conduct when he or she undertakes an action with a knowing mind. (*Smith*) (primary binding)

Rule 2: If an actor knew or should have known that his or her actions would cause serious emotional distress, intent is established. (*Phung*) (primary binding)

Application of law to facts: Mann said she intended to harm McMillan. In addition, Mann not only knew or should have known that throwing a rusty, metal bucket filled with sand at the head and face of another adult in front of the other

## ILLUSTRATION 24-6. *Continued*

adult's child resulting in the adult bleeding would cause an eight-year-old child to suffer serious emotional distress.

Conclusion: The young McMillan should be able to show intent.

Issue 2 Third Element or Subissue

Issue: Was the extreme and outrageous act the proximate cause of McMillan's emotional and physical distress?

Rule: Proximate cause exists when an act precedes and produces an injury that is likely to have occurred as a result of the act or which might have been anticipated. (*Jeffers*) (primary binding)

Application of Law to Facts: A child would be expected or likely to experience emotional distress when she witnesses her mother injured and bleeding.

Conclusion: The young McMillan will be able to show that the act was the proximate cause of her emotional and physical distress.

Issue 2 Fourth Element or Subissue

Issue: Did the child suffered from serious emotional distress?

Rule 1: To establish serious emotional distress, the mental anguish must be serious and of a nature that "no reasonable man could be expected to endure it." (*Paugh*) (primary binding) Serious emotional distress goes beyond mere upset or hurt feelings, but exists when a reasonable person is unable to cope. *Id.*

Rule 2: Physical harm need not be shown. (*Pyle*)

Rule 3: Neurosis, psychosis and phobias can establish serious emotional distress. (*Paugh*) (primary binding)

Application of Law to Facts: A psychologist found that the child suffered from post-traumatic stress syndrome and suffered anxiety and physical symptoms such as headaches and vomiting. That should be sufficient to establish serious emotion distress that is beyond mere upset or hurt feelings and that a reasonable person would be unable to cope.

Conclusion: Young McMillan can show she suffered from serious emotional distress.

Introduce Issue 3

Issue: Was Camp Cougar vicariously liable for Mann's intentional torts?

Rule 1: An entity can be held vicariously liable for the intentional actions of its agent if the entity controlled the agent's conduct and benefited from it. (*Blankenship*)

## ILLUSTRATION 24-6.   *Continued*

Application of Law to Facts: Mann may be found to be an agent for Camp Cougar. However, Mann's actions did not benefit the camp, nor did the camp exercise control over her actions.

Conclusion: Even though Mann is likely to be found liable for these intentional torts and a master can be found liable for the intentional torts of its agent, it is unlikely in this case that Camp Cougar would be found liable for Mann's torts.

Issue 3 First Element or Subissue

Issue: Is Mann Camp Cougar's agent?

Rule: A principal-agent relationship is established when one party exercises the right of control over the actions of another and those actions are for the benefit of the party exercising control. (*Hanson*) (primary binding).

Application of Law to Facts: Camp Cougar directed Mann to act as the sandbox supervisor and specifically directed her to keep people safe, exercising control over her actions and deriving benefit from her actions.

Conclusion: Mann is likely to be found to be an agent of Camp Cougar.

Issue 3 Element or Subissue 2

Issue: Is Camp Cougar, a master, vicariously liable for its agent's intentional torts?

Rule: A master can be vicariously liable for its agent's intentional tort only if the master controlled the agent's conduct and the agent's acts benefited the master. (*Hanson*) (primary binding).

Application of Law to Fact: Camp Cougar did not direct Mann to throw the bucket nor did the camp benefit from Mann's conduct.

Conclusion: Camp Cougar would not be held liable for Mann's intentional acts.

## ILLUSTRATION 24-7.   Writing from an Outline

**Outline**

First Legal Element or Subissue 1

Issue: Did a touching occur?

Rule: Objects are extensions of body parts. Contact with a substance even cigar smoke or an object can be a touching (*Leichtman*)

## ILLUSTRATION 24-7.   *Continued*

Application of law to facts: Bucket touched McMillan when Mann threw it

Conclusion: A touching occurred

**Paragraph Drafted from Outline**

I. Did a battery occur when Mann struck McMillan with a bucket and sand?

Whether Mann committed the tort of battery turns on whether an intentional touching occurred when a bucket Mann threw struck McMillan. A touching can occur when an object rather than an individual's body contacts another person. *Leichtman v. WLW Jacoc Communications, Inc.*, 92 Ohio App. 3d 232, 634 N.E.2d 697 (1994); *Smith v. John Deere Co.*, 83 Ohio App. 3d at 398, 614 N.E.2d at 1148. In *Leichtman*, one person blew cigar smoke at another person, resulting in injuries. The court found that the cigar smoke was an extension of the person and that a contact between the smoke and the nonconsenting person met the requirement of a touching for civil battery. In this case, Mann threw the bucket at McMillan, and the bucket contacted her face and head. Following the reasoning in the *Leichtman* case, the bucket would be an extension of Mann's body, and the contact between McMillan and the bucket would be considered a touching under the theory of civil battery.

## IN-CLASS EXERCISE

Review the memo in Illustration 24-8. Prepare an outline of authorities and an outline based on this memo. (This is the reverse of the process you would normally use.) Then discuss your outline. Make a list of legally significant facts and note the legal standard.

## ILLUSTRATION 24-8.   Sample Memorandum Slip-and-Fall Case

### MEMORANDUM

To: Margaret Sterner
From: Marie Main
Date: January 28, 2014
Re: *Harris v. Sack and Shop*

QUESTION PRESENTED

Is Sack and Shop, a grocery store, liable for injuries sustained by Harris, a store patron who slipped on a banana peel that had been left on the grocery store floor for two days?

## ILLUSTRATION 24-8. *Continued*

BRIEF ANSWER

Probably yes. Sack and Shop, a grocery store, probably will be liable based on negligence for injuries sustained by Harris, a store patron who slipped on a banana peel that had been left on the grocery store floor for two days.

FACTS

Our client, Sack and Shop Grocery Store, is being sued for negligence by Rebecca Harris.

Harris went to the store to purchase groceries on July 8, 2013. While she was in the produce section, she slipped on a banana peel that a grocery store employee left on the floor. The employee had dropped it on the floor two days earlier and had failed to clean it up after a patron asked him to do so.

Harris sustained a broken arm and head injuries as a result of the slip and fall.

DISCUSSION

The issue presented in this case is whether Sack and Shop Grocery Store was negligent when Rebecca Harris slipped in the store's produce section. A grocer will be found negligent if a store employee breached the store's duty of reasonable care to its patrons and, as a result of that breach, the patron was injured. *Ward v. K Mart Corp.*, 554 N.E.2d 223 (Ill. 1990). In *Ward*, the grocery store employee failed to clean up a banana peel for two days and that peel caused a patron to be injured. Similarly, in our case Sack and Shop failed to remove the banana peel for two days. Therefore, Sack and Shop is likely to be found liable for the injuries Harries sustained.

The first element to consider is whether Sack and Shop owed a duty of reasonable care to Harris. A grocery store owes a duty of care to any patron. *Ward*, 554 N.E.2d at 226. Harris was a customer in the store. Therefore, Sack and Shop owed her a duty of care.

The next question to consider is whether Sack and Shop breached its duty of reasonable care to Harris. A store will be found to have breached its duty of reasonable care to a patron if a store employee fails to properly and regularly clean the floor of the store. *Olinger v. Great Atl. & Pac. Tea Co.*, 173 N.E.2d 443 (Ill. 1961). In *Olinger*, the store was found liable because a store employee failed to clean the floor for one day and a patron slipped on a substance on the floor. 173 N.E.2d at 447. No one had told any store employee about the slippery substance. *Id.* at 447. Nonetheless, the Illinois Supreme Court found the store liable, saying that the store employees had sufficient time to notice the substance if they had used ordinary care. *Id.* In our case, Sack and Shop's employee had two days to clean the floor before Harris fell. In addition, a customer had placed the store employee on notice of the banana peel. Therefore, Sack and Shop breached its duty of care to Harris.

**ILLUSTRATION 24-8.** *Continued*

The plaintiff, however, still must establish proximate cause, that is, that the injury resulted as a natural consequence of Sack and Shop's breach of its duty. A store owner's failure to clear debris from a store floor, resulting in injury to a patron who slipped on the floor, was found to be the proximate cause of the patron's injuries. *Id.* at 449. In this case, Sack and Shop's failure to clean the peel from the floor was a breach of its duty of care to Harris. This breach resulted in injury to Harris. Sack and Shop's breach will be found to be the proximate cause of Harris's injuries.

The final element that must be established is that the plaintiff, Harris, suffered injuries. Harris sustained a broken arm and head injuries as a result of the slip and fall. Therefore, she will be able to show that she was injured.

CONCLUSION

Sack and Shop owed Harris a duty of reasonable care. The store is likely to be found to have breached that duty of reasonable care because an employee failed to remove a banana peel from the grocery store floor during the preceding two days. The injuries Harris sustained were directly caused by a slip on a banana peel. Therefore, Sack and Shop is likely to be found liable to Harris.

# CHAPTER SUMMARY

Outlining is an important component of legal writing. It helps you organize the discussion section of your legal memorandum. To outline a legal memorandum, first draft a list of legal authorities. Second, arrange the discussion sections concerning each issue and, if necessary, arrange each paragraph of the memorandum.

The list of legal authorities should include the names and citations to the authorities, a note about the legally significant facts contained in the authority, if any, and a statement that summarizes the significance of the authority.

The legal issues of the discussion should be organized in the IRAC format discussed in Chapter 22. Each element of a legal issued should be addressed in this format.

Before you can begin writing your memorandum, you must organize your thesis paragraph. The thesis paragraph is the first paragraph of your discussion. It summarizes the legal issues you will discuss in the memorandum. This paragraph also should be organized in IRAC format, if possible.

You have been shown how to draft questions presented, issues, conclusions, brief answers, facts statements, and discussion sections. In addition, you have been taught how to synthesize authorities and how to use a legal writing convention called IRAC.

## KEY TERMS

elements
list of legal authorities
outlining

thesis paragraph
threshold issue

## EXERCISES

### SHORT ANSWER

1. How do you organize a thesis paragraph?
2. How do you compile a list of legal authorities?
3. How do you determine which element to discuss first?
4. What format should each paragraph take?
5. Review the memo in Illustration 24-8 above. Prepare an outline of authorities and an outline based on this memo. (This is the reverse of the process you would normally use.) Then discuss your outline. Make a list of legally significant facts and note the legal standard.
6. Write the discussion section only for the memo below.

### MEMORANDUM

To: Ruth Abbey
From: Gail Michael
Date: January 20, 2014
Re: *Kahn v. Randall,* Civ. 95 No. 988, File No. 8988977

### QUESTION PRESENTED

Does Janice Kahn have a valid claim for intentional infliction of emotional distress against Ronnie Randall after Kahn saw Randall turn his car to strike Kahn's 11-year-old child in front of her, causing her to suffer from anxiety, headaches, and vomiting?

### CONCLUSION

Janice Kahn probably has a valid claim for intentional infliction of emotional distress against Ronnie Randall. Kahn saw Randall turn his car to strike her 11-year-old child. Seeing this accident caused Kahn to suffer from anxiety, headaches, and vomiting daily. This act could be considered extreme and outrageous conduct if it was done with intent. Several witness can testify that Randall said that he intended to harm Kahn, and Kahn states that Randall turned the car to strike her son. Two factors, however, might show that Randall lacked intent: the statement that he made to the police that he did not intend to hit the child and the fact that his blood alcohol level was .11, possibly preventing him from formulating the needed intent.

### FACTS

While driving a car Ronnie Randall struck Janice Kahn's son at 5 P.M. on August 29, 2007. It was bright and clear. No skid marks appeared on the dry street following the accident.

Janice Kahn was working in her garden about five feet from the accident scene at the time of the accident. Her son was playing a game in the street before Randall's car struck him. Kahn did not see the car strike her 11-year-old son. When she first looked up from her garden, she thought her son was dead. He was covered with blood and had several broken bones. However, Kahn's son was conscious after the accident.

Immediately after the accident, Randall, who had a blood alcohol level of .11, was cited for drunk driving and driving with a suspended driver's license. Police charged him with drunk driving and suspended his license two weeks earlier after the car he was driving struck another child at the same spot. Randall has a drinking history.

Following the accident, several witnesses said Randall was upset and wobbled as he walked. One witness said that Randall intentionally turned the steering wheel to hit Kahn's son. Kahn stated that Randall often swerved down her street to get her attention.

Rhonda Albert, Kahn's neighbor, said she heard Randall say he would get even with Kahn after Kahn broke off a ten-year relationship with him.

During Kahn and Randall's ten-year relationship, Randall was close to Kahn's son. He took him to ball games, including one in April, and attended the son's baseball games. Randall knew that Kahn's son was the most important person in her life.

Since the accident, Kahn vomits daily and suffers from anxiety and headaches. Dr. Susan Faigen, Kahn's internist, states that the anxiety, headaches, and vomiting are the result of the accident. The prevailing case is *George v. Jordan Marsh Co.*, 359 Mass. 244, 268 N.E.2d 915 (1971). In that case, the court held that one who without a privilege to do so by extreme and outrageous conduct intentionally causes severe emotional distress to another, with bodily harm resulting from such distress, is subject to liability for such emotional distress and bodily harm.

7. Write a thesis paragraph for the discussion section below.

## FACTS

Drake Industries has been leasing warehouse space at 2700 North Bosworth Avenue, in Chicago, Illinois, from the owner of the building, Michael Martin. Drake began leasing space from Martin beginning January 1, 2007 at $700 per month until the lease expired on December 31, 2007.

Martin offered a new lease to Drake on November 25, 2007, to be signed and returned by December 31, 2007. The new lease began January 1, 2008, and expired on June 30, 2008, and the rent increased to $850 per month, payable on the first of each month. Drake never signed or returned the new lease, but did pay the increased rent amount during the term of the unsigned lease ending June 30, 2008. Since then, Drake has continued paying $850 on the first day of each month. On August 15, 2008, Martin requested that Drake surrender the premises. Drake came to your firm to find out what type of tenancy he has and whether Martin gave Drake the proper notice to quit the premises.

## DISCUSSION

Is Drake Industries a holdover tenant? A holdover tenancy is created when a landlord elects to treat a tenant, after the expiration of his or her lease, as a tenant for another term upon the same provisions contained in the original lease. *Bismarck Hotel Co. v. Sutherland*, 92 Ill., App. 3d 167, 415 N.E.2d 517 (1980). In *Bismarck*, defendant Sutherland's written lease expired. Bismarck presented her with a new lease that included a rent increase. She began to pay the increase but did not sign the new lease. Sutherland could not be a holdover tenant since the terms of the old lease were not extended to the terms of the new, unsigned lease. Drake Industries was offered a new lease in 2007 that included a rent increase. Since the terms were different from the original lease. Drake could not be considered a holdover tenant.

It is the intention of the landlord, not the tenant, that determines whether the tenant is to be treated as a holdover. *Sheraton-Chicago Corp. v. Lewis*, 8 Ill. App. 3d 309, 290 N.E.2d 685 (1972). When a landlord creates a new lease and presents it to the tenant, it is clear that it was his intention that a new tenancy was created. *Holt v. Chicago Hair Goods Co.*, 328 Ill. App. 671, 66 N.E.2d 727 (1946). Martin presented Drake with a new lease to sign in November 2007, with new terms beginning January 1, 2008. It was never his intention to hold over the same lease from 2007. Therefore, Drake was not a holdover tenant and has never been one. 735 Ill. Comp. Stat. 5/9-202 (West 1993) could not apply to Drake. Martin could not demand double rental fees from Drake when it remained in possession of 2700 North Bosworth after the written lease expired on December 31, 2007.

Is Drake Industries a year-to-year tenant? When the payment of rent is annual, there arises a tenancy from year to year, even if the agreement provides for a payment of one-twelfth of the annual rental each month. *Seaver Amusement Co. v. Saxe et al.*, 210 Ill. App. 289 (1918). The terms of the 2007 written lease would have to have said "$8,400 a year rent, payable in monthly installments of $750" for it to have been considered a year-to-year lease. Since the terms of the 2007 lease only provided for monthly payments and not a yearly rental rate, Drake was not a year-to-year tenant. 735 Ill. Comp. Stat. 5/9-205 (West 1993) does not apply at all to Drake. Martin would not be required to tender 60 days' notice in writing to terminate the tenancy.

Is Drake Industries a month-to-month tenant? A month-to-month tenancy is created when a tenant remains in possession of the premises after a lease expires under different terms of tenancy. *Bismarck Hotel*, 92 Ill. App. 3d at 168, 415 N.E.2d at 517. By paying Bismarck's increased rental amount, different terms of the tenancy were established, so Sutherland's tenancy was considered month to month by the court. Drake remained at 2700 North Bosworth after its lease expired in 2007 but began paying the increased rent to Martin under the new terms of the unsigned lease. This established different terms of tenancy, so Drake has been a month-to-month tenant since 2008.

What type of notice is necessary to vacate the premises? Under 735 Ill. Comp. Stat 5/9/-207 (West 2008), notice to terminate a month-to-month tenancy must be given in writing 30 days before termination before any action for forcible entry and detainer can be maintained. Drake said that on August 15, 2008, Martin "requested" that Drake surrender the premises. An oral

request may not be sufficient and Drake may maintain that proper notice has not been made and it need not surrender the premises by September 15, 2008. A forcible entry and detainer action could not be entered and maintained and Drake need not surrender the premises until proper notice has been given.

8. Review the discussion section in the multi-issue McMillan memo above and draft a list of authorities. Then draft an outline of the discussion section.

9. Review the discussion section below and draft a list of authorities. Then draft an outline of the discussion section.

Are the Blacks entitled to special damages from Comfy Furniture for the cost of redecorating their living room? An Illinois appellate court decided that the nonbreaching party should be put back in the position that it was in when the contract was formed. *Kalal v. Goldblatt Bros.*, 368 N.E.2d 671, 673 (Ill. App. Ct. 1977). The Blacks stated their intention at the beginning concerning the fabric, the redecoration of the living room, and the family reunion. This fact was a part of their original position. The living room was redecorated. The furniture was delivered; however, the fabric was incorrect. Therefore, the Blacks have a right to recover consequential damages for the cost of the redecoration of their living room because the end result was not achieved; correctly upholstered furniture, newly redecorated living room to match, and a new living room look for the reunion. The conditions of the original contract were not met, and there was a breach of contract as embodied by the incorrectly upholstered furniture.

Under contract law, what damages are the Blacks entitled to pursue? Damages for breach of contract should place the plaintiff in a position he would have been in had the contract been performed. *Kalal*, 368 N.E.2d at 671. The plaintiffs in *Kalal* received a sofa that had been reupholstered in the wrong fabric after numerous delays, during which they had chosen three different fabrics in succession. *Id.* The court held that the defect could be remedied by the cost of reupholstering the sofa in the proper fabric. *Id.* at 674. The Blacks' chair and loveseat were improperly upholstered. Comfy Furniture upholstered their furniture with the reverse side of the fabric showing. Therefore, they were entitled to damages equal to the cost of upholstering their furniture correctly. However, the Blacks' situation is distinguished from *Kalal* in that their furniture was delivered before the date set in the contract, and it can be argued by Comfy that there was time to remedy the defect before their target date of Thanksgiving.

Are the Blacks entitled to compensation for the loss of use of their furniture? The question of compensation for the loss of use of the furniture was considered by both parties in *Kalal* to be appropriate since the plaintiffs in the case were without their furniture for several months while waiting for it to be reupholstered. *Id.* The Blacks have been similarly inconvenienced in that they, too, have been without the use of their new furniture. Thus, they are entitled to compensation for the loss of use of the furniture. However, it can be argued by Comfy Furniture that the furniture in the *Kalal* case was used and had been removed from the home for the

purpose of reupholstering it. *Id.* In the present case, the furniture was new and had never been in the Blacks' home, and Comfy may argue that the Blacks did not actually suffer loss of use of the new furniture.

Are the Blacks entitled to damages for the expense of decorating their living room to match the furniture they did not receive in the agreed-on condition? The redecorating of the living room in *Kalal* was not in the contemplation of either party at the time the contract was executed. *Kalal,* 368 N.E.2d at 671. Subsequently, the court held that the only damages that were recoverable for breach of contract are limited to those that were reasonably foreseeable and were within the contemplation of the parties at the time the contract was executed. *Id.* at 674. By the express terms of the Uniform Commercial Code, the court cannot follow tort theories to award damages. The legislative history of the U.C.C. indicates that contractual disputes should apply to the findings of the court. *Moorman Mfg. Co. v. National Tank Co.,* 435 N.E.2d 443, 453 (Ill. 1982). The Blacks only told Mr. Blaine that they needed the furniture to be completed in time for a family reunion. Comfy knew that the Blacks were under a time constraint for the delivery, but apparently there was no communication regarding the redecorating of the living room. With regard to Comfy Furniture, the redecorating of the Blacks' living room was an unforeseeable event and consequently they would not be held responsible for the expense. Because the fact that the redecorating of the living room was unforeseeable, it was not included within the terms of the contract. Therefore, Comfy only breached the express terms of the contract. The Blacks probably will not be awarded compensatory damages.

10. Finish the memorandum below. Write an outline and a discussion section based on this outline of authorities, facts, questions presented, and conclusions.

## Outline of Authorities

**1. *42 U.S.C. § 2000e* (1998):** The term "employer" means a person engaged in an industry affecting commerce who has fifteen or more employees for each working day in each of twenty or more calendar weeks in the current or preceding calendar year.

**2. *Zimmerman v. North American Signal Co.*, 704 F.2d 347 (7th Cir. 1983):** Salaried workers or full-time workers counted as employees for every day of the week on the payroll whether they were present at work or not. Hourly paid workers are counted as employees only on the days when they are actually at work or days on paid leave. (primary binding)

**3. *Musser v. Mountain View Broadcasting*, 578 F. Supp. 229 (E.D. Tenn. 1984):** "Current calendar year" is the year of discrimination. (primary persuasive)

**4. *Wright v. Kosciusko Medical Clinic*, 791 F. Supp. 1327, 1333 (N.D. Ind. 1992):** "Each working day" is literal and must be a day on which an employer conducts normal, full operations. (primary persuasive)

**5. *Norman v. Levy*, 767 F. Supp. 144 (N.D. Ill. 1991):** Part-time workers counted only on the days that they actually work. (primary persuasive)

**6.** *Knight v. United Farm Bureau Mut. Ins. Co.*, **950 F.2d 377 (7th Cir 1991):** The "economic realities" of the relationship between an employer and his or her worker must be weighted by applying five factors: (1) the amount of employer control and supervision over employee, (2) the responsibility for the operational costs, (3) the worker's occupation and the skills required, (4) the form of compensation and benefits, and (5) the length of the job commitment. *Knight,* 950 F.2d at 378. Control is the most important factor. *Id.* Knight is an insurance agent, is not permitted to sell insurance for any other companies, is required to attend weekly staff meetings in the office, and works a specified number of hours in the office (primary binding). *Knight,* 950 F.2d at 378. Company provided supplies and paid for business expenses. *Id.* Essential to company operation. *Id.* Paid commissions with no deductions. *Id.* Knight not an employee.

**7.** *Mitchell v. Tenney,* **650 F. Supp. 703 (N.D. Ill. 1986):** The "economic realities" of the relationship between an employer and his or her worker must be weighed.

**8.** *Vakharia v. Swedish Covenant Hosp.*, **765 F. Supp. 461 (N.D. Ill. 1991):** When an employee is economically dependent on an employer, the court is likely to find employment relationship. Plaintiff in *Vakharia* was a physician dependent on the hospital for business *Id.* at 463. (primary persuasive)

### MEMORANDUM: Sex Discrimination Case

To: Wallace Maine
From: Thomas Wall
Date: November 15, 2013
Re: Sex Discrimination Case against Whole In One No. C07 CIV 190, G12399990

### QUESTIONS PRESENTED

1. Under Title VII, was Whole In One an employer when 14 people, including 3 full-time and 11 part-time workers, worked on any day for 24 weeks and when 10 full-time employees were on the Whole In One payroll?

2. Under Title VII, was Walker an independent contractor rather than an employee when she worked exclusively for Whole In One, paid taxes quarterly rather than through deductions, and worked with limited company supervision?

3. Under Title VII, was Radiant an independent contractor rather than an employee when she worked with limited company supervision using company supplies and equipment and had taxes and medical deductions taken from her salary?

### CONCLUSIONS

1. Whole In One was an employer. Under Title VII, an employer has at least 15 employees working for 20 or more weeks during the relevant year: Salaried employees are included in this number for each week they are on the payroll, while hourly workers are only counted on the days they actually work.

In 2004, the year of the alleged discrimination, 14 workers, 3 full-time and 11 part-time people, worked for Whole In One on any day during the 24-week restaurant and golf season. However, 10 full-time workers were on the payroll. As these part-time workers are only counted on the days that they work, the number of part-time individuals included in the count of employees is 11 for each day of the 24-week season. Because full-time workers, however, are counted for each day of a week that they are on the payroll, all 10 of Whole In One's full-time workers would be included in the count of employees. In total, Whole In One had 11 part-time workers and 10 full-time workers "working" for 20 or more weeks during the relevant year, bringing the total count of employees to 21. Therefore, Whole In One was an employer under Title VII.

2. Walker was an employee. The Seventh Circuit will weigh five factors to determine whether she was an independent contractor or an employee for this Title VII lawsuit. The primary focus will be on the company's control of Walker. Although Walker worked from home, set her own hours, and had an impact on her commission pay, the company controlled her work by reviewing and revising it, restricting Walker's employment opportunities, and providing supplies for her. Therefore, the company exerted control over Walker and she would be considered an employee.

3. Radiant was probably an employee. To determine whether she was an employee or independent contractor for this Title VII lawsuit, the court will focus on five factors, primarily the amount of control the company exerted over Radiant's work. Whole In One provided Radiant with an office, supplies, a two-year contract, and additional training. Whole In One paid her regularly and deducted taxes from her salary. Although Whole In One did not actively supervise Radiant's work on a daily basis, she still worked in the company offices and was under the control of Whole In One. Therefore, the court probably will find that Radiant was an employee.

## FACTS

Victoria Radiant and Karen Walker, two former Whole In One Enterprises workers, brought a federal sex discrimination lawsuit based on Title VII against our client, Whole In One Enterprises, owned by Nancy and Craig Black. The lawsuit, filed in the U.S. District Court for the Northern District of Illinois, stems from the dismissal of the two women by the Blacks during 2014.

The Blacks own Whole In One Enterprises, which operates a miniature golf course and restaurant in Glenview, Illinois. During the 24-week 2012 restaurant season, 10 people worked full-time and 14 people worked part-time for Whole In One. However, no more than 14 people worked on any 1 day. Of those 14 people, only 3 were full-time employees. The other full-time employees regularly took days off during the summer restaurant and golf season.

Among the full-time workers was Karen Walker, who worked as a public relations director for Whole In One. Walker responded to an ad that said that "an employer" sought an individual to perform public relations work. Whole In One hired Walker without a contract and prohibited her from working for other firms. However, Walker worked from home and set her own hours.

Whole In One required Walker to attend weekly staff meetings at the company offices, where Whole In One would review and revise Walker's work. The company supplied Walker with paper, pencils, stamps, and telephone service and paid for her life and health insurance. Whole In One did not withhold taxes from Walker's commissions.

Victoria Radiant, who had a two-year employment contract with the company, provided marketing services to Whole In One from October of 2012 until she was fired in 2014. Although Radiant worked in the company office, Whole In One management rarely supervised her work. The company paid for her continued education, provided her with bonuses, and deducted taxes from her weekly salary.

## APPLICABLE STATUTE

The term "employer" means a person engaged in an industry affecting commerce who has 15 or more employees for each working day in each of 20 or more calendar weeks in the current or preceding calendar year. 42 U.S.C. § 2000e(b) (2004).

# LETTER WRITING

A. **BASICS OF LETTER WRITING**      530
B. **COMPONENTS OF A LETTER**      530
     1. Letterhead and Headers      530
     2. Date      532
     3. Method of Transmission      532
     4. Inside Address      532
     5. Reference Line      533
     6. Greeting      533
     7. Body of Letter      533
     8. Closing      534
     9. Copies to Others and Enclosures      535
C. **TYPES OF LETTERS**      536
     1. Confirming Letters      536
     2. Status Letters and Transaction Summary Letters      536
     3. Demand Letters      542
     4. Opinion Letters      543
     5. E-mail      545
     6. Social Media      547

## CHAPTER OVERVIEW

This chapter explains letter-writing basics, such as format and types of letters. It provides examples of a variety of letters you might use in practice.

Letter writing is one of the basic tasks you will perform as paralegals. Most letter-writing conventions apply to legal correspondence in much the same way as they do to other business communications. Paralegals should be aware of the components of basic letters as well as some special rules for legal communications.

# A. BASICS OF LETTER WRITING

The mechanics of letter writing is similar to any other legal writing project. You plan it, draft it, and revise it. In planning your communication, you must determine your audience and outline what you plan to say to your reader. When revising the letter, use proper grammar and consider any revisions that would make the letter clearer. Proofread your letter.

### ▼ What Formats Are Used?

Letters may be drafted using a variety of formats. Letters may be sent via post, facsimile, e-mail, or in a text message. Regardless of the mode of transmission, professional formatting is still required. Often the firm letterhead is set in the template for any e-mail correspondence. When in doubt as to style, always ask the supervising attorney, but it is best to always err on the side of formality. Look through the firm's correspondence file to get an idea of the format you should use. Firm style or personal taste generally determines the format of your letters. The formats are **full block, block, modified block**, and **personal style.**

In a full block letter, you do not indent the paragraphs. The paragraphs, the complimentary close, and the dateline are flush left. See Illustration 25-1. For block format, all paragraphs and notations are flush left, except for the date, the reference line, the complimentary close, and the signature lines, which are just right of the center of the page. See Illustration 25-3. In a modified block style letter, the first line of each paragraph is indented about five characters. See Illustration 25-6. In a personal style letter, often written to friends, the inside address is placed below the signature at the left margin.

# B. COMPONENTS OF A LETTER

## 1. Letterhead and Headers

A letter is divided into several sections: the date, the name and the address of the addressee called the inside address, a reference line, a greeting to the addressee, the body of the letter, and the complimentary closing.

You should draft the first page of a letter on firm letterhead. The **letterhead** is the portion of the firm's stationery that identifies the firm, generally the attorneys, and sometimes the firm's paralegals. It usually includes the firm's address and its telephone and facsimile numbers. Additional pages should not carry the firm letterhead but should be placed on matching paper with a **header** on each page.

The header identifies the letter and is generally placed on the top right side of the page. A header includes the name of the addressee, the date, and the number of the page:

Cheryl Victor
November 15, 2014
Page Two

## ILLUSTRATION 25-1.  Full Block Letter

[1]Vail McCann & Graham
888 Toledo Road
Ottawa Hills, Ohio 43606
(419) 535-7738

[2]November 7, 2014

[3]Via Federal Express
Mr. Stuart Shulman
Navarre Industries
708 Anthony Wayne Trail
Maumee, Ohio 45860

[4]Re: Settlement of Kramer v. Shulman

[5]Dear Mr. Shulman:

[6]I have enclosed a copy of the settlement agreement that we drafted and that has been signed by Mr. Kramer. Please sign the agreement and forward it to me at the above address by November 30, 2014.
If you have any questions, please feel free to call me at 419-535-7738.

[7]Sincerely,
Mara Cubbon
Legal Assistant

[8]cc: Randall Fuzzwell

[9]Enc.

[10]MAC/wlk

1. Letterhead
2. Date
3. Recipient's address and method of service
4. Reference line
5. Greeting
6. Body of the letter
7. Closing
8. Carbon copy notation
9. Enclosure of notation
10. Initials of drafter/typist

> ## ETHICS ALERT
> Check your state law as to whether your name may appear on the letterhead.

## 2. Date

The **date** should be placed at the top of the letter just below the firm's letterhead. The date is one of the key components of a letter concerning any legal matters. Date the letter with the same date as the date of mailing. This date can be crucial in determining a time line in a legal proceeding. Timing in sending documents and correspondence is often important in legal transactions and litigation matters. Therefore, be careful to include the date of mailing rather than the date of writing the letter. For example, if you prepare a letter on July 4 after the last mail pickup, you should date the letter July 5 because that is the date it would actually be mailed. This may seem like a purely technical distinction if you put the letter in the mail on July 4. However, some court cases and negotiations turn on the date of mailing. With e-mail, the date is easily discerned, but the recipient will consider the date of receipt the next business day.

## 3. Method of Transmission

If the letter is being sent by a method other than U.S. mail, it should be indicated on the top of the address and then underlined as follows:

Via E-mail and U.S. Mail
Cheryl Victor
Vice President
Arizona Currency Traders
1000 Tempe Road
Phoenix, Arizona 85038

This notation should start at least two lines below the date. See Illustration 25-1.

## 4. Inside Address

The next part of the letter, the **inside address**, should contain the name of the person to whom the letter is addressed, the individual's title if he or she has one, the name of the business if the letter is for a business, and the address.

## 5. Reference Line

The **reference line** is a brief statement regarding the topic of the letter. For example, if the letter concerns a contract for the sale of a particular property, your reference line would say:

Re: Sale of commercial property—2714 Barrington Road, Toledo, Ohio

Some firms and corporations ask that the reference line contain a client number, claim number, or case number, so investigate your firm's style.

---

### PRACTICE POINTER

If possible, review letters written by the assigning attorney. You will find the letters in the attorney's correspondence file or on the firm's intranet. Note the attorney's style for the reference line and follow it.

---

## 6. Greeting

In general, your **greeting** depends on how familiar you are with an individual. An individual whom you do not know should be addressed as "Dear Ms. White." If you know an individual well, you may address, formally, such that person by first name. If you are uncertain whether to address the individual by first name, use a title and the individual's last name. If you are addressing a letter to a particular person, such as the custodian of records, but you do not know the person's name, try to determine the person's name. If necessary, call a company or agency to determine the appropriate recipient for the letter. Your letter is more likely to be answered quickly if it is addressed to the appropriate person rather than "To whom it may concern." In addition, it may provide you with an opportunity to establish a rapport with the individual to whom the letter is addressed.

## 7. Body of Letter

The **body** of the letter follows the greeting and should begin with an opening sentence and paragraph that summarizes the purpose of the letter. Draft the body of the letter carefully. Outline the letter before writing it to be sure that you address all the necessary points. List each point you want to cover. For Illustration 25-1, your outline might read as follows:

1. enclose settlement agreement
2. ask for signature and return date
3. ask addressee to call if he has questions

Consider your audience. If you are writing to a layperson who is unfamiliar with the law, explain any legal terms you use often using definitions provided in a dictionary, or use simple language. However, do not provide any legal opinions. If you are addressing your letter to an individual who is familiar with the law, such as a judge, a paralegal, an in-house counsel, or an attorney, you do not need to explain such terms. To do so might be considered condescending.

---

## ETHICS ALERT

Do not offer any legal advice or opinions in the letter. If an attorney is not signing the letter, do not request the recipient to take any action that would change her legal position or require her to make a legal decision.

---

## 8. Closing

End your letter with a **closing** in which you invite a response, such as "Please do not hesitate to call if you have any questions," or thank the addressee for assistance, such as "Thank you in advance for your cooperation." Finally, end the letter with a complimentary closing such as "Sincerely," "Very truly yours," or "Best regards" placed two lines below the final line of the body of the letter. Place your name four lines below the closing to allow for a signature. Include your title, that is, paralegal or legal assistant.

---

## ETHICS ALERT

Be sure that your reader knows that you are a paralegal rather than an attorney. The easiest way to do this is to add your title after your name in the closing. If the letter is to be written for the attorney's signature, present the letter to the attorney for review and for her signature prior to sending.

Do not provide legal advice in your letter or represent yourself as an attorney. Ethical codes and state laws prohibit paralegals who are not licensed to practice law from providing legal opinions or from representing themselves as attorneys. To avoid any confusion or possible misrepresentation, include your title after your name when you write a letter.

## 9. Copies to Others and Enclosures

If you are copying a third party on the letter and want the original addressee to know this, note it with a "cc" at the bottom left margin of the letter following the closing. The cc indicates **carbon copy** sent to the person listed. (Although photocopies have replaced carbon copies, cc is still used.) Indicate to whom a copy of the letter was sent as "cc: Mike Sterner." See Illustration 25-2. If you do not want the original addressee to know that you copied a letter to another person, note on the draft or file copy "bcc," which means **blind carbon copy.** That notation should only appear on the draft or file copy of the letter and not on the recipient's letter.

### ILLUSTRATION 25-2.   Letter Confirming Deposition

Law Offices of Sam Farrell
2714 Barrington Road
Findlay, Ohio 45840
(419) 267-0000

January 28, 2015

Ms. Karen Dolgin
2903 W. Main Cross Street
Findlay, Ohio 45840

Re: Deposition of Robert Harrold
   Harrold v. Sofer

Dear Ms. Dolgin:

This letter is to confirm our conversation today in which you stated that you will present the plaintiff, Robert Harrold, for a deposition at the law office of Sam Farrell, 2714 Barrington Road, in Findlay, on March 18, 2015, at 2 p.m. This deposition is being rescheduled at your request because the plaintiff had a family commitment set for February 15, 2015, the date originally set for the deposition.

If you have any questions or additional problems, please feel free to call me at (419) 267-0000, extension 608.

Best regards,

Craig Black
Paralegal

cc: Sam Farrell
   Wally Sofer
CMB/klm

The next notation is for **enclosures**, such as court orders, contracts, or releases. Place the abbreviation **Enc.** or **Encs.** at the bottom left margin of the letter. See Illustration 25-1.

Finally, the letter should note your initials in all capital letters as the author of the letter and then the initials in lowercase letters of the person who typed the letter. If your initials are RAS and the typist's are HVS, then the notation under the enclosure or cc notation would read RAS/hvs.

# C. TYPES OF LETTERS

Paralegals write letters to clients to confirm deposition dates, meeting dates, hearing dates, or agreements. These letters are called confirming letters. Other letters provide a status report of a case or summarize a transaction. Some letters accompany documents, such as those for document productions, contracts, or settlement releases. These are called transmittal letters. Other letters may request information. Some letters explain the litigation process to clients. See Illustration 25-3.

## 1. Confirming Letters

**Confirming letters** reaffirm information already agreed to by you and the recipient. It is a good practice to follow up any conversation with a client or an opposing attorney or paralegal with a confirming letter that summarizes the conversation, any agreements made, or any future acts to be accomplished. See Illustration 25-2. For example, after you discuss a document production with a client and set a meeting date to review the records, send a letter summarizing the conversation. Such confirming letters provide you with a reminder of the conversation and allow anyone who reviews the file later to know what you and the client discussed should you be unavailable. Often to expedite this process, confirming letters are sent via e-mail and the billing partner and supervising attorney are copied on the correspondence.

If opposing counsel has agreed to produce documents or provide a witness for a deposition at a particular time, write a confirming letter to the opposing counsel summarizing these facts and asking to be contacted if there are discrepancies. This can be sent via e-mail with the supervising attorney's permission. Whenever a deposition is rescheduled or continued, it is imperative that a confirming letter be sent via e-mail and post to avoid future discovery disputes. Whenever your client is deposed, send him or her a copy of the deposition for review. A sample of such a letter is found in Illustration 25-4.

## 2. Status Letters and Transaction Summary Letters

Often you will be asked to provide a **status report** of a case, especially to insurance companies and other clients. See Illustration 25-5. These letters provide clients with an overview of the current activities in a court case, transaction, or other legal matter.

**ILLUSTRATION 25-3.   Letter Concerning Deposition Schedule**

Law Offices of Sam Farrell
2714 Barrington Road
Findlay, Ohio 45840
(419) 267-0000

January 28, 2015

Wally Sofer
Chief Executive Officer
1000 Hollywood Way
Houcktown, Ohio 44060

Re: Deposition of Wally Sofer
Harrold v. Sofer

Dear Mr. Sofer:

This letter is to advise you that you are required to submit to a deposition by the plaintiff's attorney at 10 a.m. on March 1, 2015, at the law office of Karen Dolgin, 2903 W. Main Cross Street in downtown Findlay. During this deposition, the plaintiff's attorney will ask you questions related to the above-referenced court case, and you will provide answers while under oath and in the presence of a court reporter. Mr. Farrell also will be present to represent you during the deposition.

Mr. Farrell and I would like to meet with you at least once before the deposition to discuss your case and this important part of your case.

I will call you Wednesday to schedule an appointment next week to prepare for your deposition.

Please bring any accident reports, citations, or other documents that relate to the accident if you have not already provided them to our office.

I look forward to speaking with you this week.

Sincerely,

Craig Black
Paralegal

cc: Sam Farrell
CMB/klm

**Transaction summary letters** often follow a business transaction such as a real estate closing. In these letters, you summarize a transaction.

## ILLUSTRATION 25-4. Letter Enclosing Deposition Transcript

Law Offices of Sam Farrell
2714 Barrington Road
Findlay, Ohio 45840
(419) 267-0000

July 11, 2014

Mr. William Gary
709 Franklin Street
Findlay, Ohio 45840

Re: Deposition on July 8, 2014

Dear Mr. Gary:

Enclosed is a copy of the transcript of your July 8, 2014, deposition. Please review the transcript carefully and note any statements that were incorrectly transcribed. You may not rewrite your testimony, but you should note any inaccurate transcriptions. You may correct the spelling of names and places. If you find any serious mistakes, please call me to discuss these problems.

When you review the deposition, please do not mark the original transcript. Instead, note any discrepancies on a separate sheet of paper. Please note the page and line of any discrepancies. I will have my secretary type a list of the discrepancies, and we will discuss these changes before we send them to the court reporter. These changes must be received by the court reporter within 30 days; therefore, I would appreciate your prompt review of the transcript and would like to review your changes by July 30, 2014. If we fail to provide the changes to the court reporter within 30 days, we will forfeit your right to correct the transcript and any inaccuracies will be part of the record.

If you have any questions, please do not hesitate to call me.

Thank you for your cooperation in advance.

Best regards,

Benjamin Farrell
Paralegal

Enc.
BSF/jas

## ILLUSTRATION 25-5.   Status Report Letter

Martin Marshall & Smith
960 Wyus Boulevard
Madison, Wisconsin 53606

June 12, 2014

Mr. Cal L. Grist
Pockets Insurance Company
10 Wausau Way
Wausau, Wisconsin 54401

Re: <u>Kelsey v. Cocoa</u>
Your claim number: C100090888

Dear Mr. Grist:

This letter is to provide you with a status report concerning the progress of the above-referenced matter. To date, we have requested that the plaintiff answer interrogatories and requests for admissions. I sent a copy of these requests to you about a week ago. The plaintiff is required to answer these requests within 30 days. We will send you a copy of the plaintiff's answers as soon as we receive them. We are scheduled to depose the plaintiff on September 1, 2014.

The plaintiff's attorney is scheduled to depose a representative of Oleo Company on October 13, 2014.

At this time, the court has not scheduled a settlement conference, but is likely to do so before the end of the year.

Please feel free to call if you have any questions.

Sincerely,

Alicia R. Samuel
Legal Assistant

ARS/yml

---

In other letters, you will **request information**, often from the custodian of records. See Illustration 25-6.

Often you will be responsible for coordinating document productions. Illustration 25-7 shows a sample **transmittal letter** to a client concerning a request to produce documents.

Many letters will be written to accompany documents, releases, and checks. See Illustrations 25-8 and 25-9.

## ILLUSTRATION 25-6.   Request for Information

Vail McCann & Morris
960 Wyus Boulevard
Madison, Wisconsin 53606

August 12, 2014

Sarah Ray
Custodian of Records
Federal Deposit Insurance Corp.
9100 Bryn Mawr Road
Rosemont, Illinois 60018

Re: Freedom of Information Act Request

Dear Ms. Ray:

Based on the Freedom of Information Act, 5 U.S.C. § 552 et seq., I am requesting that your agency provide copies of the following:

Each and every document that relates to or refers to the sale of the property located at 2714 Barrington Road, Glenview, Illinois, 60025.

The documents should be located in your Rosemont, Illinois office.

Under the act, these documents should be available to us within ten days. If any portion of this request is denied, please provide a detailed statement of the reasons for the denial and an index or similar statement concerning the nature of the documents withheld. As required by the act, Cosher, Cosher and Oleo agrees to pay reasonable charges for copying of the documents upon the presentation of a bill and the finished copies.

Thank you in advance for your cooperation in this matter.

Sincerely,

Lillian Eve Farrell
Paralegal

LEF/dag

**ILLUSTRATION 25-7.   Request to Produce Documents**

---

Carthage Katz & Kramer
1001 B Line Highway
Darlington, Wisconsin 53840

February 28, 2014

Ms. Karen Taylor
Carolton Corp.
1864 Merrimac Road
Sylvania, Ohio 43560

    Re: <u>Carolton v. Franklin</u>

Dear Ms. Taylor:

Enclosed please find a request from the defendants asking you to produce documents. The date scheduled for the production of these documents is April 1, 2014. Some documents may be protected from disclosure because they may contain confidential trade secret information, and others may be protected because they are communications between you and your attorney or the result of your attorney's work. We must respond in writing by March 25, 2014, in order to raise any of these claims.

As we must review the documents to determine whether any documents are protected, we should compile the documents no later than March 15, 2014. This will allow us time to review, to index, and to number each document.

I will be available to assist you in gathering documents to respond to this request. I will call you this week to schedule an appointment.

If you have any questions, please feel free to call.

                Sincerely,

                Eileen Waters
                Paralegal

Encs.
EDW/jnn

---

## ILLUSTRATION 25-8.   Letter Accompanying Document

Janis Max & Jordan
1600 Bradley Street
Wilmette, Illinois 60091


March 4, 2015

Eve Lilly
Lake County Recorder of Deeds
18 N. County Street
Waukegan, Illinois 60085

Re: 1785 Central Street

    Deerfield, Illinois 60015

Dear Mrs. Lilly:

Enclosed please find two original quit claim deeds, one dated December 30, 2003, and one dated January 2, 2015, relating to the above-referenced property. Both deeds have been marked "exempt" from state and county transfer tax. A check for $50.00 to cover the recording fees ($25 each) is enclosed. Please record these deeds at once and return the originals to Jacki Farrell at the 1785 Central Street address. Thank you for your assistance.

Sincerely,

Jennifer Laurence
Legal Assistant


Encs.
cc: Jacki Farrell
JML/jch

## 3. Demand Letter

A **demand letter** is a letter that states your client's demands to another party. A common letter paralegals write is a demand letter. Often the demand letter seeks to collect debts. Such a letter may need to comply with the requirements of your state's fair-debt collection laws. See Illustration 25-10.

A demand letter has several components.

Tell the reader who you are and why you are writing. This also provides credibility.

Then, state the relevant facts without adding emotional adjectives. The supervising attorney will provide guidance as to the level of detail required here.

State your client's precise demand. Follow the demand with the pertinent legal support for your demand, if suitable. Always follow the supervising attorney's instruction as to whether to include the legal support. Sometimes an attorney uses the demand letter to lay out the client's legal rights.

Clearly indicate the date compliance is expected and the consequences of failing to comply with your client's demand. Indicate the date or time frame for the demand to be met.

Always end a demand letter with: Please contact me if you have any questions or concerns.

Close the demand letter with a professional closure, even if you or the client is angry.

Ask the assigning attorney if she would be more comfortable if she signed the demand letter. An attorney must sign the letter if the demand letter will change the recipient's or your client's legal position. Short paragraphs are very effective in demand letters because each paragraph is used to state a separate point or component so that they stand out for the busy reader.

In a demand letter, you should state that your firm represents the creditor or other client, as well as the client's desire for full payment of the claim. Specify the amount demanded or state the action sought, and ask the debtor either to make payment or to contact your office within a certain number of days. Then state the action that the firm will take if the demand is not met within the specified time period.

## 4. Opinion Letters

Opinion and advice letters advise clients about the legal rules that apply to their situation. Most law firms will not have paralegals draft even a preliminary opinion letter. If your firm asks you to draft a preliminary letter, be sure not to sign the letter with your name. Always have the supervising attorney review the opinion letter carefully before it is sent to another attorney for signing. An **opinion letter** must be signed by an attorney because, as its name suggests, the letter states a legal opinion. Many firms require that opinion letters are signed only by partners, as the letter makes the firm responsible for the opinion offered.

---

### *ETHICS ALERT*

If you sign an opinion letter, this could be construed as the unauthorized practice of law. If you sign the attorney's name, without her consent, that is tantamount to practicing law.

## ILLUSTRATION 25-9.   Letter Accompanying Check

Howard & Farrell
Central and Carriage Way
Evanston, Illinois 60202


April 22, 2015

William Green
Chicago Bar Association
124 Plymouth Court
Chicago, Illinois 60611

Re: Commercial Real Estate Contract Prepared by the Real Property
   Law Committee

Dear Mr. Green:

Enclosed please find a check for $30.00 to cover the mailing fees and
the cost of a copy of the Real Estate Contract referenced above. Please
send me a copy of the contract at your earliest convenience.

Thank you for your cooperation.

Sincerely,

M. Seth Jordan
Paralegal


Enc.
cc: Rachel Jones
MSJ/ear

---

If you must draft a preliminary version of an opinion letter, the
process is similar to writing an IRAC paragraph. Start with a statement
of the legal issue. Your next sentence, however, should answer the issue.
In the paragraph following the answer to the issue, state the law and
apply the legally significant facts to the law. Provide information about
any legal issues that present problems and incorporate the legally significant facts into that discussion.

The final paragraph should state your opinion as to the conclusion
or answer to the issue presented and provide your prediction of the
outcome for the legal situation. Clients often request opinion letters
prior to entering a business transaction or to request the tax consequences of a proposed business transaction.

Discuss this letter with the attorney who will be signing it and be
sure that it is the attorney's opinion rather than your own that is conveyed to the client. Be sure that the attorney reviews the letter before
signing it. If the attorney does not initiate a discussion with you about

**ILLUSTRATION 25-10.   Demand Letter**

---

Law Office of Randall William
145 Franklin Street
Madison, Wisconsin 53606


April 1, 2015


Michelle Hunt
889 Barrington Road
Middleton, Wisconsin 53608

Re: Furniture Crafters Account 4155

Dear Ms. Hunt:

Our office represents Furniture Crafters in the collection of the $468.00 debt due on the above-referenced account. Furniture Crafters requests that you pay the full amount of the debt, $468.00, immediately.

You must pay this amount in full or contact our firm at the above telephone number or address within seven days. If we do not hear from you within seven days, we will proceed to court in this matter.

Sincerely,

Randall William
Paralegal

RAW/bgh

---

the letter, you should do so to ensure that the attorney reviewed it. Although you may draft the letter for the attorney to review, be sure that the attorney signs the letter before it is sent to the recipient. Even under direction by an attorney, a paralegal can never give legal advice, suggest a change in a legal position, or reach a legal conclusion. Opinion letters provide legal advice, suggest that a client change his legal position, and also reach a legal conclusion; this is why it is imperative for the supervising attorney to sign the letter.

## 5. E-mail

notes are now used routinely. Many of the same rules apply in the same way to an e-mail note as they would to any other letters. Professionalism is just as important in e-mail as it is in letters sent via post. Maintain a professional tone in e-mails even though the format is considered casual. Consider your audience and outline what you plan to say. Use proper grammar. Proofread your e-mail. If you would address a letter

using a title such as Mr. or Mrs., do so in the e-mail. Include your mailing address and your telephone number so that the party can contact you using methods other than e-mail. If you are sending an **attachment** such as a document to be reviewed, be sure you notify the party in advance so that the person doesn't mistakenly delete the attachment, believing it may contain a virus. Often short notes sent via e-mail are designed to fill a single screen on a smartphone or Blackberry.

---

### PRACTICE POINTER

Check with your firm concerning whether to draft any e-mails that include client confidences. E-mails can be intercepted and may not be secure. Some firms, however, have security measures in place to safeguard such communications. Most firms have a confidentiality warning as part of the firm's e-mail template. However, e-mails can still be forwarded and intercepted. If a matter is very sensitive, consider alternative transmission formats such as printed letters sent via post or even a telephone conversation.

---

When sending e-mails, remember that e-mails can be forwarded to other recipients. Also, any e-mail that you create while at work is now a permanent part of the firm or company's document files. Even if you delete the e-mail, the encryption can often be retrieved. Be very careful with what you write and how you write it when you are at work.

Most firms now include confidentiality information in the e-mail template stating that the e-mail should be viewed only by the intended recipient. Whenever writing an e-mail in any context, always make sure that it is professional, truthful, and accurate before hitting send.

---

### PRACTICE POINTER

Some e-mail programs allow you to request a return receipt that lets you know that the reader opened the e-mail. For critical e-mail it is a good idea to request such a receipt. If something is time critical and you must ensure that the party received the document, consider sending the letter by messenger.

---

Do not use all capital letters in an e-mail. That is considered screaming.

# 6. Social Media

**Social media**, such as Facebook, LinkedIn, blogs, and Twitter, are now frequently used by many legal professionals. Law firms and corporations rely on social media for marketing and networking. Client and professional correspondence have not yet adopted social media as a form of communication in the law firm environment. Most firms are adopting social media policies. Before using social media at work to communicate to clients and other parties, ask your supervising attorney if it is appropriate. Although Twitter would seem like the ideal method to quickly communicate concise information with a large group, it is still considered too informal for professional correspondence. Many senior legal professionals have not adopted social media. Twitter has a unique characteristic in that each "tweet" is limited to 140 characters. Also, with Twitter, the sender can not control where the "tweet" goes and who reads it, so many client confidentiality issues are raised.

Facebook and LinkedIn require the user to subscribe, and not everyone subscribes to such services. Always ask the supervising attorney if social media is the appropriate format for communication prior to corresponding. Always be professional in all of your communication, regardless of format.

---

*PRACTICE POINTER*

Before using any form of social media in the work environment, check if the firm or company has a social media policy in place. Remember that social media has not been adopted by everyone and that it is considered very informal for professional correspondence. Additionally, be aware of client confidentiality when using social media for professional communication.

---

## *CLASS DISCUSSION*

Please read over the following letter and find the flaws.

**Law Office**
**Attorneys at Law**
1818 Main Street
Ossining, New Jersey 07555

Mr. Ronald Tolbert
1501 South Street
Morris City, New Jersey 07345
Dear Mr. Tolbert:
Thank you for your correspondence recently. We will see where we can get this week and then write again next week. I do think we should try to get this done in the next few weeks and then put this matter to bed. As

previously indicated, I do have a substantial problem with time this week but lets see where we can get.

I don't have time now to respond to all your points and I don't know that we necessarily agree or for that matter disagree with any of the various issues, legal or other that you raise. I can respond more fully as to our position on thise various items as we go forward. I don't know that we need to get into those issues now anyway. I would like to comment on our need to receive a copy of the settlement letter.

I know that the settlement letter is important for our client. Please send the settlement letter as soon as you are able. In any event, if I am missing something, please let me know.

Sincerely,
Diane Russell
Paralegal

CHECKLIST

1. "Never give legal advice" is the first rule of letter writing for paralegals.
2. Be informative.
3. Consider your audience. If you are addressing a client, do so courteously and write at a level that the client will understand. If you were asked to answer a client's questions, be sure that you do. You should always be respectful to the addressee.
4. Choose your words carefully. You want to make certain that your words express what you intend.
5. Write succinctly and directly. Your reader is busy so you want to communicate clearly and in as few words as possible. Avoid unnecessary details.
6. Always be professional even if e-mail is the selected transmission format.
7. Proofread all correspondence.

## **CHAPTER SUMMARY**

Letter writing is an essential part of your daily routine as a paralegal. Most letter-writing conventions that apply to business communication apply to legal correspondence. However, paralegals should be careful about dating letters concerning legal matters. Letters should be dated with the date of mailing, which may or may not be the date of drafting.

A letter should contain a date, the name and address of the addressee, a reference line, a greeting to the addressee, the body of the letter, and the complimentary closing.

Confirming letters reaffirm information already agreed to between you and the recipient. Status letters provide an up-to-date review of the process of a pending matter. Transaction summary letters explain particular transactions.

Letters also are written to accompany documents, such as releases and checks, or to state your client's demands to a third party, such as for payment.

As with any written document, letters should be outlined, written, and then rewritten if necessary.

It is important to avoid the unauthorized practice of law when writing letters. Do not give any legal advice in a letter that you sign. A letter must be signed by an attorney when it contains legal advice, suggests that a client change her legal position, or states a legal conclusion. Last, in any professional communication, regardless of the format or the medium, professionalism and client confidentiality are of paramount importance.

## KEY TERMS

attachment
blind carbon copy (bcc)
block letter
body
carbon copy (cc)
closing
confirming letter
date
demand letter
e-mail
enclosure line
full block letter
greeting

header
inside address
letterhead
modified block letter
opinion letter
personal style letter
reference line
request information
social media
status report
transaction summary letter
transmittal letter

## EXERCISES

### SHORT ANSWER

1. What are the basic components of a letter?
2. What is a reference line?
3. How do you indicate that you are sending a copy of a letter to another person?
4. How do you indicate that you want someone to receive a copy, but you don't want the addressee to know that the other person received a copy of the letter?
5. What are confirming letters?
6. What is a status report letter?
7. What are transmittal letters?
8. What are demand letters?
9. Should you provide a legal opinion in a letter?

## LETTER WRITING

Prepare the following letters as if you were a paralegal with the law firm of O'Connor Hackett & Black, 1000 Madison Way, Madison, Wisconsin 53606. Addressee names are identified for you, but you may supply each one's address yourself.

10. Write a letter to Madison Insurance Corporation explaining that your law firm will be representing Carol White for a lawsuit against its insured, Harold Watson, stemming from an automobile accident that occurred on September 1. The Madison claims adjuster is Howie Mark. Harold Watson's insurance policy number is 1280. You once had a difficult time dealing with Mr. Mark and Madison Insurance in the past, so you send your letter by certified mail. Enclose a copy of the police report. Send a blind copy to your client. You write it at 5 P.M. on December 24. You realize that December 25 is a holiday and that mail will not go out until the next day.

11. Your firm represents a client, Karen Taylor, who sustained a neck injury during an automobile accident between Carter McLaughlin and Robert Carroll. Write a letter to Dr. Nancy Martin asking for a detailed report concerning the present and future medical problems of that client. Dr. Martin is an orthopedic surgeon. Indicate that you have a signed release from the client to enclose.

12. Your firm represents Margaret Weston in a divorce case. Write a short letter to her informing her of the final hearing date in her divorce case. The date is June 16, in Lucas County Domestic Relations Court, 900 W. Adams Street, Toledo, Ohio 43602.

13. Your client needs to give testimony at a deposition on November 15, at 10 A.M. at your offices. Please draft a letter asking William Hesse to be at the deposition. Explain to him that you will meet with him in advance to discuss his testimony.

14. Your firm has just settled a case involving Karen Douglas and your client, the Wentworth Industries, in Morristown, New Jersey. The case was settled for $88,000. The Wentworth corporation paid Douglas for injuries she sustained when she fell at a Mexican hotel. You do not want to admit any liability in your letter or admit any ownership interest in the Mexican hotel, the CanCan. You merely want to tender the check to Douglas in full satisfaction of any claims she or her husband have against Wentworth. You also have the signed settlement agreement to send her and the court dismissal of the action.

15. You are assigned the preparation of a letter that explains the status of a pending insurance defense litigation matter. The matter is set for trial on November 15 of this year. Two depositions have been taken—the plaintiff's and the defendant's. Interrogatories have been answered by both sides and a settlement conference is scheduled with the judge in the case on October 31. The judge is Eve G. Halsey of Ohio Common Pleas Court in Columbus, Ohio. You expect that a representative of the restaurant where the incident took place will attend the settlement conference and that an insurance company representative also will attend as required by the local court rules. Your firm will be calling several witnesses from the

restaurant to testify at the trial and you and the partner on the case, Wally Taylor, will be preparing these witnesses to testify beginning in October. Send this letter to your client, Schroeder Insurance Enterprise, 250 W. Wilson Street, Hinsdale, IL 60521. The person you deal with at the insurance company is Thomas Kennedy, a claims manager. You are sending this letter via Express Mail. The letter is being typed by Taylor's secretary Jan Marie Maggio. She will send a blind copy of the letter to an associate on the case, Janis Farrell. She also will send a carbon copy of the letter to Mr. Taylor.

16. The following letter was written and signed by a paralegal. Please list three problems that could arise from this letter.


January 1, 20_____

                                                    Sent by Mail and Fax to:

Re: Contract to purchase real estate dated December 15, 20_____

Dear Mr. Smith:

Per your request the Seller hereby agrees to extend the attorney approval contingency until 5:00 P.M., January 15, 20_____.

I specifically note to you that I am in receipt of your first amendment and its Exhibits A, B, and C.

As to paragraph 3 of your first amendment, I note to you that I am posting in the mail to you a proposed limited warranty and a Waiver and Disclaimer of Implied Warranty of Habitability. I request that you review the same after I have advised you that my client has reviewed the same. I am also posting it in the mail to them. It is specifically noted that what will be provided will be a limited warranty and that we will expect the parties to sign a waiver and disclaimer and I further note that I want to end this thing and accordingly, I provide for a date of January 15, 20_____.

I expressed to you that I was unhappy with the contingencies in paragraph 5 of the contract. In fairness, I request that if it does not appear that your client will be able to meet the contingencies, namely, either sell her home or secure financing, that she will notify us at the earliest date and to then voluntarily agree to a termination of the contract.

Looking forward to a closing with you soon.

                                                    Very truly yours,

                                                    Mary Walton
                                                    Paralegal

# SHEPARDIZING AND CITE CHECKING

▼ What Is Cite Checking, or Shepardizing, and When Is It Done?

The meaning of the term *cite checking* varies. Often, the meaning depends on the particular attorney asking you to complete the project. For some attorneys, cite checking includes three components:

1. ensuring that the cited authority in fact states what the brief or memorandum tells the reader the authority states and that the correct authority is cited;
2. making certain that the citation is placed in proper *Bluebook, ALWD,* or court format or style; and
3. checking that the authority is still current and valid law.

When some attorneys ask you to cite check your research results, they only want you to complete the final component of the cite checking process. Others may want you to complete all three tasks or just two of the three procedures.

For the first stage, you might consider using the following process:

1. Review the brief and the citation.
2. Read the cited authority.
3. Ask yourself a series of questions:
   Does the cited authority say what the brief or memorandum states that it says?
   Should quotes be placed around the text in the brief or memorandum?
   Is the correct page number for the citation listed?

What is the correct case name?
What court decided this case?
What is the date of the decision?
What is the parallel citation?

4. Make certain that you note the correct court.

For stage two, consult Appendix B. For stage three, refer to the cite checking checklist that follows.

## Cite Checking Checklist

1. Make a list of the cases, statutes, rules, or other authorities you need to cite check.
2. To be thorough, search cases in all of the following sources or services: *Shepard's* (either in hard copy with a daily update online or merely online), KeyCite, and GlobalCite.

## Shepardizing Cases in Hard-Copy Materials Checklist

1. Determine which *Shepard's* series is the appropriate one to consult. Is the case in the federal or state citators? Should you consult the regional rather than state citator?
2. Review the front cover of the most current pamphlet that accompanies the *Shepard's* citations to determine what volumes should be reviewed for your cite check.
3. Gather each of the volumes and supplements mentioned on the cover.
4. Find the appropriate reporter section in each volume.
5. Locate the volume number listed in bold. Check the top corner of the page until you find pages encompassing your volume number.
6. Find the page number.
7. Review the online *Shepard's* report.

## *Shepard's* Online Checklist for Cases

1. Click on the *Shepard's* citation button and type in the citation.
2. Check for red, orange, or yellow signals and review citing references.
3. Click on the hyperlink to review any citing authority that may challenge the validity of the case.

## KeyCite Checklist

1. Access Westlaw.
2. Click on the KeyCite button. Then type in the citation.
3. Check for red or yellow signals and review citing references.
4. Click on the hyperlink to review any citing authority that may challenge the validity of the case.

# Citechecking Statutes in *Shepard's* Print Materials

1. Determine which *Shepard's* series is the appropriate one to consult. Is the statute in the federal or state citators?
2. Review the front cover of the most current pamphlet that accompanies the *Shepard's* citations to determine what pamphlets and volumes should be reviewed for your cite check.
3. Gather each of the volumes and supplements mentioned on the cover.
4. Find the appropriate statute section in each volume and pamphlet.
5. Locate the statute. Check the top corner of the page until you find pages encompassing the statute.
6. Determine if a *Shepard's* analysis indicates whether the statute is constitutional, unconstitutional, valid, or invalid.
7. Review the online report.

# *Shepard's* Online Checklist for Statutes

1. Click on the *Shepard's* citation button and type in the citation.
2. A red exclamation point indicates that the citing reference contains strong negative treatment.
3. Review any link to documents affecting the authority.
4. Click on the hyperlinks to recently enacted legislation as well as pending bills that reference the statute that could affect its validity.

# KeyCite for Statutes

1. Enter the statute citation in the search screen.
2. Review the KeyCite report for any negative treatment. A red flag indicates that the statute has been amended in whole or in part. A yellow flag indicates that the statute has been called into question. It may be that it has been renumbered by a recent session law or that uncodified law is available that may affect the validity of the statute.

# CITATION

> ### ETHICS ALERT
>
> Always provide complete citations to anything that is not your own idea or a client's fact.

The *Bluebook* is the guide to citation form for all legal documents, whether office memos or Supreme Court briefs. The *Bluebook*, formally known as the *Uniform System of Citation*, 19th Edition, governs because of convention and tradition rather than by the mandate of the state legislature. The *ALWD Guide to Legal Citation*, 5th Edition, offers easily comprehended citations. Also, *ALWD* contains "Fast Formats" for every category of citation. These provide terrific examples of formats for all legal resources. New forms of citation are emerging due to the advent of nonproprietary cases, called public domain citations, in which the case is not attributed to a publisher. Generally, the *Bluebook* is the universal resource for citation format for all legal personnel. This appendix is designed to give you a start in your citation process. If ever in doubt as to citation format, rely on the *Bluebook*.

### ▼ What Is a Citation?

A citation is really an address indicating where the cited material can be found so that anyone reading your document can find the material if he or she wants to. The abbreviations must be consistent so that everyone knows what they

mean. We rely on a similar convention with street addresses and postal abbreviations. The abbreviation for avenue is Ave.; the postal abbreviation for New York is NY.

## ▼ What Documents Are Cited?

Any source of authority that you discuss in any legal document is cited. Any concept or idea that is not your own must be cited; this is called attributing authority to your ideas. Citing credits the source from which the idea or legal rule came. It also tells the reader where he or she can find the original source. Citations are used for all authority, whether it is primary authority such as a case or a statute, or secondary authority such as a treatise or a law review article. Also cited are looseleaf services, practitioners' materials, and newspaper articles.

The *Bluebook* has two citation formats, one for briefs and memos and the other for law review articles. *ALWD* has one format. Paralegals rely on the brief and memo format for citation.

## ▼ What Are the Components of a Citation?

Generally, the components of a cite are the name of the particular document, the volume or title where the document is located, the name of the publication that contains the document, and the specific page, section, or paragraph where the document is found. Also included is the year that a case was decided or the publication date of a book or volume of statutes. For example:

Jacobs v. Grossman, 310 Ill. 247, 141 N.E. 714 (1923)

The name of the document is the case name, *Jacobs v. Grossman*. Parallel citations are given in the example so that you can find the case in both reporters; the official reporter is always mentioned first and the unofficial reporter mentioned second. Each state has its own rules regarding the necessity of including parallel citation information for documents submitted to its court. Some states do not have state reporters and rely on the regional reporters so parallel citation is not an issue. Always check the local court rules. The first number preceding the reporter abbreviation is the volume number of the reporter. Next is the reporter abbreviation and then the page number where the case begins in the reporter. The year that the case was decided is included in parentheses. *Bluebook* **Table T.1** lists reporter abbreviations, as does *ALWD* **Appendix 1.**

Using the *Bluebook* takes practice. The *Bluebook* is organized by rules. Each rule details the citation format for each type of document. The index is very helpful in finding specific references to the citation format for an individual document such as a statute, an administrative regulation, or a law review article. For additional examples, use the Fast Formats in *ALWD*. The Fast Formats are easily located in the *ALWD* index.

The following portion of the appendix provides examples of the materials and sample cite formats. These examples will help you navigate your way. If the

illustration here does not provide adequate information, you can turn to the *Bluebook* or *ALWD* rule mentioned to obtain more detailed treatment.

## ▼ How Are Pending and Unreported Decisions Cited?

You should provide the docket number, the court, and the full date of the most recent disposition of the case, as well as the full case name.

| | |
|---|---|
| **slip opinion cite:** | Gillespie v. Willard City Bd. of Educ., No. C87-7043 (N.D. Ohio Sept. 28, 1987)—*Bluebook* format, **Rule 10.8.1**; *ALWD* format, **Rule 12.15** |
| **with page cite:** | Gillespie v. Willard City Bd. of Educ., No. C87-7043, slip op. at 3 (N.D. Ohio Sept. 28, 1987) |

According to *ALWD*, always check the local court rules to see if unpublished cases can be cited. See *ALWD* **Appendix 2**.

## ▼ How Do You Cite a State Case?

*Bluebook* **Rule 10** and *ALWD* **Rule 12.6** discuss citation formats for state cases. Also check *Bluebook* Jurisdiction-Specific Citation Rules and Style Guides at BT2 for local court citation rules. The first example below shows the citation for an Illinois case with parallel authority included. The second example shows the same case cited in a brief to an Illinois court or to the United States District Court for the Northern District of Illinois.

| | |
|---|---|
| **With parallel cites:** | Thompson v. Economy Super Marts, 221 Ill. App. 3d 263, 581 N.E.2d 885, 163 Ill. Dec. 731 (App. Ct. 1991)—*Bluebook* format |
| | Thompson v. Economy Super Marts, 221 Ill. App. 3d 263, 163 Ill. Dec. 731, 581 N.E.2d 885 (1991)—*ALWD* format |
| **In a brief:** | Thompson v. Economy Super Marts, 581 N.E.2d 885 (Ill. App. Ct. 1991)—*Bluebook* and *ALWD* formats |

Check the jurisdiction's citation rules and the firm's requirements when you use a state decision in a memorandum or a brief. See *Bluebook* **Table T.1** and *ALWD* **Appendix 2**. If you are citing a state case to a state court in which the case was decided, provide both the official citation, if one exists, and the regional citation, if court rules or the assigning partner requires it. Always list the official citation first. When you cite a state case in a memorandum addressed to a federal court or to a court of a state different from the state that decided the case, include only the regional citation as the example for citing in a brief, above, shows. If you are using only the regional citation, remember to place the abbreviation for the deciding court in parentheses. See *Bluebook* **Rule 10.4** and *ALWD* **Rule 12.6(a)**. Additionally, follow the local court rules references in *Bluebook* blue pages **BT2**, *ALWD* **Appendix 2**, and

*ALWD* **Rule 12.4**. However, if parallel citations are required, see *ALWD* **Rule 12.4** and *Bluebook* **Rule 10.3.1**.

Every state has its own rules regarding the reporter designated as "official" and whether the state has adopted public domain citations. Always check with the supervising attorney and the court rules. *Bluebook* **Table T.1** lists websites for each state, and ALWD Appendix 2 excerpts the local court citation rules. Some states, like Oklahoma, use the regional reporter as their official reporter. Increasingly, states have adopted public domain citations as their official cites that should be cited in accordance with *Bluebook* **Rule 10.3.3** and *ALWD* **Rule 12.17** (also called neutral citations). These cites are designed to allow readers to find the case in a computerized system that does not rely on commercial publishers. Cites to commercial reporters such as West's may be used to augment public domain citations.

The public domain format is as follows: case name, followed by the year of the decision, the deciding court, and the sequential number of the decision. In some jurisdictions, the sequential number of the decision is the docket number. To cite to a specific portion of the decision, you may add a reference to the paragraph. If available, a parallel cite must be listed.

**Public domain citation:**    State v. Kienast, 1996 S.D. 111, 553 N.W.2d 254
¶ 2—*Bluebook* and *ALWD* formats

Use neutral, or public domain, citations when local court rules permit according to *ALWD* **Rule 12.17**.

### ▼ How Do You Cite Decisions Found in the *Federal Reporter* or the *Federal Supplement?*

*Bluebook* Rules **10.1-10.6** and **Table T.1** and *ALWD* **Rule 12.6(c)(2)** and Appendices 1 and 4 provide detailed coverage of the citation format for cases from the *Federal Reporter* and the *Federal Supplement*. The case name is placed first and underlined. Next, place the volume number. The reporter abbreviation is next. For the *Federal Reporter*, the abbreviation is "F." The number of the series, second or third, should be placed next to the "F." For the Federal Supplement, the reporter is abbreviated "F. Supp." The page number follows the abbreviation for the reporter. Next, place an abbreviation denoting the appropriate court and the date of the decision. Be certain to include a geographic designation for the district courts.

*Federal Reporter* **case:**    Zimmerman v. North Am. Signal Co., 704 F.2d 347 (7th Cir. 1983)—*Bluebook* and *ALWD* formats

*Federal Supplement* **case:**    Musser v. Mountain View Broad., 578 F. Supp. 229 (E.D. Tenn. 1984)—*Bluebook* and *ALWD* formats

▼ How Do You Cite a Decision Contained in the *Federal Rules Decisions* Reporter?

The abbreviation for the *Federal Rules Decisions* is F.R.D. A case would be cited according to *Bluebook* **Table T.1** and *ALWD* **Appendix 1**, as follows:

> Barrett Indus. Trucks v. Old Republic Ins. Co., 129 F.R.D. 515 (N.D. Ill. 1989)

---

## *PRACTICE POINTER*

When starting an in-house memo assignment, ask the attorney about his citation preferences and look at examples in the firm's memo and brief bank. Sometimes the attorney's preferences will differ from the local court rules.

---

▼ How Do You Cite a U.S. Supreme Court Case?

According to the *Bluebook*, once a U.S. Supreme Court case is published in an advance sheet of the *U.S. Reports*, the *U.S. Reports* citation, and only the *U.S. Reports* citation, is the proper citation, without any parallel citations. See **Rule 10, Table T1.1**, and *ALWD* **Rule 12.4(c)** generally. The cite format is diagramed on page 87 of the *Bluebook*.

> Erie R.R. v. Tompkins, 304 U.S. 64 (1938)—*Bluebook* and *ALWD* formats
> Erie R.R. v. Tompkins, 304 U.S. 64, 58 S. Ct. 817, 82 L. Ed. 1188 (1938)—*ALWD* format permissible when an attorney requests it.—*ALWD* **Rule 12.4.**

However, if a Supreme Court opinion has been published in the *West Supreme Court Reporter* but not yet in the *U.S. Reports*, the *Supreme Court Reporter* citation should be used. See *Bluebook* **Table T1.1**.

If a Supreme Court opinion has not yet been published in *U.S. Reports*, *Supreme Court Reporter*, or *U.S. Reports, Lawyers' Edition*, then you should cite to *United States Law Week*. See *Bluebook* **Table T1.1**. The court designation, U.S., should be placed in parentheses with the full date. See *Bluebook* **Rule 10.4(a)**. The citation would read as follows:

> UAW v. Johnson Controls, 59 U.S.L.W. 4209 (U.S. Mar. 20, 1991)

Also see *ALWD* **Rule 12.4**. However, parallel citation of Supreme Court cases is permitted if attorneys request it.

## ▼ How Do You Use Short Citation Forms?

Short citation forms and subsequent cite formats are explained in *Bluebook* **B4.2**, and **Rule 10.9**. Also see *ALWD* **Rule 12.19**.

Full citation:

<u>Seymour v. Armstrong</u>, 64 P. 612, 613 (Kan. 1901).

Subsequent citation when there is an intervening cite:

*Seymour v. Armstrong*, 64 P. at 613. *Bluebook* **Rule 10.9**.

*Seymour*, 64 P. 613. *Bluebook* and *ALWD* **Rule 12.19** if using only the first party will not cause confusion.

A subsequent citation without an intervening cite requires the use of *Id.*:

*Id.* at 613. *Bluebook* page 14 and *ALWD* **Rule 12.19(a)**.

Use of *Id.* with parallel citations (note: follow local court rules to determine requirements for parallel citation):

Full cite:

*Thompson v. Economy Super Marts*, 221 Ill. App. 3d 263, 581 N.E.2d 885, 163 Ill. Dec. 731 (App. Ct. 1991).

Short cite without intervening citations:

*Id.* at 263, 581 N.E.2d at 887, 163 Ill. Dec. at 733—*ALWD* **Rule 12.19(d)** and *Bluebook* **B4**.

## ▼ How Do You Cite a Decision Reported on Westlaw?

*Bluebook* **Rule 18.3.1** and *ALWD* **Rule 12.13(b)** explain how an unpublished decision found only on either Westlaw or Lexis should be cited. For Westlaw, first provide the name of the case and underline it. The next part of the citation is the docket number. In the example that follows, that number is No. 82-C4585. The next part of the citation is the year that the decision was issued. Next, indicate "WL" for Westlaw and finally the Westlaw number assigned to the case. Place the date in the parentheses.

**Westlaw example:**     <u>Clark Equip. Co. v. Lift Parts Mfg. Co.</u>, No. 82-C4585, 1985 WL 2917, (N.D. Ill. Oct. 1, 1985)—*Bluebook* format

<u>Clark Equip. Co. v. Lift Parts Mfg. Co.</u>, 1985 WL 2917 (N.D. Ill. Oct. 1, 1985)—*ALWD* format, **Rule 12.13(b)**

### ▼ How Do You Cite a Decision Reported on Lexis?

For Lexis citations, first state the name of the case, the docket number, the year of the decision, the name of the Lexis file that contains the case, and the name LEXIS (using all capital letters) to indicate that the case is found on Lexis. Next place the date in parentheses.

**Lexis example:** Barrett Indus. Trucks v. Old Republic Ins. Co., No. 87-C9429, 1990 U.S. Dist. LEXIS 142 (N.D. Ill. Jan. 9, 1990)—*Bluebook* format

Barrett Indus. Trucks v. Old Republic Ins. Co., 1990 U.S. Dist. LEXIS 142 (N.D. Ill. Jan. 9, 1990)—*ALWD* format

If a decision is published in a hard-copy reporter, you should not use the Westlaw or Lexis citation. This is stipulated in *Bluebook* **Rule 18.1** and *ALWD* **Rule 12.13(b).**

### ▼ How Do You Indicate a Page or Screen Number for the Case?

An asterisk should precede any screen or page numbers. See *Bluebook* **Rule 18.3.1** and *ALWD* **12.13(b).**

**Westlaw screen no.:** Clark Equip. Co. v. Lift Parts Mfg. Co., No. 82-C4585, 1985 WL 2917, at *1 (N.D. Ill. Oct. 1, 1985)—*Bluebook* format

**Lexis screen no.:** Barrett Indus. Trucks v. Old Republic Ins. Co., 1990 U.S. Dist. LEXIS 142, at *1 (N.D. Ill. Jan. 9, 1990)—*ALWD* format

### ▼ How Do You Cite Internet Resources?

*Bluebook* **Rule 18** covers Internet materials. *ALWD* **Rule 21.5** covers electronic journals. Only rely on Internet resources if there is no other way to obtain the material, because the Internet format is transient in nature. However, if you can obtain the resource in a PDF file, then it is a reliable version. *Bluebook* **Rule 18.2.1** states that you can use sources on the Internet in lieu of the hard-copy source when the online format is the official resource for the publication or the document. This is occurring more frequently with federal, state, and municipal resources. You can use Internet sites as an additional cite when the identical information can be obtained in hard copy as well as on the Internet but the Internet resource is more accessible.

Karin Mitra, *Information v. Commercialization: The Internet and Unsolicited Electronic Mail,* 4 Rich. J.L. & Tech. 6 (Spring 1998), *available at* www .richmond.edu/jolt/v4i3/mitra.html—*Bluebook* **Rule 18.2.2**

Karin Mitra, *Information v. Commercialization: The Internet and Unsolicited Electronic Mail*, 4 Rich. J.L. & Tech. 6 (Spring 1998) www.richmond .edu/jolt/v4i3/mitra.html—*ALWD* **Rule 21.5**

## ▼ How Do You Cite Documents Retrieved in PDF Files?

Documents are widely available for retrieval in Portable Document Format, "PDF." Lexis and Westlaw now permit most resources to be saved and printed in PDF. Documents in PDF maintain the pagination from the hard-copy source and do not permit end-user manipulation.

*Bluebook* **Rules 18.1** and **18.2** and *ALWD* **Rule 30.2** address citing to PDF documents.

---

## *PRACTICE POINTER*

It is both cost- and time-efficient to attach PDF versions of cases and statutes to e-mailed memos rather than printing or photocopying the resources.

---

## ▼ How Do You Cite Federal Statutes?

Always cite to the official statutory compilation. The first entry in the citation is the title number, then the abbreviation for the statutory compilation, and then the section or paragraph number. *Bluebook* **Rule 12** and *ALWD* **Rule 14** detail all the various rules pertaining to citing statutes and codes, state or federal. Always cite to the year of the code's compilation, not the year that the particular statute section was enacted. For example:

12 U.S.C. § 211 (2012)—*Bluebook* and *ALWD* formats

If a code section is well known by a popular name, then include the name in the citation. For example:

Strikebreaker Act, 18 U.S.C. § 1231 (2012)—*Bluebook* and *ALWD* formats

You may rely on an unofficial version for updating purposes. All the following are citations to the identical statute.

26 U.S.C. § 61 (2012)—*Bluebook* and *ALWD* formats
26 U.S.C.A. § 61 (West 2011 & Supp. 2014)—*Bluebook* and *ALWD* formats
26 U.S.C.S. § 61 (LexisNexis 2010)—*Bluebook* and *ALWD* formats

As with the U.S.C., the year included in the citation is the year that the code volume was published, not the year that the statute was enacted. In the U.S.C.A. example above, the first year mentioned, 2011, is the year that the particular volume of the code was published; the second date, 2014, is the year of the pocket part supplement that updates the code volume. For the unofficial codes, the publication date is printed either on the title page of the bound volume or on the back of the title page. Note that the title and section do not change in the codes published by different companies.

---

## PRACTICE POINTER

Ask your supervising attorney if she prefers the use of "Id." for subsequent citations to the same statute or the short site format.

---

▼ How Do You Cite a Section of a Constitution, Federal or State?

*Bluebook* **Rule 11** and *ALWD* **Rule 13** outline the citation format. The United States Constitution citation refers to the particular article, section, and clause being used. For example:

U.S. Const. art II, § 2, cl. 1—*Bluebook* and *ALWD* formats

This cite is used when you are referring to the body of the Constitution. A special citation format is required when you are referring to an amendment currently in force. For example:

U.S. Const. amend. II

State constitutions are indicated by the name of the state in the *Bluebook* abbreviated format. *Bluebook* **Table T.1** and *ALWD* **Appendix 1** indicate the accepted state name abbreviation; this is not necessarily the postal abbreviation. For example, the state of Washington's postal abbreviation is WA, but the *Bluebook* abbreviation is Wash. A section of the Washington state constitution would be cited as follows:

Wash. Const. art I, § 2—*Bluebook* and *ALWD* formats

Years or dates are not included in citations to constitutions, state or federal, that are current. Parenthetical notations after the citation indicate the year a constitutional provision was repealed or amended. An example is the Eighteenth Amendment to the U.S. Constitution prohibiting the sale of liquor. The Twenty-First Amendment later repealed this. *Bluebook* **Rule 11** and *ALWD* **Rule 13.3** cover this:

U.S. Const. amend. XVIII (repealed 1933)—*Bluebook* format

U.S. Const. amend. XVIII, *repealed by* U.S. Const. amend. XXI—*ALWD* format

### ▼ How Do You Cite to a Legislative History of a Statute?

*Bluebook* **Rule 13** and *ALWD* **Rule 15** detail the citation format for all the components of the legislative process: the bill, the committee report, the debates, and transcripts of the hearings.

### ▼ How Are the *Code of Federal Regulations* and the *Federal Register* Cited?

**Rule 14** of the *Bluebook* and *ALWD* **Rule 18** provide the citation format for administrative and executive materials, which include the *Code of Federal Regulations* and the *Federal Register*. See also *Bluebook* **T.1** for each jurisdiction's administrative material. Title 21 of the C.F.R.§ 101.62 from 2014 is cited as:

21 C.F.R. § 101.62 (2014)—*Bluebook* and *ALWD* formats

A *Federal Register* entry from volume 73 beginning on page 26200, from May 8, 2008, would be cited as:

73 Fed. Reg. 26200 (May 8, 2008)—*Bluebook* and *ALWD* formats

### ▼ How Do You Cite to a Legal Dictionary?

The information for the correct citation format for dictionaries is found in **Rule 15.8** of the *Bluebook* and **Rule 22.2** of *ALWD*.

Black's Law Dictionary 712 (9th ed. 2009)—*Bluebook* format

*Black's Law Dictionary* 712 (Bryan A. Garner, ed., 9th ed. 2009)—*ALWD* format

### ▼ How Are Legal Encyclopedias Cited?

*ALWD* **Rule 22.3** and *Bluebook* **Rule 15.8** discuss legal encyclopedias. A citation to the discussion of easements would be as follows:

25 Am. Jr. 2d *Easements and Licenses* § 90 (2004 & Supp. 2014)—*Bluebook* and *ALWD* formats

28A C.J.S. *Easements* § 18 (2008 & Supp. 2014)—*Bluebook* and *ALWD* formats

▼ How Do You Cite to *American Law Reports?*

This is found in **Rule 16.7.6** of the *Bluebook* and **Rule 22.6** of *ALWD*.

William B. Johnson, Annotation, *Locating Easement of Way Created by Necessity*, 36 A.L.R.4th 769 (1985)—*ALWD* and *Bluebook* formats

▼ How Do You Cite to a Law Review or Law Journal?

*Bluebook* **Rule 16** and *ALWD* **Rule 21** indicate the citation form for a law review article, as follows:

Mitchell N. Berman, *Justification and Excuse, Law and Morality*, 53 Duke L.J. 1 (2003)—*Bluebook* and *ALWD* formats

Abbreviations for the journal names are found in **Table 13** of the *Bluebook* and *ALWD* **Appendix 5**. A legal newspaper is cited according to *Bluebook* **Rules 16.5** and **16.6**:

Wayne Smith, *Remote Access: Striking a Balance*, Law Tech. News, Jan. 2005, at 11—*Bluebook* and *ALWD* formats

*ALWD* **Rule 23.1(f)(1)** states if place of publication can't be discerned from title, include it in parentheses.

▼ How Do You Cite the Restatements?

*Bluebook* **Rule 12.9.5** and *ALWD* **Rule 23.1** indicate that the Restatements are cited as follows:

Restatement (Second) of Contracts § 235 (1979)—*Bluebook* and *ALWD* formats

Note that for *Bluebook* format the year is the year that the Restatement section was adopted. This information is given on the title page of every volume of the Restatements. When you are citing to a comment that follows the Restatement section, **Rule 3.4** of the *Bluebook* applies. For example:

Restatement (Second) of Contracts § 235 cmt. a (1979)—*Bluebook* format (date adopted)

*Restatement (Second) of Contracts* § 235 (1981)—*ALWD* format

*Restatement (Second) of Contracts* § 235 cmt. a (1981)—*ALWD* format

Note that *ALWD* format for the Restatements requires that the year is the date of volume publication—*ALWD* format, **Rule 23.1(c).**

▼ How Do You Cite an Ethics Rule Found in the *ABA Model Code of Professional Responsibility?*

The rules for citation of ethics codes are found in *Bluebook* **Rule 12.9.6** and *ALWD* **Rule 23.3.** Rule 1.10 of the *ABA Model Code* would be cited as follows:

Model Code of Prof'l Responsibility Rule 1.10 (1992)

▼ How Do You Cite an ABA Ethics Opinion?

The rules for citation of ethics opinions are contained in *Bluebook* **Rule 12.9.5** and **12.9.6** and *ALWD* **Rule 16.2.** For example:

ABA Comm. on Prof'l Ethics and Grievances, Informal Op. 88-1526 (1988)—*Bluebook* and *ALWD* formats

▼ How Do You Cite the Various Federal Rules?

Cite the federal rules in accordance with *Bluebook* **Rule 12.9.3** and *ALWD* **Rule 16.1** as follows:

Fed. R. Civ. P. 56

Fed. R. Crim. P. 1

Fed. R. App. P. 26

Fed. R. Evid. 803

Only include the year when the rule is no longer in force by providing the most recent year that it appeared and the year repealed. For example:

Fed. R. Civ. P. 9 (2006) (repealed 2008)—*Bluebook* **Rule 12.9.3** and *ALWD* **Rule16.1(d)**

NET NOTE

Go to www.suffolk.edu/law/library/19543.php for a helpful guide to using the *Bluebook*.

# CITATION EXERCISES

For the following citations, assume that these cases are being used in a brief for the U.S. District Court for the Northern District of Ohio. Correct the citation, if possible. If not, specify what is wrong. If an item is missing, note it and tell where it belongs.

1. How would you cite the following slip opinion?
   Michele Greear, et. al., plaintiffs, vs. C.E. Electronics, Inc., et. al., defendants, decided in the United States District Court for the Northern District of Ohio Western Division, docket number C 87-7749, decided by Judge Richard B. McQuade, Jr. on September 12, 1989.
2. When responding to a motion for summary judgment, the plaintiff must submit proof of each and every element of his claims so that a reasonable jury would find in his favor.
   Anderson v. Liberty Lobby, Inc., 477 U.S. 242, 105 S.Ct. 989, 10 L.Ed. 2d 1111 (1986).
3. When the relationship of the parties is so clear as to be undisputed, it can be decided as a matter of law that no apparent or actual relationship existed.
   Mateyka v. Schroeder, 504 N.E.2d 1289 (1987).
4. In a diversity action, a court must apply the conflict of law principles of the forum state. Dr. Franklin Perkins School v. Freeman, 741 F.2d 1503, 1515, n.19 (1984); Pittway Corp. v. Lockheed Aircraft Corp., 641 F.2d 524, 526 (7th Cir.); Klaxon Co. v. Stentor Electric Mfg. Co., 313 US 487, 496 (1941).
5. Gizzi v. Texaco, 437 F.2d 308 (3rd).
6. Zimmerman v. North American, 704 F.2d 347 (1983).
7. E.E.O.C. v. Dowd, 736 F.2d 1177.
8. Musser v. Mountain View Broadcasting, 578 F. Supp. 229 (1984).
9. United States v. Upjohn, 449 U.S. 383.
10. Indicate what, if anything, is missing from this citation: Consolidation Coal Co. v. Buryus-Erie Co., 89 Ill. App. 2d 103 (1982).

# CITATION PRACTICE

Provide the correct citation form for the following; use case name abbreviations found in either the *Bluebook* or the *ALWD Guide to Legal Citation*.

1. Trzcinski v. American Casualty Company
   901 Federal Reporter Second Series 1429
   Seventh Circuit Court of Appeals
   1990
2. Wade v. Singer Company
   130 Federal Rules Decisions 89
   Northern District Court of Illinois 1990

3. Pryor v. Cajda
   662 Federal Supplement 1114
   Northern District Court of Illinois 1987
4. Longman v. Jasiek
   91 Illinois Appellate Court Reports Third Series 83
   46 Illinois Decisions 636
   414 North Eastern Second Series 520
   Third District Court of Appeals 1986
5. Gulf Oil Corporation v. Gilbert
   91 Lawyers Edition 1055
   330 United States Reports 501
   67 Supreme Court Reporter 839
   1947
6. Wyness v. Armstrong World Industries Incorporated
   131 Illinois Reports Second Series 403
   546 North Eastern Reporter Second Series 568
   Supreme Court of Illinois 1989
7. Title 28 of the United States Code, section 1404(a) from the year 2006.
8. Title 42 of the Code of Federal Regulations, part 400.200 from the year 2011.

## SHORT CITATION

Write the following information in short citation format.

1. Smith v. Jones, 96 N.E.2d 17 (Ill. App. Ct. 1965).
   You are using text from p.18 of the N.E.2d.
   How would you cite this the first time?
   How would you short cite it to page 18 if it is cited in full in the immediately preceding citation?
2. Cranshaw v. Marge, 321 F.2d 97 (5th Cir. 1935).
   You need to short cite this case to reflect attributing authority to page 99 of the decision.

## CITATION FOR RESOURCES OTHER THAN CASES

1. How would you cite to a federal statute that appeared in the 2012 pocket part of Title 42 of the United States Code Annotated at section 1201 that was in a volume published in 2004?
2. How would you cite a law review article that appeared in volume 78 of the Columbia University Law Review in 1985? The article is entitled Tax Aspects of Marital Dissolution, and begins on page 1587. The author is John Reese.
3. How would you cite Megan's Law found in Title 42 of the United States Code at section 14071(e) in the 2006 Code?
4. How would you cite volume 63 of the Federal Register at page 59,231 from October 1, 1991?

5. How would you cite the Procter & Gamble 2003 annual report accessed on June 5, 2004, at pg.com/investors? Choose the "Financial Results and Events" tab, and then click the "Annual Reports" link. Click "2003 Annual Report."

## CITATIONS FOR ONLINE RESOURCES

1. How would you cite an unreported opinion available on Lexis where you are relying on a statement from page 3 of that opinion? The opinion is from 2005 and was found in the US Dist Ct file. The Lexis case number is 15976. The date of the decision is April 13, 2005. The case name is *Panera Bread Store v. Baguette Company*. The docket number is No. 05-1721.
2. You have found a new C.F.R. provision on Westlaw and you know it was printed in hard copy in the 2011 C.F.R. The provision is in Title 5 at section 12.
3. You retrieved a recent final regulation in the *Federal Register*, volume 76 at page 9080. It will be codified in the C.F.R. at 27 C.F.R. part 1. The material was accessed at www.gpoaccess.gov/fr. Please provide the citation according to the *Bluebook* or *ALWD*.
4. You have found an article in the Yale Law Journal. You know that the journal is available in hard copy at the law school library across town and the identical article is available in full text on the Web. You want to cite to both sources to improve access. What rule do you follow in the *Bluebook*?

The article is from volume 114, number 7, May 2005. The article is titled: "The Sarbanes-Oxley Act and the Making of Quack Corporate Governance" by Roberta Romana. The article begins on page 1521. The Yale Law Journal Internet site is www.yale.edu/yalelj.

# SAMPLE MEMORANDA

---

**ILLUSTRATION C-1.** **Sample Memorandum**

---

**MEMORANDUM**

To: Benjamin Joyce
From: William Randall
Date: January 28, 2014
Re: *Harris v. Sack and Shop*

## QUESTION PRESENTED

Is Sack and Shop, a grocery store, liable for injuries sustained by Harris, a store patron who slipped on a banana peel that had been left on the grocery store floor for two days?

## BRIEF ANSWER

Probably yes. Sack and Shop, a grocery store, probably will be liable based on negligence for injuries sustained by Harris, a store patron who slipped on a banana peel that had been on the grocery store floor for two days.

## FACTS

Our client, Sack and Shop Grocery Store, is being sued for negligence by Rebecca Harris.

Harris went to the store to purchase groceries on July 8, 2013. While she was in the produce section, she slipped on a banana peel that a grocery store employee left on the floor. The employee had dropped it on the floor two days earlier and had failed to clean it up after a patron asked him to do so.

## ILLUSTRATION C-1. *Continued*

Harris sustained a broken arm and head injuries as a result of the slip and fall.

### DISCUSSION

The issue presented in this case is whether Sack and Shop Grocery Store was negligent when Rebecca Harris slipped in the store's produce section. A grocer will be found negligent if a store employee breached the store's duty of reasonable care to its patrons and, as a result of that breach, the patron was injured. *Ward v. K Mart Corp.*, 554 N.E.2d. 223 (Ill. 1990). In *Ward*, the grocery store employee failed to clean up a banana peel for two days and that peel caused a patron to be injured. Similarly in our case Sack and Shop failed to remove the banana peel for two days. Therefore, Sack and Shop is likely to be found liable for the injuries Harris sustained.

The first element to consider is whether Sack and Shop owed a duty of reasonable care to Harris. A grocery store owes a duty of care to any patron. *Ward*, 554 N.E.2d at 226. Harris was a customer in the store. Therefore, Sack and Shop owed her a duty of care.

The next question to consider is whether Sack and Shop breached its duty of reasonable care to Harris. A store will be found to have breached its duty of reasonable care to a patron if a store employee fails to properly and regularly clean the floor of the store. *Olinger v. Great Atl. & Pac. Tea Co.*, 173 N.E.2d 443 (Ill. 1961). In *Olinger*, the store was found liable because a store employee failed to clean the floor for one day and a patron slipped on a substance on the floor. 173 N.E.2d at 447. No one had told any store employee about the slippery substance. *Id.* at 447. Nonetheless, the Illinois Supreme Court found the store liable, saying that the store employees had sufficient time to notice the substance if they had used ordinary care. *Id.* In our case, Sack and Shop's employee had two days to clean the floor before Harris fell. In addition, a customer had placed the store employee on notice of the banana. Therefore, Sack and Shop breached its duty of care to Harris.

The plaintiff, however, still must establish proximate cause, that is, that the injury resulted as a natural consequence of Sack and Shop's breach of its duty. A store owner's failure to clear debris from a store floor, resulting in injury to a patron who slipped on the floor, was found to be the proximate cause of the patron's injuries. *Id.* at 449. In this case, Sack and Shop's failure to clean the peel from the floor was a breach of its duty of care to Harris. This breach resulted in injury to Harris. Sack and Shop's breach will be found to be the proximate cause of Harris's injuries.

The final element that must be established is that the plaintiff, Harris, suffered injuries. Harris sustained a broken arm and head injuries as a result of the slip and fall. Therefore, she will be able to show that she was injured.

### CONCLUSION

Sack and Shop owed Harris a duty of reasonable care. The store is likely to be found to have breached that duty of reasonable care because an employee failed to remove a banana peel from the grocery store floor during the

# ILLUSTRATION C-1.   *Continued*

preceding two days. The injuries Harris sustained were directly caused by a slip on a banana peel. Therefore, Sack and Shop is likely to be found liable to Harris.

# ILLUSTRATION C-2.   Sample Memorandum: McMillan Battery Action

## MEMORANDUM

To: William Houck
From: Ivy Courier
Date: November 7, 2013
Re: McMillan Battery Action

## QUESTION PRESENTED

Did an actionable battery occur when Mann intentionally struck McMillan with a bucket, without McMillan's consent, causing McMillan to suffer physical and monetary injuries?

## CONCLUSION

Mann's intentional striking of McMillan with a bucket and sand was an actionable battery.

## FACTS

Our client, Mary McMillan, a 36-year-old bank teller, wants to bring an action for battery against Carol Mann, a 36-year-old mother, who threw a metal bucket filled with sand at McMillan at a local park. While McMillan sat on a park bench, she teased Mann's seven-year-old son. Mann did not like this teasing and threw a bucket filled with sand at McMillan. Sand landed in McMillan's eyes while she was wearing soft contact lenses. As a result, McMillan's contacts had to be replaced. The bucket also cut McMillan's eye and cheek. She had stitches in both places. McMillan asked Mann to pay for her doctor bills and for the new contacts. Mann refused and added, "I'm not sorry. I meant to hurt you."

## DISCUSSION

The issue presented is whether Mann's intentional touching of McMillan with a bucket rather than her person is an actionable battery. A battery is the intentional touching of another without consent, which causes injury. *Anderson v. St. Francis-St. George Hosp., Inc.*, 77 Ohio St. 3d 82, 671 N.E.2d 225 (1996). A touching can occur when an object rather than an individual's body contacts the other party. *Leichtman v. WLW Jacoc Communications, Inc.*, 92 Ohio App. 3d 232, 634 N.E.2d 697 (1994); *Smith v. John Deere Co.*, 83 Ohio App. 3d 398, 614 N.E.2d 1148 (1993). In this case, Mann intentionally struck McMillan with a bucket without McMillan's consent and that touching resulted in injuries. Therefore, a battery occurred.

## ILLUSTRATION C-2.  *Continued*

The threshold issue is whether a touching occurred when the bucket struck McMillan. A contact between a nonconsenting party and object rather than the actor's body can be a battery. *Leichtman v. WLW Jacoc Communications, Inc.*, 92 Ohio App. 3d 232, 634 N.E.2d 697 (1994); *Smith v. John Deere Co.*, 83 Ohio App. 3d at 398, 614 N.E.2d at 1148. In *Leichtman*, one person blew cigar smoke at another person, resulting in injuries. The court found that the cigar smoke was an extension of the person and that a contact between the smoke and the nonconsenting person met the requirement of a touching for civil battery. In this case, Mann threw the bucket at McMillan, and the bucket contacted her face. Following the reasoning in the *Leichtman* case, the bucket would be an extension of Mann's body, and the contact between McMillan and the bucket would be considered a touching under the theory of civil battery.

Next, the question to consider is whether under the statute Mann intended to touch McMillan when she struck her with the bucket. A person intends his or her conduct when he or she undertakes an action with a knowing mind. *Smith v. John Deere Co.*, 83 Ohio App. 3d 398, 614 N.E.2d 1148 (1993). In *Smith*, a police officer handcuffed the plaintiff. The court found that the officer must have intended his actions because you could not accidentally handcuff a person. *Smith*, 83 Ohio App. 3d at 399, 614 N.E.2d at 1149. In McMillan's case, Mann aimed the bucket at McMillan, purposefully trying to strike her, Mann later told McMillan that she deliberately threw the bucket at her. McMillan probably will be able to establish that Mann had the statutory intent.

The next factor to consider is whether McMillan consented to the contact. If a person consents to the touching, a battery has not occurred. *Love v. Port Clinton*, 37 Ohio St. 3d 98, 524 N.E.2d 166 (1988). In our case, McMillan did not consent to Mann's throwing of the bucket at her face. Therefore, McMillan did not consent to any contact. Finally, the question is whether McMillan suffered physical injuries. A battery occurs only if a plaintiff sustains physical injuries as a result of the touching. *Anderson v. St. Francis-St. George Hosp., Inc.*, 77 Ohio St. 3d 82, 671 N.E.2d 225 (1996). McMillan sustained cuts on her face and the sand flying out of the bucket into her eyes. McMillan will be able to show that she sustained physical injuries as a result of the contact with the bucket.

## ILLUSTRATION C-3.   Multi-Issue Memorandum: McMillan Battery Action

### MEMORANDUM

To: William Mark
From: Ivy Courier
Date: November 7, 2013
Re: McMillan Battery Action

## ILLUSTRATION C-3.   *Continued*

QUESTIONS PRESENTED

1. Did a battery occur when Carol Mann intentionally struck McMillan with a bucket, without Mary McMillan's consent, causing McMillan to suffer physical and monetary injuries?
2. Does eight-year-old Rachel McMillan have a valid claim for intentional infliction of emotional distress against Carol Mann after the child saw Mann throw a rusty metal bucket of sand at her mother's face and head, causing physical injuries to the elder McMillan and resulting in the child suffering from anxiety, headaches, and vomiting?
3. Was Camp Cougar vicariously liable for the intentional torts of Mann, a volunteer whom camp officials asked to supervise children in the sandbox?

CONCLUSIONS

1. When Mann intentionally struck McMillan on the head and in the face with a rusty, metal bucket and sand without McMillan's consent and McMillan was injured, a battery occurred.
2. Eight-year-old Rachel McMillan has a claim for intentional infliction of emotional distress against Carol Mann because the child can show that she suffered emotional distress as a result of Mann's extreme and outrageous act of intentionally throwing a rusty, metal bucket at the child's mother, causing the older McMillan to suffer physical injuries and the child to suffer from anxiety and post-traumatic stress syndrome—mental anguish no child should be expected to endure.
3. Camp Cougar will not be found vicariously liable for an intentional act of its agent, Mann, because it did not benefit from that act nor did the camp control Mann's actions.

FACTS

Our client, Mary McMillan, a 36-year-old bank teller, seeks to bring an action for battery against Carol Mann, a 36-year-old mother, who threw a rusty, metal bucket filled with sand at her at a local camp. She also wants to bring an action against Camp Cougar for vicarious liability for the intentional torts of camp volunteer Carol Mann. Camp Cougar enlisted Carol Mann, a camper's parent, to act as volunteer supervisor of the sandbox during Parent Visitor day at Camp Cougar. Camp Cougar officials told Mann to ensure that no one was injured while playing in the sandbox. Mann had handled this responsibility during Parent Visitor day in the past. Mary McMillan came to see her eight-year-old daughter, Rachel, during Camp Cougar Parent Visitor day. While McMillan sat on a camp bench, she teased Mann's seven-year-old son. Mann did not like this teasing and threw a rusty, metal bucket filled with sand at McMillan's head and face. Sand landed in McMillan's eyes while she was wearing soft contact lenses. As a result, McMillan's contacts had to be replaced. The bucket also cut McMillan's head, eye and cheek. She lost a lot of blood from her head, requiring a transfusion of one pint of blood. She had stitches

## ILLUSTRATION C-3. *Continued*

on her eyelid and cheek. After the bucket struck McMillan, Mann told McMillan in front of three witnesses, "I'm not sorry. I meant to hurt you."

Immediately after Rachel McMillan saw her mother bleeding, she began to cry and vomit. She told the camp counselors that her head hurt and she would not go with the camp director to the hospital. She said she was afraid the director would throw a bucket of sand at her if she didn't like what she said. The child missed the remainder of camp because she suffered from daily headaches and vomiting and she was afraid of the adults at the camp. A child psychologist examined the child and said she was suffering headaches, vomiting, and anxiety as a result of seeing a bucket thrown by an adult at her mother. He said she was experiencing post-traumatic stress syndrome.

### DISCUSSION

This memo first will address whether Carol Mann can be held liable for battery when she intentionally struck McMillan with a rusty, metal bucket, without McMillan's consent, causing McMillan to suffer physical and monetary injuries. Next, the discussion will consider whether eight-year-old Rachel McMillan has a claim for intentional infliction of emotional distress against Mann after the child saw Mann throw a rusty, metal bucket of sand at her mother's head and face, resulting in injury to her mother and causing the young girl to suffer from anxiety, headaches, and vomiting. Finally, the memo will explore whether McMillan can establish that Camp Cougar was vicariously liable for the intentional actions of one of its volunteers, Carol Mann, that resulted in injury to McMillan.

### 1. WAS MANN'S INTENTIONAL TOUCHING OF McMILLAN WITH A BUCKET BATTERY?

The issue presented is whether Mann's intentional touching of McMillan with a bucket rather than her person is a battery. A battery is the intentional touching of another without consent, which causes injury. *Anderson v. St. Francis-St. George Hosp., Inc.*, 77 Ohio St. 3d 82, 671 N.E.2d 225 (1996). A touching can occur when an object rather than an individual's body contacts another person. *Leichtman v. WLW Jacoc Communications, Inc.*, 92 Ohio App. 3d 232, 634 N.E.2d 697 (1994); *Smith v. John Deere Co.*, 83 Ohio App. 3d 398, 614 N.E.2d 1148 (1993). A person intends his or her conduct when he or she undertakes an action with a knowing mind. If a person consents to the touching, a battery has not occurred. *Love v. Port Clinton*, 37 Ohio St. 3d 98, 524 N.E.2d 166 (1988). A battery occurs only if a plaintiff sustains physical injuries as a result of the touching. *Anderson v. St. Francis-St. George Hosp., Inc.*, 77 Ohio St. 3d 82, 671 N.E.2d 225 (1996). In this case, Mann intentionally struck McMillan with a bucket without McMillan's consent and that touching resulted in injuries. Therefore, a battery occurred.

The threshold issue is whether an intentional touching occurred when a bucket Mann threw struck McMillan. A touching can occur when an object rather than an individual's body contacts another person. *Leichtman v. WLW Jacoc Communications, Inc.*, 92 Ohio App. 3d 232, 634

# ILLUSTRATION C-3.   *Continued*

N.E.2d 697 (1994); *Smith v. John Deere Co.*, 83 Ohio App. 3d at 398, 614 N.E.2d at 1148. In *Leichtman,* one person blew cigar smoke at another person, resulting in injuries. The court found that the cigar smoke was an extension of the person and that a contact between the smoke and the nonconsenting person met the requirement of a touching for civil battery. In this case, Mann threw the bucket at McMillan, and the bucket contacted her face and head. Following the reasoning in the *Leichtman* case, the bucket would be an extension of Mann's body, and the contact between McMillan and the bucket would be considered a touching under the theory of civil battery.

Next, the question to consider is whether under the statute Mann intended to touch McMillan when she struck her with the bucket. A person intends his or her conduct when he or she undertakes an action with a knowing mind. *Smith v. John Deere Co.*, 83 Ohio App. 3d 398, 614 N.E.2d 1148 (1993). In *Smith*, a police officer handcuffed the plaintiff. The court found that the officer must have intended his actions because you could not accidentally handcuff a person. *Smith*, 83 Ohio App. 3d at 399, 614 N.E.2d at 1149. In McMillan's case, Mann aimed the bucket at McMillan, purposefully trying to strike her, Mann later told McMillan that she deliberately threw the bucket at her. McMillan probably will be able to establish that Mann had the statutory intent.

The next factor to consider is whether McMillan consented to the contact. If a person consents to the touching, a battery has not occurred. *Love v. Port Clinton*, 37 Ohio St. 3d 98, 524 N.E.2d 166 (1988). In our case, McMillan did not consent to Mann's throwing of the bucket at her face. Therefore, McMillan did not consent to any contact. Finally, the question is whether McMillan suffered physical injuries. A battery occurs only if a plaintiff sustains physical injuries as a result of the touching. *Anderson v. St. Francis-St. George Hosp., Inc.*, 77 Ohio St. 3d 82, 671 N.E.2d 225 (1996). McMillan sustained cuts on her face and the sand flying out of the bucket into her eyes. McMillan will be able to show that she sustained physical injuries as a result of the contact with the bucket.

2. IS MANN LIABLE FOR INTENTIONAL INFLICTION OF EMOTIONAL DISTRESS?

The next issue to consider is whether eight-year-old Rachel McMillan has a claim for intentional infliction of emotional distress against Carol Mann. To successfully prove intentional infliction of emotional distress, McMillan must show that Mann intentionally committed an extreme and outrageous that caused emotional distress that no reasonable person could be expected to endure. *Yeager v. Local Union 20*, 6 Ohio St. 3d 369, 453 N.E.2d 666 (1983). *Pyle v. Pyle*, 11 Ohio App. 3d 31, 34, 463 N.E.2d 98, 101 (1983). In the case, *Rachel McMillan*, a child, saw Mann, an adult, throw the rusty, metal bucket filled with sand at her mother's head and face, causing her mother to bleed. Seeing this act caused the child to suffer from anxiety, headaches, and vomiting daily. Several witnesses can testify that Mann said that she intended to harm McMillan. A child should not be expected to

## ILLUSTRATION C-3. *Continued*

endure the pain of seeing her mother injured. Therefore, Rachel McMillan has a claim for intentional emotional distress

The threshold issue is whether Mann's act of throwing a rusty, metal bucket at the head and face of another adult in front of children was an extreme and outrageous act. An act is extreme and outrageous if it goes "beyond all possible bounds of decency," *Yeager,* 6 Ohio. St. 3d at 375, 453 N.E.2d at 672, and is regarded as "atrocious, and utterly intolerable in a civilized community." *Id.* In this case, Mann, an adult who was asked to supervise the sandbox and ensure the safety of others, threw a rusty, metal bucket filled with sand at another adult in front of young children, including her child and Rachel McMillan. The bucket struck the older McMillan causing her to bleed. That act went beyond all possible bounds of decency and was atrocious and utterly intolerable in a civilized community. This is especially true since Mann was charged with ensuring the safety of people in the sand box area. Therefore, Mann's act would be found to be an extreme and outrageous act.

Next, the young McMillan must show that the act was done with intent. A person intends his or her conduct when he or she undertakes an action with a knowing mind. *Smith v. John Deere Co.,* 83 Ohio App. 3d 398, 614 N.E.2d 1148 (1993). If an actor knew or should have known that his or her actions would cause serious emotional distress, intent is established. *Phung v. Waste Mgt., Inc.,* 71 Ohio St. 3d 408, 410, 644 N.E.2d 286, 288 (1994). In this case, Mann not only knew or should have known that that throwing a rusty, metal bucket filled with sand at the head and face of another adult in front of the other adult's child resulting in the adult bleeding would cause an eight-year-old child to suffer serious emotional distress. For those reasons, the young McMillan should be able to show intent.

The third element McMillan must establish is that the extreme and outrageous act was the proximate cause of her emotional and physical distress. Proximate cause exists when an act precedes and produces an injury that is likely to have occurred as a result of the act or which might have been anticipated. *Jeffers v. Olexo,* 43 Ohio St. 3d 140, 143, 539 N.E.2d 614, 617 (1989). In this case, the young McMillan can show that a child likely would experience emotional distress when she saw her mother injured and bleeding. Therefore, the child will be able to establish that the extreme and outrageous act was the proximate cause of her emotional distress.

Finally, the child must show that she suffered from serious emotional distress. To establish serious emotional distress, the mental anguish she suffered must be serious and of a nature that "no reasonable man could be expected to endure it." *Id.* Serious emotional distress goes "beyond trifling mental disturbance, mere upset or hurt feelings" and "may be found where a reasonable person, normally constituted, would be unable to cope adequately with the mental distress engendered by the circumstances of the case." *Paugh v. Hanks,* 6 Ohio St. 3d 72, 78, 451 N.E.2d 759, 765

**ILLUSTRATION C-3.** *Continued*

(1983). It is not necessary to prove any physical harm. *Pyle v. Pyle*, 11 Ohio App. 3d 31, 34, 463 N.E.2d 98, 101 (1983). Various neurosis, psychosis and phobias are examples of serious emotional distress. *Paugh v. Hanks*, 6 Ohio St. 3d 72, 78, 451 N.E.2d 759, 765 (1983). In this case, a psychologist examined the child and found that she suffered from post-traumatic stress syndrome and as well as physical symptoms such as headaches and vomiting after she saw an adult throw a bucket at her mother. Post-traumatic stress and anxiety coupled with these physical manifestations should be sufficient for young McMillan to establish serious emotion distress that is beyond mere upset or hurt feelings and that a reasonable person would be unable to cope.

3. WAS CAMP COUGAR VICARIOUSLY LIABLE FOR MANN'S INTENTIONAL TORTS?

The final claim to consider is whether Camp Cougar will be vicariously liable to both McMillans for Mann's intentional torts. An entity can be held vicariously liable for the actions of its agent. *Byrd v. Faber*, 57 Ohio St. 3d 56, 58-59, 565 N.E2d 584-586 (1991). A principal-agent relationship is established when one party exercises control over the actions of another and those actions are done for the benefit of the party exercising control. See Hanson v. Kynast, 24 Ohio St. 3d 171, 173, 494 N.E.2d 1091 (1986). However, a master only can be vicariously liable for its agent's intentional tort if the entity controlled the agent's conduct and the agent's acts benefited the entity. Id. In this case, Camp Cougar directed Mann to supervise a camp activity. Therefore, Mann may be found to be Camp Cougar's agent. However, Mann's actions did not benefit the camp nor did the camp exercise control over her actions. In fact, these actions may have harmed the camp. Therefore, it is unlikely that Camp Cougar would be found liable for Mann's torts.

The threshold issue is whether Mann is Camp Cougar's agent. A principal-agent relationship is established when one party exercises control over the actions of another and those actions are for the benefit of the party exercising control. See *Hanson v. Kynast*, 24 Ohio St. 3d 171, 173, 494 N.E.2d 1091 (1986). In this case, Camp Cougar directed Mann to act as the sandbox supervisor and specifically directed her to keep people safe. Therefore, Mann is likely to be found to be an agent of Camp Cougar.

The next issue to consider is whether a master can be vicariously liable for its agent's intentional torts. A master can be vicariously liable for its agent's intentional tort only if the master controlled the agent's conduct and the agent's acts benefited the master. See *Hanson v. Kynast*, 24 Ohio St. 3d 171, 173, 494 N.E.2d 1091 (1986). The camp did not direct Mann to injure McMillan, nor did the camp benefit from Mann's actions. Therefore, Camp Cougar would not be vicariously liable for Mann's act of throwing the bucket of sand at McMillan or causing young McMillan's serious emotional distress because it did not control Mann's actions nor did the camp benefit from Mann's actions.

# HELPFUL WEBSITES

**U.S. Courts: General Information**
www.uscourts.gov

**U.S. Supreme Court: Docket, Schedules, General Information, and Links to Decisions**
www.supremecourt.gov

**First Circuit Court of Appeals**
www.ca1.uscourts.gov

**Second Circuit Court of Appeals**
www.ca2.uscourts.gov

**Third Circuit Court of Appeals**
www.ca3.uscourts.gov

**Fourth Circuit Court of Appeals**
www.ca4.uscourts.gov

**Fifth Circuit Court of Appeals**
www.ca5.uscourts.gov

**Sixth Circuit Court of Appeals**
www.ca6.uscourts.gov

**Seventh Circuit Court of Appeals**
www.ca7.uscourts.gov

**Eighth Circuit Court of Appeals**
www.ca8.uscourts.gov

**Ninth Circuit Court of Appeals**
www.ca9.uscourts.gov

**Tenth Circuit Court of Appeals**
www.ca10.uscourts.gov

**Eleventh Circuit Court of Appeals**
www.ca11.uscourts.gov

**U.S. Court of Appeals for the Federal Circuit**
www.cafc.uscourts.gov

**U.S. Court of Appeals for the District of Columbia Circuit**
www.cadc.uscourts.gov

**Federal Legislation and Information**

**General Information**
thomas.loc.gov/home/thomas.php
Congress.gov

**U.S. Senate**
www.senate.gov

**U.S. House of Representatives**
www.house.gov

**Other U.S. Government Sites**

**Consumer Product Safety Commission (Recalls List)**
www.cpsc.gov

**Securities and Exchange Commission**
www.sec.gov

**Edgar (SEC Databases)**
www.sec.gov/edgar.shtml

*Federal Register*
www.federalregister.gov

*Code of Federal Regulations*
www.gpo.gov/fdsys

*List of C.F.R. Section Affected*
www.gpo.gov/fdsys

*U.S. Code*
uscode.house.gov/search/criteria.shtml

**Justice Department**
www.justice.gov

**Department of Labor**
www.dol.gov

**Internal Revenue Service**
www.irs.gov

**Patent and Trademark Office**
www.uspto.gov

**Occupational Safety and Health Administration**
www.osha.gov

**National Library of Medicine**
www.nlm.nih.gov

**Library of Congress**
www.loc.gov

## Alabama
Courts
judicial.alabama.gov
Legislature
www.legislature.state.al.us

## Alaska
Courts
www.courts.alaska.gov
Legislature
akleg.gov

## Arizona
Courts
www.azcourts.gov
Legislature
www.azleg.gov

## Arkansas
Courts
courts.arkansas.gov
Legislature
www.arkansasonline.com/news/news/legislature

## California
Courts
www.courts.ca.gov
Legislature
www.legislature.ca.gov

## Colorado
Courts
www.courts.state.co.us
Legislature
www.leg.state.co.us

**Connecticut**
>Courts
>www.jud.ct.gov
>Legislature
>www.cga.ct.gov

**Delaware**
>Courts
>www.courts.delaware.gov
>Legislature
>www.legis.delaware.gov

**Florida**
>Courts
>www.flcourts.org
>Legislature
>www.leg.state.fl.us

**Georgia**
>Courts
>www.georgiacourts.org
>Legislature
>www.legis.ga.gov

**Hawaii**
>Courts
>www.courts.state.hi.us
>Legislature
>www.capitol.hawaii.gov

**Idaho**
>Courts
>www.isc.idaho.gov
>Legislature
>www.legislature.idaho.gov

**Illinois**
>Courts
>www.state.il.us/court
>Legislature
>www.ilga.gov

**Indiana**
>Courts
>www.in.gov/judiciary
>Legislature
>iga.in.gov

**Iowa**
>Courts
>www.iowacourts.state.ia.us

Legislature
www.legis.iowa.gov

**Kansas**
Courts
www.kscourts.org
Legislature
www.kslegislature.org

**Kentucky**
Courts
courts.ky.gov
Legislature
www.lrc.ky.gov

**Louisiana**
Supreme Court
www.lasc.org
Legislature
www.legis.state.la.us

**Maine**
Courts
www.courts.state.me.us
Legislature
www.maine.gov/legis

**Maryland**
Courts
www.courts.state.md.us
Legislature
mgaleg.maryland.gov

**Massachusetts**
Courts
www.mass.gov/courts
Legislature
malegislature.gov

**Michigan**
Courts
courts.mi.gov
Legislature
www.legislature.mi.gov

**Minnesota**
Courts
www.mncourts.gov
Legislature
www.leg.state.mn.us

**Mississippi**
   Courts
   courts.ms.gov
   Legislature
   www.legislature.ms.gov

**Missouri**
   Courts
   www.courts.mo.gov
   Legislature
   www.moga.mo.gov

**Montana**
   Courts
   www.courts.mt.gov
   Legislature
   www.leg.mt.gov/css

**Nebraska**
   Courts
   supremecourt.ne.gov
   Legislature
   www.nebraskalegislature.gov

**Nevada**
   www.nevadajudiciary.us
   Legislature
   www.leg.state.nv.us

**New Hampshire**
   Courts
   www.courts.state.nh.us
   Legislature
   www.gencourt.state.nh.us

**New Jersey**
   Courts
   www.judiciary.state.nj.us
   Legislature
   www.njleg.state.nj.us

**New Mexico**
   Courts
   www.nmcourts.gov
   Legislature
   www.nmlegis.gov

**New York**
   Courts
   www.courts.state.ny.us
   Legislature

www.assembly.state.ny.us
www.nysenate.gov

### North Carolina
Courts
www.nccourts.org
Legislature
www.ncleg.net

### North Dakota
Courts
www.ndcourts.gov/court/courts.htm
Legislature
www.legis.nd.gov

### Ohio
Courts
www.sconet.state.oh.us/JudSystem/trialcourts
Legislature
www.legislature.state.oh.us

### Oklahoma
Courts
www.oscn.net
Legislature
www.oklegislature.gov

### Oregon
Courts
www.courts.oregon.gov
Legislature
www.oregonlegislature.gov

### Pennsylvania
Courts
www.pacourts.us
Legislature
www.legis.state.pa.us

### Rhode Island
Courts
www.courts.ri.gov
Legislature
www.rilin.state.ri.us

### South Carolina
Courts
www.judicial.state.sc.us
Legislature
www.scstatehouse.gov

### South Dakota
Courts
www.ujs.sd.gov
Legislature
legis.sd.gov

### Tennessee
Courts
www.tncourts.gov
Legislature
www.capitol.tn.gov

### Texas
Courts
www.courts.state.tx.us
Legislature
www.legis.state.tx.us

### Utah
Courts
www.utcourts.gov
Legislature
le.utah.gov

### Vermont
Courts
www.vermontjudiciary.org
Legislature
www.leg.state.vt.us

### Virginia
Courts
www.courts.state.va.us
Legislature
virginiageneralassembly.gov/

### Washington
Courts
www.courts.wa.gov
Legislature
www.leg.wa.gov

### West Virginia
Courts
www.courtswv.gov
Legislature
www.legis.state.wv.us

### Wisconsin
Courts
www.wicourts.gov

Legislature
legis.wisconsin.gov

**Wyoming**

Courts
www.courts.state.wy.us
Legislature
legisweb.state.wy.us/lsoweb

**Paralegal Sites**

**NFPA**

www.paralegals.org

**NALA**

www.nala.org

**ABA**

www.abanet.org

# INDEX

ABA (American Bar Association), 314
*ABA Model Code of Professional Responsibility*, 314–316, 319
  citation of, 318, 568
*ABA Model Rules of Professional Conduct*, 314, 315, 316
ABA opinions, 315–319, 568
Ability to practice, 314, 319
Active voice, 359–360, 362
Adjudicatory function, 252
Administrative agencies
  decisions, 251–252
  Ethics Alert, 274
  independent, 7, 274
  operation of, 7, 257
  police powers, 9
  Shepardizing decisions, 271–272
Administrative decisions, 251–252
Administrative law, 251–277
  *Code of Federal Regulations* and, 252–253, 256, 262, 267–271
  decisions and, 9, 251–252
  defined, 252
  federal, 252–253
  *Federal Register* and, 253–254, 256–260
  finding, 253–268
  looseleaf services and, 275–277
  as primary authority, 253
  researching summary, 276–277
  state, 5, 256

Administrative law judge (ALJ), 274, 277
Administrative rules, 11, 21, 251–253, 257
Advance sheets, 40, 54, 70. 204, 226
  Supreme Court, U.S., 38, 53
  *United States Code Annotated* (U.S.C.A.), 204, 215, 226, 231
  *United States Code Congressional and Administrative News* (U.S.C.C.A.N.), 231, 239, 240
  *United States Code Service* (U.S.C.S.), 239
Advisory ethics opinions, 316, 319
*ALWD Citation Manual*, 40, 557–568
  ABA ethics opinions, 318, 568
  *ABA Model Code of Professional Responsibility*, 318, 568
  *American Jurisprudence*, 165, 566
  *American Law Reports*, 177, 567
  cases, 40, 297, 559–561
  C.F.R., 274, 566
  C.J.S., 165–166, 566
  components, 558–559
  constitutions, 200, 565
  dictionaries, 154, 566
  Fast Formats, 557, 558
  *Federal Register*, 274, 566
  federal regulations, 274, 566
  *Federal Reporter* and *Federal Supplement*, 55, 560–561

*ALWD Citation Manual* (*continued*)
federal rules, 309, 568
*Federal Rules Decisions*, 309, 561
federal statutes, 221 564–565
FORMAT, 557
hornbooks and treatises, 180–181
Internet resources, 58, 70, 563–564
law review or law journal, 188, 563, 567
legal dictionaries, 154, 566
legal encyclopedias, 165–166, 566
legislative history, 245, 566
LEXIS cases, 58, 297–298, 562–563
public domain, 68–69, 560
restatements, 184, 567
slip opinions, 40, 559
state cases, 559–560
statutes, 221–222, 564
Supreme Court, 53, 561
Westlaw cases, 58, 297, 563
American Bar Association (ABA), 314
*American Jurisprudence* (Am. Jur.), 158–165
*American Law Reports* (A.L.R.), 170–178, 308, 311
citation, 177–178, 567
computerized method, 174
digest method, 174
illustrated, 171–173, 175–177
index method, 171, 175–177
methods of using, 172–173
rules of practice, 319
Shepardizing, 129, 174, 178
updating, 178
*Annotated Model Code of Professional Responsibility*, 315, 316
Annotated statutes, 28, 218–219, 231, 233
Appellate courts, U.S., 11–12. *See also* Circuits
appeals of decisions, 10, 11
decisions, 11–12, 23–24, 54
illustrated, 6
Internet source of decisions of, 56, 290
judicial branch, 9–12
levels of court and, 22, 23
map of, 13
rules of, 54, 311
state courts, 15
Applicable law, 315, 339, 427–428, 436, 446, 447, 451–452
Approved jury instructions, 324–325
Asserted fact, 444
Attachments, 546
Attorney deskbooks, 306, 311
Attorney directories. *See* Lawyer Directories

Attorney General, 7
Attorney supervision, 5, 374
Audience
e-mail, 545
for legal memorandums, 400
letter writing, 530
writing considerations and, 350, 352
Authorities. *See* Primary authority; Secondary authority

Background research, 334–335, 337
Balances, 6
*Ballentine's Law Dictionary*, 153
Bankruptcy courts
decisions, 56, 77
rules, 305, 306
Bills, 7
Binding authority, 23–24, 26
*Black's Law Dictionary*, 153–154
illustrated, 155
Blind carbon copy (bcc), 535
Block letter format, 530
Bluebook citation, 557–570
ABA ethics opinion, 318, 568
*ABA Model Code of Professional Responsibility*, 318, 568
*American Law Reports*, 177, 567
cases, 40, 53, 55, 58, 297, 559–561
C.F.R., 274, 566
components of, 558
constitutions, 200, 565
ethics rule or opinion, 568
*Federal Register*, 274, 566
*Federal Regulations*, 274, 566
*Federal Reporter*, 55, 560–561
federal rules, 309, 568
*Federal Rules Decisions*, 309, 561
federal statutes, 221, 564–565
*Federal Supplement*, 53–54, 560
Internet opinions, 58, 69
Internet resources, 58, 59, 563–564
law review or law journal, 188, 563, 567
legal dictionaries, 154, 566
legal encyclopedias, 165–166, 566
legislative history, 245, 566
LEXIS cases, 58, 297–298, 562–563
public domain citations, 69, 560
regional reporters, 68–69, 558, 560
Restatements, 184, 567
slip opinions, 40, 559
state cases, 68–70, 559–560
state statutes, 221, 232
Supreme Court cases, 53, 561
treatises and hornbooks, 180–181, 558
Westlaw, 58, 297, 563

Body of a letter, 533–534
Brainstorming, 83–83
Branches of government, 6–12
Brief answer, 425–429
    conclusion compared to, 426
    illustrated, 421, 426
Briefing cases. *See* Case briefing

Carbon copies (cc), 535
Case analysis, 405–412
Case briefing, 378–404
    anatomy of, 381–405
    case analysis and, 405–412
    case brief defined, 377–378
    case for sample brief, 381–382,
        396–399, 401–403, 405–409
    citation, 381
    defined, 377–378
    diagram of a decision, 379–380
    dicta, 394
    disposition, 394
    drafting, 396
    exercise, 380, 396
    facts, 389–392
    holding, 388–389
    issues, 384–386
    legal analysis, 405–414
    Net Note, 381, 396
    Practice Pointer, 381, 384, 385, 394,
        414
    procedural history, 384–386
    process of, 395
    purpose of, 377–378
    rationale or reasoning, 392–394
    relevant facts, 389–392
    sample case brief, 384, 400–401,
        403–404, 410–411
    validating cases, 384
Case citation. *See* ALWD Citation Man-
        ual; Bluebook citation; Citations
Case law, 6, 35. *See also* Digests;
        Reporters
Causes of action, 483
Certiorari, 12
Charters, 25
Checklists
    cite checking, 554
    editing, 362
    KeyCite, 544–555
    legal memorandum, 428–429
    legal authorities, 30
    letter writing, 548
    practitioner's materials, 326
    research strategy, 338–339
    Revision, 362
    *Shepard's*, 554
    *Shepard's* citator system, 554

synthesis, 493–494
    writing process, 351
Checks, 6
Chronological organization, 390–391,
        447–452
Circuits
    advance sheets, 54
    conflicting decisions between, 23–24
    federal appellate courts, 12, 13
    handbooks, 293
    levels of court and, 12, 22
    map of U.S., 13
    practitioner handbooks, 308
    Seventh Circuit material, 308, 392
Citations
    A.L.R., 177, 567
    ALWD. *See* ALWD Citation Manual
    Bluebook. *See* Bluebook citation
    case, 40, 53, 55, 58, 297, 559–561
    constitutions, 200, 565
    defined, 557–558
    documents cited, 558
    encyclopedias, 165–166, 566
    Ethics Alert, 557
    ethics rules or opinions, 568
    federal or state constitutions, 200,
        565
    federal rules, 309, 568
    federal statutes, 221, 564–565
    hornbooks and treatises, 180–181, 558
    Internet research, 58, 59, 563–564
    IRAC, 470, 471, 473
    law review or law journal, 188,
        563, 567
    legal dictionaries, 154, 566
    legislative history, 245, 566
    Net Notes, 568
    Practice Pointer, 561, 564, 565
    practice rules, 308–309
    public domain, 69, 560
    Restatements, 184, 567
    slip opinions, 40, 559
    state cases, 68–70, 559–560
    Supreme Court cases, 53, 561
    synthesis and, 484
    validating. *See* Validating. *See also*
        *specific publication or resource*
Citators, 119–151
    defined, 119–121
    as finding aid, 26, 28
    GlobalCite, 146–147
    KeyCite, 140–146, 280–281, 554–555
    *Shepard's*, 119–140, 280–283, 295
    *Shepard's* in print, 119–136
    *Shepard's* Online, 136–140
Cite checking. *See* KeyCite; *Shepard's*
        citator system; Validating

City governments, 5
Clarity, 346, 355
Closing a letter, 514
Codenotes, 47, 56
Code of ethics. *See* Ethics
*Code of Federal Regulations* (C.F.R.),
    252–273
  citation of, 274, 566
  finding administrative law, 253–273
  illustrated, 254–255, 269, 274
  Internet, 268
  old regulations, 268
  updating of, 268–269
  U.S.C.S. and, 213
  use of, 252, 267
  validating or Shepardizing,
      268–270
    *See also Federal Register*
Codification, 6–7, 17, 204, 235
Collective nouns, 371, 374
Colons, 374
Commas, 366–368, 372–373
Committee report, 235, 237–239
Common law, 6, 11
Complete sentence, 359–361
Compound subjects, 371, 374
Computerized legal research. *See also*
    Databases 280–297
  additional uses for, 279–280
  advantages of computerized citations,
      281
  benefits of, 281
  disadvantages of, 282
  efficient use of, 282, 284
  finding decisions via, 55–57, 292
  generally, 280–284
  how it works, 284–294
  integrating traditional and, 292–293
  LEXIS. *See* LEXIS
  published vs. online availability, 55–56
  query, 286–290
  Restatements, 183–184
  search, 286–290
  treatises and hornbooks, 181
  Westlaw. *See* Westlaw. *See also* Internet
      research
Computerized reporting. *See* Internet
    research
  LEXIS. *See* LEXIS
  Loislaw. *See* Loislaw
  VersusLaw. *See* VersusLaw, 437
  Westlaw. *See* Westlaw
Conclusion in a legal memorandum,
    425, 427–429
  brief answer compared to, 426
  defined, 426, 435–436
  drafting, 436–438

illustrated, 423, 437–438
  IRAC and, 471–472
  Practice Pointer, 472
Concrete verbs, 357–358, 362
Conference committee, 202, 235, 238
Confirming letters, 546, 548, 549
  illustrated, 535, 537, 538
Conflicting authorities, 23–24
Congress
  administrative agencies and, 9
  House of Representatives, 6, 7
  legislative branch, 6–7, 8
  Senate, 6, 7
  veto power of President and, 7
    *See also* Legislative process
*Congressional Index*, 239
Congressional Information Service
    (CIS), 245
*Congressional Record*, 202, 246, 249
Connectors, 280, 284, 286
Constitution, U.S., 5–6, 7, 12, 14, 21
Constitutions, 194–201
  citation of, 200, 565
  defined, 1194
  full text of, 194–195
  on LEXIS and Westlaw, 195
  primary authority, 25
  relationship between federal and
      state, 194
  Shepardizing, 195
Continuing legal education (CLE)
    materials, 321, 323, 326
Corporate Information, 323
*Corpus Juris Secundum* (C.J.S.), 158, 160,
    165, 166, 167
  illustrated, 167–169
County governments, 5
Court decisions. *See* Digests; Reporters
Court of Claims, U.S., 53
Court of International Trade, U.S.,
    12, 53
Courts of Appeals, U.S. *See* Appellate
    courts, U.S.
Cumulative Supplements (Am. Jur),
    160
*Current Law Index*, 187
Customs Court, U.S., 54

Databases, 280–297
Date, letters 532
*Decennial Digests*, 77, 78
Demand letters, 529, 543, 545, 549
  illustrated, 545
Descriptive word index method, 83–85
  illustrated, 85
Dicta, 22, 25
  case briefing and, 394

Diction, 349–351
Dictionaries, 26, 27, 153–154, 566
Digests, 74–95
  annotated codes, 213
  brainstorming, 84
  *Century Digest,* 77
  commercial case reporters and, 41, 45
  *Decennial Digests,* 77, 78
  defined, 74
  descriptive word index method and, 84, 86
  as finding tool, 26, 28, 201
  *General Digests,* 77–78
  headnotes, 75–77, 80
  illustrated, 74–75, 77–78, 79, 81, 96–90, 92–99
  key number system, 74–77, 81, 93, 115
  one good case method and, 86–87, 90–91
  online searches of, 93
  organization of, 78, 81
  overview, 73–74
  pocket parts and, 93–94
  Practice Pointer, 81
  regional, 77, 78
  rules of practice, 308
  specialized, 78
  state, 77
  step-by-step guide to, 83–114
  topical, 77
  topic outline method and, 115
  topics, 74–77
  types, 77–78
  for U.S. Supreme Court cases, 47, 77
  *West's American Digest System,* 77
  West's digest topics, 75–76
  *West's Federal Practice Digest* series, 77
  *West's Supreme Court Digest,* 77
Discussion in a legal memorandum, 427–429, 498–502, 508, 518–519
  illustrated, 500–501, 518–519. *See also* Outlining
Disposition, 394–395
District courts. *See* U.S. District Courts
Diversity cases, 11
Docket number, 37, 39, 40, 58, 61, 69
Dow Jones, 296
*Dun & Bradstreet Reports,* 326

Editing, 355–362
  diction, 357–359
  other key rules, 361–362
  paragraphs, 359
  process of, 356–357
  purpose of, 355–356
  revision checklist, 362
  sentences, 359–361
  voice, 359
Elements
  arranging the order of, 504
  defined, 501
  IRAC paragraph, 504
  legally significant facts and, 502, 520
  list of, legal authorities 498
  multi-issue memorandum, 505–519
  threshold, 503–505
E-mail, 545–550
  advance sheets, 40
  attachment, 546
  Net Note, 546
  Practice Pointer, 350
  Supreme Court Slip Opinions 39
Emotional adjectives, 446
Enabling statutes, 252
Enacted law, 5, 7
Enclosure line, 533, 535
Encyclopedias. *See* Legal encyclopedias
Ethical behavior, 314, 319
Ethics
  ABA opinions, 316, 318
  ability to practice, 314
  advisory opinions, 316
  *Annotated Model Rules of Professional Conduct 316, 318*
  decisions, 314
  ethical behavior, 299–300
  LEXIS, 303
  *Model Rules of Professional Conduct,* 314, 316, 318
  Net Note, 316
  paralegals, 2–3
  Practice Pointer, 316
  primary and annotated sources, 315
  research process, 317–318
  rules of professional responsibility. *See* Ethics rules
  sample problem, 318
  secondary sources, 316, 317
  state bar association opinions, 317
  use of annotated sources, 316
  Westlaw, 317
Ethics decisions, 314, 315, 318
Ethics rules, 313–319
  attorney supervision, 5
  citation, 318
  Ethics Alert, 314
  forms, 321–323
  jurisdiction, 9
  jury instructions, 324–325
  legal research, 2
  letterhead, 532
  letter writing, 534, 543

Ethics rules (*continued*)
  national code of ethics, 314
  paralegals, 317
  practice rules, 305
  as primary binding authority,
    314–315
  rules of professional responsibility
    313–315
  secondary sources, 315–316
  state ethical rules, 316–317
  use of annotated sources, 316
  validating, 317
  violations, 30
Executive branch, 4–7
  administrative agencies, 4, 5, 7, 12, 14
    and Chapter 9
  governor, 12
  illustrated, 4, 6
  veto power, 5
    *See also* President

Facts, 444–456
  as basis of synthesis, 483
  case analysis and, 390–391, 405, 413
  case briefing and, 389–390
  defined, 444
  legal conclusion compared to,
    446–447
  legal memorandum and, 426–427
  legal research and, 330, 338–339, 433
Facts statement, 444–456
  asserted facts and, 444
  in case briefing, 389–392
  chronological organization of, 390,
    392, 443, 447, 451
  client interview and, 447, 453, 454
  defined, 444
  drafting, 453–455
  emotional adjectives, 446
  illustrated, 411, 448–449, 450, 451, 452
  legal conclusions and, 446–447
  legally significant facts and, 414,
    433–434, 444–446
  organization, 447–453
  organization by claim or defense,
    448–449
  organization by party, 449–453
  Practice Pointer, 456
  process of writing, 453–456
  pure facts and, 444
  reverse chronological organization
    of, 447, 448, 456, 457
  rewriting, 455–456
  source of information for, 447
  topical organization of, 391
  writing, 456–457
Factual authority, 29

Federal administrative agencies, 7, 9,
    14, 244–245
Federal appellate courts. *See* Appellate
    Courts, U.S.
Federal courts, decisions of, 7, 8–10,
    21–25. *See also specific courts*
Federal Digital System, fdsys, 202, 203,
    216, 234, 235, 236, 240, 246, 249,
    263, 281, 299
Federal government, 3–14
  chart, 6
  Congress, 5
  Constitution, 3–4
  diagram, 4, 6
  executive branch, 6, 7
  issue of federal law, 9, 10, 14
  judicial branch, 7, 9, 12–13
  legislative branch, 6, 7, 12
  origin of, 3–4
  relationship between state
    governments and, 1, 4, 10, 12
  state law and, 10–12
Federal Judicial Center, 10
Federal Judicial system, 6–12
  appellate courts, 4, 8, 9, 10, 13, 14
  diversity cases, 9
  illustrated, 4, 6
  jurisdiction, 9
  Supreme Court, 10, 12, 13, 14, 15
  trial courts, 9, 14
*Federal Jury Practice Instructions Civil and
    Criminal,* 325
*Federal Local Court Forms,* 306
*Federal Local Court Rules,* 306
*Federal Practice and Procedure,* 308
*Federal Procedure Rules Service,* 307
*Federal Register,* 253, 256–260
  citation of, 274, 566
  described, 256
  finding administrative law, 253,
    256–257
  illustrated, 258–262
  Internet Search Result Page, 265
  L.S.A. and, 270–273
  updating of, 270–273
  use of, 257–265
*Federal Reporter. See West's Federal Reporter*
*Federal Rules Decisions* (F.R.D.), 55, 307
Federal Rules of Appellate Procedure,
    305, 306, 311
Federal Rules of Civil Procedure,
    304, 305, 306, 309
Federal Rules of Criminal Procedure,
    304, 305, 306, 309
Federal Rules of Evidence, 304, 305,
    306, 308, 309
*Federal Rules of Evidence Service,* 308

*Federal Supplement. See West's Federal Supplement*
Fields, 291–292
Finding tools
annotated statutes, 26, 28, 219
citators, 26, 28. *See also* Citators
digests, 26, 28
formbooks, 28, 321–323
forms, 321–323
hybrid sources of authority, 29
list of, 26
statutes, 219
*See also specific tools*
Formbooks, 28, 321–323
Forms
finding tools, 321–323
Practice Pointer, 322
Full-block letter format, 530, 531
illustrated, 531

*General Digests*, 77, 78
GlobalCite, 146–147
Governing law, 19–23
determining, 20
dicta, 25
hierarchy of authority. *See* Hierarchy of authorities
jurisdiction, 20
precedent, 20–21
Governments
city, 3
county, 3
township, 3
village, 3
Grandfathered activity, 215
Greeting, 533
Guidance, 24, 25

Handbooks, 308, 321, 324, 327
Headers, 530–532
Heading, memorandum, 423–425
Headnotes, 75–77
advance sheets, 40
defined, 40
digests, 75–77, 78, 80, 86, 91
federal court reporters, 53
illustrated, 44
in *Lawyers' Edition*, 47
quoting, 43, 47
in *Supreme Court Reporter*, 47
in *U.S. Law Week*, 39, 70
in West digests, 47, 70
Hearings, 201
Hierarchy of authorities, 21–25
conflicting decisions between circuits, 23–24

conflicts in state and federal authority, 24–25
currency, 21
determination, 20
examples, 23–24
levels of court, 22
Practice Pointer, 23
ranking of authorities, examples of, 22
state and federal decisions, 24
state court decisions, 25
Holding
case briefing and, 388–389
drafting, 388–389
legal, 20–21, 25, 378, 381, 388, 466
Home page, 264, 322
Hornbooks, 178–181, 201, 331
House committee, 197–198
House of Representatives, 4, 14. *See also* Legislative process
Hybrid sources of authority, 29
formbooks, 29
looseleaf services, 29
proof of facts, 29
Hypertext, 294

Incomplete sentence, 361, 379
Indefinite pronouns, 372, 374
*Index to Foreign Legal Periodicals*, 187
*Index to Legal Periodicals*, 187
Inside address, 532
Internet research browsers, 284
checklist, 323
citation of, 58, 59, 69, 563–564
citators online, 120, 140
*Code of Federal Regulations*, 335–338
computerized reporting, 55–57
corporate information, 325–326
encyclopedias, 170
federal court decisions, 39, 55, 56
*Federal Register*, 263
federal statutes, 234–235
forms, 322–325
hypertext, 294
jury instructions, 325
legal dictionaries, 154
legal periodicals, 187–188
legal resources, 285, 292–293, 295
LEXIS. See LEXIS
list of helpful Web sites, 584–591
Loislaw, introduced 281
*Martindale-Hubbell Law Directory*, 326–327
online services, 275
pending legislation, 231, 237, 239, 337
Practice Pointer, 57, 282, 286
primary authorities, 70, 120, 188, 294
rules of practice, 307

Internet research browsers
(*continued*)
    search engines. *See* Search engines
    searching Web, 264, 280, 294, 299
    *Shepard's*. *See Shepard's* citator system
    slip opinions, 39
    state administrative materials, 256
    state legislative information Web
        sites, 232
    state rules of practice, 309–310
    statutes, 235
    United States Supreme Court
        decisions, 39, 43, 56
    Westlaw. See Westlaw. *See also*
        Computerized legal research
IRAC (Issue, Rule, Argument,
      Conclusion), 466–473
    application, 466, 467–468, 471–472
    citations and, 470–471
    components of, 466–472
    conclusion, 472
    issues, 466, 468–469
    legal memorandum and, 428, 497
    Net Note, 466
    opinion letters, 544
    paragraphs, 466–468
    Practice Pointer, 472
    purposes of, 466
    subissue, 468
Issues, 431–434
    case briefing, 386–387
    defining, 329–330,
    IRAC and, 466, 468–469
    in memorandum, 428
    outlining, 501
    paragraph example, 466–467
    refining, 504
    researching, 434
    rules of law, 469–470
    state law, 11, 15, 16
    subissue, 165, 468
    thesis paragraph, 502–503, 505
    threshold, 500, 503, 504, 505

Judicial branch (judicial system), 4, 6, 7,
      12–13
    appellate courts, 9–10, 13
    illustrated, 4, 6
    Supreme Court, 10–11
    trial courts, 8, 9
Judicial Panel on Multidistrict
      Litigation, 53, 54
Jurisdiction, 9, 15, 20
Jury instructions, 324–326
    approved or pattern jury instructions,
      324
    Ethics Alert, 325

    finding, 325
    on Internet, 324
    LEXIS, 324
    Net Note, 323
    Practice Pointer, 322, 325
    research prior to drafting, 324, 326
    Westlaw, 324
Justice Department, 8

KeyCite
    accessing, 140–145
    *American Law Reports*, 140, 153
    case briefing and, 333, 339, 347, 384
    computerized legal research,
      281–282
    described, 140–145, 282
    flags, 140, 294
    negative history, 140, 143, 147, 295
    noting depth of treatment, 143
    rules of practice, 310
    star system, 143
    use of, 140
    Westlaw, 140, 143–147,
Key number system. *See* Digests
Key number translation table, 81, 82
    illustrated, 82

Law reviews or law journals, 26, 27, 186,
      187, 188, 229, 563, 567
Lawyer directories, 309, 326
    *Martindale-Hubbell*, 326
Legal claim, 391, 444, 445, 503
Legal conclusion, 446–447
Legal dictionaries, 26, 27, 153–154,
      566c
Legal encyclopedias, 157–170
    *American Jurisprudence*, 158–165, 542
    citation of, 165–166, 566
    *Corpus Juris Secundum*, 165–169
    defined, 157
    generally, 157–158
    LEXIS, 170
    online, 170
    research strategies, 339
    rules of practice, 307
    secondary authority, 26, 27
    state law, 170
    Westlaw, 170
Legalese, 346, 350, 356, 362, 429
Legal holding, 381, 466
Legally significant facts
    defined, 389–390, 414, 444
    facts statement and, 389–392, 427,
      444–447
    IRAC and, 471–472
    legal memorandum, 425–427,
      428–429

list of, 455
use of, 433–444
Legal meaning, 154
Legal memorandum, 420–429.
    *See also* Outlining
  audience for, 420
  brief answer, 425–426
  checklist, 428–429
  components of, 420–427
  conclusion, 425–426
  defined, 420
  discussion, 427. *See also* Outlining
  drafting tips, 429
  facts, 426–427
  facts statement and. *See* Facts
      statement
  heading, 423–424
  illustrated, 421–422, 423–425, 426
      427 487–497
  IRAC and, 428. *See also* IRAC (Issue,
      Rule, Argument, Conclusion)
  issues, 424–425, 487, 490
  memo banks, 420, 427, 428
  multi-issue, 507–519
  outlining. *See* Outlining
  Practice Pointer, 427
  questions presented, 425
  sample, 573–581
  steps in drafting, 427–429
Legal periodicals, 26, 27, 76, 185–189,
    296, 308, 567
Legal research
  goal of, 2–3, 25–29
  importance of, 3–4
  introduction, 1–14
Legal speak, 358, 362
Legal system, U.S., 3–14
  components of, 4–10
  organization of, 3–4
  relationship between federal and
      state governments, 10–12
  state government organization, 12–14
Legislation, 201–216
  pending, 237–239
Legislative branch, U.S., 4–6
  illustrated, 4, 6
  legislative process and, 201–216
Legislative history, 237–249
  citation of, 245, 566
  Congressional Information Service
      and, 245
  *Congressional Record* and, 202, 246
  defined, 237
  of laws already enacted, 240
  legislative information, 237–239
  pending legislation and, 239
  public laws and, 239

  researching, additional resources,
      241–249
  as secondary authority, 245
  state, 246
  U.S.C.C.A.N. and, 239, 240–243, 245
Legislative process, 201–216
Letterhead, 530–532
Letter writing, 530–549
  basics of, 530
  blind carbon copy, 536–537
  block, 530
  body of letter, 534–535
  carbon copy, 525–526
  closing, 525
  complimentary close, 525
  components, 531–537
  confirming letters, 536, 537
  copies to others, 535–537
  date, 533
  demand letters, 541–542, 545
  e-mail, 547
  enclosures, 545–547
  Ethics Alert, 532, 534, 543
  formats for, 531, 532
  full block, 530–531
  greeting, 534
  headers, 531–533
  inside address, 530, 532
  letterhead, 530
  method of transmission, 532
  modified block, 530
  Net Note, 546
  opinion letters, 482, 543–545
  personal style, 530
  Practice Pointer, 533, 546, 547
  reference line, 531, 533
  request for information, 539–541
  signature line, 534
  social media, 547
  status letters, 536, 539
  transaction summary letters, 536–538
  transmittal letters, 536, 539, 541
  types of, 536–547
LEXIS
  accessing other online services,
      298–299
  additional features, 298–299
  administrative agency decisions, 275
  annotated codes, 204, 218
  benefits and disadvantages, 281–282
  capitalizing proper nouns and terms,
      276
  C.F.R., 267–268
  citation, 58, 297–298, 562–563
  citators. *See Shepard's* citator system;
      Validating
  cite format, 58, 297–298

LEXIS (*continued*)
  connectors, 280, 284–289
  constitutions, 200
  continuing legal education materials, 310
  database, 280–297
  ethical rules, 317
  *Federal Register*, 265, 268, 271
  federal rules, 306
  finding cases, 55–57
  hyphenated words, 290
  jury instructions, 324–325
  legal encyclopedia, 174
  legal periodicals, 187–188
  Lexisadvance.com, 281, 294
  literal searching device, 284, 285, 286
  noise words or articles, 290, 293
  on-point information, 281–282
  organization of information, 285–286
  other services of, 298–299
  pending legislation, 231, 238, 337
  plurals, 289
  point-and-click enhancements, 294
  practice rules, 306, 310
  print citations, 58
  quotations, 174, 289, 290
  research strategy, 292, 335–338
  restrictors, 290–292, 296
  retrieving research results, 293–294
  rules of practice, 290, 293, 295
  search formulation, 286–290
  segments, 277
  *Shepard's*, 120–122, 126–127, 129, 130, 134, 139, 140 281–282, 297
  slip opinions, 36, 39
  state administrative materials, 256
  statutes, 204, 211, 215, 217–218, 229, 231
  subsequent case histories, 294
  unpublished decisions, 55–56
  uses for, 282
  using, 284–294
  Westlaw compared to, 296–297
Links, 43, 140, 186, 188, 218
*List of C.F.R. Sections Affected* (L.S.A.)
  illustrated, 269
  updating, 268–269, 270–272
List of legal authorities, 498–501
Literal searching device, 284
Local rules of court, 304–309
Loislaw
  computerized reporting, 55
  computerized research service, 280, 298
  CLE materials, 324
  federal rules, 306, 310, 311
  GlobalCite, 120, 146–147, 311
    Internet research, 281
    jury instructions, 325
    rules of practice, 306
    slip opinions, 36, 39
Looseleaf services, 262–264
  citing, 29, 57
  computerized legal research, 285, 298
  defined, 275
  federal decisions in, 55
  hybrid sources of authority, 29
  level of authority of, 276
  online, 283
  use of, 276

Mandatory authority, 23–24, 26–27
*Martindale-Hubbell Law Directory*, 326–327
Memo banks, 420–421, 428
Memorandum (memo). *See* Legal memorandum
*Model Rules of Professional Conduct* 314–315, 318
Modified-block letter format, 530, 540
Modifiers, 369
Multi-issue memorandum, 505–519, 576
  *See also* Legal memorandum

National Association of Legal Assistants (NALA), 317, 591
National Center for State Courts, 15
National Federation of Paralegal Associations (NFPA), 591
National Reporter System, 36, 59, 60, 115, 165
Net Notes
  ABA Center Professional Responsibility, 316
  administrative agencies, 9
  *American Law Reports*, 174
  bills, 7, 238, 240, 241, 248
  blogs, 299
  Bloomberg Law, 285, 296
  cabinet officials, 9
  case briefing, 381, 396
  checklists, 323
  citation, 568
  commitee reports, 238
  Congress.gov, 7, 241
  *Congressional Record*, 248
  court decisions, 57
  court rules, 10
  e-mail, 546
  ethics, 316
  ethics opinions, 316
  executive branch, 9
  executive orders, 9
  Federal Digital System, 202, 248
  Federal Judicial Center, 12

Findlaw, 187
Google Scholar, 180
IRAC, 467, 472
KeyCite, 217
law journals, 187
law reviews, 187
legal research, 330, 334, 335, 336
legal writing, 350, 466
legislative history, 238, 239
legislative information, 202, 238, 239, 241
LEXIS, 296
LexisWeb, 299
LexisAdvance, 285
National Center for State Courts, 15
research resources, 330, 334
research strategy, 330, 334
restatements, 181
secondary authority, 28, 153, 188
Senate, 246
*Shepard's*, 217
state courts, 15
state legislatures, 239
statutes, 216
statutory compilations, 217, 234
tracking federal legislation, 238
treatises, 179
United States House of Representatives, 238, 246
U.S. appellate courts, 10
U.S. bankruptcy courts, 10
U.S. Code, 217
U.S.C.A., 217
U.S.C.S., 217
U.S. district courts, 10
U.S. Senate, 246
U.S. Supreme Court, 10
WestlawNext, 285
Westlaw, 296
word selection, 347
writing, 347, 348, 350
www.fjc.gov, 12
www.gpo.gov/fdsys, 202
www.house.gov, 238, 248
www.ncsc.org, 15
www.usa.gov, 9
www.uscourts.gov, 10
www.whitehouse.gov, 9
National Center for State Courts, 15
NEWS library, 188
Newspapers, 29, 30, 31, 153, 186, 188, 232, 295, 296
NFPA (National Federation of Paralegal Associations), 317, 591
Nominalization, 357
Nonlegal sources of authority, 4, 29, 30, 31, 154

*North Eastern Reporter, Second Series. See West's North Eastern Reporter*
Note taking, 332, 336, 350

Office memorandum. *See* Legal memorandum
Official reporters, 59, 60
commercial reporters compared, 43
described, 59
On all-fours, 25
One good case method, 81, 86–92, 100. *See also* Digests
Online Digest Search, 93–114
Online research. *See* Computerized legal research; Internet research
On point, 25, 28, 29, 30, 31, 43, 81, 86 93, 101, 174, 177, 178, 180, 182, 187, 215, 219, 234, 281, 282, 284, 285, 286, 287, 290, 292, 293, 337, 338, 351, 482, 488
Opinion letters, 482, 543–545
Ordinances, 11, 25, 26, 201, 215, 245
Organization, 348–349, 356, 390, 391–392, 447–448
case brief, 391–392
Chronological, 390, 391–392, 447–448
Multi-Issue Memo, 505–516
Organization by claim or defense, 448–449
combined with other forms, 450–453
illustrated, 449, 452
Organization by party, 449–450
combined with other forms, 450–453
illustrated, 450, 452
Organization of the Legal System, 5, 14–15
Original jurisdiction, 11, 12, 16
federal trial courts, 11
Outline of Authorities, 498–499
Outlining, 498–519
of discussion, 498–504
example of, 500, 512–516
list of legal authorities, 498–499
multi-issue memorandum, 501–502, 505–516
purpose of, 498
steps to, 498–505, 516–517
thesis paragraph, 502–503

Pacer Service, 39, 55, 56
Paragraphs, 356, 360–361, 362, 468–469, 497, 501, 502, 530, 543
Paralegals, 4, 5, 28, 36, 152, 157, 237–238, 274, 314, 315, 317, 324, 330, 548, 591
Parallel construction, 370

Parentheses, 369
Passive voice, 356, 359–360
Patents, 130
Pattern jury instructions, 26, 324–325
Pending legislation, 186, 337
  finding text of, 238
  tracking, 231, 238–239
Personal-style letter format, 530
Persuasive authority, 22, 24, 27–28, 29,
      30, 153, 187, 304, 308, 314, 316,
      317, 381, 392, 427, 470
Pocket parts, 81, 93, 94, 160, 162, 163,
      164, 166, 167, 170, 174, 178, 181,
      182, 190, 204, 215, 219, 221, 226,
      230–231, 307, 310
Pocket veto, 7, 202
Police powers, 9
Popular Name Table, 219–220
Practice Pointer
  appellate court, 16
  ALWD, 385, 494
  audience, 348
  Bluebook, 385, 494
  case briefing, 385, 394
  chart of authorities, 23
  citation, 57, 153, 381, 386, 494, 565
  citecheck, 282
  commercial database, 287
  computerized legal research, 282,
    287, 340
  conclusions, 438, 472
  court form, 322
  court rules, 57
  digests, 81
  e-mail, 546
  finding tools, 28
  forms, 322
  hierarchy of authorities, 415
  highest court in state, 15
  IRAC, 472
  issues of state and federal law, 11
  jurisdiction, 14, 23
  jury instructions, 325
  KeyCite, 153, 384
  key number 81
  legal memorandum, 438, 456, 467,
    472, 505
  legislative history, 246
  letter writing, 533
  LEXIS, 282, 283
  local rules, 305
  looseleaf, 276
  memo organization, 456
  notetaking, 350
  official report, 61
  outlining, 350, 505
  pinpoint cites, 494
  persuasive authority, 27

  practice rules, 305
  prewriting, 350
  primary authority, 27, 28, 153, 276
  purpose, 348
  questions presented, 438
  regional reporter, 60
  regulations, 153
  secondary authority, 27, 28, 153
  *Shepard's*, 134, 153, 384
  social media, 547
  state reports, 60
  statutory interpretation, 153, 232
  synthesis, 485, 494
  unpublished decisions, 54, 57
  validating, 134
  West's Digest System, 81
  Westlaw, 282, 283
  where to file, 14
  writing, 348
Practice rules. *See* Rules of practice
*Practitioner's Handbook for Appeals to the
    United States Court of Appeals for
    the Seventh Circuit*, 308
Practitioner's materials, 321–325
  checklists, 323–324
  continuing legal education materials,
    323
  formbooks, 321–322
  handbooks, 324
  jury instructions. *See* Jury instructions
  other tools, 325–326
Precedent, 20–21, 392–393, 401, 414
Precedential value, 30, 137, 140, 275
Precision, 434–435
President
  administrative agencies, 7, 8
  executive branch role, 7, 8
  executive orders, 253, 256
  proclamations, 203, 253, 256
  Supreme Court appointments by, 12
  veto power of, 7, 202. *See also*
    Executive branch
Prewriting stage, 350
Primary authority, 27–28, 153, 276
  administrative opinions, 274, 276
  administrative regulations and rules,
    253
  on basis of synthesis, 482–484, 492
  binding authority, 26–27
  case law, 35
  citation to, 29
  commercial databases, 286
  legislative history, 245
  list of, 26
  mandatory authority, 26–27
  persuasive authority, 27
  research goal and, 25
  statutes, 201, 215, 492

use of, 25–27, 28, 29
  validating, 336, 347
Procedural facts, 378
Procedural history, 381, 384
Process writing, 346–351
Project Hermes, 36
Public domain citation, 68, 557, 560
Public laws, 203, 204, 216, 217, 218, 219
Punctuation, 356, 366–369
Pure fact, 444
Purpose, 347–348

Quasi-judicial function, 9, 252, 274
Quasi-legislative function, 9
Query, 181, 218, 276, 280, 281, 284,
      286–290, 291
Questions presented
  audience, 432
  defined, 425, 431–432
  drafting, 432
  first draft, 432–433
  illustrated, 425, 434
  issue in IRAC compared, 433
  legally significant facts, 433
  in legal memorandum, 425
  precision, 433–435
  research and revision of, 433–434
  specificity, 434–435
Quotation marks, 367, 369
Quotations, 289, 361

Ranking authorities, 22
Rationale, 378–379, 381, 388,
      392–393
Reasoning, 378–379, 381, 388, 392–393
Record keeping, 332–334
Reference line, 532
Regional digests, 77
Regional reporters, 59, 60
  case citation, 68–69, 560
  compared with state reporter, 59
  coverage, 59–60
  defined, 590
  illustrated, 61–68
  language compared with official
      reporter, 60
  map of National Reporter System, 60
  official state reporters vs.
      commercial, 59, 60, 68
  official vs. commercial, 60, 68
  Practice Pointer, 60
  Shepard's correlation, 132
Regulations
  administrative agencies, 9, 252
  adoption of, 9, 252, 253
  as authority, 26
  citation, 566

Code of Federal Regulations, 204, 218,
      253, 254, 262, 266–268
  defined, 252
  enabling statutes, 252
  Federal Digital System, 202, 203, 216,
      263, 264, 268, 281, 299, 306
  Federal Register, 253, 256–266, 268 270,
      271, 274
  finding, 253–254
  Internet and, 263–265
  LEXIS, 265
  Loislaw, 146
  old, 258, 268
  referenced in statutory codes, 204,
      218
  sources of, 253, 256, 257–267
  state administrative law, 256
  updating and validating, 130,
      268–273
  Westlaw, 265
Relevant facts, 83, 387, 388, 389–390,
      429, 431, 436, 437
Reporters, 35–36, 40
  advance sheets, 40
  bound, 40
  Citation, 53, 55
  computerized. See LEXIS; Loislaw;
      Westlaw
  defined, 35–36
  Federal case reports, 53–55
  Federal Appendix, 53
  Federal Reporter, 53–55
  Federal Rules Decisions, 55
  Federal Supplement, 53–55
  headnotes, 43
  illustrated, 41–42, 44–46, 48–52,
      61–68
  Internet decisions, 36, 43
  key numbers, 47
  locating cases, 47
  official vs. commercial, 43, 60, 61
  regional reporters. See Regional
      reporters
  state, 59–61
  Supreme Court, 40–43
  Supreme Court Reporter, 43–47
  syllabus, 47
  United States Reports, 40–43
  United States Supreme Court
      Reports, Lawyer's Edition, 43, 47
  West's National Reporter System, 36
Reporting systems, 36
Request for information, 540
Research Process, 317, 332–333
Research strategy, 330–337
  defining issues and area of law, 330
  diagramming the process, 332–334

Research strategy (*continued*)
  example of, 333–334
  Net Note, 330, 334, 336
  organization, 329–330
  Practice Pointer, 340
  record keeping, 329–336, 332–334
  refining, 330–332
Research vocabulary, 284, 331, 335, 336,
  337
Restatements of the Law, 181–185
  citation of, 184
  defined, 153, 181
  illustrated, 183–184
  index method, 182
  online, 182, 184
  secondary authority, 27, 30
  Shepardizing, 182
  table of cases method, 182
  table of contents from, 182
  updating, 182
  use of, 181, 182
Reverse chronological order, 447–448
Rewriting, 349, 356
Rule of law, 20
  holding and, 20, 387, 469
  IRAC and, 467
  in thesis paragraph, 502
Rules of practice,
  annotated codes. *See* United States
    Code Annotated; United States
    Code Service
  attorney deskbooks, 306
  case law, 307
  citation of, 308, 309
  defined, 304, 304
  digests, 307–308
  ensuring currency, 310–311
  Ethics Alert, 305
  federal courts, list of applicable rules,
    304, 305
  Federal Procedure Rules Service, 307
  Federal Rules Decisions, 307, 309
  Federal Rules Digest, 309
  Federal Rules of Appellate
    Procedure, 305, 306
  Federal Rules of Bankruptcy
    Procedure, 306
  Federal Rules of Civil Procedure, 304,
    305, 306
  Federal Rules of Criminal Procedure,
    304, 306
  Federal Rules of Evidence, 304, 306
  Federal Procedure Rules Service, 307
  Internet and, 306
  KeyCite, 310
  LEXIS, 306
  list of courts and applicable rules, 305
  local rules of court, 304, 305, 306
  Loislaw, 306
  Net Note, 305
  online, 306
  overview of, 304
  persuasive authorities, 304
  pocket parts, 307
  Practice Pointer, 305, 307
  practitioner handbooks, 308
  primary binding authorities, 304, 305
  researching, 307
  Rules of the Supreme Court, 305, 306
  secondary authority, 307, 308
  Shepardizing, 310–311
  sources, 306, 307, 308
  state, 304, 309–310
  steps in researching, 307–308
  treatises, 308, 310
  U.S. Courts website, 306
  Westlaw, 306
Rules of the Supreme Court, 305
Run-on sentences, 372–373

Search engines, 120, 186, 187, 299, 323
Search formation, 286–290
Secondary authority, 152–188
  ABA opinion, 315
  *American Law Reports. See American
    Law Reports* (A.L.R.)
  cite to, 28, 30, 157
  defined, 27–28
  described, 27–28
  dictionaries, 27, 153–154
  encyclopedias. *See* Legal
    encyclopedias
  ethics, 315
  ethics opinions, 315
  hornbooks, 153, 178–181
  legislative history, 245
  legal periodicals, 153, 185–188
  list of, 26
  looseleafs, 276
  Net Note, 28, 153, 158, 174, 188
  persuasive, 27
  Practice Pointer, 27, 28, 153
  Restatements of the Law, 27, 30,
    181–185
  sources of, 27, 153
  thesauri, 27, 154, 157
  treatises, 153, 178–181
  uniform codes, 28
  use of, 27–28, 131, 152
Segment, 291, 292, 293
Semicolons, 368
Senate, 6, 7, 12, 201, 202, 238, 239, 245,
    246, 249, 584. *See also* Legislative
    process

Sentences, 360–361
sentence fragments, 373
Session laws, 203, 204, 205, 217, 219,
    231, 232, 234, 246
*Shepard's* citator system, 119–140
    abbreviations, 130
    administrative agency decisions, 130,
        275
    American Law Reports, 120, 174, 178
    authorities in, 130
    case briefing and, 384
    case history, 120
    C.F.R., 271
    checklist, 554
    citing references, 130–131
    citing sources, 131
    commercial databases, 120, 130, 280,
        281–283, 294
    compared with KeyCite, 145
    constitutions, 130, 194
    daily updates, 136
    described, 119–120
    direct history, 120
    Ethics Alert, 140
    ethics rules, 317
    examples of online sources, 122–127,
        136, 137, 138–139
    examples of publications, 121, 128,
        133, 134
    federal cases, 130
    finding tools, 28, 200
    headnotes, 130
    Illustrated, 121, 122–127, 138, 129,
        133, 134
    information from, 120, 130
    LEXIS, 120, 130, 280, 281–283, 294
    Lexis Advance, 120
    Lexis headnotes, 130
    negative history, 130
    Net Note, 217
    Online, 120, 122–127, 136–140
    parallel citations, 120
    practice pointer, 135, 384
    in print, 116, 130–132, 132–136
    regional citators, 131
    regulations, 272
    reporter citations, 130
    research strategy, 130
    restatements, 130, 182
    rules of practice, 310
    signal feature, 137–139
    sources of, 120, 130
    specialized citators, 132
    state cases, 135
    state rules, 310, 311
    statutes, 217, 226–231, 234
    supplements to, 131, 133, 135

    treatment, 130, 137, 140, 226, 295,
        296
    unreported cases, 130
    use of, 119–140
    validating, 217, 226–231, 234
    West's headnotes, 130
    writing process, 331, 333
*Shepard's Code of Federal Regulations
    Citations*, 271
*Shepard's Federal Citations*, 132
*Shepard's Federal Rule Citations*, 310
*Shepard's* online, 120, 122–127, 136–140
*Shepard's Professional and Judicial Conduct
    Citations*, 317
*Shepard's Restatement of Law Citations*,
    182
*Shepard's U.S. Administrative Citations*,
    275
*Shepard's United States Citations*, 194, 310
Shepardize, 119–140, 153, 174, 178,
    182,
Short Citation Forms, 562
Signal feature of *Shepard's* Online,
    137–139
Signatures
    attorney, 534
    ethics alert, 534
Slip bills, 201–202
Slip laws, 203
Slip opinions, 39
    access to, 36, 39
    advance sheets, 40
    citation, 36, 39–40, 559
    Ethics Alert, 36, 40
    federal courts, 39
    illustrated, 37–38
    Internet, 36, 39
    LEXIS, 36, 39
    Loislaw, 36, 39
    Newspaper, 36
    PACER, 39
    state courts, 39
    Supreme Court, 36, 39
    United States Law Week, 39
    Westlaw, 36, 39
social media, 547
Specialized digests, 78
Specificity, 434–435
Sponsor, 201, 202, 203, 219, 238, 239,
    246
Star system, 143
Stare decisis, 20–21
State cases
    citation, 68–69
    digests, 77–78, 79–81
    reporters, 59
    *Shepard's*, 135

State cases (*continued*)
  unofficial reports, 59
State constitutions, 194, 200
State courts, 14, 15, 24, 25
  decisions, 25, 27, 36, 39, 55, 59
  decisions online, 55–56
  ethics rules, 314
  highest court, 15,
  issues of federal law, 16, 24
  National Center for State Courts, 15
  Net Note, 15
  persuasive authority, 25
  relationship to other state courts, 25
  rules, 304, 309
  state constitution, 194
  unofficial reports, 59
State digests, 77
State governments
  conflicts with federal authority, 24
  courts, 14, 15, 16, 25
  legislative branches, 15
  organization of, 5, 6, 14–15
  origin of, 6
  relationship with federal
    government, 5, 6, 12, 14, 16
State law encyclopedias, 157, 170
State law issues and federal courts, 14,
  16, 24
state legislative history, 246
state legislative information Web sites,
  231, 232, 234, 235, 239
State legislatures, 186, 201, 231, 232,
  238, 239, 246
State reporters, 59, 60
State rules of practice, 304, 309–310
  annotated rules, 310
  attorney deskbook, 306
  ethics alert, 305
  KeyCite, 310
  secondary authority, 307, 308
  Shepardizing, 311
  sources, 309–310
Status report, 536, 539
  illustrated, 539
Statutes,
  annotated, 28, 30, 217, 218, 219–220
  case law and, 6, 216
  citators, 120
  citation of, 158, 221, 226, 232
  constitutional, 194, 216
  Congress' role, 6
  defined, 6, 201
  enacted law, 7
  enabling, 15, 252, 253, 257, 267, 268,
    275
  Federal Digital System, 235
  finding federal, 152, 216

  finding state, 152, 232–233
  GlobalCite, 146
  hierarchy between case and, 21
  legislative process, 7, 201–202
  LEXIS, 215, 217, 218, 234–235
  Net Note, 216, 234
  online, 215, 217, 218, 234–235
  persuasive authority, 27
  Practice Pointer, 15, 232
  primary authority, 25, 26, 151–152,
    215
  reading and understanding, 215, 232
  repealed, 216
  research methods to find, 27, 28,
    151–152, 178, 180, 216, 217
  secondary authority and, 27, 151–152
  Shepardizing, updating, and validat-
    ing 120, 130, 146, 194
  state statutory compilations, 216,
    231–234, 235
  uniform codes and, 28
  U.S. Constitution and, 194
  West Codenotes, 47
  Westlaw, 215, 217, 218, 234–235
    *See also* Legislative history;
    specific codes
*Statutes at Large*, 203, 204, 205, 217, 219,
  221, 222
Statutory compilations, 217, 232, 234,
  311, 319
Subcommittee, 201
Subject and verb agreement, 370–372
Supreme Court, U.S.
  advance sheets, 40
  Bloomberg BNA, 39
  bound reporters, 40–43
  citation of cases, 40, 53
  commercial reporters, 43
  decisions, 43
  docket information, 43
  digests, 43
  function, 9, 10, 12, 15, 22
  illustrated, 10
  Internet, 36, 43
  locating cases, 36–43
  relationship to other courts, 22
  rules of, 305, 306
  slip opinions, 36, 39–40
  *Supreme Court Reporter*, 43, 44
  *United States Law Week*, 39
  *United States Reports*, 40–43
    Illustrated, 41–42
  *United States Supreme Court Reporters,*
    *Lawyer's Edition*, 43, 47
*Supreme Court Reporter*
  described, 43
  headnotes, 43, 44

illustrated, 44–46
official reporters compared, 43
syllabus, 40, 41, 42, 44
Syllabus
  defined, 36, 40, 44, 47
  illustrated, 37, 41–42, 44 48, 61
Synthesis,
  checklist for, 493–494
    defined, 482
  examples of, 482–483, 485–492, 493
  Net Note, 384
  Practice Pointer, 494
  purpose. 482
  statutes, 469, 492
  step-by-step process of, 483–484
  types of, 483

That and which, 373,
Thesauri, 26, 27, 153, 154, 157, 502
Thesis paragraph
  drafting, 502–503
  illustrated, 503
  IRAC format, 502
  issue, 502
  outline, 503
  rule of law, 505
Threshold issue, 503
Topical digests, 77
Topic outline method, 86. *See also*
    Digests
Topic sentence, 360, 468, 469
Total Client-Service Library References,
    illustrated, 171
Township governments, 5
Trademarks, 130, 303
Transaction summary letters, 536, 538
Transitions, 356, 360, 429, 506
Transmittal letters, 536, 539, 541
Treatises, 178–181
  citation to, 180
  on constitutional law, 179
  defined, 178–179
  on evidence issues, 179
  online, 181
  Net Note, 179
  noteworthy, 179
  as secondary authority, 179
  updating, 181
  use of, 179–180
Treatment, 130, 137, 140, 143, 147, 226,
    295, 296, 555
Trial courts
  decisions, 36
  district courts, 10, 11, 12, 21
  federal appellate courts and, 22
  hierarchy of authority, 21, 22
  judicial branch, 9

  opinions, 36
  original jurisdiction, 11
  practice rules, 304
  state, 15

Uniform codes, 28
*Uniform System of Citation, Nineteenth*
    *Edition. See* Bluebook citation
*United States Code Annotated* (U.S.C.A.)
  advance sheets, 219, 240
  citation, 217, 221, 226
  codes compared, 217, 218, 219–220
  constitutions and, 194
  conversion table, 221
  illustrated, 208–210, 222, 223,
    224–225, 230
  index method, 221
  KeyCite, 234
  Key numbers, 218
  legislative history, 240
  online, 215, 217, 218, 234–235
  organization, 217
  pocket parts, 219, 230
  popular name table, 219, 220
  public laws, 240
  research methods, 219
  rules and court decisions, 307–308
  Shepardizing and updating, 204,
    218–219, 226, 231, 234–235
  title outline, 221
  unofficial codes, 217, 218, 219
  U.S.C.C.A.N., 240, 241
  West Digest System, 218
  Westlaw, 215, 217, 218, 234–235
*United States Code Congressional and*
    *Administrative News* (U.S.C.C.A.N.)
  advance sheets, 231, 239
  citation of, 245
  illustrated, 242, 243–245
  legislative histories, 218, 240, 241
  U.S.C.A., 240, 241
*United States Code Service* (U.S.C.S.)
  administrative regulations
    references, 218
  advance sheets, 219, 231, 239–240
  citation, 217, 221, 226
  codes compared, 217, 218, 219–220
  constitutions and, 194
  illustrated, 211–214
  index method, 221
  LEXIS, 215, 217, 218, 234–235
  Net Note, 271
  online, 215, 217, 218, 234–235
  organization, 217
  pocket parts, 219
  popular name table, 219
  public law, 240

*United States Code Service* (U.S.C.S.)
  (*continued*)
  research methods, 219–220
  rules and court decisions, 307–308
  Shepardizing and updating, 221, 226,
    231, 234–235
  Table of U.S.C., titles 206
  title outline, 221
  unofficial codes, 217, 218
*United States Code* (U.S.C.)
  annotated versions, 217
  citation, 217, 221, 226, 228
  codification of statutes, 216–217
  constitution and, 194
  defined, 216–217
  Federal Digital System, 235
  illustrated, 207
  Internet, 216, 235
  KeyCite, 234
  Net Note, 217, 290
  as official compilation of statutes,
    216–217
  organization, 216
  research methods, 221
  rules of practice, 307–308
  Shepard's 217, 218–219
  table of titles, 206
  titles, 216
  unofficial versions of, 217, 218, 219
  updating of, 217, 218–219, 226
  Westlaw, 234
United States Constitution, 6, 12, 14
United States House of Representatives,
    238, 246
United States government. *See* Federal
    government
*United States Government Manual,*
    249
*United States Law Week,* Supreme Court
    slip opinions, 39, 53, 561
*United States Reports,* 40, 43, 47, 53, 153,
    561
  citation, 53, 561
  illustrated, 41–42, 198
  syllabus, 41
*United States Supreme Court Digest,*
    *Lawyers' Edition,* 47, 77
*United States Supreme Court Reports,*
    *Lawyers' Edition,* 43, 47, 53, 135,
    172
unofficial reports, 217
unpublished decisions, 54
U.S. bankruptcy courts, 10
U.S. Code. *See* United States Code
U.S. Constitution. *See* Constitution, U.S.
U.S. Courts of Appeals. *See* Appellate
    courts, U.S.

U.S. District Courts, 5, 8, 10, 11, 22, 23,
    24, 53, 54, 55, 69, 132, 275, 304,
    305, 559, 560
U.S.C.C.A.N. *See United States Code*
    *Congressional and Administrative*
    *News*
U.S. Supreme Court
  advance sheets, 36, 65
  appeals to, 12, 16
  bench opinions 36
  citation, 53, 561
  digests, 77
  docket, 43
  ethics, 317
  generally, 12
  hierarchy of authority, 21, 24, 25
  judicial branch, 9, 10
  Net Note, 10
  news, 186
  rules, 304, 305
  Shepard's 132, 135
  slip opinion, 36, 39
  and state law, 14
  Supreme Court Reporter, 43
  United States Reports, 40
  U.S. Supreme Court, Lawyer's
    Edition, 43
  U.S. Supreme Court Digest, 200

Validating, 119–146
  case briefing and, 384
  citators, defined, 119–120
  constitutions, 194
  Ethics Alert, 140
  ethics rules, 317
  GlobalCite, 120, 146
  internet, 235
  KeyCite, 120, 140–145, 331
    *See also* KeyCite
  Loislaw, 120, 146
  Net Note, 217
  Practice Pointer, 134, 135, 153,
    384
  practice rules, 310–311
  regulations, 268–273
  restatements, 182
  statutes, 217, 226, 231
  *Shepard's,* 119–140, 331 *See also*
    *Shepard's* citator system
  *Shepard's* in print, 116, 130–131,
    132–136, 217
  *Shepard's* online, 120, 122–127,
    136–140, 217, 234
  Westlaw, 120, 142, 143, 144, 145, 217,
    234
Verbs, 357–358, 370–371
VersusLaw, 55, 56

Vetoes, 7, 202
Village governments, 56
Voice, 350, 356, 359–360, 361
*West American Digest System,* 77
West Codenotes, 47, 56
West key number system. *See* Digests,
    key number system
Westlaw
  accessing other online services,
    294–295
  administrative agency decisions, 275
  *American Jurisprudence,* 164
  *American Law Reports,* 173, 174
  annotated codes, 204, 215
  benefits and disadvantages, 279–280,
    281–282, 285
  bill tracking, 231, 238
  capitalizing proper nouns and terms,
    290
  C.F.R., 267, 268
  citations, 58, 297, 298, 562
  citators. *See* KeyCite
  C.J.S., 165, 167, 170
  *Code of Federal Regulations,* 267, 268
  *Congressional Record,* 246
  connectors, 287–289
  constitutions, 200
  continuing legal education materials,
    324
  custom digest, 106–107
  database, 55
  digests, 78, 93, 96, 296
  ethics rules, 317
  *Federal Register,* 256, 265
  federal rules, 311
  fields, 292
  filtering, 285
  finding cases by citation, 56–57
  formbooks, 322
  full text, 290
  hyphenated words, 290
  headnotes, 282
  Internet research, 284
  irregular plurals, 289–290
  jury instructions, 325
  KeyCite 120, 140–145, 234, 280, 281,
    283, 295, 554
  key number searches, 96, 100, 101,
    102–105, 106, 107–108, 296
  legal dictionaries, 154
  legal encyclopedia services, 166, 167,
    170
  legal periodicals, 188
  legislative histories, 240
  LEXIS compared to, 292, 295, 296–297
  as literal searching device, 284
  local rules, 309–310

  natural language and, 296–297
  Net Note, 285, 296
  news information, 296
  noise words or articles, 290
  on-point information, 282
  organization of information, 56
  pending legislation, 231, 238
  plurals, 289
  point and click enhancements, 294
  Practice Pointer, 282, 283, 286
  practice rules, 311
  query formation, 218, 286–290
  quotations, 289
  regulations, 267, 268, 271
  restatements, 182, 183
  restrictors, 290–292
  retrieving research results, 293–294
  search formulation, 286–290
  *Shepard's,* 136, 145
  slip opinions, 36, 39
  state administrative materials, 256
  state legislation, 232, 234
  statutes, 204, 215, 218, 232, 234
  treatises, 181
  unpublished decisions, 55, 58, 59
  uses for, 78, 231, 282–283
  U.S.C.C.A.N., 296
  using, 280–281, 285–292, 297
  validating and updating. *See* KeyCite
WestlawNext, 56, 78,171, 174, 279–280,
    281, 283, 285, 293
*West's American Digest System. See* Digests
*West's Education Law Reporter,* 55
*West's Federal Appendix,* 53
*West's Federal Practice Digest,* 77–78, 88
*West's Federal Reporter,* 53–55, 227, 307, 560
*West's Federal Rules Decisions* (F.R.D.), 55,
    307, 309, 561
*West's Federal Supplement,* 53–55, 307, 560
*West's North Eastern Reporter,* 47, 48, 59,
    61, 78
  illustrated, 48–52, 61–69
*West's Supreme Court Digest,* 77, 78, 200
Which, 373
word selection, 347
Writing
  audience, 346–347, 348, 349, 350,
    358, 420, 530, 535, 545, 548
  checklist for writing process, 351
  clarity, 346
  clear writing and editing, 355–362
  colons, 368
  commas, 366–367, 372, 373
  concrete verbs, 357–358
  diction, 357
  double quotation marks, 369
  editing, 355–362, 388

Writing (*continued*)
emotional adjectives, 446
example of process of writing
  techniques, 350
legalese, 356, 358–359
memorandum. *See* Legal
  memorandum
modifiers, 369
Net Notes, 347, 348, 351
nominalization, 357–358
organization, 348–349, 356, 362
outlining for. *See also* Outlining
parallel construction, 370
paragraphs, 360
parentheses, 369
Practice Pointer, 348, 349, 350
preparation for, 346–347
prewriting, 350
process, 346–351
punctuation, 356. 366–369
purpose of, 347–348
quotation marks, 367, 369
revision, 346, 349, 351, 355–356, 357,
  359, 362
rewriting, 349, 356
run-on sentences, 372–373
semicolons, 368
sentences, 360–361
sentence fragments, 373
single quotation marks, 369
subject-verb agreement, 370–372
that and which, 373
topic sentence, 360, 468, 469
transitions, 356, 360, 429, 506
voice, 350, 356, 359–360, 361
word selection, 347
www.lexis.com. *See* LEXIS
www.uscourts.gov, 10